Financial Decision Making
at Retirement

Huebner School Series

Gary K. Stone, Editor

Huebner School Series

Financial Decision Making at Retirement
Second Edition

David A. Littell
Kenn Beam Tacchino
David M. Cordell

The American College/*Bryn Mawr, Pennsylvania*

This publication is designed to provide accurate and authoritative information about the subject covered. The American College is not engaged in rendering legal, accounting, or other professional advice. If legal or other expert advice is required, the services of an appropriate professional should be sought.

Library of Congress Catalog Card Number 95-75334
ISBN 0-943590-68-X

Printed in the United States of America

*To all those who have helped
to form me, both personally and
professionally*

D.A.L

To my parents

K.B.T.

*To my wife, my parents, and
my children*

D.M.C.

About the Authors

David A. Littell, JD, associate professor of taxation at The American College, received his law degree from the Boston University School of Law. He has coauthored several books and published numerous articles on pensions and employee benefits, and has an extensive background in pension planning.

Kenn Beam Tacchino, JD, associate professor of accounting and taxation and director of the Tax Institute at Widener University, is a former faculty member at and current consultant to The American College. Author of several pension books and published widely in pension journals, he earned his law degree at Western New England College School of Law.

David M. Cordell, PhD, CFA, CFP, CLU, is associate professor of finance at The American College. He holds a master's degree and a doctorate in finance from The University of Texas at Austin. He has written numerous articles on financial planning and investments and is the author of a bi-weekly newspaper column on financial planning.

Contents

Acknowledgments

The authors are grateful to many individuals for their valuable contributions to this book. We would like to express our special appreciation to the current and former American College faculty members whose help and participation were integral to the book's development. These individuals include Robert J. Doyle, Edward E. Graves, and William J. Ruckstuhl. In particular, we wish to thank Burton T. Beam for writing a large portion of the material on social security in chapters 2 and 12 and Michael J. Roszkowski for writing the section of chapter 7 on assessing risk tolerance. Dr. Roszkowski's discussion is adapted from his article, "The Psychology of Financial Planning," which appeared as a chapter in *The Financial Services Professional's Guide to the State of the Art,* The American College, 1989.

We thank Christina Hansen for her excellent production skills and her patience in deciphering, typing, and formatting this document. Without her unflagging commitment and support this project could never have been completed. We also thank Suzanne Walsh Rettew for her painstaking proofreading. And finally, we are indebted to Emily Sims for the outstanding job she did editing this manuscript. Her high standards and editorial expertise have greatly enhanced this book. Thanks, Emily.

Financial Decision Making
at Retirement

1

Retirement Planning Overview

Chapter Outline

Will you retire with financial security? Few questions generate as much anxiety as this one, yet most individuals avoid the question until it is too late to influence the answer.

Retirement planning is usually the most crucial aspect of a comprehensive financial plan. If an individual addresses the retirement planning question early enough, a competent adviser can help to accomplish the goal of a comfortable and secure retirement. When the question is ignored too long, the hope of financial security deteriorates to nothing more than a lost opportunity.

This book is directed primarily at financial advisers working with clients who have both the desire and the financial wherewithal to attain a comfortable retirement. This chapter addresses basic questions that advisers and their clients should know before beginning a retirement plan:

- What are the socioeconomic trends that have an impact on financial planning for retirement?
- What is the most overlooked stumbling block in retirement planning?
- What are the important components of retirement income?
- What is the professional's role in retirement planning?

CRITICAL TRENDS AFFECTING RETIREMENT

Describing the average retiree is like describing the average book—even if it could be done, the information would not be very useful. Retirees are wealthy and poor, male and female, old and not-so-old. They are single, married, and widowed; they have children and do not have children. They are healthy and unhealthy, happy and miserable, active and sedentary, sophisticated and naive.

Still, even though the average retiree is difficult to describe, some conditions and trends that have an impact on financial planning for retirement are worth exploring to acquire perspective before setting goals.

What Is "Retirement Age"?

No longer is 65 a magic number for retirement. Although the minimum age for full social security retirement benefits is currently 65, 1983 amendments to the Social Security Act mandated a change in this requirement. Depending on the individual's date of birth, the retirement age for full benefits now ranges from 65 to 67 as shown in table 1-1.

TABLE 1-1
Normal Retirement Age for Full Benefits

Year of Birth	Age (Years/Months)
before 1938	65/0
1938	65/2
1939	65/4
1940	65/6
1941	65/8
1942	65/10
1943–1954	66/0
1955	66/2
1956	66/4
1957	66/6
1958	66/8
1959	66/10
1960 and after	67/0

At one time, turning 65 meant mandatory retirement because of employers' policies. Now federal law specifies that such policies represent age discrimination and are illegal. Pension benefits that continue to increase after age 65, lack of success in personal investing, and longer life expectancies are among the factors that encourage older retirement ages. Also many people choose to retire long after 65 because they enjoy their work.

The availability of company-paid health benefits influences the decision regarding retirement age. Many corporations offer medical insurance at reduced rates to early retirees to bridge the gap until eligibility for medicare. However, many employers either do not offer coverage or reserve the right to cancel coverage. Recent changes in accounting rules discourage benefit plans for retirees by lowering current reported earnings in anticipation of future health care costs. Some corporations have reneged on what retirees thought was a pledge of future coverage. Retiring before age 65 while relying on employer-paid benefits can prove very costly if the employer cancels coverage and the retiree incurs a serious injury or illness during the transition between "early" retirement and medicare. Obviously this factor discourages retirement before age 65.

Several factors encourage younger retirement ages. Many people simply want to retire before age 65 and will accept a lower standard of living if necessary. Others have succeeded in saving and investing and are able to retire before 65 in comfort, even with reduced social security and retirement benefits. A trend in recent years is for corporations to trim expenses by offering incentives for older, higher-paid employees to retire early. Some corporations cut back by eliminating the older employees without offering incentives. Since older people can have trouble finding new positions, an employer cutback often amounts to the end of a worker's career—a forced retirement that is early and permanent.

What, then, is retirement age? As a practical matter the average retirement age is irrelevant to the retirement planner. What is important is the retirement age for the individual client.

Each client has a unique set of factors that influence his or her retirement age. Government and employer programs and policies are important. But also important are the client's financial and personal situations as well as his or her willingness to incur the risk of portfolio performance, inflation, and adverse changes in government and employer policies.

For most clients specification of a retirement age is based on nonfinancial criteria. If the client indicates the desire to retire at age 64, the planner's responsibility is to help determine whether that is a financially viable goal. At the same time, the planner must advise the client of negative aspects of the chosen age. Often the planner provides information that causes the client to postpone retirement.

How Long Is Retirement?

Advanced calculus is not required to estimate the length of the average individual's retirement. Many sources print actuarial tables for life expectancy based on current age. However, as with most concepts, the task is more complicated than it seems.

For the average 65-year-old in the United States, life expectancy is 17.5 years according to National Center for Health Statistics (NCHS) data for 1991.[1] This expectancy exceeds the value based on data from 1979 to 1981 by a full year. How long life expectancy will be by the time a particular client reaches age 65 is anyone's guess, but even with the AIDS epidemic life expectancy for a 65-year-old will probably continue to increase.

Life expectancy is a function of race and gender as well as age. Depending on these two factors, life expectancy for a 65-year-old is as follows according to NCHS:

TABLE 1-2 Life Expectancy for a 65-Year-Old by Race and Gender	
Race, Gender	Life Expectancy (Years)
White, Female	19.3
Black, Female	17.5
White, Male	15.5
Black, Male	14.2

While such data helps refine the estimate of a client's expected length of retirement, personal factors are also important. An obese, alcoholic smoker with diabetes, a heart condition, a family history of cancer, and multiple reckless driving citations is unlikely to reach the life expectancy. A cautious, healthy, and health-conscious individual with a good family medical history and an enthusiasm for life is likely to live beyond the expected span.

Compounding the analysis is the fact that retirement planning often involves two people: husband and wife. Typically the wife has a longer life expectancy and is younger than the husband. Basing the retirement analysis on the husband's life expectancy is likely to result in financial difficulty for his widow.

So how long will retirement last? To estimate the expected retirement period take the following steps.

- Identify the client's expected retirement age.
- Look up statistical life expectancy data—using the retirement ages of the client and his or her spouse.
- Adjust the estimate up or down for factors such as health, lifestyle, and family history.

Even after this analysis, remember this is only an estimate. Don't forget that actuarial tables represent average experience, meaning that approximately half the individuals will outlive the expectation.

Clearly, financial conservatism dictates that the planner and client should assume a longer-than-expected retirement period. Consider that it is the anxiety of possibly outliving one's money that causes clients to select life annuities or interest-only payout provisions at retirement. In effect, such clients implicitly assume a longer-than-average life span. For any reasonable life span estimate, there is some probability that the typical client will outlive his or her assets. Although this statement is mathematically obvious, if often serves as a wake-up call, further emphasizing the importance of accumulating a substantial retirement fund that the client will not outlive.

Retirement Income: The Target Replacement Ratio

Almost everyone would be happy to retire on a multimillionaire's income. Reality is that retirement income is restricted by the client's personal financial history. Sources of income emanate from the "three-legged stool" of retirement planning—comprised of social security, employer-sponsored retirement programs, and personal savings—which is discussed later in this chapter.

Most individuals are satisfied with maintaining their preretirement standard of living during retirement. Doing so does not require the retirement income to equal the preretirement income. Among the factors that reduce the income are lower taxes. Not only do retirees stop paying social security taxes, but also their social security income is subject to reduced income taxation. Some states even reduce property taxes for individuals over age 65. Another factor is that contributions to the retirement fund through 401(k) plans, 403(b) plans, IRAs, and personal savings usually stop at retirement. Disability and life insurance needs and their accompanying premiums may cease or decline. The combined cost of health care and health insurance may decrease upon the retiree's qualification for medicare. Transportation, clothing, and food expenses may be lower.

Although a precise retirement budget will differ for each client (see chapter 5 for details of the budget process), it is usually helpful to consider income replacement in retirement in percentage terms. The target replacement ratio (TRR) is equal to the amount an individual needs annually to maintain a standard of living equivalent to the preretirement standard divided by the individual's preretirement annual income:

$$\text{TRR} = \frac{\text{Postretirement annual income}}{\text{Preretirement annual income}}$$

where each income provides the same standard of living.

In general, individuals with higher incomes can have lower TRRs. One reason for this phenomenon is that there is more slack in the preretirement budgets of higher-income individuals. Some expenses can be eliminated without really changing the standard of living. (Even the wealthy are unlikely to complain about a diminished jewelry budget.)   Many types of expenses are somewhat fixed—independent of income—and represent a smaller percentage of higher incomes than lower incomes.   Another explanation for declining TRRs with increasing incomes is that higher-income individuals save more for retirement, and since that budget item disappears during retirement, the TRR falls.

Another reason for the decline in TRRs with increasing incomes is the progressivity of the income tax structure.   Individuals pay the vast majority of living expenses with aftertax dollars.   For a low-income, low-tax individual, pretax income and aftertax income are very close.   A reduction in (aftertax) expenses decreases the need for pretax income by almost the same amount because there is very little tax savings.   For the higher-income individual, a reduction in aftertax expenditures creates a greater reduction in pretax income needs because of the larger tax savings.

Trends in Target Replacement Ratios

Not only do TRRs vary according to income, but they also have risen over time, according to studies.   A presidential commission, using 1981 data on consumer spending patterns of both employed and retired people, estimated average replacement ratios needed at various income levels.[2]   The recommended TRRs ranged from 71 percent for a final preretirement annual income of $15,000 to 55 percent for final retirement incomes exceeding $50,000.

A subsequent study[3] used a similar approach and 1988 data to evaluate the impact of the Tax Reform Act of 1986 on TRRs.   This study recommended an 82 percent TRR for final preretirement annual income of $15,000, 66 percent for $50,000, and 68 percent for $80,000.

A third study, published in 1991,[4] used the *1988 Consumer Expenditure Survey*[5] to update the 1988 study.   Recommended TRRs included 90 percent for a $15,000 final preretirement annual income, 73 percent for $50,000, and 68 percent for $80,000.   Table 1-3 summarizes the suggested ratios for each of the three studies.   Note that TRRs rose over time for all but the highest income level.

The primary explanation for the increase in TRRs from the 1988 study to the 1991 study was the increase, as a percentage of income, of consumer spending. People used to spending more will generally want to continue doing so in retirement.   Unfortunately, this trend poses a serious threat to retirement security. Higher levels of spending mean less is being saved for retirement, while higher TRRs mean that more money is needed for a secure retirement.

Will the trend toward higher target replacement ratios continue?   Much depends on trends in savings.   If consumers, either on their own or with government incentives, start saving more by tightening their belts as corporate America has, the trend in TRRs could reverse itself.   If consumers continue to spend all that they earn, or even more than they earn, TRRs could continue the upward trend.

Remember, though, that the TRR is largely a macro concept—it relies on summary data for all consumers.   The information points out the collective situa-

TABLE 1-3 Target Replacement Ratios in Three Studies			
Salary	1981	1988	1991
$15,000	71%	82%	90%
$20,000	66%	75%	85%
$25,000	–	71%	82%
$30,000	60%	68%	79%
$40,000	–	67%	77%
$50,000	55%	66%	73%
$60,000	–	66%	71%
$70,000	–	–	70%
$80,000	–	68%	68%

tion, but retirement planning is ultimately a client-specific task. Each client has his or her own financial situation, which may vary greatly from the norm. For many clients a better method of calculating retirement needs is through use of the expense method shown in chapter 5.

What Is the Impact of Inflation?

The most overlooked stumbling block in retirement planning is the effect of inflation. Although financial professionals can obtain and evaluate historical inflation rates, no one knows what inflation will be in the future.

Looking at the Past

Table 1-4 shows inflation rates from 1960 through 1993 derived from the U.S. Bureau of Labor Statistics consumer price index.

Note that the first 6 years listed in the table had inflation rates under 2 percent. Subsequently factors such as government spending for social programs and the Vietnam war elevated inflation. The double-digit years were those in which energy costs—chiefly petroleum products—rose dramatically.

For the most recent 5 years (1989–1993), the average inflation rate has been 4.3 percent. Most consumers accept the current situation without much complaint. After all, it is certainly more palatable than the double-digit era. However, this comfort is like the relief of having only one child in college after having had two in college at the same time: wealth does not disappear as quickly as before, but it does continue to disappear.

Over the entire 34 years the inflation rate averaged 4.9 percent per year. A monthly retirement income of $1,000 for someone who retired at the beginning of 1960 declined in purchasing power to only $200 by the end of 1993. Of course the 65-year-old retiree in January 1960 would have aged to 99 by the end of 1993, so clients may view this example as an overstatement of their potential exposure to inflation.

TABLE 1-4			
Inflation Rates for U.S. Urban Consumers, 1960–1993			
Year	Rate (%)	Year	Rate (%)
1960	1.7	1977	6.5
1961	1.0	1978	7.6
1962	1.0	1979	11.3
1963	1.3	1980	13.5
1964	1.3	1981	10.3
1965	1.6	1982	6.2
1966	2.9	1983	3.2
1967	3.1	1984	4.3
1968	4.2	1985	3.6
1969	5.5	1986	1.9
1970	5.7	1987	3.6
1971	4.4	1988	4.1
1972	3.2	1989	4.8
1973	6.2	1990	5.4
1974	11.0	1991	4.2
1975	9.1	1992	3.0
1976	5.8	1993	3.9

Source: Bureau of Labor Statistics, *Monthly Labor Review*

Table 1-5 reveals the decline in purchasing power during various increments of the past 34 years. In each case the retiree is assumed to have received an initial monthly check of $1,000. The final column reveals how little purchasing power remained from the fixed $1,000 payment by the end of 1993.

Mitigating the loss in purchasing power is the fact that social security payments are adjusted for inflation. However, it is quite possible that legislation to improve the actuarial soundness of the system will eventually reduce benefits in some way. Any reductions are likely to fall heavily on the relatively affluent. Further, since this group receives a smaller proportion of its retirement income from social security, those inflation adjustments will provide little help.

Table 1-6 applies the historical rates from table 1-5 to show the reduction in purchasing power that those rates would impose on an individual retiring today. For example, if the inflation rate from the most recent 15-year period (5.5 percent) were to continue, an individual retiring today with a pension of $1,000 per month would see the pension's purchasing power fall to $447 in 15 years.

Although all clients are aware of inflation, few understand the degree to which it can affect them, especially over extended time periods. Showing the client the destructive capacity of inflation is one of the most important tasks for the retirement planner.

TABLE 1-5
Historical Decline in Purchasing Power of a $1,000 Initial Retirement Income through 12/31/93

Retirement Date	Years Since Retirement	Average Infla-tion through 1993	Purchasing Pow-er 12/31/93
1/1/1989	5	4.3%	$811
1/1/1984	10	3.9%	$683
1/1/1979	15	5.5%	$447
1/1/1974	20	6.1%	$305
1/1/1969	25	5.9%	$239
1/1/1964	30	5.3%	$210
1/1/1960	34	4.9%	$200

TABLE 1-6
Projected Future Purchasing Power in Dollars of a $1,000 Initial Retirement Income

Historical Inflation Rate		Dollars of Purchasing Power in					
		5 Years	10 Years	15 Years	20 Years	25 Years	30 Years
4.3%	(1989–93)	810	656	532	431	349	283
3.9%	(1984–93)	825	682	563	465	384	317
5.5%	(1979–93)	765	585	448	343	262	201
6.1%	(1974–93)	744	553	411	306	228	169
5.9%	(1969–93)	751	564	423	318	239	179
5.3%	(1964–93)	772	597	461	356	275	212

THE THREE-LEGGED STOOL

Financial needs during retirement are met from three primary sources—often referred to as the legs of a three-legged stool. The sources include social security benefits, employer-sponsored pension plan benefits, and personal savings. For each individual client, the planner must be able to pinpoint benefits available from social security and private pensions and encourage the client to maintain an adequate savings program to reach the targeted goals. This requires some general knowledge about each of the three legs and great deal of specific information about the client and his or her intentions. Below is an overview of the role of each of the three legs and an identification of the myriad of issues that must be addressed when developing a retirement plan for an individual. Each of these subjects is also covered more fully in other chapters of this book.

Social Security

The federal social security system provides retirement benefits (as well as disability benefits and survivors benefits) to a large portion of the workers—and their dependents—in the United States. Almost all employees living in the United States are covered by the program, except for certain employees of the federal government hired prior to 1984, railroad workers, and some employees of state and local governments. Eligibility for benefits is broad based—to be eligible for retirement benefits most workers must have 40 "quarters of coverage," which is approximately 10 years of employment earning at least a minimal salary ($2,520 in 1995). One statistic clearly demonstrates the importance of social security benefits: in 1990, 92 percent of all individuals over the age of 65 reported social security benefits as a source of income.

When to Retire

An essential element of any retirement plan is the age at which retirement occurs. Since social security benefits will be an important income source, the planner must understand when benefits become available and the impact of retiring at various ages. Under the retirement benefit program an individual with the prerequisite covered service will be eligible for retirement benefits as early as age 62, although benefits are actuarially reduced if they begin prior to attainment of normal retirement age. Normal retirement age is currently age 65, but for those retiring in the year 2003 or later, retirement age is gradually increased until it reaches 67 in 2027 (see table 1-1). With this changing normal retirement age, benefits will still be available at age 62, but with a greater reduction for early receipt due to the increased time period between normal and early retirement. If benefits begin after attainment of the normal retirement age, benefits are actually increased. Currently the increase is relatively small—3 percent per year; however, the percentage will be increasing up to 8 percent for those attaining age 62 in the year 2005 or after.

An additional factor to consider is whether the individual wishing to retire is going to continue working in any capacity. For individuals under the age of 70, social security benefits will be reduced if earnings exceed a specified threshold.

What Benefits Are Available

In addition to retirement benefits for workers, social security pays a number of other benefits. Retirees' spouses who are aged 62 (65 to receive full benefits) are entitled to an additional benefit. Divorced spouses are also entitled to a spousal benefit if the marriage lasted for 10 years or more. When a married (or divorced) couple includes two wage earners each wage earner will be entitled to the greater of the benefit earned on his or her own wages, or the spousal benefit that he or she is entitled to. Also eligible for an additional benefit are dependent children of a retired worker. Disability benefits are provided to those who have a physical or mental impairment that prevents them from engaging in any substantial gainful employment. Survivors benefits are eligible to widows and widowers (and divorced spouses) at age 60 and dependent children.

Higher Wages—Smaller Replacement Ratio

Calculating the actual social security benefits for an individual can be quite complicated. Fortunately, the Social Security Administration will provide benefit estimates. Without going into great detail here (chapter 2 covers this topic in depth), let us make several observations about how benefits are calculated. First note that benefits are based on the career earnings of an individual (usually 35 years of wages). Earnings are capped each year at the taxable wage base, and are also indexed for inflation. This means that benefits increase as wages increase, except that all individuals who consistently earn more than the taxable wage base will earn the same benefit.[6] Because wages are indexed in the calculation, the resulting benefit protects the individual from preretirement inflation. Additionally, benefits are protected from postretirement inflation, since benefits are indexed annually to reflect increases in the cost of living. This preretirement and postretirement inflation protection is an extremely valuable feature of the social security system.

The wage history, capped at the taxable wage base and indexed for inflation, is averaged and the result is referred to as the *average indexed monthly earnings* (AIME). To actually determine a benefit, this amount is multiplied by a formula. For an individual becoming eligible for benefits in 1995, the formula is 90 percent of the first $426 of the AIME, plus 32 percent of the next $2,141 of AIME, plus 15 percent of the AIME in excess of $2,567. The resulting amount is called the *primary insurance amount* (PIA) and most retirement, disability, and survivors benefits are based on this calculation. A worker retiring at the normal retirement age will receive 100 percent of the PIA for life.

Stepping back and looking at this formula, note that the benefits provided—as a percentage of final average salary—are lower as compensation increases. This is demonstrated in table 1-7, which describes retirement benefits for individuals at various incomes. Looking at the big picture, notice that this formula will provide retirees with larger incomes with less retirement income security, since the benefits will provide a smaller replacement ratio of preretirement earnings.

Where Social Security Fits in the Retirement Puzzle

Although social security benefits are paid to more than 9 out of 10 Americans over age 65, social security only makes up 35 percent of the income of elderly Americans compared to almost 80 percent in Sweden. Clearly, for most Americans social security benefits alone will not provide adequate retirement income. As mentioned above, this is more true for higher-income employees, whose percentage of salary replaced is lower than the nonhighly compensated.

TABLE 1-7
**Social Security as a Ratio of Final Salary for Individuals
Retiring in 1993 at Age 65**

Final Income	Single (Age 65)	Married (Age 65)*
$20,000**	39%	59%
$30,000	36%	54%
$40,000	31%	48%
$50,000	27%	41%
$60,000	23%	34%
$80,000	17%	25%
$100,000	14%	20%
$200,000	7%	10%

*assuming a nonworking spouse receiving the spousal benefit
**based upon an estimated AIME which considers annual
  salary increases of 6% up until age 65

When developing a retirement plan for any specific individual, the retirement planner will want to work with specific benefit projections provided by the Social Security Administration. However, sometimes this is not possible and, for the younger client, may not be all that relevant. Therefore the planner will want some other general projections to work with. Probably the most useful data is the information provided in table 1-7, indicating replacement ratios at various income levels. Note that when reviewing the data, you need to understand the marital status of the client and whether this is a one- or two-wage-earner family. For the client who has always earned more than the taxable wage base, the only relevant data is the maximum benefit provided by social security. Table 1-8 provides some historical data on this issue.

Recent law changes have further decreased the value of social security benefits for higher-income individuals. The Omnibus Budget Reconciliation Act of 1993 (OBRA '93) recently increased the portion of the benefit that is taxable for married individuals with provisional income (taxable income, tax-free bond income, and one-half of social security benefits) in excess of $44,000 and for single individuals with provisional income in excess of $34,000. Beginning in 1994, for those earning more than these amounts, up to 85 percent of the benefits will be taxable (up from the previous maximum of 50 percent). This change has

TABLE 1-8
Maximum Monthly Retired-Worker Benefits Payable to Individuals
Who Retired at Age 65, 1960–1993

Year of Attainment of age 65[1]	Maximum benefit			
	Original benefit payable at retirement		Benefits payable in 1992	
	Men	Women	Men	Women
1960	$ 119.00	$ 119.00	$ 674.60	$ 674.60
1961	120.00	120.00	680.00	680.00
1962	121.00	123.00	686.00	697.70
1963	122.00	125.00	691.60	708.20
1964	123.00	127.00	697.70	720.00
1965	131.70	135.90	697.70	720.00
1966	132.70	135.90	702.90	720.00
1967	135.90	140.00	720.00	741.30
1968	156.00[2]	161.60[2]	730.90	757.30
1969	160.50	167.30	752.30	784.00
1970	189.80	196.40	773.20	800.70
1971	213.10	220.40	789.10	815.60
1972	216.10	224.70	800.70	832.00
1973	266.10	276.40	821.20	853.10
1974	274.60	284.90	847.00	879.10
1975	316.30	333.70	879.10	927.40
1976	364.00	378.80	936.20	974.40
1977	412.70	422.40	997.70	1,021.00
1978	459.80	459.80	1,049.60	1,049.60
1979	503.40	503.40	1,078.90	1,078.90
1980	572.00	572.00	1,115.40	1,115.40
1981	677.00	677.00	1,155.00	1,155.00
1982	679.30[3]	679.30[3]	1,041.90	1,041.90
1983	709.50	709.50	1,013.50	1,013.50
1984	703.60	703.60	970.90	970.90
1985	717.20	717.20	956.40	956.40
1986	760.10	760.10	983.10	983.10
1987	789.20	789.20	1,007.70	1,007.70
1988	838.60	838.60	1,027.80	1,027.80
1989	899.60	899.60	1,060.10	1,160.10
1990	975.00	975.00	1,097.50	1,097.50
1991	1,022.90	1,022.90	1,092.50	1,092.50
1992	1,088.70	1,088.70	1,121.30	1,121.30
1993	1,128.80	1,128.80	. . .	. . .

1. Assumes retirement at beginning of year.
2. Effective for February 1968.
3. Derived from transitional guarantee computation based on 1978 PIA table.
Source: *Social Security Bulletin,* Annual Statistical Supplement, 1993

significant impact on affected individuals. For example, take a married couple in the 28 percent tax bracket with taxable income of $45,000 and $15,000 in social security income. Under the old law they paid $2,100 in taxes on their benefits; under the new law they will pay $3,570. This increase in taxes of $1,470 can also be characterized as a 12 percent decrease in aftertax social security benefits. Note, however, that the law did not change the tax rules for those individuals earning less than the above-mentioned threshold amounts.

Another important issue for both the planner and retiree to consider is whether the social security benefits available today will be provided at the same level in the future. The social security trust fund seems secure today, but when the baby boomer generation begins to retire, a significant strain will be put on the system. It is also not beyond Congress's control to raid the social security trust fund for other programs, or amend the program to reduce benefits. Certain changes to the system in the 1980s did reduce benefits (primarily by delaying the normal retirement age) as a means to shore up the system. These changes did help the integrity of the trust fund, but they may also portend Congress's willingness to reduce benefits prospectively. Also in the 1990s it has become popular political rhetoric to talk about reducing "entitlement programs"— including social security. Proposals are often bandied about to reduce benefits. Recent proposals include a further delay in the normal retirement age and a cap on inflation-related benefit increases.

Whether the current system remains the same or is reduced, social security cannot be relied upon too heavily. The retirement planner must understand that social security is an important stream of income but, especially for the more highly compensated worker, it will not provide anywhere near the preretirement income replacement ratio needed for a secure retirement. For lower-income individuals, social security becomes a much more central source of retirement income. However, even for the single individual retiring with an annual income of $20,000, social security provides a replacement ratio of only 39 percent—nowhere near the amount necessary for a secure retirement. Factoring in the additional possibility of future reductions in social security, everyone planning for retirement should be able to see why other sources of retirement income are necessary for a secure retirement.

Company-Sponsored Retirement Plans

A significant number of retirees will receive benefits from a company-sponsored retirement plan. As of 1990, the total number of participants, including active workers, separated vested plan participants, and retirees, was a whopping 77 million. Coverage at medium and large companies (over 100 employees) is substantial, with 78 percent of all full-time workers covered by some form of retirement plan. However, many in the workforce are employed by small companies or only work on a part-time basis. Looking at the total workforce, the U.S. Bureau of the Census in 1991 found that only 40 percent of the total active workforce is covered by a pension plan of any type.

Qualified versus Nonqualified

Company-sponsored retirement benefits come in many forms. The planner needs a basic understanding of the nature of each type of plan in order to understand the type and amount of benefits being provided—and to understand the probability of whether benefits promised will actually be paid. Chapters 3 and 4 will discuss the nature of the specific types of plans more fully, but several important trends and generalizations are discussed below.

Benefits are provided in two substantially different ways—from qualified retirement plans and from nonqualified plans. Qualified plans are plans that are entitled to special tax treatment if and when the employer meets specified qualification requirements. To qualify, plans must generally cover a wide number of employees, provide liberal vesting, and be prefunded. Contributions must be made over the life of the plan to an irrevocable trust fund (which is beyond the reach of the company's creditors), and such money must be used only to pay participants' benefits. The employer takes a deduction as it makes contributions to the trust, the trust is tax exempt, and employees are not taxed until distributions are made from the plan.

Usually (but not always) a company will maintain a qualified plan that provides a basic benefit to most full-time employees. It is not uncommon for a company to have an additional supplemental nonqualified plan that provides postretirement income for a small group of executives. These plans do not receive the same tax benefits, but plan design is more flexible. These plans come in many varieties and serve a number of goals for the employer. In many cases the plans provide significant benefits to the participating executive.

One important factor to consider with nonqualified plans is that benefits are never as secure as under a qualified plan. Because of certain tax rules, benefits cannot be prefunded through irrevocable trusts. Sometimes the benefits are not prefunded at all, while in other cases money is set aside to pay benefits but will be within the reach of corporate creditors in the case of corporate insolvency. The retirement planner needs to understand what benefits a client may be entitled to. Some probing may be necessary, since the client may not think of the nonqualified plan benefit as a retirement benefit. Nonqualified plans are discussed in depth in chapter 4. Issues discussed include benefit security, the types of plans provided, and how to determine the best time to elect benefit payments.

On the other hand, qualified plans cover a much wider group of workers and, as stated above, many retirees will benefit from payments from employer-sponsored retirement plans. Such plans come in two entirely different forms: the defined-benefit plan and the defined-contribution plan. As discussed in chapter 3, the difference between the two approaches is substantial, and every retirement planner must understand the basic nature of each.

Defined-Benefit Plans

Defined-benefit plans provide a specified benefit, usually in the form of a life annuity beginning at a specified normal retirement age. The most common type of benefit formula is one that specifies a percentage of final average earnings. The cost of most defined-benefit plans is paid by the employer—in 1991 only 5 percent of the plans required some employee contributions. Under a defined-benefit plan, contributions are required on a systematic basis so that the plan will be properly funded as benefits become due.

The major strengths of the defined-benefit plan include the following: First and foremost is that for the long-term employee, the defined-benefit plan often provides a substantial benefit for the entire life of both the retiree and his or her spouse. For example, as shown in tables 1-9 and 1-10, a 1991 Department of Labor survey for medium and large companies showed that the average benefit for an individual retiring at age 65 with a final average salary of $44,000 is a single life annuity of 29 percent of final average salary or a joint and survivor annuity of 26 percent of pay.

The majority of plans pay a benefit in the form of a life annuity—or a joint and survivor annuity for a married participant—that represents a percentage of the individual's final average compensation. By providing a benefit using final average compensation (usually the high 3 to 5 years) the benefit is protected from preretirement inflation. Note, however, that most plans do not protect against postretirement inflation—meaning that benefits are not increased to reflect the reduced earning power represented by inflation.

Another strength of the defined-benefit plan is that the employer takes the risk of the investment experience in the plan. Quite simply, the employer is responsible for contributing the amount necessary to pay for benefits. If the investment experience on amounts previously contributed is better than expected, then future contributions are reduced. On the other hand, if the investment experience is worse than expected, the employer contributes more. This is in stark contrast to the defined-contribution approach, in which the employee takes the risk of investment experience and, ultimately, the risk that the plan may or may not provide an adequate retirement income. Another important strength of the defined-benefit plan is that benefits can be based upon the employee's service prior to the establishment of the plan. This is a significant feature when a company that has not had a plan now wants to provide for the retirement income of current long-term employees.

Who Is Covered by Defined-Benefit Plans? The use of the defined-benefit plan today is much more prevalent for large and medium companies (companies with over 100 employees) than for small companies. In 1991, the majority of full-time employees of medium and large companies were covered by such a plan while only 20 percent of employees of small companies participated in defined-benefit plans. However, it is important to note that even for medium and large companies the percentage of employees covered by a defined-benefit plan has been declining. In 1980, 84 percent of full-time employees were covered by defined-benefit plans,

TABLE 1-9
Defined-Benefit Plans: Average Replacement Ratios*

Final annual salary	Straight life annuity	Joint and survivor annuity	Survivor annuity
Age 55			
$15,000	26.8	24.1	12.3
$35,000	20.4	18.3	9.3
$55,000	19.3	17.3	8.8
Age 65			
$15,000	39.3	35.1	18.5
$35,000	30.8	27.5	14.3
$44,000	29.0	26.0	13.4

*Source: 1991 Department of Labor Survey of Medium and Large Companies

TABLE 1-10
Defined-Benefit Pension Plans: Average Replacement Rates by Age and Final Salary for Medium and Large Private Establishments (1991 figures)

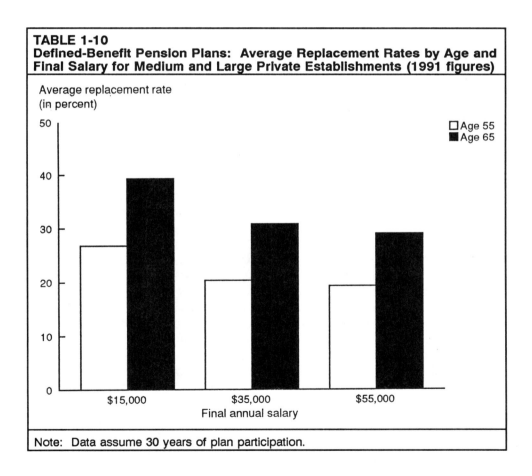

Note: Data assume 30 years of plan participation.

while by 1991 the percentage had declined to 59 percent (see table 1-11).

Another fact that demonstrates the decline of the defined-benefit plan is that the total number of private defined-benefit plans increased from 103,000 in 1975 to 175,000 in 1983, then decreased to 113,000 in 1990. Looking at the decline in plans from 1985 to 1990, one can see more of an impact on small plans than on large plans. The number of defined-benefit plans with 10 to 24 active participants decreased 36 percent between 1985 and 1990, while the number of defined-benefit plans with 500 to 999 active participants decreased 22 percent. The number of very large primary defined-benefit plans (those with 10,000 participants or more) remained stable between 1985 and 1990.

Impact of Early Retirement. Defined-benefit plans providing a life annuity benefit will make that benefit available at a normal retirement age, which under many plans is age 65. Many plans will permit early retirement, allowing benefits to begin prior to age 65, but with a reduction in benefits. The client wishing to retire prior to the normal retirement age must understand the impact on his or her benefits. Benefits are generally reduced because of three separate factors: (1) the length of service in the benefit formula is reduced, (2) the salary used in the benefit formula is lower due to the earlier retirement, and (3) the benefit amount is reduced due to the longer payout period.

In the large and medium-sized companies that sponsor the majority of defined-benefit plans, certain trends exist that have an impact on individuals retiring before normal retirement age. The statistics show that while some pension plans fully subsidize early retirement benefits (no reduction for retiring early) a typical reduction for payment at age 60 is 33 percent. A pension plan that would have provided 23 percent of final pay at age 65 might only provide 15 percent of final pay at age 60. In addition, the benefit that would have accrued between ages 60 and 65 is lost, further reducing the retirement income level. Also, the benefit level is reduced by lower salaries (assuming that salaries would continue to rise).

Impact of Changing Jobs. The one place where the defined-benefit plan shows its limitations is with the individual who changes jobs frequently. In defined-benefit plans (where the retirement benefit is based on such items as years of service and the final average salary), a worker who changes jobs four times in a career will typically receive only 50 to 60 percent of the benefit of a comparable worker who worked continuously for the same employer. This drastic impact is the result of benefit calculations that are based on the lower salaries (in the first several jobs), as opposed to a single benefit based upon the last (and presumably highest) preretirement salary. Also a worker who changes jobs frequently may lose nonvested benefits.

As well, when a worker terminates employment with a vested benefit, many defined-benefit plans will not pay out the benefit, but will rather pay a deferred retirement annuity. On the positive side, this feature forces participants to use the benefit for retirement income. However, because of the inability to roll the

TABLE 1-11
Percent of Full-time Employees Participating in Employer-Provided Retirement Plans, 1980–91

Retirement Plan Coverage	Medium and large private establishments[1]										Small private establishments[2]	State and local governments[3]	
	1980	1981	1982	1983	1984	1985	1986	1988	1989	1991	1990	1987	1990
Participants in defined-benefit pension plans[4]	84	84	84	82	82	80	76	63	63	59	20	93	90
Participants with:													
Normal retirement prior to age 65	55	56	58	64	63	67	64	59	62	55	54	92	89
Early retirement available	98	98	97	97	97	97	98	98	97	98	95	90	88
Ad hoc pension increase in last 5 yrs.	–	–	–	51	47	41	35	26	22	7	7	33	16
Terminal earnings formula	53	50	52	54	54	57	57	55	64	56	58	100	100
Benefit coordinated with social security	45	43	45	55	56	61	62	62	63	54	49	18	8
Participants in defined-contribution plans	–	–	–	–	–	53	60	45	48	48	31	9	9
Participants in plans with tax-deferred savings arrangements	–	–	–	–	–	26	33	36	41	44	17	28	45

1. From 1979 to 1986, data were collected in private-sector establishments with a minimum employment varying from 50 to 250 employees, depending upon the industry. In addition, coverage in service industries was limited. Beginning in 1988, data were collected in all private-sector establishments employing 100 workers or more in all industries.

2. Includes private-sector establishments with fewer than 100 workers.

3. In 1987, coverage excluded local governments employing fewer than 50 workers. In 1990, coverage included all state and local governments.

4. Prior to 1985, data on participation in defined-benefit pension plans included a small percentage of workers participating in money-purchase pension plans. Beginning in 1985, these workers were classified as participating in defined-contribution plans.

NOTE: Dash indicates that data were not collected in this year.

benefit into an IRA or other qualified plan, along with penalty inherent in the benefit structure for the terminating employee, defined-benefit plans are not very "portable." In today's world, where individuals are changing jobs regularly, this is a serious concern.

Defined-Contribution Plans

Defined-contribution plans come in many shapes and forms, but all have some similarities. In every defined-contribution plan, as money is contributed to the plan it is allocated to individual accounts for each worker. The accounts may actually be separate accounts, or simply bookkeeping entries in a common trust fund. In some types, such as the money-purchase plan, the employer contributes a fixed payment to each worker's account each year. In other plans, such as profit-sharing plans, the employer can contribute a discretionary amount each year. Regardless of the type, once contributions are made, any investment experience on plan assets is divided pro rata among the participants. Benefits are based on the size of the account—which equals contributions plus any gains or losses, income, expenses, and (in some cases) forfeitures allocated to the account. Defined-contribution plans almost always offer lump-sum payouts at retirement or when a worker leaves the plan before retirement. To participants, the defined-contribution plan looks simple—like a bank account—and they see their accounts increase with contributions and investment earnings.

Unlike defined-benefit plans, many defined-contribution plans include employee contributions. Today, in most cases, these contributions will be made on a pretax basis into one of three types of plans—401(k), 403(b), and salary reduction simplified employee pension (SARSEP). To encourage employee contributions, the employer may make matching employer contributions. Allowing employee participation drastically changes the nature of the plan. The distinction between personal savings and the company pension begins to disappear, and the company pension becomes a primary vehicle for employee savings.

Historically, as compared to defined-benefit plans, defined-contribution plans have often been considered the inferior cousin. From the employee's perspective, the defined-contribution plan doesn't look as desirable because the risk of the investment experience (and therefore benefit adequacy) has been shifted from the employer onto the participants. Also, since contributions are made annually and are based on current salary levels, the benefit level does not contain the preretirement inflation protection provided in a defined-benefit plan. On the other hand, in this day and age, employees change jobs regularly, and defined-contribution plan benefits have the advantage of being more portable than benefits from defined-benefit plans. Most plans allow distributions at termination of employment, at which time benefits can be rolled into a subsequent employer's plan or into an IRA. Assuming that an employee is fully vested in his or her benefit, moving from one employer to another (with similar plans) will not result in a penalty. As discussed more fully below, a major problem has been frightening numbers of employees spending—and not saving—the preretirement distributions that they receive.

Who Is Covered by Defined-Contribution Plans? Defined-contribution plans have been steadily on the rise. The total number of private defined-contribution plans (primary and supplemental) increased from 208,000 to 599,000 between 1975 and 1990. However, the rapid growth of defined- contribution plans appears to have slowed recently. Between 1989 and 1990, the total number of defined-contribution plans remained flat. The net increase in the number of primary defined-contribution plans over the whole period increased 43 percent. Most of the increase was in the plans with two to nine active participants, which increased by 66,425 plans, or 45 percent of the total increase in primary defined-contribution plans.

In medium and large companies, eligibility for defined-contribution plans has remained somewhat stable over the past few years. What has changed, however, is the percentage of employees covered by employers with cash or deferred arrangements. As of 1991, 44 percent of full-time employees were enrolled in a plan with a cash or deferred arrangement.

Early and Late Retirement. In defined-contribution plans, a participant retiring prior to normal retirement age will be eligible for the account balance accumulated at that time (or an equivalent annuity). The impact of retiring prior to normal retirement age means that the individual forgoes any additional contributions. As in the defined-benefit plan, early retirement also means that the benefit will have to be paid over a longer period of time. If an individual elects an annuity form of payment, the monthly payments will be less; if a lump-sum is elected, less will be spent each month in order to have the benefit last a lifetime. Under the law, a participant continuing work after attaining normal retirement age must continue to receive employer contributions and otherwise be treated the same as the individual who has not yet attained normal retirement age.

Changing Jobs. As mentioned above, an individual who is fully vested in his or her benefit is not necessarily penalized for moving from one company with a defined-contribution plan to another company with a similar plan. However, a problem will result if employees spend benefits that they are eligible for when they change jobs. Most plans allow participants to receive benefits as a lump sum at the time of termination. As late as 1991, almost two-thirds of plan participants were spending benefits that they were entitled to. Only slightly more than one-fourth of employees who received less than $5,000 banked the money. However, changes resulting from the Unemployment Compensation Act of 1992 may have a significant change on this behavior. Now participants must be given the option to have benefits rolled directly to an IRA or other qualified plan at the time benefits are paid. Electing the direct rollover simplifies the transaction for the participant and also means that no portion of the distribution will have to be withheld for income taxes.

Participatory Defined-Contribution Plans

The type of retirement plan that has made the most dramatic change has been the tax-favored employee-contribution plan. Although the 403(b) tax- sheltered annuity plan for nonprofit organizations and school districts has been around for a long time, a similar vehicle for the for-profit business world is relatively new. The hottest part of the retirement plan market is the 401(k) plan. According to a study by Access Research, Inc., an employee benefits consulting firm based in Windsor, Connecticut, at the end of 1993, Sec. 401(k) plans commanded $480 billion in plan assets, covered more than 17 million participants, and were offered by nearly 209,000 companies. The 1993 figure represented a 17 percent increase over that reported at the end of 1992. The average participant had an account balance of $20,000 and made annual contributions of $2,800. According to another study by Buck Consultants, an estimated 93 percent of all major companies now offer such a plan and approximately 74 percent of employees take advantage of the option.

Large companies have clearly come on board and smaller companies are following suit. Currently the largest growth area in 401(k) plans is for companies with fewer than 100 employees. According to the Access Research study, 10 percent of these smaller companies currently sponsor a plan, but the number is projected to increase to 14 percent by 1998. Also the study projects a 21 percent increase in plan formation among companies with 100 to 500 employees.

Employee Investment Direction

Along with the trend toward allowing employee pretax contributions, many defined-contribution plans now allow individual participants the opportunity to direct the investment of their account balances. This trend is significant since the long-term investment earnings will have enormous impact on the total benefit payable from the plan. Many in the retirement planning community are concerned about the choices that participants are making. One benefits consultant said, "Participants are investing in a way that almost guarantees that they won't have enough money to retire." In the early 1990s, studies were showing that participants were investing almost 70 percent of their accounts in fixed-income investments. Although investment choices have been changing, recent statistics show that 401(k) plan investments are less healthy than the funds in defined-benefit plans, which are generally professionally managed. In 1993, defined-benefit plans invested 36 percent of assets in equities. In 401(k) plans, a full 40 percent of plan assets are invested in guaranteed investment contracts (GICs), while in defined-benefit plans GIC allocation averages only 13 percent.

In the early 1990s, the benefits community began to be aware of just how conservative individual 401(k) investors really have been. In response, larger companies have begun to offer more investment education. Possibly in response to an increased awareness, participants have been moving more toward equities, generally considered a better long-term investment choice. In a survey of 813 employees, 60 percent of the respondents thought they were more knowledgeable investors today than they were one or two years ago, and 63 percent said that they were paying more attention to retirement investments. Almost 40 percent said that they had read or heard information that led them to think that a higher percentage of their retirement savings should be in stock or stock mutual funds. Less than half said that the information actually influenced them. However, the percentage of assets invested in plans is changing, and apparently employee education is making a difference.

The Role of the Private Pension

This section has clarified that the retirement planner must have substantial expertise in the private pension area to properly evaluate the benefits that a client will be entitled to. The planner must understand the difference between the defined-benefit approach and the defined-contribution approach, the impact of retiring at various ages, the affect of changing jobs, and so on. Also, as defined-contribution plans become more prominent, the retirement planner has some new accountabilities: counseling clients about appropriate investment choices under the plan and helping clients determine how much to contribute to employee pretax savings plans such as 401(k) plans. One topic that was not discussed here—but is another important role for the retirement planner—is counseling clients on the taxation of pension distributions. This important area is covered in depth in chapters 9 to 11.

The retirement planner should be aware of several significant trends that are occurring in the private pension field today. More and more companies are turning away from the defined-benefit plan and toward the defined-contribution plan as the primary retirement plan for employees. The change seems to be motivated by the cost of maintaining defined-benefit plans and not out of a concern for the retirement security of retirees. Many in the employee benefits community lament this change and are quite concerned about the impact on the retirement security of employees, although at this point it is difficult to tell exactly what the change will mean. With a more mobile workforce, it is possible that the trend toward defined-contribution plans will have its advantages. The other important trends include the rush toward 401(k) plans and the move toward giving employees individual investment choices. This all clearly means that the risk of financial security in retirement falls on the employee, and without careful choices retirement security will not be maintained. Therefore retirement planners must help their clients to make wise investment choices and maximize the opportunity to save on a pretax basis in order for their clients to get the most benefit from their plans.

Income from private pensions is an important source of retirement income. To the surprise of many, however, pension income for current retirees represents only about 19 percent of retirement income. Experts say this percentage may increase by the year 2018 to about 25 percent of total income for employees currently covered by a pension plan. On the other hand, one major concern is that pension plan coverage has been much higher for larger employers than for small employers. With 80 percent of all new jobs being added in the small business sector, future retirees will be less financially prepared unless trends change. What this means for most employees is that in combination, social security and private pensions will still fall far short of meeting retirement needs, and the third leg, private savings, will be a crucial piece of the retirement puzzle.

Personal Savings

Just from listening to the news, most of us are aware of the low savings rate for Americans today. In the 30-year period between 1950 and 1980, the U.S. savings rate exceeded 6 percent in 22 of the 30 years, *while between 1980 and 1994, the savings rate reached 6 percent only once, in 1984!* In all other 12 years the rate was lower than 6 percent.[7] As table 1-12 shows, the savings rate has generally been between 4 and 5 percent since the mid-1980s (except for a low of 3 percent in 1987). Other statistics also seem disconcerting. According to a LIMRA study called "The Baby Boomers: A Market in the Making," only 22 percent of respondents aged 22 to 37 have begun saving at all for retirement. The July 30, 1992, issue of *U.S. News & World Report* reported that in 1988, households headed by people aged 35 to 44 saved zero percent of their disposable income.

Something also looks wrong when comparing the savings rate in the United States with that of other parts of the world. Households in Europe and Japan have boosted savings dramatically in recent years. From 1988 through 1993 the savings rate in Europe increased from about 10 percent to about 13 percent, while in Japan the rate went from 14 percent to almost 17 percent. In the same time span the U.S. savings rate stayed within the 4 to 5 percent range (*Business Week,* February 21, 1994). In all, it is hard to imagine that individuals are generally saving enough to be ready for retirement.

A Successful Retirement Savings Program

The goal of any successful retirement savings program is to accumulate enough assets to combine with social security and private pensions to provide for a secure retirement. This means that at retirement the saver will want to reach some targeted amount. How this amount is calculated is quite complex, and is the subject of chapter 5. Once the accumulation goal is chosen, the saver needs a strategy of how to get there. In plotting a strategy the individual must understand that three components affect the outcome.

Length of the Accumulation Period. Accumulation of capital is impacted profoundly by the length of the accumulation period. The longer an amount is invested (and allowed to accumulate), the greater the affect of compounding. One way to illustrate this point is to calculate how much must be saved each month to accumulate a $1,000 nest egg. As table 1-13 demonstrates, at a 10 percent earnings rate, the $1,000 goal can be reached by saving $12.81 each month for 5 years, or merely saving $.75 per month for 25 years.

TABLE 1-12
Personal Savings Rate (percentage)

Year	Rate	Year	Rate
1973	9.4%	1987	3.0%
1975	7.4%	1988	4.2%
1977	5.6%	1989	4.6%
1979	5.2%	1990	4.6%
1981	6.7%	1991	4.8%
1983	5.0%	1992	5.3%
1985	4.5%	1993	4.0%

TABLE 1-13
Monthly Investment Needed to Accumulate $1,000

Years	Rate of return		
	6%	8%	10%
5	$14.26	$13.52	$12.81
10	6.07	5.43	4.84
15	3.42	2.87	2.40
20	2.15	1.69	1.31
25	1.44	1.04	0.75
30	0.99	0.67	0.44

To give your clients a realistic example of how a longer accumulation period can affect their retirement nest egg, try the following exercise. Suppose your client is Jill, a 40-year-old accountant. Her company has a 401(k) plan in which the employer matches 50 percent of each employee's pretax contribution and the rate of return on plan assets is 10 percent. You can show Jill, using table 1-13, that if she saves 6 percent of her $30,000 salary from now until retirement, she will accumulate a $300,000 nest egg!

Monthly contribution: $225 ($150 employee contribution plus a $75 employer match)

Total accumulation: Since saving $.75 a month results in a $1,000 accumulation, saving $225 a month (300 times more than $.75 a month [225/.75]) results in an accumulation of $300,000.[8]

Now show Jill what will happen if she waits until age 50 to begin building her retirement nest egg. If she starts saving 6 percent of her income at that time, by age 65 Jill will have accumulated only $93,750—a far cry from the $300,000 she could have saved simply by starting her retirement savings plan 10 years earlier.

Rate of Return. The second and possibly most important variable in any savings program is the rate of return earned on the investment. When looking at a long-term savings program, the rate of return will have an enormous impact on the amount accumulated. Take the following example:

> *Example:* George, aged 35, begins to save $2,500 a year for retirement and continues to do so until his retirement at age 65. How much will be accumulated at age 65 (disregarding taxes) assuming the following rates of return?

> An annual earnings rate of 5% $174,401
> An annual earnings rate of 10% $452,358

This illustration makes it painfully clear that the investment strategy must be considered very carefully. In this case the rate of return has doubled, but the accumulation more than doubles.

Clearly a good portfolio is diversified to reduce risk, and all investments will not earn the same rate of return. However, a well-diversified portfolio with assets that are earning a wide range of returns should still outperform the conservative, low-risk investment strategy. To illustrate, a $100,000 investment earning 5 percent over 20 years in a single investment would provide a total of $265,329; however, if the same $100,000 had been invested in five $20,000 segments, each earning the rates shown below, over 20 years the total return would be $534,946:

Each $20,000 Segment	After 20 Years
entirely lost	$ 0
0% return	$ 20,000
5% return	$ 53,066
10% return	$134,549
15% return	$327,331
Total return	$534,946

Amount Invested. Time and investment earnings can work for the benefit of your clients, but only if your clients save something! The rate of return on an investment of $0 is zero percent. Individuals saving for retirement have limits regarding how much they can spare, but they are more likely to be interested if they are shown illustrations such as the one above.

THE ROLE OF THE FINANCIAL SERVICES PROFESSIONAL

Even the mention of retirement planning evokes anxiety in most of us, and the typical reaction is to procrastinate. Although most people acknowledge that retirement planning is critical to achieve financial security, few have the knowledge, experience, and motivation to create and pursue a plan. The role of the financial services professional in retirement planning is to evaluate the client's retirement goals and financial situation, to educate the client about the realism of the goals and about alternative actions to achieve them, and to motivate the client to take action.

The financial services professional intending to offer retirement planning services needs to have a clear picture of the steps required to establish a retirement plan and how this process is related to financial planning. It is also helpful—and comforting—to see how other financial planners perceive the retirement planning part of their business. Finally, because an important goal is to motivate the client, the planner wants to be armed with an arsenal of reasons why retirement planning is crucial. Each of these issues is tackled below.

Comparison to Financial Planning

Retirement planning is a major subset of financial planning. Although a comprehensive financial plan includes retirement planning, for many clients retirement planning is the only concern.

Like financial planning, retirement planning includes six steps: (1) setting goals, (2) gathering relevant information, (3) analyzing the information, (4) developing a plan, (5) implementing the plan, and (6) monitoring the plan.

Setting Goals

Frequently the client's expressed goals are vague or imprecise. For example, a goal of retiring in comfort does not provide enough information to direct the remainder of the planning process.

The financial professional helps the client to quantify goals such as the following:

"I want to retire at age 65 with an inflation-adjusted monthly income of $4,000 in 1994 dollars without invading the principal of my savings."

Further refinement is usually necessary. For example, in the case of a married couple, will they accept a reduction in income upon the first death?

Gathering Information

Most retirement planners use commercially prepared financial planning fact finders to gather information about the client. Examples of important financial information include an inventory of assets and liabilities; securities holdings; annual income; estate planning information, including wills and trusts; relevant insurance coverages; social security retirement income estimates; and information about employer-sponsored retirement plans. Information regarding the client's risk tolerance (see chapter 7) and attitude toward financial responsibility for others is also important, as is any information that has significant financial ramifications, such as a health problem.

Analyzing Information

Retirement planners then analyze the information gathered in step 2 with respect to the goals specified in step 1. Usually the income goal is translated to an accumulation goal: "To achieve my retirement income goals I must accumulate $400,000 in personal savings over the next 22 years."

Sometimes it is obvious that the goal is not reachable, and the planner helps the client to reformulate goals. For example, the client may elect to delay retirement, to accept a lower standard of living, to work part-time during retirement, or to annuitize or draw down the retirement fund in lieu of using only investment income.

Developing the Plan

With an achievable goal and an understanding of the client's financial and personal information, the retirement planner can develop a plan of action. Sometimes the client requires little input, but more often the planner recommends restructuring the investment portfolio, changing insurance coverages, altering spending patterns, and other suggestions. Planners typically address pension alternatives including fund distribution options. Examples of these issues include whether or not to take a lump-sum distribution, and what type of annuity is most appropriate.

Many financial professionals would insert another step after developing the plan — gaining client acceptance. Even the best plan is worthless if the client does not understand it or fails to recognize its importance.

Implementing the Plan

If the client accepts the plan, the financial professional helps to implement it by facilitating changes in the portfolio and insurance coverages and taking any other necessary actions. Often commission-based planners are more successful than fee-based planners in this stage because sales commissions motivate the planner to motivate the client. Even so, the implementation step is often delayed while the client "thinks about it."

Monitoring the Plan

Retirement planners typically meet with clients at least annually to evaluate progress. Usually such meetings concentrate on measuring performance to decide if the plan is on track. However, often the client experiences changes in his or her financial or personal situation that necessitate alterations in the plan. Death of a spouse, birth of a child, and a change of jobs are just three of the important factors.

Professional Services

As a financial services professional moves into the retirement planning field, it is interesting to take note of what other professionals are doing. Robert W. Cooper[9] looked into this area by surveying three groups of practitioners, Chartered Life Underwriters (CLUs), Chartered Financial Consultants (ChFCs), and members of the Registry of Financial Planning Practitioners (Registry).

Financial Professionals' Retirement Planning Activity

Respondents to the Cooper study reported spending an average of 23 percent of their time on retirement planning activities. There was no statistical difference in this figure among the three groups. More than 75 percent expected to spend more time providing retirement planning services in the future.

Table 1-14 summarizes how CLUs, ChFCs, and Registry members allocate their retirement planning efforts among four specific activities. Note the greater emphasis for Registry members on portfolio repositioning at and during retirement.

TABLE 1-14 **Allocation of Retirement Planning Time by Area**				
Area	All Respondents	CLUs	ChFCs	Registry
Early preretirement accumulation (prior to age 55)	39.5%	41.2%	42.3%	27.0%
Late preretirement accumulation (age 55 to retirement)	30.3	31.2	30.3	28.7
Portfolio positioning at retirement	13.5	9.8	12.8	23.1
Portfolio repositioning during retirement	7.7	5.2	6.9	15.6

Table 1-15 shows, by percentage, various approaches to retirement planning used by each of the three groups. Registry members are more likely than CLUs and ChFCs to use retirement planning as a separate service or as part of a

TABLE 1-15 Percentage of Respondents Using Each Approach to Providing Retirement Planning			
Approach	CLUs	ChFCs	Registry
As part of comprehensive financial planning	38.9%	65.3%	98.2%
As part of specialized financial planning	65.5	64.8	61.8
In connection with product sales	69.9	67.6	36.4
As a separate retirement planning service	13.3	33.0	49.1
As part of a team of interrelated specialists	13.3	19.6	20.0

comprehensive financial plan. CLUs and ChFCs are much more likely to use retirement planning in conjunction with product sales.

Retirement Planning Issues: Importance to Practitioners and Perceptions of Clients

Another aspect of the Cooper study evaluated how practitioners ranked the relative importance of 42 retirement planning issues. In addition, practitioners were asked to rate the issues as they thought their clients would. Table 1-16 shows the rankings for every issue (of the 42) that was listed in the top ten by at least one practitioner group. The numbers shown represent the actual ranking of each issue.

With two exceptions, each of the practitioner groups included the same issues in their top tens. Differences among the practitioner responses are consistent with their responses in table 1-14 regarding the time spent on various retirement planning activities. Registry members ranked "selecting an appropriate investment portfolio for preservation of capital in the later preretirement years" highest, which is not surprising in light of the time Registry members spend in investment planning. Conversely, CLUs and ChFCs, both of which usually have predisposition toward life insurance, ranked "plan distribution: caring for spouse" highest.

An especially noteworthy difference between practitioner rankings and their perception of client rankings concerns retirement planning objectives. Each practitioner group perceived establishing retirement objectives and setting priorities for retirement objectives as being much more important than they felt their clients did. In fact, these steps are an integral part of a successful retirement plan. Leading the client through this process—something that clients would probably not do on their own—is an extremely valuable service practitioners provide.

Motivating Your Clients to Begin Planning for Retirement

Getting individuals to take retirement planning seriously often requires some convincing. The following list may help to motivate your clients—as well as review the important concepts described in this chapter.

TABLE 1-16
Practitioner and Client Rankings of the Importance of Retirement Planning Issues

Issue	Practitioners			Practitioners' Estimate of Importance to Client		
	CLUs	ChFCs	Registry	CLUs	ChFCs	Registry
Qualified plan distribution: Caring for spouse	1	1	10	1	1	5
Establishing retirement objectives	2	3	2	9	11	11
Minimizing taxes on distribution	3	4	3	3	4	1
Selecting an appropriate investment portfolio at retirement	4	9	4	2	2	3
Determining the amount needed for retirement	5	8	6	15	8	6
Determining the amount to save periodically for retirement	6	7	12	19	13	22
Qualified plan distribution guaranteeing a lifetime income	7	10	22	5	9	8
Setting priorities for retirement objectives	8	6	5	21	15	23
Selecting an appropriate investment portfolio for preservation of capital in the later preretirement years	9	5	1	4	3	2
Qualified plan distribution: Choosing the best option	10	2	7	11	5	4
Concern about outliving one's retirement income	12	16	16	10	16	13
Minimizing taxes	13	12	24	12	6	14
Selecting an appropriate portfolio for growth in the early preretirement years	17	14	8	16	14	7
Impact of postretirement inflation	19	15	11	8	7	9
Transferring the closely held business	20	11	17	17	10	10
Dealing with escalating health care costs after retirement	21	25	18	6	17	18
Qualified plan distribution: Choosing between a rollover and forward averaging	23	20	9	23	23	15

Notes: (a) Each number represents the actual rating by each group.
   (b) Some issues overlap and may rank higher if worded differently.
   (c) The table shows the issues identified in the top ten for any of the three groups.

- In the future, retiring at age 65 or earlier may not be so easy. Those individuals born in 1938 or later will not be entitled to full social security benefits at age 65.
- Retirement may last longer than planned. Life expectancies continue to be on the rise. In just the 10-year period from 1981 to 1991 the life expectancy for a 65-year-old increased by a full year!
- To be sure that funds are not depleted too early, everyone needs to plan on beating the odds and living beyond the average life expectancy.
- For most people today, maintaining the preretirement standard of living requires 70 to 90 percent of preretirement earnings.
- Due to inflation, a $1,000 monthly pension for the individual retiring in 1979 would have had the purchasing power of only $447 in 1993.
- Careful planning requires preparing for contingencies. Realistic possibilities include social security cutbacks, reduction in company pension benefits, periods of high inflation, and forced early retirement.
- As companies switch to defined-contribution type plans, more responsibility for retirement planning falls on employees. In many cases, participants must decide how much to save, when to start doing so, and how the company retirement money is invested.
- Americans are saving less than ever!
- Starting early can mean the difference between success and failure. Assuming a 10 percent rate of return, saving $225 a month beginning at age 40 will result in an accumulation of $300,000 at 65. Start at age 50 and only $93,750 is accumulated.
- Working with a trained professional can help an individual focus on the right issues, prepare a retirement plan, and follow through with it. The planner provides expertise, a dispassionate viewpoint, and motivation!

NOTES

1. *Statistical Bulletin,* July–September 1993, pp. 28–35.
2. President's Commission on Pension Policy, *Coming of Age: Toward a National Retirement Income Policy* (Washington, D.C.: U.S. Government Printing Office, 1987).
3. Bruce A. Palmer, *The Impact of Tax Reform on Wage Replacement Ratios* (Atlanta, Ga.: The Center for Risk Management and Insurance Research, Georgia State University, 1988).
4. Bruce A. Palmer, *1991 GSU/AACG Retirement Project Report* (Atlanta, Ga.: The Center for Risk Management and Insurance Research, Georgia State University, 1991).
5. Bureau of Labor Statistics, U.S. Department of Labor, *Consumer Expenditure Survey: Interview Survey* (Washington, D.C.: U.S. Government Printing Office, 1989).
6. This statement is true only if the individuals compared have worked over the same period of time. Since the taxable wage base goes up each year, an individual entering the workforce more recently will receive a larger benefit than one entering earlier (and obtaining normal retirement age earlier).
7. This measure of savings is based upon the Bureau of Economic Analysis, U.S. Department of Commerce, and computes savings as the difference between personal outlays and disposable personal income (after taxes and less social security contributions). Because consumer durables are regarded as current consumption and a flow of services is not imputed, some economists believe this measure underestimates actual household saving.

8. Tax-deferred accumulation is subject to income taxes as it is distributed from the plan.
9. Robert W. Cooper, "Retirement Planning: Client Needs and Professional Services," *Journal of the American Society of CLU & ChFC,* Vol. XLII, No. 6 (November 1988). Copyright 1988 by the American Society of CLU & ChFC, 270 S. Bryn Mawr Avenue, Bryn Mawr, PA 19010.

2

Social Security

Chapter Outline

Social security is the most important retirement plan in the United States. Technically, social security is the old-age, survivors, disability, and health insurance (OASDHI) program of the federal government. Most of us are aware of the substantial benefits social security pays to retired workers. But the social security system provides much more than simple retirement benefits. It also provides benefits to disabled workers and to families of workers who have died, retired, or become disabled. In addition, the hospital insurance (HI) program provides health care coverage through medicare to retirees, the disabled, and their families.

For retirement planning purposes, planners should be familiar with the entire social security system. This chapter focuses on OASDI benefits, which include old-age retirement benefits, disability benefits, and survivor benefits. Medicare, along with other retiree health care issues, will be discussed in chapter 12.

This chapter will review who is covered under the OASDI program, who pays for it, and what benefits are provided. The primary focus is on who is covered under the program and what benefits they are eligible for. However, in addition, the impact of social security taxes is discussed, as well as whether social security benefits are taxed.

EXTENT OF COVERAGE

More than 90 percent of the workers in the United States are in covered employment under the social security program. This means that these workers have wages (if they are employees) or self-employment income (if they are self-employed) on which social security taxes must be paid. The following are the major categories of workers who are not covered under the program or who are covered only if they have met specific conditions:

- civilian employees of the federal government who were employed by the government prior to 1984 and who are covered under the Civil Service Retirement System or certain other federal retirement programs. These workers are covered by government plans that provide benefits similar to those available under social security. Coverage for new civilian federal employees under the entire program was one of the most significant changes resulting from the 1983 amendments to the Social Security Act. It should be noted, however, that *all* federal employees have been covered under social security for purposes of medicare since 1983.
- railroad workers. Under the Railroad Retirement Act, employees of railroads have their own benefit system that is similar to OASDI. However, they are covered under social security for purposes of medicare. In addition, there are certain circumstances under which railroad workers receive benefits from the social security program even though their contributions were paid to the railroad program.
- employees of state and local governments unless the state has entered into a voluntary agreement with the Social Security Administration. However, this exemption applies only to those employees who are covered under their employer's retirement plan. Under an agreement with the Social Security Administration the state may either require that employees of local governments also be covered or allow the local governments to decide whether to include their employees. In addition, the state may

elect to include all or only certain groups of its employees. Prior to 1984, states and local government units were allowed to withdraw their employees from social security coverage. However, this withdrawal privilege is no longer available.

- American citizens working abroad for foreign affiliates of U.S. employers, unless the employer owns at least a 10 percent interest in the foreign affiliate and has made arrangements with the secretary of the treasury for the payment of social security taxes. However, Americans working abroad are covered under social security if they are working directly for U.S. employers rather than for their foreign subsidiaries.
- ministers who elect out of coverage because of conscience or religious principles
- workers in certain jobs, such as student nurses, newspaper carriers under age 18, and students working for the school at which they are regularly enrolled or doing domestic work for a local college club, fraternity, or sorority
- certain family employment. This includes the employment of a child under age 18 by a parent. This exclusion, however, does not apply if the employment is for a corporation owned by a family member.
- certain workers who must satisfy special earnings requirements. For example, self-employed persons are not covered unless they have net annual earnings of $400 or more. In addition, certain agricultural workers must have annual cash wages of $150 or more, and domestic workers must earn more than $50 in cash wages in a calendar quarter.

FUNDING

Part A of medicare and all the benefits of the OASDI program are financed through a system of payroll and self-employment taxes paid by all persons covered under the program. Employers of covered persons are also taxed.

In 1995 an employee and his or her employer pay a tax of 7.65 percent each on the first $61,200 of the employee's wages. Of this tax rate 6.2 percent is for OASDI and 1.45 percent is for medicare. The 1.45 percent medicare tax rate is also levied on all wages in excess of $61,200. The tax rates are currently scheduled to remain the same after 1995. However, the wage bases are adjusted annually for changes in the national level of wages. Therefore if wage levels increase by 4 percent in a particular year, the wage base for the following year will also increase by 4 percent. The tax rate for the self-employed is 15.3 percent on the first $60,600 of self-employment income and 2.9 percent on the balance of any self-employment income. This is equal to the combined employee and employer rates. An individual must continue paying FICA taxes as long as he or she continues employment, even if social security benefits have already begun.

Over the years, both the tax rate and the wage base have been dramatically increased to finance increased benefit levels under social security as well as new

TABLE 2-1			
Changes in Tax Rate and Wage Base under Social Security			
Year	Wage Base	Tax Rate	Maximum Employee Tax
1950	$ 3,000	1.50%	$ 45.00
1955	4,200	2.00	84.00
1960	4,800	3.00	144.00
1965	4,800	3.65	174.00
1970	7,800	4.80	374.40
1975	14,100	5.85	824.85
1980	25,900	6.13	1,587.67
1985	39,600	7.05	2,791.80
1986	42,000	7.15	3,003.00
1987	43,800	7.15	3,131.70
1988	45,000	7.51	3,379.50
1989	48,000	7.51	3,604.80
1990	51,300	7.65	3,924.45
1991	first 53,400	7.65	
	next 71,600	1.45	5,123.30
1992	first 55,500	7.65	
	next 74,700	1.45	5,328.90
1993	first 57,600	7.65	
	next 77,400	1.45	5,528.70
1994	first 60,600	7.65	
	additional wages	1.45	***
1995	first 61,200	7.65	
	additional wages	1.45	***
1996 and after	*	**	***

*Subject to automatic adjustment
**Same as 1994
***No determinable maximum because of unlimited wage base for medicare tax

benefits that have been added to the program. Table 2-1 shows the magnitude of these increases for selected years.

The social security program is essentially based on a system of pay-as-you-go financing with limited trust funds. This means that current payroll taxes and other contributions the program receives are used to pay the current benefits of persons who are no longer paying social security taxes because of death, old age, or disability. This is in direct contrast to private insurance or retirement plans, which are based on advance funding, whereby assets are accumulated from current contributions to pay the future benefits of those making the contributions.

All payroll taxes and other sources of funds for social security are deposited into four trust funds: an old-age and survivors fund, a disability fund, and two medicare funds. Benefits and administrative expenses are paid out of the appropriate trust fund from contributions to that fund and any interest earnings on excess contributions. The social security program does have limited reserves to serve as emergency funds in periods when benefits exceed contributions, such as in times of high unemployment. However, these reserves are currently relatively small and could pay benefits for only a limited time if contributions to a fund ceased.

In the early 1980s considerable concern arose over the potential inability of payroll taxes to pay promised benefits in the future. Through a series of changes, the most significant being the 1983 amendments to the Social Security Act, these problems seem to have been solved for the OASDI portion of the program—at least in the short run. The changes approached the problem from two directions. On the one hand, payroll tax rates were increased; on the other hand, some benefits were eliminated and future increases in other benefits were scaled back.

In times of high unemployment rates, social security disability claims normally increase in both frequency and duration. Such has been the case for the last few years. As a result, the disability trust fund will need additional resources in the near future. There are plans to strengthen this fund by transferring monies from the old-age and survivors fund.

The trust fund for old-age and survivors benefits will continue to grow and will be very large by the time the current baby boomers retire. At that time the fund will begin to decrease as the percentage of retirees grows rapidly. Until recently, projections indicated that the size of the fund would stabilize as the baby boomers died and the percentage of elderly returned to a more normal level. However, current projections indicate that the fund will be adequate only for about 35 years. Higher interest rates and lower unemployment rates in future years will act to maintain the solvency of the fund for a longer period. However, additional taxes or reduced benefits may eventually be needed.

The currently increasing size of the old-age and survivors fund has caused some concerns. The large trust fund surplus will lead to pressure for benefit increases, even though the surplus will be needed in later years. There is also the fear that Congress may decide to spend some of the surplus, thus leading to future financial problems for the OASDI program. To counter both these issues, some experts advocate a short-run decrease in the tax rate. Rather than have a stable rate of 7.65 percent, they would lower the rate by at least one percentage point and then gradually raise the rate in the future. This strategy would result in a tax rate approaching 9 percent during the retirement years of the baby boomers.

There is still concern about the medicare portion of the program. In the minds of many experts some combination of increasing contributions or decreasing benefits will be needed to keep the program viable into the next century, when the percentage of elderly persons in the population will increase dramatically. Some changes of this nature were part of recent legislation, but there is still a feeling that these changes are only short-term measures. Much more will have to be done. However, tinkering with medicare has significant political implications.

ELIGIBILITY FOR OASDI

To be eligible for benefits under OASDI, an individual must have credit for a minimum amount of work under social security. This credit is based on quarters of coverage. For 1995 a worker receives credit for one quarter of coverage for each $630 in annual earnings on which social security taxes are paid. However, credit for no more than 4 quarters of coverage may be earned in any one calendar year. Consequently a worker paying social security taxes on as little as $2,520 (that is, $630 x 4) during the year will receive credit for the maximum 4 quarters. As in the case of the wage base, the amount of earnings necessary for a quarter of coverage is adjusted annually for changes in the national level of wages. Prior to 1978 a worker could receive credit for only one quarter of coverage in any given calendar quarter. Therefore it was necessary to be earning wages throughout the year in order to receive the maximum number of credits. Now a worker with the appropriate level of wages can receive credit for the maximum number of quarters even if all wages are earned within one calendar quarter.

Quarters of coverage are the basis for establishing an insured status under OASDI. The three types of insured status are fully insured, currently insured, and disability insured.

Fully Insured

A person is fully insured under OASDI if either of two tests is met. The first test requires credit for 40 quarters of coverage. Once a person acquires such credit, he or she is fully insured for life even if covered employment under social security ceases.

Under the second test a person who has credit for a minimum of 6 quarters of coverage is fully insured if he or she has credit for at least as many quarters of coverage as there are years elapsing *after* 1950 (or *after* the year in which age 21 is reached, if later) and *before* the year in which he or she dies, becomes disabled, or reaches age 62, whichever occurs first. Therefore a worker who reached age 21 in 1982 and who dies in 1994 would need credit for only 11 quarters of coverage for his or her family to be eligible for survivors benefits. Practically speaking, note that under these rules individuals born in 1929 or later need 40 quarters of coverage to be "fully insured" for purposes of retirement benefits, even though fewer quarters of coverage are required for their families to be eligible for survivors benefits.

Currently Insured

If a worker is fully insured under OASDI, there is no additional significance to being currently insured. However, if a worker is not fully insured, certain survivors benefits are still available if a currently insured status exists. To be currently insured, it is only necessary that a worker have credit for at least 6 quarters of coverage out of the 13-quarter period ending with the quarter in which death occurs.

Disability Insured

In order to receive disability benefits under OASDI, it is necessary to be disability insured. At a minimum a disability-insured status requires that a worker (1) be fully insured and (2) have a minimum amount of work under social security within a recent time period. In connection with the latter requirement, workers aged 31 or older must have credit for at least 20 of the last 40 quarters ending with the quarter in which disability occurs; workers between the ages of 24 and 30, inclusively, must have credit for at least half the quarters of coverage from the time they turned 21 and the quarter in which disability begins; and workers under age 24 must have credit for 6 out of the last 12 quarters, ending with the quarter in which disability begins.

A special rule for the blind states that they are exempt from the recent-work rules and are considered disability insured as long as they are fully insured.

TYPES OF BENEFITS

As its name implies, the OASDI portion of social security provides three principal types of benefits:

* retirement (old-age) benefits
* survivors benefits
* disability benefits

Retirement Benefits

A worker who is fully insured under OASDI is eligible to receive monthly retirement benefits as early as age 62. However, the election to receive benefits prior to attainment of normal retirement age results in a permanently reduced benefit. (Note: Currently the normal retirement age is 65. However, beginning in 2003 the retirement age for nonreduced benefits will gradually increase until it reaches 67 in 2027. See table 1-1 in chapter 1 to determine an individual's normal retirement age.) In addition, the following dependents of persons receiving retirement benefits are eligible for monthly benefits:

* a spouse aged 62 or older. However, benefits are permanently reduced if this benefit is elected prior to the spouse's reaching age 65. This benefit is also available to an unmarried divorced spouse if the marriage lasted at least 10 years. The benefit is not payable to a divorced spouse who has remarried unless the marriage is to a person receiving social security benefits as a widow, widower, parent, or disabled child.

- a spouse of any age if the spouse is caring for at least one child of the retired worker, and the child is (1) under age 16 or (2) disabled and entitled to a child's benefit as described below. This benefit is commonly referred to as a mother's or father's benefit.
- dependent, unmarried children under 18.   This child's benefit will continue until age 19 as long as a child is a full-time student in elementary or secondary school.   In addition, disabled children of any age are eligible for benefits as long as they were disabled before reaching age 22.

It is important to note that retirement benefits, as well as all other benefits under social security, are not automatically paid upon eligibility but must be applied for.

Survivors Benefits

All categories of survivors benefits are payable if a worker is fully insured at the time of death. However, three types of benefits are also payable if a worker is only currently insured. The first is a lump-sum death benefit of $255, payable to a surviving spouse living with a deceased worker at the time of death or, if there is no such spouse, to children eligible for monthly benefits. If neither category exists, the benefit is not paid.

There are two categories of persons who are eligible for income benefits as survivors if a deceased worker was either fully or currently insured at the time of death:

- dependent, unmarried children under the same conditions as previously described for retirement benefits
- a spouse (including a divorced spouse) caring for a child or children under the same conditions as previously described for retirement benefits

The following categories of persons are also eligible for benefits, but only if the deceased worker was fully insured:

- a widow or widower at age 60. However, benefits are reduced if taken prior to age 65. This benefit is also payable to a divorced spouse if the marriage lasted at least 10 years. In addition, the widow's or widower's benefit is payable to a disabled spouse at age 50 as long as the disability commenced no more than 7 years after (1) the worker's death or (2) the end of the year in which entitlement to a mother's or father's benefit ceased.
- a parent aged 62 or over who was dependent on the deceased worker at the time of death

Disability Benefits

A disabled worker under age 65 is eligible to receive benefits under OASDI as long as he or she is disability insured and meets the definition of disability under the law. The definition of disability is very rigid and requires a mental or physical impairment that prevents the worker from engaging in any substantial gainful employment. The disability must also have lasted (or be expected to last) at least 12 months or be expected to result in death. A more liberal definition of disability applies to blind workers who are aged 55 or older. They are considered disabled if they are unable to perform work that requires skills or abilities comparable to those required by the work they regularly performed before reaching age 55 or becoming blind, if later.

Disability benefits are subject to a waiting period and are payable beginning with the sixth full calendar month of disability. Besides the benefit paid to the worker, other categories of benefits—the same as those described under retirement benefits—are available to the spouse and dependents of the workers.

As previously mentioned, certain family members not otherwise eligible for OASDI benefits may be eligible if they are disabled. Disabled children are subject to the same definition of disability as workers. However, disabled widows or widowers must be unable to engage in any gainful (rather than substantial gainful) employment.

Eligibility for Dual Benefits

In many cases a person is eligible for more than one type of OASDI benefit. Probably the most common situation occurs when a person is eligible for both a spouse's benefit and a worker's retirement benefit based on his or her own social security record. In this case and in any other case when a person is eligible for dual benefits, only an amount equal to the highest benefit is paid.

Termination of Benefits

Monthly benefits to any social security recipient cease upon death. When a retired or disabled worker dies, the family members' benefits that are based on the worker's retirement or disability benefits also cease, but the family members are then eligible for survivors benefits.

Disability benefits for a worker technically terminate at age 65 but are then replaced by comparable retirement benefits. In addition, any benefits payable because of disability cease if the definition of disability is no longer satisfied. However, the disability benefits continue during a readjustment period that consists of the month of recovery and 2 additional months.

As long as children are not disabled, benefits will usually terminate at age 18 but may continue until age 19 if the child is a full-time student in elementary or secondary school.

The benefit of a surviving spouse terminates upon remarriage unless remarriage takes place at age 60 or later.

Benefit Amounts

With the exception of the $255 lump-sum death benefit, the amount of all OASDI benefits is based on a worker's primary insurance amount (PIA). The PIA, in turn, is a function of the worker's average indexed monthly earnings (AIME), on which social security taxes have been paid.

Calculation of AIME

Even though they may initially seem rather complex, the steps in calculating a worker's AIME are relatively simple. They are outlined below and will be best understood by referring to table 2-2, which shows the computation of the AIME for a worker who attained age 30 and became disabled in 1994.

TABLE 2-2
Calculation of AIME

Year	Covered Earnings	x	Indexing Factor	=	Indexed Earnings	Earnings for Years to Be Included in Calculation
1987	$15,000	x	1.255402	=	$18,831.03	excluded
1988	16,000	x	1.196474	=	19,143.58	$19,143.58
1989	17,500	x	1.150905	=	20,140.84	20,140.84
1990	19,000	x	1.100090	=	20,901.71	20,901.71
1991	21,000	x	1.060568	=	22,271.93	22,271.93
1992	22,500	x	1.008600	=	22,693.50	22,693.50
1993	24,000	x	1.000000	=	24,000.00	24,000.00
1994	26,500	x	1.000000	=	26,500.00	26,500.00

$$\text{AIME} = \frac{\$155,651.56}{84} = \$1,852 \text{ (rounded to the next lower dollar)}$$

- First, list the earnings on which social security taxes were paid for each year beginning with 1951 (or the year in which age 22 was attained, if later) up to and including the year of death or the year prior to disability or retirement. The example in table 2-2 begins with 1987 because that was the year the worker attained age 22.
- Second, index these earnings by multiplying them by an indexing factor that reflects changing wage levels. The only years that are indexed are those prior to the indexing year, which is the year a worker turned 60 for

retirement purposes or 2 years preceding the year of death or disability for purposes of survivors or disability benefits. Therefore the indexing factor for the indexing year (1993 in the example) and subsequent years is one. For years prior to the indexing year, the indexing factor for each year is equal to the *average annual covered wages* in the indexing year divided by the average annual covered wages in the year in which earnings are to be indexed. Average annual covered wages are the average wages on which social security taxes were paid. Each year the government makes the figure for the previous year available. In the example the indexing factor for 1987 is 1.255402 because average annual covered wages were $23,132.67 in 1993 and $18,426.51 in 1987.

- Third, determine the number of years to be included in the calculation. For retirement and survivors benefits the number of years is 5 less than the minimum number of quarters necessary to be fully insured. Disability benefits, too, may be calculated by subtracting a certain number from the minimum number of quarters necessary for fully insured status. This number is five for workers aged 47 or over, four for workers aged 42 through 46, three for workers aged 37 through 41, two for workers aged 32 through 36, one for workers aged 27 through 31, and zero for workers under age 27. However, for survivors or disability benefits, at least 2 years must remain for purposes of calculating benefits. In the example the worker needs a minimum of 8 quarters to be fully insured, since 8 is the number of years after the worker reached age 21 and prior to the year of disability. Because the worker is aged 30, one year can be subtracted, which leaves 7 years to be included in the calculation. (Note: Up to 3 additional years may be dropped from the calculation if the worker had no income during the year and had a child under the age of 3 living in his or her household during the entire year.)

- Fourth, determine the years to be excluded from the calculation. These will be the years with the lowest indexed earnings. Of course, the number of years determined in the previous step must remain. In the example only one year (1987) can be excluded.

- Fifth, add the indexed earnings for the years to be included in the AIME calculation and divide the result by the number of months in these years. In the example the divisor is 84 months, which represents the 7 years of earnings included in the calculation.

As mentioned earlier, the calculation of the AIME for retirement or disability benefits excludes the year in which retirement or disability takes place. However, the indexed earning for that year can be substituted for the lowest year in the calculation if the result will be a larger AIME.

test

Determination of PIA and Monthly Benefits

Once a worker's AIME has been calculated, his or her PIA is determined by applying a formula to the AIME. The 1995 formula is as follows:

90 percent of the first $426 of AIME
plus 32 percent of the AIME in excess of $426 and less than $2,568
plus 15 percent of the AIME in excess of $2,567

The dollar figures in this formula are adjusted annually for changes in the national level of wages. The formula used to determine a worker's retirement benefit is the formula for the year in which the worker turned age 62. Therefore a worker retiring at age 65 in 1995 would use the 1992 formula rather than the 1995 formula. The formula used to determine survivors and disability benefits is the formula in existence for the year in which death or disability occurs, even if application for benefits is made in a later year.

Using the formula for 1995, a disabled worker with an AIME of $2,600 would have a PIA of $1,073.40, calculated as follows:

90 percent of $426	=	$ 383.40
plus 32 percent of $2,141	=	685.12
plus 15 percent of $33	=	4.95
		$1,073.47

(rounded to $1,073.40, the next lower $.10)

The PIA is the amount a worker will receive if he or she retires at normal retirement age or becomes disabled, and it is the amount on which benefits for family members are based. In 1995 a worker who has had average earnings during his or her lifetime can expect a PIA of about $850. A worker who has continually earned the maximum income subject to social security taxes can expect a PIA of about $1,175 for retirement purposes and a PIA of between $1,200 and $1,400 for purposes of disability and survivors benefits. The higher PIA occurs for workers who are disabled or die at younger ages.

If a worker is retired or disabled, the following benefits are paid to family members:

Category	Percentage of Worker's PIA
Spouse aged 65	50%
Spouse caring for disabled child or child under 16	50%
Child under 18 or disabled	50% each

If the worker dies, survivors benefits are as follows:

Category	Percentage of Worker's PIA
Spouse aged 65	100%
Spouse caring for disabled child or child under 16	75%
Child under 18 or disabled	75% each
Dependent parent	82.5% for one, 75% each for two

However, the full benefits described above may not be payable because of a limitation imposed on the total benefits that may be paid to a family. This family maximum will usually be reached if three or more family members (including a retired or disabled worker) are eligible for benefits. The family maximum for purposes of retirement and survivors benefits can be determined for 1995 from the following formula, which, like the PIA formula, is adjusted annually based on changing wage levels:

150 percent of the first $544 of PIA
plus 272 percent of the PIA in excess of $544 through $785
plus 134 percent of the PIA in excess of $785 through $1,024
plus 175 percent of the PIA in excess of $1,024

The family maximum for purposes of disability benefits is limited to 85 percent of the worker's AIME or 150 percent of the worker's PIA, whichever is lower. However, in no case can the maximum be reduced below the worker's PIA.

If the total amount of benefits payable to family members exceeds the family maximum, the worker's benefit (in the case of retirement and disability) is not affected, but the benefits of other family members are reduced proportionately. For example, assume a worker dies, leaving a spouse under age 65 and three children who are each eligible for 75 percent of his or her PIA of $1,000. Ignoring the family maximum, the benefits would total $3,000 ($750 for each family member). However, the family maximum using the above formula is $1,759.60 (rounded to the next lower $.10). Therefore each family member would have his or her benefit reduced to $439 (family benefits are rounded to the next lowest dollar). When the first child loses benefits at age 18, the other family members will each have benefits increased to $586 (ignoring any automatic increases in benefit amounts, including the family maximum). When a second family member loses eligibility, the remaining two family members will each receive the full benefit of $750 because the total benefits received by the family will now be less than $1,759.60.

Other Factors Affecting Benefits

Special Minimum PIA

There is a minimum PIA for workers who have been covered under OASDI for at least 10 years but at very low wages. This PIA is used only if it is higher than a worker's PIA based on actual wages. The benefit is first determined by multiplying $11.50 by the lesser of (a) the number of years of coverage minus 10 or (b) 20. This figure is then adjusted for the cumulative change in the consumer price index (CPI) since 1979. In 1995 a worker with 30 or more years of coverage under OASDI will have a minimum PIA at age 65 of just over $500.

Benefits Taken Early

If a worker elects to receive retirement benefits prior to age 65, benefits are permanently reduced by five-ninths of one percent for every month that the early retirement precedes age 65. For example, for a worker who retires at age 62, the monthly benefit will be only 80 percent of that worker's PIA. A spouse who elects retirement benefits prior to age 65 will have benefits reduced by 25/36 of one percent per month, and a widow or widower will have benefits reduced by 19/40 of one percent per month. In the latter case benefits at age 60 will be 71.5 percent of the worker's PIA. If the widow or widower elects benefits at an earlier age because of disability, there is no further reduction.

Delayed Retirement

Workers who delay applying for retirement benefits until after attainment of normal retirement age are eligible for an increased benefit. For persons born between 1917 and 1924, the increase is 3 percent for each year of delay up to age 70. The increase is 3.5 percent per year for persons born in 1925 or 1926 and 4 percent for persons born in 1927 or 1928. To encourage delayed retirement the percentage will gradually increase to 8 percent for those born in 1943 or later.

Earnings Test

Benefits are reduced for social security beneficiaries under the age of 70 if they have work wages that exceed a specified level. The rationale behind having such a reduction tied to wages, referred to as an *earnings test,* is that social security benefits are intended to replace lost wages but not other income such as dividends or interest. In 1995 social security beneficiaries aged 65 through 69 are allowed annual wages of $11,280 without any reduction in their benefits. Beneficiaries under age 65 are allowed earnings of $8,160. These figures also are adjusted annually on the basis of national wage levels. If a beneficiary earns in excess of the allowable amount, his or her social security benefit is reduced. For persons aged 65 through 69 the reduction is $1 for every $3 of excess earnings; for persons under age 65 the reduction is $1 for every $2 of excess earnings. Social security beneficiaries aged 70 or older can earn any amount of wages without a reduction of benefits.

The reduction in a retired worker's benefits resulting from excess earnings is applied to all benefits paid to the family. If large enough, this reduction may totally eliminate all benefits otherwise payable to the worker and family members. In contrast, excess earnings of family members are charged against their individual benefits only. For example, a widowed mother who holds a job outside the home may lose her mother's benefit, but any benefits received by her children will be unaffected.

Cost-of-living Adjustments

OASDI benefits are increased automatically each January as long as there has been an increase in the CPI for the one-year period ending in the third quarter of the prior year. The increase is the same as the increase in the CPI since the last cost-of-living adjustment, rounded to the nearest 0.1 percent.

There is one exception to this adjustment. In any year that the combined reserves of the OASDI trust funds drop below 20 percent of expected benefits, the cost-of-living adjustment will be limited to the lesser of the increase in the CPI or the increase in national wages used to adjust the wage base for social security taxes. When benefit increases have been based on wage levels, future cost-of-living increases can be larger than changes in the CPI to make up for the lower benefit increases in those years when the CPI was not used. However, this extra cost-of-living increase can be made only in years when the reserve is equal to at least 32 percent of expected benefits.

Offset for Other Benefits

Disabled workers under age 65 who are also receiving workers' compensation benefits or disability benefits from certain other federal, state, or local disability programs will have their OASDI benefits reduced to the extent that the total benefits received (including family benefits) exceed 80 percent of their average current earnings at the time of disability. In addition, the monthly benefit of a spouse or surviving spouse is reduced by two-thirds of any federal, state, or local government pension that is based on earnings not covered under OASDI.

REQUESTING INFORMATION & FILING FOR BENEFITS

Beginning in 1995 the Social Security Administration began to send an annual Earnings and Benefit Estimate statement to each worker aged 60 and older. By the year 2000, it is planned that this statement will be provided annually to all workers who are over age 25. In the meantime these persons should periodically check their records with the Social Security Administration.

Obtaining additional information about the social security system generally, or getting specific information about benefits is easy—simply a telephone call away. The Social Security Administration can be reached at (800) 772-1213. Forms, brochures, and even applications for benefits can be obtained by calling this number; in fact, applications can even be made by phone. While individuals are still employed, they should regularly complete and file Form SSA-7004, "Request for Earnings and Benefit Estimate Statement." The most important reason to make this request is to check the Social Security Administration's records of earnings history for accuracy. Any errors should be reported immediately. Errors are most likely to occur when an individual changes employers or has more than one employer at a time. The Social Security Administration suggests that people request the earnings and benefit estimate statement once every 3 years to ensure that errors are caught immediately—old errors may be hard to correct.

OASDI benefits will not begin until an application for benefits is made. Most applications can be taken by phone at the number mentioned above. To ensure timely commencement, clients should be encouraged to apply for benefits 3 months in advance. However, benefit claims can technically be filed up to 6 months after benefits are due to commence, since benefits can be paid retroactively for 6 months (longer in the case of a disability). If a client believes that he or she is entitled to a benefit, encourage him or her to file an application. A simple information request will not be given the same attention as a benefit application. Another important reason for filing an application is that if benefits are erroneously denied, they will be paid retroactively as of the application date once the snafu is straightened out. Also if, after benefits begin, an individual becomes aware that he or she is eligible for a second, larger benefit (for example, a spousal benefit), he or she must file an application in order to ensure receipt of the correct benefit.

TAXATION OF SOCIAL SECURITY BENEFITS

Until 1984 all social security benefits were received free of federal income taxation. Since that time, however, the rules have required that individuals with substantial additional income to pay tax on a portion of their benefits. Until 1994, the maximum amount of social security benefits subject to tax was 50 percent. However, beginning in 1994, the maximum percentage increased to 85 percent for certain taxpayers.

The portion of the OASDI benefit that is subject to tax is based on what is referred to as the individual's *provisional income*. Provisional income is the sum of the following:

- the taxpayer's adjusted gross income
- the taxpayer's tax-exempt interest for the year
- half of the social security benefits for the year

If the provisional income is less than what is referred to as the *base amount*—$25,000 for a single taxpayer and $32,000 or less for a married taxpayer filing jointly—social security benefits are not taxable. If the provisional income is between the base amount and $34,000 ($44,000 for a married taxpayer filing jointly), up to 50 percent of the social security benefit will be includible in taxable income. If the provisional amount exceeds $34,000 ($44,000 for a married taxpayer filing jointly), up to 85 percent of the social security benefit will be includable in taxable income. To summarize, the table below identifies the various cutoff points.

TABLE 2-3
Portion of OASDI Benefits Subject to Federal Income Tax

Taxpayer Filing Status	Provisional Income Threshold	Amount of Benefits Subject to Federal Income Tax
Single	under $25,000	0 percent
Single	$25,000–$33,999	up to 50 percent
Single	$34,000 or more	up to 85 percent
Married filing jointly	under $32,000	0 percent
Married filing jointly	$32,000–$43,999	up to 50 percent
Married filing jointly	$44,000 or more	up to 85 percent
Married filing separately (and living in the same household)	$0	up to 85 percent

The general description of how much is included and the various cutoffs is often sufficient for planning purposes. However, the planner may have occasion to actually calculate the specific amount of benefits that are includable as taxable income. The following explanation and example can be used to make this determination.

Step 1: Calculate provisional income.

Step 2: Determine appropriate thresholds, based on the individual's tax filing status.

Step 3: The amount of social security benefits included as taxable income is the smallest number obtained from performing the following three calculations:

(a) 50 percent of any provisional income that exceeds the base threshold plus 35 percent of any amount in excess of the second threshold

(b) 85 percent of the benefits

(c) 50 percent of the benefits, plus 85 percent of any amount in excess of the second threshold

Example: Peggy and Larry Novernstern are married and file jointly. They have an adjusted gross income of $40,000 (not considering social security benefits) plus $5,000 of tax-free bond interest, and are entitled to a $15,000 social security benefit.

Step 1: Provisional income equals:

preliminary adjusted gross income	$40,000
tax-free bond interest	5,000
50 percent of social security benefits	7,500
provisional income	$52,500

Step 2: Determine income in excess of the applicable thresholds.
Excess over base threshold:
($52,500 − $32,000) $20,500
Excess over second threshold:
($52,500 − $44,000) $8,500

Step 3: Amount includable in taxable income is the lowest of the following three amounts:

(a) 50 percent of excess over base threshold plus 35 percent of excess over second threshold
(.5 x $20,500 + .35 x 8,500)   = $13,225
(b) 85 percent of $15,000   = **$12,750**
(c) 50 percent of $15,000 +
85 percent of 8,500   = $14,725

In this case the $12,750 (85 percent of the benefit) is included as adjusted gross income.

WHEN TO TAKE EARLY RETIREMENT BENEFITS

One of the questions most frequently asked by clients considering early retirement is whether they should begin taking social security retirement benefits prior to the date that full benefits are payable. Currently a worker may retire at age 65 and receive full benefits or begin receiving reduced benefits as early as age

62. After the client looks at some threshold issues, the decision often rests on the economic issue: Are the additional benefits received in the years before age 65 sufficient to offset the benefits that will be forfeited after age 65 if retirement benefits begin early? This section will review the relevant considerations and provide a mathematical model to assist in the decision making. A table is included that is based on the model and that can be used as a guideline for determining whether your clients should elect reduced early social security retirement benefits based on their expected longevity.

Note that for some clients the solution will not be provided by the mathematical model. Other considerations, such as whether the individual is contemplating going back to work or whether he or she can really afford to retire are often more relevant. These issues are covered in more depth in "Threshold Issues" below.

Early Retirement Benefit Reduction Formulas

As described above, social security provides retirement benefits to four classes of persons. They are

- retiring employees who are fully insured and at least aged 62
- spouses, aged 62 or older, of retired workers who are receiving social security retirement benefits
- healthy surviving spouses, aged 60 or older, of deceased workers covered under social security
- disabled surviving spouses, aged 50 or older, of deceased workers covered under social security

The time that benefits can begin and the applicable benefit reductions for early commencement are different under each category. The rules for each category are summarized below.

Retiring Worker

Retirement benefits are based on a PIA. The PIA for retiring workers is the amount payable at normal retirement age, currently age 65. The PIA is based on a person's earnings history under social security. If retirement benefits commence before age 65, the retirement benefit is reduced by five-ninths of one percent (1/180 or 0.55556 percent) for each month that the retiring worker receives benefits before age 65. *Note: Benefit reductions due to early payout are generally permanent.* For example, if a person begins receiving retirement benefits when he or she is aged 62 years 9 months, the retirement benefit is 85 percent of the PIA. Since the person is receiving benefits 27 months before age 65, the PIA will be permanently reduced by 15 percent (5/9 x .01 x 27). The benefit is recalculated in only one situation—when a retired person goes back to work prior to age 65 and earns more than allowed under the earnings test ($8,160 in 1995). In this case benefits will be recalculated at normal retirement age, which will make up for some of the reduction.

Spousal Retirement Benefits

At normal retirement age a spouse is entitled to a benefit equal to 50 percent of the surviving retired spouse's PIA. However, if a spouse has worked and earned a benefit that is larger than 50 percent of the other spouse's PIA, he or she will receive the larger amount. A person whose benefit is based on a surviving retired spouse's PIA may begin receiving benefits as early as age 62. However, the benefit is reduced by 25/36 of one percent (1/144 or 0.69444) for each month before age 65 in which benefits are received. For example, a spouse electing to receive benefits beginning at age 62 will only receive 37.5 percent of his or her retired spouse's PIA. (The reduction factor is 25/36 x .01 x 36 = 25 percent. Therefore the person would receive only 75 percent of the full spouse's benefit, or 37.5 percent of the PIA.)

Spousal Benefits of Deceased Worker

The amount a surviving spouse receives after his or her spouse's death is based on the deceased spouse's PIA at the time of his or her death, unless the survivor's own PIA, based on his or her own earnings history, is higher. At normal retirement age a surviving spouse is entitled to 100 percent of the deceased spouse's PIA. However, if the deceased spouse retired early and received a reduced benefit starting before he or she reached age 65, the surviving spouse cannot receive more than the reduced benefit of the deceased spouse (or 82.9 percent of the deceased spouse's PIA if this is larger than such reduced benefit).

Note that the spousal early retirement reduction is somewhat higher than the reduction for the participant. The reason for this is that the early retirement reduction ceases at the worker's death. For example, assume a worker retires at age 65 and the spouse begins receiving the spousal benefit at age 62. The worker is entitled to 100 percent of his or her PIA while the spouse is entitled to 37.5 percent of the worker's PIA. At the worker's death the spouse is entitled to 100 percent of the worker's benefit.

Disabled Spousal Benefits of Deceased Worker

A surviving spouse may elect reduced benefits beginning at age 60 if he or she is not disabled; these benefits may begin at or after age 50 if the surviving spouse is disabled. If benefits start early, the benefit is reduced by 19/40 of one percent (0.475 percent) for each month before age 65 that benefits are received if the person is not disabled. For example, a surviving spouse who begins receiving benefits at age 62 will receive 82.9 percent of the deceased spouse's PIA. (The

reduction factor is 19/40 x .01 x 36 = 17.1 percent.) A disabled surviving spouse
who is aged 50 or older but under age 60 is entitled to 71.5 percent of the
deceased spouse's partner's PIA.

Table 2-4 summarizes these early benefit reduction rules.

TABLE 2-4 Social Security Early Benefit Reduction Formulas				
Classification				
	Retiring Worker	Spouse of Surviving Retired Worker	Healthy Surviving Spouse	Disabled Surviving Spouse Aged 50 to 60
1. Benefit at Normal Retire-ment Age	PIA	50% of spouse's PIA	100% of spouse's PIA*	100% of spouse's PIA*
2. Minimum Early Retire-ment Age	62	62	60	50
3. Reduction Formula	0.55556% x PIA x number of months early	0.34722% x PIA x number of months early	0.475% x PIA* x number of months early	28.5% of PIA* until age 60, then regular surviving spouse amount
4. Reduced Benefit Amount	PIA minus amount in Step 3	50% x PIA minus amount in Step 3	PIA* minus amount in Step 3	PIA* minus amount in Step 3
*If the deceased spouse received reduced early benefits, the surviving spouse's benefit is based on the deceased spouse's reduced benefit or, if greater, 82.9 percent of the deceased spouse's PIA.				

Threshold Issues

The decision of whether an individual should elect to receive benefits early
comes up in different contexts. For the retiring worker, it generally comes up in
three situations: as part of the decision regarding at what age to retire, as an
issue of need for the individual who has been involuntarily terminated, and as an
economic issue for the individual who has other potential sources of income in
the early years of retirement. For this third category, the primary issue is an
economic one, which is discussed in depth below. However, even for this group,
one threshold issue must be asked: Is the individual considering returning to

work at any time prior to age 70? If so, then the individual may lose benefits due to the substantial employment rules. See the next section, "Returning to Work: The Postretirement Employment Dilemma," to understand the full impact of going back to work after retirement.

For those individuals currently contemplating early retirement, the early retirement reduction factor may affect the decision to elect early retirement; more central to this decision, however, is whether the individual will have sufficient pension benefits and/or personal savings to meet retirement needs. When advising these clients, be aware that they (1) generally are not fully aware of the financial impact of having a longer retirement period, (2) do not fully understand the impact on their pension benefits when they choose to retire early, and (3) do not understand that early commencement may (or may not) substantially lower social security benefits (due to factors other than the early retirement reduction factor). Social security benefits will be most affected when the individual has a short working history or has recently seen a drastic upswing in wages. In order to determine whether early retirement will have a substantial impact on benefits, an individual can request benefit information from the Social Security Administration. Two separate information requests should be made, one indicating that early retirement will occur, and the other indicating that benefits will begin at age 65. Assuming—after considering all relevant information—that an individual can, in fact, afford to retire, then he or she will still be left with the decision of whether taking early social security benefits makes economic sense.

Another troublesome situation involves those early retirees who have been involuntarily terminated. Many in this group may feel that they do not have a choice—they need social security benefits now to meet expenses. These individuals should still consider carefully whether to begin benefits early or not. The major consideration is future employment possibilities. If they expect to go back to work, then taking benefits now means that social security benefits may be reduced or will cease during employment. As mentioned above, an individual who starts receiving benefits before age 65 and then goes back to work will have benefits recalculated at age 65. At 65, the early retirement reduction will be applied proportionately by the number of months in which benefits are curtailed by the substantial employment. However, post-65 employment can result in the permanent loss of benefits. Therefore an individual who is temporarily laid off will have to grapple with the difficult issue of how long the period will last and what his or her long-term employment prospects are likely to be. There is no easy answer for these individuals; the best an adviser can do is ensure that these clients are fully informed of the law.

When to Elect Early Benefits: The Economic Issue

As mentioned in the previous section, the primary factor in determining whether to elect reduced early benefits will be an economic one. From this perspective your clients will be better off receiving early retirement benefits if the present value of the additional benefits received before normal retirement age exceeds the present value of the higher benefits that are forgone after normal retirement age and worse off if the opposite is true. Clearly if a person does not survive to normal retirement age, electing to receive early retirement benefits is the better choice. But in most situations, a person will live past normal retirement age, and a mathematical comparison of the two options will reveal the answer. The essential factors for computing these present values are (1) the assumed real (inflation-adjusted) discount (interest) rate (which depends on both the assumed nominal discount rate and the assumed growth (inflation) rate for social security benefits), (2) the number of months before age 65 that early benefit payments will begin, and (3) the assumed life expectancy of the recipient (and sometimes that of the recipient's spouse).

The first two factors are somewhat easier to estimate with reasonable accuracy than the third one is. By equating the present value of the early benefits with the present value of the benefits forfeited after normal retirement age, one can solve for the break-even life expectancy. (This calculation is described in appendix 1.)

The break-even life expectancy can be used as a guideline when deciding whether to elect early retirement benefits. Table 2-5 presents break-even life expectancies for the four principal social security retirement beneficiary classifications for various early retirement ages and assumed real discount rates. If a person (and/or a spouse in the case of a retiring worker) is likely to live beyond the break-even age, deferring retirement benefits until the normal retirement age is optimal. Conversely if a person is unlikely to survive beyond the break-even age, electing to receive early retirement benefits is best. Armed with this information a person can decide, based on his or her own health and history of family longevity, whether he or she is likely to survive until that age and, consequently, whether to elect early benefits.

For example, assume your client, a fully insured worker, plans to begin early retirement benefits at age 62—36 months before the normal retirement age. Assuming a real (inflation-adjusted) discount factor of 4 percent, the break-even life expectancy is about age 82 years 8 months.

Analysis and Planning Guidelines

As table 2-5 shows, the break-even life expectancy increases as the assumed real discount rate rises. Figure 2-1 illustrates the increasing rate at which the break-even age rises as the assumed real discount rate increases; this is especially helpful for persons who are considering receiving reduced early retirement benefits beginning at age 62. For assumed real discount rates exceeding about 7 percent, the break-even life expectancy for retiring workers is infinite. (The same is true at discount rates of 10 percent for spouses and 6 percent for surviving spouses.) In other words, at these levels of assumed real discount rates, electing to receive reduced early social security retirement benefits is always optimal.

TABLE 2-5
Break-even Life Expectancy for Early Social Security Benefits[1]

Benefit Class	Age Early Benefits Begin	Real (Inflation-Adjusted) Discount Rate[2]			
		0%	1%	2%	3%
Retiring	62	77.00	78.00	79.02	80.08
Worker	63	78.00	79.01	80.05	82.01
	64	79.00	80.02	81.07	83.05
Spouse	62	74.00	74.07	75.03	76.00
	63	75.00	75.08	76.05	77.03
	64	76.00	76.09	77.07	78.07
Healthy	60	77.07	78.09	80.03	82.03
Surviving	61	78.07	79.10	81.06	83.09
Spouse	62	79.07	81.00	82.09	85.02
	63	80.07	82.01	84.00	86.08
	64	81.07	83.02	85.03	88.02
Disabled	50	102.08	117.00	167.02	N/A
Surviving	55	90.01	95.07	105.03	132.02
Spouse	60	77.07	78.09	80.03	82.03

1. The break-even life expectancies are expressed in a format of years and months. For example, 79.02 is age 79 years 2 months.
2. The real (inflation-adjusted) discount rate is derived by the following formula:
   real discount rate = (nominal discount rate − inflation rate)/(1 + inflation rate)
   For planning purposes, subtracting the assumed growth rate of social security benefits from the nominal discount rate is sufficient.

The Discount Rate

The discount rate is a measure of a person's preference for current benefits as compared with benefits in the future. In order to give up a dollar today most people require more than a dollar in repayment next year. Several factors affect how much additional benefit a person requires next year for deferring a benefit today.

The first and most objective factor affecting a person's personal discount rate is the currently available market rate of interest. If a person can invest at a 6 percent secure rate of return, he or she would never accept less than $1.06 next year to defer $1 of benefits today. However, market rates of interest may not be

TABLE 2-5 (cont.)

Real (Inflation-Adjusted) Discount Rate

4%	5%	6%	7%	8%	9%	10%
82.08	85.05	89.09	99.01	N/A[3]	N/A	N/A
84.03	87.06	92.11	107.01	N/A	N/A	N/A
85.11	89.08	96.05	122.10	N/A	N/A	N/A
77.00	78.01	79.07	81.07	84.07	90.01	117.01
78.04	70.09	81.06	84.01	88.02	97.09	N/A
79.09	81.04	83.06	86.09	92.07	118.05	N/A
85.00	89.03	97.05	N/A	N/A	N/A	N/A
86.10	91.10	102.08	N/A	N/A	N/A	N/A
88.08	94.07	109.08	N/A	N/A	N/A	N/A
90.08	97.98	120.00	N/A	N/A	N/A	N/A
92.08	100.12	149.03	N/A	N/A	N/A	N/A
N/A	N/A	N/A	N/A	N/A	N/A	N/A
N/A	N/A	N/A	N/A	N/A	N/A	N/A
85.00	89.03	97.05	N/A	N/A	N/A	N/A

3. N/A means the break-even life expectancy for the given assumed real discount rate is infinite. Electing to receive reduced early benefits at this discount rate is always optional.

sufficient to entice a person to defer benefits. Other, more subjective factors—such as a person's current opportunities to use the benefits today versus what he or she may perceive as more limited opportunities tomorrow; the state of a person's health and the anticipated future quality of his or her life; a person's expectations regarding his or her ability to survive and enjoy future benefits; and how willing a person is to take risks—may cause him or her to discount future benefits at more than current interest rates.

Another factor that affects discount rates is inflation. If inflation reduces the purchasing power of a dollar by 3 percent, for instance, a person would need about a 3 percent higher benefit the next year just to break even. Interest rates generally incorporate the market's expectations of inflation in the level at which the interest rates are set. However, social security retirement benefits are indexed for inflation. Consequently when current social security benefits are being compared with future social security benefits, the discount factor must be adjusted for inflation to derive the real discount rate. Although the real interest rate may not be a perfect measure of a person's personal real discount rate, real interest rates can serve as a starting point for estimating a person's real discount rate.

The real (inflation-adjusted) interest rate is computed by subtracting the anticipated inflation rate from the nominal (not inflation-adjusted) interest rate and dividing the result by the sum of one plus the inflation rate. In general, acceptable estimates of the real interest rate can be computed by subtracting the anticipated inflation rate from the nominal interest rate.

For many retirees the real rate of return on long-term corporate bonds, long-term government bonds, or Treasury bills may provide a feasible starting point for estimating their real discount rates. The real (inflation-adjusted) rate of return on a diversified portfolio of high-quality long-term corporate bonds over the period from 1926 through 1986 was 1.887 percent per year. For long-term government bonds the rate was lower—1.269 percent per year. The rate for Treasury bills, often used as an estimate of the "risk-free" rate of return, was only 0.377 percent per year, or barely above zero in real terms. Although nominal returns have often been quite high, these figures indicate that real interest rates have historically been quite low—less than 2 percent per year for any high-quality fixed-interest investment. In contrast, real compound annual returns on the S&P 500 stock portfolio, which is often cited as the best measure of the performance of the overall stock market, have averaged just under 7 percent per year over the last 60 years.

The particular characteristics of each client must be evaluated when estimating his or her real discount rate. However, based on the history of the past 60 years or so, appropriate discount rates should generally lie somewhere in the range of zero to 7 percent. Using a mixed portfolio of stocks and bonds as a benchmark for the real rate of return, 3 to 4 percent often would be an appropriate real rate of return to use as the starting point when estimating your client's real discount rate.

Planning Guidelines

Based on the values found in table 2-5, disabled surviving spouses should virtually always elect reduced early benefits since it is highly unlikely that they will live beyond the break-even age, even if one assumes a zero percent real discount factor.

Whether healthy surviving spouses should elect reduced early benefits will depend both on the assumed real discount rate and expected longevity. IRS unisex mortality factors (Table V of IRS Reg. Sec. 1.72-9 found in appendix 2) for persons aged 60 through 65 in normal health may provide a benchmark for evaluating your clients' life expectancies. According to this table, persons aged

FIGURE 2-1
Break-even Life Expectancles

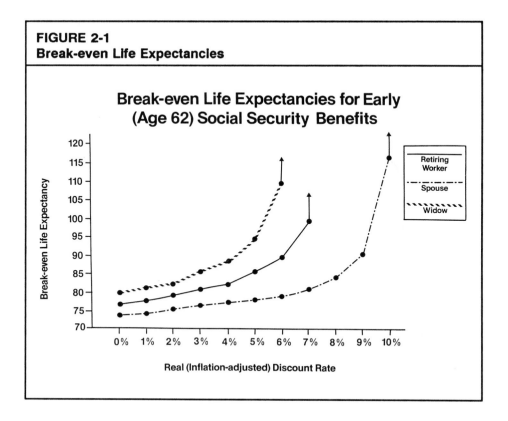

60 through 65 can expect to live to the ages of 84.2, 84.3, 84.5, 84.6, 84.8, and 85 years, respectively. However, women still have longer life expectancies for any given age than men have. Consequently a woman in normal health can expect to survive to an age somewhat beyond these ages; a man can expect to survive to an age somewhat less than these ages. Also, in each individual case, one should look at the family history to see whether there is a pattern of long or short lives, and adjust expectations accordingly.

Using the IRS mortality factors as a benchmark, the values in table 2-5 suggest that surviving spouses in normal health will generally be in a break-even position if their assumed real discount rate is between 2.5 percent and 3.5 percent, depending on the age at which they plan to take early retirement benefits. For discount factors above this range, taking reduced early retirement benefits generally will be the better choice; for discount factors below this range, deferring retirement benefits until age 65 generally will be the better choice.

The ages of married retiring workers *and* their spouses must be considered when deciding on early benefits. If a married retiring worker elects reduced early benefits, the spouse generally will receive the worker's reduced benefit after the worker's death rather than his or her full PIA. Consequently the critical benchmark life expectancy is the husband and wife's joint and last survivor life expectancy, not the worker's single life expectancy.

Joint and last survivor life expectancies depend on the ages of both the husband and wife. Each case should be evaluated using the joint and last survivor expectancy for the actual age of each spouse. These expectancies should be adjusted for the health and family longevity history of each spouse. However, we can use the IRS joint and last survivor mortality factors (from Table VI of IRS Reg. Sec. 1.72-9 found in appendix 2) for a husband and wife of the same age as a benchmark for discussion. The IRS joint and last survivor expectancies of couples of the same age for ages 62 through 65 are 89.8, 89.9, 89.9, and 90, respectively.

Based on table 2-5, couples who are the same age and are in normal health — and consequently a joint and last survivor life expectancy of almost 90 years — usually will be better off deferring the retiring worker's retirement benefits until age 65 if their real discount rate is about 5 to 6 percent (about 6 percent at age 62, declining to about 5 percent at age 64).

Single retiring workers must base the early retirement decision on their own life expectancy and assumed real discount rate. Using the IRS single life mortality factors for surviving spouses described above as a benchmark (84.5, 84.6, 84.8, and 85 years, respectively, for ages 62 through 65), single retiring workers in normal health generally will be better off deferring retirement benefits until age 65 if their assumed real discount rate is less than about 4.5 percent. In cases of real discount rates above 4.5 percent, electing reduced early benefits typically will be the better choice.

Break-even life expectancies for spouses of surviving workers who are receiving social security retirement benefits are lower than those for the other beneficiary classifications. Consequently, based solely on the life expectancy of the nonworking spouse, deferral of spousal retirement benefits until age 65 appears optimal more often for spouses of surviving workers than for surviving spouses. Once again using the IRS single life mortality factors as a benchmark, a healthy spouse with normal life expectancy appears to be better off electing to defer benefits until age 65 if his or her assumed real discount rate is less than about 8 percent at age 62, declining to about 6 percent at age 64.

However, the spousal early benefit decision does not exclusively depend on the life expectancy of the nonworking spouse. The retired working spouse's life expectancy also must be considered. Under the rules, the benefit for the surviving nonworking spouse increases to the worker's benefit after the worker dies, even when the spouse had elected to receive benefits before age 65 and was subject to the early retirement reduction. In many cases, especially when the spouse is younger than the retired worker upon whom the nonworking spouse's benefits are based, the retired worker will die before the spouse attains his or her life expectancy. Consequently a nonworking spouse who elects early spousal benefits may collect the added benefits and forfeit nothing if the retired working spouse dies before the nonworking spouse reaches his or her break-even life expectancy. Therefore the retired working spouse's life expectancy at the time the early spousal benefit will start, as well as the nonworking spouse's life expectancy, are critical values. If *either* spouse is likely to die before the nonworking spouse reaches his or her break-even life expectancy for their assumed real discount rate, the nonworking spouse will be better off electing to receive early benefits. Only if *neither* spouse is likely to die before the nonworking spouse reaches his or her break-even life expectancy should spousal benefits be deferred until the nonworking spouse is aged 65.

Simplifying somewhat, there is a 50 percent chance that any given person will die before reaching the life expectancy for his or her age and, correspondingly, a 50 percent chance that he or she will survive beyond that life expectancy. The probability that two people will *both* live beyond the life expectancy for their ages is about one in four, or 25 percent. Therefore the probability that one or the other or both will die before reaching their life expectancy is about three in four, or 75 percent.

IRS tables include mortality factors for the first death of two lives (IRS Reg. Sec. 1.72-9 Table VIA—Annuities for Joint Life Only—Two Lives— Expected Return Multiples, found in appendix 2), which can be used as benchmark life expectancies when evaluating whether a spouse of a surviving retired worker should take early benefits. For example, assume that your client is retiring at age 65, his nonworking wife is 62 years old, and both are in good health with normal life expectancies. Should the wife elect to begin early spousal retirement benefits at age 62 when her husband begins receiving normal retirement benefits?

The IRS benchmark first-death life expectancy for these current ages is 15.9 years. Therefore the spouse's "adjusted" life expectancy for use in table 5-2 is 77 years 8 months (62 plus 15.9 years). Based on this life expectancy, if your clients' real discount rate is less than about 4.75 percent, electing to defer spousal benefits is the better choice. If their real discount rate is greater than about 4.75 percent, they will probably be better off if the nonworking spouse elects to receive early benefits.

Conclusion

Whether to take reduced early social security retirement benefits is a critical decision for many retirees. Once certain threshold issues are considered, the decision is often an economic one. Will I receive more benefits (over the long run) if I begin benefits now or wait until normal retirement age? The essential factors involved in this decision are a person's life expectancy, the assumed real (inflation-adjusted) discount rate, and the number of months before normal retirement age at which the benefits will begin. Table 2-5 presents guideline break-even life expectancies based on these essential factors to assist planners in advising their retiring clients when and when not to take reduced early retirement benefits.

THE POSTRETIREMENT EMPLOYMENT DILEMMA

In many cases a client finds that retirement does not meet his or her expectations.   Such clients often seek to reenter the workforce through part-time employment.   In other cases, a client may feel the economic pressure of retirement and seek reemployment to add to his or her nest egg.

This section presents an example of such an individual reentering the workforce. The example illustrates the devastating tax penalties that await the unwary. It also illustrates many of the concepts discussed in this chapter. Finally, it offers strategies for effective planning for the client who finds himself or herself in this predicament.

> *Example:* Patty Shombert is aged 64 and single. Patty pays federal taxes at the 28 percent marginal rate, state taxes at the 3 percent marginal rate, and local taxes at the 2 percent marginal rate. Prior to going back to work Patty had an adjusted gross income of $25,000 and social security benefits of $12,000. Then, in 1995, Patty decided to take a part-time job at the local college. The job pays $20,000 per year. Patty will be disheartened to find out that she only gets to keep $3,874 of her $20,000 salary. That represents less than 20 percent of what she worked for.[1]

Here's why:

Patty will pay the normal payroll taxes that apply to all workers:

FICA tax on $20,000 salary at 7.65%	$1,530
Federal tax on $20,000 salary at 28%	5,600
State tax on $20,000 salary at 3%	600
Local tax on $20,000 salary at 2%	400
Total Payroll Taxes	$8,130

In addition, due to Patty's higher income, a larger portion of her social security benefits will be taxable (illustration 2-1). Without the job Patty would have paid tax on $3,000 worth of social security benefits ($840 in tax). With the job, Patty will pay tax on $10,200 of social security ($2,856). The increase in tax based on social security is therefore $2,016 (2,856 − 840).

Extra Tax on Social Security $2,016

Patty will also be subject to the earnings test. Since Patty is aged 64 she will lose $1 for every $2 earned over the threshold (in 1995 the threshold is $8,160 for a person under age 65). To determine the loss of social security use the following equation:

	Earnings	$20,000	
−	Threshold	8,160	
	Excess	11,840	
÷	2 (lose one dollar for every 2)	5,920	
	Lost Social Security[2]		$5,920

Total Amount of $20,000 "lost"	$16,066
Percentage Lost	80%
Total Amount of $20,000 kept	$3,934
Percentage Kept	20%

Note that the final column in illustration 2-1 shows taxes assuming that Patty was aware that her social security benefits would be reduced due to the earnings test, and that therefore she notified the Social Security Administration to reduce her benefits prospectively. This example softens the blow somewhat because she is not taxed on the higher level of benefits this year.

Planning for Returning to Work

Clearly, this example demonstrates the importance of careful planning. The retirement planner needs to emphasize to the client the impact of the decision to retire early, both economically and psychologically. If Patty had spent more time thinking through both issues maybe she would have decided either not to retire, or at least to try it before she committed to begin receiving social security benefits. If she had not started social security, Patty would have gotten to keep $11,870 of her wages when she went back to work; also she would not have been subject to the pre-age-65 reduction in social security benefits.

Note that one mitigating factor for the individual going back to work before age 65 and earning more than the earnings test allows is that lost benefits may be partially made up. Social security recalculates benefits at age 65 in this case, increasing the benefit based on how much of the pre-age-65 benefits were lost due to the reemployment. If you have a client in this situation, check with the Social Security Administration to get more information on how the increase will be calculated. Also be aware that this recalculation will make up for lost benefits only up to the individual's current normal retirement age—currently 65. Benefits lost to post-age-65 employment will be lost forever.

Other planning advice that is relevant to an individual who, like Patty, decides to go back to work includes:

- Keep income below the earnings test limit so that social security benefits are not reduced. Sometimes current earnings can be lowered by agreeing to receive partial payment as deferred compensation (after the earnings test no longer applies).
- Wait until after age 65 before going back to work, since the amount that can be earned without penalty increases from $8,160 (before age 65) to

---

ILLUSTRATION 2-1
Taxation of Social Security in Patty Shombert example

Social Security Taxation Work Sheet

Check proper box for filing status:
- ☒ A. S, HH, QW
- ☐ B. MFJ
- ☐ C. MFS and lived with spouse at any time during the year
- ☐ D. MFS and did not live with spouse at any time during the year

	No Job	$20,000/yr. Job	$20,000/yr. job; pre-payment of $5,920 benefits
1. Enter one-half of social security benefits.	$ 6,000	$ 6,000	$ 3,040
2. Adjusted gross income plus tax-exempt interest.	25,000	45,000	45,000
3. Add lines 1 and 2. (This is provisional income.)	31,000	51,000	48,040
4. Enter: $25,000 if Box A or D checked above, $32,000 if Box B checked above, or $0 if Box C checked above.	25,000	25,000	25,000
5. Subtract line 4 from line 3.	6,000	26,000	23,040
6. Divide line 5 by 2.	3,000	13,000	11,505
7. Enter the smaller of line 1 or line 6.	3,000	6,000	3,010

(If line 3 is less than $34,000 if Box A or D is checked above; $44,000 if Box B is checked above; or $0 if Box C is checked above, then enter amount from line 7 on line 15 below and skip lines 8–14.)

	No Job	$20,000/yr. Job	$20,000/yr. job; pre-payment of $5,920 benefits
8. Enter smaller of amount from line 7 above or: $4,500 if Box A or D is checked above, $6,000 if Box B is checked above, or $0 if Box C is checked above.		$ 4,500	$ 3,040
9. Enter amount from line 3 above.			
10. Enter: $34,000 if Box A or D is checked above, $44,000 if Box B is checked above, or $0 if Box C is checked above.		51,000 34,000	48,040 34,000
11. Subtract line 10 from line 9.		17,000	14,040
12. Multiply line 11 by 85%.		14,450	11,934
13. Add line 8 and line 12.		18,950	14,974
14. Multiply total social security benefits by 85%.		10,200	6,080
15. Enter smaller of line 13 or line 14. This is the amount of taxable social security.	$ 3,000	10,200	6,080

$11,280 after age 65 (in 1995). Also, the earnings test reduction is lower after age 65 — the reduction is one dollar for every three dollars of wages earned.

- The retiring worker returning to work after age 70 is not subject to a reduction in social security benefits, regardless of the amount of earnings.
- Minimize the portion of social security benefits subject to income tax by lowering nonemployment income.
- If wages are going to exceed the earnings test amount, notify the Social Security Administration in advance, so benefits can be reduced in the current year (as demonstrated in the last column of illustration 2-1). This reduction will effectively lower taxes for the current year.

NOTES

1. This example assumes that social security benefits are not taxed at the state and local level and that Patty does not notify the Social Security Administration to reduce her benefits prospectively.
2. Next year's social security will be reduced by this amount.

3

Sources of Retirement Income: Qualified Retirement Plans

Chapter Outline

Chapters 3 and 4 have two purposes. The first purpose is to help you sort through the maze of retirement plan benefits to which your clients may be entitled. The basic features of retirement plans are identified, and the typical choices that a participant has under such plans are reviewed. However, note that prior to advising a client about his or her rights under a specific retirement program, all relevant contracts, summary plan descriptions, and other descriptive documents should be reviewed.

The second purpose of the chapters is to address general retirement planning principles that may assist you when working with a client who is either self-employed or in a position to have control over the design of his or her employer's retirement program. Note that these materials are intended as an overview, and a planner will need to have a complete understanding of the complex inner workings of the various types of retirement plans prior to encouraging a client to take any specific course of action. Some suggestions for further study can be found in appendix 3.

CATEGORIZING RETIREMENT PLANS

The menu of retirement benefit programs used today is quite large—with each type of plan having its own unique characteristics. However, plans do fall within categories, and understanding how the plan is categorized goes a long way toward understanding how it works. The types of formal retirement vehicles your clients may have can be broadly classified in the following five ways:

- qualified versus nonqualified plans
- defined-benefit versus defined-contribution plans
- pension versus profit-sharing plans
- Keogh versus corporate plans
- contributory versus employer-only plans

Let's take a closer look.

Qualified versus Nonqualified Plans

Plans categorized as qualified are technically those plans subject to IRC Sec. 401(a). These types of plans include

- profit-sharing plans
- money-purchase pension plans
- target-benefit pension plans
- 401(k) plans
- defined-benefit pension plans
- stock bonus plans and ESOPs

Although the funding requirements for different types of qualified plans vary, all qualified plans are prefunded, meaning that the employer sets aside money in an irrevocable trust fund that is later used to provide benefits for the employees.[1]

In exchange for compliance with a large number of qualification requirements (see table 3-1), each of these plans is eligible for the following special tax treatment:

- The employer takes a tax deduction for contributions to the trust.
- The trust is tax exempt.
- The employee pays taxes when benefits are received.
- Plan distributions may be eligible for special income averaging.

TABLE 3-1
Major Qualification Rules for Qualified Retirement Plans

1. The plan must be in writing.
2. The plan must be permanent. (Note: Even though the intention of permanency is required, a plan can be amended or terminated.)
3. The plan must be communicated to the employees according to statutory guidelines.
4. The plan must be operated for the exclusive benefit of the employees or their beneficiaries.
5. The plan must not discriminate in terms of coverage.
6. The plan must not discriminate in terms of contributions or benefits.
7. The plan must meet funding requirements.
8. The plan's funds cannot be recaptured by the employer except when the plan is terminated and all plan liabilities are satisfied.
9. The plan must limit the amount of contributions and benefits available to participants.
10. The plan must incorporate top-heavy rules.
11. The plan must meet vesting requirements.
12. The plan can provide only "incidental" death benefits.

The qualification requirements are complex—essentially qualified plans receive the special tax treatment in exchange for covering a substantial percentage of the employees, allowing for the vesting of benefits within a limited time, and providing benefits that do not discriminate in favor of the highly compensated.

On the other side of the spectrum, nonqualified plans are generally taxed under the ordinary rules for taxing employee compensation. There are two essential components to these rules: first, the employer receives a deduction only when the employee is required to report taxable income, and second, the employee is taxed at the time the employer confers cash or other property on the employee. In most types of nonqualified plans, the objective is to promise deferred benefits and at the same time defer taxation until benefits are distributed.

This tax distinction is significant. In a qualified plan, the employer is getting the same tax treatment as if the employee received cash, while the employee defers tax—which is like getting an interest-free loan in the amount of the deferred tax. To put it another way, take, for example, John, who pays federal taxes at the 36 percent rate. In a nonqualified plan the employer picks up the tab for the employee's "interest-free loan" by deferring the deduction that would have been available the employer had paid the retirement savings to the employee in currently taxable income.

Traditional types of deferred-compensation plans discussed in chapter 4 include

- salary reduction plans
- excess-benefit plans
- supplemental employee retirement plans (SERPs)

In this text the term *nonqualified plan* also includes a number of other types of executive compensation programs. Several of the incentive plans, as discussed in the next chapter, are subject to special tax rules.

In contrast to qualified plans, nonqualified plans are generally established only for a few key employees. In fact, to ensure that certain ERISA rules do not apply, the plans must be limited to a small group of highly compensated and/or management personnel.

Two types of plans discussed in the next two chapters do not cleanly fall within either category: 403(b) tax-sheltered annuities and SEPs. Technically these plans are not qualified plans since they are not subject to all the rules of IRC Sec. 401(a). Each is authorized by its own Code section and has its own set of rules—although some of the qualified plan rules have been borrowed in each case. 403(b) plans and SEPs are closely related to qualified plans since both are employer-sponsored plans with the same special tax treatment as qualified plans—except that distributions are not eligible for special income averaging.

A third plan that does not fall within either category is the IRA. The IRA is unique in that it is a plan sponsored by the employee, not the employer. The IRA still has some similarity to a qualified plan: an individual may be eligible to take a deduction for contributions, contributions held in the IRA grow tax free, and amounts are fully taxed at the time of distribution.[2] However, IRA distributions are not eligible for special income averaging. As you will see in chapters 8 through 11, many of the distribution tax requirements and special penalty taxes that apply to qualified plans also apply to these three other tax-preferred plans—403(b)s, SEPs, and IRAs.

Retirement Planning Considerations: Nonqualified Plans

When dealing with a client who is a participant in a nonqualified plan, the planner must be aware of a number of issues. First, if benefits are paid in a single sum, the entire benefit is included as ordinary income. This is in contrast to the qualified plan, in which special 5-year or 10-year averaging may be available.

Second, retirement funds are more secure in a qualified plan than in a nonqualified plan. Promised benefits from a nonqualified plan are subject to loss for a variety of reasons.

- *The nonqualified plan may contain a severe forfeiture provision.* For example, the plan may provide that benefits are forfeited if the employee terminates employment prior to age 65. In contrast, your client's benefits are fully vested in a qualified plan after seven years or less.
- *The nonqualified plan typically will not pay benefits if the employer goes bankrupt.* In virtually all nonqualified plans today, any amounts held to satisfy benefit payments are subject to the claims of corporate creditors. Funds in a qualified plan, however, are held in an irrevocable trust outside the claims of creditors.
- *The employer may default on a promise to pay nonqualified benefits.* Unlike qualified plans, which are prefunded under stringent legal requirements, the sponsor is not required to set aside funds to pay nonqualified benefits.

Another risk to the nonqualified plan is the more tenuous timing of taxation to the employees. Although the plans are generally set up to defer taxation until benefits are distributed, the applicable tax rules are somewhat subjective and are difficult to measure with certainty.

Despite all the problems associated with them, nonqualified plans have an important role in the marketplace for upscale clients. Plans may provide benefits in excess of the qualified plan limits, as well as benefits that will not be subject to the 15 percent excise tax applicable to qualified plans (discussed in chapter 11). Thus a client with a two-tiered retirement program of both qualified and nonqualified plans is in the best position to plan for retirement. Conversely an upscale client without the second nonqualified tier may be subject to an inadequate replacement ratio because of the legislative caps placed on qualified plan benefits. Nonqualified plans are discussed further in the next chapter.

Retirement Planning Considerations: Qualified Plans

In addition to enabling your clients to have before-tax contributions made toward their retirement, a qualified plan enables the earnings on plan investments to be tax deferred no matter what investment vehicle is chosen. Therefore one important advantage available to clients in a qualified plan is that investment of qualified plan funds need not be restricted to lower-paying tax-sheltered investments.

The results of using the before-tax contribution and tax-deferred accumulation features of a qualified plan for retirement savings, as compared with having clients save on their own for retirement, are illustrated in the following case study.

Case Study: John Johnson

John Johnson is 45 years old, earns $40,000, and plans to retire at age 65. He wants to put aside 15 percent of his salary for retirement for the next 20 years. John pays federal and state taxes equal to a combined 30 percent rate.

The Current Year

	Personal Savings	Retirement Plan
Gross earnings	$40,000	$40,000
Retirement plan contribution	–	6,000
Current compensation	$40,000	$34,000
Federal and state taxes (30%)	12,000	10,200
Net pay	28,000	23,800
Living expenses	23,800	23,800
Personal savings for retirement	4,200	-0-

Immediately it is clear that by taking advantage of a retirement plan, John has $1,800 more ($6,000 − $4,200) than he would by relying solely on a savings plan. Now let's look at what happens to John's personal savings versus his retirement plan contribution when he reaches age 65.

At Age 65

	Personal Savings	Retirement Plan
Pension accumulation	10% before tax/ 7% after tax	10% before tax/ 10% after tax
Savings accumulation (annual contribution plus earnings)	$184,234	$378,015
Taxes on lump-sum distribution	-0-	$ 94,131 *
Net cash for retirement	$184,234	$283,883
Overall gain for retirement plan (Approximately 54% better than with a personal savings program)		$ 99,649

* Using 1994 tax rates and 5-year averaging

DISTINCTIONS AMONG QUALIFIED PLANS

A lot can be learned about a qualified plan by knowing how it is categorized. Every plan falls into either the defined-benefit category or the defined-contribution category. Further, every plan falls into either the pension category or the profit-sharing category. It is also important to know what type of entity sponsors the plan. Finally, the planner should know which types of plans allow pretax contributions. The following explains how plans are categorized and what the categories mean. Refer to table 3-5 at the end of this chapter for review.

Defined-Benefit versus Defined-Contribution

Qualified plans are categorized as either defined-benefit plans or defined-contribution plans. A defined-benefit plan specifies the benefits that an employee receives, and the contributions required by the employer vary annually depending on what is needed to pay the promised benefits. The maximum annual benefit that can be funded for any given employee in a qualified defined-benefit plan is 100 percent of the employee's average compensation for his or her 3 consecutive years of highest pay, up to a maximum of $120,000 per year in 1995 (indexed to inflation). Defined-benefit plans work by using a benefit formula to stipulate a promised retirement benefit. This benefit is typically geared to a percentage of the employee's final salary (for example, 50 percent of final salary). Under a defined-benefit plan, an actuary projects future benefits and then determines annual required contributions under one of several funding methods.

Defined-contribution plans, on the other hand, pay benefits based on the accumulated employer contributions, and investment experience thereon, made on the employee's behalf. In some cases employee contributions are allowed as well. Employer contributions are generally made on an annual basis. Some plans specify the amount of contribution (commonly stated as a percentage of each employee's compensation—for example 3 percent of compensation)—while others provide for a discretionary contribution (in which case the total contribution is divided among the employees' accounts). The maximum annual contribution that can be provided in a qualified defined-contribution plan on behalf of any one employee is the lesser of $30,000 or 25 percent of an employee's salary (including employee contributions). Because the contributions are allocated on behalf of each employee using separate bookkeeping accounts (similar to bank accounts), defined-contribution plans are referred to as individual account plans. The employee's account balance grows with each additional contribution and will grow (or shrink) based on the investment experience of the trust fund.

Retirement Planning Considerations

Retirement planners should be aware of the impact of their clients' retirement based on the differences between defined-contribution and defined-benefit plans.

Adequacy of Income. Under a defined-benefit plan, the employer is responsible for providing the promised benefit. If upon annual assessment the company's contributions prove inadequate to fund the promised benefits, the company must make additional contributions to make up the shortfall. On the other hand, if investments outpace expectations, contributions will decrease. In either case the risk of investment experience is on the employer. Also, since benefits are generally based on the highest salaries (usually the final 3 to 5 years of employment), benefits naturally increase with inflation — putting the risk of preretirement inflation squarely on the employer.

The opposite is true for a defined-contribution plan. The employer's obligation begins and ends with making the annual contribution. If plan investments are poor, the employee suffers the loss and may have inadequate retirement resources. In addition, contributions are based on participants' salaries for each year of their career rather than on their salary at retirement, and this may have a negative impact on the adequacy of retirement income. For example, if inflation increases sharply in the years just prior to retirement, the chances of achieving an adequate income-replacement ratio are diminished. Take the case of someone who earned an average middle-class income and whose career spanned the 1950s, '60s, and '70s. In 1950 this person earned $2,000 and received a 10 percent contribution of $200. In 1960 the employee earned $12,000 and received a 10 percent contribution of $1,200. In 1970, $24,000 was earned and there was a contribution of $2,400. During the 1970s double-digit inflation hit and salary levels increased to account for the increased cost of living. If the participant retired in 1980, he or she would be at a disadvantage because only part of the plan contributions will account for the inflationary period right before retirement. What's more, most of the annual contributions would be based on deflated salaries that occurred before the inflationary spiral. By contrast, if the participant was covered by a final-average defined-benefit plan instead, the *employer* would have to make significant contributions to account for an increased final-average salary assumption owing to higher inflation.

"Older" Employees. For clients who are business owners over age 50 with the choice of establishing a defined-benefit plan or a defined-contribution plan, the defined-benefit plan may often be the better choice. The reason for this is that more funds are earmarked for a promised benefit for older employees than for younger employees because there is less time for the plan to be funded and for interest to be earned toward the payment of a promised benefit. In addition, older employees may benefit from the fact that defined-benefit plans can fund for past service — that is, years of employment that are worked prior to the inception of the plan. Defined-contribution plans, on the other hand, may not legally provide for past service. Finally, since years to retirement are growing short, a defined-contribution plan may not have enough time to accumulate an acceptable amount of assets.

Example: New employee Bill Nelson is 55 years old and has no other retirement funds except social security. Nelson earns $50,000 annually and plans to retire at age 65. The plan's formula calls for 10 percent of salary to be deposited in Nelson's account each year. The account earns 10 percent interest. Under this accumulation scheme Nelson will have $79,687 at age 65. Even after combining this with social security, and a fair amount of private savings, Nelson's income will not be adequate to continue his preretirement standard of living.

TABLE 3-2 Defined-Benefit and Defined-Contribution Plans Compared*	
Defined-Benefit	Defined-Contribution
Specifies the benefits an employee receives—maximum, $120,000 per year in 1995 (indexed to inflation)	Specifies the contributions an employee receives—maximum, the lesser of 25 percent of salary or $30,000
Involves no individual accounts	Provides an individual account similar to a bank account
Assigns the risk of preretirement inflation, investment performance, and adequacy of retirement income to the employer	Assigns the risk of preretirement inflation, investment performance, and adequacy of retirement income to the employee
Can provide for past service	Cannot provide for past service
Maximizes the tax-shelter potential of using a qualified plan because benefits are geared to final salaries	Can be an excellent tax shelter for younger employees but is limited to providing a benefit based on career-average salaries
Can be difficult to communicate to employees	Is more easily communicated to employees
*All the qualified plans discussed in this chapter, other than the defined-benefit plan, are in the defined-contribution category. 403(b) plans, SEPs, and IRAs use a defined-contribution approach.	

Defined-contribution plans can work quite well, however, as long as the plan is established early enough.

Example: New employee Gloria Benson is 35 years old. Benson earns $50,000 annually and plans to retire at age 65. The plan's formula calls for 10 percent of salary to be deposited in Benson's account each year. The account earns a 10 percent rate of return. Under this accumulation scheme $1,355,122 will be amassed at retirement. Combined with social security and private savings, Benson's income should be adequate during the retirement years to maintain the proper standard of living.

Investment Discretion. Defined-contribution plans may afford employees the ability to choose among several different investment options. Defined-benefit plans, on the other hand, do not allow for employee investment discretion. In addition, it is the employer, not the employee, who is the beneficiary of a favorable investment performance under a defined-benefit plan.

Keogh versus Corporate Plans

All types of business entities can sponsor any kind of qualified plan. Historically plans sponsored by partnerships or sole proprietors have been referred to as "Keogh plans." At one time these plans were subject to rules that differed significantly from those that governed corporate-sponsored plans. Today the only remaining differences relate to the calculation of the deduction and availability of participant loans (see chapter 8).

Calculating the Keogh Contribution

One of the most important remaining distinctions between a Keogh and a corporate plan is that under a Keogh plan the self-employed person's contribution or benefit is based on net earnings instead of salary. This creates some complications because net earnings can be determined only after taking into account all appropriate business deductions, including the retirement plan contribution. Thus the amount of net earnings and the amount of the deduction are dependent on each other. In addition, the deduction for one-half of the social security taxes paid must be taken into account.

If a defined-benefit plan is used, an actuary is needed to straighten out this mess and to determine the plan contribution amount itself. However, if a defined-contribution plan is used, the retirement planner may be called on to calculate the maximum deduction for his or her client (see the work sheet in table 3-3).

Example: Julie is a sole proprietor. Her qualified profit-sharing plan provides that she contribute 15 percent of earned income. Julie's self-employment contribution rate is 13.0435 percent (see example in rate work sheet). Julie's net earnings from Schedule C are $150,000. Julie's deduction for self-employment tax (Form 1040) is $5,528.70. Julie's deduction for the 1993 tax year will be determined as follows:

(1) Enter self-employment rate from Line 3 of   .130435
    Step I of table 3-3.

    (2) Enter the amount of net earnings from
Schedule C (Form 1040) or from Schedule F
(Form 1040). $150,000

    (3) Enter the deduction for self-employment
tax from Line 25, Form 1040
(for 1993). $5,528.70

    (4) Subtract Line 3 from Line 2 and enter the
amount. $144,471.30

    (5) Multiply Line 4 by Line 1 and enter the
amount. This is the amount that may be
deducted by the business owner. $18,844.11

TABLE 3-3 Keogh Deduction Work Sheet	
Step I: Self-employed person's work sheet	
1. Plan contribution as a decimal (for example, 15% would be 0.15)	
2. Rate in Line 1 plus 1, shown as a decimal (for example, 0.15 plus 1 would be 1.15)	_____
3. Divide Line 1 by Line 2. This is the self-employed contribution rate. (For example, 0.15 ÷ 1.15 = .130435)	_____
Step II: Figure the deduction	
1. Enter the self-employed contribution rate from Line 3 of Step I.	_____
2. Enter the amount of net earnings that the business owner has from Schedule C (Form 1040) or Schedule F (Form 1040).	$_____
3. Enter the deduction for self-employment tax from the front page of Form 1040.	$_____
4. Subtract Line 3 from Line 2 and enter the amount.	$_____
5. Multiply Line 4 by Line 1. This is the amount that may be deducted by the business owner.*	$_____

*Note that this amount is subject to two additional limitations. First, the amount cannot exceed the $30,000 Code Sec. 415 limit. Also, the contribution cannot exceed 15 percent multiplied by $150,000 ($22,500), the maximum compensation cap.

Pension versus Profit-Sharing Plans

A third way to categorize qualified plans is to classify them as either pension plans or profit-sharing plans.   Under a pension plan the organization is committed to making annual payments to the retirement plan, since the main purpose of the plan is to provide a retirement benefit.   Under a profit-sharing plan, however, an organization can retain the flexibility necessary to avoid funding the plan annually.   What's more, a profit-sharing plan isn't necessarily intended to provide a retirement benefit as much as to provide tax deferral of present compensation.   To this end many profit-sharing plans allow employees to withdraw funds while still employed.   (The law requires that the funds be in the account for 2 or more years.)   In recent years, however, the distinction between pension and profit-sharing plans has waned somewhat due to the common practice of using profit-sharing plans in a pension-like manner   (for example, having a profit-sharing plan that requires annual employer contributions and prohibits employee in-service withdrawals).

TABLE 3-4 Pension and Profit-Sharing Plans Compared		
Characteristic	Pension Plan	Profit-Sharing Plan
Employer commitment to annual funding	Yes	No
Employer deduction	25% (or more)*	15%
Withdrawal flexibility for current employees	None	After 2 years
Investment in sponsor's own stock	limited to 10%	unlimited
*Contributions to defined-benefit plans may exceed 25 percent of compensation in some cases.		

Retirement Planning Considerations: Profit-Sharing Plans

Several factors should be kept in mind if your client has a profit-sharing plan.

- Since profit-sharing contributions are discretionary, be cautious when estimating benefits to be provided. When updating a retirement plan, be sure to review the assumptions made about the profit-sharing plan.
- The opportunity for in-service distributions opens up interesting planning opportunities.   Early distributions allow the participant to reposition

assets, take advantage of a specific investment, or meet other needs—such as purchasing life insurance as part of an estate plan.[3]

- With the lower 15 percent maximum deduction limit that applies to profit-sharing plans, the employer may want to choose a pension plan instead—or use a pension/profit-sharing combination—to allow for larger contributions.

Retirement Planning Considerations: Pension Plans

Even though pension plans are restricted from allowing employees to make in-service withdrawals, the employee may still have access to his or her retirement funds prior to retirement through the use of a plan loan provision. Plan loans are discussed further in chapter 8.

Employee Contribution versus Employer-Paid Plans

A final way of distinguishing between employer-sponsored qualified plans is to differentiate between those plans that require some form of employee contribution and plans that are fully funded by the sponsoring employer. Let's take a closer look at the plans with employee contributions.

Salary Reduction Plans

Two types of plans typically require your client to sign a salary reduction agreement so that employee contributions to the plan can be made with before-tax contributions—the 401(k) plan and the 403(b) plan. From a retirement planning perspective it is important to encourage your client to take full advantage of these tax shelters. (The before-tax nature of contributions was illustrated in the John Johnson case study.)   As well, these plans often have the added feature of employer matching contributions.   A client who turns his or her back on employer-matching contributions is forfeiting the easiest and most profitable way to save for retirement.   In addition to encouraging employee participation in an employee salary reduction plan, a retirement planner must deal with the myth held by many that salary reduction contributions are the exclusive amount of private savings they need to have for retirement.   In the first place, salary reduction contributions are often used in lieu of, not in addition to, a full retirement package from the employer. And second, the planner must point out that individual savings above and beyond the salary reductions are needed. One sobering way to accomplish this is to point toward the total amount of retirement funds needed.

Mandatory Contributions

Your client's employer may choose to require employees wishing to be covered by the plan to pay for part of their benefit with so-called mandatory contributions. Such plans are not very popular today, but a few employers still have them. Mandatory contributions generally are a feature of defined-benefit plans. In a typical contributory plan the employee contribution ranges from 2 to 6 percent of aftertax pay—that is, the employee must pay taxes on his or her compensation before the plan contribution is made.

Under most plans, an employee who fails to make mandatory contributions will be excluded from all benefits under the plan. Therefore the retirement planner should certainly encourage employees to pay required contributions.

Nondeductible Voluntary Employee Contributions

A nondeductible employee contribution is an elective contribution made by the employee with aftertax dollars. These contributions are attractive to employees because earnings on such funds are not subject to taxation until benefits are distributed, regardless of the underlying investment vehicle. Prior to 1987, aftertax contributions were a popular feature contained in many qualified plans. Beginning in 1987, however, many of these provisions were eliminated due to new nondiscrimination requirements and a new rule requiring that all such contributions count against the maximum annual contribution limit (the lesser of 25 percent or $30,000) for defined-contribution plans. Under the nondiscrimination rules, employees may not take advantage of the elective contribution feature unless there is a broad range of participation among the participant group.

Although plans may have eliminated employee contributions after 1987, employee aftertax accounts exist in many plans for contributions previously made. When these amounts are distributed from the plan, the principal amounts will constitute the nontaxable basis for your clients, and distributions of earnings on these contributions may be eligible for, along with other applicable funds, special 5-year or 10-year averaging treatment. Other rules regarding the taxation of aftertax contributions are discussed more fully in chapters 8 and 9.

Aftertax contributions are still often contained in salary reduction plans, or other savings plans, where aftertax contributions may be encouraged through the use of employer-matching contributions. If your client is in a plan containing the option to defer on either a pretax or aftertax basis, the client generally should maximize pretax contributions before considering making aftertax contributions. After maximizing pretax deferrals, your client should consider making additional aftertax contributions to take advantage of the deferral of tax on interest earnings. Also, the terms of the plan should be reviewed carefully to determine if additional aftertax contributions will entitle the client to additional employer matching contributions.

THE QUALIFIED PLAN MENU

The various types of qualified plans are in part explained by the characteristics of the categories they fall under (defined-benefit, pension, and so forth) and in part by their benefit or contribution formula. We have already discussed a significant amount about each type of plan, and the one remaining piece to the puzzle is the plan's benefit or contribution formula. Let's take a closer look at the various types of retirement plans and their benefit (contribution) formulas. At the end of the chapter, table 3-5 summarizes the characteristics of each type of plan.

Defined-Benefit Pension Plans

As its name implies, the defined-benefit pension plan has all the characteristics of defined-benefit and pension categories discussed earlier. In addition to these characteristics, a defined-benefit pension plan is characterized by the specific benefit formula used. There are four types of defined-benefit formulas — unit benefit, flat percentage of earnings, flat amount per years of service, and flat amount.

The Unit-Benefit Defined-Benefit Pension Formula

The first type of benefit formula, a unit-benefit formula, accounts for both service and salary in determining the participant's pension benefit. For example, a unit-benefit formula might read as follows:

Each plan participant will receive a monthly pension commencing at normal retirement date and paid in the form of a life annuity equal to 1.5 percent of final average monthly salary multiplied by years of service. Service is limited to a maximum of 30 years.

Example: Larry Novenstern is retiring after 25 years of service with his employer. Larry's final average monthly salary is $5,000. To determine Larry's benefit, multiply 1.5 percent by the $5,000 final average monthly salary by 25 (the number of years of service). Larry's monthly retirement benefit will be equal to $1,875, paid in the form of a life annuity. Note that a life annuity need not be the actual form of benefit. If a different annuity form is chosen, an actuarial adjustment is made to the benefit amount to account for any survivor benefits or guaranteed benefits provided under the different annuity form. Also note that if Larry had decided to stay with his employer he would have effectively stopped increasing the percentage of his final salary to be recovered at 45 percent (1.5 x 30 year cap). Retirement planners should help their clients to recognize that they are working for less if they exceed the plan's service cap. This does not mean, however, that a job change or early retirement is necessarily in order, because the final average salary component of the formula is continuing to grow.

The unit-benefit formula is the most frequently used benefit formula and provides the highest benefits to employees who

- will have or have worked for the same employer for many years, because the benefit is based in part on the years of service for the employer
- are owner-employees or high-paid employees, because the benefit is based in part on salary

The Flat-Percentage-of-Earnings Defined-Benefit Pension Formula

A second type of defined-benefit formula is the flat-percentage-of-earnings formula. This formula relates solely to a participant's salary and does not reflect an employee's service in the benefit calculation. A flat-percentage-of-earnings formula might read

> Each plan participant will receive a monthly pension benefit commencing at normal retirement date and paid in the form of a life annuity equal to 40 percent of the final average monthly salary the participant was paid.

This type of formula provides a disproportionate benefit for those employees entering the plan later in their careers. Therefore these plans have been popular for owners establishing a plan for the first time later in life. However, IRS regulations have limited the effectiveness of this type of plan design by generally requiring that under a flat-percentage-of-earnings formula any employee with less than 25 years of service will have his or her benefit proportionately reduced.

The Flat-Amount-per-Year-of-Service Defined-Benefit Pension Formula

A third type of defined-benefit formula is the flat-amount-per-year-of-service formula, which relates the pension benefit solely to the participant's service and does not reflect the participant's salary. Service is reflected by multiplying all years of service by a stated dollar amount. For example, the flat-amount-per-year-of-service formula might read as follows:

> Each plan participant will receive a monthly pension benefit commencing at normal retirement date and paid in the form of a life annuity equal to $10 for every year of service worked.

Flat-amount-per-year-of-service formulas will be common for your clients who are covered by union plans and uncommon for clients in other situations. Note that when used in union plans a flat-amount-per-year-of-service formula may relate the benefit to the actual hours a participant worked. For example, participants working 1,000 hours might receive half as much as participants working 2,000 hours. Since some union workers such as construction workers frequently have periods of unemployment (at least from the union), it is important to account for any shortfall that might occur by increasing the amount of private savings that your client makes.

The Flat-Amount Defined-Benefit Pension Formula

A final type of defined-benefit formula is a flat-amount formula. A flat-amount formula provides the same monthly benefit for each participant. A flat-amount formula might state that "each plan participant will receive a pension benefit of $200 a month, commencing at normal retirement date, paid in the form of a life annuity."

The flat-amount formula is seldom used in a plan by itself. However, plans with unit-benefit formulas often contain a minimum benefit stated as a flat amount. The minimum or "floor" benefit is used to ensure that employees can at least sustain a minimum standard of living.

Mixing Formulas

Some plans contain a mix of benefit formulas. You may encounter any number of combinations of benefit formulas when deciphering your client's plan. Each formula within the combination will represent another layer of benefits that is due to your client under the plan. In other words, although multiple formulas may confuse the issue, they typically indicate an enhanced benefit for your client.

Target-Benefit Pension Plans

Unlike defined-benefit plans a target-benefit pension plan is a defined-contribution plan. Under a target-benefit plan annual contributions are limited to the lesser of $30,000 or 25 percent of salary, and each employee is given an individual account into which funds are deposited. Target-benefit plans are a unique form of defined-contribution plan because they include some of the features associated with defined-benefit plans. One of these features is that a defined-benefit formula is used to determine the annual contribution. Under a target-benefit plan an actuary determines the amount of funds needed for a level annual contribution by using actuarial and interest assumptions in conjunction with the benefit formula. The actuary makes his or her assumptions hoping to provide a specific benefit (the target) at retirement. The determined amount is then contributed to the employee's account, at which point the investment and actuarial risks shift back to the employee. The target retirement benefit is not guaranteed by the employer. In fact, it would be unusual for the actuary to have guessed exactly right.

Like a defined-benefit flat-amount-of-earnings pension plan, target-benefit pension plans are uniquely suited for older owner-employees who are initiating a retirement program for the first time. Typically these types of owner-employees have put off retirement programs because in the early years money was tight. They have now reached a stage of fiscal maturity, and the 50- to 55-year-old owner-employee has started to think about tax shelters and retirement. The benefit formula in a target-benefit pension plan requires contributions for older employees that will be larger because there is less time to fund for the target benefit. In other words, since the time value accumulation of money is less of a factor and since contributions were not made in the early years, larger contributions are needed.

> *Example:* The Main Street Cafe has a target-benefit plan for five of its employees: Alice Bradley (aged 58), husband John Bradley (aged 60), Bob Smith (aged 47), Mary Springer (aged 28), and Sally Andrews (aged 26). The benefit formula in the plan provides for 3 percent of final average salary multiplied by years of service. At the inception of the plan the actuary takes into account final-average salary assumptions, age, mortality, interest earnings, and other assumptions in order to project the annual level contribution for each participant. Because of the comparatively advanced ages of Alice and John Bradley, their annual contribution is likely to be very high (particularly since the plan was just recently adopted). But because Mary Springer and Sally Andrews are relatively young, and there are many years to accumulate interest and to fund for the benefit, their annual contributions will be relatively low. At retirement the benefits for any employee may be lower or higher than the targeted amount, due in part to the investment performance of the employee's account.

Money-Purchase Pension Plans

A money-purchase pension plan is a form of defined-contribution plan. Under a money-purchase pension plan the company's annual contributions are mandatory and are based on a percentage of each participant's compensation. For example, the money-purchase benefit formula may provide that annual contributions will equal 10 percent of compensation for each participant. (If Karen Lamb earns $40,000, the annual contribution placed in her account is $4,000.) Under a money-purchase plan the benefits for each employee are the amounts that can be provided by the sums contributed to the employee's individual account plus investment earnings. For example, if Karen Lamb worked for 20 years and her salary remained at $40,000, she would have $80,000 plus accumulated interest of $58,876 (assuming a 5 percent annual rate) at retirement. The term *money-purchase* arose because the participant's account is traditionally used to purchase an annuity that provides monthly retirement benefits.

Profit-Sharing Plans

As its name implies a profit-sharing plan maintains all the elements attributed to the profit-sharing category discussed earlier. In addition, a profit-sharing plan is a form of defined-contribution plan. From the employee's perspective a profit-sharing plan provides a retirement benefit that is tentative at best. From the owner-employee's standpoint, however, a profit-sharing plan is a very popular choice for several reasons.

First, a profit-sharing plan can be structured to allow the owner-employee the discretion to miss annual payments from time to time (a "must" in cash-tight businesses).   In other words, as long as contributions are considered substantial and recurring by the IRS, the employer can avoid cash-flow problems by not contributing to the plan.   Second, some plans are set up so that a certain level of profits must be achieved before contributions to participant accounts will be made.   For example, the plan might state that contributions will be made from profits in excess of $100,000 (thus allowing capital for business expansion).   Third, profit-sharing plans are so flexible that they can also be used more like a pension plan, where the employer promises to make a specific contribution (generally stated as a percentage of compensation) regardless of whether the company earns any profits.   Fourth, as discussed before, a profit-sharing plan can be structured to allow employees, including owner-employees, to make in-service withdrawals—that is, plans can be designed to allow employees to withdraw funds from participant accounts as early as 2 years after they were contributed by the employer.   Fifth, profit-sharing plans are considered to be fiscally responsible because they have a high correlation to increased productivity.

Finally, a profit-sharing plan may be used to allocate contributions disproportionately to employees who (1) receive higher compensation than other employees, (2) are older than other employees, or (3) have served longer than other employees.   A plan can always allocate the employer contribution as a uniform percentage of compensation (remember that compensation for the highly paid is limited to $150,000), which results in larger contributions for the highly compensated.   Highly compensated employees can get an even larger share of the employer contribution if the plan is "integrated with social security" in the manner described later in this chapter.   Length of service (as well as level of compensation) can also be factored into the allocation method.

> *Example:* Peggy, Arthur, and Kim are three owners of a shoe store. The store declares a profit of $2,000 for 1995.   The plan's allocation formula stipulates that profits shall be allocated to participants by the ratio that the units allocated to a participant bear to the total of units allocated to all participants, with one unit allocated for each $100 of compensation and two units allocated for each year of service.   Peggy has 10 years of service and earns $20,000 (220 units), Arthur has 8 years of service and earns $15,000 (166 units), and Kim has 5 years of service and earns $10,000 (110 units).   The total units for all participants is 496.   To determine Peggy's benefit divide her units (220) by the total units and multiply the quotient by the $2,000 profit ([220 ÷ 496] x 2,000).   The contribution to Peggy's account will be $888, Arthur's contribution will be $669, and Kim's contribution will be $443.

An allocation method that takes service into consideration is valid if the average allocation rate for all highly compensated employees does not exceed the average allocation rate for non-highly compensated employees.

An allocation method that takes into consideration age can also be valid if the contributions (determined on an annual basis) on behalf of the highly compensated employees will not "purchase" a larger monthly lifetime retirement benefit than for non-highly compensated employees. This type of age weighting is a relatively new device that is referred to as an *age-weighted profit-sharing plan.* The disparity that may come about from age weighting is quite severe, resulting in an effective design strategy for the employer looking to allocate larger amounts (as a percentage of salary) to older employees.

> *Example:* Dot Matrix, aged 55, owns a software consulting business with profits that vary greatly from year to year. She has one employee, Arthur Data, aged 25. Dot's current compensation is $200,000 and Data's compensation is $40,000. Under an age-weighted profit-sharing plan, given the participants' respective ages, the rate of contribution (as a percentage of compensation) for Data can be 8.7 percent of the rate of contribution for Dot. If the company contributes 10 percent of compensation for Dot ($20,000) only .87 percent of compensation ($348) has to be contributed for Data. (Note, however, that under this scenario, a second rule, referred to as the "top heavy requirement" would require a contribution of 3 percent of compensation for Data [$1,200].)

Regardless of the design of the profit-sharing plan allocation method, the plan is subject to two limits. First, the annual employer contribution (including any employee contributions or forfeitures) for each participant in the plan may not exceed the lesser of 25 percent of compensation or $30,000. Second, the maximum deductible contribution that an employer can make to the plan is 15 percent of the aggregate of the compensation of all participants. The 15 percent limit may make it difficult to use a profit-sharing plan as the sole retirement plan when the employer wants to make the maximum contribution (25 percent/$30,000) for key management employees. A profit-sharing plan may still provide the desired result using one of the allocation methods discussed above which results in a higher rate of contribution for the highly compensated. A second alternative is for the employer to establish two plans, one a discretionary profit-sharing plan and the second a money-purchase pension plan with a specified annual contribution (generally 10 percent of compensation). This dual plan design allows the employer to make deductible contributions of up to the 25 percent/$30,000 limit, while also giving the employer a significant amount of flexibility if the employer wants to make smaller contributions for a particular plan year.

Stock Plans

Stock bonus plans and employee stock ownership plans (ESOPs) are derived from profit-sharing plans and are therefore similar to them in many ways. For example, stock bonus plans, ESOPs, and profit-sharing plans are all forms of defined-contribution plans—contributions need not be fixed or made every year, and contribution levels to any one employee (even owner-employees) typically will not exceed 15 percent (the amount of the business's deduction). However, stock bonus plans and ESOPs differ from profit-sharing plans in that they typically invest plan assets primarily in the employer stock, whereas profit-sharing plans are usually structured to diversify investments.   From a retirement planning standpoint this can be disastrous because without any diversity of investment, participants are exposed to potential disaster if the employer stock drops in value. There is, however, some relief available for ESOP participants. The law requires that once an ESOP participant attains age 55 and completes at least 10 years of participation, the participant may elect (between the ages of 55 and 60) to diversify the retirement benefit by moving up to 50 percent of his or her account balance into other investments. Planners should recommend that their clients take advantage of this in all but a few cases where the stability of the employer stock is unquestioned. There is a trade-off for diversification, however, in the loss of the tax-timing strategy (discussed next).

Tax-Timing Strategy for Stock Plans

Stock bonus plans and ESOPs can allow distributions to participants in the form of employer stock. Stock distributed as part of a lump-sum distribution (see chapter 8) is eligible for special tax deferral. When stock is distributed, the tax on the distribution is determined based on the value of the stock at the time it was purchased by the plan—not on the value at the time of distribution. This unrealized appreciation is not subject to tax until the stock is later sold by the participant.

> *Example:* Steve Gilchrist has 10,000 shares of his company's stock, each with a basis of $10 a share. In 1993, when Steve retires, the stock is worth $12 a share. Steve elects to take the ESOP distribution in stock. Steve's tax liability will be determined on the plan's cost of $100,000 (10,000 shares x $10 per share), not on the actual value of $120,000. When Steve sells the stock in 1995 at $12 a share, he will then pay taxes on the $20,000 appreciation ($2 a share x 10,000 shares). By taking the distribution in employer stock Steve acquired a valuable tax-timing strategy that could effectively lower the actual amount paid in taxes. What's more, if Steve at some later date sells the stock back to the ESOP and uses the proceeds to purchase "qualified replacement property," he may be able to further delay paying taxes on the gain. (This advantage has several significant qualification requirements; for more information see Code Sec. 1042).

Put Options for Stock Plans

One potential disadvantage for stock plans might have been the lack of liquidity of stock from a closely held business. In a stock plan, however, the employer is required to offer a repurchase option (also known as a put option). This option must be available for a minimum of 60 days following the distribution of the stock and, if the option is not exercised in that period, for an additional 60-day period in the following year. The repurchase option creates an administrative and cash-flow problem for your clients who are business owners, but significant protection for your clients who are employees.

401(k) Plans

One of the most popular types of qualified plans is the 401(k) plan. As discussed previously a 401(k) plan allows employees to elect deferral of taxation on current salaries or bonuses simply by putting money into the plan. Participants who forego receiving a portion of their salary or bonuses enjoy abundant tax savings. In order to understand the state of 401(k) plans today, it is important to look at their history. For many years employers who felt they could not adequately fund their employees' (and their own) retirement needs provided thrift plans (if employer matching contributions were not involved, the plans were called savings plans). Under thrift plans employees become partners of the employer in providing for their own retirement needs. A thrift plan calls for employees to contribute a fixed percentage of salary to the plan and for the employer to make a contribution "matching" either the entire employee contribution or a portion thereof. Thrift plans, however, are not tax efficient because the employee's contribution is made with aftertax dollars. The Revenue Act of 1978 included provisions allowing employees to make before-tax thrift contributions to qualified plans, but the provisions under which plans qualified were unclear. In November 1981 the IRS issued proposed regulations covering these statutory provisions, and plan sponsors began to adopt the new 401(k) plans.

At first the 401(k) plan could be structured to allow an individual participant to reduce his or her salary by an amount equal to the defined-contribution limit of the lesser of 25 percent of salary or $30,000. In time, however, the legislature realized that (1) salary reductions were siphoning off much-needed tax revenue and (2) employers were shifting too much of the retirement burden to employees by using 401(k) plans in lieu of, rather than in addition to, other qualified plans. To rectify this Congress enacted a $7,000 annual limit (indexed annually—in 1995 the limit is $9,240).

In today's market many employers, even those with defined-benefit, target-benefit, or money-purchase plans, opt for a complementary 401(k) plan. These plans are still highly regarded, despite the $9,240 limit, because they provide a substantial employee benefit at a small employer cost.

From a retirement planning perspective you may run into clients whose employer plans followed the same course as the history of 401(k) plans—that is, they have made taxable thrift contributions, followed by large 401(k) contributions, followed by limited 401(k) contributions. For those clients who were originally involved in the thrift plan, it is likely they will have some "basis" for annuity distribution purposes.

Other 401(k) Retirement Planning Considerations

401(k) plans differ from their parent profit-sharing plans in the following four ways:

- 401(k) salary reductions may affect other benefit programs and may reduce benefits available under a group life or health insurance plan.
- 401(k) salary reductions are immediately 100 percent vested and cannot be forfeited.
- Withdrawals under 401(k) plans are different from those under profit-sharing plans, and, in general, money placed in a 401(k) plan is used more for retirement purposes since substantial restrictions curtail withdrawals before retirement.
- Because of their special tax advantage, 401(k) plans are subject to an extra nondiscrimination test called the actual-deferral-percentage test. The actual-deferral-percentage test ensures that higher-paid employees don't use the 401(k) plan to stockpile contributions unless lower-paid employees are also significantly involved in the plan. Pursuant to this test some of your higher-paid clients may have before-tax retirement contributions either recharacterized as nondeductible contributions or returned to them.

403(b) Plans

A 403(b) plan (sometimes referred to as a tax-sheltered annuity [TSA] or tax-deferred annuity [TDA]) is similar to a 401(k) plan in many respects. Both plans permit an employee to defer taxes on income by allowing before-tax contributions to the employee's individual account, by allowing deferrals in the form of salary reduction, and by allowing the plan's use in conjunction with, or in lieu of, most other retirement plans. However, 403(b) plans are distinguishable from 401(k) plans in several ways.

- The 403(b) market includes only tax-exempt organizations and public schools, and only certain types of tax-exempt organizations qualify for 403(b) status. These are the so-called 501(c)(3) tax-exempt organizations.
- 403(b) plans can be funded only through annuity contracts or mutual funds.

TABLE 3-5
Employer-Sponsored Plans with Special Tax Treatment

Type of Plan	Sample Formula	DB/DC**	Pension/ Profit-Sharing	Employee Contributions	Special Rules
Defined-Benefit	1% x FAC* x years of service	DB	pension	• mandatory after tax • voluntary after tax	• plan must describe plan benefits
Money-Purchase Pension	10% annual employer contribution	DC	pension	• voluntary after tax	• contribution must be definite
Target-Benefit Pension	employer contributes amount needed to fund defined-benefit described above	DC	pension	• voluntary after tax	• calculate contribution using specified actuarial method
Profit-Sharing	discretionary contribution is allocated pro rata based on compensation	DC	profit-sharing	• voluntary after tax	• allocation method must be definitely determinable
401(k)	employee makes contributions; employer matches	DC	profit-sharing	• voluntary before tax • voluntary after tax	• hardship and age 59 1/2 in-service withdrawals • maximum deferral election of $9,240 • ADP and ACP testing
Stock Bonus	same as for profit-sharing plan	DC	profit-sharing	• voluntary after tax	• pay distributions in stock • put option • voting pass-through • dist. within 5 years
ESOP	same as for profit-sharing plan; plan must invest primarily in employer securities	DC	profit-sharing	• voluntary after tax	• leveraged loan • put option • appraisal • diversification • voting pass-through • dist. within 5 years
403(b)	can look like profit-sharing plan and/or 401(k) plan	• 401(k)-like withdrawal rules • sponsored by charitable organization or public school • voluntary pretax employee contribution up to maximum of $9,500			• nonforfeitable (immediate vesting) • one deferral election each year • invest only in annuities or mutual funds • exclusion allowance

* Final average compensation
** DB: defined-benefit; DC: defined-contribution

- If a salary reduction is used, the amount of the 403(b) contribution that can be made by an employee is restricted to the lesser of a complicated figure referred to as the "exclusion allowance" or $9,500. The total contribution, including employer contributions, is subject to the same maximum contribution limit of 25 percent of salary or $30,000, whichever is lower.

- Unlike most 401(k) plans, 403(b) salary reduction agreements may not be changed during the plan year (except to discontinue salary reductions). For example, Sam cannot elect to reduce his salary by 7 percent and subsequently change the reduction to 4 percent during the same year. However, Sam may elect to discontinue salary reductions entirely (on a prospective basis). From a planning perspective, you should help your client make a realistic choice regarding the level of salary deferral, so that he or she is not required to discontinue deferral elections at some later date.

Summary

Table 3-5 summarizes the categories each plan falls into and briefly reviews some of the special requirements that apply to each type of plan. This chart can be a helpful tool for learning the rules that apply to each type of plan.

QUALIFIED PLANS:
WHAT YOU DON'T KNOW CAN HURT YOU

The qualified plans (and 403(b) annuities) that we've discussed are part of what is generally considered a complex area typically reserved for pension specialists. However, every retirement planner must be aware of the following areas in order to best serve their clients' retirement needs:

- plan termination
- plan provisions relating to early retirement
- plan provisions relating to deferred retirement

The Impact of a Qualified Plan Termination on the Participant

Even though the law requires that qualified plans be intended to be permanent, employers may cease making future contributions by terminating the plan (a formal process involving IRS approval and, in the case of defined-benefit plans, PBGC approval). If your client's plan is terminated, contingency savings plans must be made to account for the loss of employer-provided retirement funds. In some cases, however, employers may replace the terminated plan with a different plan. Under this scenario the retirement planner should assess the new plan and evaluate its place in the overall retirement picture.

If your client's plan is terminated after he or she is retired, no change will generally occur. If your client's qualified plan is terminated while he or she is still employed, however, your client will be affected in several ways with regard to his or her rights under the terminated plan. One of the most important ways that your client will be affected is that he or she becomes 100 percent vested in his or her account balance (defined-contribution plans) or accrued benefit (defined-benefit plans). One hundred percent vesting occurs even if the participant was zero percent vested on the day before the termination.

> *Example:* Jane is in a defined-contribution money-purchase plan. The plan is terminated. At the point when the plan is terminated Jane was 60 percent vested in her $10,000 retirement account. Upon plan termination Jane will be 100 percent vested in the $10,000 retirement account.

> *Example:* John Jones is in a defined-benefit plan that promises him an annual benefit equal to 50 percent of his final annual salary. John's accrued benefit (the present value of his anticipated future benefit) is calculated by the plan actuary to be $7,000. John is 40 percent vested in this amount. Upon termination of the plan John will be 100 percent vested in his $7,000 accrued benefit. (Retirement planners may be able to determine their client's accrued benefit from the annual benefit statement distributed by the employer or by contacting the plan's administrator.)

In addition to becoming fully vested under the plan your clients may be forced to deal with a plan distribution. If such a distribution occurs, your client will be issued election forms that will ask for payout preferences and outline the tax consequences of each alternative. In most cases your client will be given the option to receive a deferred annuity contract, payable at normal retirement age, or a single-sum distribution. A deferred annuity will not result in immediate taxation and will preserve the amount to be used for retirement. If the single sum is elected, the plan is required to give your client an option to have the amount transferred directly to another qualified plan or an IRA account. For two reasons, the client should almost always make this election. First, by transferring the money into another tax-deferred vehicle, the individual can continue to defer taxes until the money is actually needed at retirement. Although your client might be tempted to take (and spend) the lump sum, this amount has been earmarked for retirement and, if spent, will be hard to replace. Also, the tax implications of spending the money now can be severe. In addition to paying income taxes on the distribution, an individual under age 59 1/2 generally will be required to pay a 10 percent early distribution excise tax.

Second, your client actually has the option to receive the lump sum and roll the benefits into an IRA or other qualified plan or elect to have the plan directly transfer funds to one of these plans. The direct transfer option is the better choice because with this method no income tax withholding is required. If the participant elects to actually receive the lump-sum payment, the amount may be rolled into another qualified plan or an IRA within 60 days from the date of the distribution. However, the employer is required to withhold 20 percent of the distribution for federal income taxes—requiring the participant who wishes to roll over the entire benefit to come up with the cash for the additional 20 percent out of his or her own pocket. Of course, the 20 percent will be refunded after the tax return is filed, but the taxpayer has just made a no-interest short-term loan to the federal government.

In addition to, or in lieu of, distributing plan funds the employer may end up purchasing annuity certificates from an insurance carrier. Under this option the insurer assumes the employer's liability (up to the point of termination) and guarantees payment of the vested benefit under an annuity certificate. The annuity certificate your client will receive will contain information regarding the annuity's starting date (typically the date your client would have been eligible to retire under the plan), the amount of the annuity, and the annuity options available. It should be noted that the insurer does not guarantee all promised benefits, just benefits that accrued to the point of termination. Therefore in the John Jones example, John's annuity would reflect his $7,000 accrued benefit, not his 50 percent of final salary benefit promise.

A third aspect of plan termination is appropriate only for your clients who belong(ed) to a defined-benefit plan. For participants in a defined-benefit plan the consequences of plan termination trigger PBGC protection. The PBGC's primary function is to protect the plan participants. If the employer is unable to make benefit payments, the PBGC will guarantee the payment of certain benefits known as basic benefits (special or unusual benefits are generally not covered). Most notably, basic benefits do not include those benefits that become vested due to the plan termination. The PBGC insurance covers only up to a maximum benefit level. The maximum insured benefit equals the lesser of

- $2,573 (limit for 1995) a month, adjusted upward each year to reflect changes in the social security wage base, or
- 100 percent of average monthly wages during the participant's 5 highest-paid consecutive years

Example: The Ajax defined-benefit plan terminates because the employer is seriously underfunded and cannot meet benefit payments. The PBGC has removed the plan's trustee and is currently administering the plan. Al Abernathy has a plan benefit of $3,000 per month, and his average monthly wage during his highest-paid consecutive years was $5,000. The actual benefit Al will receive will be $2,573 (the PBGC guarantee).

A final consequence that plan termination has on the plan participant is applicable if life insurance policies are involved. The plan document should be written permitting participants to acquire their policies. (Policies are typically purchased by younger participants, whose premiums will be very attractive, or by older participants who may have become uninsurable.) The participant will be taxed on the value of the policy less any basis and will assume premium payments thereafter. Since IRAs cannot invest in insurance contracts, a participant wanting both to defer taxes—by rolling benefits into an IRA—and maintain the policy has a problem. The best solution is for either the trustee or the participant to strip the policy of cash value (except for the participant's PS 58 "cost basis")[4] and roll the additional cash into the IRA. Even if the participant does not want to maintain the policy, he or she may want to use this approach so that the amount that had been taxed as PS 58 costs can be received tax free. The law requires that the policy actually be distributed in order to recover PS 58 costs.

Plan Provisions Relating to Early Retirement

In addition to addressing yourself to your client's benefit at normal retirement age, the following factors should be considered with regard to his or her benefit at an early retirement age:

- Sometimes (especially in defined-benefit plans) age is not the only determinant of early retirement; rather, both age and service dictate the early retirement age. One typical early retirement provision requires that the employee be aged 55 with at least 10 years of service (in pension parlance, this is known as 55 and 10). It is therefore important to verify whether your client has met any service requirement for early retirement age.
- Early retirement benefits may end up being very costly to your client. While it is true that retirement benefits will be paid out over a longer period of time (the difference between early retirement age and normal retirement age) there are several mitigating factors.

  - For clients in a defined-benefit plan, early retirement benefits are typically actuarially reduced to reflect the longer payout period.
  - For clients in a defined-contribution plan, early retirement causes your client to lose several years of contributions based on a higher salary. By cutting out what could have been the 5 to 10 years of highest salary that a client would have earned, the shortfall in contributions may be dramatic.
  - For clients in a defined-benefit plan in which the final average salary formula is used, an early retirement could substantially reduce the final average salary factor from what it could have been had your client not taken early retirement, thus causing a lower benefit.

— Clients who take early retirement have lost the inflation protection offered by increasing salaries, thus extending their inflation exposure during retirement.

— Sometimes, even though they are actuarially reduced, early retirement benefits from a defined-benefit plan are partially subsidized by the employer. If early retirement is partially subsidized, the actuarial reductions don't reflect the true cost of providing the benefit, and the difference represents an additional employer-provided benefit.

The following items should be reviewed with a client who is considering early retirement:

- What is the earliest age at which early retirement is possible?
- What is the plan's service requirement for early retirement?
- Have lost earnings from early retirement been considered?
- What is the actuarial reduction for early retirement benefits?
- Is the actuarial reduction reflective of a true reduction for time value of money, or is early retirement partially subsidized by the employer?
- Has lost purchasing power occurring during the early retirement been considered?
- Has the lost income from a reduction in final average salary been considered?
- Is there a cap on years of service in the benefit formula?
- Are any early retirement incentives (such as golden handshakes) available?

Plan Provisions Relating to Deferred Retirement

One growing concern among retirement planners is dealing with their clients who elect to stay employed past normal retirement age. There has been a recent upswing in this area, due in part to a 1986 amendment to the Age Discrimination Employment Act (ADEA), which generally prohibits involuntary retirement, and in part to an increasing realization of the impact that postretirement inflation can have on financial security. Keep the following items in mind when dealing with a client who chooses to defer retirement:

- Clients in a defined-contribution plan will continue to receive contributions to their individual account until actual retirement.
- Clients in a defined-benefit plan may or may not continue to accrue benefits under the plan. If the plan specifies full accrual after a specified period of service (for example, 30 years of service is the maximum amount of service in which accruals are permitted), accruals for clients will cease based on service at that point. If, however, no service accrual cap applies, a client will continue to accrue benefits even after normal retirement age.

- Clients who work beyond age 70 1/2 will be forced to start taking plan distributions. Ironically employer contributions or benefit accruals may still be forthcoming even as distributions are being paid out.
- For clients in a defined-benefit plan the employer may actuarially increase the benefit payout to reflect the shorter payout period.
- The longer a client continues to work the shorter his or her exposure will be to postretirement inflation problems.

QUALIFIED PLANS: WHERE TO FIND OUT MORE

Employers provide many sources of information that are essential tools for the retirement planner. Let's take a closer look.

The Summary Plan Description

A summary plan description (SPD) is an easy-to-read booklet that explains your client's pension and other employer benefit plans. A summary plan description bridges the gap between the legalese of the pension plan and the understanding of the average participant by effectively communicating how a plan works, what benefits are available, and how to get these benefits.

A well-drafted summary plan description will be fair and even-handed — that is, it won't be a sales or promotional tool. However, some SPDs spend more time "selling" the employer's benefit package than explaining the employees' rights. This type of SPD is specifically prohibited by regulations that mandate that an SPD cannot downplay the negative consequences of involvement — for example, it cannot gloss over plan terms that may cause a participant to lose benefits or fail to qualify for them. Any limitations, exceptions, reductions, or other restrictions on plan benefits must also be duly noted. The SPD, however, is not prescreened to assure compliance. Instead, copies are filed with the Department of Labor, where they are checked for noncompliance only when problems have been raised by plan participants.

If there is a conflict between the plan and the SPD, disclaimers in the SPD will typically indicate that the plan provisions will be controlling. Despite these disclaimers, however, courts are increasingly ruling that the summary plan description's provisions are binding on the employer. Thus if an important conflict arises, the advice of an attorney should be sought.

Here is a list of the most important things you can learn about your client's retirement plan from his or her summary plan description:

- the plan administrator's name and address
- the plan's benefit or contribution formula
- an explanation of the plan's eligibility requirements for participation and benefits
- an explanation of any joint and survivor benefits

- an explanation of any terms that could result in a participant's losing benefits
- a description and explanation of the plan provisions for determining years of service for eligibility, vesting, breaks in service, and benefit accrual
- the investment options available under the plan
- procedures for presenting claims for benefits under the plan and remedies for benefits denied under the plan
- a statement of ERISA rights (this statement is standard text promulgated by the Department of Labor)
- whether the plan is protected by PBGC insurance

Other Information Resources

In addition to the summary plan description the employer will supply the following resources:

- *annual benefit statements*—Under most circumstances employers provide these statements annually as a matter of course, but if this is not the case, upon written request each plan participant or beneficiary is entitled to receive a statement of the individual's own accrued benefit or account balance under the qualified plan. This statement need not be furnished more than once in any 12-month period but must be furnished upon a participant's termination of employment.
- *1099R Forms*—These forms are filed with the IRS and sent to any participant or participant's beneficiary who receives a distribution.

The following checklist should be used to help you in your fact-finding process.

Employer-Provided Documents **Used for Retirement Planning**	
Name of Plan Administrator_____ Phone Number_____	
1. Summary Plan Description	[ ]
2. Annual Benefit Statements	[ ]
3. 1099R Form	[ ]
4. Withholding Form	[ ]

NOTES

1. A plan that is fully funded with insurance contracts does not need a trust fund.
2. Except for nondeductible contributions.
3. Distributions prior to age 59 1/2 are subject to a 10 percent excise tax—which can often be avoided with careful planning (see chapter 8).
4. As discussed in chapter 8, each year a policy is held by the plan, the cost of the current year's insurance is taxable using what are called the PS 58 rates. At the time of the distribution, the PS 58 costs are considered cost basis and will not be taxed a second time. However, to actually treat the PS 58 costs as basis, the insurance policy must be distributed.

4

Sources of Retirement Income: Nonqualified Plans, IRAs, and SEPs

Chapter Outline

NONQUALIFIED PLANS—OVERVIEW

Nonqualified deferred-compensation plans are retirement plans that do not burden the employer with the qualification requirements applicable to a qualified plan but also do not entitle the employer to an immediate deduction for deferred compensation. Instead, as a trade-off for being permitted unrestricted design and use of the plan, the employer must wait to take a tax deduction until the employee is taxed on the benefit (generally at the time of the employee's retirement).

Nonqualified plans are found most often among executives in large and medium-sized corporations, but many small closely held businesses also use them. Nonqualified plans are often used for the following reasons:

- to bring executive retirement benefits up to desired levels by adding a second tier of benefits to the qualified plan
- to circumvent the nondiscrimination requirements for a qualified plan
- to exceed the maximum benefit and contribution limits of a qualified plan
- to provide a stand-alone benefit that allows highly compensated employees to defer current income as a means of supplementing retirement income
- to shift income to later years
- to encourage long service

There are three basic types of nonqualified plans: the salary reduction plan, the excess-benefit plan, and the supplemental executive retirement plan.

Salary Reduction Plans

Under a *nonqualified salary reduction plan,* your client has the option to forgo receipt of currently earned salary, bonuses, or commissions for retirement purposes. You may run into situations where a salary reduction plan is offered as part of a package of perks to selected managers or highly compensated employees, or you may want to consider having your client negotiate with his or her employer during contract negotiations to institute such a plan. This type of plan is most beneficial when the employee's income is currently taxed at the highest marginal rates and he or she anticipates being in a lower tax bracket after retirement, but it is often employed as a means of income leveling for highly compensated employees whose income would otherwise drop sharply after retirement.

When establishing a salary reduction plan or, for that matter, a SERP (discussed below), the employer will want to be sure that the plan is exempt from the requirements of ERISA. To do this the employer must limit participation to a select group of management or highly compensated employees. This exception is referred to as the top-hat exception, and a plan that satisfies these conditions is often referred to as a *top-hat plan.*

Excess-Benefit Plans

A second type of nonqualified plan is the *excess-benefit plan,* so called because it satisfies the employer objective of exceeding the Code Sec. 415 limits ($120,000 defined-benefit/$30,000 defined-contribution dollar limits applicable in 1995). In other words, an excess-benefit plan picks up where the maximum contribution and benefit limits for a qualified plan leave off. Thus from a retirement planning perspective this type of plan may be essential to those clients who are effectively restricted from receiving the proper income-replacement ratio by the Sec. 415 limits.

Excess-benefit plans are considered a type of employer-provided *salary continuation plan* (as opposed to an employee-elected *deferred-compensation plan*). In other words, under a salary continuation plan the executive does not forgo receipt of currently earned income, but instead receives an additional retirement benefit (or contribution). In operation, excess-benefit plans are dovetailed into an underlying qualified plan to provide the benefit or contribution that is blocked out by the Sec. 415 limits.

Technically the excess-benefit plan satisfies another exception to the ERISA rules. Unlike the top-hat plan, an excess-benefit plan can cover any employees as long as the plan is designed only to provide benefits in excess of the 415 limits.

Supplemental Executive Retirement Plans (SERPs)

Perhaps the most popular type of nonqualified plan is the supplemental executive retirement plan. A supplemental executive retirement plan satisfies the employer objective of complementing an existing qualified plan that is not already stretched to the maximum limits by bringing executive retirement benefits up to desired levels.

SERPs, much like excess-benefit plans, are generally dovetailed into an underlying qualified defined-contribution or defined-benefit plan. The major difference, however, is that SERPs may complement qualified plan limitations that are below the Sec. 415 limits. Like the salary reduction plan, the SERP must be maintained only for a select group of management or highly compensated employees in order to satisfy the top-hat exception to ERISA.

Retirement Planning Concerns

One question raised by retirement planners who have some control over their clients' participation in nonqualified plans is whether it is wise to defer compensation if tax rates are expected to increase. At first it might seem that deferring compensation in this situation will never make sense. Why defer if taxes will be higher later? However, in some circumstances this decision might make sense. When the individual elects to defer, the full amount deferred is allowed to grow instead of being subject to taxes now, in which case only the post-tax dollars would accumulate earnings. The rate of growth on the pretax deferral may offset the higher rate of tax. Three factors will have an impact on whether deferring will work in a particular situation:

- the tax rate when funds are distributed
- the length of the deferral
- the rate of return that deferred funds earn

Table 4-1 can help you with this decision under a number of different assumptions. The table assumes that the individual is currently in the 36 percent tax bracket, and uses future projected tax rates of 39, 45, and 50 percent. Now, looking at the table, you can identify the length of deferral required in order for deferral to make sense for each of these tax rates and at a number of different rates of return. The "break-even points" identify the length of deferral at which deferring or not deferring will result in equal total dollars saved. If the length of deferral is longer, deferral will result in greater savings, and if the period of deferral is shorter, paying taxes now would make more sense.

TABLE 4-1
Years until Breakeven for Deferred Compensation
Assuming Tax Rates Will Increase and Current Rate Is
36 Percent (Federal)

Current Tax Rate	36%	36%	36%
Projected Tax Rate	39%	45%	50%
Before-Tax Return on Plan Investments	Number of Years to Breakeven*		
3%	2.71	7.55	11.11
4%	2.04	5.69	8.38
5%	1.64	4.57	6.73
6%	1.37	3.83	5.63
7%	1.18	3.29	4.85
8%	1.04	2.90	4.27
9%	0.93	2.58	3.81
10%	0.84	2.34	3.44
11%	0.77	2.13	3.14
12%	0.71	1.96	2.89
13%	0.65	1.83	2.69

$$\text{*Number of years} = \frac{\text{Natural log of (new tax rate/current tax rate)}}{\text{Natural log of (1 + interest rate)}}$$

Example: Employee Charles Able has a current effective tax rate of 36 percent and has the options of either deferring $10,000 under his company's nonqualified top-hat plan or having the money paid out under a currently taxable executive bonus agreement. If Able projects that a 50 percent individual tax rate will apply when his distribution occurs and that he can earn an aftertax interest rate of 8 percent on deferred funds, he will be better off under the nonqualified plan as long as the deferral period is longer than 4.2 years. If, however, the deferral period is less than 4.2 years, Able will be better off from a tax standpoint under an executive bonus plan.

EXECUTIVE-BONUS LIFE INSURANCE PLANS

An alternative that can be used in combination with, or in lieu of, the previously discussed deferred-compensation plans is the executive bonus life insurance plan (also known as a Sec. 162 plan). Like a deferred-compensation plan, an executive bonus insurance plan can be provided on a discriminatory basis to help business owners and selected executives save for retirement. The executive bonus life insurance plan, however, does not provide for the deferral of income. Under an executive bonus life insurance plan the corporation pays a bonus to the executive for the purpose of purchasing cash-value life insurance. The executive is the policyowner, the insured, and the person who makes the beneficiary designation. The corporation's only connection (albeit a major one) is to fund premium payments and, in a few cases, to secure the application for insurance. Bonused amounts can be paid out by the corporation in one of two ways: the corporation can pay the premiums for the policy directly to the insurer or the bonus can be paid to the employee, who then pays the policy premiums. In either case the corporation deducts the contribution from corporate taxes and includes the amount of the payment in the executive's W-2 (taxable) income.

Concern over the receipt of additional taxable income from executive bonus life insurance plans has caused many employers to provide a second bonus to alleviate any tax that the business owner or executive may pay (these plans are typically called *double-bonus plans*).

EXECUTIVE INCENTIVE OR BONUS PLANS

In addition to the various qualified and nonqualified plans already described, many of your clients—especially highly paid executives—may participate in executive incentive or bonus plans. The purpose of these plans is to reward the executive based on the performance of the company stock or, in some cases, on the basis of certain financial objectives, such as cumulative growth and earnings per share or improvement in return on investment. There is typically no tax to the executive at the time the rights to future stock appreciation or future benefits are granted; in most cases the executive has considerable flexibility as to when benefits will be realized and subject to tax. Consequently, for executives who hold these rights as they approach retirement, one of the more important planning issues is planning for the timing of the exercise of these rights. In particular, planners should recognize that the tax rate in the year before, the year of, and the year after retirement can vary dramatically. Let's look at the characteristics of some of the more commonly used forms of executive incentive plans.

Nonqualified Stock Options (NQSOs)

Nonqualified stock options are options to purchase shares of company stock at a stated price over a given period of time (frequently 10 years). The option price normally equals 100 percent of the stock's fair market value on the date the option is granted, but it may be set below this level. Typically the executive may exercise the options by paying cash equal to the exercise price or by tendering previously owned shares of stock.

At the time the option is exercised the excess of the fair market value of the stock over the option price is taxed as ordinary income and is subject to withholding. The company receives a tax deduction in the amount of the executive's income from the exercise of the option in the year the executive is taxed if withholding requirements are met.

> *Example:* The employer grants to Ellie Executive the right to purchase 500 shares of common stock at the market price at the time of issuance ($20) at any time over the next 5 years. After 3 years, the market price has risen to $60 per share. Ellie purchases all 500 shares at $20 per share ($10,000). She now has $20,000 ($40 x 500) of ordinary income, which is the difference between the purchase price ($10,000) and the current market value ($30,000).

Clearly these options will be valuable to the executive only if the price of stock has risen since the date the option was issued, but there is a possibility of large gains if the price is increased substantially. The executive typically may choose to exercise the options to maximize gains at any time before or after retirement without limitation; however, there *is* a limitation for executives who are considered "insiders" under SEC rules. Essentially, an insider is any executive who would have access to information that is not available to the general public. Insiders are subject to an insider-trading rule that limits the sale of stocks by the executive to within 6 months of the time he or she has been issued the option. Therefore the 6-month period begins when the option is issued and ends when the stock is sold. This matching rule was adopted in 1991 and is less burdensome than the previous rule that measured the 6-month period from the time the option was exercised to the date of sale.

In order to exercise the options the executive needs cash to pay the option price for the stock. Although this often will require borrowing, once the options are exercised the executive may sell a sufficient number of the shares to repay the loan. If the executive prefers to hold the shares for their potential future appreciation, devising a method to raise the cash necessary to purchase shares becomes an important part of retirement planning. In addition, if employer stock constitutes a disproportionate share of a retiring executive's investment portfolio, planning for the systematic repositioning of the portfolio is another consideration for the practitioner.

Stock Appreciation Rights (SARs)

Stock appreciation rights normally are granted in tandem with an option whereby the executive, in lieu of exercising the option, can receive a payment equal to the excess of the stock's market value at exercise over the option price. SARs may be attached to incentive stock options or nonqualified stock options or may be granted on a "stand alone" basis without an option. When the SARs are exercised, payment may be in the form of cash, stock, or a combination of the two.

> *Example:* Start with same situation as in the above example. Now assume, however, that Ellie can choose either to exercise all the options or to trade in up to half the options for cash. Assume that she decides to exercise 250 options and cash in on the SAR value on the other 250. Therefore Ellie will receive $10,000 ($40 x 250) in cash, and will have to pay out $5,000 to purchase the other shares ($20 x 250). She can use the remaining $5,000 to pay her tax liability.

The value of the rights is taxed in the year of exercise as ordinary income and is subject to withholding. The company may take a tax deduction in the amount of the executive's income from exercise of these rights in the year the executive is taxed.

As in the case of nonqualified stock options, the executive has the possibility of receiving large gains. Noninsiders may choose the timing of exercise to maximize gains, but insiders must follow the insider-trading rules.

SARs have two features that make them different from nonqualified stock options. First, since the executive is paid the difference between the option price and the market value of the stock at the time the SAR is exercised, the executive does not have to raise the cash necessary to actually purchase the shares at the option price as he or she would with an NQSO. However, in some cases the gains of SARs may be capped by a company-imposed maximum designed to limit the company's potential cost. This is never the case with nonqualified stock options.

Incentive Stock Options (ISOs)

An incentive stock option is an option to purchase shares of the company stock at 100 percent or more of the stock's fair market value on the date that the option is granted for a period of up to 10 years. ISOs are taxed more favorably to the participant than nonqualified stock options but are less flexible. There are certain limits on the value of options that can become exercisable annually, and there are certain holding period requirements before sale. In addition, any option granted to a shareholder of 10 percent or more of a company's voting stock must be priced at 110 percent or more of the stock's fair market value, with an option term of no more than 5 years. As in the case of nonqualified stock options, the options may be exercised by paying cash or by tendering previously owned shares of stock.

When the executive exercises the ISO there is no regular income tax owed. However, the excess of the stock's fair market value at the time of exercise over the option exercise price—that is, the "spread"—is a tax preference item that may trigger an alternative minimum tax obligation. If the shares are held for at least 2 years from the date the option was granted and at least one year from exercise, the tax on sale is payable at a long-term capital-gains rate on the increase in the stock's value from the date of the grant of the option to the date of sale of the stock. If the holding period requirements are not met, the gain to the extent realized from the time the option is granted to the time of exercise of the option is taxed as ordinary income; the remainder is taxed as capital gain.

Although capital gains are currently taxed at the same rate as ordinary income, the distinction may still be important when repositioning your client's portfolio of investments at and after retirement. Capital gains on the sale of stocks acquired through incentive stock options can be used to offset capital losses from the sale of other securities. Therefore the timing of the sale of stock acquired through incentive options (and nonqualified stock options) is an important part of investment planning at and after retirement. Since many executives acquire sizable blocks of stock in their company through various incentive plans, one important planning consideration is often the systematic liquidation of this stock and the purchase of other securities to better diversify the executive's investment portfolio at retirement.

As with NQSOs, ISOs provide the executive with the possibility of large gains. In addition, SARs can be attached to the options if they have the same terms as the underlying option. Within limits the executive can choose the timing of exercise of the options to maximize gains; however, options granted prior to December 31, 1986, must be exercised in the order in which they were granted.

Phantom Stock

Phantom stock is the name given to what is essentially just a bookkeeping entry on behalf of the executive as if the executive had been given stock in the company. Units analogous to company shares are granted to the executives, and the value of the units generally equals the appreciation and market value of the stock underlying the units. Phantom units are valued at a fixed date, typically at retirement or 5 to 15 years after the grant of the phantom stock. When the phantom stock "matures," that is, at its valuation date, the company may pay the executive in cash, stock, or some combination of both. In many cases, dividend equivalents may be credited to the units just as dividends would be paid to the underlying stock. Phantom stock mirrors the tax, accounting, and insider-trading treatment of SARs.

> *Example:* Employer grants Executive A 100 shares of phantom stock, the value of which is $5,000 ($50 per share). The phantom stock matures, and 5 years later its value has increased to $7,500 ($75 per share). At that time, the employer pays the employee $2,500, the difference between the value at time of the grant and the value at the time of maturity.

On the payment date the value of the units is taxed to the executive as ordinary income and is subject to withholding. The company takes a tax deduction in the amount of the executive's taxable income from the units.

As with other incentive plans, the executive has the possibility of large gains. Although one advantage of phantom stock over stock options is that the executive avoids the financing cost associated with exercise of the options, in some cases gains may be capped by company-imposed maximums designed to limit the company's potential payment, and, since payment is typically triggered by retirement, the executive generally has no flexibility in choosing when to value the award. In cases where the executive can control the form or timing of the unit's valuation or settlement, trading restrictions, similar to those applying to stock options and SARs, will apply to insiders.

Restricted Stock

In a restricted stock plan, the participant is given (usually at no cost) shares of company stock. The shares are actually stamped with specific restrictions, which require that the participant give the shares back to the company upon a specified event. Most commonly, the restriction is that if the employee stops working prior to some specified date, the individual will have to forfeit the shares. Another common restriction is a clause that would require forfeiture if the individual terminated employment and went to work with the competitor (commonly called a noncompete clause). Dividends on the stock are usually paid to the participant during the entire period in which he or she holds the stock.

> *Example:* Company grants to Billy Bigshot 200 shares of stock worth $10,000. The stock will be forfeited unless Billy works until age 65, at which time the stock becomes freely transferable by Billy. At age 65 Billy retires and decides to hold the stock, which is now valued at $8,000.

For the employer, restricted stock plans are another way to tie the employee to the company, through the vesting provision, and to tie the benefit to the performance of the company stock. From the employee's perspective, this type of deferred compensation is relatively secure, since the stock is titled in the executive's name, meaning that creditors cannot get to this asset if the company performs badly. Another advantage is that the employee does not have to pay anything in order to get stock ownership, unlike stock option plans. The biggest limitation, from the employee's perspective, is the possibility of forfeiture.

From a tax perspective, the shares of stock are generally not taxed until the substantial limitations on the stock lapse. At that time, the value of the stock will be treated as ordinary income to the participant and will be deductible as compensation expense to the employer. Any dividends paid to the participant will also be treated as compensation income—both includible as income to the participant and deductible as compensation by the employer.

Participants under a restricted stock plan can make an election, within 30 days of the time of the stock grant, to be taxed sooner—at the time of the grant. Making this election is a big gamble since the stock could be forfeited later, and the taxpayer would not be able to recoup the taxes paid. However, an individual who (1) does not expect to lose the stock, (2) has the money to pay taxes at the time of the grant, and (3) expects the stock to greatly appreciate in value may want to consider the election. When the participant later sells the stock, he or she will be concerned about whether the sale will be eligible for the 28 percent long-term capital gains rate. Under the rules, the one-year holding period begins at the time taxes are paid. So paying taxes earlier starts the clock ticking and gives the participant a better chance of being eligible for long-term capital gains when the restrictions lapse.

Performance Unit/Performance Cash

A performance unit is an award granted in the form of a contingent number of units or as a contingent cash award. Units may be granted with a fixed-dollar payment value, with the number of units earned varying on the basis of performance achievements. Alternatively, a fixed number of units may be granted, the payment value of which will vary on the basis of performance achievements.

The duration of the performance cycle may vary but is typically from 3 to 5 years. The financial objectives that serve as the basis for performance achievements may relate to such items as cumulative growth and earnings per share or improvement on return in investment.

Example: Company promises Paully President that if the company's earnings per share increase by 5 percent over the next 3 years, he will receive $50,000. If earnings per share increase by 10 percent, he will receive $100,000.

The company may pay the award in cash and/or stock of equivalent value. On the payment date, the value of the award paid in cash or unrestricted stock is taxed as ordinary income and is subject to withholding. The company takes a tax deduction in the amount of the executive's taxable income from the award.

Since performance units virtually never survive beyond an executive's retirement, they are not an important item in retirement planning per se. However, since they may provide sizable bonuses to executives who meet the performance achievements desired, they may play a very important role in deciding when an executive chooses to retire. Consequently, performance units are an important factor in preretirement planning for executives who are approaching retirement age.

Performance Shares

A performance share is a contingent performance award granted in the form of a fixed number of common shares at the beginning of a performance cycle. The number of shares payable at the end of the cycle depends on the extent to which objectives have been achieved. The value received by the executive depends both on the number of shares earned and their market value at the time of payment. As with performance units, the duration of the performance cycle may vary but is typically from 3 to 5 years, and financial objectives may relate to such items as cumulative growth and earnings per share or improvement in return on investment. Also like performance units, payout may be in the form of shares of stock and/or cash of equivalent value. On the payment date, the value of the award paid in cash or unrestricted stock is taxed as ordinary income to the executive and is subject to withholding. The company takes a tax deduction in the amount of executive's income from the award.

As in the case of performance units, performance shares are an important consideration for executives approaching retirement in deciding when they should retire.

Performance units or performance shares are sometimes granted simultaneously with nonqualified stock options granted at market value. The payout from performance units or performance shares may enable the executive to pay taxes on the exercise of the option or may help finance the exercise of the options.

Book-Value Purchase Rights

Book-value purchase rights are an executive incentive plan commonly used in closely held companies. The executive is offered the opportunity to purchase shares of stock, the price of which is determined by reference to book value. Shares must be resold to the company at a later date at the per share book value at that time. Shares for a book-value plan are often a separate, nonvoting class of stock; the holders of this class of stock typically receive dividends as paid to regular shareholders.

These purchase rights usually must be exercised within a limited amount of time, generally no more than 3 to 6 months. At the time the executive exercises the right to purchase, there are no tax consequences. When the shares are sold back to the company, the increase in book value from the date of purchase is taxed as a long-term capital gain if held for the required holding period; otherwise it is taxed as ordinary income.

> *Example:* Bob Bonus has the opportunity to buy a special class of nonvoting stock at $40 per share within the next 3 months. Bob decides to buy 1,000 shares. Under the terms of the sale, Bob will sell back the shares of stock 5 years from the date of purchase at whatever the book value is then. Bob will receive dividends. The book value after 5 years in $50. Bob has a long-term capital gain of $10,000.

Like other incentive plans, this plan offers the executive the possibility of large gains if the book value of the company increases substantially. However, since the stock may be resold to the company only, book-value stock lacks the open-market stock price appreciation potential of marketable stock. Although the executive may usually sell the stock back to the company at any time prior to retirement, many book-value plans give the company the option to call the stock (that is, force the executive to sell the stock back to the company) when the executive retires or otherwise ceases employment with the company.

The principal retirement planning issue with book-value stock is the timing of the redemption of the stock. If all stock must be redeemed by retirement, the stock should be systematically redeemed before retirement to avoid a large increase in taxable income in the year of retirement. Even if the stock does not have to be redeemed at retirement, book-value stock is typically not the type of security that should be held in a retirement investment portfolio because it lacks the potential for the open-market stock price to appreciate and because the closely held companies that typically issue these shares are much more likely to suffer financial hardship than larger companies whose shares are traded in the open market.

Junior Stock

Junior stock is a restricted stock that is convertible at a one-to-one ratio into the regular common stock shares of the company if specific performance goals are achieved. Due to the junior stock's nonassured conversion feature and inferior rights, the fair "market" value of junior shares is considerably below that of the shares into which they could convert. Junior stock typically pays no dividends, has no voting rights, and is subordinate to all other issues of the company, including the common stock, in a liquidation. Junior stock is nontransferable: it can only be converted into common stock—if the performance conditions are achieved—or sold back to the issuing corporation, usually at the original purchase price. In some cases junior stock may be sold at a discount from fair value or granted at no cost to the executive, but this affects the tax treatment to the executive.

> *Example:* Arthur Accountant, controller of XYZ Corp., is given the option to purchase 500 shares of junior stock at $15 per share (at the time, the market value of common stock is $30 per share). Each share can be converted after 2 years to a share of common stock, but only if the earnings per share on common stock have increased by 20 percent. During the waiting period the junior stock is nontransferable. If the price of the common stock drops below $15, or if the company does not meet the performance goals, XYZ Corp. will buy back the junior stock at $15 per share.

When the executive purchases junior stock he or she will be taxed on any difference between the fair value of the junior stock and the price paid (typically, however, there is no difference since usually the stock is sold at fair market value). When the junior stock is converted into regular stock there is no tax, and when the common stock is sold, the difference between the original junior stock purchase price and the common stock price at the time of sale is taxed as a capital gain.

The principal advantages of junior stock to the executive include

- the possibility of large gains
- the purchase price is lower than the cost of common stock
- taxation is delayed until the common stock is sold
- the executive's downside risk is limited by the company's repurchase provisions

The principal disadvantage of junior stock is that the performance goals may never be reached, which means the executive may never be able to convert the junior stock into the common stock. In this case the executive has lost the opportunity to participate in the appreciation of the common stock and, in fact, has basically lost the interest he or she could have earned by investing in some other alternative since he or she may generally redeem the junior stock only for the amount originally paid.

Under this plan the principal planning issue for executives approaching retirement is deciding on when to retire. Executives who own junior stock and are likely to meet the performance objectives probably will not want to retire until the performance objectives have been met and the junior stock may be converted to the common stock of the company.

IRAS—THE GROUND RULES

One of the most important discretionary sources of retirement income that retirement planners can counsel their clients about is an individual retirement account (IRA). Individual retirement accounts are similar to qualified plans in many respects. Both are tax-favored savings plans that encourage the accumulation of savings for retirement by allowing contributions to be made with pretax dollars (if the taxpayer is eligible) and earnings to be tax deferred until retirement. This windfall for taxpayers comes at the government's expense in both cases. The federal government and most state and local governments postpone collecting taxes on accumulated interest and/or contributions to encourage people to plan for their retirement. Also, both plans have stringent rules to ensure that the goal of encouraging retirement savings is achieved and that the revenue loss is minimized.

An IRA is a savings program into which many of your clients can make yearly tax-deductible contributions. The IRA document itself is a written trust or a custodial account whose trustee or custodian must be a bank, a federally insured credit union, a savings and loan association, or a person or organization that receives the IRS's permission to act as the trustee or custodian (for example, an insurance company).

IRAs are subject to certain limitations. These limitations include the following:

- Contributions to an IRA cannot exceed $2,000 a year or 100 percent of compensation, whichever is smaller. (There are two exceptions to this rule: a spousal IRA can be set up, and rollover contributions of any amount can be placed in an IRA.)
- IRA contributions cannot be made during or after the year your client reaches age 70 1/2.
- IRA funds may not be commingled with your client's other assets; the funds can contain only IRA contributions and rollover contributions.
- IRA funds may *not* be used to buy a life insurance policy.
- Funds contributed to an IRA cannot be invested in collectibles.
- No loans may be taken from these savings programs.

Individual retirement accounts also have certain ground rules regarding eligibility, contribution and deduction limits, and distributions. In general, these rules ensure that the federal government is promoting retirement savings, not merely providing a tax shelter. These rules also protect against the loss of excess federal revenue by limiting the amount of contributions, prescribing the dates by which distributions must occur, and limiting participation to those who are not considered active participants in a pension program or who are considered middle class or below.

Who Is Eligible for IRAs?

Any person under age 70 1/2 who receives compensation (either salary or self-employment earned income) can make a contribution to an IRA. For some the contribution will *not* be deductible, but the interest earnings will be tax deferred. For others the contribution (as well as any interest earnings) will be tax deferred through an income tax deduction. Deductible IRA contributions are permitted if your client (or your client's spouse) is not an active participant in an employer-maintained retirement plan or if your client's adjusted gross income falls below prescribed limits, which are designed to approximate a middle-class income. In other words, if either your client or your client's spouse (whether filing jointly or separately) is an active participant in an employer plan, the IRA deduction is available only if their adjusted gross income is below certain limits.

Active Participant

For the retirement planner, the first issue that arises under the eligibility question is identifying whether your client is an active participant in an employer-maintained plan. The plans that are considered basically take into account every type of qualified plan: defined-benefit pension plans, money-purchase plans, target-benefit plans, profit-sharing plans, stock plans, tax-sheltered annuity plans, and even simplified employee pension plans (SEPs). Federal, state, or local government plans are also included. Not included, however, are nonqualified retirement arrangements and executive incentive or bonus plans. An employee who is covered only by a nonqualified plan and/or an executive incentive or bonus plan will not be considered an active participant and therefore can make deductible IRA contributions.

Simply being associated with an employer-sponsored plan does not affect your client's ability to make deductible IRA contributions. Deductibility of IRA contributions is jeopardized only if your client is an active participant in the employer-sponsored plan. *Active participant* has a specific meaning depending on the type of plan involved.

Defined-Benefit Plans. Generally a person is an active participant in a defined-benefit plan unless excluded under the eligibility provisions of the plan for the entire plan year. This is true even if the employee elects not to participate in the plan. For example, ABC Company has a plan that requires employees to contribute in order to participate. Since Kim does not feel she can afford to make contributions, she does not participate. However, Kim is still considered an active participant for IRA purposes, even though she is not active in the plan.

On the other hand, a client will not be considered an active participant in a defined-benefit plan in the following situations:

- if your client is not covered under the plan's eligibility provisions (for example, employees who are not currently eligible or who will never be eligible for plan participation)
- if the defined-benefit plan is frozen—meaning that no additional benefits are accruing currently for any participant

Defined-Contribution Plans. In general, a person is an active participant in any type of defined-contribution plan if the plan specifies that employer contributions must be allocated to the individual's account. In a profit-sharing or stock plan where employer contributions are discretionary, the participant must actually receive some contribution (even if the contribution amounts to a reallocated forfeiture) for active-participant status to be triggered. Furthermore, mandatory contributions, voluntary contributions, and contributions made pursuant to a salary reduction, 403(b), 401(k), or SEP (discussed later) arrangement will also trigger active-participant status.

A special rule applies when contributions are completely discretionary under the plan (like a profit-sharing plan) and contributions are not made until after the end of the plan year (ending with or within the employee's tax year in question). In this case, to recognize that a plan participant may not know whether he or she is an "active participant" by the time the IRA contribution deadline arrives, the employer's contribution is attributable to the following year.

> *Example:* Sally first becomes eligible for XYZ Corporation's profit-sharing plan for the plan year ending December 31, 1992. The company is on a calendar fiscal year and does not decide to make a contribution for the 1992 plan year until June 1, 1993. Sally is not considered an active participant in the plan for the 1992 plan year. However, due to the 1992 contribution, she is an active participant for the 1993 plan year.

Several other important rules apply to both defined-benefit and defined-contribution plans. The first addresses the issue of which calendar year an individual is considered an active participant, when he or she is a plan participant in a plan with a plan year overlapping two calendar years. The rule provides that the individual will be an active participant for the calendar year in which the plan year ends.

> *Example:* Susan first becomes eligible for the ABC money-purchase pension plan for the plan year June 1, 1994 to May 30, 1995. Susan is an active participant for 1995 (but not 1994) because the plan year ended during calendar year 1995.

The second rule addresses the situation in which an individual is a participant only for part of a plan year. In this case the person is considered a plan participant for the entire plan year in question, even if eligible for a only a short period of time. Finally, note that when determining active participant status, it does not matter whether or not the participant is vested in the benefit.

Income Level

The second issue that arises under the eligibility question is determining whether your client can make deductible contributions under the income-level rules. In general, people who are not active participants can deduct contributions to an IRA regardless of what they earn. For an active participant, however, fully deductible contributions are allowed only if he or she has adjusted gross income below a specified level. If the adjusted gross income exceeds the specified limit but falls below a maximum level, the $2,000 IRA limit is proportionately reduced by a formula (table 4-2).

TABLE 4-2
Limits for Deductible IRA Contributions for Active Participants

Filing Status	Full IRA Deduction	Reduced IRA Deduction	No IRA Deduction
Individual or head of household	$25,000 or less	$25,000.01 – $34,999.99	$35,000 or more
Married filing jointly	$40,000 or less	$40,000.01 – $49,999.99	$50,000 or more
Married filing separately	Not available	$0.01 – $9,999.99	$10,000 or more

---

The level for unreduced contributions depends upon your client's filing status. Married couples filing a joint return will get a full IRA deduction if their adjusted gross income is $40,000 or less, whereas marrieds filing separately cannot get a full IRA deduction. Individual taxpayers and taxpayers filing as head of household will get a full IRA deduction if their adjusted gross income is $25,000 or less.

The maximum level for deductible contributions is $49,999.99 for marrieds filing jointly; $9,999.99 for marrieds filing separately; and $34,999.99 for those using head-of-household or individual filing status. In other words, if an active participant's adjusted gross income exceeds these levels, no part of an IRA contribution can be deducted.

For taxpayers whose adjusted gross income falls between the no-deduction level and the full-deduction level, their reduced deduction can be computed by using the following formula:

$$\text{Deductible amount} = \$2,000 - \frac{\text{adjusted gross income} - \text{filing status floor}}{5}$$

Example: Ken and Patty Jenkins (a married couple filing jointly) are both working and have a combined adjusted gross income of $46,000. Ken and Patty can each make the full IRA contribution of $2,000 (total $4,000). The following formula shows that each can deduct $800 (total $1,600):

$$\text{Ken and Patty's deductible amount} = \$2,000 - \frac{\$46,000 - \$40,000}{5}$$

Ken and Patty's deductible amount = $800 each

Therefore of the $4,000 contributed to an IRA, $2,400 will be on an aftertax basis.

Example: Anne Le Flamme (filing as a single taxpayer) has an adjusted gross income of $30,000; she too can make a $2,000 contribution, but only $1,000 will be deductible:

$$\text{Anne's deductible amount} = \$2,000 - \frac{\$30,000 - \$25,000}{5}$$

Anne's deductible amount = $1,000

After Anne consults with her retirement planner, however, she might choose to limit her contribution to the $1,000 deductible permitted and then seek tax shelter elsewhere for the other $1,000 that she has targeted for retirement savings.

Three important rules apply to taxpayers who fall into the reduced IRA contribution category. First, the IRS allows the adjusted limitation to be rounded up to the next $10 increment. For example, if the formula for Kay shows her eligible to make a deductible contribution of $758.43, her deductible contribution is rounded up to $760. The second rule concerning the reduction formula is that there is a $200 floor. This floor means that even if, for example, Ed's deductible IRA contribution works out to $57, Ed is still entitled to make a $200 deductible contribution. If Ed's deductible amount is zero, however, no deductible contribution is allowed, not even the $200 floor amount. Note that a one-cent difference can mean the loss of a $200 deduction. For example, Faye and Roger Maloney (marrieds filing jointly) have $50,000 in adjusted gross income, which means no deductible IRA. If Faye and Roger could reduce the amount of adjusted gross income by one cent, to $49,999.99, they would be entitled to a $200 deductible IRA contribution. The third rule is that a taxpayer can designate contributions as nondeductible even when they are actually deductible so that he or she will be able to receive distributions tax free. This strategy is useful only if your client has little or no taxable income or if your client anticipates large tax increases in the future.

Contribution Limits

The limit for annual contributions to an IRA is the lesser of $2,000 or 100 percent of compensation. It is important to remember that a contribution cannot exceed a client's *compensation.* Compensation is defined as earnings from wages, salaries, tips, professional fees, bonuses, and any other amount a client receives for providing professional services. In addition, alimony and separate-maintenance payments are considered compensation for IRA purposes. Compensation does not include earnings and profits from property, such as rental interest or dividend income, or amounts received as a pension or annuity. Thus retirees will need a part-time job in order to make IRA contributions even if they would like to save a portion of their pension distribution for later in their retirement.

Self-employeds who have a net loss from self-employment can still make a $2,000 IRA contribution if they have at least $2,000 of employment compensation from another employer. On the other hand, if there are both employment income and net income from self-employment, the two amounts are added together to determine the amount that can be contributed.[1]

> *Example:* In his first year in business Donald, a self-employed creator of computer software, has a net loss of $17,000, largely because of start-up costs. However, he did receive $4,000 from part-time teaching at a university. Donald may contribute up to $2,000 to an IRA because his salary will not be reduced by his self-employment loss.

> *Example:* Marge, an aspiring self-employed artist and part-time day-care worker, received only $1,000 in salary income from her day-care job, but her net self-employment income from paintings she sold was $3,000. Marge may contribute up to $2,000 for an IRA because the combination of salary income and self-employment income exceeds $2,000.

Timing of Contributions

Contributions to an IRA can be made at any time. The year for which a contribution can be deducted, however, depends on when the contribution is made. If the contribution occurs between April 16 and December 31, it is deductible only for the year in which it is made. If the contribution is made between January 1 and April 15 (the tax-return due date not including extensions), it may be deductible either for the year in which it is made or the preceding year (assuming that contributions have not already been made for that year). This means that a contribution to an IRA can be made after the tax year is over up until the tax-filing deadline for the preceding year (April 15). During this period your client can contribute $4,000 at one time. For example, on January 15 a $4,000 contribution can be made with $2,000 applying to the prior year and $2,000 applying to the current year.

Spousal IRAs

Spousal IRAs provide an opportunity to save an additional $250 and to arrange favorable distribution of IRA assets. A spousal IRA may be set up under the following conditions:

- The taxpayer is married at the end of the year.
- The taxpayer receives compensation (no passive or retirement income may be contributed).
- The taxpayer's spouse has received no compensation during the tax year. (If the taxpayer's spouse has received compensation, the spouse can set up his or her own IRA.)
- A joint tax return is filed for the tax year in which the contribution is made.

Spousal IRAs are quite flexible. Up to $2,000 may be contributed on behalf of either spouse (but the total for both spouses may not exceed $2,250). However, no amount has to be contributed on behalf of either spouse. Specifically, the taxpayer may contribute $2,000 to his or her spouse's account, and none to his or her own, or vice versa. Since no more than $2,000 can be placed in either IRA for any year, two IRAs must be set up in order to take full advantage of the $2,250 spousal limit.

Spousal IRAs are subject to the same deductibility rules that apply to nonspousal IRAs—active participants in an employer plan are barred from deducting a spousal IRA unless they fall under the prescribed income ranges that were discussed earlier. In other words, nonactive participants may deduct spousal IRAs, active participants whose adjusted gross income is $40,000 or less can take a full spousal IRA deduction of $250, and active participants whose adjusted gross income is $40,000.01−$49,999.99 can take a reduced spousal deduction. As with the nonspousal IRA, the spousal IRA requires a mathematical formula to determine the appropriate deductible amount. The formula is as follows:

$$\text{Deductible amount for spousal IRA} = \$250 - \frac{\text{adjusted gross income} - \$40,000}{40}$$

Example: Joe and Jane Morgan would like to contribute to a spousal IRA in addition to their regular IRA. Joe and Jane have an adjusted gross income of $46,000, which enables them to make an $800 deductible contribution under the regular IRS deduction limits (see table 4-2). Jane stays home with the children and has no income. Joe and Jane want to maximize their deductible contribution by setting up a spousal IRA.

$$\text{Deductible amount for spousal IRA} = \$250 - \frac{\$46,000 - \$40,000}{40}$$

Deductible amount for spousal IRA = $100

Note that the total deductible limit will be $900 ($800 for the nonspousal IRA and $100 for the spousal IRA) and that the spousal IRA is *not* subject to the $200 floor.

In addition to allowing an extra $250 in savings, a spousal IRA provides a valuable opportunity to split contributions to meet retirement and tax needs.

Example: Greg and Diane LeRose meet all the requirements for a spousal IRA. Greg is 50 years old and Diane is 53. If the LeRoses wish to withdraw their contributions as soon as possible without penalty, the $2,000 should be deposited in Diane's IRA and the spousal $250 in Greg's. The reason is that Diane will reach the age that withdrawals are allowed without penalty—age 59 1/2—before Greg and will therefore be able to withdraw her account 3 years before Greg. However, if the LeRoses desire to postpone paying tax on the money as long as possible by delaying the distribution of the account, the $2,000 contribution should be placed in Greg's account since he will turn 70 1/2 (when distributions must start) 3 years after Diane. Of course, if Greg and Diane want to hedge their bets, they can split the contributions evenly or place a substantial amount in Greg's account to delay taxation, while also placing enough in Diane's account to start adequate withdrawals during the 3-year period when she can make penalty-free withdrawals and he cannot.

Excess Contributions

An excess contribution is any amount contributed to an individual retirement arrangement that exceeds the $2,000 limits or $2,250 spousal limit. One common way of falling into the excess-contribution trap is to make a rollover that does not meet the prescribed rules. An improper rollover on other excess contributions will result in an excise tax of 6 percent on the excess. If the excess amount (plus interest) is withdrawn by the tax deadline for the year the excess contribution is made, however, the taxpayer does not have to pay the penalty. The taxpayer does have to include the excess amount in his or her gross income for that year and may have to pay a 10 percent premature distribution penalty on the interest. However, there is no premature distribution penalty on the principal amount.

INVESTMENTS

Types of Investments

Individual retirement accounts can be invested in a multitude of vehicles running the gamut from annuities to limited partnerships, from investments with minimal risk and modest returns to speculative investments with promises of greater return. IRAs are typically invested in certificates of deposit, money market funds, mutual funds, limited partnerships, income bond funds, corporate bond funds, and common stocks and other equities. Self-directed IRAs (IRAs in which the taxpayer is able to shift investments between general investment vehicles offered by the trustee) are also popular because they allow the investor to have investment flexibility and to anticipate or react to interest-rate directions and market trends.

Choosing the best investment for an individual retirement arrangement is similar to choosing any other investment. You must consider your client's lifestyle, other financial resources, and degree of risk aversion.

Individual Retirement Annuities

An individual retirement annuity (IRA annuity) is an annuity contract typically issued by insurance companies. IRA annuities are similar to IRAs except that the following additional rules apply because of their annuity investment feature:

- The IRA annuity is nontransferable. In other words, unlike the proceeds from other annuities, the IRA annuity proceeds must be received by either the taxpayer or a beneficiary. Individuals cannot set up an IRA annuity and then pledge the annuity to another party or put the annuity up as a security for a loan. For example, if a loan were made under an automatic premium-loan provision, the plan would be disqualified.
- IRA annuities may not have fixed premiums. However, charging an annual fee for each premium or having a level annual premium for a supplementary benefit, such as waiver of premium in case of disability, is allowable.

Investment Restrictions

Investment of IRA funds is generally open to all the investment vehicles available outside IRAs. There are, however, a few exceptions.

Clients cannot invest IRA funds in

- life insurance

- collectibles
- prohibited transactions

Life Insurance

Investment in life insurance is not allowed for an IRA even though defined-benefit and defined-contribution retirement plans allow an "incidental" amount of life insurance. IRAs, however, are not subject to the same rules (or underlying logic) and are considered to be strictly for retirement purposes. Therefore no incidental insurance is available.

Collectibles

If an IRA is invested in collectibles, the amount invested is considered a distribution in the year in which the amount is invested. This eliminates the tax advantages of IRAs. If the investment is made prior to age 59 1/2, a 10 percent excise tax will also be applicable unless the payment is made in the form of a life annuity or its equivalent. Collectibles include works of art, Oriental rugs, antiques, gold, rare coins, stamps, rare wines, and certain other tangible property.

There is one exception to the prohibition on investments in collectibles. Any gold or silver coin issued by the United States government can be bought with IRA funds. However, gold and silver coins of other countries are still prohibited as an IRA purchase.

Prohibited Transactions

A prohibited transaction for purposes of an IRA or IRA annuity is any improper use of the account or annuity, such as borrowing money from the account or annuity, selling property to the account, and using the account or annuity as security for a loan. If a nonexempt prohibited transaction occurs, the IRA will be "disqualified" and the taxpayer must include the fair market value of all of the IRA assets in his or her gross income for tax purposes in the year in which the prohibited transaction occurs. There also may be a 10 percent premature distribution penalty if the prohibited transaction occurred prior to age 59 1/2. In effect, prohibited transactions are treated as distributions from the plan.

Other Investments

Although there is no general restriction on investing in tax-sheltered vehicles such as municipal bonds, such investments are imprudent for IRA purposes because the tax shelter is not necessary. Since an IRA already provides for tax deferral, the overkill of investing in a tax-free bond will not make it worthwhile for an investor to take the lower yield that municipal bonds typically offer.

Advantages of Individual Retirement Annuities

The primary reason for choosing one IRA funding vehicle over another is the investor's desired return balanced against the amount of risk the investor is willing to accept. There are, however, secondary reasons that make IRA annuities worth considering when the return/risk factors are comparable with other investments: the waiver-of-premium coverage in case of disability and the lifelong payments that are provided. The waiver-of-premium coverage provides an investor with valuable protection should disability occur, which is especially important for those relying on individual-retirement-arrangement funds as a major source of retirement income. The lifetime payments offered by an annuity are a second reason for choosing an IRA annuity. As with any annuity, the investor is betting he or she will outlive the mortality table. If the investor does, the excess payments represent mortality gain, which can be thought of as an additional return on investment. The IRA annuity also quells a common fear of retired persons—running out of funds and becoming dependent on others. Ideally, investors would like to live off the interest provided by their personal savings and IRAs; however, this is not possible for many. Life annuities provide a structured way to use up both principal and interest without the danger of running out of funds.

INDIVIDUAL RETIREMENT ACCOUNTS AND THE RETIREMENT PLANNER

For the retirement planner understanding IRAs requires more than just knowing their various rules, restraints, and tax implications. The retirement planner must also analyze whether a current client's interests are best served by making IRA contributions and must identify potential clients who need IRA assistance. Retirement planners should even ask themselves whether selling IRAs is appropriate for them.

Should Your Client Make an IRA Contribution?

There are any number of valid reasons why people do not make IRA contributions:

- IRA contributions are unaffordable because of present income level or current cash flow.
- Large expenses, such as a child's college education, are close at hand and the money would have to be withdrawn shortly after deposit.
- Tax rates for the client are very low (for example, for someone in graduate school), and it is reasonable to assume he or she will be in a much higher bracket at retirement.

- Savings cannot be tied up because of insecure prospects for future income (for example, for someone involved in a speculative employment situation).

If, however, your client's excuse for not contributing is lack of knowledge about IRAs or lack of interest in them, being too young, or having an adequate retirement plan, then careful reconsideration is warranted. For example, does your client who is "too young" know that by making just nine $2,000 contributions from age 18 to age 26—and no contributions thereafter—an IRA at age 65 will be larger than an IRA funded with a $2,000 contribution each year from age 27 to age 65 (table 4-3)? Has your client whose retirement plan is "adequate" considered that postretirement inflation at a modest increase of 4 percent per year means that a $1 loaf of bread at age 65 will cost $2.19 at age 85?

One of the most important considerations in deciding whether to put money into an IRA is whether your client can deduct the initial contribution. Taxpayers who can make contributions on a before-tax basis have a huge advantage over those whose only benefit is the interest accumulation on a tax-sheltered basis. Those whose only advantage is tax-deferred interest accumulation must look carefully at net aftertax investment return and the desirability of keeping the contributions tied up until the break-even point, where the benefit of tax-deferred accumulation exceeds the 10 percent penalty in the event that funds must be withdrawn prior to age 59 1/2.

Regardless of whether pretax contributions can be made, it is important to know if the "risk" of tying up income justifies the return of the IRA tax advantage(s). Generally the risk is justified if the client is committed to saving for retirement, but it will not be justified if the client is likely to raid the IRA before the appropriate time. Undisciplined IRA withdrawals represent ineffective money management, and planners who feel withdrawals are too great a temptation for their clients may want to avoid the IRA in the first place. On the other hand, some planners believe the lock-in of retirement funds is a hidden advantage of IRAs because the client is coerced into leaving savings for retirement and will not be tempted to withdraw funds under marginal circumstances. In either case, knowing your client's financial habits and forecasting his or her willpower are the deciding factors.

SIMPLIFIED EMPLOYEE PENSION PLANS (SEPs)

A simplified employee pension plan (SEP) is a retirement plan that uses an individual retirement account as the receptacle for contributions. The word *pension* in *simplified employee pension plan* is actually a misnomer. A SEP is not a pension plan; it is an alternative to a profit-sharing or 401(k) plan. The SEP alternative is often encountered with clients who work for small businesses. Under a SEP, each participant's IRA can be funded up to a maximum of 15

TABLE 4-3
IRA Funding Plans*

Plan One			Plan Two		
Age start		18	Age start		27
Age end		26	Age end		65
Amount per year		$2,000	Amount per year		$2,000
Rate of return		10%	Rate of return		10%
Value at age 65		$1,229,194	Value at age 65		$883,145
Total amount contributed		$8,000	Total amount contributed		$78,000
Age	Amount	Value	Age	Amount	Value
18	$2,000	$ 2,200	18	$ 0	$ 0
19	2,000	4,620	19	0	0
20	2,000	7,282	20	0	0
21	2,000	10,210	21	0	0
22	2,000	13,431	22	0	0
23	2,000	16,974	23	0	0
24	2,000	20,872	24	0	0
25	2,000	25,159	25	0	0
26	2,000	29,875	26	0	0
27	0	32,862	27	2,000	2,200
28	0	36,149	28	2,000	4,620
29	0	39,763	29	2,000	7,282
30	0	43,740	30	2,000	10,210
.	.	.	.	.	.
.	.	.	.	.	.
.	.	.	.	.	.
60	0	763,233	60	2,000	540,049
61	0	839,556	61	2,000	596,254
62	0	923,512	62	2,000	658,079
63	0	1,015,863	63	2,000	726,087
64	0	1,117,449	64	2,000	800,896
65	0	1,229,194	65	2,000	883,185

*This comparison is hypothetical; no guarantees are implied for specific investments. The interest rate is assumed to remain unchanged for the entire period.

percent of compensation or $30,000, whichever is less. Typically the employer funds the SEP. Other clients will have employers who have a salary reduction SEP. If a salary reduction SEP is used, the maximum by which an employee can reduce his or her salary to fund the SEP is the lesser of 25 percent of compensation or $9,240 in 1995 (or as indexed). The SEP may be designed to accommodate both employer contributions and salary reduction employee contributions.

Technically a SEP is not a qualified plan (an Internal Revenue Code Sec. 401 plan) but instead is a form of individual retirement arrangement (an Internal Revenue Code Sec. 408 arrangement). In spite of the fact that SEPs are not qualified, they have a "qualified flavor." Employers who set up SEPs

- must make contributions on a nondiscriminatory basis (for example, contributions cannot discriminate in favor of the prohibited group)
- must assure that contributions bear a uniform percentage of compensation (only compensation up to $150,000 can be taken into account) except that the plan may be integrated with social security
- may not disallow participation because of age if the employee is 21 or older
- are subject to the top-heavy rules

SEPs, on the other hand, are designed differently from qualified plans because they contain many of the IRA rules, such as the following:

- No loans are permitted from a SEP.
- The IRA rules relating to distributions and early or late withdrawals apply.
- Investment in collectibles (except for U.S. government gold coins) is prohibited.
- There is no 5-year or 10-year averaging.
- All amounts contributed to a SEP (even employer contributions) are immediately 100 percent vested in the participant.

SEPs are also subject to the following special design rules that do not apply to either a qualified plan or an IRA:

- SEPs may not disallow participation if an employee has performed service for the employer during at least 3 of the immediately preceding 5 years (performing service means receiving $400 [as indexed for 1995] or more in compensation for the year).
- Contributions must be made under a written allocation formula that specifies how the amount allocated is to be computed.
- The maximum salary reduction that can be taken under a SEP is $9,240 (as indexed for 1995).
- A salary reduction SEP can be maintained only if the plan has 25 or fewer participants, 50 percent of the eligible participants make salary deferral elections, and special nondiscrimination requirements are satisfied.

NOTES

1. In other words, the employment earnings are not reduced by the self-employment loss.

5

Determining Retirement Needs

Chapter Outline

Arguably the most important part of any comprehensive plan for retirement is the estimate of the client's retirement income needs, along with the calculation of the savings rate necessary to meet those needs. Retirement income needs are typically defined as the amount needed throughout retirement that allows a client to sustain the standard of living enjoyed just prior to retirement. Generating the income needed requires accumulation of a sufficient retirement fund—the bankroll for the retirement years. The savings rate needed is the percentage of salary that a person must put aside during his or her working years to achieve the retirement goal.

The methods for accomplishing a needs and savings analysis can vary considerably. There are a variety of work sheets and computer models that accomplish this objective. In addition, most work sheets and computer models make room for the planner to insert his or her unique perspective. It is the purpose of this chapter to provide you with an understanding of the process involved in arriving at the bottom line figure needed. While it would be impossible to review each work sheet and computer model individually, it is possible to focus on common characteristics of the process. An understanding of the process distinguishes a professional planner from the crowd and allows for a more accurate prediction to be made. To foster insight into the needs and savings analysis, this chapter will

- examine the assumptions that must be made in order to arrive at a skillful prediction regarding a client's unique circumstances
- probe into the common features contained in the myriad work sheets and computer models by looking at three different methods for determining need

One caveat is in order before we begin. All too often clients and planners alike hold the retirement target generated from a work sheet or computer package as gospel. The amount needed to maintain a client's preretirement standard of living is not etched in stone, however. Successful planners realize that the number generated is an approximation that is only as valid as its underlying assumptions and methodology. Therefore the target set should be tempered with common sense and realistic expectations. After all, it is more prudent to motivate a client to action (albeit inadequate) than to scare a client into inaction or apathy.

ASSUMPTIONS REQUIRED IN WORK SHEETS AND COMPUTER MODELS

Many work sheets and computer models enable the planner to tailor the retirement prediction to a client's unique situation by choosing assumptions for future contingencies. Others make the assumption for the planner and lock out the ability to fine-tune a prediction. Since retirement planning is an art form, not a science, the better models allow the most flexibility by giving the planner control over assumptions. Planners, however, must be up to the complex task of effectively choosing assumptions. A thorough understanding of the details underlying the assumptions can make the difference between a child's finger painting and a master's portrait.

Assumptions that are typically required in most work sheets and computer models include

- the rate of inflation the client will experience
- the age at which the client will retire
- the age at which the client will die
- the replacement ratio that a client will need

- the tax rate applicable now and in the future
- the investment return the client can expect
- the step-up rate (the rate at which the client will increase annual savings allocations)

Each work sheet and computer model may treat these assumptions differently. For example, many work sheets break down inflation into time categories (preretirement and postretirement). Others are content to make one inflation assumption for both periods and still others brush back inflation by focusing on the real rate of return (actual rate of return less *inflation*). Regardless of how the assumptions are treated, however, the planner and the client must be comfortable with the numbers to be plugged in if they want to get a realistic projection. Let's take a closer look at how to choose the best numbers for your client's situation.

Inflation Assumption

One of the most critical assumptions that a planner must make concerns the inflation rate that will apply to the client. As we saw in chapter 1, inflation erodes the client's purchasing power over time, making it difficult to maintain economic self-sufficiency during retirement. The effects of this erosion are dramatically illustrated when different inflation assumptions are plugged in to work sheets and computer models. Consider this: By changing the inflation rate from 4 to 6 percent in one model the client's target increases from $825,000 to $1,008,000—a $183,000 (20 percent) difference. The same change (4 to 6 percent) in another model almost doubled the amount the client needed to save (from 28 to 54 percent of salary!). For this reason it is essential to be as accurate as possible when forecasting the rate of inflation that will apply to your client.

Forecasting Inflation

Forecasting inflation for your client would not be an easy task even if you had a crystal ball. The reason for this is that even if an accurate prediction of the national inflation rate could be made, other factors come into play. For example:

- A retiree's personal buying habits will affect his or her actual inflation rate.
- Retirees buy more services than goods. Historically services have inflated at a higher rate than goods. Thus the national average of inflation is understated for retirees (based on this logic).
- There are significant regional variations in inflation from the national rate.
- Long-term inflation is the appropriate variable, but published statistical data focuses on the annual inflation rate (for example, 2.7 percent in 1994), not the long-term rate.
- Medical inflation is twice the national average. Certain retirees (generally people who fall into what demographers call the "old-old" category) will

have extensive medical expenses, whereas others (the "young-old" category) do not use as many medical services.

- Inflation accounts heavily for housing costs. For many retirees this may be a moot point because they own their house outright or live under rent control. In addition, the average market basket of goods and services that comprises the consumer price index (which is used to determine inflation) may not be the *average* goods and services used by a retiree.
- Planning for the younger client (in late 20s to early 30s) can be troublesome because inflation over 60 years or more must be considered.

Planners should not despair, however; despite uncertainty and disagreement over the best estimate for inflation, some concrete thinking exists. For one thing, most planners feel comfortable using a long-term view of inflation because preretirement and postretirement planning can encompass a long period of time. For example, for the period from December 1951 to December 1986 inclusive, the average compound increase in prices was 4.3 percent. Successful planners are not getting caught up in today's relatively low inflation rates nor were they overly concerned with the double-digit inflation of the late '70s and early '80s. Planners therefore help their clients prepare for the financial troubles that lie ahead by having them focus on a long-term rate.

A second issue that is generally agreed upon is that a client's tolerance tendencies should be factored in. A risk-averse client will probably want a more conservative figure projected, whereas a risk taker may feel comfortable with a relatively low inflation assumption.

A third factor to consider is that the proxy used for inflation can be changed over time to reflect changes in the long-term rate and the client's actual experience. This is not to say that each year the planner should reinvent the wheel, but it does provide flexibility in planning because the retirement model is constantly evolving.

**YOUR FINANCIAL SERVICES PRACTICE:
MONITORING ASSUMPTIONS**

Planners cannot take a once-and-done attitude toward clients when it comes to sculpting a retirement plan. The plan should be revisited periodically to check the accuracy of assumptions and the effectiveness of the client in meeting goals.

Which Rate Is Best?

Most planners use inflation assumptions between 3 and 6 percent. The actual rate chosen for a client will vary depending on spending habits, current age, and risk-tolerance tendencies. From our experience 4 percent is a common choice. This is a widely held view of economists for long-term inflation. Consider, however, that one prudent way to operate is to run several calculations using different rates in a narrow range. The higher the inflation rate, the greater the percentage of salary that your client needs to save. Clients who choose the lowest realistic rate will have the least amount of sacrifice now. They should be warned, however, that their future behavior will be affected — if for no other reason than to limit their "personalized" rate of inflation.

Retirement Age Assumption

Many planners automatically pencil in age 65 as the starting date for retirement despite the fact that the average retirement age in the United States is 62. Consider that only 67 percent of men 55 to 65 years old were still in the workforce in 1987 compared to 90 percent in 1947, and you get a fairly good picture of a growing trend — clients are retiring early. In fact, one Life Insurance Marketing and Research Association (LIMRA) survey showed that roughly 80 percent of people in large companies with pension plans retired before age 65. Another important statistic: 51 percent of all 64-year-olds are retired.

Reasons for Early Retirement

Some clients approach retirement planning as financial independence planning. For these people the assumption of retirement age turns into the goal for financial independence. For example, these clients approach the problem as, "What percentage of my salary do I need to save to retire at age 55?" It is generally easy to adjust computer models and work sheets to fit these clients' needs.

In addition to retiring early for financial independence, many look at the issue of health in order to help make the early retirement decision. Some look to retire early while they are still in good health. Others are forced to retire early because of their health (for example, one diabetic client retired early to pursue a 10-mile-a-day walking regimen that would keep his blood sugar low). And in many cases a client is forced to retire early because of the health of his or her spouse. In other words, such a client is forced to retire early to become a caregiver to the spouse (or in some cases a parent).

Another reason for early retirement is the recent trend of corporate downsizing. In some cases office politics force a premature departure. In others retirement packages known as golden handshakes are offered to cut payroll costs attributable to older employees. In a 1992 Charles D. Spencer & Associates Survey of 71 large companies, 32 percent of early retirements during the tested year were the result of golden handshakes (up from 26 percent in 1990). No matter what the company's motivation, planners must face the fact that people are being shown the door (pushed out?) earlier and earlier.

Other reasons that retirement prior to age 65 remains the preferred exit time for employees include the following:

- *The phenomenon of the two-wage-earner family.* In many cases normal retirement of one spouse may prompt early retirement of the younger spouse. One study showed that the profile of the individual most likely to retire was a married person whose spouse was retired.
- *Death of the spouse.* Statistics show that another group likely to retire early is widows—perhaps because they received death benefits and other inheritance from their partners.
- *Laborers and manual workers.* This group often retires early as well—perhaps because of the physically demanding nature of their jobs.

Reasons against Early Retirement

Despite the trend toward early retirement, the planner must be ready to point out the downside of leaving too early. Factors include the following:

- Social security normal retirement age is slated to increase from 65 to 67 for some baby boomers and over 65 but before age 67 for others (see chapter 2).
- The impact of early retirement on pension benefits can be devastating. In a final-average-salary defined-benefit plan, the pension is lowered because the peak earning years are shortchanged. (In other words, the pension would be higher because it would have been based on higher earnings had the worker stayed on the job.) The same holds true for the account balance in a defined-contribution plan.
- Pensions are often adjusted downward to reflect the longer payout that comes with early retirement.
- Early retirement means increased exposure to inflation.
- Early retirement may have to wait for the payoff of fixed long-term liabilities such as mortgage and college tuition for the kids. Many baby boomers had children later in life, exacerbating this problem.

What Age Is Best?

Considering that a myriad of factors must be examined, one can see that the choice of a retirement date is not the easy task that it appeared to be at first blush. The planner's role, with the aid of work sheets and computer models, is to make the retirement age as realistic as possible for the client. Often a client will seek to retire on what he or she considers to be a large amount of money. Unfortunately, however, it is typically not going to be enough. It is up to the planner to point out that because of inflation and longevity, delaying retirement may be the most logical situation. In other words, one of the chief functions of the planner and the retirement work sheet/printout is to foster a realistic attitude in the client. This attitude will then enable the planner to better forecast the intended retirement date of the client.

YOUR FINANCIAL SERVICES PRACTICE:
ESTIMATES VERSUS HABITS

At this point it has become clear that there is an interplay between the assumptions used in the work sheets and computer models and the current and future habits of retirees. In some instances the work sheet will help a person to "see the light" and change his or her habits to accommodate financial security in the future. In other cases assumptions need to be changed, in part because retirement goals are not etched in stone and in part because clients are not willing to alter their behavior. Astute planners will use the work sheet or computer software as a reality check for their clients—a way to show clients that decisions they make today have a direct correlation to their quality of life tomorrow. *For this reason, assumptions are part of the educational process for the client (and the planner) and subject to manipulation by both.*

Longevity Assumption

Ideally, clients would accumulate enough assets to allow them to live on the interest alone and never have to liquidate the principal. For many clients, however, this is not a viable strategy. These clients must liquidate their retirement savings throughout the retirement period. We have already discussed the uncertainty of the inauguration of retirement. Imagine our dilemma over the uncertainty concerning the end of retirement—death! As ghoulish as it may sound, the impossible task of predicting the demise of their clients is a real issue that planners face. Severe mistakes in either direction can tend to grossly overstate or understate the amount of savings needed to meet a particular retirement goal. As a case in point, consider the unlucky client who retires at age 64 and dies at age 66; for this client only a modest sum is actually needed. Had the client known that his postretirement life span would be short, both the planner and client would have been spared the needless headaches of trying to squeeze the most out of every penny prior to retirement. On the other hand, take Joe "Methuselah" Brown, who retired at age 64 and just sent you an invitation to his 105th birthday party. Not only have the extra years of life formed a planning problem, but Joe has had an increased exposure to inflation as well.

Notwithstanding the potential for error, planners must make their best educated guess concerning their clients' (both spouses if applicable) life expectancies in order to complete a retirement work sheet or computer model. In many cases this assumption is generated by the ages at which parents and grandparents have died. This is generally sound thinking because medical studies show a strong relationship between genetics and life expectancy. In addition to family history, factors that should be considered include

- The physical condition of the client, including the client's personal medical history
- Life expectancy tables (see table 5-1; also see table 1-2 in chapter 1). Make note, however, that insurance tables tend to understate life expectancy and annuity tables tend to overstate life expectancy. What's more, even if tables are accurate, *one-half of the people outlive the tables' projections.*
- The tendency of higher socioeconomic groups to have longer life expectancies. Many believe this is due in part to easy access to medical care.
- The fact that the average number of years until the second death in a couple is longer than the individual life expectancy of either person alone. For example, based on one table of life expectancies for all races (not reproduced in this text), the husband of a married couple where each spouse is aged 65 has a life expectancy of about 14.1 years while the wife has a life expectancy of 18.3 years. However, the average number of years until the second death of a husband and wife who are each aged 65 is about 21.3 years—3 years, or over 16 percent, longer than the wife's expectancy of 18.3 years. In other words, although each spouse has less than a 50 percent chance of living an additional 21.3 years when each life is considered alone, there is about an even chance that one of the two will live at least an additional 21.3 years when you consider their joint (second-to-die) life expectancy.

What's a Planner to Do?

Many planners feel comfortable adding a fudge factor to their life expectancy estimate. If the client lives longer than can be anticipated the fudge factor will make up for the additional years. If the client does not live as long, some excess assets will be left for heirs (which generally is a viable planning goal anyway). At the extreme, some planners use a life expectancy assumption of age 100 since statistically very few people will live beyond this point. Using this as a conservative estimate will save the planner from the fatal (pun intended) error of understating life expectancy.

Another way to fudge this decision about life span is to divide assets into different classes. For example, X fund will be used for the normal expected life expectancy and Y fund can be reserved for heirs, but consumed if longevity necessitates it. In many cases the reserve fund will be a home's value (or equity) or the value of a vacation home.

Note, however, that whatever fudge factor is used, planners must guard against overstating the retirement need to the extent that the annual amount of savings needed is unattainable. In other words, using unrealistically high life expectancies will create unreasonably high demands on the percentage of salary a client needs to save and ultimately scare the client into inaction because of inability to meet savings schedules.

TABLE 5-1
Expectancies of Life at Single Years of Age, by Color and Sex: United States: 1980*

Age	All races			White			All other					
							Total			Black		
	Both Sexes	Male	Female	Both Sexes	Male	Female	Both Sexes	Male	Female	Both Sexes	Male	Female
50	27.8	24.9	30.6	28.1	25.2	30.9	25.5	22.6	28.3	24.5	21.6	27.3
51	27.0	24.1	29.7	27.2	24.3	30.0	24.8	21.9	27.5	23.8	21.0	26.5
52	26.1	23.3	28.8	26.4	23.5	29.1	24.0	21.2	26.7	23.1	20.3	25.7
53	25.3	22.5	28.0	25.6	22.7	28.2	23.3	20.6	25.9	22.4	19.7	24.9
54	24	21.7	27.1	24.8	21.9	27.4	22.6	19.9	25.1	21.7	19.0	24.2
55	23.7	21.0	26.3	23.9	21.2	26.5	21.9	19.3	24.4	21.0	18.4	23.4
56	22.9	20.2	25.4	23.1	20.4	25.7	21.2	18.6	23.6	20.3	17.8	22.7
57	22.2	19.5	24.6	22.4	19.6	24.8	20.5	18.0	22.9	19.7	17.2	22.0
58	21.4	18.8	23.8	21.6	18.9	24.0	19.9	17.4	22.1	19.0	16.6	21.3
59	20.6	18.0	23.0	20.8	18.2	23.2	19.2	16.8	21.4	18.4	16.0	20.5
60	19.9	17.4	22.2	20.1	17.5	22.4	18.6	16.2	20.7	17.8	15.5	19.8
61	19.2	16.7	21.4	19.3	16.8	21.6	17.9	15.7	20.0	17.2	14.9	19.2
62	18.5	16.0	20.6	18.6	16.1	20.8	17.3	15.1	19.3	16.6	14.4	18.5
63	17.8	15.4	19.8	17.9	15.4	20.0	16.7	14.6	18.6	16.0	13.9	17.8
64	17.1	14.7	19.1	17.2	14.8	19.2	16.1	14.0	18.0	15.4	13.4	17.2
65	16.4	14.1	18.3	16.5	14.2	18.5	15.5	13.5	17.3	14.8	12.9	16.5

TABLE 5-1 (Continued)
Expectancies of Life at Single Years of Age, by Color and Sex: United States: 1980

Age	All races			White			All other					
							Total			Black		
	Both Sexes	Male	Female	Both Sexes	Male	Female	Both Sexes	Male	Female	Both Sexes	Male	Female
66	15.7	13.5	17.6	15.8	13.6	17.7	15.0	13.0	16.7	14.3	12.4	15.9
67	15.1	12.9	16.9	15.2	13.0	17.0	14.4	12.5	16.0	13.7	11.9	15.3
68	14.4	12.3	16.1	14.5	12.4	16.2	13.8	12.0	15.4	13.2	11.4	14.6
69	13.8	11.8	15.4	13.9	11.8	15.5	13.3	11.5	14.8	12.6	10.9	14.0
70	13.2	11.3	14.8	13.3	11.3	14.8	12.8	11.1	14.2	12.1	10.5	13.4
71	12.6	10.7	14.1	12.7	10.7	14.1	12.2	10.6	13.6	11.6	10.0	12.9
72	12.0	10.2	13.4	12.1	10.2	13.5	11.7	10.2	13.0	11.1	9.6	12.3
73	11.5	9.7	12.8	11.5	9.7	12.8	11.3	9.7	12.5	10.6	9.2	11.8
74	10.9	9.3	12.1	10.9	9.3	12.2	10.8	9.3	12.0	10.1	8.8	11.2
75	10.4	8.8	11.5	10.4	8.8	11.5	10.3	8.9	11.4	9.7	8.3	10.7
76	9.9	8.4	10.9	9.9	8.3	10.9	9.8	8.5	10.9	9.2	7.9	10.2
77	9.3	7.9	10.3	9.3	7.9	10.3	9.4	8.1	10.4	8.8	7.5	9.7
78	8.9	7.5	9.7	8.8	7.5	9.7	8.9	7.7	9.9	8.3	7.1	9.2
79	8.4	7.1	9.2	8.4	7.1	9.2	8.5	7.3	9.4	7.9	6.7	8.7
80	7.9	6.7	8.6	7.9	6.7	8.6	8.1	6.9	9.0	7.4	6.3	8.2
81	7.5	6.3	8.1	7.4	6.3	8.1	7.7	6.5	8.5	7.0	6.0	7.7
82	7.0	6.0	7.6	7.0	6.0	7.6	7.3	6.2	8.1	6.6	5.6	7.3
83	6.6	5.7	7.2	6.6	5.6	7.1	6.9	5.8	7.7	6.2	5.2	6.9
84	6.2	5.3	6.8	6.2	5.3	6.7	6.6	5.5	7.3	5.8	4.9	6.5
85	5.9	5.0	6.4	5.9	5.0	6.3	6.3	5.3	7.0	5.5	4.5	6.1

*From the Department of Health and Human Services, Public Health Service, annual report, Vital Statistics of the United States, for the year 1980.

Income Requirement Assumption

The income requirement assumption represents the planner's estimation of the level of income needed by retirees to sustain the standard of living they enjoyed just prior to retirement throughout their retired life. In some cases it can be measured as a percentage of final salary (called the *replacement-ratio approach*). In other cases it is the projected retirement budget for a client (called the *expense method*).

Replacement-Ratio Approach

Some experts believe that 80 percent of a person's final salary will keep him or her in the style to which he or she is accustomed throughout retirement. Note that postretirement inflation is not factored into the replacement ratio. Instead it is treated separately. In other words, the work sheets and computer models account for an inflation-protected stream of income separate from the replacement ratio that will be needed in the first year of retirement.

Factors That Influence a Replacement Ratio of Less Than 100 Percent. Support for a replacement ratio of less than 100 percent of final salary rests upon the elimination of some employment-related taxes and some expected changes in spending patterns that reduce the retiree's need for income (such as expenditures that will either decrease or disappear in the retirement years).

Reductions in Taxation. In many circumstances, retirees can count on a lower percentage of their income going to pay taxes in the retirement years. Some taxes are reduced or eliminated, and retirees may enjoy special favorable tax treatment in other areas, too. Let's take a closer look at the potential reductions in taxation that are granted to retirees.

Social Security Taxes. FICA contributions (old-age, survivors, disability, and hospital insurance) are levied solely on income from employment. Distributions from pensions, IRAs, retirement annuities, and other similar devices are not considered income subject to FICA or SECA taxes. Hence for the retiree who stops working entirely, social security taxes are no longer an expenditure.

Increased Standard Deduction. For a married taxpayer aged 65 or over, the standard deduction is increased by an additional $750 (in 1994). If the taxpayer's spouse is also 65 or older, yet another $750 increase in the standard deduction can be taken ($750 for each spouse, or $1,500 total). For a taxpayer over 65 who is not married and does not file as a surviving spouse, $950 is added to the standard deduction (in 1994). Note that for taxpayers who itemize deductions (using schedule A), this will be a moot point. In other words, clients have the option of doing one thing or the other—itemizing or using the standard deduction.

Social Security Benefits Exclusion. A married taxpayer can exclude all social security benefits from his or her income for tax purposes if the taxpayer's modified adjusted gross income (which includes interest earned on state and local government securities) plus one-half of the social security benefits does not exceed the base amount of $32,000 ($25,000 for single taxpayers). For others, only part of their social security benefit will be untaxed. See chapter 2 for a thorough discussion of how social security is taxed.

Some examples will help to show just what the social security benefits exclusion means in tax savings for a retiree.

Example 1: Paul and Peggy are married and file jointly. They receive $20,000 in pension income and $10,000 in social security income. All of their social security income is received tax free. Since they are in the 28 percent tax bracket this amounts to a tax savings of $2,800.

Example 2: Arthur and Ann are married filing jointly. They receive $30,000 in pension income and $20,000 in combined social security benefits. Arthur and Ann will pay taxes on $4,000 of their social security income and will receive $16,000 of their social security income tax free. Since they are in the 28 percent tax bracket this amounts to $4,480 in tax savings.

Example 3: James and Julie are married filing jointly. They receive combined pensions of $200,000 and combined social security of $20,000. James and Julie will pay taxes on $17,000 of their social security benefit and receive $3,000 tax free. Since they are in the 36 percent tax bracket they will save $1,080 in taxes.

State and Local Income Taxation. In some states social security benefits are fully exempt from state income taxation; in others some taxation of these benefits might occur if the state's income tax is assessed on the taxpayer's taxable income as reported for federal income tax purposes. In addition, some states grant extra income tax relief for the elderly by providing increased personal exemptions, credits, sliding scale rebates of property or other taxes (the amount or percent of which might be dependent on income), or additional tax breaks such as

- exemption of all or part of retirement pay from the state income tax base
- exemption of all or part of unreimbursed medical expenses from the state income tax base
- freezing of taxes at the level for the year the taxpayer reaches 65
- deferring real estate taxes until after the death of the retiree

Deductible Medical Expenses. Due to the reduced retirement income level and the increased medical expenses that retirees often face, it might be easier for taxpayers who itemize deductions to exceed the 7.5 percent threshold for deductibility of qualifying medical expenses.

Reduced Living Expenses. In addition to the possible reductions in taxation, certain reduced living expenses may permit retired individuals to maintain their standard of living on a lower income. Let's take a closer look at some of the reduced living expenses.

Work-Related Expenses. The costs of proper clothing for work, commuting, and meals purchased during work hours are eliminated when a person retires. In addition, other expenses, such as membership dues in some professional or social clubs, may be reduced because of retired status or may be eliminated if no longer necessary.

Home Ownership Expenses. By the time of retirement, many homeowners have "burnt the mortgage" and no longer have this debt reduction expenditure. (*Planning Note:* It may be worthwhile for a client to pay off the mortgage at or near the date of retirement. This mortgage redemption not only eliminates the debt repayment expenditure but also reduces income from interest or dividends on assets used to pay the mortgage, thereby reducing income for federal and state tax purposes. For taxpayers of modest means, the income reduction might place them just below the threshold for taxation of social security benefits. Also, most of the monthly mortgage payments typically are applied to principal reduction; thus interest deductibility would be a minor tax benefit. Furthermore, the interest being paid could exceed the rate of earnings on invested funds, thereby producing a real saving for the retiree.)

Absence of Dependent Children. The expense of supporting dependent children is usually completed by the time a client enters retirement. Be cautious, however, because retirees, especially those who married later in life, occasionally have children who are not self-supporting and will require continued financial support during some of the clients' retirement years.

Senior Citizen Discounts. Special reductions in price are given to senior citizens. Some reductions, such as certain AARP discounts, are available at age 50. Many businesses, however, require proof of age 65 (usually by having a medicare card) to qualify for discounts on prescriptions, clothing, and restaurant meals. Discounts typically range from 5 to 15 percent of an item's cost.

No Longer Saving for Retirement. For many retirees retirement is not a time to continue to save for retirement. Cessation of payments to contributory pension plans, lack of eligibility for IRA or Keogh plan contributions, and just the psychological fact of being retired can help to weaken retirees' motivation to save for the future. Note that a retired worker's income can fall by the amount being saved with no concurrent reduction in standard of living. Therefore a retired worker who has been saving 10 percent of income needs only to maintain an "inflation protected" 90 percent (before tax) of income to enjoy the same purchasing power.

ILLUSTRATION 5-1
Justification of Less Than 100 Percent Replacement Ratio

Patty and Ken Tailor (both aged 64) have a combined salary of $100,000 ($50,000 each) and would like to maintain their current purchasing power when they retire next year. If their anticipated reduced nonwork expenses are offset by increased living expenses (see below), they can maintain their purchasing power by having a retirement income of 80 percent of their salary, as illustrated below.

Working salary		$100,000
Less FICA taxes[1]	$ 7,650	
Less increase in standard deduction[2]	0	
Less tax savings on tax-free part of social security[3]	840	
Less state and local tax reduction[4]	1,400	
Less deductible medical expenses[5]	0	
Less reduced living expenses[6]	0	
Less retirement savings[7]	10,000	
Reductions subtotal		19,890
Total purchasing power needed		$ 80,110
Percentage of final salary needed (approximate)		80%

1. Since each earns $50,000, each pays $3,825 in FICA taxes.
2. No increase in standard deduction will occur because they itemize using Schedule A.
3. Patty and Ken will get $20,000 in social security. $3,000 will be received tax free for a savings of $840 at the 28 percent tax bracket.
4. The Tailors will get a sliding scale rebate on their property taxes equal to $1,400.
5. They will not take a medical deduction.
6. The Tailors figure any reduced living expenses in retirement from work will be offset by increased retirement expenses (see below).
7. The Tailors had been saving 10 percent of their salary in a 401(k) plan (5 percent each).

Increased Living Expenses. Some retirement planners are rather uncomfortable with recommending a planned reduction in income in the first year of retirement. These planners believe that certain factors suggest that during the first year of retirement at least as much if not more income will be required to maintain the preretirement standard of living. Let's take a closer look at these factors.

Medical Expenses. Without question, medical expenses will increase over time for virtually all clients. The mere act of aging and the associated health problems generate additional demands for medical services. Even if advancing age does not create an increase in an individual's demands for medical services, inflation in these costs will. Furthermore, increases in inflation are not evenly distributed in the various medical care disciplines, and those services that will potentially affect retirees have been hit hardest. For example, over the past 20 years, the cost of hospital rooms rose 719 percent, professional medical services rose 406 percent, and prescription drugs rose 196 percent. This final increase does not consider the prices for some of the newer, more costly wonder drugs. Although retirees are often covered by medicare and other health insurance, the trend in these coverages has been toward cost containment—defined by the government and the insurance companies as that of shifting more of the medical cost to the insured by means of larger deductibles and coinsurance payments. These higher medical expenses would be in addition to the increased premiums for the insurance.

Travel, Vacations, and Other Lifestyle Changes. Many clients expect to devote considerably more time to travel and vacations upon retirement than they did during their working years. Increased leisure time, once a scarce commodity, now provides the opportunity to travel. Unfortunately vacationing can be an expensive activity. Indeed, an increase in vacation activities represents a rise in the standard of living and will require additional income.

Dependents. As previously stated, parents usually need less income during the first year of retirement because they no longer financially support their children, who typically become self-supporting prior to parental retirement. However, many retirees still have dependents to support. Many parents have children with mental or physical problems who will require long-term custodial and financial care throughout the retirement years. Because medical care, surgical techniques, and drugs are helping to prolong life, other retirees may have to provide for their aged parents who no longer possess the wherewithal to do so themselves.

Additional Services. As people age, they often need to hire others to perform services that they previously performed themselves. This can include a wide number of physically demanding activities such as cutting the lawn, working on the car, painting the house, climbing ladders to make repairs, and shoveling snow. It may also include hiring individuals for housecleaning or caring for an infirm spouse or other family member. Some physical impairments may require a change in transportation mode—such as a change from public transportation to taking taxis—which will mean an increased expense.

**YOUR FINANCIAL SERVICES PRACTICE:
WARNING YOUR CLIENTS ABOUT THE RISKS**

Whether your clients accept an 80 percent replacement ratio or feel something more is necessary, it should be stressed that there is no definitive answer to determine absolutely if the postretirement income should be less than, equal to, or greater than that of the preretirement years.

Estimating financial needs during the first year of retirement is like trying to hit a moving target when you are blindfolded: Your aim is obscured by many unknown variables and the target is hard to draw a bead on.

Expense Method

A second way planners can estimate their client's retirement needs in the first year of retirement is by using the expense-method approach. The expense method of retirement planning focuses on the projected expenses that the retiree will have in the first year of retirement. For example, if the 64-year-old near-retiree expects to have $3,000 in monthly bills ($36,000 annually), then the retirement income for that retiree should maintain $36,000 worth of purchasing power in today's dollars. If, however, a younger client is involved, more speculative estimates of retirement expenses must be made (and periodically revised).

A list of expenses that should be considered includes expenses that may be unique to the particular client as well as other, more general expenses. As noted for the replacement-ratio approach, expenses that tend to increase for retirees include the following:

- utilities and telephone
- medical, dental, drugs, health insurance
- house upkeep, repairs, maintenance, property insurance
- recreation, entertainment, travel, dining
- contributions, gifts

YOUR FINANCIAL SERVICES PRACTICE:
RATIO VERSUS EXPENSE METHOD

If your work sheet or computer model gives you a choice of whether to use a replacement ratio or expense amount consider the following:

- The expense method usually works well for clients at or near retirement since they have a handle on their projected retirement budget.
- The replacement-ratio method usually works well for younger clients since they do not have a handle on their retirement expenses but can sometimes gauge the standard of living they want to enjoy.
- To predict final salary for the replacement ratio of a younger client, one can do the following:

  - Put a growth factor onto current salary and do a time value calculation (this is sometimes done for you by the work sheet).
  - Examine the salaries of those retiring today who hold the position the client feels he or she will attain by retirement.
  - Look at salary scales when applicable.

Conversely, some expenses tend to decrease for the retiree. These include the following:

ILLUSTRATION 5-2
Understanding the Expense Method

Your clients, Bob and Betty Smith, both aged 64, would like to maintain their current purchasing power when they retire next year. They can do this by having an annual income of $40,860 as illustrated below. Note that the figures are estimates of their expenses during retirement (some are higher than their current expenses and some are lower than their current expenses). Also note that postretirement inflation will be accounted for later.

Estimated Retirement Living Expenses (in Current Dollars)

		Per Month x 12 =	Per Year
1.	Food	$ 500	$ 6,000
2.	Housing:		
	a. Rent/mortgage payment	400	4,800
	b. Insurance (if separate payment)	25	300
	c. Property taxes (if separate payment)	150	1,800
	d. Utilities	180	2,160
	e. Maintenance (if owned)	100	1,200
3.	Clothing and Personal Care:		
	a. Wife	75	900
	b. Husband	75	900
4.	Medical Expenses:		
	a. Doctor (HMO)	75	900
	b. Dentist	20	240
	c. Medicines	75	900
5.	Transportation:		
	a. Car payments	130	1,560
	b. Gas	50	600
	c. Insurance	50	600
	d. Car maintenance (tires and repairs)	30	360
6.	Miscellaneous Expenses:		
	a. Entertainment	150	1,800
	b. Travel	200	2,400
	c. Hobbies	50	600
	d. Other	100	1,200
	e. Club fees and dues	20	240
7.	Insurance	100	1,200
8.	Gifts and contributions	50	600
9.	State, local, and federal taxes (if any)	800	9,600
10.	Total expenses (current dollars)	3,405	40,860

- mortgage payments
- food
- clothing
- income taxes
- property taxes
- transportation costs (car maintenance, insurance, other)
- debt repayment (charge accounts, personal loans)
- child support, alimony
- household furnishings

Other Assumptions

In addition to making assumptions concerning inflation, retirement age, longevity, and the amount/percentage of final salary to be deemed the appropriate standard of living (replacement ratio), planners must make predictions on tax rates and investment returns. Some factors to consider that might help in this process are

- the risk-return characteristics of the retirement portfolio that a client is comfortable with
- the ability of a client to use tax-sheltered qualified plans and IRAs
- the potential future income the retiree is expecting (Note that past thinking has been to assume that a retiree's tax rate will decline because his or her income has declined; however, this will not be the case if the planner has done a good job!)
- the propensity to invest more conservatively (and consequently have a lower rate of return) as a client approaches retirement and after a client retires
- the propensity of clients to invest too conservatively in their qualified plan at work
- the inevitable federal tax law changes that are likely to occur
- the state income taxes that may be applicable to a relocated client
- the planner's investment recommendations

These and other considerations can help a planner to tailor his or her assumptions to a client's specific situation.

Many models look at savings as a percentage of income. If this is the case, the amount that you save each year increases as your salary increases. Some models have the added flexibility of a step-up rate, which is the percentage growth in the client's annual allocation to savings. The step-up rate typically corresponds to the client's projected growth rate in compensation, thus keeping the rate of savings a constant percentage. In other words, clients can increase retirement savings in a painless way by bolstering savings with future salary increases. To best predict this assumption, contracts, salary scales, and salary history should be reviewed. Such a review will tell the planner about expected increases in income.

HOW WORK SHEETS AND COMPUTER MODELS WORK

Now that we have examined the assumptions used in many work sheets and computer models, it is time to turn to an examination of the models themselves. Given the variety of packages available, each having its own unique features, we are presented with a daunting task. There is a manageable solution to this problem, however. In the next few pages we will take a four-step approach to acquainting you with work sheets and computer models. The first step is to discuss the theory behind a generic computer model. This will de-mystify the process and allow you to understand the common theory that is utilized in most software. The second step is to introduce a shorthand formula that can be used to identify the retirement need. This formula will give you the ability to show clients a quick estimate of their need. It also can be used in conjunction with other models to give a range of possible targets (thus dispelling the myth that the numbers are etched in stone). The third step is to introduce you to a consumer work sheet. The work sheet we have chosen first appeared in *U.S. News and World Report* several years ago and is widely used. The fourth step is to introduce you to our version of a planner's work sheet. The model can be used in your practice to create a target savings amount for your client. In steps two through four we will use a case study approach to demonstrate how a retirement needs analysis is conducted.

The Theory behind a Generic Computer Model

Computer software packages use many different approaches for calculating retirement fund needs. The following steps are typical of the internal workings of these models.

Step 1: Projecting Retirement Income from Existing Resources

One essential element in any retirement needs analysis is knowing where a client stands now. Planners usually use a fact finder in conjunction with their software. Information from the fact finder that must be input into the computer includes social security estimates (typically in current dollars), defined-benefit pension estimates (typically in current dollars), defined-contribution retirement plan estimates (the current account balance), and private savings (including IRAs, annuities, and other investment funds earmarked for retirement).

Step 2: Comparing What a Client Has to What a Client Needs

Many models determine a retirement income shortfall (RIS). Determining the RIS is a simple matter of subtracting the annual income projected from existing resources from the annual income needed at retirement (arrived at by either a replacement-ratio or expense approach). To produce the income shortfall requires a "pot of money" that the planner must help the client fill.

Example: Patty (aged 60) has a $100,000 salary. After using the replacement-ratio approach Patty and her planner feel that an $80,000 (80 percent) target will meet her desired living standards. (Note that the $80,000 figure will have to be increased after her first year of retirement to account for inflation.) In addition, Patty and her planner determine that her social security, pension, and *current* savings will provide $60,000 per year. Patty therefore has a shortfall of $20,000 ($80,000 need minus $60,000 resources). The computer software will effectively calculate the amount necessary at retirement to produce this stream of income over her projected lifetime. This amount becomes one target for which the planner and Patty must save.

Step 3: Providing Inflation Protection for Income Provided from Existing Resources

Determining this income shortfall is only one part of the picture. In addition, any computer model must take into consideration the decline in purchasing power that is the result of continued inflation. For example, a $25,000 company pension that is not increased for inflation will have significantly less purchasing power at age 75 than at age 65.   Most sources of income (other than social security, which is subject to an annual cost-of-living adjustment, or COLA) will be subject to a decline in purchasing power (or DIPP). To make up for this DIPP, the computer model will determine an additional amount needed to be saved in order to keep up with the increasing needs during retirement.   This additional "pot of money" that the planner must help to fill is sometimes called an existing-resources DIPP fund.

Example: Patty's pension at retirement was $40,000 annually and her other savings at retirement were converted to a $10,000-a-year annuity. Due to the effects of the DIPP, her pension and annuity must be bolstered each year to maintain a level purchasing power—she must maintain her own COLA fund for these amounts. The $10,000 that she will receive from social security is already adjusted for inflation and need not be considered for this calculation.

Step 4: Computing the Sum Needed at Retirement

Once the RIS is calculated and all the sources of income that need DIPP protection have been identified, the program will calculate the sum the client will need to have saved by the time he or she retires. The following describes what the computer actually calculates.

- *RIS Calculation.* Most programs will calculate a single sum representing the amount needed to provide the RIS stream of income over the expected lifetime of the retiree. To reflect the impact of DIPP, the program will actually calculate the amount needed to provide an increasing stream of income so as not to lose ground against inflation. Technically speaking, the number calculated is the present value (at retirement) of the inflation-protected RIS stream of income over the projected lifetime or payment period. Note that with this method the amount calculated will be exhausted at the end of the expected lifetime.

- *DIPP Fund Calculation.* In the previous calculation the impact of DIPP was actually taken into account for determining the amount needed to meet the RIS needs. A second calculation is needed to provide an inflation-protected supplement for other sources of income that are subject to DIPP. An additional amount is needed from which to make increasing payments to supplement the fixed payment stream. Technically, the number calculated represents the sum of the present values (at retirement) of all the inflation adjustments needed for all existing-resource income that will not automatically adjust for inflation.

  Example: To protect against a 4 percent inflation rate, the $50,000 first-year retirement income from existing non-inflation-adjusted resources must grow to $52,000 in the second year ($50,000 x 1.04), to $54,080 in the third year ($50,000 x 1.04^2), and to $56,243 in the fourth year ($50,000 x 1.04^3), and must continue to grow at 4 percent a year. Thus the inflation adjustments above the $50,000 first-year retirement income are $2,000 in the second year, $4,080 in the third year, $6,243 in the fourth year, and so on for the projected life of the client. It is these inflation adjustments that are discounted back to the retirement year and added together to calculate the existing-resource DIPP fund.

- *Add RIS and DIPP Numbers.* This "retirement target" amount represents the additional amount that the individual needs to save by retirement age in order to meet his or her financial objectives.

Step 5: Determining an Annual Savings Amount to Achieve the Targeted Amount

Some programs will stop after step 4. However, most will also figure out the stream of contributions (annual savings) needed to meet the target. This calculation may either provide an answer expressed as a level savings stream or as a stepped-up stream that increases with a person's salary.

Determining the Retirement Need Using a Shorthand Formula

The goal of the shorthand formula is to calculate the capital needed at retirement that will sustain a person at a constant standard of living until death. In other words, it tells a client how much he or she needs to save in order to have enough annual income each and every year of retirement to maintain his or her current standard of living. The assumptions used in the formula method are the replacement ratio needed, expected inflation, anticipated rate of return, and the duration of retirement. The formula used is

$$C_r = E_r \left[\frac{1 - a^n}{1 - a} \right]$$

where

C_r = capital needed at retirement in then-current dollars

E_r = income needed in the first year of retirement in then-current dollar

$a = \dfrac{1 + i}{1 + r}$

i = inflation rate

r = aftertax rate of return

n = duration of retirement

It is important to emphasize that E_r (income needed in the first year of retirement) and C_r (capital needed at retirement) are in then-current dollars. One approach to calculating E_r is to specify the retirement income needed in today's dollars and adjust for the inflation anticipated between today and the year of retirement. Using future value concepts,

$$E_r = E_t (1 + i)^b$$

where

E_t = target retirement income in today's dollars

b = number of years until retirement

Some examples will help to illustrate.

Example 1: After analyzing the replacement ratio needed (using our prior discussion) the planner feels that Stan and Judy need $48,000 in then-current dollars in their first year of retirement to maintain their standard of living. In addition, the planner specifies that

- a 5 percent inflation assumption should be used
- a 7 percent rate of return assumption should be used
- retirement is projected to last 20 years

Step 1: Assign numbers to the variables.

$$E_r = \$48,000$$
$$i = 5\%$$
$$r = 7\%$$
$$n = 20 \text{ years}$$

Step 2: Solve for a.

$$\frac{1 \ + \ .05}{1 \ + \ .07} \ = \ .9813$$

Step 3: Solve the formula.

$$C_r \ = \ E_r \left| \frac{1 \ - \ a^n}{1 \ - \ a} \right|$$

$$= \ \$48,000 \ \left[\frac{1 \ - \ (.9813^{20})}{1 \ - \ .9813} \right]$$

$$= \ \$48,000 \ \left[\frac{1 \ - \ .6855}{.0187} \right]$$

$$= \ \$48,000 \ \left[\frac{.314}{.0187} \right]$$

$$= \ \$48,000 \ \text{x} \ \ 16.813$$

$$= \ \$807,024$$

Stan and Judy need $807,024 for retirement.

   Example 2: Fred and Wilma also need a replacement ratio of $48,000. They are, however, more optimistic about living longer than Stan and Judy (example 1) and feel they need to use the following assumptions:

- 5 percent inflation (same as example 1)
- 7 percent rate of return (same as example 1)
- 35 years for life expectancy (15 years longer than example 1)

Step 1: Assign numbers to the variables.

$$E_r \ = \ \$48,000$$
$$i \ = \ 5\%$$
$$r \ = \ 7\%$$
$$n \ = \ 35$$

Step 2: Solve for a.

$$\frac{1 \ + \ .05}{1 \ + \ .07} \ = \ .9813$$

Step 3: Solve the formula.

$$C_r = E_r \left| \frac{1 - a^n}{1 - a} \right|$$

$$= \$48,000 \left| \frac{1 - (.9813^{35})}{1 - .9813} \right|$$

$$= \$48,000 \left[\frac{1 - .5165}{.0187} \right]$$

$$= \$48,000 \left[\frac{.4835}{.0187} \right]$$

$$= \$48,000 \text{ x } 25.855$$

$$= \$1,241,040$$

Fred and Wilma need \$1,241,040 for retirement. This is \$434,016 more than Stan and Judy because of the 15 years of additional life expectancy.

Determining Retirement Needs Using a Consumer Work Sheet

The work sheet that follows can be used to illustrate the percentage of salary a person needs to save each year. Conceptually this work sheet makes most of the assumptions for you—for example, an 80 percent replacement ratio (step 2) and a 25-year life expectancy (see line 8 explanation). While this simplicity can be a limitation for a planner (as discussed earlier) it may be a blessing for the weary client. For this reason planners may want to use this type of work sheet as an informational piece in a client mailer (with strong comments about its limitations).

Example: The following financial information applies to Bob and Donna.

- They are 15 years from retirement.
- Their current salary is \$100,000.
- They have a defined-benefit plan of \$2,000 a month (\$24,000 annually).
- Their combined social security benefits are estimated to be \$18,000.
- They have \$130,000 in IRAs, 401(k) plans, and mutual funds.

Using the work sheet below Bob and Donna can see that they need to save 25 percent of their current salary.

TABLE 5-2
Work Sheet: Calculation of Retirement Expenses—Alternative 2[*]

	Your Circumstances	Example
1. Current annual gross salary	$_____	$ 100,000
2. Retirement-income target (multiply line 1 by 0.8—80 percent target)	$_____	80,000
3. Estimated annual benefit from pension plan, not including IRAs, 401(k)s, 403(b)s, or profit-sharing plans[1]	$_____	24,000
4. Estimated annual social security benefits[1]	$_____	18,000
5. Total retirement benefits (add lines 3 and 4)	$_____	42,000
6. Income gap (subtract line 5 from line 2)[2]	$_____	38,000
7. Adjust gap to reflect inflation (multiply line 6 by factor A, below)	$_____	68,400
8. Capital needed to generate additional income and close gap (multiply line 7 by 16.3)[3]	$_____	1,114,920
9. Extra capital needed to offset inflation's impact on pension (multiply line 3 by factor B, below)	$_____	204,000
10. Total capital needed (add lines 8 and 9)	$_____	1,318,920
11. Total current retirement savings (includes balances in IRAs, 401(k)s, profit-sharing plans, mutual funds, CDs)	$_____	130,000
12. Value of savings at retirement (multiply line 11 by factor C, below)	$_____	416,000
13. Net capital gap (subtract line 12 from line 10)	$_____	902,920
14. Annual amount in current dollars to start saving now to cover the gap (divide line 13 by factor D, below)[4]	$_____	25,578
15. Percentage of salary to be saved each year (divide line 14 by line 1)[5]	_____ %	25%

(Continued on following page)

Factors for Work Sheet Calculations Assuming 4 Percent Inflation and 8 Percent Rate of Return

Years to Retirement	Factor A	Factor B	Factor C	Factor D
10	1.5	7.0	2.2	17.5
15	1.8	8.5	3.2	35.3
20	2.2	10.3	4.7	63.3
25	2.7	12.6	6.9	107.0
30	3.2	15.3	10.1	174.0

[1]   Lines 3 and 4: Employers can provide annual estimates of your projected retirement pay; estimates of social security benefits are available from the Social Security Administration at (800) 937-2000. Both figures will be stated in current dollars, not in the high amounts that you will receive if your wages keep up with inflation. The work sheet takes this into consideration.

[2]   Line 6: Even if a large pension lets you avoid an income gap, proceed to line 9 to determine the assets you may need to make up for the erosion of a fixed pension payment by inflation.

[3]   Line 8: This calculation includes a determination of how much capital you will need to keep up with inflation after retirement and assumes that you will *deplete the capital over a 25-year period.*

[4]   Line 14: Amount includes investments earmarked for retirement and payments by employee and employer to defined-contribution retirement plans such as 401(k)s and 403(b)s. The formula assumes you will increase annual savings at the same rate as inflation.

[5]   Line 15: Assuming earnings rise with inflation, you can save a set percentage of gross pay each year, and the actual amount you stash away will increase annually.

*Reprinted with permission from U.S. News & World Report, August 14, 1989, page 62.

Determining Retirement Needs Using a Planner's Work Sheet

The work sheets that follow allow the planner to focus on tailoring a retirement needs analysis to a particular client. The first step is to list a variety of assumptions (these are discussed with the clients prior to filling out the work sheets). The second step is to list factors generated from time-value-of-money tables. An explanation of how each factor was determined follows the work sheets in the commentary for tables 5-7 through 5-14. The third step is to calculate the amount the clients need to save in the initial year.

Case Study Facts

Ann (aged 44 in 1995) and Robert (aged 46 in 1995) are married and have two children. Ann and Robert both plan to retire in 19 years (the year 2014) unless their planner counsels otherwise. Robert will be 65 and Ann will be 63 when they retire. Pertinent financial data includes the following:

- Ann earns $35,000 as a school teacher.
- Robert earns $140,000 as an engineer.
- Ann has $64,000 in her 403(b) retirement plan.
- Ann will receive a pension of $1,400 a month at age 63.
- Robert has a 401(k) plan with $120,000 in it.
- Robert has no defined-benefit plan at work.
- Robert will receive $1,100 a month from social security when he retires at age 65.
- Ann will receive $800 a month from social security when she retires at age 63.
- Both social security amounts are in today's dollars and, where applicable, reflect early retirement reductions.
- They have joint savings of $50,000 earmarked for retirement.
- They have sufficient savings to meet their other long-term financial goals, including sending their children to college.

After an initial interview with the planner it was decided that the following assumptions will be used:

- an inflation rate of 4 percent
- an expected duration of retirement of 25 years (Note that the Stacks have decided to set aside the potential gain from the sale of their home and vacation home to cover them should they live longer than the 25-year period—if not, this will be part of the legacy they leave their children.)
- an aftertax rate of return of 8 percent prior to retirement
- an aftertax rate of return of 7 percent after retirement
- an 80 percent replacement ratio
- a savings step-up rate of 6 percent (This means that the annual allocation to savings will increase by 6 percent each year until retirement.)

TABLE 5-3
Planner's Work Sheet
Step 1: List Assumptions

	ASSUMPTIONS	
A1.	Inflation rate prior to retirement	4%
A2.	Inflation rate after retirement	4%
A3.	Number of years until retirement	19 Yrs.
A4.	Expected duration of retirement	25 Yrs.
A5.	Rate of return prior to retirement	8%
A6.	Rate of return after retirement	7%
A7.	Savings step-up rate	6%

TABLE 5-4
Planner's Work Sheet
Step 2: Calculate Factors

The following factors were calculated using tables 5-7 through 5-14, which follow your blank work sheet in this book. Each table has a detailed explanation (and example) of how to extract the appropriate factor.

	FACTORS		Assumptions (from table 5-3)
F1.	Preretirement inflation factor	2.11	Table 5-7; years = A3, rate = A1
F2.	Retirement needs present value factor	17.936	Table 5-8; years = A4, rate = A6 minus A2
F3.	Current assets future value factor	4.32	Table 5-7; years = A3, rate = A5
F4.	Defined-benefit income present value factor	12.469	Table 5-8; years = A4, rate = A6
F5.	Savings rate factor	0.01435	Table 5-12; years = A3, rate = A7 minus A5

TABLE 5-5
Planner's Work Sheet
Step 3: Computation of Retirement Need and Amount to Be Saved

		COMPUTATIONS	
L1.		Projected annual retirement budget	$140,000 (80% of $175,000)
L2.	−	Social security benefit	22,800 (Ann and Robert annual total)
L3.	=	Net annual need in current dollars	$117,200
L4.	×	F1 factor	2.11
L5.	=	Inflation-adjusted annual retirement need	247,292
L6.	×	F2 factor	17.936
L7.	=	Total resources needed for retirement	$4,435,429
L8.		Total in defined-contribution plans	184,000
L9.	+	Total private savings earmarked for retirement	50,000
L10.	=	Current assets available for retirement	234,000
L11.	×	F3 factor	4.32
L12.	=	Future value of current assets	$1,010,880
L13.		Annual income from defined-benefit plan	16,800 (Ann's annual pension)
L14.	×	F1 factor	2.11
L15.	=	Inflation-adjusted annual income from defined-benefit plan	35,448
	×	F4 factor	12.469
L17.	=	Lump-sum value of defined-benefit plan	442,001
L18.		Total resources available for retirement (line 12 and line 17)	1,452,801
L19.		Additional amount you need to accumulate by retirement	2,982,628
L20.	×	F5 factor	0.01435
L21.	=	Amount you need to save—first year	$42,801 (24% of salary)
		(Savings in each subsequent year must increase by the savings step-up rate, 6%)	

TABLE 5-6
Retirement Planning Work Sheet

ASSUMPTIONS

A1.   Inflation rate prior to retirement
A2.   Inflation rate after retirement
A3.   Number of years until retirement
A4.   Expected duration of retirement
A5.   Rate of return prior to retirement
A6.   Rate of return after retirement
A7.   Savings step-up rate

FACTORS

F1.   Pre-retirement inflation factor
F2.   Retirement needs present value factor
F3.   Current assets future value factor
F4.   Defined-benefit present value
        factor
F5.   Savings rate factor

COMPUTATIONS

L1.   Projected annual retirement budget
L2.   −   Social security benefit
L3.   =   Net annual need in current dollars
L4.   x   F1 factor
L5.   =   Inflation-adjusted annual retirement need
L6.   x   F2 factor
L7.   =   Total resources needed for retirement

L8.   Total in defined-contribution plans
L9.   +   Total private savings earmarked for
             retirement
L10. =   Current assets available for retirement
L11. x   F3 factor
L12. =   Future value of current assets
L13.   Annual income from defined-benefit plan
L14. x   F1 factor
L15. =   Inflation-adjusted annual income from
             defined-benefit plan
        x   F4 factor
L17. =   Lump-sum value of defined-benefit plan

L18.   Total resources available for retirement
             (line 12 and line 17)
L19.   Additional amount you need to
             accumulate by retirement
L20. x   F5 factor
L21. =   Amount you need to save—first year

(Savings in each subsequent year must increase by the savings step-up
rate, 6%)

THE INFLATION AND FUTURE VALUE FACTORS

Table 5-7 is used to select the appropriate Preretirement Inflation Factor (F1) and Current Assets Future Value Factor (F3) for use in the Retirement Planning Work Sheet. An explanation of the use of the table follows the table.

TABLE 5-7
Future Value Factors

Yrs	0%	1%	2%	3%	4%	5%	6%
1	1.00	1.01	1.02	1.03	1.04	1.05	1.06
2	1.00	1.02	1.04	1.06	1.08	1.10	1.12
3	1.00	1.03	1.06	1.09	1.12	1.16	1.19
4	1.00	1.04	1.08	1.13	1.17	1.22	1.26
5	1.00	1.05	1.10	1.16	1.22	1.28	1.34
6	1.00	1.06	1.13	1.19	1.27	1.34	1.42
7	1.00	1.07	1.15	1.23	1.32	1.41	1.50
8	1.00	1.08	1.17	1.27	1.37	1.48	1.59
9	1.00	1.09	1.20	1.30	1.42	1.55	1.69
10	1.00	1.10	1.22	1.34	1.48	1.63	1.79
11	1.00	1.12	1.24	1.38	1.54	1.71	1.90
12	1.00	1.13	1.27	1.43	1.60	1.80	2.01
13	1.00	1.14	1.29	1.47	1.67	1.89	2.13
14	1.00	1.15	1.32	1.51	1.73	1.98	2.26
15	1.00	1.16	1.35	1.56	1.80	2.08	2.40
16	1.00	1.17	1.37	1.60	1.87	2.18	2.54
17	1.00	1.18	1.40	1.65	1.95	2.29	2.69
18	1.00	1.20	1.43	1.70	2.03	2.41	**2.85**
19	1.00	1.21	1.46	1.75	**2.11**	2.53	3.03
20	1.00	1.22	1.49	1.81	2.19	2.65	3.21
21	1.00	1.23	1.52	1.86	2.28	2.79	3.40
22	1.00	1.24	1.55	1.92	2.37	2.93	3.60
23	1.00	1.26	1.58	1.97	2.46	3.07	3.82
24	1.00	1.27	1.61	2.03	2.56	3.23	4.05
25	1.00	1.28	1.64	2.09	2.67	3.39	4.29
26	1.00	1.30	1.67	2.16	2.77	3.56	4.55
27	1.00	1.31	1.71	2.22	2.88	3.73	4.82
28	1.00	1.32	1.74	2.29	3.00	3.92	5.11
29	1.00	1.33	1.78	2.36	3.12	4.12	5.42
30	1.00	1.35	1.81	2.43	3.24	4.32	5.74
31	1.00	1.36	1.85	2.50	3.37	4.54	6.09
32	1.00	1.37	1.88	2.58	3.51	4.76	6.45
33	1.00	1.39	1.92	2.65	3.65	5.00	6.84
34	1.00	1.40	1.96	2.73	3.79	5.25	7.25
35	1.00	1.42	2.00	2.81	3.95	5.52	7.69
36	1.00	1.43	2.04	2.90	4.10	5.79	8.15
37	1.00	1.45	2.08	2.99	4.27	6.08	8.64
38	1.00	1.46	2.12	3.07	4.44	6.39	9.15
39	1.00	1.47	2.16	3.17	4.62	6.70	9.70
40	1.00	1.49	2.21	3.26	4.80	7.04	10.29
41	1.00	1.50	2.25	3.36	4.99	7.39	10.90
42	1.00	1.52	2.30	3.46	5.19	7.76	11.56
43	1.00	1.53	2.34	3.56	5.40	8.15	12.25
44	1.00	1.55	2.39	3.67	5.62	8.56	12.99
45	1.00	1.56	2.44	3.78	5.84	8.99	13.76

TABLE 5-7 (Continued)
Future Value Factors

Yrs	7%	8%	9%	10%	11%	12%	15%	20%
				Rate				
1	1.07	1.08	1.09	1.10	1.11	1.12	1.15	1.20
2	1.14	1.17	1.19	1.21	1.23	1.25	1.32	1.44
3	1.23	1.26	1.30	1.33	1.37	1.40	1.52	1.73
4	1.31	1.36	1.41	1.46	1.52	1.57	1.75	2.07
5	1.40	1.47	1.54	1.61	1.69	1.76	2.01	2.49
6	1.50	1.59	1.68	1.77	1.87	1.97	2.31	2.99
7	1.61	1.71	1.83	1.95	2.08	2.21	2.66	3.58
8	1.72	1.85	1.99	2.14	2.30	2.48	3.06	4.30
9	1.84	2.00	2.17	2.36	2.56	2.77	3.52	5.16
10	1.97	2.16	2.37	2.59	2.84	3.11	4.05	6.19
11	2.10	2.33	2.58	2.85	3.15	3.48	4.65	7.43
12	2.25	2.52	**2.81**	3.14	3.50	3.90	5.35	8.92
13	2.41	2.72	3.07	3.45	3.88	4.36	6.15	10.70
14	2.58	2.94	3.34	3.80	4.31	4.89	7.08	12.84
15	2.76	3.17	3.64	4.18	4.78	5.47	8.14	15.41
16	2.95	3.43	3.97	4.59	5.31	6.13	9.36	18.49
17	3.16	3.70	4.33	5.05	5.90	6.87	10.76	22.19
18	3.38	4.00	4.72	5.56	6.54	7.69	12.38	26.62
19	3.62	4.32	5.14	6.12	7.26	8.61	14.23	31.95
20	3.87	4.66	5.60	6.73	8.06	9.65	16.37	38.34
21	4.14	5.03	6.11	7.40	8.95	10.80	18.82	46.01
22	4.43	5.44	6.66	8.14	9.93	12.10	21.64	55.21
23	4.74	5.87	7.26	8.95	11.03	13.55	24.89	66.25
24	5.07	6.34	7.91	9.85	12.24	15.18	28.63	79.50
25	5.43	6.85	8.62	10.83	13.59	17.00	32.92	95.40
26	5.81	7.40	9.40	11.92	15.08	19.04	37.86	114.48
27	6.21	7.99	10.25	13.11	16.74	21.32	43.54	137.37
28	6.65	8.63	11.17	14.42	18.58	23.88	50.07	164.84
29	7.11	9.32	12.17	15.86	20.62	26.75	57.58	197.81
30	7.61	10.06	13.27	17.45	22.89	29.96	66.21	237.38
31	8.15	10.87	14.46	19.19	25.41	33.56	76.14	284.85
32	8.72	11.74	15.76	21.11	28.21	37.58	87.57	341.82
33	9.33	12.68	17.18	23.23	31.31	42.09	100.70	410.19
34	9.98	13.69	18.73	25.55	34.75	47.14	115.80	492.22
35	10.68	14.79	20.41	28.10	38.57	52.80	133.18	590.67
36	11.42	15.97	22.25	30.91	42.82	59.14	153.15	708.80
37	12.22	17.25	24.25	34.00	47.53	66.23	176.12	850.56
38	13.08	18.63	26.44	37.40	52.76	74.18	202.54	1020.67
39	13.99	20.12	28.82	41.14	58.56	83.08	232.92	1224.81
40	14.97	21.72	31.41	45.26	65.00	93.05	267.86	1469.77
41	16.02	23.46	34.24	49.79	72.15	104.22	308.04	1763.73
42	17.14	25.34	37.32	54.76	80.09	116.72	354.25	2116.47
43	18.34	27.37	40.68	60.24	88.90	130.73	407.39	2539.77
44	19.63	29.56	44.34	66.26	98.68	146.42	468.50	3047.72
45	21.00	31.92	48.33	72.89	109.53	163.99	538.77	3657.26

Selecting the Preretirement Inflation Factor (F1)

The appropriate F1 factor depends on the assumed annual inflation rate prior to retirement (line A1 of the Retirement Planning Work Sheet) and the number of years until retirement (line A3 of the Retirement Planning Work Sheet). The F1 factor is found in table 5-7 by looking in the column with the interest/inflation rate equal to the inflation rate specified in line A1 and the row with the number of years equal to that specified in line A3 of the Retirement Planning Work Sheet. For example, if you assume inflation will average 6 percent per year until retirement (A1) and you expect to retire in 18 years (A3), the appropriate preretirement inflation factor (F1) is 2.85.

Selecting the Current Assets Future Value Factor (F3)

The appropriate F3 factor depends on the assumed rate of return on investment prior to retirement (line A5 of the Retirement Planning Work Sheet) and the number of years until retirement (line A3 of the Retirement Planning Work Sheet). The F3 factor is found in table 5-7 by looking in the column with the interest/inflation rate equal to the rate of return specified in line A5 and the row with the number of years equal to that specified in line A3 of the Retirement Planning Work Sheet. For example, if you assume you can invest at a rate of 9 percent per year until retirement (A5) and you expect to retire in 12 years (A3), the appropriate current assets future value factor (F3) is 2.81.

ANNUITY FACTORS

Table 5-8 is used to select the appropriate Retirement Needs Present Value Factor (F2) and Defined-Benefit Present Value Factor (F4) for use in the Retirement Planning Work Sheet presented. An explanation of the use of the table follows the table.

TABLE 5-8 Present Value of an Annuity Factors							
	Rate						
Yrs	0%	1%	2%	3%	4%	5%	6%
1	1.000	1.000	1.000	1.000	1.000	1.000	1.000
2	2.000	1.990	1.980	1.971	1.962	1.952	1.943
3	3.000	2.970	2.942	2.913	2.886	2.859	2.833
4	4.000	3.941	3.884	3.829	3.775	3.723	3.673
5	5.000	4.902	4.808	4.717	4.630	4.546	4.465
6	6.000	5.853	5.713	5.580	5.452	5.329	5.212
7	7.000	6.795	6.601	6.417	6.242	6.076	5.917
8	8.000	7.728	7.472	7.230	7.002	6.786	6.582
9	9.000	8.652	8.325	8.020	7.733	7.463	7.210
10	10.000	9.566	9.162	8.786	8.435	8.108	7.802
11	11.000	10.471	9.983	9.530	9.111	8.722	8.360
12	12.000	11.368	10.787	10.253	9.760	9.306	8.887
13	13.000	12.255	11.575	10.954	10.385	9.863	9.384
14	14.000	13.134	12.348	11.635	10.986	10.394	9.853
15	15.000	14.004	13.106	12.296	11.563	10.899	10.295
16	16.000	14.865	13.849	12.938	12.118	11.380	10.712
17	17.000	15.718	14.578	13.561	12.652	11.838	11.106
18	18.000	16.562	15.292	14.166	13.166	12.274	11.477
19	19.000	17.398	15.992	14.754	13.659	12.690	11.828
20	20.000	18.226	16.678	15.324	14.134	13.085	12.158
21	21.000	19.046	17.351	15.877	14.590	13.462	12.470
22	22.000	19.857	18.011	**16.415**	15.029	13.821	12.764
23	23.000	20.660	18.658	16.937	15.451	14.163	13.042
24	24.000	21.456	19.292	17.444	15.857	14.489	13.303
25	25.000	22.243	19.914	17.936	16.247	14.799	13.550
26	26.000	23.023	20.523	18.413	16.622	15.094	13.783
27	27.000	23.795	21.121	18.877	16.983	15.375	14.003
28	28.000	24.560	21.707	19.327	17.330	15.643	14.211
29	29.000	25.316	22.281	19.764	17.663	15.898	14.406
30	30.000	26.066	22.844	20.188	17.984	16.141	14.591
31	31.000	26.808	23.396	20.600	18.292	16.372	14.765
32	32.000	27.542	23.938	21.000	18.588	16.593	14.929
33	33.000	28.270	24.468	21.389	18.874	16.803	15.084
34	34.000	28.990	24.989	21.766	19.148	17.003	15.230
35	35.000	29.703	25.499	22.132	19.411	17.193	15.368
36	36.000	30.409	25.999	22.487	19.665	17.374	15.498
37	37.000	31.108	26.489	22.832	19.908	17.547	15.621
38	38.000	31.800	26.969	23.167	20.143	17.711	15.737
39	39.000	32.485	27.441	23.492	20.368	17.868	15.846
40	40.000	33.163	27.903	23.808	20.584	18.017	15.949
41	41.000	33.835	28.355	24.115	20.793	18.159	16.046
42	42.000	34.500	28.799	24.412	20.993	18.294	16.138
43	43.000	35.158	29.235	24.701	21.186	18.423	16.225
44	44.000	35.810	29.662	24.982	21.371	18.546	16.306
45	45.000	36.455	30.080	25.254	21.549	18.663	16.383

TABLE 5-8 (Continued)
Present Value of an Annuity Factors

Yrs	7%	8%	9%	10%	11%	12%	15%	20%
1	1.000	1.000	1.000	1.000	1.000	1.000	1.000	1.000
2	1.935	1.926	1.917	1.909	1.901	1.893	1.870	1.833
3	2.808	2.783	2.759	2.736	2.713	2.690	2.626	2.528
4	3.624	3.577	3.531	3.487	3.444	3.402	3.283	3.106
5	4.387	4.312	4.240	4.170	4.102	4.037	3.855	3.589
6	5.100	4.993	4.890	4.791	4.696	4.605	4.352	3.991
7	5.767	5.623	5.486	5.355	5.231	5.111	4.784	4.326
8	6.389	6.206	6.033	5.868	5.712	5.564	5.160	4.605
9	6.971	6.747	6.535	6.335	6.146	5.968	5.487	4.837
10	7.515	7.247	6.995	6.759	6.537	6.328	5.772	5.031
11	8.024	7.710	7.418	7.145	6.889	6.650	6.019	5.192
12	8.499	8.139	7.805	7.495	7.207	6.938	6.234	5.327
13	8.943	8.536	8.161	7.814	7.492	7.194	6.421	5.439
14	9.358	8.904	8.487	8.103	7.750	7.424	6.583	5.533
15	9.745	9.244	8.786	8.367	7.982	7.628	6.724	5.611
16	10.108	9.559	9.061	8.606	8.191	7.811	6.847	5.675
17	10.447	9.851	9.313	8.824	8.379	7.974	6.954	5.730
18	10.763	10.122	9.544	9.022	8.549	8.120	7.047	5.775
19	11.059	10.372	9.756	9.201	8.702	8.250	7.128	5.812
20	11.336	10.604	9.950	9.365	8.839	8.366	7.198	5.843
21	11.594	10.818	10.129	9.514	8.963	8.469	7.259	5.870
22	11.836	11.017	10.292	9.649	9.075	8.562	7.312	5.891
23	12.061	11.201	10.442	9.772	9.176	8.645	7.359	5.909
24	12.272	11.371	10.580	9.883	9.266	8.718	7.399	5.925
25	**12.469**	11.529	10.707	9.985	9.348	8.784	7.434	5.937
26	**12.654**	11.675	10.823	10.077	9.422	8.843	7.464	5.948
27	12.826	11.810	10.929	10.161	9.488	8.896	7.491	5.956
28	12.987	11.935	11.027	10.237	9.548	8.943	7.514	5.964
29	13.137	12.051	11.116	10.307	9.602	8.984	7.534	5.970
30	13.278	12.158	11.198	10.370	9.650	9.022	7.551	5.975
31	13.409	12.258	11.274	10.427	9.694	9.055	7.566	5.979
32	13.532	12.350	11.343	10.479	9.733	9.085	7.579	5.982
33	13.647	12.435	11.406	10.526	9.769	9.112	7.591	5.985
34	13.754	12.514	11.464	10.569	9.801	9.135	7.600	5.988
35	13.854	12.587	11.518	10.609	9.829	9.157	7.609	5.990
36	13.948	12.655	11.567	10.644	9.855	9.176	7.617	5.992
37	14.035	12.717	11.612	10.677	9.879	9.192	7.623	5.993
38	14.117	12.775	11.653	10.706	9.900	9.208	7.629	5.994
39	14.193	12.829	11.691	10.733	9.919	9.221	7.634	5.995
40	14.265	12.879	11.726	10.757	9.936	9.233	7.638	5.996
41	14.332	12.925	11.757	10.779	9.951	9.244	7.642	5.997
42	14.394	12.967	11.787	10.799	9.965	9.253	7.645	5.997
43	14.452	13.007	11.813	10.817	9.977	9.262	7.648	5.998
44	14.507	13.043	11.838	10.834	9.989	9.270	7.650	5.998
45	14.558	13.077	11.861	10.849	9.999	9.276	7.652	5.998

Selecting the Retirement Needs Present Value Factor (F2)

The appropriate F2 factor depends on the assumed annual inflation rate after retirement, the expected duration of retirement, and the assumed rate of return on investment after retirement (lines A2, A4, and A6, respectively, of the Retirement Planning Work Sheet [table 5-3]). The F2 factor is found using a two-step process. First, you must determine the inflation-adjusted interest rate. This is estimated by subtracting your assumed inflation rate after retirement (A2) from your assumed investment rate of return after retirement (A6).

Specifically,

Value from A6	−	Value from A2	=	Inflation-Adjusted Rate
	−		=	

Next, you can find the appropriate F2 factor by looking in table 5-8 in the column with the inflation-adjusted interest rate equal to that just computed and the row with the number of years equal to that specified in line A4 of the Retirement Planning Work Sheet. For example, if you assume inflation will average 5 percent per year after retirement (A2) and you expect to earn 8 percent on your investments after retirement (A6), your inflation-adjusted interest rate would be

Value from A6	−	Value from A2	=	Inflation-Adjusted Rate
8%	−	5%	=	3%

If your expected duration of retirement is 22 years (A4), the appropriate retirement needs present value factor (F2) is found by looking in the 3 percent column and the 22 year row of table 5-8. In this case, F2 is 16.415.

Selecting the Defined-Benefit Present Value Factor (F4)

The appropriate F4 factor depends on the assumed rate of return on investment after retirement and the expected duration of retirement (lines A6 and A4 of the Retirement Planning Work Sheet, respectively). The F4 factor is found in table 5-8 by looking in the column with the interest rate equal to the rate of return specified in line A6 and the row with the number of years equal to that specified in line A4 of the Retirement Planning Work Sheet. For example, if you assume you can invest at a rate of 7 percent per year after retirement (A6) and you expect your retirement needs to last 26 years (A4), the appropriate defined-benefit present value factor (F4) is 12.654.

THE SAVINGS RATE FACTOR

Tables 5-9 through 5-14 are used to select the appropriate Savings Rate Factor (F5) for use in the Retirement Planning Work Sheet. An explanation of the use of the tables follows the tables.

TABLE 5-9
Yearly Savings Rate Factors
0% Savings Step-up Rate (A7)

Yrs	Assumed Rate of Return (A5)					
	1%	2%	3%	4%	5%	6%
1	0.99010	0.98039	0.97087	0.96154	0.95238	0.94340
2	0.49259	0.48534	0.47826	0.47134	0.46458	0.45796
3	0.32675	0.32035	0.31411	0.30803	0.30210	0.29633
4	0.24384	0.23787	0.23207	0.22643	0.22096	0.21565
5	0.19410	0.18839	0.18287	0.17753	0.17236	0.16736
6	0.16094	0.15542	0.15009	0.14496	0.14002	0.13525
7	0.13726	0.13187	0.12671	0.12174	0.11697	0.11239
8	0.11950	0.11423	0.10918	0.10435	0.09974	0.09532
9	0.10568	0.10051	0.09557	0.09086	0.08637	0.08210
10	0.09464	0.08954	0.08469	0.08009	0.07572	0.07157
11	0.08560	0.08057	0.07580	0.07130	0.06704	0.06301
12	0.07807	0.07310	0.06841	0.06399	0.05983	0.05592
13	0.07170	0.06678	0.06216	0.05783	0.05377	0.04996
14	0.06624	0.06137	0.05682	0.05257	0.04859	0.04489
15	0.06151	0.05669	0.05220	0.04802	0.04414	0.04053
16	0.05737	0.05260	0.04817	0.04406	0.04026	0.03675
17	0.05372	0.04899	0.04461	0.04058	0.03686	0.03344
18	0.05048	0.04579	0.04146	0.03749	0.03385	0.03053
19	0.04758	0.04292	0.03865	0.03475	0.03119	0.02794
20	0.04497	0.04035	0.03613	0.03229	0.02880	0.02565
21	0.04260	0.03802	0.03386	0.03008	0.02666	0.02359
22	0.04046	0.03591	0.03179	0.02808	0.02473	0.02174
23	0.03850	0.03399	0.02992	0.02626	0.02299	0.02007
24	0.03671	0.03223	0.02820	0.02460	0.02140	0.01857
25	0.03506	0.03061	0.02663	0.02309	0.01995	0.01720
26	0.03353	0.02912	0.02518	0.02170	0.01863	0.01595
27	0.03212	0.02774	0.02385	0.02042	0.01742	0.01481
28	0.03082	0.02646	0.02261	0.01924	0.01631	0.01377
29	0.02960	0.02527	0.02147	0.01815	0.01528	0.01281
30	0.02846	0.02417	0.02041	0.01714	0.01433	0.01193
31	0.02740	0.02313	0.01942	0.01621	0.01346	0.01112
32	0.02641	0.02217	0.01849	0.01534	0.01265	0.01038
33	0.02547	0.02126	0.01763	0.01452	0.01190	0.00969
34	0.02459	0.02041	0.01682	0.01376	0.01120	0.00906
35	0.02377	0.01961	0.01606	0.01306	0.01054	0.00847
36	0.02298	0.01886	0.01534	0.01239	0.00994	0.00792
37	0.02225	0.01814	0.01467	0.01177	0.00937	0.00741
38	0.02155	0.01747	0.01404	0.01118	0.00884	0.00694
39	0.02088	0.01683	0.01344	0.01064	0.00835	0.00650
40	0.02025	0.01623	0.01288	0.01012	0.00788	0.00610
41	0.01965	0.01566	0.01234	0.00963	0.00745	0.00572
42	0.01908	0.01511	0.01184	0.00917	0.00704	0.00536
43	0.01854	0.01460	0.01136	0.00874	0.00666	0.00503
44	0.01802	0.01411	0.01090	0.00833	0.00630	0.00472
45	0.01753	0.01364	0.01047	0.00794	0.00596	0.00443

TABLE 5-9 (Continued)
Yearly Savings Rate Factors
0% Savings Step-up Rate (A7)

Yrs	7%	8%	9%	10%	11%	12%	15%	20%
1	0.93458	0.92593	0.91743	0.90909	0.90090	0.89286	0.86957	0.83333
2	0.45149	0.44516	0.43896	0.43290	0.42697	0.42116	0.40445	0.37879
3	0.29070	0.28522	0.27987	0.27465	0.26956	0.26460	0.25041	0.22894
4	0.21049	0.20548	0.20061	0.19588	0.19129	0.18682	0.17414	0.15524
5	0.16251	0.15783	0.15330	0.14891	0.14466	0.14054	0.12897	0.11198
6	0.13065	0.12622	0.12194	0.11782	0.11385	0.11002	0.09934	0.08392
7	0.10799	0.10377	0.09972	0.09582	0.09209	0.08850	0.07857	0.06452
8	0.09109	0.08705	0.08319	0.07949	0.07596	0.07259	0.06335	0.05051
9	0.07802	0.07415	0.07046	0.06695	0.06361	0.06043	0.05180	0.04007
10	0.06764	0.06392	0.06039	0.05704	0.05388	0.05088	0.04283	0.03210
11	0.05921	0.05563	0.05224	0.04906	0.04605	0.04323	0.03571	0.02592
12	0.05224	0.04879	0.04555	0.04251	0.03966	0.03700	0.02998	0.02105
13	0.04640	0.04308	0.03997	0.03707	0.03437	0.03185	0.02531	0.01718
14	0.04144	0.03824	0.03526	0.03250	0.02994	0.02756	0.02147	0.01408
15	0.03719	0.03410	0.03125	0.02861	0.02618	0.02395	0.01828	0.01157
16	0.03351	0.03053	0.02780	0.02529	0.02299	0.02088	0.01561	0.00953
17	0.03030	0.02743	0.02481	0.02242	0.02024	0.01826	0.01336	0.00787
18	0.02749	0.02472	0.02221	0.01994	0.01788	0.01602	0.01147	0.00650
19	0.02500	0.02234	0.01994	0.01777	0.01582	0.01407	0.00986	0.00539
20	0.02280	0.02023	0.01793	0.01587	0.01403	0.01239	0.00849	0.00446
21	0.02083	0.01836	0.01616	0.01420	0.01247	0.01093	0.00732	0.00370
22	0.01907	0.01670	0.01459	0.01273	0.01109	0.00965	0.00632	0.00307
23	0.01749	0.01521	0.01319	0.01143	0.00988	0.00854	0.00546	0.00255
24	0.01606	0.01387	0.01195	0.01027	0.00882	0.00756	0.00472	0.00212
25	0.01478	0.01267	0.01083	0.00924	0.00787	0.00670	0.00409	0.00177
26	0.01361	0.01158	0.00983	0.00833	0.00704	0.00594	0.00354	0.00147
27	0.01255	0.01060	0.00893	0.00751	0.00630	0.00527	0.00307	0.00122
28	0.01158	0.00971	0.00812	0.00677	0.00564	0.00468	0.00266	0.00102
29	0.01070	0.00891	0.00739	0.00612	0.00505	0.00416	0.00231	0.00085
30	0.00989	0.00817	0.00673	0.00553	0.00453	0.00370	0.00200	0.00071
31	0.00916	0.00751	0.00613	0.00500	0.00406	0.00329	0.00174	0.00059
32	0.00848	0.00690	0.00559	0.00452	0.00364	0.00293	0.00151	0.00049
33	0.00786	0.00634	0.00510	0.00409	0.00327	0.00261	0.00131	0.00041
34	0.00729	0.00584	0.00466	0.00370	0.00294	0.00232	0.00114	0.00034
35	0.00676	0.00537	0.00425	0.00335	0.00264	0.00207	0.00099	0.00028
36	0.00628	0.00495	0.00389	0.00304	0.00237	0.00184	0.00086	0.00024
37	0.00583	0.00456	0.00355	0.00275	0.00213	0.00164	0.00074	0.00020
38	0.00542	0.00420	0.00325	0.00250	0.00191	0.00146	0.00065	0.00016
39	0.00503	0.00388	0.00297	0.00226	0.00172	0.00131	0.00056	0.00014
40	0.00468	0.00357	0.00272	0.00205	0.00155	0.00116	0.00049	0.00011
41	0.00435	0.00330	0.00248	0.00186	0.00139	0.00104	0.00042	0.00009
42	0.00405	0.00304	0.00227	0.00169	0.00125	0.00093	0.00037	0.00008
43	0.00377	0.00281	0.00208	0.00153	0.00113	0.00083	0.00032	0.00007
44	0.00351	0.00259	0.00191	0.00139	0.00101	0.00074	0.00028	0.00005
45	0.00327	0.00240	0.00174	0.00126	0.00091	0.00066	0.00024	0.00005

Yrs	1%	2%	3%	4%	5%	6%
1	0.99010	0.98039	0.97087	0.96154	0.95238	0.94340
2	0.48773	0.48058	0.47360	0.46677	0.46009	0.45356
3	0.32035	0.31411	0.30803	0.30210	0.29633	0.29071
4	0.23671	0.23096	0.22538	0.21997	0.21470	0.20959
5	0.18656	0.18115	0.17590	0.17083	0.16592	0.16116
6	0.15317	0.14800	0.14301	0.13820	0.13355	0.12907
7	0.12934	0.12437	0.11958	0.11498	0.11056	0.10631
8	0.11149	0.10669	0.10208	0.09766	0.09343	0.08938
9	0.09764	0.09297	0.08852	0.08426	0.08020	0.07633
10	0.08657	0.08203	0.07772	0.07361	0.06970	0.06599
11	0.07753	0.07311	0.06892	0.06495	0.06119	0.05762
12	0.07001	0.06571	0.06164	0.05779	0.05415	0.05072
13	0.06367	0.05946	0.05550	0.05177	0.04826	0.04496
14	0.05824	0.05413	0.05028	0.04665	0.04326	0.04008
15	0.05355	0.04953	0.04577	0.04226	0.03898	0.03592
16	0.04945	0.04553	0.04186	0.03845	0.03527	0.03232
17	0.04585	0.04201	0.03843	0.03511	0.03204	0.02920
18	0.04266	0.03890	0.03541	0.03218	0.02920	0.02646
19	0.03981	0.03613	0.03272	0.02958	0.02670	0.02405
20	0.03726	0.03365	0.03032	0.02727	0.02448	0.02192
21	0.03495	0.03142	0.02817	0.02520	0.02249	0.02003
22	0.03286	0.02940	0.02623	0.02334	0.02071	0.01834
23	0.03097	0.02757	0.02447	0.02166	0.01912	0.01682
24	0.02923	0.02591	0.02288	0.02014	0.01767	0.01546
25	0.02764	0.02438	0.02142	0.01876	0.01637	0.01423
26	0.02618	0.02298	0.02009	0.01750	0.01518	0.01312
27	0.02483	0.02170	0.01887	0.01635	0.01410	0.01211
28	0.02359	0.02051	0.01775	0.01529	0.01311	0.01120
29	0.02243	0.01942	0.01672	0.01432	0.01221	0.01036
30	0.02136	0.01840	0.01576	0.01343	0.01138	0.00960
31	0.02036	0.01746	0.01488	0.01261	0.01062	0.00890
32	0.01943	0.01658	0.01406	0.01185	0.00992	0.00826
33	0.01856	0.01576	0.01330	0.01114	0.00927	0.00767
34	0.01774	0.01500	0.01259	0.01049	0.00868	0.00713
35	0.01697	0.01429	0.01193	0.00988	0.00813	0.00664
36	0.01625	0.01362	0.01131	0.00932	0.00762	0.00618
37	0.01558	0.01299	0.01073	0.00879	0.00714	0.00576
38	0.01494	0.01240	0.01019	0.00830	0.00670	0.00537
39	0.01434	0.01184	0.00969	0.00784	0.00629	0.00501
40	0.01377	0.01132	0.00921	0.00742	0.00591	0.00467
41	0.01323	0.01083	0.00876	0.00702	0.00556	0.00436
42	0.01272	0.01036	0.00834	0.00664	0.00523	0.00408
43	0.01224	0.00992	0.00795	0.00629	0.00492	0.00381
44	0.01178	0.00951	0.00758	0.00596	0.00463	0.00356
45	0.01134	0.00912	0.00723	0.00565	0.00436	0.00333

TABLE 5-10 Yearly Savings Rate Factors 2% Savings Step-up Rate (A7) — Assumed Rate of Return (A5)

TABLE 5-10 (Continued)
Yearly Savings Rate Factors
2% Savings Step-up Rate (A7)

| Yrs | \multicolumn{8}{c}{Assumed Rate of Return (A5)} |

Yrs	7%	8%	9%	10%	11%	12%	15%	20%
1	0.93458	0.92593	0.91743	0.90909	0.90090	0.89286	0.86957	0.83333
2	0.44717	0.44092	0.43480	0.42882	0.42296	0.41722	0.40072	0.37538
3	0.28522	0.27987	0.27466	0.26957	0.26461	0.25976	0.24592	0.22496
4	0.20463	0.19980	0.19511	0.19055	0.18612	0.18181	0.16959	0.15134
5	0.15656	0.15210	0.14779	0.14361	0.13956	0.13564	0.12460	0.10836
6	0.12475	0.12059	0.11657	0.11269	0.10894	0.10533	0.09524	0.08065
7	0.10223	0.09830	0.09453	0.09091	0.08742	0.08407	0.07480	0.06161
8	0.08550	0.08179	0.07823	0.07483	0.07157	0.06845	0.05989	0.04795
9	0.07263	0.06911	0.06575	0.06254	0.05949	0.05658	0.04867	0.03783
10	0.06246	0.05911	0.05592	0.05290	0.05004	0.04732	0.03999	0.03016
11	0.05424	0.05105	0.04803	0.04518	0.04249	0.03995	0.03316	0.02425
12	0.04749	0.04445	0.04158	0.03889	0.03636	0.03398	0.02769	0.01961
13	0.04186	0.03896	0.03624	0.03369	0.03131	0.02908	0.02326	0.01595
14	0.03711	0.03434	0.03176	0.02935	0.02711	0.02503	0.01964	0.01302
15	0.03307	0.03042	0.02796	0.02569	0.02358	0.02163	0.01665	0.01067
16	0.02959	0.02706	0.02472	0.02257	0.02059	0.01877	0.01416	0.00876
17	0.02657	0.02416	0.02194	0.01990	0.01804	0.01634	0.01208	0.00722
18	0.02394	0.02164	0.01953	0.01760	0.01585	0.01426	0.01033	0.00595
19	0.02164	0.01943	0.01743	0.01561	0.01396	0.01248	0.00885	0.00492
20	0.01960	0.01750	0.01559	0.01388	0.01233	0.01094	0.00760	0.00407
21	0.01780	0.01579	0.01398	0.01236	0.01091	0.00961	0.00653	0.00337
22	0.01620	0.01428	0.01256	0.01103	0.00967	0.00846	0.00562	0.00280
23	0.01477	0.01294	0.01130	0.00986	0.00858	0.00746	0.00485	0.00232
24	0.01349	0.01174	0.01019	0.00882	0.00763	0.00658	0.00418	0.00193
25	0.01234	0.01067	0.00920	0.00791	0.00679	0.00581	0.00361	0.00160
26	0.01130	0.00971	0.00831	0.00710	0.00605	0.00514	0.00312	0.00133
27	0.01037	0.00884	0.00752	0.00638	0.00539	0.00455	0.00270	0.00111
28	0.00952	0.00807	0.00681	0.00574	0.00482	0.00403	0.00234	0.00092
29	0.00875	0.00737	0.00618	0.00516	0.00430	0.00358	0.00203	0.00077
30	0.00806	0.00673	0.00561	0.00465	0.00385	0.00317	0.00176	0.00064
31	0.00742	0.00616	0.00509	0.00419	0.00344	0.00282	0.00152	0.00053
32	0.00684	0.00564	0.00463	0.00378	0.00308	0.00250	0.00132	0.00044
33	0.00631	0.00517	0.00421	0.00341	0.00276	0.00222	0.00114	0.00037
34	0.00583	0.00474	0.00383	0.00308	0.00247	0.00198	0.00099	0.00031
35	0.00539	0.00435	0.00349	0.00279	0.00222	0.00176	0.00086	0.00025
36	0.00498	0.00399	0.00318	0.00252	0.00199	0.00156	0.00075	0.00021
37	0.00461	0.00366	0.00290	0.00228	0.00178	0.00139	0.00065	0.00018
38	0.00426	0.00337	0.00264	0.00206	0.00160	0.00124	0.00056	0.00015
39	0.00395	0.00309	0.00241	0.00187	0.00144	0.00110	0.00049	0.00012
40	0.00366	0.00285	0.00220	0.00169	0.00129	0.00098	0.00043	0.00010
41	0.00339	0.00262	0.00201	0.00153	0.00116	0.00088	0.00037	0.00009
42	0.00315	0.00241	0.00183	0.00139	0.00104	0.00078	0.00032	0.00007
43	0.00292	0.00222	0.00168	0.00126	0.00094	0.00070	0.00028	0.00006
44	0.00271	0.00205	0.00153	0.00114	0.00084	0.00062	0.00024	0.00005
45	0.00252	0.00188	0.00140	0.00103	0.00076	0.00055	0.00021	0.00004

TABLE 5-11
Yearly Savings Rate Factors
4% Savings Step-up Rate (A7)

Yrs	Assumed Rate of Return (A5)					
	1%	2%	3%	4%	5%	6%
1	0.99010	0.98039	0.97087	0.96154	0.95238	0.94340
2	0.48298	0.47592	0.46902	0.46228	0.45568	0.44924
3	0.31411	0.30803	0.30210	0.29633	0.29071	0.28522
4	0.22980	0.22428	0.21891	0.21370	0.20864	0.20372
5	0.17932	0.17418	0.16920	0.16439	0.15972	0.15520
6	0.14575	0.14090	0.13623	0.13172	0.12736	0.12316
7	0.12184	0.11724	0.11282	0.10856	0.10446	0.10052
8	0.10396	0.09958	0.09537	0.09134	0.08747	0.08375
9	0.09011	0.08592	0.08190	0.07807	0.07440	0.07089
10	0.07908	0.07505	0.07122	0.06756	0.06407	0.06075
11	0.07009	0.06622	0.06255	0.05905	0.05573	0.05258
12	0.06264	0.05892	0.05539	0.05205	0.04888	0.04589
13	0.05636	0.05278	0.04940	0.04620	0.04318	0.04033
14	0.05102	0.04757	0.04431	0.04125	0.03836	0.03565
15	0.04641	0.04309	0.03996	0.03702	0.03426	0.03168
16	0.04241	0.03920	0.03619	0.03337	0.03073	0.02827
17	0.03890	0.03580	0.03291	0.03020	0.02768	0.02533
18	0.03580	0.03281	0.03002	0.02742	0.02501	0.02277
19	0.03305	0.03016	0.02748	0.02498	0.02267	0.02054
20	0.03059	0.02781	0.02522	0.02282	0.02061	0.01857
21	0.02839	0.02569	0.02320	0.02090	0.01878	0.01683
22	0.02640	0.02380	0.02139	0.01918	0.01715	0.01529
23	0.02460	0.02209	0.01977	0.01764	0.01569	0.01392
24	0.02296	0.02053	0.01830	0.01626	0.01439	0.01270
25	0.02147	0.01913	0.01697	0.01500	0.01322	0.01160
26	0.02011	0.01784	0.01576	0.01387	0.01216	0.01062
27	0.01886	0.01667	0.01466	0.01285	0.01120	0.00973
28	0.01771	0.01559	0.01366	0.01191	0.01034	0.00893
29	0.01665	0.01460	0.01274	0.01106	0.00955	0.00820
30	0.01567	0.01369	0.01190	0.01028	0.00883	0.00755
31	0.01476	0.01285	0.01112	0.00956	0.00818	0.00695
32	0.01392	0.01208	0.01041	0.00891	0.00758	0.00641
33	0.01314	0.01136	0.00975	0.00831	0.00703	0.00591
34	0.01242	0.01069	0.00914	0.00775	0.00653	0.00546
35	0.01174	0.01007	0.00857	0.00724	0.00607	0.00504
36	0.01111	0.00950	0.00805	0.00677	0.00564	0.00467
37	0.01052	0.00896	0.00757	0.00633	0.00525	0.00432
38	0.00997	0.00846	0.00712	0.00593	0.00489	0.00400
39	0.00945	0.00800	0.00670	0.00555	0.00456	0.00371
40	0.00897	0.00756	0.00631	0.00521	0.00425	0.00344
41	0.00851	0.00715	0.00594	0.00488	0.00397	0.00319
42	0.00808	0.00677	0.00561	0.00459	0.00371	0.00296
43	0.00768	0.00641	0.00529	0.00431	0.00346	0.00275
44	0.00730	0.00608	0.00499	0.00405	0.00324	0.00256
45	0.00695	0.00576	0.00471	0.00380	0.00303	0.00238

TABLE 5-11 (Continued)
Yearly Savings Rate Factors
4% Savings Step-up Rate (A7)

Yrs	\multicolumn{8}{c}{Assumed Rate of Return (A5)}
	7%	8%	9%	10%	11%	12%	15%	20%
1	0.93458	0.92593	0.91743	0.90909	0.90090	0.89286	0.86957	0.83333
2	0.44293	0.43676	0.43072	0.42481	0.41902	0.41336	0.39706	0.37202
3	0.27987	0.27466	0.26957	0.26461	0.25977	0.25504	0.24154	0.22107
4	0.19893	0.19429	0.18977	0.18538	0.18111	0.17695	0.16516	0.14753
5	0.15082	0.14658	0.14247	0.13849	0.13463	0.13090	0.12036	0.10485
6	0.11910	0.11518	0.11140	0.10775	0.10422	0.10082	0.09129	0.07749
7	0.09673	0.09308	0.08957	0.08620	0.08295	0.07983	0.07117	0.05881
8	0.08019	0.07678	0.07351	0.07038	0.06738	0.06450	0.05658	0.04549
9	0.06754	0.06433	0.06128	0.05836	0.05558	0.05292	0.04567	0.03568
10	0.05758	0.05457	0.05171	0.04899	0.04640	0.04394	0.03729	0.02830
11	0.04959	0.04675	0.04407	0.04152	0.03911	0.03684	0.03073	0.02263
12	0.04306	0.04038	0.03786	0.03548	0.03324	0.03112	0.02551	0.01823
13	0.03765	0.03512	0.03275	0.03052	0.02843	0.02647	0.02131	0.01476
14	0.03311	0.03072	0.02849	0.02640	0.02445	0.02264	0.01790	0.01200
15	0.02926	0.02701	0.02491	0.02295	0.02114	0.01945	0.01510	0.00980
16	0.02598	0.02385	0.02187	0.02004	0.01834	0.01678	0.01278	0.00802
17	0.02315	0.02114	0.01928	0.01756	0.01598	0.01452	0.01085	0.00659
18	0.02071	0.01880	0.01704	0.01543	0.01396	0.01261	0.00924	0.00542
19	0.01857	0.01677	0.01512	0.01361	0.01223	0.01098	0.00789	0.00447
20	0.01670	0.01500	0.01344	0.01202	0.01074	0.00958	0.00675	0.00369
21	0.01506	0.01344	0.01198	0.01065	0.00945	0.00838	0.00578	0.00305
22	0.01361	0.01208	0.01070	0.00945	0.00834	0.00734	0.00496	0.00252
23	0.01232	0.01087	0.00957	0.00841	0.00737	0.00644	0.00427	0.00209
24	0.01117	0.00980	0.00858	0.00749	0.00652	0.00566	0.00367	0.00173
25	0.01015	0.00885	0.00770	0.00668	0.00578	0.00498	0.00316	0.00144
26	0.00924	0.00801	0.00692	0.00596	0.00512	0.00439	0.00273	0.00119
27	0.00842	0.00726	0.00623	0.00533	0.00455	0.00387	0.00235	0.00099
28	0.00768	0.00658	0.00562	0.00478	0.00405	0.00342	0.00203	0.00082
29	0.00702	0.00598	0.00507	0.00428	0.00360	0.00302	0.00176	0.00068
30	0.00642	0.00543	0.00458	0.00384	0.00321	0.00267	0.00152	0.00057
31	0.00588	0.00494	0.00414	0.00345	0.00286	0.00237	0.00131	0.00047
32	0.00538	0.00450	0.00374	0.00310	0.00255	0.00210	0.00114	0.00039
33	0.00494	0.00410	0.00339	0.00279	0.00228	0.00186	0.00099	0.00033
34	0.00453	0.00374	0.00307	0.00251	0.00204	0.00165	0.00085	0.00027
35	0.00417	0.00342	0.00279	0.00226	0.00182	0.00146	0.00074	0.00023
36	0.00383	0.00312	0.00253	0.00203	0.00163	0.00130	0.00064	0.00019
37	0.00352	0.00285	0.00230	0.00183	0.00146	0.00115	0.00056	0.00016
38	0.00324	0.00261	0.00209	0.00165	0.00131	0.00102	0.00048	0.00013
39	0.00299	0.00239	0.00190	0.00149	0.00117	0.00091	0.00042	0.00011
40	0.00276	0.00219	0.00172	0.00135	0.00105	0.00081	0.00036	0.00009
41	0.00254	0.00201	0.00157	0.00122	0.00094	0.00072	0.00032	0.00008
42	0.00235	0.00184	0.00143	0.00110	0.00084	0.00064	0.00027	0.00006
43	0.00217	0.00169	0.00130	0.00099	0.00076	0.00057	0.00024	0.00005
44	0.00200	0.00155	0.00118	0.00090	0.00068	0.00051	0.00021	0.00004
45	0.00185	0.00142	0.00108	0.00081	0.00061	0.00045	0.00018	0.00004

TABLE 5-12
Yearly Savings Rate Factors
6% Savings Step-up Rate (A7)

Yrs	Assumed Rate of Return (A5)					
	1%	2%	3%	4%	5%	6%
1	0.99010	0.98039	0.97087	0.96154	0.95238	0.94340
2	0.47831	0.47134	0.46453	0.45788	0.45137	0.44500
3	0.30803	0.30211	0.29633	0.29071	0.28522	0.27987
4	0.22312	0.21781	0.21265	0.20763	0.20276	0.19802
5	0.17236	0.16748	0.16276	0.15818	0.15375	0.14945
6	0.13867	0.13414	0.12976	0.12553	0.12144	0.11749
7	0.11473	0.11048	0.10639	0.10246	0.09866	0.09501
8	0.09688	0.09289	0.08905	0.08536	0.08182	0.07843
9	0.08309	0.07932	0.07571	0.07225	0.06894	0.06577
10	0.07214	0.06858	0.06517	0.06191	0.05881	0.05584
11	0.06325	0.05988	0.05666	0.05359	0.05067	0.04789
12	0.05591	0.05271	0.04967	0.04677	0.04402	0.04141
13	0.04976	0.04672	0.04384	0.04110	0.03851	0.03606
14	0.04454	0.04166	0.03892	0.03634	0.03390	0.03159
15	0.04007	0.03732	0.03473	0.03229	0.02998	0.02782
16	0.03619	0.03359	0.03113	0.02882	0.02664	0.02460
17	0.03282	0.03034	0.02801	0.02582	0.02376	0.02184
18	0.02985	0.02750	0.02529	0.02321	0.02127	0.01946
19	0.02724	0.02500	0.02290	0.02093	0.01910	0.01740
20	0.02492	0.02278	0.02079	0.01893	0.01720	0.01559
21	0.02284	0.02082	0.01892	0.01716	0.01552	0.01401
22	0.02099	0.01906	0.01726	0.01559	0.01404	0.01261
23	0.01932	0.01748	0.01578	0.01419	0.01273	0.01138
24	0.01781	0.01607	0.01445	0.01294	0.01156	0.01029
25	0.01645	0.01479	0.01325	0.01183	0.01052	0.00932
26	0.01521	0.01364	0.01217	0.01082	0.00958	0.00845
27	0.01409	0.01259	0.01120	0.00992	0.00875	0.00768
28	0.01306	0.01163	0.01031	0.00910	0.00799	0.00699
29	0.01212	0.01077	0.00951	0.00836	0.00731	0.00636
30	0.01126	0.00997	0.00878	0.00769	0.00670	0.00580
31	0.01047	0.00925	0.00812	0.00708	0.00614	0.00530
32	0.00975	0.00858	0.00751	0.00653	0.00564	0.00484
33	0.00908	0.00797	0.00695	0.00602	0.00518	0.00443
34	0.00846	0.00741	0.00645	0.00556	0.00477	0.00406
35	0.00790	0.00690	0.00598	0.00514	0.00439	0.00372
36	0.00737	0.00642	0.00555	0.00476	0.00404	0.00341
37	0.00688	0.00598	0.00515	0.00440	0.00373	0.00313
38	0.00643	0.00558	0.00479	0.00408	0.00344	0.00287
39	0.00602	0.00520	0.00446	0.00378	0.00318	0.00264
40	0.00563	0.00485	0.00415	0.00351	0.00293	0.00243
41	0.00527	0.00453	0.00386	0.00325	0.00271	0.00224
42	0.00493	0.00424	0.00360	0.00302	0.00251	0.00206
43	0.00462	0.00396	0.00335	0.00281	0.00232	0.00190
44	0.00433	0.00370	0.00313	0.00261	0.00215	0.00175
45	0.00406	0.00346	0.00292	0.00243	0.00199	0.00161

TABLE 5-12 (Continued)
Yearly Savings Rate Factors
6% Savings Step-up Rate (A7)

Yrs	Assumed Rate of Return (A5)							
	7%	8%	9%	10%	11%	12%	15%	20%
1	0.93458	0.92593	0.91743	0.90909	0.90090	0.89286	0.86957	0.83333
2	0.43877	0.43268	0.42671	0.42088	0.41516	0.40957	0.39347	0.36873
3	0.27466	0.26957	0.26461	0.25977	0.25505	0.25044	0.23726	0.21726
4	0.19342	0.18894	0.18459	0.18035	0.17624	0.17223	0.16086	0.14383
5	0.14529	0.14125	0.13734	0.13355	0.12988	0.12631	0.11626	0.10144
6	0.11368	0.11000	0.10644	0.10300	0.09968	0.09647	0.08749	0.07443
7	0.09149	0.08810	0.08484	0.08170	0.07868	0.07577	0.06768	0.05610
8	0.07516	0.07203	0.06903	0.06615	0.06338	0.06073	0.05341	0.04311
9	0.06273	0.05983	0.05705	0.05440	0.05186	0.04944	0.04280	0.03362
10	0.05301	0.05031	0.04774	0.04529	0.04296	0.04074	0.03471	0.02651
11	0.04525	0.04273	0.04035	0.03808	0.03594	0.03390	0.02842	0.02109
12	0.03894	0.03660	0.03438	0.03229	0.03031	0.02844	0.02345	0.01690
13	0.03375	0.03156	0.02950	0.02756	0.02573	0.02402	0.01947	0.01362
14	0.02942	0.02738	0.02546	0.02367	0.02198	0.02040	0.01625	0.01103
15	0.02578	0.02388	0.02209	0.02042	0.01886	0.01741	0.01363	0.00897
16	0.02269	0.02091	0.01925	0.01770	0.01626	0.01492	0.01148	0.00732
17	0.02005	0.01839	0.01684	0.01540	0.01407	0.01284	0.00970	0.00598
18	0.01778	0.01622	0.01478	0.01344	0.01221	0.01108	0.00822	0.00491
19	0.01582	0.01435	0.01301	0.01177	0.01063	0.00959	0.00698	0.00403
20	0.01411	0.01274	0.01148	0.01033	0.00928	0.00832	0.00595	0.00332
21	0.01261	0.01133	0.01016	0.00909	0.00812	0.00724	0.00507	0.00274
22	0.01130	0.01010	0.00901	0.00802	0.00712	0.00630	0.00434	0.00226
23	0.01015	0.00903	0.00801	0.00708	0.00625	0.00550	0.00371	0.00187
24	0.00913	0.00808	0.00713	0.00627	0.00550	0.00481	0.00318	0.00155
25	0.00823	0.00724	0.00635	0.00556	0.00485	0.00422	0.00273	0.00128
26	0.00743	0.00650	0.00568	0.00493	0.00428	0.00370	0.00235	0.00106
27	0.00672	0.00585	0.00508	0.00439	0.00378	0.00325	0.00202	0.00088
28	0.00608	0.00527	0.00455	0.00391	0.00334	0.00285	0.00174	0.00073
29	0.00551	0.00475	0.00408	0.00348	0.00296	0.00251	0.00150	0.00061
30	0.00500	0.00429	0.00366	0.00311	0.00263	0.00221	0.00129	0.00050
31	0.00454	0.00387	0.00329	0.00277	0.00233	0.00195	0.00112	0.00042
32	0.00413	0.00350	0.00296	0.00248	0.00207	0.00172	0.00096	0.00035
33	0.00376	0.00317	0.00266	0.00222	0.00184	0.00152	0.00083	0.00029
34	0.00343	0.00288	0.00240	0.00199	0.00164	0.00134	0.00072	0.00024
35	0.00313	0.00261	0.00216	0.00178	0.00146	0.00119	0.00062	0.00020
36	0.00285	0.00237	0.00195	0.00160	0.00130	0.00105	0.00054	0.00017
37	0.00261	0.00215	0.00176	0.00143	0.00116	0.00093	0.00047	0.00014
38	0.00238	0.00196	0.00159	0.00129	0.00103	0.00082	0.00040	0.00012
39	0.00218	0.00178	0.00144	0.00116	0.00092	0.00073	0.00035	0.00010
40	0.00199	0.00162	0.00130	0.00104	0.00082	0.00065	0.00030	0.00008
41	0.00183	0.00147	0.00118	0.00094	0.00074	0.00057	0.00026	0.00007
42	0.00167	0.00134	0.00107	0.00084	0.00066	0.00051	0.00023	0.00006
43	0.00153	0.00123	0.00097	0.00076	0.00059	0.00045	0.00020	0.00005
44	0.00141	0.00112	0.00088	0.00068	0.00053	0.00040	0.00017	0.00004
45	0.00129	0.00102	0.00080	0.00062	0.00047	0.00036	0.00015	0.00003

TABLE 5-13
Yearly Savings Rate Factors
8% Savings Step-up Rate (A7)

	Assumed Rate of Return (A5)					
Yrs	1%	2%	3%	4%	5%	6%
1	0.99010	0.98039	0.97087	0.96154	0.95238	0.94340
2	0.47373	0.46685	0.46013	0.45356	0.44713	0.44084
3	0.30211	0.29633	0.29071	0.28522	0.27987	0.27466
4	0.21666	0.21155	0.20659	0.20176	0.19707	0.19251
5	0.16568	0.16105	0.15657	0.15222	0.14800	0.14392
6	0.13192	0.12768	0.12358	0.11961	0.11578	0.11207
7	0.10801	0.10409	0.10031	0.09666	0.09315	0.08976
8	0.09023	0.08660	0.08310	0.07974	0.07650	0.07339
9	0.07656	0.07317	0.06992	0.06681	0.06382	0.06096
10	0.06574	0.06258	0.05956	0.05667	0.05391	0.05126
11	0.05700	0.05405	0.05124	0.04855	0.04599	0.04354
12	0.04981	0.04706	0.04444	0.04194	0.03956	0.03729
13	0.04382	0.04125	0.03880	0.03647	0.03426	0.03216
14	0.03877	0.03636	0.03408	0.03190	0.02985	0.02790
15	0.03446	0.03221	0.03007	0.02805	0.02613	0.02433
16	0.03076	0.02865	0.02665	0.02477	0.02298	0.02131
17	0.02755	0.02558	0.02371	0.02195	0.02029	0.01873
18	0.02475	0.02291	0.02116	0.01952	0.01798	0.01653
19	0.02230	0.02058	0.01895	0.01741	0.01597	0.01463
20	0.02014	0.01853	0.01700	0.01557	0.01423	0.01298
21	0.01823	0.01672	0.01530	0.01396	0.01271	0.01155
22	0.01653	0.01512	0.01379	0.01254	0.01138	0.01029
23	0.01502	0.01370	0.01245	0.01129	0.01020	0.00920
24	0.01367	0.01243	0.01127	0.01018	0.00917	0.00823
25	0.01245	0.01130	0.01021	0.00920	0.00825	0.00738
26	0.01136	0.01028	0.00926	0.00832	0.00744	0.00663
27	0.01038	0.00937	0.00842	0.00753	0.00672	0.00596
28	0.00949	0.00854	0.00766	0.00683	0.00607	0.00537
29	0.00868	0.00780	0.00697	0.00620	0.00549	0.00484
30	0.00795	0.00713	0.00636	0.00564	0.00498	0.00437
31	0.00729	0.00652	0.00580	0.00513	0.00451	0.00395
32	0.00669	0.00597	0.00530	0.00467	0.00410	0.00357
33	0.00614	0.00547	0.00484	0.00426	0.00372	0.00323
34	0.00564	0.00502	0.00443	0.00389	0.00339	0.00293
35	0.00518	0.00460	0.00405	0.00355	0.00308	0.00266
36	0.00477	0.00422	0.00371	0.00324	0.00281	0.00241
37	0.00439	0.00388	0.00340	0.00296	0.00256	0.00219
38	0.00404	0.00356	0.00312	0.00271	0.00233	0.00199
39	0.00372	0.00328	0.00286	0.00248	0.00213	0.00181
40	0.00342	0.00301	0.00263	0.00227	0.00195	0.00165
41	0.00316	0.00277	0.00241	0.00208	0.00178	0.00150
42	0.00291	0.00255	0.00222	0.00191	0.00163	0.00137
43	0.00268	0.00235	0.00204	0.00175	0.00149	0.00125
44	0.00247	0.00217	0.00188	0.00161	0.00136	0.00114
45	0.00228	0.00200	0.00173	0.00147	0.00125	0.00104

TABLE 5-13 (Continued)
Yearly Savings Rate Factors
8% Savings Step-up Rate (A7)

Yrs	*Assumed Rate of Return (A5)*							
	7%	8%	9%	10%	11%	12%	15%	20%
1	0.93458	0.92593	0.91743	0.90909	0.90090	0.89286	0.86957	0.83333
2	0.43469	0.42867	0.42278	0.41701	0.41137	0.40584	0.38994	0.36550
3	0.26957	0.26461	0.25977	0.25505	0.25044	0.24594	0.23307	0.21354
4	0.18807	0.18376	0.17956	0.17548	0.17151	0.16765	0.15667	0.14023
5	0.13996	0.13612	0.13239	0.12878	0.12528	0.12189	0.11230	0.09814
6	0.10849	0.10503	0.10168	0.09845	0.09532	0.09230	0.08382	0.07147
7	0.08650	0.08336	0.08033	0.07740	0.07459	0.07188	0.06433	0.05349
8	0.07040	0.06753	0.06478	0.06213	0.05958	0.05714	0.05038	0.04083
9	0.05821	0.05558	0.05306	0.05065	0.04835	0.04614	0.04008	0.03164
10	0.04873	0.04632	0.04401	0.04181	0.03972	0.03772	0.03226	0.02480
11	0.04121	0.03899	0.03688	0.03487	0.03296	0.03114	0.02623	0.01961
12	0.03514	0.03309	0.03115	0.02931	0.02757	0.02592	0.02149	0.01563
13	0.03017	0.02828	0.02650	0.02482	0.02323	0.02173	0.01773	0.01253
14	0.02606	0.02432	0.02268	0.02113	0.01968	0.01832	0.01471	0.01010
15	0.02262	0.02102	0.01951	0.01809	0.01676	0.01552	0.01226	0.00817
16	0.01973	0.01824	0.01685	0.01555	0.01434	0.01321	0.01026	0.00664
17	0.01727	0.01590	0.01462	0.01342	0.01231	0.01128	0.00862	0.00541
18	0.01517	0.01390	0.01272	0.01163	0.01061	0.00967	0.00726	0.00442
19	0.01337	0.01220	0.01111	0.01010	0.00917	0.00831	0.00614	0.00362
20	0.01181	0.01073	0.00972	0.00880	0.00795	0.00716	0.00520	0.00297
21	0.01046	0.00946	0.00853	0.00768	0.00690	0.00619	0.00441	0.00244
22	0.00929	0.00836	0.00751	0.00672	0.00601	0.00536	0.00376	0.00201
23	0.00826	0.00741	0.00662	0.00590	0.00524	0.00465	0.00320	0.00166
24	0.00737	0.00657	0.00584	0.00518	0.00458	0.00404	0.00273	0.00137
25	0.00658	0.00584	0.00517	0.00456	0.00401	0.00352	0.00233	0.00113
26	0.00588	0.00520	0.00458	0.00402	0.00352	0.00307	0.00200	0.00093
27	0.00527	0.00464	0.00406	0.00355	0.00309	0.00268	0.00171	0.00077
28	0.00472	0.00414	0.00361	0.00314	0.00272	0.00234	0.00147	0.00064
29	0.00424	0.00370	0.00321	0.00278	0.00239	0.00205	0.00126	0.00053
30	0.00381	0.00331	0.00286	0.00246	0.00211	0.00179	0.00108	0.00044
31	0.00343	0.00297	0.00255	0.00218	0.00186	0.00157	0.00093	0.00036
32	0.00309	0.00266	0.00228	0.00194	0.00164	0.00138	0.00080	0.00030
33	0.00279	0.00239	0.00204	0.00172	0.00145	0.00121	0.00069	0.00025
34	0.00252	0.00215	0.00182	0.00153	0.00128	0.00107	0.00060	0.00021
35	0.00227	0.00193	0.00163	0.00137	0.00114	0.00094	0.00051	0.00017
36	0.00206	0.00174	0.00146	0.00122	0.00101	0.00083	0.00044	0.00014
37	0.00186	0.00157	0.00131	0.00108	0.00089	0.00073	0.00038	0.00012
38	0.00169	0.00141	0.00117	0.00097	0.00079	0.00064	0.00033	0.00010
39	0.00153	0.00127	0.00105	0.00086	0.00070	0.00057	0.00029	0.00008
40	0.00138	0.00115	0.00095	0.00077	0.00062	0.00050	0.00025	0.00007
41	0.00126	0.00104	0.00085	0.00069	0.00056	0.00044	0.00021	0.00006
42	0.00114	0.00094	0.00077	0.00062	0.00049	0.00039	0.00019	0.00005
43	0.00104	0.00085	0.00069	0.00055	0.00044	0.00035	0.00016	0.00004
44	0.00094	0.00077	0.00062	0.00050	0.00039	0.00031	0.00014	0.00003
45	0.00086	0.00070	0.00056	0.00044	0.00035	0.00027	0.00012	0.00003

TABLE 5-14 Yearly Savings Rate Factors 10% Savings Step-up Rate (A7)					
Assumed Rate of Return (A5)					
Yrs	1%	2%	3%	4%	5%	6%
1	0.99010	0.98039	0.97087	0.96154	0.95238	0.94340
2	0.46924	0.46245	0.45581	0.44932	0.44297	0.43676
3	0.29634	0.29071	0.28522	0.27987	0.27466	0.26957
4	0.21041	0.20550	0.20072	0.19607	0.19155	0.18716
5	0.15927	0.15487	0.15061	0.14648	0.14247	0.13859
6	0.12550	0.12152	0.11768	0.11396	0.11037	0.10689
7	0.10165	0.09804	0.09454	0.09117	0.08792	0.08478
8	0.08401	0.08070	0.07751	0.07444	0.07149	0.06864
9	0.07048	0.06745	0.06453	0.06173	0.05904	0.05645
10	0.05984	0.05705	0.05438	0.05181	0.04935	0.04700
11	0.05129	0.04872	0.04627	0.04392	0.04167	0.03952
12	0.04430	0.04194	0.03968	0.03753	0.03547	0.03351
13	0.03851	0.03633	0.03426	0.03228	0.03040	0.02860
14	0.03365	0.03165	0.02974	0.02793	0.02620	0.02456
15	0.02954	0.02770	0.02595	0.02428	0.02269	0.02119
16	0.02604	0.02434	0.02273	0.02119	0.01974	0.01837
17	0.02302	0.02146	0.01998	0.01857	0.01724	0.01598
18	0.02042	0.01898	0.01762	0.01632	0.01510	0.01395
19	0.01816	0.01683	0.01558	0.01439	0.01327	0.01221
20	0.01618	0.01496	0.01381	0.01272	0.01169	0.01072
21	0.01445	0.01333	0.01227	0.01126	0.01032	0.00943
22	0.01292	0.01189	0.01092	0.01000	0.00913	0.00832
23	0.01158	0.01063	0.00974	0.00889	0.00809	0.00735
24	0.01039	0.00952	0.00869	0.00792	0.00719	0.00651
25	0.00933	0.00853	0.00778	0.00706	0.00639	0.00577
26	0.00839	0.00766	0.00696	0.00631	0.00569	0.00512
27	0.00755	0.00688	0.00624	0.00564	0.00508	0.00455
28	0.00680	0.00619	0.00560	0.00505	0.00453	0.00405
29	0.00613	0.00557	0.00503	0.00453	0.00405	0.00361
30	0.00553	0.00502	0.00452	0.00406	0.00363	0.00322
31	0.00500	0.00452	0.00407	0.00365	0.00325	0.00288
32	0.00451	0.00408	0.00367	0.00328	0.00291	0.00257
33	0.00408	0.00368	0.00330	0.00295	0.00261	0.00230
34	0.00369	0.00333	0.00298	0.00265	0.00235	0.00206
35	0.00334	0.00300	0.00269	0.00239	0.00211	0.00185
36	0.00302	0.00272	0.00243	0.00215	0.00190	0.00166
37	0.00274	0.00246	0.00219	0.00194	0.00171	0.00149
38	0.00248	0.00222	0.00198	0.00175	0.00154	0.00134
39	0.00225	0.00201	0.00179	0.00158	0.00138	0.00120
40	0.00204	0.00182	0.00162	0.00143	0.00125	0.00108
41	0.00185	0.00165	0.00146	0.00129	0.00112	0.00097
42	0.00167	0.00149	0.00132	0.00116	0.00101	0.00087
43	0.00152	0.00135	0.00120	0.00105	0.00091	0.00079
44	0.00138	0.00123	0.00109	0.00095	0.00083	0.00071
45	0.00125	0.00111	0.00098	0.00086	0.00075	0.00064

TABLE 5-14 (Continued)
Yearly Savings Rate Factors
10% Savings Step-up Rate (A7)

Yrs	\multicolumn{8}{c}{Assumed Rate of Return (A5)}

Yrs	7%	8%	9%	10%	11%	12%	15%	20%
1	0.93458	0.92593	0.91743	0.90909	0.90090	0.89286	0.86957	0.83333
2	0.43068	0.42474	0.41892	0.41322	0.40765	0.40219	0.38647	0.36232
3	0.26461	0.25977	0.25505	0.25044	0.24594	0.24155	0.22898	0.20991
4	0.18289	0.17873	0.17469	0.17075	0.16692	0.16320	0.15261	0.13672
5	0.13482	0.13117	0.12762	0.12418	0.12085	0.11761	0.10847	0.09493
6	0.10352	0.10027	0.09712	0.09408	0.09113	0.08829	0.08029	0.06862
7	0.08176	0.07884	0.07602	0.07331	0.07069	0.06817	0.06112	0.05099
8	0.06591	0.06328	0.06075	0.05831	0.05597	0.05373	0.04749	0.03865
9	0.05397	0.05159	0.04931	0.04712	0.04502	0.04302	0.03748	0.02974
10	0.04475	0.04259	0.04053	0.03855	0.03667	0.03487	0.02995	0.02316
11	0.03747	0.03551	0.03364	0.03186	0.03017	0.02855	0.02416	0.01821
12	0.03164	0.02986	0.02816	0.02655	0.02502	0.02357	0.01966	0.01442
13	0.02690	0.02528	0.02374	0.02228	0.02090	0.01960	0.01610	0.01150
14	0.02300	0.02153	0.02013	0.01881	0.01756	0.01639	0.01326	0.00922
15	0.01977	0.01842	0.01716	0.01596	0.01483	0.01378	0.01098	0.00742
16	0.01707	0.01584	0.01469	0.01360	0.01258	0.01163	0.00913	0.00600
17	0.01479	0.01367	0.01262	0.01164	0.01072	0.00986	0.00762	0.00486
18	0.01286	0.01184	0.01089	0.00999	0.00916	0.00838	0.00638	0.00396
19	0.01122	0.01029	0.00942	0.00861	0.00785	0.00715	0.00536	0.00323
20	0.00981	0.00896	0.00817	0.00743	0.00675	0.00612	0.00451	0.00264
21	0.00860	0.00783	0.00710	0.00643	0.00582	0.00525	0.00381	0.00216
22	0.00756	0.00685	0.00619	0.00558	0.00502	0.00451	0.00322	0.00177
23	0.00665	0.00601	0.00541	0.00486	0.00435	0.00388	0.00273	0.00145
24	0.00587	0.00528	0.00473	0.00423	0.00377	0.00335	0.00232	0.00120
25	0.00519	0.00465	0.00415	0.00369	0.00328	0.00290	0.00197	0.00099
26	0.00459	0.00410	0.00364	0.00323	0.00285	0.00251	0.00168	0.00081
27	0.00407	0.00362	0.00320	0.00283	0.00248	0.00217	0.00143	0.00067
28	0.00361	0.00320	0.00282	0.00248	0.00217	0.00189	0.00122	0.00055
29	0.00320	0.00283	0.00249	0.00217	0.00189	0.00164	0.00104	0.00046
30	0.00285	0.00251	0.00219	0.00191	0.00166	0.00143	0.00089	0.00038
31	0.00254	0.00222	0.00194	0.00168	0.00145	0.00124	0.00076	0.00031
32	0.00226	0.00197	0.00171	0.00148	0.00127	0.00108	0.00065	0.00026
33	0.00202	0.00176	0.00152	0.00130	0.00111	0.00095	0.00056	0.00022
34	0.00180	0.00156	0.00135	0.00115	0.00098	0.00083	0.00048	0.00018
35	0.00161	0.00139	0.00119	0.00102	0.00086	0.00072	0.00041	0.00015
36	0.00144	0.00124	0.00106	0.00090	0.00076	0.00063	0.00036	0.00012
37	0.00129	0.00111	0.00094	0.00079	0.00067	0.00055	0.00031	0.00010
38	0.00115	0.00099	0.00084	0.00070	0.00059	0.00049	0.00026	0.00008
39	0.00103	0.00088	0.00074	0.00062	0.00052	0.00043	0.00023	0.00007
40	0.00093	0.00079	0.00066	0.00055	0.00046	0.00037	0.00020	0.00006
41	0.00083	0.00070	0.00059	0.00049	0.00040	0.00033	0.00017	0.00005
42	0.00075	0.00063	0.00053	0.00043	0.00036	0.00029	0.00015	0.00004
43	0.00067	0.00056	0.00047	0.00039	0.00031	0.00025	0.00013	0.00003
44	0.00060	0.00050	0.00042	0.00034	0.00028	0.00022	0.00011	0.00003
45	0.00054	0.00045	0.00037	0.00030	0.00025	0.00020	0.00009	0.00002

Selecting the Savings Rate Factor (F5)

The appropriate F5 factor depends on the number of years until you plan to retire, the average annual rate of return you expect to earn on investment until retirement, and your savings step-up rate (lines A3, A5, and A7 of table 5-6, the Retirement Planning Work Sheet, respectively). To find the appropriate F5 factor you must first select the table corresponding to your savings step-up rate (A7). The tables correspond to step-up rates ranging from 0 percent to 10 percent, with the step-up rate increased by 2 percentage points in each successive table.

The savings step-up rate is the rate at which you plan to increase or step up the amount you save each year. Frequently, the step-up rate is set equal to the rate at which a person expects his or her annual earnings to grow. If the step-up rate is set equal to the earnings growth rate, the amount that must be saved each year remains a fixed proportion of those growing earnings. Therefore the "burden" of saving for retirement remains the same each year relative to your growing income. For example, if you expect your earnings to grow at an average annual rate of 6 percent per year and want your required savings each year to be constant relative to your earnings, you would use the table showing a 6 percent savings step-up rate.

Once you have selected the table corresponding to your desired step-up rate, you would find your savings rate factor (F5) in the column and row corresponding to your assumed investment rate of return prior to retirement (A5) and the number of years until you plan to retire (A3), respectively. For example, if your step-up rate is 6 percent (A7), your assumed rate of return is 8 percent (A5), and you plan to retire in 10 years, your savings rate factor (F5) is 0.05031.

Remember, line 21 of the Retirement Planning Work Sheet (table 5-6) calculates the amount you need to save the first year. In each subsequent year you must increase the amount you save by your assumed savings step-up rate if you are to reach your goal. For example, assume your savings step-up rate is 5 percent and the amount calculated in line 21 of the Retirement Planning Work Sheet is $1,000. In the second year you would have to save $1,050; in the third year, $1,102.50; in the fourth year, $1,157.62; and so on.

The amount you must save each year is calculated by multiplying the prior year's savings amount by (1 + the step-up rate). For example, if your savings step-up rate is 6 percent, you would compute each subsequent year's savings amount by multiplying the previous year's savings amount by 1.06.

If you specify a 0 percent savings step-up rate, you will reach your retirement accumulation goal by saving the same level amount each year as determined in line 21 of the Retirement Planning Work Sheet (table 5-6), assuming your actual investment rate of return matches your assumed rate of return.

CONCLUSION

The planner's work sheet that you have just reviewed, as well as the other material in this chapter, will help you and your client to set goals and to better understand the retirement needs analysis. Properly utilizing the tools provided and properly analyzing the assumptions needed will assist clients immeasurably. We feel it bears repetition, however, that this is an art form, not a science. The numbers are not absolute. Your best judgment should be used in conjunction with what this chapter has given you to achieve the best results for your client.

6

Investing—Part I

Chapter Outline

Everyone wants to invest for high returns with low risk. However, as every student of investments is taught, if you want high returns you must bear correspondingly high risks. But is this always so? And how is risk related to returns?

This chapter reviews two important concepts in the risk-return arena. The first topic relates to the most important concept of this half-century—*modern portfolio theory* (MPT). MPT revolutionized security and portfolio analysis by quantifying the concept of risk. In the process, MPT added science to the art of portfolio management.

The second topic concerns the evaluation of risk over time. Specifically, research shows that while stocks are riskier than bonds and money-market instruments in the short run, stocks are clearly less risky over the long run even though their return is higher. Since retirement planning usually involves a long time horizon, stock investments are especially valuable in the retirement portfolio.

MODERN PORTFOLIO THEORY: WHAT THE RETIREMENT PLANNER SHOULD KNOW

The empirical tests of the random walk hypothesis (that security prices move in a manner that cannot be predicted by prior price changes) and the efficient market hypothesis (that new information is quickly incorporated into security prices) have given tremendous support to the primary conclusion of these theories, which is that most investors cannot expect to outperform the market on a risk-adjusted basis consistently. Prices in the market quickly reflect relevant information and, in that sense, are generally fair.

These developments do not imply, however, that one investment is just as good as any other investment for any investor. Each investor must still assess his or her own investment objectives and design an investment portfolio that will meet these needs and risk preferences. This section will introduce the concepts of modern portfolio theory that have dominated both academic and practitioner discourse regarding the risk-return trade-off. With this understanding retirement planners may be better able to help their clients select portfolios that suit their needs and objectives.

Early Development of Portfolio Theory

In the 1950s Harry Markowitz published his classic book, *Portfolio Selection*. The essential conclusion of Markowitz's theory was that portfolios of risky stocks could be put together in such a way that the portfolio as a whole actually could be less risky than any one of the individual stocks in it. Assuming that people prefer higher expected returns and less dispersion or likelihood of deviations from the expected return, Markowitz showed theoretically that among all portfolios of risky assets, there is a set of efficient portfolios. Each of these portfolios is efficient in the sense that for its expected return, there is no portfolio with less risk (variance) and for its risk, there is no portfolio with greater expected return. How does this work? The mathematical development is rather complex, but it depends essentially on two basic principles: *covariance* and *diversification.*

Covariance—The Concept

What is covariance? As the term suggests, covariance means varying together. Covariance is a measure of the degree to which random variables move in a systematic way, either positively or negatively.

Perfect Positive or Negative Covariance. Let us look at what could be considered variables that are perfectly covariable. For a given policy type and age at issue, an insurance agent knows what first year commission to expect for whatever face amount is sold. The face of the policy and the commission are perfectly dependent—the higher the face amount, the larger the commission; the lower the face amount, the smaller the commission. Therefore the face amount and the commission are perfectly and positively covariable.

Another example of dependence, and thus covariability, is perfect negative covariance. That is, if one variable is larger, the second is smaller; if one is positive, the other is negative. For instance, in a perfect bond market we would find that the interest rate and the price of a bond are perfectly negatively covariable. Interest rates and prices are related; the price must adjust to equate the bond's yield with the market rate of interest. For any randomly selected market rate of interest there exists a bond price that will equate the yield on a bond having a fixed coupon with the market rate of interest. As the market interest rate goes up, the price of the bond must go down.

What does this have to do with Markowitz's portfolio theory? Let us create a very simplistic but informative example. Suppose an individual has an opportunity to purchase shares in two businesses. The first is a suntan lotion manufacturer. The second is a manufacturer of umbrellas. Each of these businesses is affected by the weather. If the summer season is rainy, the umbrella manufacturer will have a return of 25 percent. If it is sunny, however, the umbrella manufacturer will lose 10 percent. In contrast, the suntan lotion manufacturer will get a return of 25 percent if the summer season is sunny and will lose 10 percent if the summer season is rainy. If, on the average, one-half of the seasons are sunny and one-half are rainy, the investor who has purchased stock in the umbrella manufacturer will find that half of the time he or she earns a 25 percent return and the other half of the time he or she loses 10 percent of the investment. On the average the investor will earn a return of 7.5 percent. (This is called the *expected return,* meaning the return the investor expects after averaging all possible outcomes.)[1] In a similar manner, the investor who has purchased stock in the suntan lotion company will also get an average return of 7.5 percent, but the incidence of the gains and losses will be reversed. Investing in only one business or the other would be fairly risky because there could be several sunny or rainy seasons in a row.

Suppose, however, that the individual invests equal amounts in each company. Whether the sun shines or the rain falls, he or she will earn 25 percent on half of the investment and −10 percent on the other half; the net return will be 7.5 percent. Therefore the investor can eliminate all risk and still get the same expected return, 7.5 percent. Obviously the portfolio combination of equal shares in each company is the best possible choice since it minimizes the risk (variability of possible outcomes) for the given level of expected return. Using the same example, the following is a simplified version of Markowitz's portfolio theory:

Investment:	100% in Umbrella Co.	100% in Suntan Lotion Co.
If Sunny	−10%	25%
If Rainy	25%	−10%
Expected Return	7.5%	7.5%

Investment:	50% in	plus	50% in	Certain
	Umbrella Co.		Suntan Lotion Co.	Return
If Sunny	−10% x 50%	+	25% x 50%	7.5%
If Rainy	25% x 50%	+	−10% x 50%	7.5%
Expected Return	7.5%		7.5%	7.5%

This representation of Markowitz's portfolio theory demonstrates that investors should choose the combination of securities that minimizes the risk of the entire portfolio for a specified expected return. Any one security may have great variability of outcomes by itself, but when combined with the other securities in a portfolio the important factor is covariance.

Independence—The Opposite of Perfect Covariability. Covariance is a measure of the degree to which random variables move in a systematic way, either positively or negatively. Two random variables are independent if they exhibit no covariance. That is, one variable is not dependent upon or related to the other in any systematic way. For example, each roll of a fair die is independent of any other roll. The outcome of a flip of a coin is unaffected by any previous flips.

Covariance and Independence Combined. Unfortunately the real world offers very few opportunities for perfect covariability or independence. Most real-world variables are neither completely dependent (perfectly covariable) nor completely independent. For instance, the weight and height of humans have positive covariance. The taller an individual is, the more likely it is that his or her weight is greater. In contrast to our previous examples, however, knowing an individual's height or weight alone does not allow us to know or predict the other factor with certainty, although we could probably make a better guess than if we knew nothing about the individual. Other independent factors, such as bone structure, muscle tone, and so forth, will affect the relationship between height and weight.

Most real-world securities have some common factor or factors that influence them mutually and many other factors that affect each independently. For example, many common economic factors will influence the earnings of Ford and General Motors in similar ways. However, each company's earnings will also be influenced by many independent factors that will have no effect whatsoever on the other company—for example, the company president's health or a fire in a warehouse. Consequently we would expect the earnings of Ford and GM to have very positive covariability, but not perfect covariability.

The real world has instances of negative covariability as well. Higher oil and gasoline prices may mean greater earnings for Exxon but lower earnings for Consolidated Trucking. Obviously both Exxon and Consolidated are influenced by a number of factors other than the price of gasoline, but many of those factors will be independent events unrelated to most other events affecting either firm.

Diversification

Why is it important to distinguish those factors that covary from those that do not? Because the risk resulting from the independent factors—the factors that do not covary—can be eliminated by *diversification.* The principle of diversification is probably intuitively understood by almost everyone and yet it is difficult to explain without technical jargon and mathematical analysis. In simple terms, diversification is the process of combining securities in such a way that the variability of the independent factors tends to be canceled out, leaving only the covariability between the securities' returns. For example, when a dart is thrown at a target, chances are not good that the dart will hit the bull's-eye. However, as more and more darts are thrown, those darts hitting above the bull's-eye will tend to equal in number those below it, and those to the right will tend to equal those to the left, so that, on average, the errors cancel. Therefore the larger the "portfolio" of throws, the more likely it is that the average throw will be a bull's-eye.

A similar process describes the diversification of a portfolio of securities. As more and more securities are added to the portfolio, the random and independent factors that cause one security to perform poorly are likely to be offset by other independent factors that cause another security to perform above average. These independent factors, like the scattering of darts, tend to offset one another. The variability of the portfolio will depend less and less on the independent factors and more and more on the covariances between the securities as the number of securities in the portfolio increases.

Is it necessary for the average investor to hold hundreds of securities to gain the advantages of diversification? Most individuals are surprised when they discover how few securities they need to virtually eliminate the diversifiable risk (the independent variability) from their portfolio. By the time the 20th security is added, about 90 percent of all the independent variability is eliminated. Different securities and different industries have different proportions of diversifiable variability but, on the average, the diversifiable variability makes up 50 to 75 percent of a stock's total variability. The relatively few securities that are required to eliminate so much risk (variability) at no loss of expected return indicates the power and importance of this principle. A well-diversified portfolio will always be preferred to a less diversified portfolio with the same expected return because the variability of outcomes will be reduced with no loss in expected returns.

Systematic (Market) and Unsystematic (Diversifiable) Risk. Other researchers soon realized that Markowitz's principles would have significant implications if applied to asset pricing in the marketplace. If investors *do* seek to minimize risk for any given level of expected returns, as Markowitz suggested, then prices in the stock market should tend to reflect these risk-reducing activities. These researchers suggested that each security should be valued on the basis of its covariability with the market as a whole. On the basis of Markowitz's principles, the only risk (or variability) the investor could not diversify away was that part directly related to the overall market variability. That is, even if an investor diversified as completely as possible by buying some shares of all securities in the market, he or she could not eliminate all risk or variability since the market as a whole is variable. The part of a security's total risk or variability that relates to the market as a whole is called its *systematic* or *market* risk. The remaining risk that results from factors exclusive to the company itself, such as a new product or a warehouse fire, is called its *unsystematic, diversifiable,* or *residual risk.*

Systematic Risk, Residual Risk, and Diversification. Systematic risk is price fluctuation related to fluctuations in the overall market. Figure 6-1 shows two securities, C and D, whose price changes are completely dependent upon the market. Stock C rises twice as far as the market when the market is up and falls twice as far as the market when the market is down. In contrast, stock D moves only half as far as the market in either direction. Both stock C and stock D are perfectly covariable with (dependent upon) the market and each other. Note, however, that since stock D is only half as volatile as the market and stock C is twice as volatile as the market, stock C is four times as volatile as stock D. So, although stocks may be perfectly covariable (dependent), one stock may show considerably greater magnitude of price fluctuations.

Residual (or *unsystematic) risk* is the stock price fluctuation that is independent of movements in the general market. Stock E is an example of a stock whose price movements are completely independent of the market.

Most stocks, however, have some combination of systematic and residual risk. Stock F is an example of a stock that moves generally with the market but also has residual price fluctuations caused by independent factors.

Figure 6-2 demonstrates that as the number of securities in a portfolio increases, the total risk (total variability of outcome) is reduced. However, diversification eliminates only the unsystematic risk, which results from the independent factors affecting each security separately. It does not affect the systematic risk.

Beta and the Capital Asset Pricing Model

William Sharpe was one of the leading formulators of the *capital asset pricing model* (CAPM), which further defined the relationship between risk and return. CAPM holds that in an efficient market an investor should receive reward for bearing systematic risk but not for bearing unsystematic risk. Since diversification eliminates unsystematic risk, the unsystematic risk of a security added to a diversified portfolio is irrelevant. The result is that securities are priced according to their systematic risk. The statistical measure that indicates the level of a stock's (or a portfolio's) systematic risk or sensitivity to overall market fluctuations is called its *beta coefficient.*

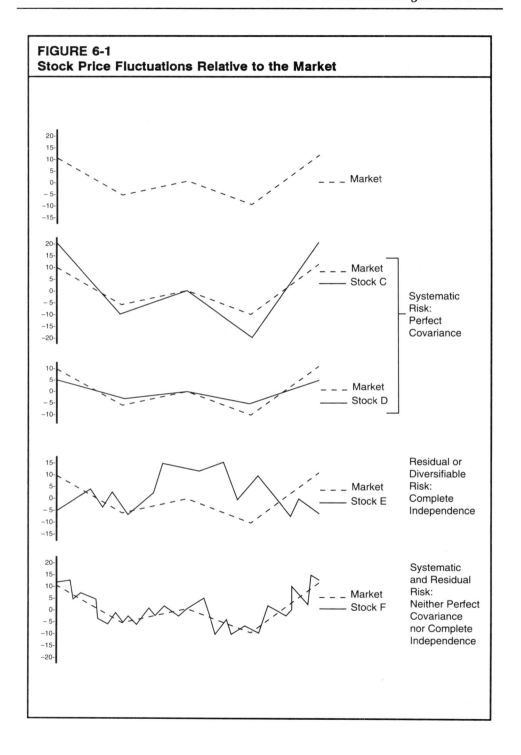

FIGURE 6-1
Stock Price Fluctuations Relative to the Market

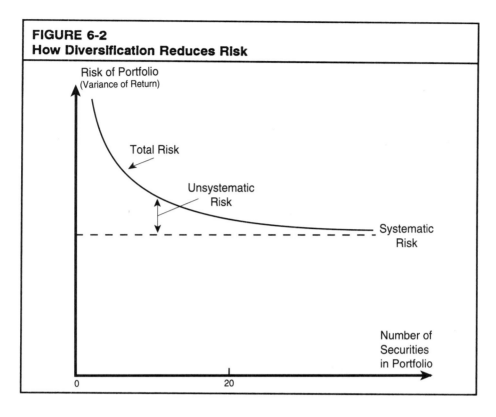

FIGURE 6-2
How Diversification Reduces Risk

Beta

The beta coefficient is defined mathematically as the ratio of the security's covariance with the market portfolio and the market's variance. In other words, the beta coefficient is a proportional measure of the systematic risk of a stock or portfolio relative to the market's total variability. The market portfolio, by this definition, has a beta of one. If a security has a beta coefficient greater than one, this security will tend to move up more than the market when the market is up and move down more than the market when the market is down. For example, a security with a beta coefficient of 1.5 will tend to move up 15 percent when the market moves up 10 percent, and down 15 percent when the market moves down 10 percent. In contrast, a security with a beta coefficient of .75 will tend to fluctuate only 75 percent as widely as the market. In figure 6-1 stock C has a beta of 2 and stock D has a beta of 0.5.

The Capital Asset Pricing Model

If people are rational and the market is efficient, the price of a security should be related to its risk. Markowitz formulated his portfolio theory on the basis that individuals would minimize risk for any given level of expected return. Theoreticians and practitioners all agree that investors can be induced to accept greater risk only with the lure of greater potential returns. Therefore stock prices must adjust to offer higher expected returns when more risk is perceived. This means that investors will pay lower prices for securities with higher systematic risk and higher prices for securities with lower systematic risk, all else being equal. As the prices for securities with lower systematic risk are bid up, the expected returns will fall. Similarly the prices of securities with higher systematic risk will be bid down and the expected returns will rise. Since all unsystematic risk can be diversified away, people will be rewarded only for bearing systematic risk (covariance with the market).

Let us consider an example. Suppose two securities have equal expected earnings per share but that one security has half the systematic variability (covariance with the market) of another. That is, security A has a beta of .75, while security B has a beta of 1.5. However, assume that the total variability (the total of the systematic and unsystematic variability) of each security as measured by standard deviation is equal. If variability rather than covariability mattered, the securities would be priced identically, since they have equal expected earnings and equal variability. However, a wise investor who holds a broadly diversified portfolio of many securities would realize that if he or she purchased security A he or she could diversify away a great deal of the unsystematic risk. The contribution of security A to the overall variability of the portfolio would be half as great as the contribution of security B. Therefore for this investor's purposes security A is more valuable. The investor would be willing to pay a higher price for security A than for security B, even though the expected earnings per share and total variability are equal.

As a result of the actions of this and other investors, the price of the security with the lowest systematic risk (lowest ratio of covariability to total variability of the portfolio) would be bid up in the market and the price of the security with the highest systematic risk would be bid down. Since earnings per share are equal, a higher price for security A implies a lower expected rate of return, while a lower price for security B implies a higher rate of return. Since all securities in the market portfolio must be held by someone, the price (and implicitly the expected rate of return) of every security in the market must be related to its systematic risk relative to the market. That is, security prices should reflect a consistent risk-return trade-off, where risk is not variability (standard deviation) but rather covariability (beta) relative to the market as a whole.

The Linear Risk-Return Relationship. The previous discussion indicates that the beta coefficient measures the relevant systematic risk. Sharpe's CAPM indicates that there is a simple relationship between risk and return. The CAPM says that the return one can expect from a security is *linearly* related to its beta. That is, the additional return one can expect above the return one could get for holding a riskless security, such as a Treasury bill, is proportional to its beta (see figure 6-3). If an investor exclusively purchased Treasury bills, which are about as risk-free as any investment on earth (and which are virtually unaffected by market fluctuations), he or she would receive a minimum risk-free rate of return. As investments become more risky (greater beta), the expected return should increase. The fact that other longer-term federal bonds, state and local bonds (adjusted for tax-exempt feature), corporate bonds, preferred stocks, and common stocks have historically had higher expected returns than Treasury bills[2] and are progressively more covariable with overall market fluctuations gives support to this theory.

Figure 6-3 describes the relationship between systematic risk (beta) and expected return. The equation for the straight line from the risk-free rate through M, called the security market line, is

Expected rate of return =
   Risk-free rate + Beta x (Expected return on the market − Risk-free rate)

For example, a security that has a beta of zero—no covariance with the market, such as stock E in figure 6-1—will sell so that its expected return equals the risk-free rate (Treasury bill rate) even though it may have some independent variability. If a security with a zero beta sold for a premium above the risk-free rate, a wise investor could buy a portfolio of such securities and diversify away the independent variability. This virtually would assure the investor that he or she would get a higher return than the risk-free rate while bearing no additional risk. The action of this and other investors would bid up the price of these zero-beta securities causing their expected returns to fall until the expected return from the zero-beta securities just equaled the risk-free rate.

Many investors are willing to bear additional risk if they can expect higher returns on the average. But, as was demonstrated earlier, only the nondiversifiable systematic risk will be compensated with higher expected returns, since the nonsystematic risk can be diversified away.

The shaded region of figure 6-3 demonstrates how the range of actual after-the-fact returns gets larger as systematic risk increases. The graph is a two-dimensional representation of a three-dimensional concept. The curved lines are bell-shaped to approximate normal distributions of rates of return (the vertical axis) relative to systematic risk, or beta (the horizontal axis). In three dimensions, the end-points of the curves would be on the surface of the page, but the rest of the curves would rise vertically off the page like cross-sections of a mountain. The security market line—the ridge of the mountains—represents the expected risk-return relationship while the spread of the mountains shows how the actual return may differ from the expected. For higher beta securities—represented as points farther to the right on the security market line—the spread of the distribution increases, suggesting a broader range of potential returns and therefore more risk.

The return in the market has, over long periods of time, exceeded the risk-free rate of interest, but not in all periods. An investment could hardly be called risky,

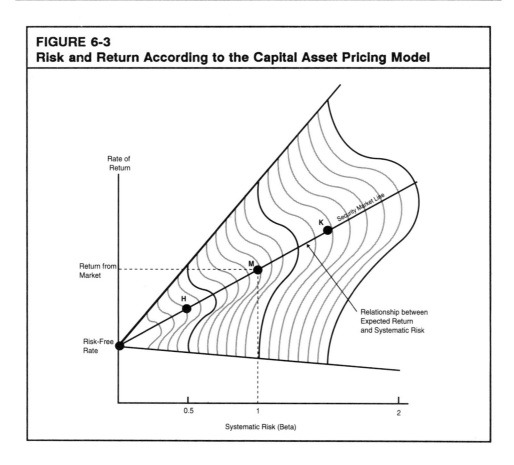

FIGURE 6-3
Risk and Return According to the Capital Asset Pricing Model

or warrant higher expected (average) returns, if it did not involve the possibility of loss in some periods. Although diversification eliminates unsystematic risk, the investor who holds a higher-beta portfolio bears the risk (which cannot be eliminated) that the market as a whole will deviate from its expected return.

Figure 6-3 also shows that any number of different expected returns are possible simply by adjusting the beta of the portfolio. If an investor is willing to bear the same risk as the market, he or she simply needs to purchase a broadly diversified portfolio that has a beta of one. His or her expected return will be the same as the market's return. A simple way to achieve this objective is to purchase shares in an index fund.

An individual who desires an investment with less systematic risk than the market can simply split the investment in the proper proportions between Treasury bills and a market-index fund. For example, if an individual puts half of his or her investment into Treasury bills and half into an index fund, the portfolio would be at point H on the security market line, where the beta is 0.5 and the expected return is halfway between the return on Treasury bills and the return on the market as a whole.

The theory of asset pricing asserts very simply that to get a higher average long-term rate of return an investor should just increase the beta of his or her portfolio. An investor could get a portfolio with a beta larger than one by buying high-beta stocks. Alternatively, the investor could use leverage to increase the portfolio's beta. Point K on the security market line represents the beta and expected return if the investor invests in portfolio M and then borrows at the risk-free rate and invests the borrowed money in portfolio M. Of course, the risk-free rate is not a reasonable borrowing rate. Extensions of the model show the effect of higher borrowing rates.

Tests and Criticisms of Modern Portfolio Theory and the Capital Asset Pricing Model

Anyone can theorize about how security markets work. Modern portfolio theory and the capital asset pricing model are just more theories. The really important questions follow: Do they work? Is beta a useful measure of risk? Do high-beta portfolios always fall farther in down markets than low-beta portfolios? Is it always true that over the long term high-beta portfolios provide larger overall returns than low-beta portfolios? Does a beta of a portfolio today provide any useful information about the beta in the future?

Empirical Evidence Supporting the CAPM

Researchers have subjected these theories to considerable empirical testing. The results of these tests show remarkable support for most aspects of the theories, yet these theories are far from perfect descriptions of reality.

For example, investors should be skeptical of beta estimates based upon historical data. The history of a stock's beta relative to the market may not be a good estimate of its *future* systematic risk. Beta estimates for individual stocks are not very accurate. The beta estimated in one period may differ significantly from one estimated in a later period.

However, thanks to the law of large numbers, several inaccurate beta estimates on individual stocks can be combined to form surprisingly accurate estimates of the beta for a portfolio. The process involved is similar to the principle of diversification. While the beta estimates for some securities will be too high, the estimates for others will be too low, tending to offset one another. The result is that the beta of a portfolio with a sufficient number of individual stocks will be a good estimate of the portfolio's actual beta and will be a good predictor of performance. Similarly betas or covariances of market segments, such as large common stocks, small stocks, corporate bonds, futures contracts, and so forth, are relatively stable. Therefore using betas or covariances for these segments when making asset allocation decisions with regard to various market segments within the overall portfolio will usually provide reliable and stable results.

Tests have also shown that future betas for larger portfolios (25 or more securities) were remarkably well predicted on the basis of past experience. Future betas for very small portfolios or individual stocks were not as well predicted by past experience. Therefore for sufficiently large portfolios an investor can expect a stable risk-return relationship over time as indicated by the estimated beta.

Tests of the capital asset pricing model itself have tried to determine whether security returns are in fact directly related to beta. Tests of a large number of professionally managed portfolios have shown a remarkable consistency with the theory. First, returns are basically related to beta in a straight-line manner, just as the theory predicts. Second, over the long term high-beta portfolios have provided larger average returns than low-beta ones; in up years high-beta portfolios have outperformed the low-beta portfolios, while in down years the high-beta portfolios have performed much worse than the low-beta portfolios. Therefore although the high-risk (high-beta) portfolios have had higher average returns, over some down periods in the market they have performed much worse than low-risk (low-beta) portfolios. The possibility of this outcome is exactly what is meant by the concept of risk, as illustrated by figure 6-3, and is precisely why betas for diversified portfolios seem to be a very useful risk measure.

Empirical Evidence not Supporting the CAPM

The empirical evidence indicates indisputably that security and portfolio returns are related to risk as measured by beta, but some empirical tests have found shortcomings in the models. For example, beta does not always perform well in the short run. There have been some up market years where low-beta stocks have gone up more than high-beta stocks, and vice versa. The conclusion drawn from these results is that beta can predict well for long-run relationships, but that over shorter periods (under a year) the relationship between beta and return might not be as regular.

A second deviation from the theory is revealed by evidence that demonstrates that over the long term the average returns on high-beta stocks, although higher than the average return on low-beta stocks, is not quite as high as would be predicted by the theory. It seems that people may tend to overbet on long shots. They apparently are willing to pay somewhat more than what the theory predicts for securities with a high probability of low or moderate returns and a low probability of exceptional returns. In other words, people may be willing to accept a little less in expected returns for a remote chance of exceptional gains.

Some empirical studies done on individual stocks have shown that both systematic risk (beta) and unsystematic risk (residual or diversifiable risk) are related to security returns. The theory holds that unsystematic risk should command no premium since it can be diversified away, and therefore returns should be unrelated to unsystematic risk. Other studies have found unsystematic risk unrelated to returns. The statistical problems in testing certain aspects of the theory may be the source of this ambiguity. Perhaps also, as above, people are willing to assume some additional unsystematic risk on the remote chance of exceptional gains. Nearly everyone has heard a story about someone who purchased the shares of a small, unknown company and then accumulated a fortune as the company grew and prospered.

In addition, studies of individual behavior indicate that many people do not act consistently when risk is perceived in terms of loss rather than potential gains. In the aggregate this concept may be reflected in market prices as an undervaluing of the potential upside gain and overdiscounting of the potential losses relative to what the capital asset pricing theory predicts.

Finally, despite the theoretical and empirical evidence in support of a policy of diversification, empirical studies of individual investors' portfolios show that most investors are woefully underdiversified. This does not mean that security prices do not conform with the theory, but it does mean that a significant number of investors do not behave as though they subscribe to the theory. The effect that this behavior by individual investors has upon market prices is difficult to determine, but it is clear that most investors could reduce risk while maintaining the same level of return if they diversified more broadly.

There is still much debate in the academic and financial community on risk measurement. There is a great deal of evidence that supports certain aspects of modern portfolio theory and the capital asset pricing model. However, there is also sufficient evidence that beta is not a perfect risk measure. Undoubtedly, there will be future improvements in risk measurements. For the present, beta is a measure that is available and easily used, and it *can* be of enormous help to investors.

Review of MPT Concepts

The essence of modern portfolio theory is that risky stocks can be combined into portfolios in such a way that they are risk-return efficient. Risk-return efficiency means that for any given level of desired return one can find a portfolio with the least dispersion or variance about its expected return. This development depends basically upon two principles: covariance and diversification.

Covariance is a measure of the degree to which random variables move in a systematic way, either positively or negatively. By combining securities that are negatively covariable, investors can reduce the variability of outcomes without sacrificing expected returns.

Most real-world securities have some common factor or factors that are covariable and many other factors that influence each security independently. The independent factors increase the variability of each security, but if many securities are combined these independent factors tend to offset one another. This process of combining securities in such a way that the independent variability cancels out is called diversification. As more and more securities are added to a portfolio, the portfolio's total variability will depend more and more upon the covariability between the securities and less and less upon the variability of the independent factors. Therefore when considering the purchase of a security to add to an already broadly diversified portfolio, a wise investor will be concerned only about the covariance of the stock with his or her portfolio. Covariance, rather than variance, represents the increment of risk to an investor's portfolio.

Using these principles, Markowitz demonstrated that out of all possible portfolios consisting of all stocks in the marketplace one could, by analyzing covariances, theoretically construct a subset of portfolios that would provide the least variability of outcomes for any possible level of expected return.

Other researchers soon realized that Markowitz's principles would have significant implications if applied to the pricing of capital assets in the market-place. On the basis of Markowitz's principles, the only risk (variability) that an investor could not diversify away was that part directly related to overall market variability. That part of a security's total risk or variability related to the market as a whole is called its systematic or market risk. The remaining risk, which results from independent factors, is called the unsystematic, diversifiable, or residual risk.

The statistical measure that indicates the level of a stock's (or portfolio's) systematic risk is called its beta coefficient. Beta is a proportional measure of the systematic risk of a stock relative to the market's total variability. A portfolio with a beta of 1.5 will tend to move up 15 percent when the market moves up 10 percent and move down 15 percent when the market moves down 10 percent.

Sharpe's capital asset pricing model holds that a security return is related linearly with its beta. People are induced to accept greater risk as represented by beta only if they are rewarded with greater expected returns.

Empirical tests of the capital asset pricing model have supported many aspects of this theory, but support has not been universal. Beta estimates for individual stocks are unreliable, whereas betas for well-designed portfolios are reliable and are good predictors of risk-return performance. Tests of the relationship between returns and beta have shown that portfolio returns are related to beta linearly, as the theory predicts. Over the long run high-beta portfolios have provided larger average returns than low-beta portfolios, while also demonstrating greater yearly fluctuations.

In the short run, however, beta does not always perform as well in predicting risk-return relationships according to the capital asset pricing theory. In addition, the long-term average returns on high-beta stocks are not quite as high as would be predicted by the theory. Also some studies of individual stocks indicate that both systematic risk and unsystematic risk are related to returns. This is in contradiction to the theory, which asserts that only systematic risk should be related to returns since the unsystematic risk can be diversified away.

Unfortunately a perfect measure of risk does not exist. Nevertheless, beta is a serviceable and useful risk estimate when applied to well-diversified portfolios rather than to individual stocks. There will assuredly be future improvements in risk measurements, but for the present beta can be of enormous help to investors.

RISK, RETURN, AND THE PLANNING HORIZON: WHAT THE RETIREMENT PLANNER SHOULD KNOW

As the following discussion will demonstrate, risk, as measured by potential deviations or fluctuations from the expected or average return for a given class of investment assets, depends critically on the investor's planning horizon or expected holding period. As an investor's planned holding period increases, the risk of substantial deviations from the expected or average return for any given type of investment declines. More important, as the holding period increases, risk (as measured by the range of worst possible outcomes) decreases. For longer holding periods the so-called riskier investments, such as common stocks, have historically had higher or better "worst" performances than those considered less risky, such as T-bills and bonds. Armed with a solid understanding of the relationship between risk and holding-period returns, financial planners can help their clients achieve their accumulation objectives for various planning horizons by selecting investments that maximize potential returns within acceptable risk levels.

Historical Perspective—Nominal and Real Returns

Historically, investments with greater risk have provided higher returns. Table 6-1 shows total annual compound and simple nominal returns (with reinvestment of cash flows), standard deviations (a measure of risk that is essentially the average amount by which any given period's return varies from the average return for all periods) for common stocks (based upon the Standard & Poor's [S&P] composite index), small capitalization stocks (the bottom 20 percent of the stocks listed on the New York Stock Exchange ranked by capitalization), long-term AAA-rated corporate bonds, long-term government bonds, U.S. Treasury bills, and the consumer price index for the period 1926 through 1990. Table 6-2 shows real (inflation-adjusted) returns for the same period.[3]

Small stocks, which have experienced the greatest yearly fluctuation of returns as indicated by the standard deviation of 36.3 percent, have provided the highest annual compound return over this period. U.S. Treasury bills, which have had the lowest yearly fluctuation in returns, have also had the lowest annual compound return. Each of the other investments rank as expected with respect to their return given their risk, as measured by the fluctuation (standard deviation) in their annual returns. These results confirm that in the long run returns are positively related to the risk associated with the investment. In other words, the more risk there is, the greater the potential reward.

Over any short-term holding period, however, an investor cannot expect returns on the high-risk investments to necessarily exceed the returns on the low-risk investments. Of course, that is exactly why the high-risk investments are considered risky. Since the high-risk investments have widely fluctuating returns year by year, an investor with a 5-year investment horizon who invests in small stocks, for instance, may experience low or negative returns over that relatively short time period. The investor may lose money relative to an equivalent

TABLE 6-1 1926–1990 Nominal Returns (Not Adjusted for Inflation)			
Series	Compound Return	Simple Return	Standard Deviation
Small stocks	11.632%	17.070%	35.41
Common stocks	10.091	12.148	20.17
Long-term corporate bonds	5.212	5.515	8.41
Long-term government bonds	4.545	4.862	8.54
Intermediate government bonds	4.992	5.126	5.50
U.S. Treasury bills	3.673	3.726	3.38
Inflation	3.141	3.248	4.75

TABLE 6-2 1926–1990 Real Returns (Adjusted for Inflation)			
Series	Compound Return	Simple Return	Standard Deviation
Small stocks	8.233%	13.516%	34.74
Common stocks	6.739	8.833	20.95
Long-term corporate bonds	2.009	2.462	9.87
Long-term government bonds	1.363	1.831	10.07
Intermediate government bonds	1.788	2.016	6.96
U.S. Treasury bills	0.516	0.610	4.35
Inflation	0	0	0

investment in Treasury bills. Similarly returns on small stocks over that relatively short time period may be exceptionally high and exceed the long-term average return for small stocks many times over.

In general, investors can expect that as their investment horizon lengthens, the returns they realize will tend to deviate less from the long-term average for the type of investment they have selected. The practical implication of this result is that investors with long-term investment objectives should be willing to invest in what are considered higher-risk, higher-return instruments than they would tolerate for short-term objectives. Investors who can tolerate the high-risk investments for short-term objectives must understand that they may realize extraordinary results—either high returns or high losses.

Historical Perspective—Risk Premiums

Table 6-3 presents risk premiums for the six basic asset classes introduced in table 6-1 for the period of 1926 through 1990. A *risk premium* is the average additional return an investor receives for bearing the additional risk of a given investment relative to a given safer alternative.

The *real riskless interest rate* serves as the basis for all the other risk premiums. The real riskless interest rate is based on the difference in returns between consumer goods (inflation as measured by the CPI) and U.S. Treasury bills, which

TABLE 6-3 Risk Premiums			
Series	Compound Return	Simple Return	Standard Deviation
Real interest rates (T-bills to inflation)	0.52%	0.61%	4.54
Maturity premiums (LT gov't. bonds to T-bills)	0.84	1.14	8.39
Default premiums (LT corp. to gov't. bonds)	0.64	0.65	3.14
Equity risk premiums (stocks to T-bills)	6.19	8.42	21.26
Small stock premiums (small stocks to stocks)	1.40	4.92	22.10

are a very short-term, almost risk-free asset (using risk of capital and income as the criterion).

The *bond maturity premium* measures the additional return investors receive for bearing the interest-rate risk of long-term but essentially default-free government bonds relative to Treasury bills. Since long-term bond prices fluctuate more than prices of short-term bonds for a given change in interest rates, long-term bondholders face the risk of capital loss if they must sell before the bonds mature.

The *bond default premium* measures the additional return investors receive for bearing the risk of default on corporate bonds relative to government bonds of equal maturity. The total risk premium for corporate bonds relative to Treasury bills may be approximated by adding the bond maturity premium to the default premium.

The *equity risk premium* is a measure of the additional return an investor receives from an investment in common stocks relative to an investment in Treasury bills.

The *small stock premium* is a measure of the additional return from an investment in small capitalization stocks relative to an investment in S&P 500 stocks. The total risk premium for an investment in small stocks relative to Treasury bills may be approximated by adding the equity risk premium for S&P stocks to the small stock premium.

One of the most startling observations from table 6-3 is that the real riskless compound rate of return has been only about one-half of one percent (0.5 percent). These historical data suggest that investors who invest exclusively in Treasury bills can expect little more than a break-even return after inflation. In contrast, based on 65 years of experience, investors in common stock can expect a long-term compound real rate of return that is about 6.2 percent higher than the return on Treasury bills and 6.7 percent higher than inflation. Investors in small stocks can expect a compound long-term real (inflation-adjusted) rate of return of more than 8 percent.

Note in tables 6-1 and 6-2 that simple returns are always larger than compound returns. The reason for this relationship is that compound returns are based on geometric means, while simple returns are based on arithmetic means. A series of examples will help explain.

Consider an investment of $100 that grows to $200 after one year and then falls back to $100 after the second year. In the first year the return is 100 percent ([200 − 100] ÷ 100), and in the second year the return is −50 percent ([100 − 200] ÷ 200). The simple return (arithmetic average) of the 2 years' returns is 25 percent per year ([100% + (−50%)] ÷ 2). Yet the investment was worth the same value at the end of 2 years as it was at the beginning. The simple return overstates the actual return received by the investor.

Compound returns are calculated from a geometric mean of wealth relatives. A wealth relative is simply the end-of-period value divided by the beginning-of-period value. Geometric means are calculated by multiplying the years' wealth relatives and then taking them to the 1/N power where N is the number of periods. Subtracting 1.0 from the geometric mean gives the compound annual return in decimal form. Thus the compound annual rate is

$$r = [R_1 \times R_2 \times \dots R_N]^{1/N} - 1$$

when r is the compound rate in decimal form, R_t is the wealth relative in period t, and N is the number of time periods.

For the previous example, the wealth relatives are 2.0 (200/100) and 0.50 (100/200) for the 2 years. Thus according to the formula above

$$\begin{aligned} r &= (2.0 \times 0.50)^{0.5} - 1 \\ &= (1)^{0.5} - 1 \\ &= 0 \end{aligned}$$

Note that the compound return of 0 percent makes sense since the example had an ending value that was equal to the beginning value—nothing was gained.

Wealth relatives are equal to 1.0 plus the rate of return, as the following demonstrates:

$$\text{Wealth relative} = \frac{\text{ending value}}{\text{beginning value}}$$

$$= \frac{\text{ending value} - \text{beginning value} + \text{beginning value}}{\text{beginning value}}$$

$$= \frac{\text{ending value} - \text{beginning value}}{\text{beginning value}} + \frac{\text{beginning value}}{\text{beginning value}}$$

$$= \text{percentage increase} + 1.0$$

$$= 1.0 + r$$

In any series of wealth relatives the compound return (calculated from the geometric mean) will be equal to the simple return (the arithmetic mean) if there is no variability in the series. For example, for 2 consecutive years of 10 percent returns the simple return is 10 percent ([10% + 10%] ÷ 2) and the compound return is 10 percent ([1.10 x 1.10]$^{0.5}$ − 1).

If there is variability in the series, however, the compound return will be smaller than the simple return. For example, if returns are 5 percent and 15 percent in consecutive years, the simple return is 10 percent ([5% + 15%] ÷ 2), while the compound return is only 9.89 percent ([1.05 x 1.15]$^{0.5}$ − 1). The more variable the series of returns, the smaller the compound rate is relative to the simple rate. For example, if the returns are 0 percent and 20 percent in consecutive years, the simple rate is still 10 percent ([0% + 20%] ÷ 2) but the compound rate falls to 9.54 percent ([1.0 x 1.20]$^{0.5}$ − 1).

Common Stock (S&P Composite) Returns

Over the period from 1926 through 1990, nominal stock returns were positive in 45 out of 65 years or almost 70 percent of the time. Real (inflation-adjusted) returns were positive about two-thirds of the time (43 out of 65 years). The longest period over which an investor would have had a negative nominal total return (unadjusted for inflation) on an S&P composite common stock investment was the 14-year period of 1929 through 1942. However, during the 18-year period from June 1964 through September 1982, a common stock investor would have had a negative real rate of return (adjusted for inflation). Although real returns were negative over this period, in nominal terms the value of investment would have more than tripled.

Five-Year Holding-Period Returns

Looking at all possible 5-year holding periods from 1926 through 1990, the average nominal annualized simple return was 10 percent. Nominal annualized compound rates of return were positive in 54 out of 61 of the 5-year holding periods, or almost 90 percent of the time. They ranged from a high of 23.5 percent from 1950 to 1954 to a low of −12.5 percent from 1928 to 1932—a min-max range (computed as the difference between the minimum and maximum values) of 36.4 percent. There is about a 99 percent probability that any given 5-year nominal annualized simple return will fall between −15.35 and 35.31 percent.

The average real annualized simple return was more than 6.5 percent. Real compound annualized returns were positive in 47 out of 61 of the 5-year holding periods, about 77 percent of the time. They ranged from a high of 23.5 percent from 1932 to 1936 to a low of −9.3 percent from 1937 to 1941—a min-max range of 32.8 percent. Based on the historical distribution of returns, the real annualized 5-year return should fall within the range of −17.33 to 30.40 percent about 99 percent of the time.

Ten-Year Holding-Period Returns

The average nominal annualized simple return was 10.3 percent for all 10-year holding periods over the period 1926 to 1990. Nominal annualized compound returns were positive in 54 out of 56, or over 96 percent, of the 10-year holding periods. They ranged from a high of 20.1 percent from 1948 to 1958 to a low of −0.9 percent from 1928 to 1938—a min-max range of 21 percent. This range is about half the size of the 5-year holding period min-max range. Based on the historical distribution of returns, the 10-year nominal annualized return should fall within the range of −6.10 to 26.62 percent 99 percent of the time.

The average real annualized simple return was 6.5 percent. Real annualized compound returns were positive for 88 percent of the 10-year periods (49 out of 56). They ranged from a high of 17.9 percent from 1948 to 1958 to a low of −3.8 percent from 1964 to 1974—a min-max range of 21.7 percent, or about two-thirds the size of the 5-year min-max range. The 10-year real annualized return should fall between −10.17 and 23.15 percent about 99 percent of the time.

Twenty-Year Holding-Period Returns

For 20-year holding periods the average nominal annualized simple return was 10.5 percent. Nominal annualized returns were positive for all 46 of the 20-year holding periods. They ranged from a high of 16.9 percent from 1942 to 1961 to a low of 3.1 percent from 1928 to 1948—a min-max range of 13.8 percent. This range is about one-third the size of the 5-year holding period min-max range. Approximately 99 percent of the time, 20-year nominal annualized returns should fall between 0.33 and 20.66 percent.

The average real annualized simple return was 6.6 percent. Real annualized returns were positive in all 46 of the 20-year holding periods. They ranged from a high of 13.0 percent from 1942 to 1961 to a low of 0.8 percent from 1965 to 1984—a min-max range of 12.2 percent, or about one-third the 5-year range. Based on the historic distribution of returns, the real 20-year annualized return has a 99 percent chance of falling within the range of −4.82 to 18.09 percent.

Holding Period and Min-Max Range

These results demonstrate that investors can generally expect both the real and nominal returns they realize on a portfolio of common stocks to deviate less from the long-term average return for common stocks the longer their anticipated holding period. In other words, common stocks become less risky (with no reduction in expected return) the longer an investor plans to hold them. Perhaps more important, the downside risk, as measured by the probability of negative average annual compound returns that are less than zero, declines as the holding period increases. Specifically, the probability of earning a negative real return for a one-year investment in S&P stocks is about 34 percent (or 1 in 3). For a 20-year holding period, the probability that the average real annual compound return

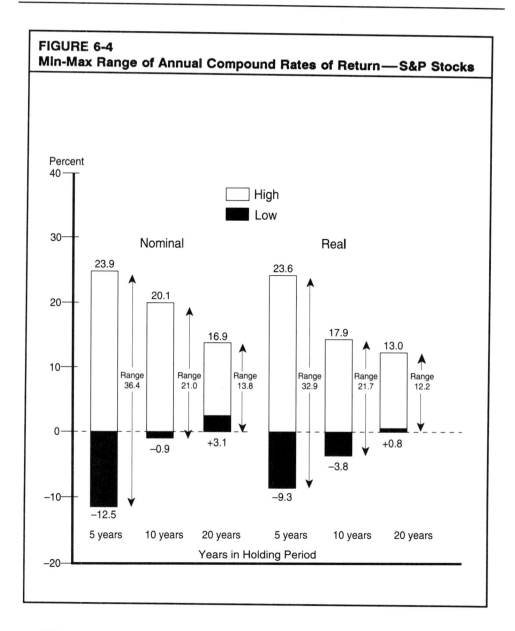

FIGURE 6-4
Min-Max Range of Annual Compound Rates of Return—S&P Stocks

will be negative is less than 4 percent (or 1 in 25). Consequently common stocks may be suitable investments for long-term accumulation objectives for many investors who would be unwilling to bear the risk of common stocks for short-term accumulation objectives. Figure 6-4 graphically demonstrates this point for nominal and real rates of return.

Table 6-4 shows total nominal and real compound and simple annualized rates of return for S&P 500 stocks for holding periods ranging from one year to 50

TABLE 6-4
Holding-Period Risk-Return Analysis for S&P 500 Stocks (1926–1990)

Nominal Returns

Yrs. in Holding Period	Annualized Average Return				Min-Max Range (%)	Percent HPR>0	Standard	Prob. HPR<0	99% Probability Range		
	Compound Return (%)	Simple Return (%)	Maximum Value (%)	Minimum Value (%)					Minimum (%)	Maximum (%)	Range (%)
1	10.09	12.15	53.99	-43.34	97.33	69.23	20.79	27.96	-50.23	74.53	124.76
2	10.09	11.28	41.70	-34.77	76.47	81.25	15.00	22.61	-33.73	56.29	90.02
3	10.09	10.65	30.86	-26.95	57.82	85.71	11.57	17.88	-24.06	45.35	69.41
4	10.09	10.20	31.62	-22.66	54.28	88.71	9.81	14.92	-19.22	39.63	58.85
5	10.09	10.01	23.92	-12.47	36.38	88.52	8.45	11.82	-15.35	35.36	50.71
7	10.09	10.07	24.23	-3.49	27.72	93.22	6.65	6.49	-9.87	30.01	39.88
10	10.09	10.26	20.06	-0.89	20.95	96.43	5.45	3.00	-6.10	26.62	32.72
15	10.09	10.22	18.24	0.64	17.60	100.00	4.56	1.26	-3.47	23.91	27.38
20	10.09	10.49	16.86	3.11	13.75	100.00	3.39	0.10	0.33	20.66	20.34
25	10.09	10.31	15.02	5.94	9.08	100.00	2.49	0.01	2.83	17.80	14.97
30	10.09	10.97	13.49	8.47	5.02	100.00	1.42	0.01	6.71	15.23	8.52
40	10.09	10.83	12.49	8.85	3.63	100.00	1.10	0.01	7.53	14.13	6.60
50	10.09	10.18	11.97	7.69	4.28	100.00	1.35	0.01	6.14	14.22	8.08

Real (Inflation-Adjusted) Returns

Yrs. in Holding Period	Compound Return (%)	Simple Return (%)	Maximum Value (%)	Minimum Value (%)	Min-Max Range (%)	Percent HPR>0	Standard	Prob. HPR<0	Minimum (%)	Maximum (%)	Range (%)
1	6.74	8.83	53.39	-37.37	90.76	66.15	20.95	33.67	-54.03	71.70	125.73
2	6.74	7.90	42.69	-29.25	71.94	71.88	15.05	29.99	-37.25	53.04	90.28
3	6.74	7.22	32.14	-22.94	55.08	77.78	11.38	26.29	-26.91	41.34	68.25
4	6.74	6.75	29.45	-17.28	46.73	74.19	9.40	23.64	-21.45	34.94	56.39
5	6.74	6.54	23.51	-9.34	32.85	77.05	7.95	20.56	-17.33	30.40	47.73
7	6.74	6.51	22.31	-7.27	29.58	84.75	6.48	15.74	-12.92	25.94	38.86
10	6.74	6.49	17.87	-3.76	21.63	87.50	5.55	12.14	-10.17	23.15	33.32
15	6.74	6.33	14.64	-0.58	15.22	92.16	4.73	9.03	-7.85	20.52	28.37
20	6.74	6.63	13.04	0.84	12.20	100.00	3.82	4.12	-4.82	18.09	22.91
25	6.74	6.76	11.75	2.60	9.14	100.00	2.92	1.03	-2.00	15.53	17.53
30	6.74	7.33	10.58	4.45	6.13	100.00	1.85	0.01	1.77	12.89	11.12
40	6.74	7.10	9.15	5.70	3.44	100.00	0.95	0.01	4.25	9.95	5.70
50	6.74	6.26	7.04	4.77	2.27	100.00	0.67	0.01	4.25	8.27	4.02

years. It also shows the maximum and minimum values for each holding period, the min-max range, and the standard deviation of the holding period returns. Smaller standard deviations suggest a lower beta, implying less risk. Finally, based on the historical distribution of returns, it shows the range into which you can expect annualized holding period returns to fall 99 percent of the time.

Small Capitalization Stocks

Returns on small stocks, similar to returns on S&P common stocks, were positive in about two-thirds of the years from 1926 through 1990 (44 out of 65). The simple one-year nominal average return was 17.07 percent. The one-year nominal average compound return was 11.63 percent. The 15-year period from 1928 to 1942 was the longest period over which an investor would have earned a negative return in either real or nominal terms. During the 18-year period (1964–1982) when the real returns on S&P common stocks were negative, small stocks grew at an 8.2 percent annual compound rate of return—enough to increase investor wealth in real terms fourfold. The simple real (inflation-adjusted) one-year average return was 13.52 percent. The one-year real average compound return was 8.23 percent.

Five-Year Holding-Period Returns

For 5-year holding periods the average nominal annualized simple return was 13.5 percent. Nominal annualized compound returns were positive in about 85 percent of the periods (52 of 61). They ranged from a high of 45.9 percent from 1941 to 1945 to a low of −27.5 percent from 1928 to 1932—a min-max range of 73.4 percent. Based on this history, an investor could expect nominal 5-year annualized rates of return to fall between −34.36 and 61.43 percent 99 percent of the time.

The average real annualized simple return was 9.8 percent. Real annualized compound returns were positive in over 80 percent of the periods (49 of 61). They ranged from a high of 47.1 percent from 1932 to 1936 to a low of −23.4 percent from 1928 to 1932—a min-max range of 70.5 percent. The real 5-year annualized compound rate of return should fall between about −32.48 and 52.03 percent 99 percent of the time.

Ten-Year Holding-Period Returns

For 10-year holding periods the average nominal annualized simple return was 14.36 percent. Nominal annualized returns were positive in 55 of 57 periods. They ranged from a high of 30.4 percent from 1975 to 1984 to a low of −5.7 percent from 1929 to 1938—a min-max range of 36.1 percent, or half the 5-year range. Ten-year nominal annualized compound returns can be expected to fall between −8.94 and 37.66 percent 99 percent of the time.

The average real annualized simple return was 10.4 percent. Real 10-year holding-period annualized returns were positive in 51 of 57 periods. They ranged from a high of 21.5 percent from 1975 to 1984 to a low of −3.8 percent from 1929 to 1938—a min-max range of 25.3 percent, or about one-third the 5-year range. Real 10-year annualized compound returns should fall within −8.6 and 29.32 percent 99 percent of the time.

Twenty-Year Holding-Period Returns

For 20-year holding periods nominal annualized simple returns averaged 14.36 percent and were positive in all 47 of the 20-year holding periods. Nominal annualized compound returns ranged from a high of 21.1 percent from 1942 to 1961 to a low of 5.7 percent from 1929 to 1948—a min-max range of 15.4 percent, or almost five times less than the 5-year range. Similarly, the range in which the 20-year annualized compound return can be expected to fall 99 percent of the time is 4.02 to 24.7 percent, again about one-fifth the size of the 5-year range.

The average real annualized simple return was 10.35 percent. Real annual compound returns for 20-year holding periods were positive in all 47 periods. They ranged from a high of 17.2 percent from 1942 to 1961 to a low of 4 percent from 1929 to 1948—a min-max range of 13.2 percent, or more than five times smaller than the 5-year range. There is a 99 percent chance that the real 20-year annualized return will fall between .25 and 20.44 percent.

Holding Period and Min-Max Range

Similar to the results for S&P stocks, the rate of return realized on a portfolio of small capitalization stocks generally has deviated less from the long-term average expected return the longer the investor's holding period.

The min-max range of returns for any given holding period is greater for small capitalization stocks than for S&P stocks. Therefore although small capitalization stocks become less risky the longer the investor's expected holding period (in the sense that the investor's actual return is less likely to deviate substantially from the long-term expected averages), the returns on small capitalization stocks still fluctuate more on average for any given holding period than returns on S&P common stocks.

However, the risk of small stocks decreases more than the risk of S&P stocks as the holding period increases. Specifically, the historical 5-year min-max range of returns for small stocks was more than twice as large as the range for S&P stocks (73.4 percent nominal and 70.4 percent real for small stocks versus 36.4 percent nominal and 32.9 percent real for S&P stocks). In contrast, the historical 20-year min-max ranges for small stocks and S&P stocks are almost identical (15.4 percent nominal and 13.2 percent real for small stocks versus 13.7 percent nominal and 12.2 percent real for S&P stocks). And for all holding periods of 20 years or longer, small capitalization stocks have absolutely dominated S&P stocks

TABLE 6-5
Holding-Period Risk-Return Analysis for Small Stocks (1926–1990)

Yrs. in Holding Period	Annualized Average Return					Nominal Returns			99% Probability Range		
	Compound Return (%)	Simple Return (%)	Maximum Value (%)	Minimum Value (%)	Min-Max Range (%)	Percent HPR>0	Standard	Prob. HPR<0	Minimum (%)	Maximum (%)	Range (%)
1	11.63	17.07	142.87	−58.01	200.87	67.69	35.41	31.49	−89.15	123.29	212.45
2	11.63	15.16	73.69	−45.15	118.84	71.88	26.21	28.16	−63.47	93.79	157.26
3	11.63	14.24	71.31	−46.73	118.04	77.78	21.42	25.31	−50.02	78.51	128.54
4	11.63	13.64	64.17	−38.50	102.68	79.03	18.79	23.40	−42.73	70.00	112.73
5	11.63	13.54	45.90	−27.54	73.44	85.25	15.97	19.83	−34.36	61.43	95.79
7	11.63	13.90	35.78	−18.22	54.00	89.83	11.44	11.21	−20.41	48.21	68.62
10	11.63	14.36	30.38	−5.70	36.08	96.43	7.77	3.23	−8.94	37.66	46.60
15	11.63	14.40	23.33	−1.30	24.63	94.12	5.71	0.59	−2.74	31.54	34.29
20	11.63	14.36	21.13	5.74	15.39	100.00	3.45	0.01	4.02	24.70	20.68
25	11.63	13.90	19.62	7.16	12.46	100.00	2.99	0.01	4.94	22.87	17.93
30	11.63	14.47	18.83	8.84	10.00	100.00	2.72	0.01	6.32	22.62	16.30
40	11.63	14.45	17.90	11.10	6.80	100.00	2.01	0.01	8.42	20.48	12.05
50	11.63	14.30	17.46	9.80	7.66	100.00	2.48	0.01	6.86	21.73	14.87
Real (Inflation-Adjusted) Returns											
1	8.23	13.52	141.63	−59.27	200.90	67.69	34.74	34.87	−90.72	117.75	208.47
2	8.23	11.51	71.52	−43.47	114.99	70.31	25.30	32.46	−64.38	87.41	151.79
3	8.23	10.54	67.12	−43.80	110.92	73.02	20.11	30.02	−49.79	70.86	120.64
4	8.23	9.89	59.80	−34.22	94.02	74.19	17.11	28.17	−41.45	61.22	102.67
5	8.23	9.78	47.06	−23.38	70.44	80.33	14.08	24.38	−32.48	52.03	84.51
7	8.23	10.09	25.30	−14.46	39.76	81.36	9.68	14.88	−18.96	39.13	58.09
10	8.23	10.36	21.47	−3.80	25.27	89.29	6.32	5.06	−8.60	29.32	37.91
15	8.23	10.32	19.31	−0.42	19.74	96.08	4.93	1.82	−4.47	25.11	29.58
20	8.23	10.35	17.18	3.96	13.22	100.00	3.36	0.11	0.25	20.44	20.19
25	8.23	10.22	16.21	5.27	10.94	100.00	2.75	0.01	1.98	18.46	16.48
30	8.23	10.70	15.40	6.08	9.33	100.00	2.50	0.01	3.21	18.20	15.00
40	8.23	10.60	13.64	8.24	5.40	100.00	1.50	0.01	6.11	15.09	8.98
50	8.23	10.22	12.83	7.35	5.49	100.00	1.67	0.01	5.20	15.25	10.05

in terms of nominal returns. The maximum *and* minimum annualized nominal compound returns for small stocks for any holding period of 20 years or more were always greater than the corresponding maximum and minimum values for S&P stocks.

Looking at real inflation-adjusted returns, small capitalization stocks similarly dominated S&P stocks for all holding periods of 10 years or more. Consequently, for long-term accumulation objectives, investors can capture a substantial expected annual return premium (1.4 percent compound small stock premium) with virtually no increase in risk by shifting from a portfolio of S&P stocks to a portfolio of small capitalization stocks. Figure 6-5 compares real (inflation-adjusted) min-max ranges for both S&P stocks and small capitalization stocks for holding periods ranging from one year to 50 years.

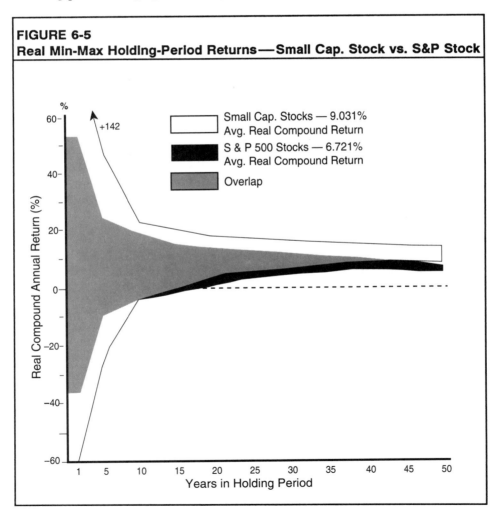

FIGURE 6-5
Real Min-Max Holding-Period Returns—Small Cap. Stock vs. S&P Stock

When only downside risk—the likelihood of loss—is considered, small stocks look even better relative to S&P stocks for longer holding periods. For holding periods of up to 5 years, small stocks have a higher probability than S&P stocks of earning an average real compound annual return that is negative. However, for longer holding periods the probability of negative returns is less for small stocks than for S&P stocks. For instance, for 20-year holding periods the probability of negative returns for small stocks is .11 percent, or about one in 1,000. In contrast, for S&P stocks, the probability is 4.12 percent, or about 40 times greater than for small stocks.

Long-Term Corporate Bonds

The average annual nominal simple rate of return and the average annual inflation-adjusted real simple rate of return on long-term corporate bonds were 5.21 percent and 1.887 percent, respectively, over the period from 1926 through 1990. In 50 out of the 65 years, long-term corporate bonds had positive nominal compound returns, ranging from 43.8 percent to −8.1 percent. Based on history, an investor should expect nominal annual returns to fall within −19.70 and 30.73 percent 99 percent of the time. Long-term corporate bonds had positive inflation-adjusted real annual compound returns in 41 out of the 65 years. Real returns ranged from a high of 38.48 percent to a low of −15.43 percent.

Five-year, 10-year, and 20-year nominal annualized compound returns for long-term corporate bonds ranged from 22.41 percent, 14.07 percent, and 9.53 percent, respectively, on the high side, to −2.22 percent, 0.98 percent, and 1.34 percent, respectively, on the low side. Therefore the respective min-max ranges were 24.64 percent, 13.09 percent, and 8.24 percent.

Real annualized compound returns ranged from 18.51 percent, 9.9 percent, and 5.44 percent to −10.27 percent, −5.18 percent, and −2.67 percent, respectively, for 5-, 10-, and 20-year holding periods. Therefore the respective real min-max ranges were 28.78 percent, 15.08 percent, and 8.11 percent. These results are perfectly consistent with expectations regarding risk level and holding periods relative to the other asset categories. Perhaps one of the most notable items is the consistently high probability of negative real returns for all holding periods. The chance for negative real returns stays at around 40 percent (or 2 in 5) regardless of the holding period.

Stocks and Bonds Compared

Although the long-term corporate bond min-max ranges for holding periods were smaller than the corresponding ranges for either S&P stocks or small capitalization stocks, both S&P stocks and small capitalization stocks absolutely dominated long-term corporate bonds for longer holding periods.

TABLE 6-6
Holding-Period Risk-Return Analysis for Corporate Bonds (1926–1990)

Yrs. in Holding Period	Annualized Average Return					Percent HPR>0	Standard	Prob. HPR<0	99% Probability Range		
	Compound Return (%)	Simple Return (%)	Maximum Value (%)	Minimum Value (%)	Min-Max Range (%)				Minimum (%)	Maximum (%)	Range (%)
Nominal Returns											
1	5.21	5.51	43.79	-8.09	51.88	76.92	8.41	25.60	-19.70	30.73	50.44
2	5.21	5.36	25.25	-3.40	28.65	81.25	6.34	19.87	-13.64	24.37	38.01
3	5.21	5.24	22.23	-3.59	25.82	87.30	5.37	16.49	-10.88	21.35	32.23
4	5.21	5.16	23.06	-2.66	25.72	88.71	4.87	14.49	-9.46	19.78	29.24
5	5.21	5.14	22.41	-2.22	24.64	95.08	4.57	13.05	-8.57	18.85	27.42
7	5.21	4.98	17.19	-0.63	17.81	98.31	3.91	10.15	-6.76	16.73	23.49
10	5.21	4.63	14.07	0.98	13.09	100.00	3.04	6.41	-4.50	13.75	18.24
15	5.21	4.21	10.56	1.02	9.54	100.00	2.43	4.18	-3.09	11.50	14.58
20	5.21	3.93	9.58	1.34	8.24	100.00	2.01	2.53	-2.10	9.95	12.05
25	5.21	3.49	7.13	1.34	5.79	100.00	1.41	0.68	-0.75	7.74	8.49
30	5.21	3.65	6.88	1.79	5.09	100.00	1.33	0.32	-0.35	7.66	8.01
40	5.21	3.69	5.50	2.64	2.86	100.00	0.82	0.01	1.22	6.16	4.94
50	5.21	4.12	4.90	3.47	1.43	100.00	0.45	0.01	2.76	5.48	2.72
Real (Inflation-Adjusted) Returns											
1	2.01	2.46	38.46	-15.43	53.89	63.08	9.87	40.16	-27.15	32.08	59.23
2	2.01	2.26	22.27	-14.40	36.67	64.06	7.85	38.66	-21.28	25.80	47.07
3	2.01	2.09	18.73	-12.67	31.40	60.32	6.79	37.93	-18.29	22.47	40.76
4	2.01	1.97	18.51	-11.60	30.12	54.84	6.16	37.45	-16.50	20.44	36.93
5	2.01	1.92	18.51	-10.27	28.78	54.10	5.77	36.99	-15.39	19.23	34.62
7	2.01	1.64	13.10	-5.55	18.65	54.24	5.05	37.26	-13.50	16.79	30.29
10	2.01	1.06	9.90	-5.18	15.08	48.21	3.85	39.15	-10.49	12.62	23.11
15	2.01	0.52	7.96	-3.86	11.82	52.94	2.63	42.10	-7.36	8.41	15.77
20	2.01	0.28	5.44	-2.67	8.11	45.65	1.75	43.74	-4.97	5.52	10.49
25	2.01	0.15	3.37	-1.95	5.32	43.90	1.24	45.16	-3.58	3.88	7.46
30	2.01	0.24	2.90	-1.52	4.42	47.22	1.22	42.11	-3.43	3.92	7.35
40	2.01	0.20	2.38	-1.89	4.27	53.85	1.17	43.10	-3.31	3.71	7.02
50	2.01	0.42	1.56	-0.30	1.86	75.00	0.61	24.46	-1.40	2.24	3.64

Figure 6-6 compares nominal min-max ranges for both S&P stocks and long-term corporate bonds for holding periods ranging from one year to 50 years. For any holding period of 15 years or longer, the maximum nominal annualized compound holding-period returns for S&P stocks were always considerably higher than the corresponding values for long-term bonds while the S&P stock's minimum nominal annualized compound holding period returns were essentially equal to or greater than the corresponding values for long-term bonds. In fact, for holding periods of 25 years or more, the *minimum* values for S&P stocks were always greater than the *maximum* values for long-term bonds. Note, however, that for shorter holding periods (5 or fewer years), minimum values for S&P stocks were significantly lower than for corporate bonds while maximum values for S&P stocks were only slightly higher than for corporate bonds.

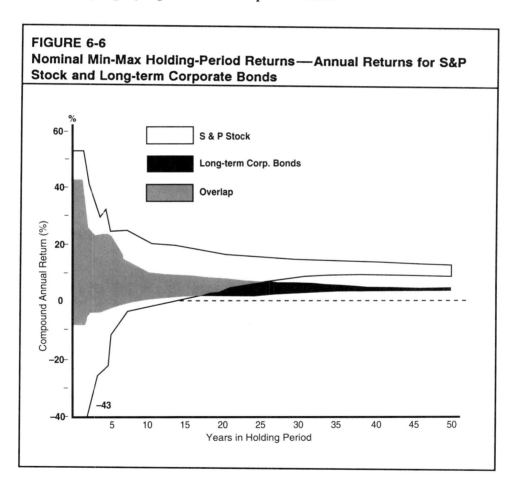

FIGURE 6-6
Nominal Min-Max Holding-Period Returns—Annual Returns for S&P Stock and Long-term Corporate Bonds

Given that the average nominal compound rate of return for S&P stocks over the period from 1926 through 1990 (10.091 percent) was 4.88 percent greater than for corporate bonds (5.212 percent), investors with longer-term investment horizons can apparently capture a sizable annual return premium with virtually no increase in risk (as measured by the worst downside performance) by investing in S&P stocks rather than long-term corporate bonds.

Long-Term U.S. Government Bonds

Over the entire period from 1926 through 1990 compound annual real (inflation-adjusted) long-term government bond returns were only 1.0 percent. Nominal long-term government bond returns were positive in 47 out of the 65 years. Nominal annual returns ranged from 40.4 percent in 1982 to −9.2 percent in 1967. Real long-term government bond returns were positive in slightly more than half the years (40 out of the 65 years). Real annual returns ranged from 35.13 percent in 1982 to 15.6 percent in 1946.

Over this entire period the highest *nominal* annualized compound returns were 21.6 percent for 5-year holding periods, 9.7 percent for 10-year holding periods, and 9.0 percent for 20-year holding periods. The lowest nominal annualized returns were −2.1 percent, −0.07 percent, and 0.7 percent for 5-, 10-, and 20-year holding periods, respectively. The nominal min-max ranges for 5-, 10-, and 20-year holding periods were 23.7 percent, 13.9 percent, and 8.3 percent, respectively.

The highest *real* annualized compound return for 5-year holding periods was 17.7 percent; it was 8.9 percent for 10-year holding periods and 4.5 percent for 20-year holding periods. The lowest real annualized compound returns were −10.2 percent, −5.35 percent, and 3.06 percent respectively for 5-, 10-, and 20-year holding periods. The real min-max ranges for 5-, 10-, and 20-year holding periods were 27.8 percent, 14.2 percent, and 7.6 percent, respectively. Notable, once again, is the consistently high probability of negative real returns over any given holding period. The probability of negative real returns ranges from about 40 percent for shorter holding periods to more than 60 percent for longer holding periods.

Stocks and U.S. Government Bonds Compared

Once again, the min-max annualized compound return range declines as the holding period increases. And consistent with their risk rating, the min-max annualized compound return range for long-term U.S. government bonds for any given holding period is smaller than for either S&P common stocks or small capitalization stocks. However, similar to corporate bonds, for longer holding periods (about 15 years or longer) long-term government bonds have been absolutely dominated by both S&P stocks and small capitalization stocks in that the maximum and minimum annual compound returns for these assets have been greater than the corresponding values for long-term government bonds.

U.S. Treasury Bills and Inflation

The inflation-adjusted U.S. Treasury bill return over the entire period from 1926 through 1990 was only 0.516 percent compounded annually. The nominal rate was 3.673 percent. The real riskless interest rate is often reported as being between 3 and 4 percent, which does not seem to be supported if we define the real riskless interest rate as the premium on T-bills over the rate of inflation.

The studies that have measured the real riskless interest rate at 3 to 4 percent have typically used high-grade long-term corporate bond yields to measure the riskless rates. Since long-term corporate bond yields incorporate both promised future maturity premiums and default premiums, as well as promised future real interest rates, measures of the real riskless rate that use high-grade long-term corporate bond yields probably overstate the real rate of return.

Throughout the entire period from 1926 to 1990, U.S. Treasury bill returns often tracked inflation rates very closely. However, in certain subperiods, such as the deflationary period between 1926 and 1932, when the annual rate of inflation was −0.4 percent while bills returned 2.7 percent annually, this close relationship has broken down.

Five-year annualized *nominal* compound returns from rolling over one-month bills ranged from a high of 11.1 percent (1979−1983) to a low of 0.1 percent (1937−1941), for a min-max range of 11 percent. For 10-year periods the nominal compound returns ranged from a high of 9.2 percent (1977−1986) to a low of 0.2 percent (1933−1942), for a min-max range of 9 percent. For 20-year periods the highest nominal compound rate was 7.7 percent (1967−1986), and the low was 0.4 percent (1931−1950), for a min-max range of 7.3 percent.

The 5-, 10-, and 20-year annualized real compound returns ranged from 8.4 percent, 4.7 percent, and 1.3 percent on the high side to −6.08 percent, −5.08 percent, and −3.04 percent on the low side, respectively. The real min-max ranges for these holding periods were 14.5 percent, 9.7 percent, and 4.4 percent, respectively. The probability of experiencing negative real rates of return starts at an incredibly high 44 percent for one-year holding periods and increases consistently for longer holding periods to more than 90 percent for 50-year holding periods.

Treasury Bill Rates versus Inflation

Five-year, 10-year, and 20-year annualized inflation rates ranged from a high of 10.1 percent in 1977 through 1981, 8.7 percent in 1973 through 1982, and 6.4 percent in 1965 through 1984, respectively, to a low of −5.4 percent in 1928 through 1932, −2.6 percent in 1926 through 1935, and 0.07 percent in 1926 through 1945, respectively.

In 1973 through 1980 the real riskless rate of return averaged −.7 percent per year. In the more recent period of 1981 through 1990 Treasury bill returns stayed historically high, with an average nominal annual rate of 8.5 percent. Over the

TABLE 6-7
Holding-Period Risk-Return Analysis for Long-Term Government Bonds

Yrs. in Holding Period	Compound Return (%)	Annualized Average Return				Percent HPR>0	Standard	Prob. HPR<0	99% Probability Range		
		Simple Return (%)	Maximum Value (%)	Minimum Value (%)	Min-Max Range (%)				Minimum (%)	Maximum (%)	Range (%)
Nominal Returns											
1	4.54	4.86	40.35	-9.19	49.53	72.31	8.54	28.46	-20.76	30.48	51.24
2	4.54	4.68	27.71	-4.83	32.54	79.69	6.26	22.73	-14.10	23.46	37.56
3	4.54	4.53	23.49	-4.91	28.41	84.13	5.17	19.09	-10.99	20.04	31.03
4	4.54	4.45	20.90	-2.84	23.74	87.10	4.67	17.07	-9.57	18.47	28.04
5	4.54	4.44	21.62	-2.14	23.76	90.16	4.46	15.99	-8.94	17.81	26.75
7	4.54	4.29	16.07	-0.88	16.95	98.31	3.80	12.99	-7.13	15.70	22.83
10	4.54	3.97	13.75	-0.07	13.82	98.21	2.91	8.68	-4.78	12.71	17.49
15	4.54	3.62	9.78	0.40	9.39	100.00	2.34	6.12	-3.41	10.65	14.06
20	4.54	3.37	9.01	0.68	8.32	100.00	1.95	4.21	-2.48	9.23	11.71
25	4.54	2.96	6.65	0.82	5.83	100.00	1.36	1.49	-1.13	7.04	8.17
30	4.54	3.08	6.43	1.53	4.90	100.00	1.28	0.79	-0.74	6.91	7.66
40	4.54	3.12	4.92	2.26	2.66	100.00	0.80	0.01	0.73	5.52	4.78
50	4.54	3.54	4.46	2.80	1.65	100.00	0.59	0.01	1.78	5.31	3.53
Real (Inflation-Adjusted) Returns											
1	1.36	1.83	35.13	-15.46	50.59	58.46	10.07	42.79	-28.39	32.05	60.44
2	1.36	1.59	24.67	-13.69	38.35	59.38	7.62	41.73	-21.27	24.45	45.71
3	1.36	1.38	19.96	-12.27	32.23	60.32	6.37	41.41	-17.74	20.50	38.24
4	1.36	1.26	16.42	-10.98	27.40	54.84	5.65	41.17	-15.68	18.21	33.89
5	1.36	1.22	17.73	-10.10	27.83	49.18	5.30	40.91	-14.69	17.13	31.82
7	1.36	0.95	12.02	-5.68	17.71	50.85	4.58	41.75	-12.77	14.68	27.45
10	1.36	0.41	8.86	-5.35	14.22	41.07	3.36	45.12	-9.68	10.51	20.19
15	1.36	-0.04	6.54	-4.46	11.00	33.33	2.35	50.72	-7.09	7.00	14.09
20	1.36	-0.26	4.53	-3.06	7.58	26.09	1.62	56.39	-5.11	4.59	9.70
25	1.36	-0.37	2.58	-2.46	5.03	26.83	1.15	62.59	-3.80	3.07	6.87
30	1.36	-0.31	2.12	-2.00	4.12	38.89	1.13	60.63	-3.70	3.09	6.79
40	1.36	-0.34	1.63	-2.27	3.90	46.15	1.05	62.70	-3.48	2.80	6.28
50	1.36	-0.14	0.82	-0.81	1.63	25.00	0.52	60.22	-1.70	1.43	3.13

TABLE 6-8
Holding-Period Risk-Return Analysis for T-Bills

Nominal Returns

Yrs. in Holding Period	Annualized Average Return					Percent HPR>0	Standard	Prob. HPR<0	99% Probability Range		
	Compound Return (%)	Simple Return (%)	Maximum Value (%)	Minimum Value (%)	Min-Max Range (%)				Minimum (%)	Maximum (%)	Range (%)
1	3.67	3.73	14.71	-0.02	14.73	98.46	3.38	13.54	-6.42	13.87	20.29
2	3.67	3.70	12.96	0.00	12.96	100.00	3.33	13.32	-6.28	13.67	19.95
3	3.67	3.66	12.15	0.00	12.14	100.00	3.27	13.15	-6.15	13.48	19.63
4	3.67	3.63	11.70	0.02	11.69	100.00	3.24	13.07	-6.07	13.34	19.42
5	3.67	3.61	11.12	0.07	11.05	100.00	3.21	13.08	-6.03	13.25	19.28
7	3.67	3.56	10.44	0.10	10.34	100.00	3.17	13.08	-5.96	13.09	19.05
10	3.67	3.49	9.17	0.15	9.03	100.00	3.08	12.89	-5.76	12.74	18.50
15	3.67	3.32	8.29	0.22	8.07	100.00	2.79	11.70	-5.04	11.68	16.72
20	3.67	3.21	7.66	0.42	7.23	100.00	2.51	10.09	-4.33	10.75	15.08
25	3.67	2.93	6.89	0.57	6.32	100.00	2.12	8.41	-3.44	9.29	12.73
30	3.67	3.09	6.51	0.94	5.57	100.00	1.92	5.40	-2.68	8.86	11.53
40	3.67	3.11	5.37	1.52	3.85	100.00	1.33	0.99	-0.89	7.11	8.00
50	3.67	3.26	4.38	2.33	2.06	100.00	0.72	0.01	1.11	5.41	4.31

Real (Inflation-Adjusted) Returns

Yrs. in Holding Period	Compound Return (%)	Simple Return (%)	Maximum Value (%)	Minimum Value (%)	Min-Max Range (%)	Percent HPR>0	Standard	Prob. HPR<0	Minimum (%)	Maximum (%)	Range (%)
1	0.52	0.61	12.55	-15.07	27.62	61.54	4.35	44.43	-12.45	13.67	26.13
2	0.52	0.55	12.13	-11.51	23.64	59.38	4.00	44.51	-11.46	12.56	24.02
3	0.52	0.49	11.07	-8.41	19.48	58.73	3.71	44.78	-10.63	11.60	22.23
4	0.52	0.43	9.40	-6.81	16.21	56.45	3.46	45.10	-9.96	10.82	20.78
5	0.52	0.38	8.42	-6.08	14.50	57.38	3.31	45.49	-9.55	10.30	19.85
7	0.52	0.21	7.45	-6.72	14.17	54.24	3.02	47.19	-8.85	9.28	18.13
10	0.52	-0.08	4.65	-5.08	9.73	51.79	2.50	51.23	-7.57	7.41	14.98
15	0.52	-0.36	2.98	-3.71	6.69	60.78	1.88	57.55	-6.00	5.28	11.29
20	0.52	-0.43	1.32	-3.04	4.36	56.52	1.44	61.83	-4.75	3.89	8.64
25	0.52	-0.41	1.16	-2.31	3.48	48.78	1.15	64.05	-3.85	3.03	6.88
30	0.52	-0.31	1.31	-1.75	3.07	36.11	0.96	62.70	-3.20	2.58	5.78
40	0.52	-0.36	1.04	-1.21	2.25	26.92	0.73	68.96	-2.54	1.82	4.37
50	0.52	-0.41	0.04	-0.87	0.91	6.25	0.26	94.07	-1.20	0.38	1.58

same period the real riskless rate was 3.73 percent. Since the depression era real interest rates reached a monthly high of 13.9 percent (annualized) in March 1982.

Although Treasury bill rates and inflation rates have been closely correlated over the period from 1926 to 1990, in some periods real rates of return have been substantially negative or substantially positive. Since nominal interest rates are never negative, real rates of return will always be significantly high in periods of deflation. The exceptionally high real rates of return experienced in the period from 1981 to 1990 may be attributable to exceptionally high premiums for the uncertainty of inflation after the unprecedented rise in inflation in the late 1970s.

Conclusions and Implications

Table 6-9 summarizes the relationships between holding periods and min-max ranges of annualized compound rates of return for the various asset categories discussed above. Figure 6-7 graphically shows real min-max ranges for holding periods ranging from 5 to 50 years.

Table 6-9 presents very useful information. Looking at real inflation-adjusted returns, S&P stocks have historically performed better than what are called less

TABLE 6-9
Summary: Holding-Period Returns

Asset	Years in Holding Period	Annualized Compound Rates of Return %							
		Nominal				Real			
		Simple Average	High	Low	Range	Simple Average	High	Low	Range
S&P Stocks	5	10.0	23.9	−12.5	36.4	6.5	23.5	−9.3	32.9
	10	10.3	20.1	−0.9	21.0	6.5	17.9	−3.8	21.7
	20	10.5	16.9	3.1	13.8	6.6	13.0	0.8	12.2
Small Cap. Stocks	5	13.5	45.9	−27.5	73.4	9.8	47.1	−23.4	70.4
	10	14.4	30.4	−5.7	36.1	10.4	21.5	−3.8	25.3
	20	14.4	21.1	5.7	15.4	10.4	17.2	4.0	13.2
L-T Corp. Bonds	5	5.1	22.4	−2.2	24.6	1.9	18.5	−10.3	28.8
	10	4.6	14.1	1.0	13.1	1.1	9.9	−5.2	15.1
	20	3.9	9.6	1.3	8.2	0.3	5.4	−2.7	8.1
L-T U.S. Gov't Bonds	5	4.4	21.6	−2.1	23.8	1.2	17.7	−10.1	27.8
	10	4.0	13.8	−0.1	13.8	0.4	8.9	−5.4	14.2
	20	3.4	9.0	0.7	8.3	−0.3	4.5	−3.1	7.6
U.S. T-Bills	5	3.6	11.1	0.1	11.0	0.4	8.4	−6.1	14.5
	10	3.5	9.2	0.1	9.0	−0.1	4.7	−5.1	9.7
	20	3.2	7.7	0.4	7.3	−0.4	1.3	−3.0	4.4
Consumer Price Index	5	3.3	10.1	−5.4	15.5	NA	NA	NA	NA
	10	3.6	8.7	−2.6	11.1	NA	NA	NA	NA
	20	3.7	6.4	0.1	6.3	NA	NA	NA	NA

risky long-term corporate and government bonds for investment horizons (holding periods) as short as 5 years. Although the min-max range for S&P stocks is larger than the min-max ranges for these "safer" investments, the worst 5-year performance for S&P stocks (−0.3 percent annual compound rate of return) over the period 1926 to 1986 was still slightly better than the worst performance for long-term corporate and government bonds (−0.4 percent and −0.2 percent, respectively). At the same time, the average performance and the best performance for S&P stocks were vastly better than for either long-term corporate or government bonds. In fact, in terms of downside risk (worst 5-year period), T-bills did only slightly better than S&P stocks (−0.2 percent for T-bills versus −0.3 percent for S&P stocks).

For 10-year investment horizons or longer, S&P stocks have dominated corporate and government bonds and T-bills in real inflation-adjusted terms. In fact, in real inflation-adjusted terms small capitalization stocks have dominated S&P stocks and all other investment categories for 10-year investment horizons or longer.

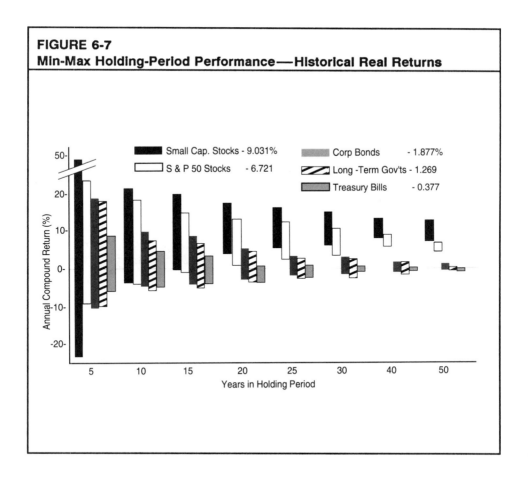

FIGURE 6-7
Min-Max Holding-Period Performance—Historical Real Returns

The fact that the worst performance for a given holding period over the entire 1926 to 1990 period for S&P stocks or small stocks was better than the worst performance for the other investment categories does not mean that S&P stocks or small stocks outperformed the other categories in each period. For example, in the 10-year period between 1969 and 1978 the real compound annual return on small stocks was −0.144 percent as compared with only −0.488 percent for long-term government bonds.

The most important conclusion to be drawn from these analyses is that the actual risk—in the most important sense of downside performance— associated with what are considered the riskier investments (S&P stocks or small stocks) may be less than that associated with the "safer" investments (corporate and government bonds and T-bills) when the investment planning horizon is longer term. Investors looking to fund their Keoghs or IRAs or to otherwise invest for retirement or long-term accumulation objectives and who have at least a 10-year investment horizon will almost certainly be better off investing in stocks than in bonds or money market investments. These analyses further suggest that variable life insurance or variable deferred annuities invested in equity portfolios should be considered by many healthy people with longer-term accumulation and protection objectives. Although yearly returns will vary much more widely for stocks than for bonds or money-market instruments, the up years should more than offset the down years. The investor should expect superior overall returns with very little risk that the stock investment will underperform a longer-term bond investment.

For shorter-term objectives, such as education funding for a child who will attend college in the next 5 years, bonds or money market instruments present much less risk than stocks. Also all long-term investment goals ultimately become short-term goals as the target date approaches. Investors who invested in stocks for their long-term goals but who are unwilling to bear the additional risk of stock investments for short-term goals should typically begin to shift assets from stocks to bonds and money market instruments within 5 years of their target. By carefully choosing when they shift the investments they can essentially "lock in" the almost certainly higher returns earned on stocks over the major part of the accumulation period and reduce the risk of major losses in the years the funds are needed.[4]

NOTES

1. The expected return of 7.5 percent is calculated as follows: There is a 50 percent probability of a 25 percent return; that is, 0.5 x 25% = 12.5%. There is a 50 percent chance of −10 percent return (loss); that is, 0.5 x (−10)% = −5%. Adding the two, 12.5 + (−5) = 7.5, or 7.5 percent return, on the average.

2. In some short periods Treasury bills have given investors higher returns than alternative investments. However, when comparing Treasury bills with alternative longer-term investments such as stocks or bonds we are actually comparing a sequence of Treasury-bill investments over a longer holding period. Although for short periods Treasury bills may have

higher returns, when we average Treasury-bill returns over longer periods, returns to a sequence of Treasury-bill investments are generally less than returns to longer-term bond or stock investments.

3. Data for these analyses come from the *SBBI/PC* Software package, Ibbotson Associates, Inc., 8 South Michigan Avenue, Chicago, Illinois 60603 (1991).

4. For more information regarding risk, return, investment holding periods, and other aspects of investment and financial planning refer to *The Tools and Techniques of Financial Planning,* 4th edition, Stephan R. Leimberg, et al. The National Underwriter Company, 420 East 4th Street, Cincinnati, OH 45202.

7

Investing—Part II

Chapter Outline

As shown in the previous chapter, investment analysis involves many complex and quantitative concepts. A significant aspect of portfolio management is making sure that the investments are appropriate for the investor. This chapter begins with a discussion of the investor and continues with a discussion of the investment process.

The first section reviews critical concepts of the investor's risk tolerance—the relative willingness to incur investment risk in pursuit of return. The second section discusses life-cycle investing, which holds that clients in different phases of life usually have different investment objectives and risk-taking capacity, especially in regard to the retirement portfolio.

With a solid understanding of risk tolerance and life-cycle investing, practitioners can pursue building and managing the retirement portfolio—the topic of the third section of this chapter. The final section addresses financial decisions at retirement, concentrating on the little-used variable life annuity.

RISK TOLERANCE CONSIDERATIONS

Risk tolerance has always been a central concept in the financial planning process. Although there are many mathematical models of risk tolerance in the academic literature of the field, many financial services practitioners have assumed that, for most practical purposes, determining a client's propensity toward risk is an easy task. Many have simply asked the client a question like, "On a scale of 1 to 10, with 10 being the greatest inclination toward risk taking, where would you place yourself?" Or, even more simply, "Are you risk tolerant?" Until recently, practitioners saw little need to explore the complexity of these questions.

People are often not fully aware of their true level of risk tolerance or of the factors that influence their perception of the riskiness of a situation. When a person's self-ascribed level of risk tolerance is compared to his or her actual behavior, quite often it becomes clear that the risk-taking propensity is overstated. One major reason for this overstatement is that our culture considers risk taking to be a valued characteristic. Since most people want to present themselves in the best possible light to others by emphasizing strong points and downplaying faults, they often attempt to enhance their status by claiming that they possess such a valued characteristic—few people think of themselves as less willing to take risks than their peers. Psychologists refer to this tendency to overstate the degree to which one has a favorable personality trait as *inflation bias* or *social desirability bias*. Because the term "risk-averse" is emotionally laden, some authorities recommend that instead, words and phrases such as "conservative" or "interested in asset preservation" be used to avoid offending a person with low proclivity for risk taking.

Financial services professionals, especially those involved in retirement planning, are becoming increasingly aware of the need to understand the concept of risk tolerance. This heightened awareness can be attributed to several related factors, including (1) a growing sophistication and professionalism within the financial planning industry, (2) practitioners' desire to help clients better understand their risk-taking propensity in order to develop "comfortable" investment portfolios for them, (3) various regulatory mandates that require financial services professionals to "know the client," and (4) the litigious nature of our society, which makes it important to be able to prove that due diligence was exercised regarding the element of risk employed in relation to the client's risk-taking character.

Furthermore, continuing research on risk tolerance has refined our under-standing of the concept. Many of the early mathematical models of risk tolerance were based on the premise that a person always acts rationally in financial matters. It has become increasingly obvious over the years, however, that this premise is incorrect—at best, we act within a given boundary of rationality. Researchers in various fields have identified a number of situations in which irrational behavior is likely to occur. Here are a few examples: (1) Based on their long run performance, initial public offerings of common stock are overpriced. (2) Most investors assign too much importance to recent information when revising their estimates about the future. (3) Investors often exhibit "herd" mentality. Earlier risk-tolerance models are being revised to account for these findings.

The following sections briefly summarize some of the major scientific findings about risk tolerance and indicate the implications of these results. Increased awareness of these factors and their implications allows the practitioner to understand and serve his or her clients, better benefiting both the client and the practitioner.

Personal Definitions of Risk

The definition of "risk" a client may have in mind does not necessarily fit the formal definition of risk as volatility. Personal definitions of risk usually focus on how much will be potentially lost or how much will be potentially gained.

Is Risk Viewed as a Good Thing or a Bad Thing?

The term *risk* can carry neutral, positive, or negative connotations. While some people relate risk to *uncertainty* (which has a neutral connotation), in most people's minds, the word *risk* is associated with negatives such as *danger* or *possible loss*. The term *risk* may also connote positives such as *challenge, opportunity,* or *thrill,* but only a minority of clients will associate risk with these terms. In addition to varying interpretations and varying personal definitions of *risk,* the extent to which people perceive the riskiness of a situation and their willingness to accept a risk can vary depending upon the individual and the situation.

Perceived Risk and Purchasing Behavior

Every purchase, including that of investment products, gives rise to concern about whether the wrong choice is being made. The greater the perceived risk in a purchase, the more the client will try to reduce this concern. Consequently the greater the risk

- the more likely that people will buy products or services with which they (and their peers) are familiar and from sources that have a high recognition factor (brand loyalty)
- the more likely that buyers will seek information about the product before reaching a decision to buy (public relations and advertising have more impact)
- the less likely people will be to make a purchase without prolonged deliberation (no impulse purchasing)
- the more likely that after making the purchase people will try to reduce the attractiveness of the unselected alternatives in their own minds by

searching for information that supports their choice. Research suggests that people are more likely to agree with information that supports the selection than with information that fails to support it (thus advertising to a past purchaser may reduce concern about a purchase)

Types of Risk Taking

When discussing risk taking, it is necessary to realize that a client can be risk-taking in one situation, yet risk-averse in another. Upon analysis, it is evident that there are some systematic reasons underlying this inconsistent behavior. The section that follows will consider this issue in more detail.

Is Risk-Taking Propensity Situation Specific or a General Personality Trait?

Psychologists are still debating the question of whether most people's pattern of risk taking is consistent in all aspects of their lives or whether their degree of risk tolerance is dependent upon the nature of any given situation. Although some evidence suggests that individuals do have a slight predisposition to act consistently in either a risk-taking or risk-averse manner in a variety of situations, this predisposition is very strong primarily for persons with the personality type known to psychologists as the *thrill seeker*. In general, a person's risk-taking behavior will be more constant the more similar two risk-taking situations are.

Research has shown that there are essentially four major categories of life situations that involve risk taking:

- *monetary:* situations that involve investments, gambling, job changes, and so on
- *physical:* situations such as mountain climbing or skydiving that could result in bodily harm
- *social:* situations that could lead to loss of self-esteem or of another's respect. For example, "call reluctance" comes from the unwillingness to take a social risk.
- *ethical:* situations that involve the prospect of compromising society's or one's own moral or religious standards. For example, insider trading could be a violation of both personal and societal standards.

There is greater consistency in risk-taking behavior *within* each of these four categories than *across* them. For example, knowing that someone is a risk taker in a certain physical activity provides an idea about how the individual will feel about other situations that involve potential bodily harm. A person who scuba dives is likely to be willing to try skiing. However, knowing that a person scuba dives gives fewer clues about whether the person will be willing to invest in a financially risky venture. The latter is better determined through a knowledge of the person's typical behavior in other monetary risk-taking situations. Thus a financial consultant who mails a promotion for an "aggressive" mutual fund to a sky divers' club should not be surprised if the responses to the ad are not dramatically greater than they would have been if the mailing had been made to the public at large.

Even within the domain of financial risk tolerance, an individual may express inconsistent attitudes and behaviors. For instance, a speaker at the 1993 ICFP retreat related a story about a client who described himself as a "conservative" investor, yet had a considerable investment in a gold mine in French Guinea.

While a clear understanding of a client's risk tolerance in the monetary category should be of primary concern to the financial services professional, there may be some value in looking at the client's risk-taking disposition in the other three categories as well. First, this information could help make clients aware that they do not necessarily have the same propensity for risk in money matters as in physical activities; clients often assume that there is a strong general predisposition to the same level of risk across the four categories. Second, a social risk-taking propensity becomes relevant in a circumstance where a client believes that a poor investment decision could reflect poorly on him or her from a social perspective. Third, a consistently high level of risk taking across the four categories may alert the planner to a client with a thrill-seeking personality type. A discussion of this distinction appears later in this chapter.

Situational Influences on the Willingness to Take Risks

Practitioners must be aware that risk tolerance does not necessarily remain constant throughout life. It can rise or fall with changes in health, family size, job situation, cash flow, or world events. Even something as seemingly insignificant as a person's mood on a given day can affect his or her evaluation of the riskiness of a given situation. Studies have shown that when in a bad mood, a person tends to see greater risk, while a good mood decreases the level of perceived risk. There is a related phenomenon with economic cycles. In times of economic optimism, people tend to have a greater willingness to take risks.

Clients tend to be most risk averse when a decision's outcome affects not only themselves but the people they care about as well. Conversely, clients are somewhat less risk averse if the decision affects only themselves. The most risk-prone decisions are made when *neither* the decision maker nor his or her loved ones would suffer from a poor choice—people take the greatest risks when strangers will bear the consequences of their actions. For example, managers seem to be more likely to take risks with investments of their company's money than with their own funds. Similarly, according to studies of stock market traders, investors using their own money transact fewer trades and require more information before making a transaction.

The *amount* at risk is a primary factor in determining whether a person will be risk taking or risk averse in a given situation. The larger the amount of money at stake (relative to the decision maker's total assets), the greater the risk averseness.

A decision about a risky matter is also influenced by the lag between the time of making the decision and the time the decision reaches fruition. Generally if the consequences of the decision will be known right away, the decision maker will be relatively more risk averse than if the consequences of the decision will be unknown for some time. Often people make very risk-averse decisions because they have a short-term perspective on their financial status; if these people were to adopt a more long-term perspective, such as considering the value of their investments at retirement, they might opt for an investment with greater risk but with a higher potential payoff in the long run. As noted in the previous chapter, another good reason to adopt a long-term perspective is that many investments that are risky in the short run are less risky when the investment horizon is lengthened. Investors willing to accept more short-term risk are rewarded with higher returns and, in the long run, less risk.

Some authorities contend that the dangers of inflation, known as inflation risk, should be as much a concern to preretirees as the risk of loss of capital. An article in the December 1994 issue of *Financial Planning* magazine describes a case in which a trustee was sued for being too conservative. The plan earned an annual return of 7 percent, using a portfolio composed primarily of Treasury bonds. But a bull stock market returned 13 percent during this period, and the trustee was taken to task for not matching this return rate.

If clients learn to adopt a long-term investment perspective, then more aggressive investments become more palatable. One approach is to have the client, over time, reduce the frequency with which he or she examines the performance of the investment. While the natural inclination may be to look at it on a daily basis, perhaps the client can be gradually weaned from this practice so that he or she at first looks at the performance every week. Next, the schedule can be changed so that the client examines the investment's performance only at month end. The next steps would be a quarterly schedule and finally a semi-annual schedule. An annual system of analysis would follow. This way, short-term volatilities in performance would not trigger anxiety. (A formal term for this type of gradual progression toward a desired behavior is "shaping.")

However, the financial adviser needs to realize that studies on fears and phobias show that even after an individual overcomes a fear through training, the fear does not disappear entirely. Thus a risk-averse investor will never completely be free of the fear of losing the principal, because the individual is predisposed to focus on the threat. To keep any type of phobia from recurring, the person must mentally rehearse the fear reduction strategies to keep from relapsing.

A variety of other methods may help a person teach himself or herself to become more risk tolerant. One technique that should lead to greater client risk tolerance is to increase knowledge of financial matters. Research on risk taking shows that individuals who engage in a risky activity report a greater understanding of the risks involved as well as less fear of the risks. Unknown risks loom larger than known risks, and experience with the activity reduces this fear. Although education may not always be a substitute for experience, it is at the very least the next best thing to it. A survey of 401(k) participants sponsored by New York Life Insurance Company and conducted by the Gallup Organization in 1992 found that there is widespread ignorance regarding basic investment concepts.

Increasing the client's sense of control over the investment is another method that can be used to foster greater risk taking. It has been demonstrated in a variety of studies that people have less fear of, and therefore are more risk taking in, activities that they view as being under control. So, for instance, people who fear flying on an airplane may not be afraid to drive to the airport because they view the latter as something they can control. Yet, from an actuarial standpoint, the risks of driving far outweigh the risks of flying on a commercial airline. It's noteworthy that even an illusion of control leads to a reduction of the fear.

The "illusion of control" concept was first identified by a social psychologist who compared depressed individuals and normal persons on their ability to accurately estimate their own chance of success at different tasks. This research-er's expectation was that the depressed persons would estimate their probability of success as lower than normal individuals and, moreover, that their estimates would be less accurate. Her expectations were confirmed on the first point, but not on the second. In other words, while the depressed individuals did rate their chance of success lower than normal individuals, they were actually more accurate in their self-estimates. The normal people tended to be overconfident in their self-appraisals, doing much worse on the tasks than they estimated.

It has been proposed that this illusion of control is necessary for our mental health. We need to have a feeling that we are in charge of our destiny.

Practitioners who give presentations to groups—for example, to married couples—should be aware of a phenomenon known as the *risky shift,* which has been the subject of many psychological studies. When the members of a group are polled individually about a choice between a risky and a safe course of action, most individuals will opt for the safe alternative, but if the group is then allowed to discuss the issues to reach a consensus, it will most often choose the riskier option.

The risky-shift phenomenon has been observed in almost all situations. In one notable experiment that demonstrated the risky shift in an investment context, finance students taking courses in investments or securities analysis were asked to make investments in products that ranged from high quality (secure, certain returns, no variability in pattern of returns in previous years) to low quality (uncertain returns, with high returns in some years and low returns in other years). Students first made their choices individually and later took part in a group discussion in which they had to reach a consensus on which investments to make. The students tended to favor the safer, high-quality investments when polled individually, while the group favored the riskier, low-quality investments.

There are at least two possible explanations for a shift toward the riskier choice: (1) the risk-tolerant members of the group are more influential and convince the less risk-prone members to take risks they otherwise might not, and (2) responsibility for the consequence of a risky course of action can be diffused among the members of the group. The practitioner should recognize that after a group consensus decision of this type, some portion of the group may be unhappy if they have been persuaded to select an option that they might not have selected otherwise.

Attributes of Risk Takers

Research has been conducted to identify the demographics and personality characteristics associated with individuals who are risk averse or risk seeking. Some characteristics do seem to consistently differentiate between various levels of risk taking, as the discussion below will show.

Demographic Characteristics and Risk Tolerance

Most people are risk averse in most situations most of the time. Risk aversiveness increases with age and is more common among retired individuals, the oldest child in a family, and public sector employees.

The issue of sex differences in risk tolerance has been researched extensively. Early studies on this topic usually have found that women are more likely to exhibit greater levels of risk aversion than men. More recent investigations of this issue have either found smaller differences than before or even no differences. Because some studies have failed to reveal a sex difference in risk taking, it has been suggested that the notion of women having lower risk-taking proclivities than their male counterparts is a myth. It is probably better to conclude that women's risk tolerance is undergoing a radical transformation due to their changing role in society, and that they are more risk tolerant than in the past.

A very comprehensive analysis of women's attitudes toward financial matters was recently completed by the National Center for Women and Retirement Research Center in conjunction with the *Working Woman* magazine, which published the results in its February 1995 issue. It was found that the greatest obstacles to women's financial success were their fear of failure and fear of the unknown. More than half of the women delayed making financial decisions for these reasons. Even when they made a decision, close to 60 percent indicated that they second-guessed their choice.

Men tend to blame their advisers or luck for bad investment decisions, whereas women are more likely to blame themselves, according to one psychologist quoted in the article. Part of this fear of putting money into risky investments is the belief that if the investments perform poorly, it will be difficult to replace the lost funds. As the article points out, this fear is based on reality, given that women's earnings are generally lower than men's.

The study identified personality characteristics that allow women to make good financial decisions: "assertiveness, optimism, an adventurous spirit, and optimistic outlook." These characteristics were found among the women who made retirement planning a priority, set financial goals, and saved and invested on a regular basis. For example, nearly twice as many women who are optimistic set a specific savings goal as women who are pessimists (40 percent compared to 21 percent). This characteristic is related to how long a woman has worked (the longer, the more likely she is to save). Nearly all the women surveyed (94 percent) acknowledged that in order to get above-average profits, one has to take some risk.

Greater-than-average risk taking, in contrast, is found among young people, people who are paid on commission, those with high incomes, the wealthy, those who have liquid assets, those without dependents, and those who are successful in their jobs. Sophistication in business also seems to be associated with greater financial risk taking. Experts have suggested that baby boomers as a generation are greater risk takers than their parents.

The adviser must never rely solely on demographic characteristics as the means for assigning a level of risk tolerance to a given client. Allocation of assets on the basis of a demographic profile, without any further assessment of the client's actual tolerance, is unacceptable. An analysis of demographic factors should serve primarily as a means for developing some hunches about a client, which are to be confirmed or disconfirmed through additional and more direct means of assessment.

Personality and Lifestyle Characteristics of the Risk Taker

A majority of studies on the personality traits of risk takers have been conducted with the assumption that risk taking is a general personality trait rather than a behavior that varies from situation to situation. Therefore the measures of risk taking used in studies have consisted of attitudes toward physical, social, ethical, and monetary risk taking in the *aggregate*. One should exercise caution in utilizing these findings in financial planning since they may apply more to another category of risk taking (particularly physical risk taking) than to monetary risk taking.

The risk taker's profile includes both positive and negative characteristics (note that not *every* characteristic will necessarily be found in every risk taker). The person willing to take risks has been found to be persistent, self-confident, independent, creative, self-accepting, dominant, masculine, aggressive, irresponsible, status-seeking, clever, imaginative, manipulative, outgoing, and opportunistic. Risk taking is also associated with greater job satisfaction, lesser feeling of guilt for wrong-doing, strong leadership ability, strong social presence, inability to accept other people's decisions, little need for an ordered environment, and the ability to handle stress. The risk taker generally has a broad perspective, sees mistakes as setbacks rather than as personal failures, and believes that being unsuccessful today will not necessarily mean being unsuccessful tomorrow. In an ambiguous situation the risk taker will see less uncertainty and will foresee fewer grave consequences from the possibility of making a bad decision. The risk taker prefers people who are risk tolerant to those who are risk averse. Risk takers feel that they are in control of their own destiny.

An analysis of the risk taker's life experiences shows that he or she: (1) smoked, drank, and had sexual intercourse at a young age; (2) took dares, fought frequently, and participated in sports while growing up; (3) learned to drive a car earlier than usual; and (4) enjoys hazardous activities such as motorcycling, hang gliding, scuba diving, skateboarding, skydiving, and car racing. Interestingly, the risk taker does not consider these activities to be as dangerous as most people do. There is evidence to show, for example, that neither investment speculators nor skydivers consider their behavior to be as hazardous as most people do.

Risk takers are highly represented in dangerous jobs (for example, as police officers and fire fighters), though any jobs that require independent decisions will appeal to risk takers. Risk takers place more emphasis on merit than on seniority in job promotions and, in comparison to more cautious colleagues, risk-taking managers rise more rapidly through the corporate ranks. Risk takers require less time to make a major decision and do so with less information, though evidence suggests that they process information more carefully and accurately.

The risk taker tends to complete timed tests very quickly, attempting to compensate for the greater number of mistakes by answering more questions. When taking tests like the Scholastic Aptitude Test (which in years past had a greater penalty for answering a question incorrectly than for not answering), the risk taker is likely to take a chance by guessing.

Variables that fall under the monetary lifestyle category, and therefore relate more specifically to risk taking in financial matters than to risk taking in general, include the following:

- *ratio of low-risk to high-risk investments.* Look at the riskiness of clients' previous investment portfolios, their awareness of the risk, *and* their satisfaction with their portfolios.
- *ratio of liabilities to gross assets (the debt ratio).* It has been suggested that a debt ratio over 23 percent is risk tolerant whereas below 8 percent is risk averse.
- *ratio of liabilities to gross income*
- *ratio of life insurance to annual salary*
- *number of voluntary job changes relative to number of years of work experience.* This is particularly important if one job was terminated before a replacement was found, or if the job was a promotion involving relocation. A recent Roper poll found that job security is the top priority for most workers. Faced with a choice between greater job security with a modest pay increase and greater pay but lower job security, 83 percent would take the former.
- *length of tenure in present position.* It has been observed that the longer an employee remains in one position, the less likely it is that he or she

will advance. Risk takers will change employers when no advancement opportunities appear.

* *percentage of annual salary spent on recreational gambling*

It is now recognized that frequent stock market trading in high-risk investments may be indicative of compulsive gambling. *Smart Money* magazine (January 1995) contains an article titled "All the Wrong Moves" about a 60-year-old lawyer who spent 3 decades trying to outsmart the market. Using easily available credit, such as credit card advances, this gentleman was able to amass a whopping $670,000 in losses. This led to bankruptcy before a social service agency was able to diagnose the compulsive gambling. He laments that not one of the financial advisers he dealt with over the years even suggested that his frequent trading might be a psychological problem.

Dangers in Dealing with the "Thrill Seeker"

As indicated earlier, the thrill seeker is the personality type most likely to *consistently* take risks. Although a distinction is sometimes made between the physical and nonphysical categories of thrill seekers, all thrill seekers are similar in that they abhor routine, both mental and physical. These individuals are always on the lookout for experiences that offer novelty, ambiguity, complexity, and intensity. If a thrill seeker can't find excitement, he or she will create it. In-and-out trading in the stock market, for example, provides many of the same quick thrills as do the use of options, short selling, and margin buying. For the thrill seeker, the uncertainty of an investment decision may hold as much enticement as, if not more than, the anticipated monetary payoff.

How can a financial professional identify the thrill seeker? To a certain extent, the thrill seeker is a caricature of a risk taker, showing many of the same basic traits in a markedly exaggerated form. It is important to realize that not everyone who consistently takes risks is a thrill seeker, although by definition every thrill seeker must be considered a risk taker. There is some research indicating that thrill seekers have a biologically based need for greater-than-normal levels of arousal. In addition to those already mentioned, studies have shown thrill seekers to have the following characteristics:

* They tend to like loud parties.
* They are extroverted and impulsive, and are fast decision makers.
* They often participate in risky sports.
* They like to gamble, especially in games with a quick turnaround like blackjack.
* They tend to associate with unconventional people and to intensely dislike boring people.
* They look for variety in their sex lives, have had more sexual partners and encounters than usual, and have a greater-than-average interest in erotic

and pornographic materials.

- They tend to use recreational drugs, and quite often use a variety of drugs (there is no conclusive evidence to suggest a preference for stimulants over sedatives).
- They often drive recklessly and have a history of speeding tickets and traffic violations.
- They enjoy spicy and sour foods.
- They like to travel.
- They enjoy social drinking.
- They often volunteer for medical or psychological experiments.

Although thrill seekers constitute a relatively small portion of the population, they pose a serious potential threat to the financial consultant. While they may appear to be perfect candidates for risky investments, their very love for uncertainty and their desire for novel, intense, and varied experiences may lead thrill seekers to pursue legal action should an investment go sour. To this type of personality, suing can be a thrilling experience, especially if it has not been tried before. With a thrill seeker as a client, you must take particular care in documenting due diligence.

Need for Achievement versus Need to Avoid Failure

When encountering a new client, a practitioner should look for clues regarding the primary motivation guiding that client's behavior. Psychologists have long been aware that some people are motivated primarily by a need to achieve, whereas others are most strongly influenced by a need to avoid failure.

Persons with a need to achieve like to strive, compete, and win and want to be responsible for their behavior. They tend to set specific goals and to measure their performance against these goals. Conversely individuals with a strong need to avoid failure find disapproval extremely painful and would rather not engage in any activity that could potentially lead to criticism.

These two types of personalities prefer different degrees of risk in activities in which their abilities can be questioned. For example, persons with a high need for achievement prefer tasks with moderate levels of risk. In contrast, those with a high need to avoid failure favor tasks that are either *very* risky or *very* safe, since these extreme levels allow them to avoid the pain of failure; that is, they are likely to succeed with the safe tasks, and failure on the risky tasks can be easily excused as simply due to chance factors beyond anyone's control.

Investors with a strong need to avoid failure are quite likely to experience immense difficulty in cutting losses for fear that doing so would prove them incompetent. They would no longer be able to call a decline in the price of a stock merely a paper loss. When dealing with clients of this type, the term *cutting losses* and similar terms that connote failure should be avoided. Instead, the client should be counseled to "transfer assets" or "move to better opportunities."

A client with a strong need to avoid failure is one for whom you need to set formal upper and lower limits for buying and selling securities. There should be an agreement that the security will be sold if the upper price limit is realized or if the price drops to a certain agreed-upon level.

Risk Perception

The objective level of risk inherent in a situation can be either underestimated or overestimated, depending on how the risk is perceived. Perception does not always equal reality. The section that follows considers the factors that may distort the objective risk.

Looking at Risk Objectively

Logically, the two most important determinants of whether a person will be risk tolerant or risk averse in a given situation should be (1) the odds of winning and losing and (2) the potential payoffs and losses. Much of the time, however, people decide on a gamble by an intuitive "gut feeling." It is possible to evaluate a complicated decision more objectively with a simple formula that requires only multiplication and subtraction skills. To illustrate, suppose you want to determine which of the following two gambles offers you a better bet:

Bet 1: A 25 percent chance (probability) of gaining $8,000 and a 75 percent chance of losing $1,000

Bet 2: A 50 percent chance (probability) of gaining $6,000 and a 50 percent chance of losing $2,000

To determine the better bet, follow this simple four-step procedure:

Step 1: *Compute the expected value of gain.* Multiply the probability of the gain by the potential monetary reward.

Step 2: *Compute the expected value of loss.* Multiply the probability of the loss by the potential monetary loss.

Step 3: *Compute the net expected value of the gamble.* Subtract the expected value of the loss (result of step 2) from the expected value of the gain (result of step 1).

Once you have calculated these values, you can go on to step 4.

Step 4: *Compare the overall values of the two gambles.* Compare the results of step 3 and take the risk that has the highest value.

Plugging in the numbers from the example generates an expected value of bet 1 is as follows:

Gain: .25 (probability of gain) x $8,000 (amount of reward)   = $2,000
Loss: .75 (probability of loss) x $1,000 (amount of loss)   = $ 750

Expected Value of bet 1: $1,250

Using the same procedure, the expected value of bet 2 is as follows:

Gain: .50 (probability of gain) x $6,000 (amount of reward)   = $3,000
Loss: .50 (probability of loss) x $2,000 (amount of loss)   = $1,000

Expected Value of bet 2: $2,000

When the expected values of bet 1 and bet 2 are compared, it can be seen that bet 2 has a higher net expected value. Based on that one objective factor, bet 2 is the better choice. However, a number of studies have demonstrated that not everyone looks at the net expected value (or "bottom line") when making a decision subjectively. Some people minimize the *expected loss* (de-emphasizing the expected gain), while others do the reverse.

Cautiousness When Winning and Adventurousness When Losing

Many conventional financial models contain the underlying assumption that most people are uniformly risk averse in all kinds of financial decisions. This assumption is being challenged because the probability distributions in most studies include only sets of potential gains. In real life most investments also include the possibility of loss. For example, many studies include bets of the following type, in which a choice must be made between a certain event offering a relatively low payoff and one offering the probability, albeit small, of a relatively greater payoff:

Choice 1: a certain gain of $1,000
Choice 2: a 30 percent chance of gaining $4,000

The expected value of choice 1 is $1,000 (1 x $1,000 = $1,000), while the expected value of choice 2 is a slightly larger amount, $1,200 (.30 x $4,000 = $1,200). Despite the higher expected value of choice 2, most people are risk averse in a gamble that pits a sure gain against a probable gain that has a theoretically more attractive expected value. That is, most people would select choice 1. Those people who prefer to take the choice with the low odds (choice 2) are considered risk tolerant for this particular gamble.

Let us assume that we now present the same group of people with other probability and payoff figures. As the probable gain of the gamble increases in expected value, more and more people will be willing to play it over the certain gain. The point at which people are willing to take a chance and go for the bet with the uncertain outcome differs from individual to individual. At some point, almost everyone will go for the gamble (for example, the choice between a certain payoff of $1,000 and a 30 percent chance of winning $4 million).

In the example above, the two possibilities (winning $1,000 or $4,000) were both gains. But what happens when people are presented with the choice between two losses, one of which is a small but certain loss and the other of which is a gamble where the individuals will either suffer a greater loss or lose nothing? For example, consider the following two choices:

Choice 1: a certain loss of $1,000
Choice 2: a 30 percent chance of losing $4,000 (and therefore a 70 percent chance of losing nothing)

Even though the expected value of the loss in choice 2 is greater (.30 x $4,000 = $1,200), most people are inclined to take the 70 percent chance that they will lose nothing rather than experience the smaller but definite loss of $1,000. But, as in the last example, at some point the potential loss will be so large that most people will take the certain loss of the smaller amount.

The implications that can be drawn from studies of this nature are that (1) most people are risk averse when faced with a choice between gains, but (2) they are risk tolerant in situations in which the choice is between one or more losses—that is, people do not find it easy to cut their losses. However, if a loss could result in financial ruin, people are usually risk averse. Also, the risk taking involved in a choice between two or more unpleasant events is more extreme than the risk aversion experienced in a choice between two or more pleasant events.

These laboratory-type findings have received support from observations of betting patterns at a race track. These observations show that a person losing at the track tends to place large bets and bet on long shots in an attempt to hit it big to recoup the day's losses. Conversely if a person is ahead, the bets are more in line with that individual's characteristic risk tolerance. In other words, when losing, a client is likely to make substantial changes in risk preferences, but when winning, risk taking usually follows expected patterns.

The Thrill of Victory versus the Agony of Defeat

Suppose that you made a successful investment that produced a return of $2,000. Provided that this return was better than expected, it will make you happy to some degree. Of course, if you lost $2,000 on this same type of investment, you would be somewhat unhappy. Do winning and losing the same amount produce the same intensity of emotional reaction? Research findings suggest that for most people the answer is no. The loss of $2,000 produces a higher degree of displeasure than the gain of $2,000 produces pleasure. Do not be surprised if clients are more upset with you about losses than pleased with you about equivalent gains.

The Importance of How an Issue Is Framed

It was noted earlier that people are more likely to be risk averse in a choice between two or more possible gains and more risk taking in a choice between two or more possible losses. Frequently, however, it is possible to describe something in terms of *either* gains or losses, just as it is possible to describe a glass as either half empty or half full. What happens under these circumstances? The following is from a recent experiment (R. Hogarth. *Judgment and Choice: The Psychology of Decisions.* 1987. John Wiley & Sons, 605 Third Ave., New York, NY 10158. Phone (212) 850-6000) that may help answer this question.

In this experiment, each subject was presented with one of the following two scenarios.

Scenario 1: Imagine you have just learned that the sole supplier of a crucial component is going to raise prices, and that the price increase is expected to cost your company $6 million. Two alternative plans have been formulated to counter the effect of the price increase. The anticipated consequences of these plans are as follows: (1) If plan A is adopted, the company will save $2 million; and (2) if plan B is adopted, there is a 33.33 percent probability that the company will save $6 million, and a 66.66 percent probability that it will save nothing.

Question: Do you favor plan A or plan B?

Scenario 2: Imagine that you have just learned that the sole supplier of a crucial component is going to raise prices and that the price increase is expected to cost your company $6 million. Two alternative plans have been formulated to counter the effect of the price increase. The anticipated consequences of these plans are as follows: (1) If plan C is adopted, the company will lose $4 million; and (2) if plan D is adopted, there is a 33.33 percent probability that the company will have no loss, and a 66.66 percent probability that the company will lose $6 million.

Question: Do you favor plan C or plan D?

If you read the two scenarios carefully, you will see that they are identical except that in scenario 1 the consequences are worded in terms of how much will be *saved,* whereas in scenario 2 the consequences are expressed in terms of how much will be *lost.* Theoretically the same proportion of people should pick plan A as plan C, and the same proportion should pick plan B as plan D. This was not the case, however. Most people (75 percent) picked choice A in scenario 1, and most (80 percent) selected choice D in scenario 2. In fact, most people responded oppositely in the two problems: the majority went for the risk-averse choice when the scenario was given in terms of *gains* or *savings* and for the risk-taking choice when the scenario was stated in terms of *losses*.

The lesson is that you must frame questions to clients with extreme care. The answers provided by clients could be significantly different depending on how the facts are couched in the question. It is suggested that you present questions both in terms of gains and losses to help the client understand the risk from both perspectives.

The "Sure Thing" Principle

It has been repeatedly observed that when making decisions, people tend to place too much emphasis on selecting a choice with an outcome that is certain, and too little on choices that have outcomes with moderate or high probability. For example, when offered a 100 percent chance of winning $4,000 and a 90 percent chance of winning $5,000, most people will take the $4,000 sure thing despite the fact that the expected value of the second choice is $500 greater (.9 x $5,000 = $4,500). Even a probability difference as small as 99 percent versus 100 percent seems to be significant in many people's minds. While this sort of decision is easier to understand when the choices are of the one-shot or once-in-a-lifetime variety, such behavior also occurs in situations in which the individual is presented with a continuous series of choices. There is no doubt that in the long run, a person profits more from choosing an alternative with a higher expected value, even if the outcome is uncertain. Unfortunately many clients may not consider choices in terms of their long-term outcomes.

Understanding the sure thing principle helps the adviser present concepts in terms that are most likely to encourage action by the client. For example, consider that an insurance policy that offers coverage against a peril (such as fire) can be viewed as (1) *full protection* against that specific risk or (2) a *reduction* in the overall probability of property loss. From a psychological standpoint, there is an advantage to describing this insurance in terms of the former. This fact is based on the results of a number of studies that show that a disproportionately high value is placed on the complete elimination of a risk relative to the value placed on the reduction of risk.

Preference Reversals

Which of the following two bets would most people favor?

Choice 1:   a high probability of winning a relatively small amount of money (for example, a 90 percent chance of winning $5)

Choice 2:   a low probability of winning a moderate amount of money (for example, a 9 percent chance of winning $50)

Both bets have the same expected value (both .9 x $5 and .09 x $50 equal $4.50), but the first has a much higher probability of paying off, while the second has a much larger potential payoff.

The choice most people will make depends on whether they are asked to (1) identify which of the two bets they would play, or (2) identify the amount of money they would be willing to pay for the bet. Most people would rather play the bet with the higher probability of winning a small amount, but when a cash equivalent is assigned to the two bets, most people tend to reverse their preference—they assign the higher price to the bet with the low probability of winning a moderate amount. For example, if Amy is asked to name the price at which she would sell someone else the lottery ticket in her pocket for each of these two bets, she tends to put a higher price on choice 2, the choice with a low probability of winning a moderate amount of money.

What is the source of this bias? In selecting a bet, the center of one's attention is the probability of a win, but when pricing a bet, one focuses on the potential payoff. Evidence suggests that people tend to *overprice* the low-probability bet.

How does this relate to investment decisions for retirement? Investment decisions can be framed as either *direct choices* (should I buy stock A or stock B?) or *pricing* (at what price should I buy stock A?). The answers to these two questions may differ.

Mental Accounts

A growing body of evidence indicates that people may not always judge the value of gains and losses by the standard of absolute monetary value. Simply put, in deciding whether or not it is worth it to do something, people use *relative* rather than absolute standards. Consider a scenario presented by D. Kahneman and A. Tversky in 1984 (D. Kahneman and A. Tversky. "Choices, Values, and Frames." *American Psychologist,* 1984, vol. 39, pp. 341—350). In the scenario, a person goes to a store to buy a $125 jacket and a $15 calculator. The store clerk informs the customer that a branch store 20 minutes away has the calculator on sale for $10. How many people do you think would be willing to go to the branch store to save the $5? The answer is 68 percent of those polled.

Now let us change the prices in the scenario so that the $5 difference is in the price of the jacket ($120 at the branch store and $125 at the main store). How many people would take the extra drive to save $5 on the jacket? According to the results of the study, only 29 percent would be willing to go to the branch store under these circumstances.

The moral of the story? An amount of money to be lost or gained will not be valued in isolation. The extent to which the loss or gain will please or displease will be judged relative to a subjective standard. For example, the appreciation of one's stock may be evaluated relative to how another stock is doing or relative to how one's friend or neighbor has fared in the stock market.

Our mental accounting system also makes it more difficult to (1) make a decision to sell a particular investment than to buy it, and (2) abandon a particular investment decision than to create one. Consequently it is very easy for people to continue in poor investments despite the "obvious" availability of better alternatives.

Words That Communicate the Certainty of Success and Failure

It would be nice if financial services professionals could always communicate the certainty of success of a given investment strategy in terms of numbers, such as, "I'm 68 percent certain that this investment strategy will produce a yield of 20 percent." Instead, practitioners usually have to communicate their level of confidence in less exact language. What words indicate low certainty and what words indicate high certainty? A study reported by P.G. Moore in 1977 offers some answers to this question (P.G. Moore. "The Manager Struggles with Uncertainty." *Journal of the Royal Statistical Society, Series A (General)*, 1977, vol. 140, pp. 129–148). The subjects in this study were a group of managers who were asked to rank the order of frequently used terms from *most certain* (a rank of 1) to *least certain* (a rank of 10). The terms ranked were: doubtful, expected, hoped for, likely, not certain, not unreasonable that, possible, probable, quite certain, and likely.

In table 7-1 these words are listed in terms of the average rank assigned to them by the subjects. This information provides some idea about how each expression will be understood by the average client. Remember, however, that "average" is an abstraction and does not describe everybody: the *range* column in the table indicates that the ranks assigned to these expressions were far from unanimous. For example, take a look at both the average and range for *probable*. On average, *probable* was interpreted as the fourth most certain word on the list, but the range data indicate that some people considered it to convey a large degree of certainty and ranked it second, while others thought it conveyed a large degree of uncertainty and ranked it ninth. The lesson here is clear—make certain that your understanding of the words you use to express a probability statement is the same as that of your clients!

Research exists to suggest that even presenting numbers to indicate the degree of risk is not infallible. There are different formats to present the same numbers, and the format may influence how the information is interpreted. For example, in one study, the chance of experiencing one disabling injury in a car while driving without a seatbelt was presented as either (a) .00001 for each trip or (b) .33 over 50 years of driving. The two are mathematically equivalent, yet more people indicated that they would wear a seatbelt when the chance of injury was described as .33. The reason for this effect is that people have very poor comprehension of the significance of low probabilities. Subjectively, they either dismiss the significance of low probabilities or inflate it to a level that is more familiar.

TABLE 7-1 Differences in Uncertainty Expressions		
Average Rank	Range	Expression
1.1	1–3	Quite certain
3.0	1–4	Expected
3.9	2–7	Likely
4.3	2–9	Probable
4.7	3–7	Not unreasonable that
6.1	3–9	Possible
7.2	3–10	Hoped for
7.8	3–10	Not certain
8.6	7–10	Doubtful
8.8	3–10	Unlikely

Use Care in Generalizing

This section provided an overview of research on risk tolerance. Through a combination of established facts and the latest information on this complex and dynamic construct, you may be able to identify some of the situations that increase or decrease a person's level of risk tolerance and some of the personality and demographic characteristics that relate to an above-average or below-average risk-taking propensity.

The information in this section should help bridge the gap between research and practice, allowing financial services professionals to be more sensitive to client needs. However, do not forget that these findings relate to group differences that are seldom absolute: what applies to the group as a whole does not apply to each member of that group. This point is especially important considering that the financial services professional deals with people on an *individual* basis. For example, although on the average men are more risk tolerant than women, keep in mind that this generalization may not apply to the man or woman you will be doing a financial plan for tomorrow.

LIFE-CYCLE INVESTING

Life-cycle investing (LCI) is the process of tailoring the investment portfolio to fit the client's phase in the life cycle. LCI also prescribes adjusting the investment portfolio to meet changes in objectives as the client passes through the phases.

Usually LCI involves reducing risk and emphasizing income as the individual grows older. However, LCI does not stress age differences to the exclusion of other factors, such as wealth and risk tolerance. Rather, LCI provides a framework within which the planner can integrate those factors.

Reasons for the Emerging Emphasis on LCI

Although life-cycle investing is an old concept, there are many reasons for the increased emphasis on it.

1. *More knowledgeable population.* With the proliferation of journalistic coverage of business topics, people are more informed than ever of investment issues. Armed with more information, they are not afraid to ask questions of their financial advisers.

2. *Longer life span.* As the expected life span lengthens, individuals need to plan for longer retirements, which requires the accumulation of more funds. Another aspect of longer lives is the potential need for financing expensive long-term health care.

3. *Greater variety of personal financial goals.* In the post-war period, financial demands have risen. Especially among baby boomers, expectations frequently include vacation homes, extensive travel, and an expensive lifestyle, in addition to college education for children.

4. *Changing personal financial goals, needs, attitudes, and knowledge.* As aging occurs, different goals gain or diminish in importance, and we experience changes in attitude toward the need to accumulate. With greater exposure to investment information, people become more knowledgeable and therefore desire a greater variety of investment techniques. Even the baby boomer generation is changing focus from instant gratification to saving for education and retirement.

5. *Changing potential to save/invest.* At different periods in the life cycle people have more funds available for investment (for example, after completion of children's education expenses). Many people experience higher real incomes, especially those in two-income families.

6. *Increased variety, complexity, and risks of investment instruments.* New investment products appear on the horizon almost daily, some of which are designed to enhance achievement of either a general or specific goal. A complicating factor is the frequency of tax law changes.

7. *Persistent inflation.* Although it appears that the recurring inflation/deflation sequence has disappeared, the economy is still experiencing a long-term, continuous inflation, albeit at lower levels. The need to accommodate inflation in financial plans is as strong as ever.

8. *Growth of financial planning profession.* As the financial planning profession has grown, practitioners have sought techniques that meet client needs. Clients have become increasingly aware of the importance of LCI as their advisers have introduced them to the concept.

Changes in Emphasis over Time

Figure 7-1 shows graphically the change in emphasis of investment characteristics as people age.

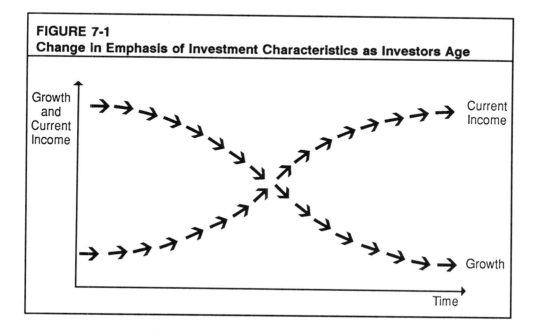

FIGURE 7-1
Change in Emphasis of Investment Characteristics as Investors Age

The Income-Growth Trade-off

As investors age they reduce the emphasis on growth. Viewed another way, they restructure their portfolios to provide more current income as they get older. Note that the investor's emphasis on growth at younger ages is not because of a desire for risk. Rather, the investor seeks a higher total return and must endure more risk to achieve it.

Older individuals typically recognize that they have a reduced opportunity to recover from investment setbacks, and their willingness to take the risk required for growth seems to decrease with age. They can achieve this change in the portfolio's characteristics by either (1) concentrating their annual additions to the portfolio in higher-current-income, lower-risk investments or (2) shifting money realized from maturing or sale of assets into lower-risk, higher-current-income investments.

Factors other than Age

Age is only one of the factors to consider in life-cycle investing. Personal characteristics and portfolio objectives weigh heavily in the LCI approach and will influence the shapes and relative positions of the portfolio growth and current income lines of figure 7-1.

Personal Characteristics

At least five types of personal characteristics or conditions affect the income-growth trade-off in life-cycle investing. These characteristics are

- stability, amount, and sources of income
- family situation
- the client's balance sheet
- the client's investment experience and knowledge
- risk attitudes and propensities

Each of these characteristics is discussed below.

Stability, Amount, and Sources of Income. A client with a fluctuating income, such as a commissioned salesperson, typically should not select a very high-risk portfolio because of the possibility of a prolonged down period of employment income. If more than one spouse is employed, a higher-risk, lower-income portfolio can be selected. Higher income permits greater portfolio risk, since high-income individuals have the potential to save proportionately more than low-income individuals. If an individual has numerous sources of income, such as salary from secure position, dividends, interest, and so on, greater portfolio risk can be taken due to the stability of the income flow.

Family Situation. A young, married investor with children should avoid aggressive, high-portfolio-risk investments until family obligations are met. Those with aged or handicapped dependents who might need long-term care and its attendant costs should opt for a conservative portfolio. It is important, too, to note that marriage plans, plans involving career changes, and so on can affect portfolio risk, and that at any age, larger families may have greater need for current income from the portfolio.

The Client's Balance Sheet. In looking at the client's balance sheet, the planner should be sure to take into account the client's debt relative to his or her net worth and his or her attitudes toward debt. Also keep in mind the obvious fact that individuals with large net worth relative to assets (or debt) are in better a position to own higher-risk portfolios.

The Client's Investment Experience and Knowledge. Recognize that neophytes are more likely to make investment mistakes and hence should initially place only a small portion of their investment money into any one high-risk instrument. Remember, too, that a disastrous investment loss early on can seriously hinder implementing an effective, long-term investment program.

Risk Attitudes and Propensities. Generally investors are risk averse—that is, they will accept high risk only if they will obtain more than proportionate increases in investment return. If individual investors are risk averse, they will opt for safer investments with a higher current income flow, such as CDs, Treasury bills, and bonds, rather than those with greater long-term growth potential and less current income.

Factors for assessing an individual's monetary risk-taking propensities include the following:

- ratio of high risk to low risk investments in portfolio
- ratio of liabilities to net worth (or gross assets)
- ratio of liabilities to gross income
- ratio of life insurance to annual salary
- number of voluntary job changes relative to total work experience
- percent of annual income spent on recreational gambling

Portfolio Objectives

Another set of factors influencing portfolio decisions within the LCI approach relates to the client's portfolio objectives. These factors are

- the client's current income needs
- safety, or capital preservation
- growth
- tax aspects

Each of these factors is discussed below.

Current Income Needs. Is the portfolio objective to generate high current income? If so, the gap between the growth and income lines in figure 7-1 will be narrower prior to retirement and will separate further after retirement. Conversely, a desire for higher current income could lead to taking higher risk.

Capital Preservation. When focusing on capital preservation, a smaller portion of the portfolio is invested in riskier investments, leading to the same result as when trying to generate high current income. Note, too, that the portfolio is more susceptible to the ravages of inflation because concentrating on capital preservation limits growth potential.

Growth. In contrast to other portfolio objectives, this objective is future oriented. With the attendant problems of forecasting, the result is a large portion of portfolio invested in higher-risk securities. When the emphasis is on future growth, current income is not often sought as an objective.

Tax Aspects. Some tax-oriented portfolios, for example, holding investment-grade municipal bonds, are relatively conservative. Alternatively, portfolios with investments that employ leverage and deferral as important elements of their tax strategy tend to have higher risk and lower current income.

Portfolio Design Principles

Several portfolio principles are important in life-cycle investing. These portfolio design concepts are

- a quantitative approach
- diversification
- matching maturities
- the relative importance and deferrability of the objective
- the time frame, or time horizon, of the investment objective
- the relative importance of consistency versus market timing

Each of these aspects is discussed below.

A Quantitative Approach. Portfolio objectives must be set in target dollar amounts in order to enable plans to be set and to provide a basis for evaluation of portfolio performance. The objectives must have time frame for when funds are needed in order to assist in selection. As well, portfolio objectives must be prioritized to determine which ones should receive greater emphasis.

Diversification. For the different types of investment assets, relative emphasis might be different for different investors' objectives, risk attitudes, age, and so on. Within a category of investments, one growth-oriented mutual fund will achieve diversification, in contrast to only *one* growth stock; and a client should purchase several mutual funds to (1) diversify over the inability of one fund to select and prune its portfolio and (2) to protect against the risk that the fund's portfolio manager departs and the fund's performance drastically changes.

Matching Maturities. Through this approach, it is possible to link the maturity date of the instrument with the date on which funds are needed. It also helps avoid a possible forced sale at a disadvantageous (distressed) price.

Relative Importance and Deferrability of the Objective. The greater the importance of the objective to the individual, the greater the emphasis (amount of saving and effort) devoted to its achievement should be. If the objective is not deferrable, the commitment to annual funding for goal achievement should be greater. The less deferrable an objective is, the more cautious the investment strategy should be.

Time Horizon. The shorter the available time frame in which to accumulate the funds, the more critical the plan. The longer the time frame, the greater the latitude in portfolio design. Planners should also advise their clients to make the most of compounding by beginning to save and/or invest as soon as possible, even if only a small amount is available; selecting a risk-return ratio that is consistent with their risk profile; and contributing regularly and, if possible, consistently in order to take advantage of compounding.

Relative Importance of Consistency versus Market Timing. In general, adopting a consistent, logical investment approach is more appropriate than attempting market timing. Many researchers have studied the likely gains from market timing. Most have concluded that while successful market timing can improve performance, the likelihood of success is small. When transaction costs and taxes are considered, the benefits of market timing do not outweigh the disadvantages.

Life-Cycle Periods

There are five distinct periods of life in life-cycle investing. Although some clients will not experience all phases or will spend more or less time in a phase, the vast majority of clients go through the following phases: (1) early career, (2) career development, (3) peak accumulation, (4) preretirement years, and (5) retirement.

The early career phase normally encompasses age 25 (or under) to 35. Often the individual is newly married and has young children, and one or both of the spouses are establishing employment patterns. The client is probably concerned about accumulating funds for a home purchase if he or she has not already done so. As the children grow older, the parents begin to think about saving for college, and many will accumulate funds to start a business. Job-related geographic relocation can put a strain on the family as well as the budget. There is generally little consideration of retirement planning, particularly in the early years of this period.

The career development phase normally encompasses ages 35 to 50 and is often a time of career enhancement, upward mobility, and rapid growth in income from profession or business. The phase usually includes accumulation and expenditure of funds for children's college education. Clients make greater efforts to coordinate employee benefits of the spouses and to integrate employee benefits with investment strategies. Geographic relocation is still a possibility, and the client becomes increasingly concerned about financial independence and retirement income planning. The most successful clients will begin general wealth building beyond their basic objectives and may purchase a second home or travel extensively.

In the peak accumulation phase, the client is usually moving toward maximum earnings and has the greatest opportunity for wealth accumulation. The phase may include accumulating funds for other objectives, but is usually a continuation of retirement income planning, coordination of employee benefits with investment and retirement strategies, and saving for a vacation home or travel. Most clients begin reducing investment risk to emphasize income production for retirement (particularly near the end of this period) and become increasingly concerned about minimizing taxes.

Preretirement years are the 3 to 5 years prior to planned retirement age. This phase often includes winding down both the career and income potential. Clients begin restructuring the portfolio to reduce risk and enhance income. There is further emphasis on tax planning and the evaluation of retirement plan distribution options relative to income needs and tax consequences.

Retirement is the final phase in the cycle. For the successful client, it is a time of enjoyment with a comfortable income and sufficient assets to preserve purchasing power. It may involve a geographical relocation. Many clients become more active socially, and taking up new hobbies and volunteer work is common. Some seek a new career, and many will look for a job (part-time or full-time) that has less stress.

Two additional concerns may be appropriate to any phase, but the timing varies considerably. First, depending on the family situation, the need to provide for long-term health care may become apparent. Second, some clients will need to devote resources to care for parents or a disabled child for a long period of time.

Portfolio Selection in the Phases of the Life Cycle

As already noted, a number factors other than age influence decisions in life-cycle investing. However, many practitioners and clients find it helpful to see guidelines that relate investment choices to the phases in the life cycle.

TABLE 7-2
Investment Allocation Percentages

Life-Cycle Stage	Investment Categories		
	low risk, safe, secure	medium risk, growth type	high risk, high growth
Early career	0% to 30%	60% to 80%	0% to 30%
Career development	10% to 40%	50% to 70%	0% to 20%
Peak accumulation	20% to 50%	40% to 60%	0% to 20%
Preretirement	30% to 80%	20% to 50%	0% to 20%
Retirement	40% to 90%	10% to 50%	0% to 10%

Table 7-2 demonstrates a set of proportions that individuals in different phases of the life cycle might allocate to assets with specific risk-return characteristics.

Where an individual's portfolio allocations should fall within the ranges is dependent on factors mentioned earlier. For example, consider a client who is single, wealthy, debt free, and risk tolerant and who has a high, stable income and extensive knowledge and experience in investments. This person can appropriately select asset categories that maximize growth and de-emphasize risk avoidance.

Conversely, consider a client who has a young family, minimal assets, considerable debt, and an unstable income and who is a risk avoider with little knowledge or experience in investments. This person is likely to take the most conservative path, emphasizing safety and de-emphasizing growth.

BUILDING AND MANAGING THE RETIREMENT PORTFOLIO

Life-cycle investing is a general approach to asset management. It encompasses a multitude of goals, such as education funding, purchase of a business or second home, travel, and retirement funding.

The topic of building and managing an investment portfolio is also very broad, and much of the information depends on the investor's goal. Almost every possible goal has merit; however, this book is concerned with retirement funding, so the following discussion is limited to the building and managing of the retirement portfolio. Many concepts are universal, but it is important to recognize that many are unique to retirement planning.

An Organized Approach

Most individual investors adopt an ad hoc approach to investing. They might read a bit about a possible investment, although they would never read a prospectus. They hear about their friends' successes and attempt to emulate them by investing in the same opportunities, usually after the investment has already experienced its greatest growth.

Unusually high potential returns are especially enticing to most individual investors, but few of these investors are competent to evaluate the risk they are facing. Most people give little thought to how an investment fits into their existing portfolio, much less their investment goals or philosophies—if they have any.

Financial professionals who advise or sell products to individuals cannot take such a haphazard approach to investment management, especially when retirement money is involved. Legal, regulatory, and ethical issues aside, a sloppy strategy is simply unprofessional.

A logical, organized, consistent, and defensible framework for building and managing the retirement portfolio is necessary. Such a framework is delineated below; it includes the following steps: (1) setting goals, (2) gathering and analyzing client data, (3) developing an investment policy, (4) determining asset allocation, (5) specifying industry weightings, (6) selecting companies, and (7) monitoring the portfolio. Most readers will note the similarity between this approach and the six steps in financial planning.

This framework includes some important assumptions. First, it is limited to retirement investments; there is no secondary use for the money. Second, it is directed at individuals rather than at groups. As a comparison, managing a portfolio for a corporate pension plan with 100 plan participants involves additional issues such as actuarial concepts. Third, it is directed at clientele of moderate to substantial means to whom retirement planning is a primary goal. The centi-millionaire usually has minimal concern about retiring comfortably and has a broader set of techniques to accomplish his or her investment goals. Fourth, liquidity is not a major consideration, although many people view borrowing or cashing in retirement accounts as a potential source of liquidity. Fifth, the money is invested in tax-deferred accounts such as IRAs, 401(k)s, and deferred annuities. Sixth, all portfolio income is reinvested in the retirement portfolio.

Steps in Building and Managing the Retirement Portfolio

1. Setting goals
2. Gathering and analyzing client data
3. Developing investment policy
4. Determining asset allocation
5. Specifying industry weightings
6. Selecting companies
7. Monitoring the portfolio

Step 1: Setting Goals

As Laurence J. Peter said in *The Peter Principle*, "If you don't know where you're going, you will probably end up somewhere else." Although goal setting is critical to creating a successful retirement portfolio, few people actually set clearly defined goals. By leading the client through the goal setting exercises, the financial professional not only helps establish reasonable goals, but also helps set a tone for the entire investment management process.

Practitioners should query the client to learn what he or she is trying to accomplish. Usually the response is couched in general terms such as, "Well, we want to have a comfortable standard of living when we retire." At first glance this seems to be a reasonable goal, but a closer evaluation reveals that it is far too vague. When do they want to retire? What is meant by "comfortable"? Do they want to consider inflation?   Do they want to retire on "interest only" or draw down their accumulated portfolio over their expected lives?

Skillful questioning by the practitioner may reveal a more precise goal such as, "We want to retire in 20 years with an aftertax income of $60,000 per year in current dollars, and we want the income to continue as long as we live without depleting the principle."

Note that, while we now have a reasonable financial planning goal, the subject of this section is building and managing the retirement portfolio. We need an investment goal! Going through the second step will allow us to modify the goal to make it useful in investment management.

Step 2: Gathering and Analyzing Client Data

The first aspect of data gathering and analyzing is to identify financial resources. How large is the current portfolio and how large will the future additions to the portfolio be? A more subtle piece of information is how much retirement income will be provided from sources other than the retirement portfolio, such as social security and an employer-sponsored pension or profit-sharing plan. (Chapter 5 describes in detail the process of calculating retirement fund needs.)

The second aspect of data gathering and analysis to identify is any potential constraints. Of primary concern is evaluating the client's risk tolerance, a process described earlier in this chapter. For example, an extremely risk-averse individual may not be willing to utilize equity investments that may be necessary to earn a high enough rate to reach his or her financial goal.

The client's possible liquidation of the retirement portfolio is a critical assumption also. If the client intends to liquidate or "spend down" the portfolio over a specified number of retirement years, he or she will need less money than if the interest-only approach is used. However, spending down the portfolio also means that a smaller estate will be left at death, and it involves higher risk because if the client lives longer than expected he or she could run out of funds.

Another constraint is the individual's phase in the life cycle. For an older client, attaining the goal may not be possible without devoting a higher percentage of the portfolio to risky assets than is usually suggested.

Closely related is the client's relative inflexibility with regard to a retirement date. If the client is adamant about retiring at a particular time—age 65, for example—the management of the portfolio is less flexible because the stock market cycle may not cooperate with the client's plan. Any portfolio decisions in the years immediately before the retirement year will be dominated by the proximity of the retirement year, possibly making the decisions more conservative. A more flexible client might be willing to ride out a valley in the stock market. This could mean postponing retirement or simply postponing any massive liquidation of the portfolio.

If the primary vehicle for retirement saving is a 401(k) plan, the plan may offer investment possibilities that are especially conservative, again inhibiting the client from attaining the needed rate of return.

Knowledge of the constraints will allow the practitioner to make a rough estimate of a rate of return. First, calculate the amount that must be accumulated at retirement to generate the needed income using the procedure in chapter 5.

Second, use the risk profile and other constraints to create portfolio weightings in the major asset categories (stocks, bonds, cash equivalents). Then, using the projected rates of return for those categories, calculate a weighted average projected rate of return. Assume, for example, that the client's risk profile and other factors suggested portfolio allocations of 60 percent in stock, 30 percent in bonds, and 10 percent in cash equivalents. If projected rates of return for stocks, bonds, and cash equivalents were 10 percent, 6 percent, and 4 percent, the projected portfolio return would be as follows:

Asset Category	Rate of Return	Weight	Product
Stock	10%	.60	6.0
Bonds	6%	.30	1.8
Cash equivalents	4%	.10	0.4
	Projected portfolio return		8.2%

Third, apply this rate to both the current total of invested assets and the projected future contributions to determine whether the needed accumulation can be reached. For example, assume that the client currently has invested assets of $200,000 and intends to contribute $10,000 per year and that the procedure in chapter 5 reveals a need for a $1.2 million retirement fund in 20 years. Using the rate of 8.2 percent, $200,000 accumulates to $967,331 and $10,000 per year accumulates to $467,885 for a total of $1,435,216.

Reevaluating the Goal. At this point the original portfolio goal can be revisited. (Recall that the goal was not couched in terms appropriate to portfolio management.) Since the projected retirement accumulation exceeds the required $1.2 million, the client could consider the following four choices among many others.

First, he or she can select a goal of accumulating a larger fund over the 20 years, perhaps the $1,435,216 figure calculated above. This approach would provide a higher level of retirement lifestyle than originally planned. Second, he or she could select a goal of $1.2 million, and lower the annual contribution to $4,973. This makes more money available to support a modest increase in the current lifestyle while still achieving the goal. Third, he or she could set the goal at $1.2 million, but manage the portfolio more conservatively. This would allow the client to reach the goal with a rate of return of only 7.09 percent. (That is, the internal rate of return that equates the $1.2 million terminal value with the

$200,000 current portfolio and the $10,000 per year additions is 7.09 percent.) Since 7.09 percent is less than the 8.2 percent projected return, the client can reduce risk by changing the asset weights as long as the projected rate of return does not fall below 7.09 percent. For example, the following weights produce a projected rate of return of 7.12 percent, which would generate a terminal value of $1,206,849. The client could reduce risk by changing the asset proportions to the following, for example:

Asset Category	Rate of Return	Weight	Product
Stock	10%	.33	3.30
Bonds	6%	.57	3.42
Cash equivalents	4%	.10	0.40
	Projected portfolio return		7.12% >7.09%

In other words, the client could reduce the stock portion from 60 percent of the portfolio to only 33 percent of the portfolio and still exceed the $1.2 million goal.

A fourth alternative is to retire early. However, the calculations would have to include reductions in pension payments and social security as well as a longer retirement period. In other words, $1.2 million will not be enough if the client wants to retire early.

Often, of course, the options are not so pleasant. What should the client do if the projected accumulation is less than the required accumulation? Actually, the options are the mirror image of the prior case.

Assume the same situation as above, except that the client has only $100,000 in invested assets rather than $200,000. The projected accumulation in 20 years is $483,666 for the current portfolio and, again, $467,885 for the $10,000 per year additions, for a total of $951,551.

As before, the client has a multitude of options, but three are very clear. First, the client can set a lower, more reasonable goal, accepting a lower-than-desired lifestyle during retirement. Note that the reduction in the accumulation is almost 20 percent. While this seems very large at first, it actually represents a reduction of only 20 percent of that portion of retirement income that comes from the personal portfolio. It has no effect on the retirement income from a pension or profit sharing-plan or from social security. If, for example, 40 percent of retirement income was to come from personal savings, the reduction in total retirement income would be only 8 percent (20% x 40%).

Second, the client can set the goal at the required accumulation of $1.2 million and invest more money annually to reach the goal. In this case, the contribution would have to increase to $15,310 per year, 53 percent more than planned. As an aside, note that even the $10,000 figure is beyond the maximum employee contribution to a 401(k) plan. So unless the client has control over a qualified plan—as a self-employed person, for example—all the extra annual additions will be in aftertax dollars.

Third, the client can set the goal at $1.2 million but accept more risk to achieve a higher return to meet the goal. In this case, the rate of return would have to be more than 9.76 percent to accumulate $1.2 million. This would require that more than 90 percent of the portfolio be invested in stock under the return assumptions above.

Fourth, the client can make use of principal. Many clients adopt an "interest-only" approach toward retirement income. Since they plan never to spend their principal, they must accumulate a larger fund to generate the necessary cash flow. Clients who are willing to "spend down" principal or to purchase a life annuity at retirement can lower their funding needs significantly.

There is also a fifth important option—delaying retirement. By waiting almost 3 extra years before retiring, the client can attain the $1.2 million mark without additional risk. By that point, the client probably will not need the entire $1.2 million for several reasons. First, the pension income will be higher, reflecting more years of service and probably a higher average income. Second, social security will probably be slightly higher. Third, if the required accumulation was based on a spend-down model, as opposed to an interest-only model, less accumulation will be necessary because the client's older retirement age implies financing fewer years of retirement.

Alternative Actions If Retirement Fund Projection Is Too Low

1. Accept a lower retirement standard of living.
2. Increase annual savings.
3. Seek a higher return by accepting more risk.
4. Make use of principal by a spending down or purchasing a life annuity at retirement.
5. Delay retirement.

Note that the calculations implicitly assume that the rates of return will remain constant, suggesting that the proportions in the investment categories will remain constant also. This belies the life-cycle concept, which suggests that the equity portion will decline over time all the way to (and past) the retirement date. Remember, though, that this process was undertaken to establish a retirement portfolio goal that is reasonable in light of the client's financial wherewithal, risk tolerance, and other constraints; it was not meant to limit flexibility in setting future asset proportions.

Clients frequently mention other goals relating to such topics as education planning or estate creation. Again, these are valid financial planning topics, but they are not retirement portfolio goals. Education funding has a different time horizon and different tax factors, for example. Estate creation can usually be incorporated in the retirement planning goal as an increase in the needed accumulation or as a constraint—the decision to plan for an interest-only approach rather than spending-down.

Recall that, while this is step 2, we have actually gone back through step 1. Although there are five more steps in building and managing the retirement portfolio, the most important part—the foundation—has been laid. Taking the client through this process of stating a goal, restating it in quantifiable portfolio management terms, reevaluating it in light of client information, and then setting a realistic goal is the practitioner's most important service.

Step 3: Developing an Investment Policy

Few practitioners who assist clients in retirement planning recognize the importance of developing an investment policy. To many the task sounds cumbersome, if not esoteric, and appears to be time-consuming overkill.

The truth is that developing an investment policy is easy, and having a policy clarifies the client's understanding of the plan and helps keep him or her on the right track. For the practitioner an investment policy provides a framework for advising the client and explaining the advice. Having a reasonable, client-approved policy—and following the policy—also helps protect the practitioner in the event of misunderstandings or legal action. In short, developing an investment policy is an integral part of a professional approach.

The Investment Policy Statement. There is plenty of latitude in setting a policy statement. In general, a good statement should be brief and put in writing. It should provide enough information to reveal the policy but not enough information to be overly constraining. Points worthy of inclusion in the statement are a portfolio objective, investment characteristics, risk-return objectives, and any other factors the practitioner deems worthy of mention.

The *portfolio objective* differs from the client's accumulation goal, described earlier. The best way to understand portfolio objectives is to review some mutual fund prospectuses. Every prospectus contains a statement of the fund's investment objective, and phrases typically used include:

"seeks maximum capital gains"
"obtain long-term growth of invested capital"
"significant income along with long-term growth"
"current income and capital appreciation"
"seeks current income; capital growth is secondary"
"seeks above-average income and preservation of capital"

A second worthwhile component of a policy statement is that regarding the *investment characteristics* of the major portfolio components. For example, common stocks and/or their underlying companies may be further defined by terms such as *growth-oriented, medium- to large-sized, well-established, small-*

capitalization, emerging, and *dividend-paying.* Bonds may be further defined by terms such as *U.S. government, U.S. agency, high-grade corporate, investment grade,* and *intermediate maturity.*

An indication of the *risk-return trade-off* sought for the portfolio is beneficial, although it should not be quantified. Sometimes the description of the trade-off is very explicit, such as "maximum total return consistent with moderate portfolio volatility." Other descriptions imply the risk-return trade-off. For example, using the word "aggressive" suggests that the portfolio seeks a high rate of return and will incur a high degree of risk. Note that there is always an assumption that risk and return are positively related. It would be inappropriate to state an objective of "maximum possible return and minimum possible risk."

Many practitioners mention other factors in the policy statement, especially if there is a strong commitment to a particular investment philosophy or strategy such as those noted in the following section. For example, if the client is committed to a passive strategy—similar to an index mutual fund—or a strategy of investing only in mutual funds, it is reasonable to include that information. Remember, though, that it is best not to provide too much information in the policy statement.

The following is a typical example of a policy statement:

This tax-deferred portfolio seeks long-term capital appreciation subject to moderate volatility, primarily through investment in common stock of stable but growth-oriented companies.

Retirement Portfolio Management Methods. Managers of retirement portfolios for individuals have a multitude of approaches, strategies, and techniques available to them. These methods are apt to change more frequently than the investment policy statement but, since they reflect the philosophy adopted by the client, they are still somewhat stable.

Practitioners should determine which methods are appropriate for the client and present them to the client for approval. As with the policy statement, the list of methods should be committed to writing. However, most practitioners find it helpful to provide a bit of latitude by stating before the list that "the following methods *may* be used" in the management of the portfolio.

International Diversification. Unlike a sector-type mutual fund, retirement portfolios for individuals should be diversified not only among companies but also among industries. Most managers believe that at least some degree of international diversification is appropriate also. For the vast majority of investors, international diversification is accomplished by purchasing international or global mutual funds rather than individual securities.

Many investors view international investing as a source of returns that are higher than those available in this country and become disillusioned when international stocks underperform domestics. While it is true that there are excellent opportunities in other countries, the major benefit from international investing is diversification. The fact that foreign markets operate in cycles that do not coincide with the U.S. markets means that international investing reduces the variability—the risk—of the portfolio.

Fundamental versus Technical Analysis. Fundamental analysis refers to the process of identifying investments that will have high risk-adjusted returns by evaluating their underlying economic factors. (See "top-down" and "bottom-up" analysis below.) *Technical analysis* refers to the process of identifying underpriced stocks by looking at the stock market itself and especially at the supply and demand for stock. The underlying principle is that stock's value is simply a function of supply and demand for the stock in the marketplace rather factors such as the company's ability to generate earnings and pay dividends. Of special interest to the technical analyst is comparison of the stock's current price and trading volume to historical data for the stock. Individual stock data are also compared to data for the market as a whole. Technical analysts typically use charts, graphs, and regression models of past performance to try to predict future performance.

"Top-down" Analysis. This classic approach to fundamental analysis is a three-step process. First, the analyst looks at aggregate economic and market factors. According to the top-down approach, it is extremely difficult for a stock to increase in value when the economy and market are faltering. However, if the future of the economy and market are bright, the analyst evaluates different market sectors, or industries, to determine which are likely to perform especially well. Finally, the analyst looks at individual companies in the industry to decide which are most likely to provide the best risk-return combination.

"Bottom-up" Analysis. Proponents of bottom-up analysis are not as concerned about economic, market, and industry factors as proponents of top-down analysis are. They believe that there are always undervalued assets, regardless of the economic or industry outlook, and surmise that the real value will eventually be recognized by the market, causing prices to rise. Devotees of this approach are sometimes called *stock pickers*.

Contrarian Investing. Investors who are willing to buck trends are good candidates for *contrarian investment strategies*. These approaches attempt to identify generally accepted views and then do just the opposite. If most people feel that the market is headed down, or if an industry is out of favor, or if a company has performed poorly in recent years, a contrarian would be inclined to invest.

Probably the most widely known indicator for contrarians is odd-lot trading. This tenet holds that unsophisticated small investors trade in odd lots (fewer than

100 shares) and have bad investment timing. If odd-lot buy orders exceed odd-lot sell orders, small investors must believe that the market is headed up. The contrarian infers that since small investors are usually wrong, the market is about to turn down.

Special Situation Analysis. Sometimes an unusual investment opportunity called a *special situation* presents itself. Proponents of this approach believe that some unusual investments offer high potential return with lower-than-commensurate risk because the market is inefficient in evaluating them. For example, companies that are in bankruptcy will be completely avoided by most investors, and many institutional investors are legally forbidden from buying their stock. Investors willing to consider such companies often find that the lack of demand for the stock causes the price to be lower than justifiable by fundamental analysis.

Special situation analysis is primarily the domain of specialized security analysts rather than the generalist retirement planning practitioner. Any portion of the portfolio allocated to this approach should be relatively small and diversified, preferably using mutual funds.

Market Timing. In this approach managers attempt to anticipate major value changes in asset categories — especially common stock — and make major changes in the allocation of the portfolio accordingly. Market timers are proponents of equity investing. However, while the traditional investment credo is "buy low, sell high," market timers follow a "sell high, buy back low" approach.

In the extreme, if the market-timing manager strongly believes that the stock market has reached a peak and will soon drop precipitously, he or she may elect to sell all common stock in the portfolio and purchase money market securities with the proceeds. Of course, while a total sell-off may be possible for small portfolios or for mutual fund investors, it is not realistic for large portfolios.

Although promoters of market timing services and newsletters make convincing arguments on behalf of this approach, academic research indicates that likely gains from market timing are minimal.

There are several problems with market timing. Often the technical indicators that signal market movement in one direction or the other are simply incorrect. In other cases, the indicators are correct on the direction of the movement, but the degree of movement is too small to be profitable.

A subtle problem associated with market timing is its effect on investor psychology. The investor who adopts a buy-and-hold strategy rarely makes a "killing" in the market, but rarely loses his or her shirt. In contrast, market timers are more likely to have larger successes and larger failures. Unfortunately, when investors get burned, their common reaction is to withdraw from the market in favor of less volatile investments. The result is lower long-term returns.

Mutual Fund Investing. The vast majority of individual investment for retirement utilizes mutual funds or variable deferred annuities rather than individual stocks. Most practitioners recommend a family of mutual funds or an annuity product that offers a broad range of risk-return possibilities. These investments offer professional management and instant diversification, even for very small initial contributions.

Increasingly, practitioners are recommending diversification among portfolio managers. The rationale for this approach, which is consistent with the efficient market concept, is that some managers in a particular fund category will perform better during one period, while others will perform better in the next. Using more than one family of funds helps to diversify this "manager risk." One point to consider in this approach is that fund loads are usually lower for larger purchases. If spreading the money around too much causes the client to pay higher loads, this diversification may not be worth the cost.

Passive Investing. Another offshoot of the efficient market concept, passive investing ignores most of the approaches previously mentioned. Essentially, passive investors assume that attaining consistently high risk-adjusted returns is impossible because of the market's efficiency, so they do not even try.

Instead, passive investors usually attempt to duplicate the risk/reward characteristics of a well-known stock indicator series by creating a portfolio that is nearly identical to that implied by the indicator series. For example, the manager may create a portfolio that has the same stocks in the same proportions as the stocks represented in the Standard & Poors 500. Rather than spending money on fundamental or technical analysis, the manager merely maintains the appropriate proportions for each stock in the portfolio by reinvesting dividends appropriately.

Of course, to set up and maintain such a 500-stock, properly proportioned portfolio, the asset base must be rather large. For that reason the passive strategy for an individual investor saving for retirement normally involves an index mutual fund.

Dollar-Cost Averaging. Dollar-cost averaging is actually less a technique than a result. The concept usually involves investing a specified amount monthly into a specific security, mutual fund, or variable annuity regardless of whether the recent trend of the investment has been up or down. If this approach is followed and the current stock price declines, the fixed payments actually buy more shares so that the average purchase price per share for the portfolio declines. For a long-term investor the presumption is that the price will eventually rise, so a lower average purchase price means a greater total profit.

In the following example of the potential effect of dollar-cost averaging, the investor buys $100 of stock in each month, regardless of the stock's price. The average price paid per share is $700 ÷ 22 shares or $31.82. Even though the price in July is the same as it was in January, suggesting no change in value at first glance, the value of the portfolio has actually increased by $400.

Month	Purchase Price	Shares Purchased	Total Shares	Total Invested	Current Value
January	50	2	2	100	100
February	40	2.5	4.5	200	180
March	25	4	8.5	300	212.50
April	20	5	13.5	400	270
May	25	4	17.5	500	437.50
June	40	2.5	20	600	800
July	50	2	22	700	1,100

Retirement portfolios typically use dollar-cost averaging implicitly—especially in 401(k) plans—since regular, stable contributions are made and since individuals usually maintain the investment mix for their contributions. Mutual funds and variable annuities are especially appropriate since purchase of fractional shares is allowed, so the contribution is completely utilized.

Step 4: Determining Asset Allocation

Asset allocation is the process of setting the portfolio proportions for the major asset categories. For most retirement portfolios, the categories are limited to stocks, bonds, and money market instruments, but other categories such as real estate can be included also.

As discussed previously, individual retirement portfolios normally have little need for liquidity and much need for growth. Unless the time horizon until the client begins liquidating the portfolio is short, asset allocation will emphasize stock heavily and money market instruments lightly. The earlier discussion of risk tolerance also implicitly addressed the asset allocation question—those who are less risk tolerant should invest less in stock. After considering the time horizon and risk tolerance aspects, portfolio managers who take an active approach seek more information before making the final asset allocation decision. They frequently use aspects of technical analysis, but fundamental analysis—especially the top-down version—is the primary method. The first stage in the top-down approach is economic analysis.

Economic Analysis. The primary purpose in economic analysis is to identify factors that will influence security markets. Analysts typically forecast quarterly values for the following 2 years and annual values for 3 additional years. Any projections beyond 5 years provide so little reliability that many analysts consider them a waste of effort.

Some of the most commonly used data in the economic analysis step are the following:

- Gross national product (GNP)
- Gross domestic product (GDP)

- Money supply
- Unemployment rate
- Personal and disposable income
- Personal savings rate
- Consumer price index (CPI)
- Producer price index (PPI)
- Department of Commerce's Index of Leading Economic Indicators (See table 7-3)
- Federal Reserve Board Index of Industrial Production
- Corporate profits
- Interest rates
- Construction activity
- Automobile production
- Foreign exchange rates
- Business spending plans

Using the data, the analyst attempts to identify the economy's position in the normal economic cycle. Further economic data analysis, projections of fiscal and monetary policy, and evaluation of the social, political, and international environment help the analyst predict the direction and extent of economic growth or contraction in the foreseeable future.

TABLE 7-3
Index of Leading Economic Indicators

The index of leading economic indicators is used to project the economy's performance 6 months or a year ahead. The index is made up of 11 measurements of economic activity that tend to change direction long before the overall economy does.

- Average work week of production workers in manufacturing
- Average weekly claims for state unemployment insurance
- New orders for consumer goods and materials, adjusted for inflation
- Vendor performance (companies receiving slower deliveries from suppliers)
- Contracts and orders for plant and equipment, adjusted for inflation
- New building permits issued
- Change in manufacturers' unfilled orders, durable goods
- Change in sensitive materials prices
- Index of stock prices
- Money supply: M-2, adjusted for inflation
- Index of consumer expectations

Source: Bureau of Economic Analysis, U.S. Department of Commerce

---

Two major factors that the analyst forecasts are interest rates and corporate profits. Interest rate projections are important for several reasons. First, decisions to invest in stock, bonds, and money market instruments are obviously dependent on the interest rates available on the latter two. Second, projected interest rate movements could have a significant impact on investment values, especially for bonds, whose values vary inversely with interest rates. Third, interest rates exert a major force on consumer spending and corporate investment, both of which strongly influence profitability and growth. Fourth, interest paid by corporations is an extremely important part of the corporation's total expenses, which obviously affect profits.

Not only do interest rates affect corporate profits, they also affect stock prices. All other factors being equal, lower projected profits cause lower stock prices. Further, higher interest rates encourage stockholders to sell stock in favor of bonds or money market instruments. This increase in the supply of stock decreases stock prices.

Another aspect of the relationship between interest rates and stock prices is the discount rate. A stock's price is equal to the discounted value of its associated cash flows. Specifically, the market discounts the projected future dividends and projected future sale price of the stock to calculate the current price of the stock. The appropriate discount rate is a function of the risk-free interest rate and an upward adjustment for the relative riskiness of the cash flows. Lower interest rates result in lower discount rates, and lower discount rates result in higher stock prices. Of course, at the same time, the interest rate scenario affects bonds—lower rates increase bond prices.

Making the Asset Allocation Decision. Before making the asset allocation decision the portfolio manager often reviews a set of economic forecasts rather than just one. Usually the analysts *may* present the forecasts with associated probabilities. For example, interest rates, corporate profits, and stock values may be forecast for three economic scenarios: best, worst, and most likely. Another approach may be to state that

> "we project a 60 percent probability that the T-bill rate in 12 months will be between 4 and 5 percent, a 20 percent probability that it will be between 3 and 4 percent, and a 20 percent probability that it will be between 5 and 8 percent."

Armed with an understanding of the implications of the forecasts on stock and bond values and knowing the client's risk tolerance and time horizon, the portfolio manager decides what percentage to allocate to each asset category.

The vast majority of advisers of individual retirement planning investors have minimal expertise in security analysis. Most advisers use analysis provided by brokerage firms or subscribe to independent forecasting services to help in the asset allocation process.

Many advisers suggest so-called asset allocation mutual funds, in which the funds' portfolio managers decide the proportions. However, fund managers make their decisions independently of an individual investor's risk tolerance and life-cycle phase. Further, a large fund does not have the flexibility to reshape the portfolio radically if market conditions change quickly. A financial planner with knowledge of the market and the client's personal situation is better equipped to make the optimal asset allocation decision for that client than is the mutual fund manager. Still, for the vast majority of retirement planning clients, especially those under 45 years of age, a fairly high percentage should be allocated to stocks because they will outperform bonds and money market instruments over a long time period.

Step 5: Specifying Industry Weightings

A portfolio manager's use of economic analysis does not end with asset allocation. After deciding the proportion of the portfolio to invest in stocks, and before selecting individual stocks, managers evaluate data to decide how much of the stock portfolio to invest in various industries.

In general, industries and stocks tend to move in the same direction as the market. After all, the market consists of the stocks—it goes up because they go up. But different industries perform differently in different economic conditions. For example, profitability in some industries is especially interest sensitive, such as in the utility industry. Political, regulatory, and international factors also affect industries in varying degrees. For example, a presidential proposal for health-care reform has much greater implications for the pharmaceutical industry than for the automobile industry. The dissolution of the Soviet empire has greater influence on the defense industry than on the cosmetics industry.

Portfolio managers are always conscious of what percentage of the market value of all companies is represented by companies in each industry. For example, perhaps the market value of all companies in the widget industry equals 3 percent of the total market value of all companies. When a manager is convinced that the widget industry will outperform the market, he or she will decide to invest relatively heavily in that industry—more than 3 percent of the portfolio.

Except for sector funds, which concentrate investments in specific industries, management of industry allocations is rather subtle. Even if a portfolio manager thinks that the widget industry will outperform the market by 50 percent, it is imprudent to invest too much of the portfolio in that one industry. If the forecast turns out to be wrong, the impact of over-investing in that industry may be severe.

Step 6: Selecting Companies

The rationale for analyzing industries before companies is that companies within an industry are subject to similar external influences. Steel prices are critical to all automobile companies; oil prices are critical to all airline companies.

Still, each company has its own strengths and weaknesses relative to its industry. Two appliance manufacturers may have different degrees of financial leverage, making one more susceptible to the vagaries of interest rates. Even if they have the same degree of financial leverage, one may have more short-term debt, leaving it more exposed to interest-rate fluctuations because of the imminent need for refinancing.

Another important factor is the company's operating characteristics. Analysts compare companies to the industry standard for liquidity ratios (for example, current ratio = current asset + current liabilities), activity ratios (inventory turnover = total sales + average inventory), debt ratios (times interest earned = earnings before interest and taxes + interest charges), and profitability ratios (profit margin = net income + total sales). Evaluating these and many other ratios in light of industry averages and projected economic conditions helps the analyst identify companies likely to outperform the industry.

A company's research and development program is an important precursor of growth, especially in high-tech industries. A biotech company that does not invest heavily in high-quality R&D is unlikely to maintain or increase market share. Future earnings growth is a most important aspect of the manager's assessment of a company. However, looking at past growth may be an imprecise or even incorrect indicator. Buying IBM in the early 1980s based on its growth in the previous 10 or 20 years would have yielded more pain than gain. It is the evaluation of all the other economic, industry, and company factors that helps the analyst to predict future growth.

Many of these characteristics are implicit indicators of a company's management quality. But most analysts want to know more about the senior-level managers themselves. The chief executive's experience, track record, and reputation are important. For different companies a technical, marketing, financial, or legal background may be most valued. A particularly noteworthy point is the chief executive's emphasis on building a management team and grooming potential successors.

International exposure differs markedly among companies within industries. One oil company may have far greater reliance on Middle East oil reserves than another company, making the supply line more vulnerable. However, the international factor can be a positive as well. A consumer products manufacturer with substantial international market penetration is likely to have less earnings volatility than a similar manufacturer that distributes only within the United States.

A relatively recent emphasis for portfolio managers is so-called *socially responsible,* or *socially directed, investing.* Some clients prefer not to invest in companies or industries involved in certain activities. For example, an investor may want to avoid investing in cigarette manufacturers, defense contractors, or nuclear-oriented utilities. The investor may object to any company that invests in a particular country—companies involved in South Africa felt this pressure prior to the demise of apartheid.

Obviously economic, industry, and company analysis—steps 4, 5, and 6—are covered in much more detail in books that concentrate on these topics. Again, most financial planners do not perform sophisticated security analysis, relying instead on the analysis of sophisticated, knowledgeable, and experienced experts.

Still, the savvy financial planner who limits recommendations to mutual funds should be familiar with the portfolio analysis process, if for no other reason than to answer client questions.

Step 7: Monitoring the Portfolio

A financial adviser's involvement with the investment portfolio does not end when the portfolio is first selected. The adviser must monitor the suitability and performance of the portfolio continually.

Since dividends flow in constantly, investment decisions continue forever. Economic and market conditions change, suggesting a review of asset allocation of the existing portfolio. Industries fall in and out of favor. And a company that was yesterday's sure thing sometimes becomes today's has-been. In short, all the factors used in selecting the original portfolio change on a daily basis.

For the adviser to an individual retirement planning investor, all six prior steps are repeated continually. Of particular note is any change in the client's risk tolerance or any change in the goals. A death in the family or an unexpected cash drain can have major impact on the client's financial situation with important ramifications throughout the portfolio management process. The mere passage of time gives rise to managerial decisions—the closer to retirement, the less portfolio risk most clients can accept.

Evaluating the performance of the portfolio is another aspect of the monitoring process. Typically, a portfolio manager uses quantitative techniques to measure performance on a risk-adjusted basis. Two such approaches are the Sharpe method, in which the portfolio's return in excess of the risk-free rate is divided by the portfolio's standard deviation, and the Treynor method, in which the return in excess of the risk-free rate is divided by the portfolio's beta. The higher the ratio, the greater the excess return relative to portfolio risk. The result is then compared to the value calculated for other portfolios.

$$
\begin{array}{c}
\text{Portfolio Performance Measures} \\[1em]
\text{Sharpe Factor} = \dfrac{\text{Portfolio Excess Return}}{\text{Standard Deviation}} \\[1em]
\text{Treynor Factor} = \dfrac{\text{Portfolio Excess Return}}{\text{Portfolio Beta}}
\end{array}
$$

A common and less complicated approach for evaluating mutual funds is to compare the fund's return to the return for funds with similar objectives, for example, ranking an income mutual fund with all the other income funds. However, comparing, say, a growth fund to a balanced one is inappropriate since the portfolios have completely different objectives and risk profiles.

Many advisers and their clients are perplexed by the myriad of rankings of funds in the popular press. Each publication has its own approach and none should be used without a thorough understanding of the methodology. One consideration in fund evaluation is that a relatively new fund may have had excellent performance for a short period, but have no experience in different economic or market conditions. Also note that a relatively small fund may lack efficiencies of scale, making its performance seem lower until it grows to the point that its fixed costs shrink as a percentage of total assets.

Probably the most inappropriate use of such rankings is to select the fund that has the best return, overall or within its classification, for the most recent quarter or year. Returns for such short periods are unreliable indicators of long-term performance, which is much more important to the retirement investor. Sometimes the highest-ranking fund for a quarter is a sector fund or precious metals fund, neither of which should represent a large proportion of a retirement portfolio.

If your fund underperformed its competitors over the past year, should you unload it? Not necessarily. Again, long-term performance is the more appropriate indicator. However, beware if a highly successful fund loses its portfolio guru. Perhaps the manager's legacy is sufficient to ensure that subsequent managers will perform well, but do not assume that the past is indicative of the future.

INVESTMENT DECISIONS AT RETIREMENT

Retirement presents more than an enormous adjustment in lifestyle. The financial decisions at retirement are enormous, too, often involving hundreds of thousands of dollars.

Faced with personal financial decisions that dwarf those from previous experience, retirees tend to select the path that appears most conservative. Unfortunately, the "safe" path—a fixed-income approach—is actually the riskiest because of inflation.

An actuarially average 65-year-old retiree can look forward to a 17-year life span. At an inflation rate of 4 percent, a fixed income of $1,000 per month at the start of retirement will decline in purchasing power to only $500 by the time the retiree reaches expected mortality.

A related problem is volatility in interest rates. Many who retired in the early 1980s during high interest rates have seen their "fixed" income from certificates of deposits or bonds fall by more than 50 percent in nominal terms—without even considering inflation. To maintain income, retirees often draw down principal, but doing so is equivalent to killing the goose that lays the golden eggs, albeit slowly. Eventually the income and the principal disappear.

An alternative to maintaining a fixed-income portfolio is to purchase a life annuity. One advantage of a life annuity is that the payment is not affected by changes in interest rate; it is truly fixed. Another advantage is that the payment is larger than would be received from a comparable interest-bearing investment because, in effect, the principal is allocated to the payments.

Life annuities are not without shortcomings. First, monthly payments are fixed, which means that an interest rate decline will not lower the payment, but neither will the payment rise with inflation. Second, if interest rates are low when the life annuity is purchased, the monthly payment will be relatively low and, again, will never rise. Third, the client effectively signs over all the principal to the insurer, immediately decreasing the amount available to heirs. The fact that all payments stop at the annuitant's death is troublesome to most people because of the concern that neither they nor their heirs will "get their money back." Of course, many forms of the life annuity are available to protect heirs. For example, a "life annuity with 10 years certain" assures that the contractual payment will continue for at least 10 years, but the initial payment will be actuarially smaller to adjust for the guarantee.

For clients who are concerned about inflation and who refuse to purchase a life annuity, maintaining an equity-based portfolio is a valid option. Historically dividends have grown with inflation, so the client's income from the portfolio grows. However, many people are uncomfortable with an equity-based portfolio because they fear that its value may fall.

The Variable Life Annuity

An increasingly attractive alternative to an equity-based portfolio or a traditional fixed life annuity is the variable life annuity, which involves use of an equity-based portfolio as an investment vehicle for the annuitant's contribution. As the value of the portfolio grows with the economy, the monthly payments to the annuitant grow.

Relative to a comparable equity portfolio, a variable life annuity provides higher monthly income because of the effective allocation of principal to the monthly payments. However, as is the case with a traditional life annuity, the annuitant loses ownership of the principal.

Compared to a traditional life annuity, the variable version offers a lower initial monthly payment. Even more detrimental is the prospect that a decline in the equity portfolio will cause a decline in the monthly payments. This possibility makes the fixed annuitization seem more palatable for most retirees.

However, retirees who fear inflation, trust in the long-term growth of equities, and want to maximize monthly income over the long run should consider placing a portion of their retirement funds in a variable life annuity.

A Look at the Record

Table 7-4 summarizes data for fixed and variable annuity payouts for Aetna Life Insurance and Annuity Company, which has offered variable life annuities for 26 years. The data includes 15-, 10-, and 5-year periods.

Two versions of the company's equity-based variable life annuity are included. The first uses an assumed net investment rate of 3 1/2 percent, and the second uses an assumed net investment rate of 5 percent. Clients select one of these two

TABLE 7-4
Summary of Comparison of Fixed and Variable Immediate Annuities

	15 Year*	10 Year*		5 Year*		
	10/78–9/93	10/78–9/88	10/83–9/93	10/78–9/83	10/83–9/88	10/88–9/93
Annuity price	$137,741.05	$137,741.05	$137,741.05	$137,741.05	$137,741.05	$168,350.17
Initial payment						
Fixed	1,225.90	1,225.90	1,257.58	1,225.90	1,257.58	1,506.51
Variable 3 1/2%	1,000.00	1,000.00	1,000.00	1,000.00	1,000.00	1,000.00
Variable 5%	1,123.97	1,123.97	1,123.97	1,123.97	1,123.97	1,148.15
End-of-period payment						
Fixed	1,225.90	1,225.90	1,257.58	1,225.90	1,257.58	1,506.51
Variable 3 1/2%	4,397.80	2,820.91	2,409.35	1,804.90	1,545.44	1,515.07
Variable 5%	3,988.20	2,749.01	2,347.93	1,890.10	1,618.39	1,620.71
Total payments						
Fixed	220,662.00	147,108.00	150,909.60	73,554.00	75,454.80	90,390.60
Variable 3 1/2%	446,347.33	219,695.27	203,114.14	75,601.49	78,942.18	78,082.80
Variable 5%	439,164.70	226,687.24	210,419.07	81,746.76	85,329.39	86,345.91
Number of months in which variable payments exceeded fixed payment						
Variable 3 1/2%	150/180	90/120	93/120	30/60	33/60	2/60
Variable 5%	162/180	102/120	99/120	42/60	39/60	24/60

*Each of these is a life annuity evaluated over the time frame specified.

rates at the inception of the payout period. Future payments depend on the performance of the equity fund relative to the assumed rate.

Selection of the 3 1/2 percent rate results in a smaller initial monthly payment than that generated by the 5 percent rate. However, since the equity portfolio will perform better relative to a 3 1/2 percent assumption than to a 5 percent assumption, future payments will grow faster under the 3 1/2 percent assumption. Also with the 3 1/2 percent assumption, payments will shrink less when the equity portfolio performs poorly.

The 15-Year Record. Table 7-4 includes historical data for the 15-year period from October 1978 to September 1993 for a male annuitant at age 65. A graph of the raw data appears in figure 7-2. An initial premium of $137,741.05 produced an initial monthly payment of $1,000 for the 3 1/2 percent option, $1,123.97 for the 5 percent option, and $1,225.90 for the company's fixed annuity.

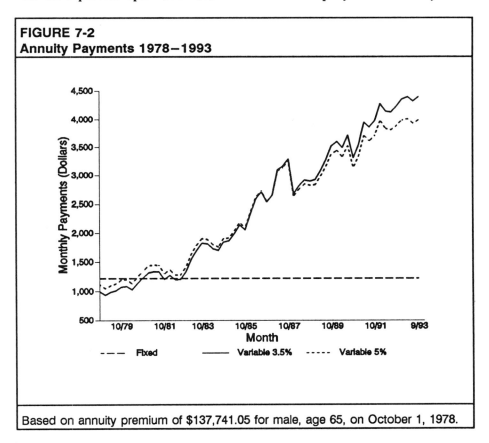

FIGURE 7-2
Annuity Payments 1978—1993

Based on annuity premium of $137,741.05 for male, age 65, on October 1, 1978.

During the 15 years the monthly payment for the 3 1/2 percent option grew by more than 339 percent to $4,397.80. In 150 of the 180 months the payment was higher than that of the fixed version. The total received during the 15 years was $446,347.33 for the 3 1/2 percent option, which was 102 percent more than the $220,662 for the fixed version.

The monthly payment for the 5 percent option grew by more than 254 percent to $3,988.20. Its monthly payment was higher than that of the fixed version in 162 of the 180 months. The total payments were $439,164.70, or 99 percent larger than the fixed version's total.

The 10-Year Record. Table 7-4 also summarizes historical data for the 10-year period from October 1983 to September 1993 for a unisex table and age 65. Figure 7-3 gives a graphic depiction. An initial premium of $137,741.05 produced an initial monthly payment of $1,000 for the 3 1/2 percent option, $1,123.97 for the 5 percent option, and $1,257.58 for the company's fixed annuity.

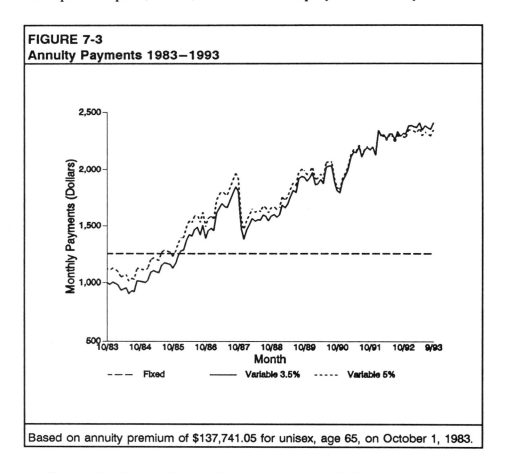

FIGURE 7-3
Annuity Payments 1983–1993

Based on annuity premium of $137,741.05 for unisex, age 65, on October 1, 1983.

During the 10 years the monthly payment for the 3 1/2 percent option grew by more than 140 percent to $2,409.35. In 93 of the 120 months the payment was higher than that of the fixed version. The total received during the 10 years was $203,114.14 for the 3 1/2 percent option, 35 percent higher than the $150,909.60 for the fixed version.

The monthly payment for the 5 percent option grew by more than 108 percent to $2,347.93. This payment was higher than that of the fixed version in 99 of the 120 months. The total payments were $210,419.07, or 39 percent larger than the total for the fixed version.

We can also examine the 10-year period from October 1978 to September 1988. The monthly payment for the 3 1/2 percent option grew by more than 182 percent to $2,820.91. In 90 of the 120 months the payment was higher than that of the fixed version. The total received during the 10 years was $219,695.27 for the 3 1/2 percent option, 49 percent larger than the total of $147,108.00 for the fixed version.

During the same period the monthly payment for the 5 percent option grew by more than 144 percent to $2,749.01 and it was higher than that of the fixed version in 102 of the 120 months. The total payments were $226,687.24, which was 54 percent larger than the total for the fixed version.

The 5-Year Record. Table 7-4 also shows historical data for the 5-year period from October 1988 to September 1993 for a unisex table and age 65. The raw data are graphed in figure 7-4. A premium of $168,350.17 produced an initial monthly payment of $1,000 for the 3 1/2 percent option, $1,148.15 for the 5 percent option, and $1,506.51 for the company's fixed annuity.

During the 5 years the monthly payment for the 3 1/2 percent option grew by more than 51 percent to $1,515.07. In only 2 of the 60 months the payment was higher than that of the fixed version. The total received during the 5 years was $78,082.80 for the 3 1/2 percent option, 14 percent less than the $90,390.60 for the fixed version.

The monthly payment for the 5 percent option grew by more than 41 percent to $1,620.71. Its monthly payment was higher than that of the fixed version in 24 of the 60 months, and total payments were $86,345.91, which was 4 percent less than the fixed version's total.

We can also examine the 5-year period from October 1983 to September 1988 and the 5-year period from October 1978 to September 1983 in table 7-4. For the period from October 1983 to September 1988, the monthly payment for the 3 1/2 percent option grew by more than 54 percent to $1,545.44. In 33 of the 60 months the payment was higher than that of the fixed version. The total received during the 5 years was $78,942.18 for the 3 1/2 percent option, 5 percent more than the $75,454.80 for the fixed version. The monthly payment for the 5 percent option grew by more than 43 percent to $1,618.30. Its monthly payment was higher than that of the fixed version in 39 of the 60 months, and total payments of $85,329.39 were 13 percent larger than the fixed version's total.

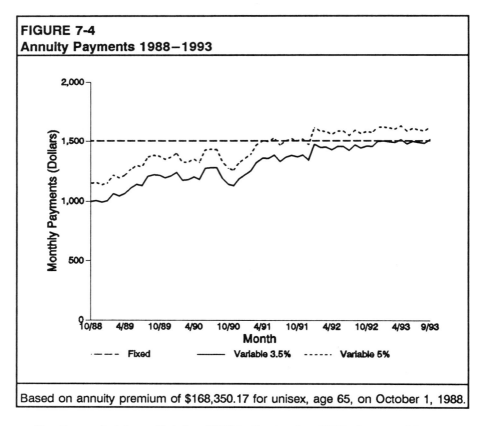

FIGURE 7-4
Annuity Payments 1988—1993

Based on annuity premium of $168,350.17 for unisex, age 65, on October 1, 1988.

For the period from October 1978 to September 1983, the monthly payment for the 3 1/2 percent option grew by more than 80 percent to $1,804.90. In half of the 60 months the payment was higher than that of the fixed version. The total received during the 5 years was $75,601.49 for the 3 1/2 percent option, which was 3 percent larger than the total of $73,554 for the fixed version. The monthly payment for the 5 percent option grew by more than 68 percent to $1,890.10. Its monthly payment was higher than that of the fixed version in 42 of the 60 months, and total payments of $81,746.76 were 11 percent larger than the total for the fixed version.

It is apparent that the relative sizes of the fixed and variable payments at the annuity's inception are critical. For the most recent 5-year period the initial payment for the 3 1/2 percent option was 33 percent lower than for the fixed option. The greater this discount, the longer it will normally take for the variable payment to catch up to the fixed. Obviously a small discount at the beginning of a bull market is optimal.

If a 5-year period were the appropriate criterion, consultants would be wise to ignore variable immediate annuities based on the historical record. Performance for the most recent 5-year period for the 3 1/2 percent option is especially weak. However, life annuities for retirement income are typically in place for longer than 15 years.

As the 15-year data in figure 7-2 show, a client would have received approximately the same total income in the first 5 years if he or she had chosen a variable instead of a fixed annuity. The same client would have fared much better in the second 5 years with the variable alternative. By the end of 15 years, the variable payment with the 3 1/2 percent option was three times as large as the payment under the fixed option.

Of course, past performance is not necessarily an accurate predictor of future performance. A prolonged market slump could cause the variable options to fall behind the fixed option for an extended period.

Still, a client who lives to full life expectancy is likely to benefit greatly from selection of a variable option. Healthy, health-conscious people with good medical family histories will probably benefit even more with the continued growth of the economy and the stock market.

Not every client is a good candidate for a variable life annuity. For instance, it is not a good choice for someone in poor health, but neither is a fixed life annuity. Clients who cannot tolerate market volatility are poor candidates, as are those who do not have faith in the future growth of the economy and the market. Clients with limited means may need more monthly income than the initially low monthly income from the variable option. Ironically they stand to gain the most from the variable option since it will probably help them leap ahead of inflation in the long run. Another unlikely candidate is a client with a substantial portfolio and an understanding of investments. This person can create a withdrawal program that may provide more flexibility and greater returns than the variable annuity option.

As with any investment, consultants should avoid trying to commit a high percentage of the client's funds to variable life annuities. However, the variable option represents a useful tool that is highly likely to provide better returns than its most popular competitor, the fixed life annuity. For the right candidate, variable annuity payouts and variable life annuities are excellent retirement planning alternatives.

8

Planning for Distributions from Retirement Plans — Part I

Chapter Outline

OVERVIEW OF DISTRIBUTION PLANNING

Proper planning for the distribution of benefits from qualified plans (and other tax-sheltered plans, including SEPs, IRAs, and 403(b) plans) is an extremely important and complex subject. A great deal of wealth is being accumulated in tax-sheltered plans today, and individuals want to receive benefits in the most tax-efficient manner. Making sure that taxes are minimized — and benefits are maximized — requires careful planning and a great deal of knowledge.   In addition, other distribution rules, such as the minimum distribution rules and the qualified joint and survivor rules, must be contended with.

Due to the enormity of this subject area, the next four chapters are devoted to it. Since the focus of this book is retirement planning, the materials primarily center on income taxes and the other restrictions that apply to pension distributions. However, since estate planning is also important — and tied closely with the income tax planning — this subject is also discussed briefly in chapter 11. Before getting into the details let's begin by looking at the big picture.

Income Taxation of Pension Distributions

From the employee's perspective, the advantage of tax-sheltered retirement plans is that taxes are deferred until benefits are distributed — the day of reckoning.   Generally, the entire value of a distribution will be included as ordinary income in the year of the distribution. If the individual has made aftertax contributions or receives an insurance policy and has paid PS 58 costs, he or she will have a "cost basis" that will not be taxed. When an individual with a cost basis receives the benefit over a number of years, the cost basis will be recovered using the exclusion ratio methodology discussed later in this chapter.

If the benefit is distributed in a single sum, the cash basis will be recovered at once, and the taxable portion will be treated as ordinary income unless the benefit qualifies as a lump-sum distribution and is eligible for the special tax treatment discussed in chapter 9. Individuals born before 1936 may be eligible for 10-year forward averaging or special capital-gains treatment. These individuals, as well as those born on or after January 1, 1936, may also be eligible for special 5-year averaging or the deferral of unrealized appreciation on distributed employer stock.

Distributions may also be subject to one or two additional excise taxes. First, as discussed later in this chapter, the taxable distributions from tax-sheltered retirement plans (qualified plans, 403(b) plans, IRAs and SEPs) made prior to age 59 1/2 will be subject to an additional 10 percent excise tax.   Second, as discussed in chapter 11, a 15 percent excise tax (referred to as the excess distributions excise tax) applies when distributions from all tax-sheltered plans exceed $150,000 for a calendar year.   These complex taxes each have numerous exceptions, and a special grandfathering election may reduce the excess distributions excise tax in some cases.

In many cases, all taxes, including the excise taxes, can be avoided by rolling—or directly transferring—the benefit into an IRA or other qualified plan. Today, most distributions are eligible for rollover treatment. The primary rule that prohibits indefinite income tax deferral is the minimum distribution rule, which requires distributions to begin at age 70 1/2, discussed further in chapter 10.

Limitations and Restrictions

In addition to the taxation of benefits, pension distributions are subject to certain restrictions and limitations, which are also covered in the next four chapters.

Some of the restrictions include

- limitations on in-service distributions
- plan loans
- distributions in the form of a qualified joint and survivor annuity
- requirements of minimum distributions beginning at age 70 1/2

As discussed later in this chapter, only profit-sharing type qualified plans (as well as SEPs and 403(b) plans) are allowed to provide in-service distributions—pension plans (including defined-benefit, money-purchase and target-benefit plans) cannot. The in-service distribution rules for profit-sharing plans are quite liberal—except for 401(k) plans and 403(b) plans, in which the participant must demonstrate a financial hardship. All qualified plans and 403(b) plans can allow for plan loans, within certain restrictions.

The form of payout is often restricted by the qualified joint and survivor annuity rules. A married individual receiving benefits from a qualified retirement plan generally must distribute the benefit in the form of a joint and survivor annuity, unless the participant and his or her spouse agree to an alternative form of distribution.[1]

Finally, the minimum distribution rules require that payouts commence by April 1 of the year following the year in which the participant attains age 70 1/2.

When studying the various rules that apply to pension distributions, *be sure to keep in mind that the timing of benefits, form of payout, and the availability of in-service withdrawals or loans are always subject to the terms of the specific plan involved.* The legal restrictions discussed here provide only a framework within which a plan can operate. Before advising a client of his or her rights or obligations, it is imperative to review the specific plan provisions.

Estate Taxation of Pension Accumulations

Qualified plan and other tax-sheltered benefits payable to a beneficiary at the death of the participant will be included in the participant's taxable estate. In addition, if the benefits exceed a specified threshold an additional 15 percent excess accumulations estate tax will apply to the difference between the value of benefits and the tax threshold.[2] The impact of the tax is reduced somewhat by the ability to deduct the tax on the estate tax return. Benefits payable to beneficiaries will still be subject to income tax, although the benefit amount is treated as income in respect to the decedent, meaning that the income taxes will be reduced by the estate taxes paid as a result of the pension benefit.

Planning for Individual Needs

Proper distribution planning is more complicated than simply knowing, in isolation, the various taxes and legal requirements. Planning must look at the big picture, taking into consideration the individual's needs and desires. Any strategy selected must account for the following factors:

- the client's needs and goals
- the variety of distribution options that are available in your client's particular situation
- the implications of choosing one option over another from a tax perspective
- the implications of choosing one option over another from a cash-flow perspective
- the implications of choosing one option over another from a death benefit and estate tax perspective
- the ability to delay the receipt and taxation of a distribution by rolling the distribution over into an IRA or another qualified plan
- the relative benefit of a lump-sum distribution compared to some form of periodic payment from the plan

All too often planners feel that reducing the taxation on a client's retirement distribution is the only consideration when making a distribution decision. Tax planning is only part of the process. The ultimate goal is to maximize wealth while meeting the client's cash-flow and other needs, not merely to save taxes.

DISTRIBUTIONS PRIOR TO RETIREMENT

Clients should be discouraged from taking distributions from retirement plans prior to retirement. These distributions may reduce retirement resources to unacceptable levels by undermining the objective of maximizing retirement savings on a tax-advantaged basis. Nevertheless, distributions prior to retirement are common, and planners must know the rules and tax ramifications involved so that they can provide comprehensive financial services for their clients. Let's look at an overview of these rules and their tax ramifications.

In-Service Distributions

Whether or not an individual can obtain a distribution while still employed depends on the type of plan involved. Pension plans prohibit these so-called in-service withdrawals altogether. If a pension plan (defined-benefit, cash-balance, target-benefit, or money-purchase plan) permits an employee to receive a distribution while employed, the plan will generally lose its tax-sheltered status.

Profit-sharing plans, stock bonus plans, and employee stock ownership plans (ESOPs), on the other hand, may be designed to permit employees to receive in-service withdrawals after funds have been in the client's account for 2 years. In addition, 401(k) plans and 403(b) TDA plans may be designed to allow in-service withdrawals if the employee has a financial hardship. Finally, IRAs and simplified employee pension plans (SEPs) allow withdrawals with absolutely no plan impediments. *(Planning Note:* Plans may distribute funds to former employees who become disabled or distribute funds to the beneficiary of a deceased employee.)

Loans from Qualified Plans

In some cases, an alternative available to a preretirement distribution is a plan loan. A loan (within allowable limits) allows for the tax-free use of plan benefits, avoiding both income tax and the 10 percent penalty tax. All qualified plans and 403(b) annuity plans may provide for loans, although no plan is required to do so. Loan provisions are more common in defined-contribution type plans, especially profit-sharing, 401(k) and 403(b) plans. IRAs and SEPs may not permit loans.

A small business owner who wants to take advantage of the plan loan opportunity has to consider several things before including a plan loan provision. First, plan loans are available only to owners of C corporations. Neither S corporation employees who are shareholders owning more than 5 percent in the corporation nor owner-employees (that is, sole proprietors or partners owning more than 10 percent of an unincorporated business) are eligible for plan loans. Also, if a C corporation owner wants to take a loan, other plan participants must also have access.

If the employer still wants to provide a loan program, the program has to satisfy certain ERISA requirements so that the loans will not be treated as prohibited transactions. To avoid penalties all loans must

- be made available to participants and beneficiaries on a reasonably equivalent basis
- be adequately secured
- be made in accordance with specific plan provisions
- bear a reasonable (market) rate of interest

A loan will not be taxable as long as several requirements are satisfied, including the following:

- The loan must not exceed the lesser of 50 percent of the participant's vested account balance or $50,000.
- The $50,000 loan limitation must be reduced by the highest outstanding balance of all loans in the previous year.
- Loans must be repaid in equal installments, no less frequently than quarterly.
- Loans cannot exceed 5 years except when the loan is used to purchase the participant's principal residence.

Under the tax rules, a participant may borrow up to $10,000 even if this is more than one-half of the vested benefit. For example, a person having a vested benefit of $13,000 could still borrow up to $10,000. However, in practice, employers do not allow loans in excess of the 50 percent limit, since DOL regulations would require security other than the participant's vested account balance—which would be complex to administer.

The second rule can be illustrated with the following example.

Example: Venus Value has an outstanding loan balance of $7,500 on January 1, 1995. She finishes paying off the loan on December 30, 1995, and wants to take a new maximum loan on December 31, 1995. Assuming that Venus is otherwise eligible for a $50,000 loan, the maximum loan she can take on December 31, 1995, is $42,500 ($50,000 minus $7,500, the largest outstanding loan balance in the last year).

Interest on a plan loan will be treated as consumer interest that is not deductible by the employee as an itemized deduction unless the loan is secured by a home. Even if the loan is secured by a home, interest deductions are specifically prohibited in two situations—if the loan is (1) to a key employee, as defined by the Code's rules for top-heavy plans (Sec. 416), or (2)secured by a Sec. 401(k) or TDA (Sec. 403(b)) plan account attributable to employee elective deferrals.

Loans that do not comply with these rules are treated as in-service distributions to the extent that the loan exceeds the maximum permissible limit. For example, an individual with a vested account balance of $60,000 taking a loan in the amount of $35,000 will have $5,000 of taxable income ($5,000 more than the $30,000 limit [1/2 of $60,000]). When repaid, the taxable portion of the loan is treated as a nondeductible employee contribution that may be recovered tax free at a later time.

In general, spouses of participants must give written consent before a loan may be granted from the plan. The spousal consent rules are described below.

Taxation of Distributions Prior to Retirement

In the case of a plan that allows for preretirement distributions, it is not atypical for a participant to receive an in-service distribution on a portion of his or her benefit in order to meet financial hardships or to pay for other expenses. If the participant's entire benefit consists of pretax contributions, any distribution will be included in the participant's taxable income and may also be subject to the 10 percent excise tax on early distributions. However, if a portion of the benefit is attributable to amounts that have already been taxed (referred to as the investment in the contract), some or all of such distribution will not be taxed. Investment in the contract includes employee aftertax contributions and PS 58 costs as well as other amounts.

Prior to 1987, an amount up to the participant's investment could be withdrawn prior to the annuity starting date (the time retirement benefits begin) without income tax consequences. The Tax Reform Act of 1986 changed this rule significantly. A grandfather provision still allows a participant to withdraw an amount equal to the pre-1987 investment in the contract without tax as long as the plan provided for in-service distributions on May 5, 1986. Post-1986 amounts attributable to the investment in the contract, however, are now subject to a pro rata rule. The general rule is that the amount of the distribution that is excluded from tax is based on a ratio, with the numerator being the investment in the contract and the denominator being the total account balance at the time of the distribution. However, when determining the ratio, an individual may treat employee aftertax contributions and the investment experience thereon separately from the rest of the participant's benefit. This rule still allows a participant to withdraw aftertax contributions with limited tax liability. This principle can be best illustrated with an example.

> *Example:* Joe has an account balance of $1,000, $200 of which is attributable to post-1986 employee contributions and $50 of which is attributable to investment earnings on the $200 contribution. Joe takes an in-service distribution of $100. The exclusion ratio is $200/$250 or 80 percent. Therefore Joe will receive $80 income tax free and will owe tax on $20.

Distributions When Changing Employers

When an employee leaves employment prior to retirement for reasons other than death or disability, the provisions of the plan will dictate whether a distribution of retirement funds can occur. Many plans have adopted a cash-out provision and will permit employees to take funds in a lump-sum payout when they terminate employment prior to retirement. If the plan has such a provision, an employer is entitled to cash out the former employee's benefit if the value of the benefit is $3,500 or less, regardless of the employee's request to the contrary. If the value of the vested benefit is over $3,500, however, an employee can opt to have his or her funds remain in the former employer's plan until retirement. This option is seldom chosen because most clients do not want to deal with a former employer. (*Planning Note:* Clients should compare the investment performance of plan funds when making distribution decisions. If the former employer's plan earns a better rate of return than the new employer's plan, your client may want to consider leaving his or her plan assets in the former employer's plan.) Also remember that clients may roll balances over to IRAs where they may have considerable flexibility in how the balances are invested. However, they also lose some tax advantages and flexibility in other regards (as will be discussed later).

Some employers do not provide a cash-out provision. An employer may design a plan to hold the funds of employees who leave the company before normal retirement age until retirement age. (*Planning Note:* Regardless of your client's situation advise him or her not to squander a distribution at termination. Funds often should be rolled over into an IRA or, if permitted, into the new employer's plan.)

Early-Distribution Penalty

Despite the fact that clients may legally be allowed to obtain their retirement funds prior to retirement, either as an in-service distribution or when changing employees, the government imposes penalties on those who do. A 10 percent penalty will be imposed on the taxable amount of a preretirement distribution in most cases (commonly referred to as the Sec. 72(t) penalty). In addition, taxpayers must include the appropriate amount of the distribution in their taxable income.

The 10 percent tax applies only to the "taxable portion" of the distribution. If a distribution includes amounts that have been previously subject to tax, such as aftertax employee contributions, the nontaxable portion of the distribution is exempt from the 10 percent penalty tax.

The 10 percent penalty applies to distributions that are made from a qualified plan, a Sec. 403(b) plan, an individual retirement account, and a SEP. The rule is stated in such a way that the penalty is supposed to apply to all preretirement distributions. However, a distribution can escape the 10 percent penalty if it qualifies under one of several exceptions. To escape the 10 percent penalty the distributions must be

- made on or after attainment of age 59 1/2, or, if made from a qualified plan or 403(b) annuity (but not an IRA or SEP), after separation from service after age 55
- made to a beneficiary or to a participant's estate on or after the participant's death
- attributable to disability
- part of a series of substantially equal periodic payments made at least annually over the life or life expectancy of the participant or the joint lives or life expectancies of the participant and beneficiary. (If the distribution is from a qualified plan, the employee must separate from service.)

- to cover medical expenses deductible for the year under Code Sec. 213 whether or not actually deductible (not applicable to distributions from IRAs)

The following examples should help to illustrate when the 10 percent penalty applies and when it does not.

Example: Greg Murphy, aged 55, takes a $50,000 lump-sum distribution from his profit-sharing plan. The $50,000 lump-sum distribution will be subject to a $5,000 penalty unless Greg has taken the distribution upon termination of employment.

Example: Jane Goodall, aged 45, takes a life annuity from Biological Researchers, Inc., when she quits and goes to work for the Primate Institute. Jane's distribution is not subject to penalty because of the periodic payments exception.

Example: Ed Miller, aged 35, takes a distribution from his 401(k) plan to meet an extreme financial hardship. Ed's distribution is subject to the 10 percent penalty.

Avoiding the Early Distributions Excise Tax

In some cases, a client might need to make withdrawals prior to age 59 1/2 to pay personal or business expenses or, in some cases, to make an investment. With downsizing in the early 1990s, many middle-aged workers have been forced to take early retirement. Many of these individuals look for other employment, but may have a period in which they have to tap their nest eggs. Within the list of exceptions to the early distribution excise tax, some planning opportunities do exist. Of limited use is the age 55 exemption. To be eligible for this exemption, the individual must actually terminate employment on or after attaining age 55. The exception applies to qualified plans and 403(b) plans, but not to IRAs. Therefore, if IRA money is needed, even losing a job does not qualify for an automatic exemption from the tax.

Of more use is the substantially equal periodic payment exception. Under this exception, payments can begin at any age, as long as payments are set up to last for the life of the participant or the joint lives of the participant and his or her beneficiary. Note that if the distribution is from a qualified plan, the individual must have separated from service before distributions begin. For the individual who needs the withdrawals to meet ongoing financial needs, periodic distributions may be just the ticket. If, on the other hand, a large single-sum amount is needed, this strategy may still work. The individual can borrow the sum needed and repay the loan from the periodic distributions.

A client going down this road needs to be aware of potential potholes. The largest is that once payments have begun, they must continue for a specified period in order to avoid the tax. Failure to make the required number of payments means that the 10 percent penalty will be due on all distributions made before age 59 1/2, as well as interest on the tax obligation that was avoided during the years that distributions were made.

Fortunately the rules do not actually require that payments continue for life. Payments can be stopped without penalty after the later of 5 years after the first payment or age 59 1/2. For example, an individual who begins distributions in substantially equal payments at age 56 in January 1994 must continue taking the distributions until January 1999. Or take the example of an individual beginning withdrawals at age 47. In this case, payments must continue until he or she attains age 59 1/2, which is a period of 12 1/2 years.

The other concern is determining how much has to be withdrawn in order to constitute a substantially equal periodic payment. The withdrawals must be calculated under one of three IRS-approved methods: (1) life expectancy, (2) amortization, or (3) annuitization. The methods for determining an appropriate payment are extremely flexible. Payments may be made monthly, quarterly, or annually, and a range of interest rates and mortality tables may be used. The flexibility allowed can be demonstrated with the following example.

> *Example:* Assume Sara, aged 50, has an IRA account of $200,000. All the following represent withdrawal amounts that satisfy one of the calculation methods described by the IRS.

Life expectancy (33.1 years)	$ 6,042
Annuitization (33.1 years, 5% interest)	$11,888
Amortization (33.1 years, 8% interest)	$16,073

Note that under the life expectancy method, the distribution will fluctuate each year. Generally larger distributions are required as time goes on. The IRS has indicated that the distribution amount can be based on any of the methods of calculating a minimum distribution under IRC Sec. 401(a)(9) (see chapter 10 for more information about this subject). The simplest way to make this calculation is to divide the current account balance by the participant's life expectancy. The amortization method works the same way as amortizing a loan—the loan payments are amortized over the life expectancy of the individual. With the annuitization method, the account balance is divided by a life annuity factor. Both the annuitization and the amortization methods will give the same results given the same mortality and interest assumptions. For more on the mechanics of selecting a number that complies with the IRS guidelines, see appendix 4.

RETIREMENT DISTRIBUTIONS: AN OVERVIEW

Choosing the best distribution at retirement can be a rather complex decision. This decision involves personal preferences, financial considerations, and an interplay between tax incentives and tax penalties. Planners must keep in mind a myriad of factors in order to render effective advice.

For example, typical considerations include whether

- the periodic distribution will be used to provide income necessary for sustaining the retiree or whether the distribution will supplement already adequate sources of retirement income
- the client has properly coordinated distributions from several different qualified plans and IRAs
- the retiree will have satisfactory diversification of his or her retirement resources after the distribution occurs
- the client has complied with the rules for minimum distributions from a qualified plan
- the client is receiving "too much" from the retirement plan, thereby subjecting his or her distributions to a success tax (the 15 percent excise tax on excess distributions and excess accumulations, which is discussed in a later chapter)

REQUIRED SPOUSAL BENEFITS

Qualified plans must conform with requirements under the Retirement Equity Act of 1984, which gives the spouse of a plan participant certain legal rights in the participant's plan benefit. Unless expressly waived by both the participant and spouse in accordance with strict rules, qualified plans must automatically provide the following two forms of survivorship benefits for a spouse:

- *qualified preretirement survivor annuity* (QPSA) for the surviving spouse of a participant who dies before the annuity starting date
- *qualified joint and survivor annuity* (QJSA) for the participant and the spouse at the annuity starting date

Generally speaking, the annuity starting date is the date retirement benefits commence in accordance with the plan.

All pension plans (including defined-benefit, money-purchase, target-benefit, and cash-balance plans) must conform with these requirements. Other defined-contribution plans (including profit-sharing plans, stock bonus plans and ESOPs) must conform unless all the following requirements are met:

- The plan pays a death benefit in the amount of the participant's nonforfeitable benefit (vested benefit prior to death) to the surviving spouse or to another designated beneficiary with the spouse's consent.

- The participant has not elected to receive benefits in the form of a life annuity.
- If the qualified plan is the recipient of a direct plan-to-plan transfer from a plan subject to the spousal benefit rules, then the general rules must apply to the transferred benefits.

The QJSA requirements also do not apply (in any type of plan) when the value of a participant's vested benefit does not exceed $3,500.

The rules effectively require qualified plans to provide minimum preretirement death benefits to married participants with vested benefits (unless the participant and spouse waive such benefit). The rules do not require any such preretirement benefit for unmarried participants. For example, it is not unusual in defined-benefit plans with large numbers of participants for the plan to provide preretirement death benefits only for married participants.

Qualified Preretirement Survivor Annuity (QPSA)

Once a participant has earned a vested interest in the plan benefit, the nonparticipant spouse acquires the right to a QPSA, payable in the event of the death of the participant prior to the annuity starting date. The QPSA requirement applies whether or not the vested participant is employed at the time of death.

In a defined-contribution plan the QPSA must be payable as a life annuity purchased with 50 percent of the participant's vested account balance, and the spouse must have the opportunity to elect to have payments begin within a reasonable time after the participant's death. The vested account balance includes amounts that become vested on account of the participant's death and amounts payable from life insurance proceeds.

In a defined-benefit plan, the survivor annuity payable is somewhat more complicated to calculate. The amount is based on the fictional presumption that the participant terminated employment (on the day before death), survived until the earliest retirement age under the plan, elected a qualified joint and survivor annuity, and died the day after the annuity began. The QPSA is the survivor portion of such a benefit beginning on the earliest age that the participant could have begun retirement benefits. Note that in a defined-benefit plan, no survivor benefit is required if the participant was not vested prior to death.

The plan administrator generally must give the participant notice of the right to waive the QPSA beginning on the first day of the plan year during which the participant reaches age 32 and ending on the close of the plan year preceding the plan year in which the participant reaches age 35 (with some exceptions for employees terminating earlier or hired later). The actual election period begins on the first day of the plan year in which the participant attains age 35 and ends on the date of the participant's death. Any valid waiver has to be in writing, with written consent by the participant's spouse.

The plan does not have to give the participant the opportunity to waive the QPSA if the employer "fully subsidizes" the benefit. A QPSA is fully subsidized if the participant's failure to waive the benefit will not cause a reduction in any plan benefit with respect to the participant and will not create increased contributions by the participant.

Qualified Joint and Survivor Annuity (QJSA)

When a married participant survives to the time retirement benefit payments begin (the annuity starting date), the required form of benefit is a qualified joint and survivor annuity (QJSA). Under the QJSA a monthly benefit is paid to the participant for the duration of his or her life, and payments continue for the life of a spouse if he or she outlives the participant. The amount of the spousal survivor benefit cannot be less than 50 percent or more than 100 percent of the joint benefit.

The participant has to be given the right to waive the QJSA benefit during the 90-day period prior to the annuity starting date. The plan administrator must give the participant notice of this election within a reasonable period prior to the annuity starting date, and the notice must contain complete information notifying the participant of the right to waive the QJSA, the economic effect of such an election, and the spouse's rights under such an election. Any valid waiver has to be in writing, with written consent by the participant's spouse as well.

Required Consent

Elections to waive QPSA or QJSA benefits must be made in writing by the participant and must be consented to by the participant's spouse. The spouse's consent does not have to be irrevocable. However, the plan may require irrevocable waivers. The spousal consent is in favor of a particular beneficiary. If the participant wishes to choose a different beneficiary, a new spousal consent must be obtained.

The participant's election and spousal consent must be "informed" consent, meaning that they are given adequate counsel about the effect of such election, and they must acknowledge that they understand the impact of their election on benefit rights. In addition, the consent must be witnessed by a plan representative or a notary public.

Waivers for Loans

When a participant obtains a loan from a plan, the loan is most often secured with the participant's account balance. From the standpoint of the plan, this is adequate security, since the plan can easily "foreclose" on the participant's vested account balance in the case of a default on the loan balance. However, from the standpoint of the participant's spouse, a loan default reduces the participant's benefit from the plan, reducing the promised QPSA or QJSA that the spouse is otherwise entitled to receive. To avoid such conflicts, the rules provide that a plan subject to the QJSA and QPSA requirements must obtain the spouse's consent in writing within 90 days of the commencement of the loan.

Planning Considerations

A participant making an election for the form of retirement benefits should be careful to coordinate the preretirement death-benefit election. For example, suppose a couple wishes to name a child as the beneficiary of the participant's postretirement benefits after the participant dies, since the spouse has adequate income from other sources. The participant and spouse must be sure to sign both preretirement QPSA consent forms as well as postretirement QJSA consent forms in case the participant dies prior to commencement of his or her retirement benefits.

DISTRIBUTION OPTIONS

As described above, qualified plans must generally provide a joint and survivor annuity as the normal retirement benefit for married participants. For a single person the normal benefit is typically a life annuity (or in contributory plans, a modified cash-refund annuity).

Many plans allow participants to select some other form of benefit from a list of options in the plan, with the appropriate spousal consent, if needed. If a desired option is not among those offered by the plan, participants can usually elect to roll benefits over into another plan or into an IRA, where they then have complete flexibility as to how benefits are distributed. (The rollover rules are discussed later in this chapter.) Options for distributions include

- various annuity arrangements
- discretionary installment payments
- lump-sum distributions

The remainder of this chapter deals with the two forms of periodic distributions—annuities and discretionary installment payments. The advantage of taking a periodic distribution as opposed to a lump-sum distribution is the continued deferral of taxation on the retirement plan balances and earnings until benefits are actually received. However, lump-sum distributions may also qualify for favorable tax treatment. Determining which option is better depends on a number of factors and is the subject of a subsequent chapter. For now, let's take a closer look at the various types of periodic payment options and when they might be most appropriate.

Annuity Distributions

Annuity contracts provide for the payment of income on a monthly basis. These contracts are basically the distribution or liquidation of a sum of money (the plan's benefit) on an actuarial basis. The amount of the benefit that is payable depends on several factors. These factors include

- the amount used to fund the annuity—called the annuity's purchase price (which is a function of the plan's contribution or benefit formula)
- the age of the client (annuitant)
- the number of lives covered by the annuity (if the annuity covers two lives, the amount of the benefit is dependent on the ages of both people)
- any minimum guarantees that are offered (refund or minimum payment period—for example, a 10-year guarantee)
- the interest assumption used

Each annuity payment is comprised of part payback of the annuity purchase price, part investment earnings on the purchase price, and some benefit of survivorship to surviving annuitants from other annuitants who died before receiving a full return of their original benefit balances. In addition, part of the forfeited funds will be pooled with funds from other annuitants to provide extended benefits for those annuitants who live beyond their life expectancy.

There are several types of annuity forms from which the planner can choose.

Life Annuity

A life annuity provides monthly payments to your client during his or her lifetime. Payments from a life annuity completely stop when your client (annuitant) dies, and no other benefit is paid to any beneficiary. Since all of the annuity funds are being applied toward providing the monthly benefit and none toward providing a survivor benefit or a refund of premium (as is the case in any other type of annuity), a life annuity provides the largest monthly benefit for a given amount of money (table 8-1).

A life annuity is an ideal choice for persons trying to stretch their assets as far as possible while still guaranteeing a lifetime income because a life annuity maximizes the amount of the monthly benefit. Typically individuals who are not concerned about providing retirement income to a spouse or other dependent choose a life-annuity option. Caution is advised, however, because even if an annuitant receives only one payment under the contract before he or she dies, all the remaining value in the contract is forfeited. If your client is seeking a minimum payback guarantee to be provided for a beneficiary and does not need to squeeze the maximum income out of his or her annuity, he or she should be advised to reject the straight life annuity because of the possibility of forfeiture in the event of early death.

Life Annuity with Guaranteed Payments

A life annuity with guaranteed payments (sometimes referred to as a life annuity with a period-certain guarantee) provides monthly benefit payments to your client during his or her lifetime. Similar to a life annuity, payments stop when your client dies. Unlike a life annuity, however, if an agreed-upon minimum amount of guaranteed payments has not been paid to the annuitant, these payments (or their lump-sum commuted value) will be paid out to your client's (annuitant's) beneficiary. Any length of guarantee is available. Typical guarantee periods are for 5, 10, or 20 years. For longer period-certain guarantees the monthly benefit that your client will receive will be lower (table 8-1). This decrease occurs because the underwriter must allocate part of the annuity funds toward the guarantee feature. If the guarantee is for a long period of time, a greater amount of assets must be shifted away from the pooled assets providing current monthly benefits.

A life annuity with no guarantees will often be the best choice for clients who have no need to provide retirement income to a spouse or other dependent. If, however, there is a need to provide for the continuation of retirement income, a joint and survivor annuity is typically used. In some cases a life annuity with some level of guarantee may be appropriate, such as when a person does not have to provide for the needs of a spouse yet wishes to leave some legacy to heirs in the event of an early death, but cannot afford to give up too much income. A life annuity with guaranteed payments is used by clients who would like to make sure that a portion of their retirement accruals will be recovered either as a benefit to themselves or to a beneficiary.

Life annuities with guaranteed payments may also be used to provide a limited survivor benefit to an unhealthy spouse. For example, assume a retiring husband is in good health and his wife is in poor health. In this case a life annuity with a minimum guarantee might be used rather than a joint and survivor annuity to provide the wife with income in the unlikely (but possible) case of the husband predeceasing the wife. The period chosen should to some extent reflect the best medical estimate of the wife's maximum life expectancy and, if applicable, the husband's desire to pass on wealth.

The selection of a life annuity with a period-certain guarantee should be used with caution in these cases, however. There is always some chance, despite the severity of an illness, that an ill spouse will recover or survive long beyond the expected period. In such cases the spouse could be left with no income. As an alternative to a life annuity with guaranteed payments, planners should consider advising their clients to elect the single life option with no guarantees and to purchase life insurance, if they are insurable. The insurance may provide the required benefits in the event that the client predeceases his or her ill spouse. If the client survives the ill spouse, as anticipated, the insurance may be terminated or held to provide benefits for another beneficiary after the client's death.

Modified Cash-Refund Annuity

A modified cash-refund (MCR) annuity is typically the normal form of benefit in a defined-benefit plan with mandatory contributions. An MCR is a life annuity with a guaranteed payment. In this case the guarantee or refund is a specified dollar amount, generally the client's contributions to the plan with interest. This type of annuity ensures that the clients' contributions to the pension plan will not be lost because of premature death. As with a life annuity with guaranteed payments, the refund feature of an MCR costs the participant in the form of lower monthly benefits (see table 8-1).

Conventional Joint and Survivor (J&S) Annuity

As previously mentioned, the normal form of benefit paid to a married individual from a qualified plan is a joint and survivor annuity. The beneficiary under a joint and survivor annuity does not have to be the spouse. If the participant is married, however, the spouse must consent to allow someone else to be the beneficiary. A J&S annuity provides monthly payments to the participant during his or her lifetime. The retirement income continues after the participant's death with payments made to the client's beneficiary (the survivor). Typically the amount of the survivor payment can be

- the same amount that was being paid out to the client (J&S 100)
- three-fourths of the amount that was being paid out to the participant (J&S 75)
- two-thirds of the amount that was being paid out to the participant (J&S 66 2/3)
- one-half of the amount that was being paid out to the participant (J&S 50)

Payments cease when both the participant and beneficiary have died. No death benefit or refund of premiums will be paid.

A conventional J&S annuity with a survivor benefit ratio of less than 100 percent pays the reduced benefit only if the participant dies first. If the survivorship beneficiary dies first, the unreduced benefit is paid to the surviving participant as long as he or she lives.

When assessing the suitability of a joint and survivor annuity the planner should consider the following:

- In general, the younger the beneficiary is, the lower the monthly benefit that will be paid.
- As a general rule, when the survivor benefit ratio is higher (that is, 100, 75, 66 2/3, or 50 percent), the monthly benefit will be lower. For example, a joint and survivor annuity with 100 percent survivor benefits will be

more costly in a given case (that is, provide lower monthly payments) than a joint and survivor annuity that provides a two-thirds survivor annuity.

- The life expectancy, based on the health of your client and his or her spouse, must be considered. For example, if the plan participant is not healthy and there is a great likelihood that the beneficiary will outlive the plan participant, a 100 percent joint and survivor annuity may be appropriate.

- Any life insurance coverage that is in force on the life of the participant should be considered when determining the need for a survivor option. Depending on the circumstances, a better benefit package may sometimes be created by combining the single life annuity option with the purchase of life insurance on the participant's life to provide the survivor benefit rather than by electing the J&S annuity from the plan.

- The amount of income needed by the surviving spouse will help to determine the percentage of the survivorship benefit that will be chosen. For example, retirement income needs may drop radically if one party dies (for example, in the case where one party was disabled or sickly and required expensive medical attention).

"First-Death" Reduction J&S Annuity

Since the income needs of the survivor are usually less than those of the couple, some plans now offer an option where the benefit is reduced upon the first death, regardless of who dies first. The advantage of this option is that the benefit payable while both live will be greater than that payable with a conventional J&S annuity for any given survivor benefit ratio. Alternatively the plan will be able to pay a higher benefit to the survivor than with a conventional J&S annuity for a given level of benefit payments while both live.

J&S Annuity with "Pop-Up" Feature

Another J&S annuity option commonly seen in government and public pension plans, such as those offered by school districts, is a J&S annuity with a "pop-up" feature. Like conventional J&S annuities where a survivor benefit ratio of less than 100 percent is elected, these annuities pay a specified joint benefit while both the participant and the participant's beneficiary survive and a reduced benefit (equal to the elected percentage of the joint benefit) to the surviving beneficiary in the event that the participant predeceases the beneficiary. In contrast, with a conventional J&S annuity, if the beneficiary dies before the participant, the monthly benefit "pops up" to what it would have been had the participant chosen a single-life annuity rather than the joint and survivor annuity. The pop-up feature comes at a cost. Generally the joint benefit paid on an annuity with the pop-up feature will be less than what would be paid on a conventional J&S annuity without the pop-up feature. Consequently in the general case where both the participant and beneficiary are in reasonably good health, the choice of the pop-up feature in effect shifts benefits away from the couple, when benefits are presumably most needed, to the participant, but *only if* he or she survives the beneficiary.

The pop-up feature can be somewhat attractive, however, in cases where the participant's spouse/beneficiary, for instance, is in poor health. The J&S annuity will provide benefits for the spouse in the unlikely event that the participant predeceases the spouse, but, in the more likely event that the unhealthy spouse dies first, the benefits paid to the participant are equal to what he or she would have had under the single-life option.

Despite its appeal in such circumstances, other options might be better suited and more cost effective. For example, a single-life annuity with a guaranteed period equaling the spouse's maximum likely longevity may provide higher benefit payments. Alternatively a single-life annuity combined with the purchase of life insurance on the participant (assuming insurability) might often be a more cost-effective and flexible strategy.

Other Annuities

In addition to the typical forms of annuities, your client's plan may contain one or more of the following less frequently used annuity forms.

Full Cash Refund. A full cash-refund annuity pays back the benefit balance at the time of retirement as a guaranteed minimum benefit. Under this annuity, if the client dies before receiving monthly benefits equal to the original benefit balance, the difference between the original benefit balance and the aggregate monthly payments already received is refunded to the client's beneficiary.

Temporary Annuity. A temporary annuity makes payments over a period that expires at the earlier of death or a specified date. Participants who retire prior to age 65 may wish to elect a temporary annuity in conjunction with a regular annuity. The temporary annuity is set so that it is equal to the amount the participants will receive at age 65 from social security payments. Thus it provides the participants with a level total annual benefit both before and after age 65. The temporary annuity will pay an amount before age 65 that is equal to what will be received as a social security benefit after age 65. Temporary annuities are also useful for a client who expects to receive a trust fund distribution at a known future date. The temporary annuity can provide income until the trust fund begins distributions.

Annuity Certain. This annuity (also called a term-certain annuity) provides a specified amount of monthly guaranteed payments for a specified period (for example, payments for 20 years). There is no life contingency element. An annuity certain continues to be paid whether your client survives to the end of the annuity period or not.   If the client dies before the specified period runs out, payments will be made to the client's beneficiary.   This type of annuity can also be used as a pre-social-security benefit supplement.

TABLE 8-1 Comparison of Annuity Forms ($200,000 Benefit Balance for Client Aged 65, Spouse Aged 62)	
Annuity Form	Monthly Benefit
Life	$1,818
Life annuity/10-year guarantee	1,710
Life annuity/20-year guarantee	1,560
Modified cash refund (10 percent contributions)	1,720
Modified cash refund (25 percent contributions)	1,700
Joint and survivor (50 percent)	1,696
Joint and survivor (66 2/3 percent)	1,626
Joint and survivor (100 percent)	1,504

Variable Annuities

Some employer plans offer variable annuity contracts as well as the fixed-dollar annuity contracts just discussed.   The variable annuity contracts are designed to provide fluctuating benefit payments over the payout period that may provide increasing benefits during periods of inflation.   The assets backing these contracts are generally invested in higher-risk securities than are used for fixed-dollar annuity contracts and usually (but not necessarily) keep pace with inflation.   The benefits paid to your client depend on the investment performance of the underlying assets.   Variable annuities have historically enabled annuitants to maintain some degree of the purchasing power of their benefits.   Clients who are financially able to undertake the additional risk should seriously consider a variable annuity.

The types of benefit arrangements available under variable annuity contracts are the same as those available under fixed-dollar annuities.   The only thing that changes is the fluctuating nature of the actual benefit payments.

Operation of a Variable Annuity

Under a variable annuity contract your client will have a given number of annuity units as of the date the contract is annuitized, and that number of units will not change during the benefit payout period.   However, the value of annuity units does change in direct relationship to the net asset value of the annuity assets managed by the insurance company. As the value of the invested assets increases, the value of the annuity units will also increase. Likewise, decreases in the investment portfolio for the contracts will lead to decreases in the value of annuity units. The actual benefit payment each month will depend on the current value of the annuity unit multiplied by the number of units owned.

Under most variable annuity contracts there is an assumed investment rate (AIR) that the investment portfolio must earn in order for benefit payments to remain level. If the investment performance exceeds that AIR, then the level of benefit payments will increase. On the other hand, if the investment performance falls below the AIR, then the level of benefit payments will decrease.

Example: Your client, Frank Jackson, has a variable annuity contract that was issued with a 6 percent AIR and a beginning unit value of $20. Frank owns 100 units. The investment yield during the first month in Frank's contract was 12 percent; during the second month the investment yield was 4 percent. Frank can calculate his monthly benefit by monitoring the changes in the unit value and by comparing the actual performance with the assumed 6 percent interest rate. During the first month the 12 percent return on portfolio doubles the assumed 6 percent AIR and leads to a 6 percent increase in the $20 unit value. The new unit value is now $21.20 ($2,120 per month). During the subsequent month, because the actual return is only 4 percent, which is 2 percent less than the AIR, there will be a 2 percent reduction in the unit value to $20.77 ($2,077 per month). The unit value could actually drop below the beginning $20 value ($2,000 per month) if investment performance remains below the assumed 6 percent level for an extended period of time.

Selecting the AIR

Under some contracts the purchaser is able to select the AIR from a narrow range of possible rates. It is much easier to receive an increasing stream of benefit payments by selecting a lower AIR even though it is initially more expensive. The effect of choosing a different AIR can be demonstrated by returning to the Frank Jackson example.

Example: If Frank Jackson had chosen an AIR of 8 percent rather than 6 percent, the benefit increase in the first month would have been 4 percent instead of 6 percent. The unit value would have changed to $20.80 instead of $21.20. The next month's decrease in benefits would have been a more drastic 4 percent reduction rather than the 2 percent reduction. The unit value would have decreased to $19.96 instead of $20.77 from the lower AIR. By choosing the less costly higher AIR the client increases the likelihood that benefit payments will increase less rapidly and decrease more rapidly.

If your client has a variable annuity, keep in mind that although variable annuity contracts are intended to provide a hedge against inflation and protect the purchasing power of the benefits, these increases have not always occurred at exactly the same time that prices increase. Often prices go up significantly before the level of benefits increases. These temporary mismatches between price increases and benefit increases are inevitable and can lead to a temporary loss of purchasing power.

TAXATION OF PERIODIC DISTRIBUTIONS

Periodic payments (annuity or installment payments) made from qualified plans, IRA accounts, and 403(b) annuities are generally taxable as ordinary income. However, if some of the participant's benefit under the plan is attributable to dollars in the plan that have already been subject to taxation, such as employee contributions and amounts attributable to term insurance premiums (PS 58 costs), then a portion of each annuity payment will be exempt from tax until the total nontaxable amount has been distributed.

Different rules apply depending upon whether the recipient has begun to receive periodic payments as a retirement benefit or whether an in-service preretirement distribution is being made. The rules applicable to preretirement in-service distributions have already been discussed. This section will review the rules applicable to retirement distributions.

If the participant has an investment in the contract (cost basis), each annuity payment is multiplied by an exclusion ratio. The exclusion ratio is determined by dividing the distributee's investment in the contract by the expected benefit from the annuity. The exclusion ratio is then multiplied by the amount of the distribution in order to determine the taxable and nontaxable amount.

Investment in the Contract

The first step in determining the tax is to determine the amount of the distribution that is not subject to tax. This amount is referred to as the *investment in the contract* or *cost basis*.

The primary amounts recoverable tax free as a participant's cost basis include

- the total aftertax contributions made by the employee to a contributory plan
- the total cost of life insurance actually reported as taxable income on federal income tax returns by the participant (the PS 58 costs) if the plan distribution is received under the same contract that provides the life insurance protection. (If the plan trustee cashes in the life insurance contract before distribution, this cost basis amount is not available. For a person who is now or was self-employed, no PS 58 costs are available.)

The Regular Method for Calculating Exclusion Amounts

The exclusion ratio may be computed in either of two ways: the regular method or the safe harbor method. Calculation of the regular exclusion ratio for single or joint and 100 percent survivor life annuities (without a refund or guarantee feature) is rather easily described. The ratio is a fraction, where the numerator is the investment in the contract (cost basis) and the denominator is the expected benefits from the contract.

$$\text{Exclusion ratio} = \frac{\text{Investment}}{\text{Expected benefits}}$$

The exclusion ratio is rounded to three decimal places when used to compute the amount excludible.

In order to calculate the exclusion ratio the expected benefit must first be determined. The expected benefit is determined by multiplying the annual benefit payable under the contract by the number of years that the benefits are expected to be paid. This life expectancy in years is found in Table V for single life annuities and Table VI for joint and survivor annuities under IRC Reg. Sec. 1.72-9 (see appendix 2). If the participant does before the cost basis is fully recovered, a deduction for the unrecovered basis is allowed on the final income tax return.

The exclusion ratio continues to apply until the cost basis is fully recovered. Payments received subsequently are taxable in full.

Example: John Thomas is scheduled to receive $12,000 per year in monthly installments of $1,000 from his qualified plan paid in the form of a life annuity. The payments will begin in the first month after his retirement. John is aged 61 and has a life expectancy of 23.3 years (Table V). John has made aftertax contributions to the plan amounting to $24,000. John's exclusion is determined as follows:

Investment in contract   = $24,000
Expected benefits   = $12,000 x (23.3) = $279,600

Exclusion ratio   = $\dfrac{\$ 24,000}{\$279,600}$

= 0.0858 = 0.086 (rounded to three places), or 8.6%

When John receives his first monthly benefit of $1,000, he will not have to pay taxes on $86 (1,000 x 8.6%) and will pay taxes on the remaining $914. The $86 portion of the payment is considered a return of John's previously taxed basis. If John is still receiving benefits after 23.3 years, all subsequent benefit payments will be taxable as ordinary income since he will be deemed to have recovered all of his nontaxable basis from the annuity contract.

The regular method is easy to apply when calculating exclusion ratios for single or joint and 100 percent survivor life annuities without a refund or guarantee feature, but can become quite involved if other types of annuity arrangements are used. For those interested in determining exclusion ratios in more complex situations, see appendix 5.

The Safe Harbor Method for Calculating Exclusion Amounts

The safe harbor method may be used for distributions of annuity payments that commence after July 1, 1986. According to the IRS most annuitants will be able to exclude from taxable income a larger portion of their annuity payments than if they used the regular method for computing exclusion ratios. The following three conditions must be met in order to use this method:

1. The annuity payments must depend on the life of the distributee or the joint lives of the distributee and beneficiary.

2. The annuity payments must be made from an employee plan qualified under Sec. 401(a) of the Code (a pension, profit-sharing, or stock bonus plan), an employee annuity under Sec. 403(a), or a 403(b) tax-deferred annuity plan (IRAs and SEPs are excluded).

3. The distributee must be under age 75 when annuity payments commence or, if the distributee is aged 75 or older, payment may not be guaranteed for more than 5 years.

Under the safe harbor method the total number of monthly annuity payments expected to be received is based on the distributee's age at the annuity starting date rather than according to the life expectancy tables in IRC Reg. Sec. 1.72-9. The same expected number of payments applies to a distributee whether he or she is receiving a single life annuity or a joint and survivor annuity. The number of payments to be used is set forth in table 8-2.

The investment in the contract is the aggregate amount of aftertax contributions to the plan (plus other aftertax amounts such as PS 58 costs and repayments of loans previously taxed as distributions) minus the aggregate amount received before the annuity starting date that was excluded from income. No refund feature adjustment is required. In addition, when the distributee is entitled to the $5,000 death benefit income tax exclusion, he or she can increase the amount of the investment in the contract by the $5,000 amount.

TABLE 8-2 Number of Months for Safe Harbor Exclusion Method	
Age of Distributee	Number of Payments
55 and under	300
56–60	260
61–65	240
66–70	170
71 and over	120

The distributee recovers his or her investment in the contract in level amounts over the number of monthly payments determined in the table above. The amount excluded from each payment is calculated by dividing the investment by the set number of monthly payments determined in the table above. That is,

$$\frac{\text{Investment}}{\text{Number of monthly payments}} = \frac{\text{Tax-free portion}}{\text{of monthly annuity}}$$

The dollar amount determined using the safe harbor method will be excluded from each monthly annuity payment, even where the amount of the annuity payments changes. For example, the amount to be excluded as determined at the annuity starting date remains constant, even if the amount of the annuity payments increases due to cost-of-living increases, or decreases in the case of a reduced survivor benefit annuity. If the amount to be excluded from each monthly payment is greater than the amount of the monthly annuity (such as might be the case for decreased survivor payments), then each monthly annuity payment will be completely excluded from gross income until the entire investment is recovered. Similar to the regular rules, once the entire investment is recovered, each monthly payment is fully taxable; if annuity payments cease before the entire investment is recovered, the unrecovered investment may be deducted on the last tax return.

Example: John Thomas from the previous example elects the safe harbor method for computing his exclusion amount. The set number of months used to compute the exclusion amount is 240 (for age 61 from table 8-2). Since his investment in the contract is $24,000, the amount excluded from each payment is $100 ($24,000/240). This exclusion amount is $14 more than the exclusion amount computed using the regular exclusion ratio for a single life annuity in the previous example.

How to Elect the Safe Harbor Method

A person may elect the safe harbor method on his or her own tax return even if the payer does not use it. When the participant receives a benefit, the payor is required to report the total amount and the taxable amount of the distribution on IRS Form 1099R. The payor can either use the regular or the safe harbor method of determining the taxable portion of the distribution. The participant is not bound by the payor's method of determining the taxable amount, and is permitted to elect either approach on his or her tax return.

When to Use the Safe Harbor Method

In addition to its convenience and simplicity, the safe harbor method is generally the better method for computing exclusion amounts because it frequently provides a higher aftertax value than the regular method. At worst, the safe harbor method and the regular method give almost identical results. This will occur when the individual is at the high end of the age categories shown in table 8-2 and is receiving either a single life annuity or 100 percent joint and survivor annuity with no guaranteed payments. Therefore, as a general statement, choosing the safe harbor method is a safe bet. However, it is never a bad idea to run the numbers using both methods, just to make sure that the highest exclusion amount is chosen. The higher the exclusion ratio, the longer taxes are deferred.

Installment Payments

When the distribution is in the form of periodic installment payments, the expected benefit for determining the exclusion ratio is the total of all expected installment payments.

> *Example:* Sally elects to receive monthly installment payments of $200 a month for 10 years, for a total of $24,000 ($200 x 12 x 10). Her cost basis is $1,200. The exclusion allowance is $1,200/$24,000 = .05 (5 percent). Therefore Sally will not pay tax on $10 of each $200 installment payment.

ROLLOVERS AND TRANSFERS

Certain types of distributions from qualified plans, IRAs, SEPs, and Sec. 403(b) tax-deferred annuity plans may be rolled over tax free to an IRA account as long as the rollover is made within 60 days of the receipt of the distribution. Distributions from a qualified plan can also be rolled over into another qualified plan. A rollover means that the participant physically receives the distribution and subsequently deposits the amount into an appropriate plan. Failure to roll the distribution over within 60 days from the receipt of the distribution will subject the participant to income tax and, if applicable, the 10 percent early withdrawal penalty on the entire taxable portion of the distribution.

Since a plan participant could inadvertently fail the 60-day rollover requirement, the Emergency Unemployment Act (P.L. 102-318), effective for distributions made beginning in 1993, requires qualified plans and Sec. 403(b) tax-sheltered annuities to give participants the option to have eligible benefit distributions transferred directly from one plan trustee to the trustee of an IRA (or in the case of a qualified plan distribution, another qualified plan).

The law also encourages direct transfers (versus rollovers) by requiring 20 percent of any distribution that is not directly transferred to be withheld for federal income tax purposes. In other words, a participant planning to roll over a distribution will receive only 80 percent of the distribution; 20 percent is withheld for taxes. If an individual wants to roll over the entire distribution, he or she has to come up with the additional cash to deposit into the new plan and must request a tax refund. Since both direct transfers and rollovers defer income tax on the distribution, a participant in a qualified plan or Sec. 403(b) tax-sheltered annuity should take advantage of the direct transfer option—thus avoiding the 20 percent income tax withholding.

Distributions from a qualified plan can also be rolled over (or transferred directly) into another qualified plan. In general, a rollover into another qualified plan may be preferable to a rollover into an IRA because the preferential tax treatment may be preserved with regard to 5-year or 10-year forward income averaging, capital-gain treatment, and certain other features, such as loan provision. IRAs, SEPs, and 403(b) annuity plans are not eligible for 5-year or 10-year forward averaging treatment, and IRAs may not provide loans. If an individual is not immediately eligible for participation into another qualified plan, he or she may roll/transfer the benefit into a conduit IRA (see discussion below) and later roll the benefit back into a qualified plan.

Distributions Qualifying for Rollover Treatment

As mentioned above the Emergency Unemployment Act liberalized the rollover rules. The current rules provide that

any portion of *any* (taxable) distribution from

- a qualified plan
- or a tax-sheltered annuity

may be rolled tax free into

- an individual retirement plan
- a qualified plan (only for distributions from qualified plans)
- or an annuity plan (only for distributions from annuity plans)

The only distributions excepted from the general rule are

- minimum required distributions (see chapter 10)
- distributions of substantially equal periodic payments made

    — over the participant's remaining life (or life expectancy)
    — over the joint lives (or life expectancies) of the participant and a beneficiary
    — over a period of more than 10 years

The maximum permissible amount that can be rolled over is the taxable portion of the distribution. In other words, aftertax contributions cannot be rolled over.

When to Use Direct Transfers or Rollovers

The direct transfer (or rollover) is an important tool for distribution planning because a client's plan may not provide a distribution option that meets his or her needs. In such cases plan balances or the accrued benefits may often be rolled over to another plan or to an IRA designed to provide the distribution option desired. In addition, rollovers are used when

- a participant in a qualified plan, 403(b) annuity plan, or IRA would like to continue to defer taxes on the money in the plan, but wants to change the form of investment or gain greater control over it
- a participant in a retirement plan receives a large plan distribution upon retirement or termination of employment and wants to defer taxes on part or all of the distribution beyond the normal starting date for the plan or to avoid the 10 percent early distribution penalty
- a participant in a qualified retirement plan or a 403(b) annuity plan that is being terminated by the employer wishes to defer taxes on the distribution from the terminated plan
- the spouse of a deceased employee wants to defer taxation on a lump-sum distribution of the deceased spouse's benefit or prefers a distribution option not provided as a survivor benefit option under the plan

The entire amount qualifying for a transfer or rollover need not be rolled over. However, any amount not rolled over will be subject to income tax and the 10 percent early-withdrawal penalty, if applicable.

Conduit IRAs

Conduit IRAs are IRAs that are used to hold qualified plan funds for transfer from one qualified plan to another when an employee changes employers and the transfer to the new qualified plan cannot be completed either directly or within 60 days of the distribution from the original plan. When the transfer between two qualified plans can be completed either directly or within 60 days, it is generally more convenient to roll the funds directly from one plan to the other. The initial transfer from the qualified plan to the IRA is tax free if completed within 60 days. The amount in the conduit IRA may subsequently be transferred tax free to another plan if the conduit IRA contains no assets other than those attributable to the distribution from the original qualified plan.

Conduit IRAs may also be used to transfer funds between two Sec. 403(b) annuity plans, if the plans permit such transfers. However, the conduit IRA may not be used to transfer funds between a qualified plan and a Sec. 403(b) annuity plan, or vice versa.

Distribution of Annuity Contracts

In some cases qualified plans may distribute an annuity contract to a participant instead of a cash distribution. Assuming the annuity contract has the desired features, the annuity can serve the same purposes as an IRA rollover, since the participant will not be taxed until distributions are made under the annuity contract. The annuity contract does not have to meet the requirements of an IRA, but the tax implications and the distribution requirements and restrictions (such as the minimum distribution rules) are generally similar.

CASE STUDIES

Ralph and Dora Archer

Ralph Archer, aged 65, is nearing retirement and must choose the form of his retirement distribution. His wife, Dora, is independently wealthy. Both Ralph and Dora have families from previous marriages. Essentially all of Dora's wealth will be distributed to her children upon her death. Ralph earns a modest income and is concerned about outliving his own financial resources if he survives Dora. The marriage is very solid, and Ralph will have no financial difficulties as long as Dora is alive.

Ralph's two main objectives are to maximize his retirement benefits and to guarantee that his benefits will be lifelong. Ralph may be well advised to delay the inception of his retirement benefits until the earlier of age 70 1/2 or Dora's death. When Ralph starts receiving his benefits, he would be wise to select a life annuity, with Dora's consent, since he does not need to provide survivor benefits for Dora and is not bothered by the prospect of forfeiting unpaid benefits at death. Ralph's $200,000 fund balance can provide him with $1,818 a month for the rest of his life, starting at age 65. This payment is 20 percent more than he would receive if he were to elect a joint survivor annuity benefit providing equal payments to Dora after his death.

Jerry and Joan Davenport

Jerry and Joan Davenport have no children and have been completely dependent on Jerry's modest income for their financial support. They are both aged 65, and Jerry must now select the form of his retirement distribution. Joan has been fighting cancer for the last year, and the doctors do not expect her to live more than 8 months. Jerry is in extremely good health and comes from a long-lived family. He is concerned about having an adequate income and wants to make sure that he does not exhaust his resources before his death. Jerry can maximize his guaranteed lifetime income by selecting a life-annuity option. In addition, Jerry might consider buying term insurance, which would be helpful in the event that he dies before his wife.

Larry and Sheila Richardson

Larry and Sheila Richardson are preparing for Larry's retirement at age 65. They have no children and are both in good health. Because Sheila is only 50 years old, selection of a survivorship annuity will significantly decrease the monthly benefit available from the pension plan. Larry and Sheila are wondering whether they should take the joint and survivor benefit or elect out of the survivorship benefit and apply the difference to the purchase of life insurance on Larry with the benefits payable to Sheila. This decision depends on Larry's insurability and the cost of coverage relative to the benefit it provides. If the death benefit provided is greater than the cost of the life annuity for Sheila, the purchase of life insurance is a viable alternative.

NOTES

1. Certain profit sharing type plans—which include 401(k) plans—are exempt from these requirements.
2. The threshold amount depends upon the participant's age and year of death.

9

Planning for Distributions from Retirement Plans — Part II

Chapter Outline

Instead of taking periodic payments from a qualified plan, employees are frequently permitted to receive their retirement benefit in a lump-sum distribution. Employees may choose to have lump-sum distributions from their qualified plans taxed in an advantageous manner by selecting either 5-year or 10-year income averaging; by having distributions attributable to pre-1974 participation subject to lower capital-gain tax rates; and/or by excluding from gross income the net unrealized appreciation of distributed employer securities. Alternatively employees may choose to forego this tax treatment and instead receive installment or annuity payments from the plan or roll the distribution over into an IRA where the taxes on the distribution will be delayed until proceeds are received.

From a planning standpoint several key questions arise when clients consider taking a lump-sum distribution.

- Should clients who qualify for 10-year averaging (that is, clients born before January 1, 1936) choose to use 10-year or 5-year averaging for lump-sum distributions?
- What should clients do with distributions of employer's stock with net unrealized appreciation?
- When should clients elect to use the capital-gain provision for pre-1974 accruals?
- When is one of the averaging provisions better (or worse) than receiving installment payments from the plan or from an IRA rollover account?

LUMP-SUM DISTRIBUTION DEFINED

Before evaluating those four questions, let us define what qualifies as a lump-sum distribution, indicate what conditions are necessary to make an averaging election, and discuss the potential tax advantages of lump-sum distributions.

Qualifying Plans

To qualify for special tax treatment the lump-sum distribution must come from a pension, profit-sharing, 401(k), stock bonus, or employee stock ownership plan. Distributions from SEPs, IRAs, and 403(b) annuity plans do not qualify.

Qualifying Distributions

In order to qualify for special averaging treatment, capital-gain treatment, or the special net unrealized appreciation treatment for employer securities, a distribution must qualify as a *lump-sum distribution*. In order to qualify the following four conditions must apply:

- The client must have been a plan participant for at least 5 years.

- The funds must be distributed to your client within one taxable year.
- The distribution must represent your client's entire account balance or benefit.
- The amount distributed must be payable only if the client dies, attains at least age 59 1/2, separates from service, or is disabled.

These conditions, as well as some special issues, need further explanation. Many questions exist in the interpretation of each of these requirements, and the IRS, as well as the Federal Courts, continually provides guidance. The material below describes much of this guidance; however, given the organic nature of this area of the law, determining whether any specific distribution qualifies requires a careful review of the current law.

Plan Participation for at Least 5 Years

In some cases, participation in two plans can be aggregated for determining whether the 5-year requirement has been satisfied. The IRS has ruled that service can be aggregated if the benefit from one plan is transferred directly (from the trustee of that plan) to the trustee of the distributing plan. However, aggregation is not allowed when a participant simply rolls over the benefit from one plan to the other. Also, the 5-year participation rule does not apply to a beneficiary electing special averaging upon the death of the employee. In other words, the employee does not have to have 5 years of participation for the beneficiary to be eligible for special averaging.

Funds Distributed within One Taxable Year

To qualify as a distribution within one taxable year the distribution does not have to be made in a single payment as long as the complete balance is distributed within one taxable year.

Distribution Represents Entire Benefit

According to Internal Revenue Code jargon, the distribution must be the "balance to the credit" of an employee that becomes payable to the recipient. Basically, this means that the distribution is the entire benefit earned by the employee at the time of payment. However, there are a lot of questions as to what the balance to the credit means. First, note that when making this determination, any nonvested amounts that are forfeited at the time of the distribution are not counted.

Second, when determining whether a benefit constitutes the balance to the credit, the Code requires that certain plans be aggregated. If an individual participates in more than one pension plan, these plans will be aggregated. Similarly, profit-sharing plans are aggregated and stock bonus plans are aggregated. For example, an individual with a benefit in a money-purchase pension plan and a defined-benefit pension plan only receives a lump-sum distribution if benefits from both plans are distributed during the year. On the other hand, if the individual has benefits in both a money-purchase pension plan and a profit-sharing plan, the individual can receive the profit-sharing benefit and be eligible to get lump-sum treatment without also receiving the money-purchase benefit.

Another issue that arises regularly is what happens when a person receives the entire benefit due to him or her at the time, and then later is entitled to additional benefits. When additional amounts are paid in a subsequent year due to calculation errors, the IRS has ruled that the additional payments will not necessarily cause the loss of lump-sum treatment (on the previous payments). However, the additional payments are not eligible for lump-sum treatment.

Another common issue is whether a distribution constitutes the balance to the credit when the individual had previously received distributions from the plan. In this case, the IRS has indicated that the balance to the credit includes all amounts in the participant's account (including any nondeductible employee contributions) as of the time of the first distribution received after the triggering event (see next section). For example, assume an individual withdraws nondeductible contributions prior to age 59 1/2 and then receives the remaining benefit after attaining age 59 1/2. In this case the participant has received the balance to the credit since the nondeductible distributions were made prior to attaining age 59 1/2.

Distribution on Account of Death, Age 59 1/2, Separation from Service, or Disability

To qualify as a lump-sum distribution, the payment of the benefit must be on account of one of these four events (referred to as *triggering events*): distribution on account of death, age 59 1/2, separation from service, or disability. Many difficult issues arise in this area, and the IRS has published numerous revenue rulings and private letter rulings to address them. One especially troublesome issue is the determination of whether a separation from service has occurred. On this issue, the IRS has indicated that a separation does not occur when an employee (1) continues employment in any capacity (even if part-time or noncompensated); (2) continues employment in the same job with a new employer after a liquidation, merger, or consolidation; or (3) continues as an "independent contractor" if the services provided are essentially the same as when the individual was employed. On a more liberal note, the IRS has indicated that a distribution can be treated as "on account of separation from service" even if it is made several years after the year that separation from service occurred.

Special Issues

Disqualified Plans

The federal courts are divided on the issue of tax treatment of distributions from disqualified plans (plans that have lost their qualified status through an IRS determination). The Tax Court has generally held that the favorable tax treatment for lump-sum distributions is available with respect to contributions made to a qualified plan before the date the plan became disqualified. The courts of appeal have been split on the issue, with most holding that no portion of a distribution made from a disqualified plan qualifies for favorable lump-sum treatment. Therefore the tax treatment for distributions from disqualified plans is uncertain and may vary depending on the circuit in which the taxpayer resides.

Qualified Domestic Relations Orders

If a distribution of the balance to the credit of an employee would constitute a lump-sum distribution, then a distribution of the balance to the credit of an alternate payee under a qualified domestic relations order (QDRO) constitutes a lump-sum distribution. An alternate payee may include the participant's spouse, former spouse, child, or other dependent.

ELIGIBILITY FOR SPECIAL TAX TREATMENT

5-Year Averaging

An individual can elect 5-year averaging only if *all* the following conditions are met:

- The distribution qualifies as a lump-sum distribution.
- The distribution is received after the employee attains age 59 1/2.
- The election for 5-year averaging has not been made before (only one election per taxpayer).
- The taxpayer elects to treat all such amounts received during the year in the same manner.

The second requirement can be confusing since attaining age 59 1/2 is a triggering event for a distribution to qualify as a lump sum. What happened is that under the Tax Reform Act of 1986 (TRA '86) the requirements for special averaging treatment became more strict. Before TRA '86, averaging was available for any distribution made on account of one of the four triggering events (termination of employment, disability, death, or age 59 1/2). Now, 5-year averaging treatment is available only upon attainment of age 59 1/2. This requirement applies even for payment of a death benefit. The IRS has indicated that the employee had to be at least aged 59 1/2 at death in order for the beneficiary to be eligible for 5-year averaging treatment. TRA '86 did contain a grandfathering rule that allows individuals born before 1936 to receive distributions before attainment of age 59 1/2.

After TRA '86 individuals can make only one election to use forward averaging treatment. However, TRA '86 contained another grandfather rule allowing those who had elected lump-sum treatment on a distribution before January 1, 1987, to make one more special averaging election from a different plan after January 1, 1987.

Clients may aggregate distributions from one or more employers, and the aggregate distribution may qualify for lump-sum treatment if each of the separate distributions would alone qualify for lump-sum treatment and each distribution is received in the same taxable year. In fact, an individual electing special lump-sum tax treatment on one lump-sum distribution is required to treat all lump-sum distributions received in that year in the same manner.

10-Year Averaging

TRA '86 replaced 10-year averaging with 5-year averaging. However, TRA '86 grandfathered 10-year averaging for individuals born prior to January 1, 1936. If such an individual is eligible for 5-year averaging he or she is also eligible for the grandfathered 10-year averaging. He or she may make the election even though the employee is not aged 59 1/2 at the time, and can make only one election (of either 5- or 10-year averaging). As under the 5-year averaging rule, if the election is made it must apply to all lump-sum distributions made in the taxable year.

Capital-Gains Election

Clients born before January 1, 1936, can elect to treat the portion of a lump-sum distribution attributable to pre-1974 plan participation as capital gain. If this election is made, the amount subject to capital gain is taxed at a special grandfathered rate of 20 percent. A recipient may make only one such election. Employees born after January 1, 1936, do not have this option.

Unrealized Appreciation

Whenever a recipient receives a lump-sum distribution, he or she may elect to defer paying tax on the net unrealized appreciation in employer securities. If the distribution is not a lump-sum distribution, unrealized appreciation is excludible only to the extent that the appreciation is attributable to nondeductible employee contributions.

COMPUTING THE 5-YEAR OR 10-YEAR FORWARD AVERAGING TAX

The idea behind both the 5-year and 10-year averaging methods is to separate a lump-sum payment from the recipient's other taxable income and to tax this payment as if it had been received evenly over a 5-year or 10-year period, respectively.

Both averaging taxes are computed in an analogous manner that can be briefly described with an example using 5-year averaging.

Five-year averaging works as follows: The first step is to reduce the benefit by the *minimum distribution allowance*. The distribution allowance is calculated by (1) determining the lesser of $10,000 and one-half of the total taxable amount and then (2) reducing the number calculated in (1) by 20 percent of the total taxable amount in excess of $20,000. When you do the math, you can see that the minimum distribution allowance becomes $0 for taxable distributions of $70,000 [(1) $10,000—which is the lesser of $10,000 and one-half of $70,000 (2) is reduced by $10,000—which is 20 percent of $50,000, the total taxable amount in excess of $20,000]. There is no minimum distribution allowance for taxable distributions in excess of $70,000.

After determining the minimum distribution allowance, the remaining taxable amount is divided by five and a separate tax is determined on this portion, based on the single taxpayer rate for the current tax year without any deductions or exclusions. The actual tax is this amount multiplied by five.

Example: Assume that Waldo receives a $40,000 lump-sum distribution in 1995. What is the tax using 5-year averaging?

1.	Total taxable amount	$40,000
2.	Minimum distribution allowance	
	[$10,000 − (20% x $20,000)]	$6,000
3.	Balance	$34,000
4.	1/5 of balance	$6,800
5.	Tax on line 5 (15%)	$1,020
6.	Tax (5 x line 5 amount)	$5,100

The taxpayer elects and reports this calculation on Form 4972, reproduced in appendix 6, which is filed with the tax return for the year. Form 4972 includes detailed instructions and a work sheet for making the calculation.

Averaging Tax Schedules

Planners do not need to perform the entire computation each time a client desires tax planning advice concerning distributions from a qualified plan. Tables can be used, such as the ones shown in tables 9-1 and 9-2; as well, computer programs making these calculations are available. Table 9-1 shows the 5-year averaging tax table for 1995. Five-year averaging uses current tax rates (in this case 1995 rates). Obviously, the calculations will be different for years after 1995—slightly as inflation pushes up tax brackets and drastically if tax rates change. Table 9-2 shows the 10-year averaging tax table. Under this grandfathering method, 1986 tax rates are used to calculate the tax. The calculations stay the same regardless of the year of distribution.

To compute the 5- or 10-year tax on a lump-sum distribution using these tables the planner must first compute the *adjusted total taxable amount*. The adjusted total taxable amount is equal to the total amount of the distribution, less all the following:

- any nontaxable portions, such as portions that are attributable to nondeductible employee contributions or PS 58 costs (see the discussion on investment in the contract in chapter 8)
- the unrealized appreciation in the employer's stock that is included in the distribution
- the amount subject to tax as capital gain if the capital-gain provision is elected
- up to $5,000 of employee death benefits in the case of a deceased participant

(*Planning Note:* If an annuity contract is distributed as part of a lump-sum distribution, certain adjustments must be made in the averaging-tax calculation. In such cases a planner should not use table 9-1 or table 9-2 to compute the averaging tax, but rather should use Form 4972 to properly account for these adjustments.)

Using the Tables

The best way to explain how to use these tables would be to use an example. Assume your client receives a lump-sum distribution of $150,000. For simplicity assume that the entire distribution is taxable, and that there are no plan accumulations attributable to pre-1974 service. The 5-year averaging tax is determined by using table 9-1 to find the range of values into which the adjusted total taxable amount falls. In this case the $150,000 distribution falls in the range between $116,750 and $282,750. Therefore the tax on this distribution is equal to $17,512.50 plus 28 percent of the amount of the distribution in excess of $116,750. The amount of the distribution in excess of $116,750 is $33,250; 28 percent of $33,250 is $9,310. Thus the entire tax on the distribution is equal to $17,512.50 plus $9,310, or $26,822.50. Note that your client would have to pay $42,000, or $15,177.50 more in tax on this distribution, if he or she was in the 28 percent tax bracket and did not elect to use 5-year averaging.

If your client was born before 1936, he or she would qualify for 10-year averaging. The 10-year averaging tax on the $150,000 distribution is found by

TABLE 9-1
5-Year Averaging (Lump-sum distributions received in 1995 or later)*

If the adjusted total taxable amount is:		the separate tax is	plus this %	of the excess over
at least	but not more than	the separate tax is	plus this %	of the excess over
. . .	$ 20,000	$ 0	7.5	$ 0
$ 20,000	70,000	1,500	18.0	20,000
70,000	116,750	10,500	15.0	70,000
116,750	282,750	17,512.50	28.0	116,750
282,750	589,750	63,992.50	31.0	282,750
589,750	1,282,500	159,162.50	36.0	589,750
1,282,500	. . .	408,552.50	39.6	1,282,500

*Based on the 1995 single tax rate schedule. In future years these amounts will shift slightly upward, corresponding to the indexation of tax rates for inflation.

using table 9-2 in the same way as we used table 9-1 to calculate the 5-year averaging tax. The $150,000 distribution falls in the range between $137,100 and $171,600 in table 9-2. Therefore the tax on the $150,000 distribution is equal to $21,603 plus 23 percent of the excess over $137,100. The excess over $137,100 is $12,900; 23 percent of $12,900 is $2,967. Thus the total 10-year averaging tax on a $150,000 distribution is equal to $21,603 plus $2,967, or $24,570. Clearly, if your client qualifies, he or she should use 10-year averaging rather than 5-year averaging since he or she would save $2,252.50.

When Qualifying Taxpayers Should Elect 10-Year rather than 5-Year Averaging

In 1995 10-year averaging is more favorable than 5-year averaging when the adjusted total taxable amount is less than or equal to $367,687 (assuming no portion qualifies for capital-gain treatment). If some portion of the distribution qualifies for capital-gain treatment (taxed at a 20 percent rate), 10-year averaging is more favorable than 5-year averaging for even larger distributions. Table 9-3 shows the tax differentials under 5-year and 10-year averaging for 1995. This table clearly demonstrates the superiority of 10-year averaging for smaller distribution amounts and the superiority of 5-year averaging for larger distribution amounts. In future years the crossover point at which 5-year averaging will be more favorable than 10-year averaging will fall as the tax rate schedule used when computing 5-year averaging is adjusted upwards for inflation.

TABLE 9-2				
10-Year Averaging (Using 1986 tax rates)*				
If the adjusted total taxable amount is:				
at least	but not more than	the separate tax is	plus this %	of the excess over
. . .	$ 20,000	0	5.5	0
$ 20,000	21,583	$ 1,100	13.2	$ 20,000
21,583	30,583	1,309	14.4	21,583
30,583	49,417	2,605	16.8	30,583
49,417	67,417	5,769	18.0	49,417
67,417	70,000	9,009	19.2	67,417
70,000	91,700	9,505	16.0	70,000
91,700	114,400	12,977	18.0	91,700
114,400	137,100	17,063	20.0	114,400
137,100	171,600	21,603	23.0	137,100
171,600	228,800	29,538	26.0	171,600
228,800	286,000	44,410	30.0	228,800
286,000	343,200	61,570	34.0	286,000
343,200	423,000	81,018	38.0	343,200
423,000	571,900	111,342	42.0	423,000
571,900	857,900	173,880	48.0	571,900
857,900	. . .	311,160	50.0	857,900

*Persons electing 10-year averaging must use the 1986 single tax rate schedule regardless of the year in which they actually receive the distribution.

There is another potential tax advantage to lump-sum averaging. The 15 percent excise tax on excess distributions, which is discussed in chapter 11, applies differently when a taxpayer elects 5- or 10-year averaging. In this case, the exemption from the 15 percent excise tax for the lump-sum distribution is equal to five times the applicable annual exemption for regular distributions where averaging is not elected. The impact of the 15 percent tax on excess distributions is discussed in chapter 11.

EMPLOYER SECURITIES WITH NET UNREALIZED APPRECIATION

The net unrealized appreciation in the employer's stock that is included in a lump-sum distribution is excluded when computing the income tax on the distribution. (The appreciation is included, however, when computing the 15 percent excess distributions tax.) The net unrealized appreciation is the difference between the value of the stock when credited to the participant's account and its fair market value on the date of distribution. This unrealized appreciation is

TABLE 9-3 Differences in Tax under 5-Year and 10-Year Forward Averaging (No capital gain)				
Taxable Distribution Amount	Tax Using 5-Year Forward Averaging (1995 tax rates used)	Tax Using 10-Year Forward Averaging (1986 tax rates used)	Differential (5-year minus 10-year averaging)	% of Increase or Decrease
$ 100,000	$ 15,000	$ 14,471	$ 529	37.0
150,000	26,822	24,570	2,252	9.2
200,000	40,822	36,922	3,900	10.6
250,000	54,822	50,770	4,052	7.9
300,000	69,340	66,330	3,010	4.5
350,000	84,840	83,602	1,238	1.4
367,687	90,323	90,323	(0)	0.0
400,000	100,340	102,602	(2,262)	−2.3
450,000	115,840	122,682	(6,842)	−5.9
500,000	131,340	143,682	(12,342)	−9.4
550,000	146,840	164,682	(17,842)	−12.2
600,000	162,852	187,368	(24,515)	−15.1
750,000	216,852	259,368	(42,515)	−19.6
1,000,000	306,852	382,210	(75,357)	−24.5
1,500,000	507,552	632,210	(124,658)	−24.6

taxable as long-term capital gain to the recipient when the shares are sold, even if sold immediately. If the recipient holds the shares for a period of time after distribution, any additional gain (above the net unrealized appreciation) is taxed as long- or short-term capital gain, depending on the holding period.

The participant may elect at the time of the distribution to pay tax on the net unrealized appreciation (versus taking advantage of the opportunity to defer taxes). Since the capital-gain tax rate (28 percent) may be substantially higher than the rates under special averaging, this is a viable choice for the individual who anticipates selling the stock soon after the distribution. Deferring taxes under the unrealized appreciation rules means forgoing the opportunity to have the distribution taxed under the averaging rules or at the special 20 percent capital-gain rate.

Example: Randi receives a distribution including $1,000 of net unrealized appreciation, and she is eligible for 10-year averaging treatment. The marginal tax rate under the 10-year averaging (based on the amount of her total distribution) is 18 percent. In the following year she sells the stock and pays 28 percent capital-gain tax on the unrealized appreciation. Randi paid $280 in tax instead of the $180 she would have paid if she had included the amount in income at the time of the distribution.

In contrast, if the recipient plans to hold the stock for a period of time, the tax deferral on the unrealized appreciation of the distributed stock may provide a significant benefit. In fact, if the stock is held until death, any gain on the stock subsequent to the distribution will escape tax altogether because of a step-up in basis.

THE CAPITAL-GAIN PROVISION

Persons born before January 1, 1936, may elect to treat the portion of a lump-sum distribution that is attributable to pre-1974 participation in a plan as capital gain.   If a person elects capital-gain treatment, the existing capital gain—that is, the pre-1974 plan accruals—is taxed at a flat 20 percent rate.   If the capital-gain provision is elected, the capital-gain portion of a lump-sum distribution is then excluded when the person calculates either the 5- or 10-year averaging tax.   Therefore the total tax payable on a lump-sum distribution when a person elects capital-gain treatment for pre-1974 plan accruals is equal to 20 percent of the portion of the distribution attributable to the pre-1974 plan accruals plus the averaging tax on the remainder.

The portion of a lump-sum distribution attributable to pre-1974 plan accruals is determined by finding the ratio of the person's months of plan participation before 1974 to the total months of plan participation. However, participation for any part of a calendar year prior to 1974 counts as 12 months of participation.

For example, if your client began his or her participation in the plan on July 1, 1970, and retires on June 30, 1988, with continuous service, the number of months of plan participation before 1974 is 48 (participation in 4 calendar years prior to 1974), and the total months of participation comes to 222 (48 months pre-1974 and 174 months post-1973).   Therefore the capital-gain portion is calculated as follows:

$$\text{Capital-gain portion} = \frac{\text{Months of pre-1974 participation}}{\text{Total months of participation}}$$

$$= \frac{48}{222}$$

$$= 22\%$$

Assuming that the lump-sum distribution is equal to $150,000, the capital-gain portion would be $33,000. If your client elects capital-gain treatment, only the portion of the distribution not attributable to the capital-gain portion (in this case, $117,000) is included in the adjusted total taxable amount when computing the averaging tax.

When Should a Person Born before January 1, 1936, Elect the Capital-Gain Provision?

Clearly a client born before January 1, 1936, should elect the capital-gain provision for pre-1974 plan accruals whenever the adjusted total taxable amount after subtracting the capital-gain portion is taxed at an effective rate of more than 20 percent. In table 9-1, for example, we can see that in 1995 a person will always benefit by electing the capital-gain treatment for pre-1974 plan accruals if the adjusted total taxable amount after subtracting the capital-gain portion equals or exceeds $116,750. (This amount will increase in future years as a result of the inflation adjustment to the tax rate schedule.) At that level all additional amounts are taxed at a 28 percent, and perhaps a 31 percent, tax rate. Since the capital-gain portion is taxed at a flat 20 percent rate, a person in these circumstances would pay less tax by electing the capital-gain treatment.

If we look at table 9-2, we can see that a person who elects 10-year averaging will always benefit by electing the capital-gain treatment for pre-1974 plan accruals if the adjusted total taxable amount after subtracting the capital-gain portion is equal to or greater than $137,100. At that level each additional dollar of adjusted total taxable amount is taxed at a rate of 23 percent or higher.

For example, suppose your client receives a taxable distribution of $170,000, of which $30,000 may be treated as capital gain. Your client is eligible for 10-year averaging. Since under the applicable averaging formula any amount over $137,100 is taxed at a rate of 23 percent or higher, your client should elect capital-gain treatment. With capital-gain treatment the last $30,000 of the distribution—the capital-gain amount—will be taxed at a rate of only 20 percent instead of 23 percent or more.

The capital-gain election may only be used once. If the capital-gain election is used either in conjunction with an averaging election for a lump-sum distribution or when the person does not otherwise qualify for 5- or 10-year averaging, no forward averaging election for any other lump-sum distribution may be used in the future.

Capital Gain for Persons Born on or after January 1, 1936

No persons born on or after January 1, 1936, are allowed to elect capital-gain treatment on any portion of a distribution.

Summary of Special Tax Treatment

We have now addressed and answered three of the four questions raised in planning for lump-sum distributions. First, clients who were born before January 1, 1936, should choose 10-year averaging for lump-sum distributions in 1995 only if the adjusted total taxable amount is less than $367,687. Above this amount 5-year averaging is more favorable. In years after 1995 this crossover point will fall as the tax rate schedule for 5-year averaging is adjusted upward for inflation.

Second, your clients should elect capital-gain treatment for pre-1974 accruals whenever the adjusted total taxable amount is taxed at an effective rate of more than 20 percent (tables 9-1 and 9-2).

Third, your clients who will be receiving employer securities with net unrealized appreciation and who plan to sell the securities soon after they receive the distribution should consider whether they may be better off paying tax using 5- or 10-year averaging versus deferring taxation. By doing so their cash will be treated as part of the distribution qualifying for favorable averaging and/or capital-gain treatment.

AVERAGING VERSUS PERIODIC PAYOUTS

One critical question remains to be answered. When should your clients elect to receive lump-sum distributions, a situation in which they may enjoy the tax benefits of averaging and capital-gain treatment, rather than periodic payouts from their plans (or from IRA rollover accounts), where the tax is deferred? Although this decision involves many variables unique to each client, the decision depends on the following factors. If the aftertax proceeds from the lump-sum distribution can be invested outside the plan to generate a payment stream that is at least as great as the aftertax periodic payments from the plan, the lump-sum distribution is the better choice; if not, the periodic payout is the better choice.

The factors that enter this decision include

- the ages of the participant and the beneficiary
- the health of the participant and the beneficiary—that is, their life expectancies
- the anticipated rate of return on investment
- the amount of the lump-sum distribution
- the portion of the distribution (pre-1974 plan accruals) qualifying for capital-gain treatment
- the anticipated taxable income from sources other than the retirement plan during the payout period
- the client's need for immediate versus deferred retirement income
- objectives regarding lifetime benefits versus bequests for heirs

Averaging and Joint and Survivor Annuities

To understand whether the client is better off receiving periodic payments or taking a lump-sum and investing outside the plan, in this section we will look at an example. The example is fact specific, but the analysis will help you to understand the decision-making process.

Table 9-4 shows the crossover points for taxable retirement benefit levels at which a married participant is equally well off from an economic standpoint with either the inside or outside annuity. A client whose adjusted total taxable amount *exceeds* the table values corresponding to his or her circumstances should choose the annuity from the plan. On the other hand, a client whose adjusted total taxable amount *is less than* the table values will be better off if he or she elects a lump-sum distribution, uses averaging, and invests the aftertax proceeds in a joint and survivor annuity outside the plan. Because of the tax deferral on the earnings, a commercial annuity contract will generally provide higher aftertax benefits than other investments available outside the plan that earn the same before-tax rate of return.

The values in table 9-4 were computed assuming the following:

- Both the participant and spouse are aged 65.
- Both spouses are in normal health, and payouts are made over their joint and survivor life expectancy of 25 years.
- The survivor benefit ratio is 100 percent.
- Neither has any dependents.
- 1993 tax rates are used, including standard deduction and elderly deduction.
- The participant was born before January 1, 1936, and may elect 10-year averaging (if optimal).
- The investment rate of return is the same both inside and outside the plan. (This assumption presumes that if rates of return on commercial annuities outside the plan are better than those implicitly offered inside the plan, the participant will roll the distribution over into an IRA and purchase an annuity with competitive rates.)

The amount of tax the couple will pay on their retirement benefits from either the inside or outside annuity depends on their total taxable income. Table 9-4 shows crossover points for all levels of taxable income from sources other than retirement benefits during retirement.

An example is helpful in order to understand what is going on in table 9-4. Adolph, aged 65, is retiring from XZY, Inc. He has been a participant in XYZ's money-purchase pension plan and is eligible to receive a lump-sum payment of $200,000 or a joint and survivor annuity. Adolph is eligible for 5- and 10-year averaging, but no portion of the benefit is eligible for the special capital-gain election. If he elects the lump sum, Adolph will pay $41,212 in taxes using 5-year averaging (20.6 percent), or $36,922 under 10-year averaging (18.5 percent). He will also have $40,000 a year in taxable income outside the plan.

Assume that Adolph knows that he needs this retirement money to meet expenses during retirement and he wants to provide an adequate stream of income to himself and his spouse throughout retirement. In this scenario, it makes sense for him to elect a joint and survivor annuity, since this form of payment will provide a specified stream of income over his own lifetime and that of his spouse.

TABLE 9-4								
Outside versus Inside Annuity Crossover Points for a Married Client with Payout over 25-Year Period*								
Taxable Income Excluding Retirement Benefits	Assumed Rate of Return							
	0% Capital Gain				25% Capital Gain			
	6%	8%	10%	12%	6%	8%	10%	12%
$ 0	$ 29	$ 24	$ 21	$ 0	$ 29	$ 24	$ 21	$ 0
10	29	24	21	0	29	24	21	0
20	29	24	21	0	29	24	21	0
30	29	24	21	0	29	24	21	0
40	155	94	56	43	170	94	56	43
50	155	94	56	43	170	94	56	43
60	155	94	56	43	170	94	56	43
70	155	94	56	43	170	94	56	43
80	185	94	56	43	248	94	56	43
90	206	144	86	55	259	147	86	55
100	206	144	86	55	259	147	86	55
110	206	144	86	55	259	147	86	55
120	206	144	86	55	313	147	86	55
130	299	225	86	55	443	294	186	55
140	319	227	164	116	471	315	188	116
150	333	249	180	130	490	337	220	130
160	337	249	180	137	490	337	220	137
170	337	249	180	137	490	337	220	137
180	337	249	180	137	490	337	220	137
190	337	249	180	137	490	337	220	137
200	337	249	180	137	490	337	220	137
210	337	249	180	137	490	337	220	137
220	337	249	180	137	765	361	220	137
230	373	286	180	137	785	466	321	137
240	470	324	246	187	774	469	331	230
250	470	324	250	187	763	455	331	230
260	440	315	250	187	750	431	314	222
270	400	303	246	176	712	413	286	199
280	383	294	223	167	712	413	286	191
*Values computed using 1993 tax rate schedule for married persons filing jointly with no dependents.								

Given these circumstances, there are two ways that Adolph can receive a joint and survivor annuity. He can receive the benefit under the terms of the plan, or he can take the lump-sum benefit, pay taxes now under 10-year averaging, and purchase a commercial annuity that is payable in the same benefit form. With the commercial annuity, the only additional taxes he will pay (as he receives periodic payments) will be on the interest earnings. If he elects the joint and survivor annuity from the plan, he will pay ordinary income taxes on the amount distributed each year.

At first glance, Adolph might be tempted to take a lump sum using 10-year averaging since the tax rate is a favorable 18.5 percent. However, from a purely economic viewpoint, he should only choose the lump sum if the aftertax monthly annuity benefit from the commercial annuity exceeds the aftertax annuity benefit that he will receive from the plan.

To help him make the decision, table 9-4 can be helpful. As we know, Adolph is eligible to receive a lump sum of $200,000, none of which will be treated as capital gain. To read the chart, look at the numbers in the $40,000 taxable income row as it intersects with the 0 percent capital-gain column(s). Whether or not he is better off taking the annuity will be affected by the assumed rate of interest earned on the outside annuity. Using 6 percent, table 9-4 says that for any lump-sum value under $155,000 Adolph should pay taxes now and buy the outside annuity. On the other hand, for any lump-sum amount in excess of $155,000, it makes more sense for him to receive the benefit from the plan. As the interest rate goes up the value in which the outside annuity makes sense becomes lower. For example, at 12 percent interest the crossover point is $43,000.

It is important to note that table 9-4 is fact specific. It only works with the specified interest rates, joint and survivor form of benefit, capital-gain choices, and specified mortality assumptions. One important assumption in the analysis is that tax rates will remain the same into the future. If an individual assumes that tax rates will go up or down, this assumption also will play into the decision-making process.

For those interested in going into more depth with this topic, appendix 7 provides the mathematical model used to make the crossover analysis. With the model, a variety of assumptions can be pumped into the equation to help determine whether paying taxes now or deferring makes the most sense.

Deciding Whether to Take the Lump Sum or Defer— General Considerations

The analysis described in table 9-4 points out the complexity of determining whether it makes sense to pay taxes now under the averaging rules, or whether deferring will have better tax results. The model reviewed in table 9-4 helps in this analysis; other models and computer software are available as well. However, as demonstrated in table 9-4, the answer is closely connected to the assumptions used, making it difficult to rely entirely on a mathematical analysis. Before choosing a model or software package the planner must be familiar with the various factors that influence the end result. The materials below review the many relevant factors that affect this analysis.

The Length of the Expected Payout Period from the Plan

The longer the period of tax deferral, the more likely that deferring taxes and taking a stream of payments from the plan over time will result in a larger total payout than paying lump-sum taxes currently. The length of the payout period can be affected by a number of factors. If the benefit is being paid out over the life expectancies of the participant and a beneficiary, the individuals' ages will affect the length of the payout period. The client's need may also affect the length of the payout period. For example, a client might know that he or she will need the money over a short period of time in order to make a particular investment or because of other special needs. On the other end of the scale is the individual who has other assets to live on and has the option to defer distributions as long as necessary to ensure proper tax planning. The law does require minimum distributions beginning at age 70 1/2, but under these rules only modest amounts need to be distributed and the length of the payout period is substantial (see chapter 10 for more details).

Amount of the Lump-Sum Averaging Tax

Of course, when determining whether to pay taxes now or defer, the amount of taxes paid under the lump-sum tax rules is crucial. As described above, for larger distributions the amount of tax savings for lump-sum averaging is almost nil. Also, eligibility for 10-year averaging will result in lower taxes when the distribution is $367,687 or less. In addition, if a portion of the distribution is treated as capital gain, the special grandfathered 20 percent tax rate may reduce the total tax due. All factors that act to reduce taxes will favor paying taxes now and purchasing an outside annuity.

Amount of Outside Income

As an individual's taxable income from sources outside of the plan (and along with it the marginal tax rate) rises, the ability to have benefits taxed at the special averaging tax rate becomes more attractive. Therefore the lump-sum value at which paying taxes now and buying an outside annuity will rise as outside taxable income rises.

Interest Rate Assumptions

As interest rates go up, the outside annuity becomes less attractive. This is because the advantages of delaying taxation and letting the larger amount grow in value are more pronounced as interest rates rise. This phenomenon is demonstrated in table 9-4, where you can see the crossover point decreasing as the interest rate goes up.

Changes in the Tax Rates

Whether an individual wants to elect special averaging will also depend on his or her outlook regarding tax rates. If the individual expects tax rates to go up, then the results of averaging will look even better. On the other hand, if the client expects tax rates to go down, deferral will be favorable. However, be aware that the advantages of tax deferral can be powerful, and even a substantial increase in the tax rate in the future may not offset the advantages of deferring taxes.

SUMMARY

Persons approaching retirement face a myriad of options regarding how they will receive their retirement benefits. To select the best option, a person must consider trade-offs in the timing and amount of taxation and economic benefits. This chapter addressed four critical questions many retirees must answer if they are considering a lump-sum distribution from their qualified plan. Although there may be mitigating factors in each case, the decision rules may be summarized as follows.

The first question was whether those persons who qualify should elect to use 10-year or 5-year averaging. The answer: Based on 1995 tax rates, a person should use 10-year averaging whenever the taxable amount subject to averaging is less than about $367,687; otherwise 5-year averaging is more favorable.

The second question addressed what a person should do with distributions of employer's stock with net unrealized appreciation. The answer: When a person is planning to sell the stock when received, he or she should consider asking the plan administrator to sell the stock and distribute cash instead (if permitted) if the tax on the appreciation using the averaging formula is lower than that which would be paid under the regular tax rules. Generally if a person does not plan to sell the stock immediately, he or she will be better off taking the stock distribution.

The third question dealt with when a person should elect capital-gain treatment for pre-1974 accruals. The answer: For persons born before January 1, 1936, the capital-gain election is beneficial whenever the portion qualifying for the election would be taxed at a rate higher than 20 percent under the averaging formula elected. The election is always advisable when 10-year averaging is used if the taxable amount excluding the capital-gain portion is greater than $137,100. Based on current tax rates the critical value when 5-year averaging is used is $116,750. For persons born on or after January 1, 1936, the capital-gain election has been phased out and is no longer applicable.

The fourth question had to do with when a person is better off electing a lump-sum distribution using averaging rather than electing periodic distributions from the plan. The answer: This is the most difficult question to answer because of the many factors involved. However, appendix 7 provides a method for evaluating this complex problem. If a planner wants to use the methodology in the appendix or available software solutions, he or she needs to understand what factors the particular approach considers and compare them to the list of relevant factors described at the end of this chapter. For example, the planner should understand whether the model considers factors such as future tax rate changes, taxable income from sources other than the pension plan, and a variety of interest assumptions.

10

Required Minimum Distributions from Qualified Plans, IRAs, and 403(b) Plans

Chapter Outline

The minimum distribution rules contained in IRC Sec. 401(a)(9) are designed to limit the deferral of taxation on plan benefits. The primary reason for allowing the deferral of taxes is to encourage savings for retirement. This tax-preferred item comes at a great cost to the government; in fact, recent surveys by the Treasury Department have indicated that pension plans are the most costly tax preference item (even more costly than health care). Therefore the minimum distribution rules have been designed both to ensure that a significant portion of a participant's benefit is paid out during retirement and to limit the period for benefits paid after death. The rules cover all tax-preferred retirement plans including qualified plans, IRAs (including SEPs), 403(b) annuity plans, and even IRC Sec. 457 plans.

The minimum distribution requirements will have the most impact on those individuals who do not need the tax-sheltered retirement income to live and who wish to defer the payment of tax as long as possible. The rules provide optional methods of calculating the minimum payments, each method having its advantages and disadvantages. The retirement planner needs to have an understanding of these rules so that his or her client can make the best choice. When choosing the appropriate method of distribution, relevant considerations include the client's objectives, the amount of tax-sheltered income involved, the ages and life expectancies of the client and his or her beneficiary or beneficiaries, and the availability of any death benefits.

However, the rules will also impact on a much broader spectrum of the retiring population. The minimum distribution rules apply on a year-by-year basis, and a minimum distribution is always required once the individual has reached the *required beginning date* (April 1 of the year following the attainment of age 70 1/2). Therefore the minimum distribution rules have an ongoing impact on any retiree who has attained age 70 1/2 with a benefit due from a qualified retirement plan, an IRA, a Sec. 457 deferred-compensation plan, or a 403(b) tax-sheltered annuity plan. If the rules are not met, a 50 percent excise tax must be paid by the participant. If the client has rolled all tax-sheltered benefits into an IRA, there will be very few places to turn for advice on calculating the minimum distribution amount. In many cases IRA sponsors will not take the responsibility of ensuring compliance. A retirement planner who can help explain these rules and ensure compliance will be much appreciated by the client.

The chapter first addresses the mechanics of the minimum distribution rules and goes on to discuss planning considerations.

OVERVIEW OF THE LAW

The minimum distribution requirements of IRC Sec. 401(a)(9) generally require that distributions from qualified retirement plans be made within a specified time period beginning when a participant becomes 70 1/2 or earlier if he or she dies before reaching 70 1/2. Essentially the same rules apply to IRAs, SEPs, Sec. 457 deferred-compensation plans, and Sec. 403(b) annuity plans.

In general, distributions have to begin by the April 1 following the year in which the participant reaches age 70 1/2, referred to as the required beginning date. If the entire benefit is not distributed at that time, the benefit must be distributed over a period no longer than the joint expected lifetime of the participant and a chosen beneficiary. There are several options for determining the minimum distribution amount, and all participant elections must be made by the required beginning date. After the participant's death any remaining benefit payable to beneficiaries must be paid out at least as rapidly as during the participant's lifetime, using the same calculation method.

A separate rule applies if the participant dies before the required beginning date. In this case, the general rule is that distributions must be made within 5 years of death. However, broad exceptions apply that allow payments to be made over the expected lifetime of a beneficiary as long as payments begin in a timely fashion.

In the materials below these two rules are discussed separately, and to avoid confusion always remember this distinction: *One minimum distribution rule applies when the participant dies prior to the required beginning date, and another applies for the individual who lives until that date.* Also note that proposed Treasury Regulation Sec. 1.401(a)(9) provides extremely comprehensive guidance on the minimum distribution requirements. These regulations should be consulted when actually calculating any minimum distributions.

Several other key concepts introduced in this chapter have an impact on the application of the minimum distribution rules. First is the minimum distribution incidental benefit (MDIB) requirement, which is intended to ensure that most retirement benefits are paid to the retiree and that postretirement death benefits remain incidental. However, in practice, the rule has limited application, only altering the result of the general minimum distribution rules in the case of an individual who chooses a nonspousal beneficiary more than 10 years younger than himself or herself.

YOUR FINANCIAL SERVICES PRACTICE:
WHAT ACTUALLY NEEDS TO BE DONE

As you will learn reading this assignment, taking full advantage of the opportunity to maximize the deferral of income taxes under the minimum distribution rules requires both knowledge and planning. Periodically sit down with clients who have not yet attained age 70 1/2 and review their beneficiary election forms. As you will learn, a spouse often makes the best beneficiary, an estate should never be the chosen beneficiary, and electing a trust as beneficiary can be tricky. When your client attains age 70 1/2, once again sit down and review beneficiary election forms for all plans subject to the rules. In almost all cases the beneficiary designated on the election form at the required beginning date is the one used for determining the all required subsequent minimum distributions. This means that this is your last opportunity for careful planning—don't miss it!

Second is the interplay between the spousal rollover rule and the minimum distribution rules. Code Sec. 402 allows a spouse the option to roll over a benefit received at the death of the participant into an IRA in his or her own name. As discussed later in this chapter, the rollover is treated as a complete distribution from the participant's plan, meaning that the minimum distribution rules no longer apply to that plan. After the rollover, the minimum distribution rules will have to be satisfied—treating the spouse as the participant. This rule provides planning opportunities, but can also be confusing. The summary table at the end of the chapter can help to identify all applicable options in any specific situation.

PENALTIES FOR FAILURE TO COMPLY

Under IRC Sec. 4974, if the minimum distributions are not made in a timely manner, the plan participant is required to pay a 50 percent excise tax on the amount of the shortfall between the amount actually distributed and the amount required to be distributed under the minimum distribution rules described above. The Internal Revenue Service is authorized to waive the 50 percent excise tax if the taxpayer establishes that the failure to make the minimum required distribution is due to reasonable error, and reasonable steps are being taken to remedy the shortfall. The payment of tax is accompanied by Form 5329. An individual who wants to protest must pay the tax and request a refund on Form 5329.

If the plan is a qualified plan, it may lose its tax-favored status if the minimum distribution rules are not satisfied. The same result applies to an IRA if "a pattern or regular practice of failing to meet the minimum distribution requirements" appears.

MINIMUM DISTRIBUTIONS AT AGE 70 1/2

The next several pages describe the minimum distribution rules that apply when the individual has lived until the required beginning date (generally April 1 of the year following attainment of age 70 1/2). The rules are quite complex and contain several key terms and concepts that you will need to remember. The rules for determining the minimum distribution are different depending upon whether the distribution is from an individual account plan or is payable as an annuity—either from a defined-benefit plan or from a commercial annuity. The account plan rules apply to all IRAs, 403(b) plans, SEPs, Sec. 457 plans, and qualified plans of the defined-contribution type, unless a commercial annuity is purchased prior to required beginning date. The account plan rules are reviewed below, followed by a discussion of the annuity distribution rules.

Account Plan Distributions

The date benefit payments must begin is called the required beginning date. This date is generally April 1 of the year following the calendar year in which the covered participant becomes age of 70 1/2. However, there are two important exceptions:

- Any participant in a government or church plan who remains an employee after reaching age 70 1/2 will not have to begin distributions until the April 1 following the later of the calendar year in which the participant reaches age 70 1/2 or the calendar year in which he or she retires.
- Any qualified plan participant who reaches 70 1/2 prior to 1988 and who is not considered a 5 percent owner of the entity sponsoring the plan will not have to begin distributions until April 1 following the later of the year of attainment of age 70 1/2 or the year in which the participant retires.

The required beginning date is somewhat of a misnomer since a minimum distribution is required for the year in which the participant attains age 70 1/2 (referred to as the "first distribution year") and for every subsequent year. The distribution for the first distribution year can be delayed until the following April 1, but all subsequent distributions must be made by December 31 of the applicable year.

> *Example 1:* Shelley turned age 70 on March 15, 1991. On September 15, 1991, she turned 70 1/2. The first distribution is for the year ending December 31, 1991, but the required beginning date is April 1, 1992. If she takes the first minimum distribution on April 1, 1992, she will have to take the minimum distribution for the second distribution year by December 31, 1992.

As you can see, delaying the first distribution into the second year doubles up the required distribution for that year and increases taxes for that year—not a desirable result in some cases.

First Distribution Year Calculation

The minimum distribution calculation for the first distribution year is quite simple. It is the participant's benefit as of the end of the year prior to the first distribution year, divided by the life expectancy of the participant and a chosen beneficiary as of the last day of the distribution year (referred to as the "applicable life expectancy" [ALE]).

$$\frac{\text{Benefit}}{\text{ALE}} = \text{required minimum distribution}$$

Participant's Benefit. The participant's benefit in a defined-contribution plan, 403(b) plan, or IRA is based on the participant's account balance. In an IRA account the benefit for a distribution year is the IRA account balance at the end of the previous calendar year. For qualified plans and 403(b) plans, the employee's benefit is his or her individual account balance as of the last valuation date in the calendar year immediately preceding the distribution year.

TABLE 10-1
Table V—Ordinary Life Annuities;
One Life—Expected Return Multiples*

Age	Multiple	Age	Multiple
40	42.5	66	19.2
41	41.5	67	18.4
42	40.6	68	17.6
43	39.6	69	16.8
44	38.7	70	16.0
45	37.7	71	15.3
46	36.8	72	14.6
47	35.9	73	13.9
48	34.9	74	13.2
49	34.0	75	12.5
50	33.1	76	11.9
51	32.2	77	11.2
52	31.3	78	10.6
53	30.4	79	10.0
54	29.5	80	9.5
55	28.6	81	8.9
56	27.7	82	8.4
57	26.8	83	7.9
58	25.9	84	7.4
59	25.0	85	6.9
60	24.2	86	6.5
61	23.3	87	6.1
62	22.5	88	5.7
63	21.6	89	5.3
64	20.8	90	5.0
65	20.0		

Source: A portion of Table V from Reg. Sec. 1.72-9.

Calculation of the ALE. The ALE for the first distribution year is going to be the actuarial single or the actuarial joint life and last survivor expectancy period of the covered participant and his or her designated beneficiary as of the last day of the first distribution year. The ALE is determined by use of the expected return multiples in Tables V and VI of Treas. Reg. Sec. 1.72-9 (portions of these tables are reproduced in tables 10-1 and 10-2 and complete tables are reproduced in appendix 2). In subsequent years the applicable life expectancy is determined in one of several ways, based upon the participant's election. The methods are described below.

Example 2: Suppose Sidney is aged 71 and Nancy, his sister, is aged 69 on the last day of the first distribution year. The ALE is 20.7 (see table 10-2). Assuming the applicable benefit is $150,000, the minimum distribution is $7,246.37 ($150,000/20.7).

TABLE 10-2
Table VI—Ordinary Joint Life and Last Survivor Annuities;
Two Lives—Expected Return Multiples*

Ages	65	66	67	68	69	70	71	72	73	74
68	23.6	23.3	22.8	22.3	21.9	21.5	21.2	20.8	20.6	20.2
69	23.4	22.9	22.4	21.9	21.5	21.1	20.7	20.3	20.0	19.6
70	23.1	22.5	22.0	21.5	21.1	20.6	20.2	19.8	19.4	19.1
71	22.6	22.2	21.7	21.2	20.7	20.2	19.8	19.4	19.0	18.6
72	22.5	21.9	21.3	20.8	20.3	19.8	19.4	18.9	18.5	18.2
73	22.2	21.6	21.0	20.5	20.0	19.4	19.0	18.5	18.1	17.7
74	22.0	21.4	20.8	20.2	19.6	19.1	18.6	18.2	17.7	17.3
75	21.8	21.1	20.5	19.9	19.3	18.8	18.3	17.6	17.3	16.9
76	21.6	20.9	20.3	19.7	19.1	18.5	18.0	17.5	17.0	16.5
77	21.4	20.7	21.1	19.4	18.8	18.3	17.7	17.2	16.7	16.2
78	21.2	20.5	19.9	19.2	18.6	18.0	17.5	16.9	16.4	15.9

Source: A portion of Table VI from Reg. Sec. 1.72-9.

Minimum Distribution Incidental Benefit Rules. The ALE calculation is modified in one case—when the beneficiary is a nonspouse who is more than 10 years younger than the participant. In this case the "applicable divisor" under the MDIB rules is substituted for the ALE. The applicable divisor is taken from a table included in the Proposed Regulations, and is shown in table 10-3. The applicable divisor is based upon the participant's attained age on the last day of the first distribution year.

Example 3: Ralph attained age 70 on August 1, 1990. He had an IRA account balance of $200,000 on December 31, 1990. The account is growing (from interest earnings and capital growth) at an annual rate of 8 percent. He is unmarried, and his chosen beneficiary is his niece, Alice, who was aged 51 on December 31, 1991. Calculate the minimum distribution for Ralph for year one.

Step 1: Determine first distribution year and required beginning date:

Ralph attained age 70 1/2 on February 1, 1991. Therefore the first distribution year is the year ending December 31, 1991. Payments may be delayed until the required beginning date, which is April 1, 1992.

TABLE 10-3
Table for Determining Applicable Divisor for Installment Payments and Maximum Period Certain for Term Annuities

Age of the Employee	Applicable Divisor	Age of the Employee	Applicable Divisor
70	26.2	93	8.8
71	25.3	94	8.3
72	24.4	95	7.8
73	23.5	96	7.3
74	22.7	97	6.9
75	21.8	98	6.5
76	20.9	99	6.1
77	20.1	100	5.7
78	19.2	101	5.3
79	18.4	102	5.0
80	17.8	103	4.7
81	16.8	104	4.4
82	16.0	105	4.1
83	15.3	106	3.8
84	14.5	107	3.6
85	13.8	108	3.3
86	13.1	109	3.1
87	12.4	110	2.8
88	11.8	111	2.6
89	11.1	112	2.4
90	10.5	113	2.2
91	9.9	114	2.0
92	9.4	115 and older	1.8

Source: Proposed Treas. Reg. Sec. 1.401(a)(9)-2

Step 2: Determine the attained ages:

Ralph is aged 71 and Alice is aged 51 on the last day of the first distribution year.

Step 3: Determine the applicable joint life expectancy:

Looking at Table VI for Ralph, aged 71, and Alice, aged 51, the ALE is 43 years.

Step 4: Determine the MDIB applicable divisor:

The applicable divisor for a participant at age 71 is 25.3.

Step 5: Determine the benefit:

The benefit in an IRA is the account balance on the last day of the year preceding the distribution year. Since the distribution year is 1991, the account balance on December 31, 1990, is used. In this case, that amount is $200,000.

Step 6: Calculate the minimum distribution:

Divide the benefit by the lesser of the numbers in Steps 3 and 4. $200,000 divided by 25.3 equals $7,905.

Required Distributions for Subsequent Years

The methodology for calculating the minimum distribution is essentially the same for each subsequent distribution year. The required distribution is the applicable benefit divided by the appropriate ALE or, when applicable, the MDIB applicable divisor.

   The benefit used in the calculation is the value of the benefit as of the end of the prior distribution year, as described above for the first year's distribution. The only special case is when the required distributions for the first and second distribution years are made in the second distribution year. In this case, the first distribution may be subtracted from the balance when calculating the benefit for the second distribution year.

   The ALE for subsequent years will depend upon whether the individual elects to have life expectancies recalculated or not. The Proposed Regulations provide that the life expectancies of the participant and/or a spousal beneficiary may be recalculated each year (as long as the plan provides for such elections). When the beneficiary is not the spouse, the beneficiary's life expectancy may not be recalculated.

When the election is made not to recalculate any life expectancies, the ALE is determined for each distribution year simply by subtracting one from the previous ALE. When life expectancies are not recalculated, the length of the distribution period is a fixed period, regardless of when the participant or his or her designated beneficiary dies.

Example 4: Assume that there is no recalculation of life expectancies and that the same facts apply as in example 2. The ALE for Sidney and Nancy in the second distribution year is 19.7 (20.7 − 1). If the applicable account balance is $152,000, the minimum distribution is $152,000/19.7, or $7,715.74. In each subsequent year the ALE is reduced by one until the ALE is zero, regardless of whether Sidney or Nancy continue to live. If they both die in year 12, any remaining account balance can continue to be distributed over the remaining 8.7 years.

When the beneficiary is the participant's spouse, then either one life or both lives can be recalculated in determining the ALE. If both lives are recalculated, the ALE is calculated using the actual ages of each person in the distribution year based on Table VI. This means that payments will be accelerated at the time of death. The impact of recalculation on the stream of distributions is discussed in the section on planning considerations. Tables 10-5 and 10-6 demonstrate the impact of recalculation over a period of time. Once the decision is made to recalculate life expectancies, the recalculation must be used in all subsequent years.

Example 5: Assume Aristotle is required to take a minimum distribution from a qualified plan. On the last day of the first distribution year he is aged 70 and Sylvia, his wife and beneficiary, is aged 71. Table VI in the Regulations (table 10-2) shows that the ALE for the first distribution year is 20.2. If both life expectancies are recalculated, the ALE for the second distribution year (when Aristotle is aged 71 and Sylvia is aged 72) is 19.4.

When both life expectancies are recalculated, the ALE is reduced by less than one each year. This means that the minimum required distribution is going to be smaller than under the fixed period method. However, a price is paid for recalculation. In the year following the death of an individual whose life expectancy is being recalculated, his or her life expectancy becomes zero. After the first death, the ALE is now calculated based upon the single life expectancy of the remaining person. After the second death, the entire remaining benefit must be distributed in the year following the second death. The implications of this rule are discussed further in the planning section below.

In some cases only one of the two measuring lives will be recalculated. With a spousal beneficiary, the participant can elect to have either life recalculated.

With a nonspousal beneficiary, the participant can choose recalculation for his or her own life, but not for the beneficiary. When only one life expectancy is recalculated, the methodology for calculating the ALE is more complicated. For the first distribution year, the calculation of life expectancy is the same as described above. For the second year, the ALE is calculated using the actual age of the participant as of the last day of the second distribution year and the "adjusted age" of the beneficiary. Calculating the adjusted age of the beneficiary is a two-step process. The beneficiary's adjusted age is computed, starting with his or her age in the first distribution year. The beneficiary's ALE is calculated based on this age by consulting Table V in the Proposed Regulations for single life expectancy. Then, in the next year, one is removed from the ALE. The beneficiary's adjusted age is then calculated by using Table V in reverse— comparing the adjusted ALE to the comparable age (rounded up to the next age). That age is the beneficiary's adjusted age for that year. The same process is used to recalculate life expectancies in all subsequent years. Example 4 on page 325 demonstrates the methodology for recalculating life expectancies.

> *Example 6:* Assume that Sonny, a participant in an IRA, was born on January 15, 1925, and that his spouse and beneficiary, Cher, was born on March 15, 1945. Sonny elects to recalculate his life expectancy but not the life expectancy of his spouse. He has received the appropriate first-year distribution (during 1995, the first distribution year) and wants you to help him calculate the required minimum distribution for 1996, the second distribution year. His benefit as of December 31, 1995, is $216,000.

Step 1:   Calculate Cher's adjusted age for the second distribution year:

Cher is aged 50 at the end of the first distribution year. According to IRS Table V (table 10-1) her life expectancy for that year is 33.1. To calculate her adjusted age, reduce 33.1 by one (32.1) and find the matching age on table 10-1. Note that 32.1 does not match a specified life expectancy on the table. Age 51 has a 32.2 year life expectancy and age 52 has a 31.3 year life expectancy. When the life expectancy falls between two numbers on the table, go to the life expectancy that goes with the higher of the two corresponding ages. In this case, Cher's adjusted age is 52.

Step 2:   Calculate Sonny and Cher's joint life expectancy for the second distribution year:

Sonny's age on December 31, 1996, the second distribution year, is 71, and Cher's adjusted age is 52. Therefore—again looking at IRS Table VI—their joint life expectancy is 32.2.

Step 3:   Calculate the required minimum distribution:

Divide $216,000 by the ALE of 32.2. The minimum required distribution is $6,708.

When only one life expectancy is recalculated, what happens at death depends upon who dies first. If the first death is that of the person whose life is being recalculated, that person's life expectancy becomes zero in the following year. For the remaining person (the nonrecalculated one), the remaining life expectancy is based upon the single life expectancy table (IRS Table V). The way this works is that the life expectancy of that person is determined back as of the first distribution year. Then one is removed for each subsequent distribution year that has passed, up to and including the year of death of the first to die. For an example, see the case illustrated in table 10-7. The number of remaining years becomes a fixed period in which the distribution must be made, and distributions may continue over this period regardless of when the remaining beneficiary dies.

The situation is much simpler when the person whose life expectancy is not being recalculated dies first. In this case, the methodology for calculating the minimum continues undisturbed, using the same methodology as described above.

MDIB in Subsequent Years. As described above, when the beneficiary is a nonspouse who is more than 10 years younger than the participant, the ALE is replaced by the MDIB applicable divisor. This rule continues to apply in subsequent distribution years as long as the participant is alive. After the participant's death the MDIB applicable divisor no longer applies. For an example of how this works, see table 10-7.

Calculating the Minimum Distribution with No Beneficiary

The minimum distribution may also be calculated by assuming that the distribution will be made simply over the lifetime or expected lifetime of only the participant. The methodology for calculating the minimum distribution is similar to that described above. The attained life expectancy is calculated using the single life table (Table V in the Regulations). The participant may elect either to recalculate or not recalculate his or her life expectancy each year. When a single life is used to determine the minimum payout, the MDIB rules have no impact. Although this approach is allowed, there is essentially no advantage to this method of calculation.

Annuity Payments

When a defined-benefit pension plan pays out a benefit in the form of an annuity, or if a commercial annuity is purchased to satisfy benefit payments, a separate minimum distribution rule applies. These rules are quite straightforward and, unlike the account plan rules, the determination only has to be made one time, when the distribution begins.

In most cases life annuities and joint and survivor annuities satisfy the minimum distribution rules. In order to satisfy the rules, all the following requirements must be met:

- The annuity must begin on or before the required beginning date.
- Payments must be made at intervals that occur at least annually.
- The stream of payments must be "nonincreasing."

The term *nonincreasing* is defined broadly in the regulations, and both variable annuities and annuities that increase due to cost of living increases fit within the definition.

Joint and survivor annuities with a survivor benefit of up to 100 percent are generally allowed. The only exception is for nonspousal beneficiaries who are more than 10 years younger than the participant. In this case the MDIB rules kick in and the maximum survivor benefit will be something less than 100 percent. To determine the applicable survivor percentage see the IRS Table reproduced in table 10-4. The example below explains how this works.

> *Example 7:* Sandra wants to elect a 100 percent joint and survivor benefit from her company's defined-benefit plan beginning at age 70. She is considering her son, Albert, aged 45, as the contingent beneficiary. Looking at table 10-4, notice that the maximum survivor benefit for a beneficiary who is 25 years younger than the participant (70 − 45 = 25) is 66 percent.

Annuities that contain a period certain also satisfy the rules if the period does not exceed the joint life expectancy of the participant and beneficiary, as calculated in IRS Table VI. However, if the beneficiary is a nonspouse who is more than 10 years younger than the participant, then once again the MDIB rules limit the life expectancy to the factors contained in table 10-3.

> *Example 8:* Suppose that Herb, aged 70 (at the end of the first distribution year), chooses a joint and survivor annuity with Sally, aged 80, as the contingent beneficiary. Herb wants to have a period-certain feature and wants to know if there are limitations on the length of the period certain. Given their attained ages for the first distribution year, Table VI in the Regulations (appendix 2) indicates that their ALE is 17.6. This is

TABLE 10-4
Table for Determining the MDIB Maximum Applicable Survivor Annuity Percentage

Excess of Age of Employee over Age of Beneficiary	Applicable Percentage	Excess of Age of Employee over Age of Beneficiary	Applicable Percentage
10 years or less	100%	28	62%
11	96	29	61
12	93	30	60
13	90	31	59
14	87	32	59
15	84	33	58
16	82	34	57
17	79	35	56
18	77	36	56
19	75	37	55
20	73	38	55
21	72	39	54
22	70	40	54
23	68	41	53
24	67	42	53
25	66	43	53
26	64	44 years and more	52
27	63		

Source: Proposed Treas. Reg. Sec. 1.401(a)(9)-2

the maximum length for period-certain payments for an annuity beginning at age 70.

PRERETIREMENT DEATH BENEFITS

When the particpant dies after the required beginning date, then distributions must continue in the manner described in the section above. However, when the participant dies prior to the required beginning date, then a separate rule applies for determining the maximum length of the distribution period.

The general rule is that distributions must be made within 5 years after the participant's death. This means that the participant's entire interest must be distributed as of December 31 of the calendar year that contains the fifth anniversary of the date the participant dies. However, the rule has significant exceptions. The 5-year rule does not have to be satisfied if one of these exceptions is satisfied. A plan will meet the minimum distribution rules as long as distributions satisfy the general rule or one of the exceptions.

Two major exceptions apply to the 5-year rule. One applies when the beneficiary is the participant's spouse and the other applies when the beneficiary is a nonspouse. In the case of nonspouse beneficiaries the minimum distribution rule is also satisfied if the distribution is made over the lifetime or expected lifetime of the beneficiary, as long as the benefit begins by December 31 of the year following death. When the beneficiary is the participant's spouse, the distribution may be made over the life of the spouse, as long as payments begin on or before the later of (1) December 31 of the calendar year immediately after the calendar year in which the participant died, or (2) December 31 of the calendar year immediately after the year in which the participant would have reached age 70 1/2. However, if the spouse dies prior to the commencement of benefit payments, then benefits may be distributed to his or her beneficiary under the same rules that would apply to the participant.

SPECIAL RULES

Beneficiary Issues

All the minimum distribution rules involve identification of the participant's beneficiary. The rules are quite complex in this regard to accommodate all of the possible selections. The following questions and answers highlight the relevant rules. In the planning section that follows, the practical significance of these rules discussed.

Who Are the Beneficiaries when Multiple Beneficiaries Are Elected?

When the participant has identified more than one individual as the beneficiary, the general rule is that the oldest beneficiary is used to determine joint life expectancy. If, after the initial determination of life expectancy, a new beneficiary is added (replacing or sharing benefits with the previous beneficiary), the new beneficiary will be substituted for the old in determining life expectancies only if the new beneficiary has a shorter life span. In other words, a new beneficiary may decrease the calculation of joint life expectancy but cannot increase it.

What Happens If a Nonperson Is Chosen as the Beneficiary?

Choosing a beneficiary that is a nonperson can be quite problematic. *Having the estate be the beneficiary is the same as having chosen no beneficiary.* Electing a trust as beneficiary *will have the same result* unless

- the trust is valid under state law
- the trust is irrevocable at the earlier of death or the required beginning date
- the beneficiaries under the trust are identifiable
- the trust document is provided to the plan's administrator

In the case of a trust that conforms with the rules, the beneficiaries of the trust will be treated as the beneficiaries for purposes of the minimum distribution rules.

Participant Elections and the Role of the Plan Document

Each plan must specify that the plan will meet the minimum distribution provisions. Also the plan can have additional optional language addressing two specific issues: (1) whether or not life expectancies are recalculated under the account plan method, and (2) whether the 5-year distribution rule or one of the alternative methods applies when calculating the preretirement distribution minimum. How the plan addresses these issues will affect the participants' options under a specific plan. These issues can be addressed in a number of ways, described below.

Recalculation of Life Expectancies

- Default provision—if the plan does not address whether life expectancies can be recalculated, all lives will be recalculated.
- The plan can give participants the option to elect to recalculate or not.
- The plan can require that life expectancies not be recalculated.
- The plan can require recalculation.

Preretirement Death Benefits

- Default provision—if the plan does not address this issue, a spousal beneficiary will be subject to the spousal exception to the 5-year distribution rule. All other beneficiaries are subject to the 5-year rule.
- The plan can give participants (and beneficiaries) the option to elect whether the 5-year rule or the applicable exception to the 5-year rule applies.
- The plan can require that the 5-year rule applies.
- The plan can require that the exceptions apply.

Multiple Plans

Generally the required minimum distributions must be calculated—and distributed—separately for each plan subject to the rules. Since this requirement can be quite onerous for the individual with multiple plans, the IRS has relented somewhat for individuals with multiple IRAs or 403(b) plans. In Notice 88-38 the IRS specified that the minimum distributions calculated separately for each IRA can be aggregated and taken from any of the covered plans. The notice allows 403(b) plans to be aggregated in a similar way (although IRAs and 403(b) plans may not be aggregated). The aggregation rule doses not apply to qualified plans.

Rollovers and Transfers

As discussed in chapter 10, liberal rules allow participants the right to roll or transfer benefits from one type of tax sheltered plan to another plan. This transaction is relatively simple except in the case of the individual rolling over the benefit after attainment of age 70 1/2. In order to ensure that the minimum distributions are made, the rules clarify what to do in this special situation.

Special rules apply to amounts rolled (or transferred) from one tax-sheltered retirement plan to another. From the perspective of the distributing plan, the amount distributed (to be rolled over or transferred) is credited towards determining the minimum distribution from the plan. However, if a portion of the distribution is necessary to satisfy the minimum distribution requirements, that portion may not be rolled (or transferred) into another plan.

> *Example 9:* Shirley, aged 71 1/2, receives a single-sum distribution from a qualified retirement plan. She intends to roll the distribution into an IRA. She may not roll the portion of the lump-sum distribution that represents the minimum distribution for the current distribution year into the IRA.

Once the amount is rolled into the second plan, it will count toward determining the participant's benefit for determining the minimum distribution. However, since the minimum distribution is based on the benefit in the previous year, the amount rolled over does not affect the minimum until the following year.

Spousal Rollovers

When the spouse is the sole beneficiary of the participant's retirement plan benefit, the spouse has a unique opportunity—to roll the benefit into an IRA in his or her own name. Under the minimum distribution rules, the rollover is treated as a complete distribution of the participant's benefit, satisfying the minimum distribution rules from the perspective of the participant's plan. Once the benefit is in the spouse's name, the minimum distribution rules have to be satisfied with the spouse treated as the participant. The spouse has the opportunity to name a beneficiary and calculate future minimum distributions based upon the joint life expectancy of the spouse and the beneficiary.

This is a powerful planning opportunity that will be discussed more fully later in the chapter. There are several other practical concerns that have to be considered when the spouse wants to take advantage of this opportunity:

- The spouse has to be the sole beneficiary of the retirement benefit.
- The benefit does not actually have to be rolled over into another plan. It can be simply retitled in the spouse's name.
- The opportunity to roll over is available regardless of either the age of the participant at death or the age of the spouse at that time.
- When the participant has attained age 70 1/2 at death, calculating the required minimum distribution for the year in which the rollover takes place is somewhat tricky. As described above in the rollover section, in the rollover year, the minimum is based on the participant's minimum distribution elections. The first distribution year for the spouse's plan is the year following the rollover.

TEFRA 242(b) ELECTIONS

Although 1983 seems long ago, certain elections made prior to 1984 may have an impact on the calculation of a participant's minimum distribution under a qualified plan. (This special rule does *not* apply to IRA distributions.) The Tax Equity and Fiscal Responsibility Act (TEFRA) substantially changed the minimum distribution requirements for qualified plans (the rules were changed again to essentially their current form under the Tax Reform Act of 1984 (TRA)). The changes made in TEFRA included a grandfathering rule that allowed participants with accrued benefits as of December 31, 1983, to sign an election form (prior to January 1, 1984) indicating the time and method of distribution of their plan benefit. The benefit election form had to be specific and had to conform to pre-TEFRA rules, which allowed distributions to be deferred much later than age 70 1/2. These grandfather provisions were contained in Sec. 242(b) of TEFRA and are generally referred to as Sec. 242(b) elections.

These Sec. 242(b) elections continue to be valid if benefits are being paid from the original plan in which the election is made, and if the plan distributions follow the Sec. 242(b) distribution election. If it is not followed exactly with regard to the form and timing of the payments, the election is considered "revoked." A substitution or addition of a beneficiary generally does not result in the revocation of the election. If the benefit election is changed or revoked after the individual has reached the required beginning date under the current rules, the participant will be forced to "make up" distributions that would otherwise (absent the Sec. 242(b) election) have been required under the current rules.

Sec. 242(b) elections can delay the timing of required distributions substantially. The retirement planner should be sure to ask if the client has retained an election form in his or her files. As noted above, the election has to be followed exactly in order to avoid having to take a potentially large distribution at some later date.

PLANNING CONSIDERATIONS

The financial adviser in the role of planner should take leadership around the minimum distribution planning decision. In many cases, especially in IRAs and 403(b) plans, no other professionals are keeping track of this issue. Failure to make a minimum distribution carries a stiff penalty to the participant. Also, with careful planning, the amount of deferral can be lengthened.

Taking full advantage of the opportunity to maximize the deferral of income taxes under the minimum distribution rules requires both knowledge and planning.

Most important is avoiding simple mistakes. Below is a list of common distribution errors that should be avoided at all costs:

- not making a required minimum distribution, resulting in a 50 percent excise tax
- failing to do tax planning at age 70 1/2, the last time that proper planning can be considered!
- failing to read the plan to find out the distribution method options allowed under *this* plan
- choosing the life expectancy recalculation method for an individual who has a short life expectancy at age 70 1/2
- choosing the estate or a nonconforming trust as beneficiary—the same as choosing no beneficiary, foreshortening the period of distributions

Clearly, advising in this area requires a broad understanding of the rules. To help you master the major rules, page 336 provides, in a single table, a comprehensive look at the rules discussed in this chapter.

On the practical side, several decisions have to be made over the life of the participant's plan participation. The first issue that will arise is the choice of beneficiary for any death benefits. As described earlier, choosing the estate or a nonqualifying trust as a beneficiary is the same as choosing no beneficiary. Under the rules applicable when death occurs prior to the required beginning date, having no beneficiary means that all distributions have to be paid out within five years of death—not over the life expectancy of a chosen beneficiary. The spouse generally makes the best beneficiary because of his or her opportunity to either follow the minimum distribution rules that apply to the participant or roll the benefit into his or her own IRA and start over.

The second issue that must be addressed is choosing the method for calculating the minimum distribution at the required beginning date. If the benefit is an annuity from a defined-benefit plan or from the purchase of a commercial annuity, the annuity must simply conform with the applicable rules. However, when the payment is from an individual account plan, the participant will generally have the option to recalculate applicable life expectancies. Don't forget that availability of choice depends entirely on the terms of the applicable plan, *meaning that the plan must be read carefully.* The impact of the recalculation decision will be discussed below.

Also remember that the beneficiary on the plan's beneficiary designation form at the required beginning date is the one used for calculating all future minimum distributions. If no beneficiary election has been made, or if the estate or a non-conforming trust is chosen, then only the participant's life is taken into consideration—*which is never to the advantage of the participant.* A beneficiary change after the required beginning date may shorten the payout period, but it will never lengthen it. *This means that the required beginning date is the last opportunity to do appropriate distribution planning!*

Making Minimum Distribution Elections

Although the minimum distribution rules provide substantial flexibility in determining the required minimum, an individual's distribution options are always controlled by the terms of the retirement plan. Most qualified plans and 403(b) plans limit the individual's choice among several options, which may include life annuities, period certain installment payments, or a lump sum. So the first step is to understand the various plan options. If an individual wants to maximize flexibility, he or she should consider a lump-sum distribution (if it is available under the plan)—and rolling the benefit into an IRA. In the IRA, distributions can be made at the participant's discretion, allowing distribution as slowly as allowed by law or more quickly if required.

Second, some clients will want to consider annuitization, either in a qualified plan or in an IRA after a rollover. When the annuity is purchased before the required beginning date, annuitization has one important strength—simplicity. With a 50 percent excise tax for failing to satisfy the minimum distribution rules, some clients will prefer not having to worry about calculating the minimum distribution amounts on an annual basis. On the other hand, annuitization may not be the best choice for the individual who wants to defer payments as long as possible in order to leave substantial benefits to future generations. Traditionally, the annuity has been a way to liquidate assets over covered individuals' lifetimes. Annuities spread payments evenly (or with some growth in a variable annuity) over the payout period, while the account plan minimum distribution rules allow smaller payments in the beginning and larger payments later. In any event, it is unwise to make snap judgments about the appropriateness of annuitization. For example, in some cases, annuitization, combined with life insurance planning, can be a valid estate planning approach. Be careful, however, when purchasing an annuity after the required beginning date. In this case, the account plan rules apply until the annuity is purchased. The type of annuity that can be purchased

Minimum Distribution Rules Overview

Death Prior to the Required Beginning Date

General rule is that the entire amount must be distributed prior to the 12/31 following the 5th anniversary of participant's death. Exceptions apply—depending upon whether the beneficiary is the participant's spouse or not.*

Spousal beneficiary	Nonspousal beneficiary
If the distribution begins by the 12/31 following the date on which the participant would have attained age 70 1/2, benefits can be paid over the spouse's lifetime.	If the distribution begins by 12/31 of the calendar year following the year of death, benefits can be paid over the beneficiary's lifetime.
Methodology for determining the minimum distribution under the lifetime exception is the same as for post -70 1/2 nonannuity distributions. Spouse's life expectancy can be recalculated.	Methodology for determining the minimum distribution under the lifetime exception is the same as for post -70 1/2 nonannuity distributions. Nonspouse beneficiary's life expectancy cannot be recalculated.
Spouse has a second option, to roll over the benefit into his or her own IRA in which case the death distribution rules no longer apply. (Spouse may treat as own without actual rollover.)	

Notes

*The plan document can eliminate or limit the choice of calculation method. If the plan fails to address which distribution method applies, then the lifetime exception applies for spouses and the 5-year rule applies for nonspouses.

Participant Lives to the Required Beginning Date

General rule is that the distributions must be payable over the joint life expectancies of the participant and a chosen beneficiary beginning by the required beginning date (April 1 of the year following the attainment of age 70 1/2). Although distributions can begin as of that April 1, a minimum distribution must be made for the first distribution year (year attaining age 70 1/2) and for every subsequent year. Calculation of the minimum depends upon whether the distribution is in the form of a commercial annuity or an individual account and whether or not the beneficiary is a spouse.

Purchase annuity		Do not purchase annuity	
Spousal beneficiary	Nonspousal beneficiary	Spousal beneficiary	Nonspousal beneficiary
Must begin annuity payments by the required beginning date (payable in intervals of one year or less). The annuity payments can extend as long as a joint and 100% survivor annuity with a period certain that does not exceed the joint life expectancies of the participant and the beneficiary.	If beneficiary is more than 10 years younger than the participant the MDIB rules limit the period certain payments and the maximum survivor percentage of the annuity.	Required distribution for first distribution year (year of attainment of age 70 1/2) is the account balance as of the previous 12/31 divided by the joint life expectancy of the participant and the beneficiary as of the last day of the first distribution year. Similar rules apply for calculating minimum distribution for subsequent years (see below).	If the beneficiary is more than 10 years younger than the participant the MDIB rules provide a factor that is substituted for the actual joint life expectancy.
The MDIB rules do not apply to a spousal beneficiary.		The MDIB rules do not apply to a spousal beneficiary.	
		At the time distributions begin, individual may elect to recalculate life expectancy of either (or both) the participant and the spouse in subsequent years.	At time distributions begin, an election can be made to recalculate participant's life expectancy for subsequent years. Cannot recalculate beneficiary's life expectancy.

In all cases, distributions after death must continue at least as rapidly as prior to the death of the participant. Spouse retains the option to roll benefits into his or her own IRA.

will be limited by the participant's recalculation decision under the account plan rules. For example, the regulations prohibit the purchase of a life annuity when the participant elected not to recalculate life expectancies.

Although annuitization is an option, many individuals wanting to maximize the opportunity to control — and defer — pension distributions will not annuitize. Therefore most will be subject to the account plan rules. When the account plan rules apply, the individual will be faced with two choices: a beneficiary election and whether or not to elect to recalculate applicable life expectancies.

Because of the importance of the beneficiary issue, the planner must pay close attention to details. The beneficiary for purposes of determining all future minimum distributions is the person identified on the plan's beneficiary designation form at the required beginning date. If the participant has not named a beneficiary, the default beneficiary under the terms of the plan will be considered the beneficiary. Changes in the beneficiary election after this date generally are ignored for calculating required minimums unless a new beneficiary is older, in which case the new beneficiary's life expectancy is substituted for the previous one. As mentioned above, choosing the estate as the beneficiary is treated as electing no beneficiary. A trust will be treated the same way unless the trust is irrevocable at the required beginning date, and several other provisions have been satisfied.

Recalculating Life Expectancies

Another important decision is whether or not to recalculate life expectancies. Remember that this choice requires affirmative action. If the participant does not want to use the plan's default provisions the plan administrator has to be notified of the selection prior to the required beginning date.

The choice to recalculate is a gamble on the individual's life expectancy. If the individual lives beyond the expected lifetime, recalculation stretches out the minimum distribution payments. However, if death occurs before the individual's anticipated life expectancy (as of the first distribution year), distributions will be made more rapidly than if recalculation is not elected. Therefore if the participant is in good health at the required beginning date, recalculation should be strongly considered. Clearly this decision is a gamble, but an informed participant can make an intelligent choice. If the beneficiary is the spouse — and recalculation can be chosen for either life — the decision about whether to recalculate should be made separately for each life based on each person's health at the required beginning date.

For the participant with an average expected lifetime, whether to recalculate is truly a toss-up. The clearest situation is for the individual who is in poor health at the required beginning date. In this case, recalculation should not be elected. When the spouse is the beneficiary, the danger of a short distribution period due to the early death of the participant can be offset by the spouse's special opportunity to roll benefits into his or her own IRA account at the participant's death.

TABLE 10-5
Minimum Required Distribution Computation without
Recalculation of Life Expectancies

Assumptions

Participant's age at first distribution year	70
Spouse/beneficiary's age at first distribution year	68
Participant's age at death	78
Beneficiary's age at death	83
Do not recalculate life expectancies.	
Current account balance	$400,000
Assumed rate of return on balance	7%

Distribution occurring on last day of each distribution year:

Age Parti-cipant	Age Bene-ficiary	Beginning Balance	ALE	Minimum Distribution	Ending Balance
(1)	(2)	(3)	(4)	(5)	(6)
70	68	$400,000.00	21.5	$18,604.65	$409,395.35
71	69	$409,395.35	20.5	$19,970.50	$418,082.52
72	70	$418,082.52	19.5	$21,440.13	$425,908.17
73	71	$425,908.17	18.5	$23,022.06	$432,699.67
74	72	$432,699.67	17.5	$24,725.70	$438,262.96
75	73	$438,262.96	16.5	$26,561.39	$442,379.97
76	74	$442,379.97	15.5	$28,540.64	$444,805.93
77	75	$444,805.93	14.5	$30,676.27	$445,266.07
78	76	$445,266.07	13.5	$32,982.67	$443,452.02
	77	$443,452.02	12.5	$35,476.16	$439,017.50
	78	$439,017.50	11.5	$38,175.44	$431,573.29
	79	$431,573.29	10.5	$41,102.22	$420,681.21
	80	$420,681.21	9.5	$44,282.23	$405,846.66
	81	$405,846.66	8.5	$47,746.67	$386,509.26
	82	$386,509.26	7.5	$51,534.57	$362,030.34
	83	$362,030.34	6.5	$55,696.98	$331,675.49
		$331,675.49	5.5	$60,304.63	$294,588.14
		$294,588.14	4.5	$65,464.03	$249,745.28
		$249,745.28	3.5	$71,355.79	$195,871.65
		$195,871.65	2.5	$78,348.66	$131,234.01
		$131,234.01	1.5	$87,489.34	$52,931.05
		$52,931.05	0.5	$56,636.22	($0.00)
		($0.00)	0		

TABLE 10-6
Minimum Required Distribution Computation Using Recalculation of Both Life Expectancies

Assumptions

Participant's age at first distribution year	70
Spouse/beneficiary's age at first distribution year	68
Participant's age at death	78
Spouse's age at death	83
Recalculate life expectancies.	
Current account balance	$400,000
Assumed rate of return on balance	7%

Distribution occurring on last day of each distribution year:

Age Participant	Age Beneficiary	Beginning Balance	ALE	Minimum Distribution	Ending Balance
(1)	(2)	(3)	(4)	(5)	(6)
70	68	$400,000.00	21.5	$18,604.65	$409,395.35
71	69	$409,395.35	20.7	$19,777.55	$418,275.47
72	70	$418,275.47	19.8	$21,125.02	$426,429.73
73	71	$426,429.73	19	$22,443.67	$433,836.14
74	72	$433,836.14	18.2	$23,837.15	$440,367.52
75	73	$440,367.52	17.3	$25,454.77	$445,738.48
76	74	$445,738.48	16.5	$27,014.45	$449,925.72
77	75	$449,925.72	15.8	$28,476.31	$452,944.21
78	76	$452,944.21	15	$30,196.28	$454,454.02
	77	$454,454.02	11.2	$40,576.25	$445,689.55
	78	$454,454.00	11.2	$40,576.25	$445,689.50
	79	$445,689.50	10.6	$42,046.18	$434,841.60
	80	$434,841.60	10.0	$43,484.16	$421,796.40
	81	$421,796.40	9.5	$44,399.62	$406,922.50
	82	$406,922.50	8.9	$45,721.63	$389,685.50
	83	$389,685.50	8.4	$46,391.13	$370,572.30
		$370,572.30	7.9	$46,907.89	$349,604.50
		$349,604.50	0	$349,604.00	0

When a distribution is made from an account plan, recalculating—versus not recalculating—life expectancies has a significant impact on the flow of distributions. Take, for example, Jonathan and his wife, Josephine. Table 10-5 shows the required stream of distributions, assuming there are no recalculations of life expectancies. Under this method the stream of payments steadily increases throughout the 21.5-year period. In this example, Jonathan and Josephine are not particularly long-lived. Their beneficiaries may continue to receive distributions over a 6-year period after Josephine's death.

Table 10-6 shows the required stream of distributions, assuming recalculation of both lives. If this method is used while both are alive, the stream of distributions is slightly smaller than without recalculation. For example, in the year that Jonathan reaches 76, the required minimum distribution is $27,014.45 versus $28,540.64 under the nonrecalculation method. However, the distributions are accelerated at the time of death. This can be seen both by the significant increase in the minimum distribution in the year following Jonathan's death (jump from $30,196.28 to $40,576.25) and the fact that the remaining account balance of $313,707.94 must be distributed in the year following Josephine's death.

If the individual is concerned about maximizing the amount left to his or her heirs, *under these specific facts* the recalculation method is probably not the best solution. However, this determination is fact specific, and must be based on assumptions about the actual life expectancies of the individuals involved. For example, if we expect Jonathan and Josephine to live substantially longer than the 21.5-year life expectancy, recalculation will extend the payout period.

The only way to really understand the impact of the various choices is to work with a particular fact pattern and create a chart as we have done in the Jonathan and Josephine example. A simple program can be written with any spreadsheet software, or commercial programs can be purchased that calculate the minimum distribution amount, using a specific set of assumptions.

Planning for Maximum Deferral

As mentioned above, recalculating life expectancies can result in a significant amount of deferral. If an individual is married with a spouse the same age or younger and both are in good health, recalculation will result in a payout period that extends to the end of the survivor's life. The younger the spouse, the longer this payout period is likely to be. Since recalculation does carry the risk of continued life, the participant with a younger spouse may consider electing not to recalculate the life expectancy of the spouse. This will guarantee that the minimum payout period (regardless of who lives) will extend for the life expectancy (at the time payments begin) of the spouse. For example, assume that the spouse is aged 50 in the first distribution year. If the spouse's life is not recalculated the payout period will be 28.6 years, the life expectancy of a 50-year-old.

The spouse's ability to roll the benefit into his or her own IRA and then choose another beneficiary also makes the spouse an excellent beneficiary choice. Choosing the spouse allows maximum flexibility: the opportunity either to continue payments under the previously chosen death benefit rules or to start over with the benefit in the spouse's name. The spouse can then take advantage of the next strategy—choosing a young beneficiary to maximize deferral.

Another effective strategy to maximize deferral is to elect a young non-spousal beneficiary. This strategy can result in extremely long periods of deferral. As mentioned above, in this case the life expectancy of the nonspousal beneficiary cannot be recalculated. Also, the MDIB rules limit the life expectancy (size of the denominator) during the period in which both the participant and the beneficiary are alive. However, the regulations clearly indicate that the MDIB rules do not apply after the death of the participant. This means that after the participant's death, the denominator in the calculation becomes the remaining life expectancy of the beneficiary.

Table 10-7 contains an example showing a client's ability to defer the distributions in a case in which a younger nonspousal beneficiary is selected. The table contains the theoretical minimum distribution pattern over a period of years for a participant, aged 70 in the first distribution year, who has selected a beneficiary, aged 50 in the first distribution year. In this example, the amount of the minimum distribution is controlled in the first few years by the MDIB requirements. However, once the participant dies (at age 78 in this example), the minimum distribution is actually smaller in the following year. This result occurs because the minimum distribution at age 78 is $1,847,653/19.2 (the MDIB applicable divisor), while in the following year the minimum distribution is $1,880,757/24.1 (the remaining life expectancy of the beneficiary). Remember that the remaining life expectancy, when the beneficiary's life expectancy is not recalculated, is the life expectancy in the first distribution year minus the number of years that have elapsed (33.1 − 9 = 24.1). Also note that since the beneficiary's life expectancy is not recalculated, the distribution may continue over the 24.1-year period regardless of whether the beneficiary lives over this entire period.

Preparing Retirement Needs Analysis

Retirement (and estate) planners may be involved in comparing income sources to anticipated retirement needs. In this process it may be determined that amounts in tax-sheltered retirement plans are not needed to meet current needs. In performing such an analysis, the planner must remember to consider that distributions may be required under the minimum distribution rules. Amounts distributed earlier than expected will be taxed sooner, which will affect the results of the analysis.

Looking at the Whole Picture

Tax planning for retirement plan distributions can be a complicated process. The minimum distribution rules are just one piece of the puzzle. Another consideration is whether or not to take lump-sum averaging on a distribution. Also, the impact of the 15 percent excise tax on excess distributions and the 15 percent excess accumulations tax paid by the estate has to be considered.

TABLE 10-7
Minimum Required Distribution Computation Recalculation of Participant's Life Expectancy

Assumptions

Participant's age at first distribution year	70
Beneficiary's age at first distribution year	50
Participant's age at death	78
Beneficiary's age at death	70
Recalculate participant's life expectancies.	
Current account balance	$1,500,000
Assumed rate of return on balance	7%

Distribution occurring on last day of each distribution year:

Age Participant	Age Beneficiary	Beginning Balance	ALE	MDIB	Minimum Distribution	Ending Balance
(1)	(2)	(3)	(4)	(5)	(6)	(7)
70	50	$1,500,000	34.0	26.2	$57,251	$1,547,748
71	51	$1,547,748	32.2	25.3	$61,175	$1,594,914
72	52	$1,594,914	31.2	24.4	$65,365	$1,641,193
73	53	$1,641,193	30.3	23.5	$69,838	$1,686,238
74	54	$1,686,238	29.4	22.7	$74,283	$1,729,991
75	55	$1,729,991	28.5	21.8	$79,357	$1,771,733
76	56	$1,771,733	27.6	20.8	$84,771	$1,810,983
77	57	$1,810,983	26.7	20.1	$90,098	$1,847,653
78	58	$1,847,653	25.8	19.2	$96,231	$1,880,757
	59	$1,880,757	24.1		$78,039	$1,934,370
	60	$1,934,370	23.1		$83,738	$1,986,037
	61	$1,986,037	22.1		$89,865	$2,035,194
	62	$2,035,194	21.1		$96,454	$2,081,203
	63	$2,081,203	20.1		$103,542	$2,123,344
	64	$2,123,344	19.1		$111,169	$2,160,809
	65	$2,160,809	18.1		$119,381	$2,192,684
	66	$2,192,684	17.1		$128,227	$2,217,944
	67	$2,217,944	16.1		$137,760	$2,235,440
	68	$2,235,440	15.1		$148,042	$2,243,878
	69	$2,243,878	14.1		$159,140	$2,241,809
	70	$2,241,809	13.1		$171,130	$2,227,606
		$2,227,606	12.1		$184,099	$2,199,438
		$2,199,438	11.1		$198,147	$2,155,251
		$2,155,251	10.1		$213,397	$2,092,728
		$2,092,728	9.1		$229,970	$2,009,249
		$2,239,219	8.1		$248,055	$1,901,841
		. . . . .	. . .		. . . .	. . . . .

Example 10: Assume that Alex, aged 65, begins to receive an annual pension from a qualified defined-benefit plan in the amount of $90,000. In addition, assume that he also received a distribution of $950,000 from a profit-sharing plan, which he rolled into an IRA. The IRA benefit will have to be distributed beginning at age 70 1/2. If Alex chooses to delay distributions until 70 1/2 and minimize the required distributions in early years, the result may be that in later years distributions (along with the $90,000 pension) will exceed the $150,000 threshold, triggering the 15 percent excise tax on excess distributions. In this example, Alex should consider either starting distributions prior to age 70 1/2 or receiving distributions in excess of the minimum in early years to avoid the impact of the 15 percent excise tax.

These choices can be complex, and they involve making assumptions about future tax rates and potential interest earnings. The retirement planner needs to have a handle on each of the components in order to help guide the client. The final—and, for the wealthy client, possibly the most important—part of this analysis is the impact of estate taxes. The income tax planning process may effectively delay distributions and minimize income taxes, which may also result in staggering estate taxes. To have the income tax planning work properly the estate tax issue must also be addressed. The estate planning issue is similar to other cases where the estate's assets are liquidated. Although beyond the scope of this book, the solution in this case is often life insurance planning. Commercial software packages are available to help sort out these various components for the retirement planner. These interrelated considerations are discussed further in the following chapter, and several available resources will be identified.

11

The Impact of the 15 Percent Excess Distributions and Excess Accumulations Taxes on Retirement Accumulation and Distribution Planning

Chapter Outline

OVERVIEW

The Tax Reform Act of 1986 (TRA '86) created two "excise" taxes that apply to taxpayers who have accumulated significant benefits within qualified retirement plans, IRAs, SEPs, Keogh plans and 403(b) tax-deferred annuities. The first tax, referred to here as the *excess distributions excise tax*, imposes an additional income tax of 15 percent on annual distributions from any of the above-named plans in excess of a specified threshold ($150,000 in 1995). The second tax, which is closely tied to the first, is a 15 percent additional estate tax on the amount of remaining plan benefits at the time of death that exceed another specified threshold (the threshold depends upon the individual's age at death). This second tax is referred to herein as the *excess accumulations estate tax.*

When the law was first enacted in 1986, individuals who had accumulated more than $562,500 in plan benefits as of August 1, 1986, were eligible to make a special grandfather election limiting their exposure to these two new excise taxes. The election had to have been made on a pre-1989 tax return. Many wealthier taxpayers made the election at that time, and this decision still affects them today—requiring that retirement planners be familiar with both the taxes and the grandfather election. In fact, virtually all participants in qualified plans must assess their potential future exposure to the taxes and take steps to minimize their effects.

However, techniques employed to avoid or minimize one or both taxes generally involve some trade-offs or costs. For example, often the benefits of income tax deferral can outweigh the cost of paying the 15 percent excise tax in the future. In addition, taxpayers are placed in a catch-22 position where strategies designed to minimize the excess distribution excise tax will often expose them to a higher potential excise tax bite on their accumulations at death (the excess accumulations estate tax), and vice versa. Strategies that are implemented to reduce the impact of these excise taxes must weigh the relative tax benefits and costs in terms of both lifetime distributions and accumulations at death and consider the timing of these costs and benefits. Although the nominal tax rate on either excess lifetime distributions or excess retirement accumulations at death is 15 percent, the estate excise tax is deductible when computing the estate tax. Consequently the effective estate excise tax rate on excess accumulations may be significantly lower than 15 percent and, as a result, may shift the weight of one's planning emphasis in favor of minimizing the excess distributions excise tax.

Planning for the consequences of these excise taxes ultimately involves all aspects of retirement plan accumulation and distribution planning. An individual's health and family longevity, investment philosophy, estate plan, selection of beneficiaries and distribution options, and concerns for potential long-term income tax rate changes, as well as the economy, will directly or indirectly influence decisions regarding this tax. More specifically, every technique employed to reduce exposure to the excise taxes must take into account the client's overall financial situation as well as the relevant income and estate tax considerations.

Ultimately, the impact of the excise tax must be considered when making all decisions about the distribution: the timing of the distributions, the form of payment, and the choice of beneficiary. The tax may even affect the continued viability of some plans where key employees and owners have already amassed such sizable benefit balances that additional contributions or benefit accruals will inevitably be subject to the tax. In these cases, nonqualified deferred-compensation arrangements or tax-favored investments outside qualified plans may present attractive alternatives. The list of planning issues can go on and on.

THE EXCESS DISTRIBUTIONS EXCISE TAX

The basic rule imposes a 15 percent excise tax on all distributions from covered plans, with certain limited exclusions, to the extent that the total of such distributions received in any year exceeds the *applicable annual exemption*, or what is also called the *annual threshold amount*. The applicable annual exemption is $150,000. After 1995, it will be indexed each year for inflation.

To illustrate the basic rule, assume that Sheila receives annuity payments in the amount of $68,000 in 1995 from a qualified plan. Also in 1995 she withdraws $98,000 from an IRA. In addition to paying income taxes on the distributions, she will pay $2,400 (($166,000 − $150,000) x .15) in excise tax.

A special rule applies to distributions in which the taxpayer elects special lump-sum averaging treatment. The applicable annual exemption for lump-sum distributions where 5-year or 10-year averaging or capital-gain treatment for pre-1974 plan participation is elected is equal to five times the applicable annual exemption for regular distributions. For example, in 1995 the lump-sum exemption was $750,000 (five times the $150,000 annual exemption for regular distributions).

The exemptions for regular distributions and for lump-sum distributions apply separately. That is, a person who received both a lump-sum distribution from one plan and regular distributions from other plan(s) in 1995 was entitled to both the $750,000 exemption for the lump-sum distribution and the $150,000 exemption for the regular distributions—a total exemption of $900,000. However, any extra "unused" exemption for one type of distribution may not be used to shelter excess distributions of the other type.

Exclusions

Almost all distributions from qualified retirement plans, IRA, SEPs, and 403(b) tax-deferred annuities (referred to as *covered plans*) are subject to the tax. There are only six exclusions. These exclusions include

- distributions of the participant's aftertax investment in the plans
- distributions that are rolled over to an IRA or another qualified plan

- distributions to an alternate payee under a qualified domestic relations order, but only if the payments are included in income by the alternate payee (and are therefore included with other distributions for the alternate payee in determining the alternate payee's excess distributions)
- health coverage or any distribution of medical benefits provided under an arrangement described in IRC Sec. 401(h)
- distributions payable to a beneficiary as a death benefit (since these payments are subject to the 15 percent excise tax on excess retirement accumulations)
- distributions of annuity contracts to the extent that they are not includible in income at the time of the distribution. However, later annuity payments from the contract are subject to the excise tax.

In the event that a person incurs the 10 percent Sec. 72(t) penalty for early withdrawals, the 15 percent excise tax, if any, is reduced to the extent of the early withdrawal penalty. In other words, the total excise on any distributions subject to the early withdrawal penalty will not exceed 15 percent.

The Grandfather Election

To protect themselves from the full impact of the new taxes, many individuals with the requisite $562,500 or more in accumulated benefits on August 1, 1986, made the grandfather election. How the grandfather election impacts on an individual's ability to protect large distributions from the excise tax will depend on the total amount that was grandfathered and on which "grandfather recovery method" the participant elected.

Back on August 1, 1986, an individual's initial *grandfather amount* was equal to the total taxable balance in all of his or her qualified plans, IRAs, SEPs, and 403(b) tax-deferred annuities. All distributions made on or after January 1, 1987, have the impact of reducing the remaining grandfather amount—by an amount that is also dependent upon the individual's grandfather recovery method.

Grandfather Recovery Methods

Persons making the grandfather election were permitted to choose between two methods for computing the grandfather recovery amount—the discretionary method and the attained age method. Because of its flexibility almost everyone elected the discretionary method of recovery.

Under the *discretionary method,* all distributions are subject to what is referred to as the 10 percent recovery method, until such time that an individual elects to switch to the 100 percent recovery method. The election to change to the 100 percent method is permanent, and all future distributions are subject to this method of recovery.

Under the 10 percent recovery method, the remaining grandfathered amount is reduced in the amount of 10 percent of each distribution. For example, assume Rollo has a grandfathered amount of $1 million and takes a $100,000 distribution for the year. The remaining grandfathered amount is $990,000, since only $10,000 (10 percent of $100,000) is removed. Therefore the obvious advantage of the 10 percent method is that it preserves the grandfathered amount. On the other hand, the disadvantage of the 10 percent method is that it provides no effective protection from the excise tax. The amount of a distribution protected from tax is the greater of 10 percent of the distribution or the applicable threshold amount (which is $150,000 in 1995). For example, assume instead that Rollo took a distribution of $200,000. Rollo would be subject to pay the 15 percent tax ($7,500) on the difference between $200,000 and $150,000, since $150,000 is greater than $20,000 (10 percent of the $200,000 distribution).

Under the 100 percent recovery method the advantages and disadvantages are reversed. In this case 100 percent of each distribution is protected from the excise tax and the remaining grandfathered amount is reduced by 100 percent of each distribution. For example, if Rollo had elected to switch to the 100 percent recovery method, and he received a distribution of $200,000, his remaining grandfathered amount would be $800,000, and he would not be subject to any excise tax.

The *attained age method* is the alternative grandfather recovery method. Under this method the amount of each distribution that is considered a recovery of the grandfather amount is determined using a complicated formula that varies with a person's age. However, experts generally agreed that this method provided no advantages over the discretionary method, and virtually no one elected this form of recovery method, meaning that practitioners should not encounter this election in practice today. Therefore this recovery method will not be discussed further.

Practical Considerations

While these rules seem complex, the decision making is quite straightforward. First, the election period has ended and no new grandfather elections may be made. If your client had a large pension and/or IRA accumulations in 1986, ask whether he or she made the election. If the answer is yes, then look at the election form to determine whether the individual elected the 10 percent or the accelerated 100 percent method. Assuming the 10 percent method was elected, at the time distributions begin the decision must be made whether or not to accelerate to 100 percent. If the amount of the distribution is less than the annual exemption ($150,000) the acceleration election should not be made. The individual does not need protection from the tax and will want to save the grandfathered amount. Remember that in this case the grandfathered amount is reduced by 10 percent of the distributed amount. If the distribution exceeds the annual exemption and the excise tax may apply, the acceleration election should be considered. If the individual receives his or her entire benefit, he or she should make the acceleration election to protect the distribution from the excise tax. If the distribution constitutes only a portion of the benefit and the amount is only slightly higher than the annual exemption ($150,000), the decision is more difficult. Accelerating protects the current distribution from the excise tax but uses up the grandfathered amount quickly. Furthermore, since the remaining grandfather amount is used when determining the excise tax on excess retirement accumulations at death, choosing to accelerate the recovery rate to shelter lifetime distributions may increase a person's exposure to the tax at death.

THE EXCESS ACCUMULATIONS ESTATE TAX

Since a person could obviously avoid the excise tax by minimizing lifetime distributions (within the limits imposed by the uniform minimum distribution rules), the law provides that excess retirement accumulations at death are subject also to a 15 percent excise tax. This *death excise tax* is imposed in addition to any federal estate or gift taxes and may not be offset by the lifetime unified credit or by any deductions, such as the marital deduction or deductions for charitable contributions. However, it is deductible when computing the federal estate tax.

Also, under a provision enacted under the Technical and Miscellaneous Revenue Act of 1988 (TAMRA), if virtually all the decedent's retirement balances (defined by committee reports as at least 99 percent) go to the surviving spouse, the surviving spouse may elect to treat the balances as his or her own for purposes of the excise tax. In this case, the excise tax is not imposed on the excess retirement accumulations at the first death.

Excess retirement accumulations are defined as the amount by which the value of a person's plan balances (less certain limited exclusions) exceed a stated threshold. The threshold amount varies based on the person's age at death. This is because the threshold is based on the present value of a *hypothetical single life annuity;* the amount of the annuity is equal to the applicable annual exemption in the year of death multiplied by a life annuity factor based on the decedent's attained age in the year of death. The annuity factor is based on the interest rate and mortality assumptions for valuing life annuities as provided in IRS Regs. 20.2031-7.

For some examples, see table 11-1. In the table the annuity tax threshold was calculated using the applicable annual exemption for 1994 and the applicable interest rate as of October 1994. The excess accumulations tax threshold is shown for individuals who die at age 60, 65, 70, 75, or 80 in October 1994. The table also demonstrates what the threshold would be for such individuals if they were to die in 5, 10, or 15 years. Note that as individuals age, the life annuity factor will be smaller—reducing the threshold. However, at the same time the applicable annual exemption will increase for inflation. As you look across the rows in table 11-1, you can see these two forces competing.

TABLE 11-1 Excess Accumulations Estate Tax Threshold Amount				
Age in 1994	Death in 1994 ($150,000)	Death in 1999 ($180,673)	Death in 2004 ($219,816)	Death in 2009 ($267,440)
60	$1,282,890	$1,410,333 (65)	$1,529,458 (70)	$1,613,599 (75)
65	$1,170,900	$1,257,105 (70)	$1,326,260 (75)	$1,345,491 (80)
70	$1,043,685	$1,090,091 (75)	$1,105,894 (80)	$1,087,973 (85)
75	$ 905,025	$ 908,966 (80)	$ 894,233 (85)	$ 864,366 (90)
80	$ 754,650	$ 734,996 (85)	$ 710,445 (90)	$ 684,138 (95)
Assumptions: (1) annuity valuation interest rate: 8.6% (Oct. 1994); (2) annual threshold amount: $150,000 in 1994 and increasing for inflation 4% each year				

A remaining grandfathered amount at the time of death can provide protection from the excess accumulations tax. In this case the amount of accumulations that exceed the greater of the applicable threshold or the remaining grandfathered amount would be subject to the 15 percent tax. For example, if an individual had $2 million accumulated in applicable plans, the accumulations tax threshold was $1.25 million, and the remaining grandfathered amount was $1.4 million, the estate would be subject to a 15 percent tax on $600,000 ($2 million − $1.4 million). However, if in the same example the remaining grandfathered amount was $1 million, then the tax would be 15 percent of $750,000 ($2 million − $1.25 million).

Exclusions

As is the case with the 15 percent excise tax on excess distributions, exclusions from the excise tax on excess accumulations are few. In addition to the exclusions mentioned above for excess distributions, the amounts excluded from the excess accumulations tax include the value of any death benefits payable immediately after death with respect to the decedent to the extent that the sum of such death benefits plus other benefits payable exceed the total value of benefits payable immediately prior to death. Basically this means that life insurance benefits within a plan payable at death that are in excess of the amount the decedent could have received just prior to death if he or she had terminated or redeemed the policies are not subject to the 15 percent death excise tax. The *net amount at risk* (the pure term insurance portion of the death benefit) in life insurance policies is excludible.

Figure 11-1 summarizes how to calculate the excess accumulations estate tax.

FIGURE 11-1
Calculating the Excess Accumulations Estate Tax

The amount of the tax is 15 percent of the value of

- IRA, qualified plan, 403(b), and SEP benefits that will be payable to the participant's beneficiaries at the time of the participant's death *excluding* (1) investment in the contract, (2) amounts payable to an alternate payee, and (3) life insurance proceeds in excess of the cash value of the contract

in excess of a specified threshold:

- The threshold is (1) the annual applicable threshold ($150,000) multiplied by an annuity factor that is based on the individual's age as of the date of death or (2) the remaining grandfathered amount—if larger.

Example: Rocky dies in October 1994 at age 70 with $2 million in benefits that will be payable to beneficiaries. Calculate the excess accumulations estate tax.

$$\$150,000 \times 6.9579 = \$1,043,685$$
$$\$2,000,000 - \$1,043,685 = \$956,315$$
$$\$956,315 \times .15 = \$143,447 \text{ in excise tax}$$

STRATEGIES TO REDUCE THE EXCESS DISTRIBUTIONS EXCISE TAX

Clearly, planning for the excess distributions excise tax is involved, and many factors must be considered. A person's health and family longevity, investment philosophy, estate plans, and selection of beneficiaries and distribution options, along with the potential for long-term income tax rate changes and economic changes, may directly or indirectly influence decisions regarding this tax. More specifically, every technique employed to reduce exposure to the excise tax must take into account the client's overall financial situation as well as the relevant income and estate tax considerations.

Your clients who are likely to pay the excise tax on excess distributions should consider the following strategies to manipulate the timing of distributions and to minimize the effect of the tax.

Extending the Distribution Period

Extending the payout period will reduce exposure to the excess distribution excise tax in two ways. First, extending the payout period reduces the annual payments for a given benefit balance. For example, a benefit balance of

$1,473,000 paid out over 10 years will provide annual payments of $229,587 per year, assuming a 9 percent rate of return. If the payout period is extended to 25 years, the annual benefit payment is reduced to $150,000 a year. Extending the period of payout reduces the potential annual tax by almost $12,000 (the $79,587 in excess of $150,000 taxed at 15 percent).

Second, extending the payout period allows inflation to push the annual exemption amount higher, thus reducing the excess amount subject to tax. This will be especially effective for persons who have made the grandfather election. For example, assuming a 4 percent annual inflation adjustment, the 1995 indexed annual exemption of $150,000 will grow to the following values over the coming years:

Year	Years Until	Exemption
1995	0	$150,000
2000	5	182,498
2005	10	222,037
2010	15	270,142
2015	20	328,668

Inflation alone is no panacea. When a person's current benefit accruals are at the level where lifetime distributions or accumulations at death are likely to be incurred, the excise tax can offer little relief from inflation. Without significant withdrawals, plan balances can be expected to grow faster than the rate of inflation, and exposure to the tax can only be expected to increase over time. However, by employing the techniques discussed below to extend the period over which distributions are received and thereby reduce annual payments, a person may have a fighting chance against this onerous "success" tax.

Electing Life Annuity Payments

This option stretches out the payments over the anticipated life expectancy.

Electing Payments Based on Two Lives

The expected payout period will always be longer, and annual payments lower, when they are based on two lives rather than one.

Structurally, the benefit distribution options available are determined by the particular plan document. Generally a participant will have the opportunity to receive the benefit in the form of a contingent annuity (in many plans a married participant must have the option to receive a qualified joint and survivor annuity; see chapter 3). In some situations the participant may have the opportunity to make the minimum required distribution under the discretionary installment method (see chapter 10), using a designated beneficiary to determine the minimum distribution. In either case, the distributions are subject to the minimum distribution rules, and if the beneficiary is not the spouse, the minimum incidental death benefit rules (described in chapter 10) also apply. This general concept is discussed in more depth on pages 354 through 356.

The decision to name a nonspouse as beneficiary should be made with caution because of potentially adverse estate and gift tax consequences. When the spouse is the beneficiary of the retirement plan benefit, the federal estate tax marital deduction will always apply. However, leaving qualified plan benefits directly to a nonspouse beneficiary will result in either gift or estate taxes. If the election of the beneficiary is irrevocable, a gift is made as of the time of the election. However, if the beneficiary election is revocable until death (as is the case in most retirement plans), the actuarial value of survivor's interest will be included in the taxable estate. With gift and estate tax rates ranging as high as 55 percent, choosing a nonspousal beneficiary simply to minimize the effects of the 15 percent excess distributions excise tax may not be the best idea. The only way to leave a nonspouse some of the benefit without estate tax consequences (at the time of the participant's death) is through the use of a qualified terminable interest properties (QTIP) trust. With this strategy, the beneficiary is the QTIP trust, and the spouse receives a lifetime interest in the assets of the trust. The remainder can be left to a beneficiary of choice. Of course, if this strategy is used the trust must be drafted properly to ensure qualification for the marital deduction. This issue illustrates how numerous complex considerations must be balanced when planning for retirement distributions.

Electing Joint and Survivor Annuity Payments

Since the benefits paid under various annuity options are generally actuarially equivalent to one another, the larger the benefit payable to the survivor beneficiary after the participant's death, the smaller the amount paid while both annuitants are alive. Consequently electing either a 100 percent survivor benefit when the spouse is named as the beneficiary or the maximum allowable survivor benefit under the minimum distribution incidental benefit rules when someone other than the spouse is named as the beneficiary (rather than the commonly offered 75 percent, 66 percent, or 50 percent survivor benefit) will reduce exposure to the 15 percent excise tax on excess distributions.

Electing Guaranteed Payments on Life Annuity Options

When a participant elects a period of guaranteed payments under a life annuity option, there is an actuarial cost; thus the monthly benefit is lowered. The reduced payments reduce exposure to the excess distributions excise tax. At the same time, guaranteed payments provide the benefit of income protection for heirs in the event of an early demise.

Electing Discretionary Payments under the Minimum Distribution Rules

Individuals with large benefit accumulations who have attained age 70 1/2 could be required to take minimum distributions that potentially exceed the excise tax threshold. When this is the case, the method used for calculating the minimum distribution must be chosen carefully. If the qualified plan allows for only annuity and/or lump-sum payments and does not permit discretionary annual payments (most plans will not allow this option), an individual should consider rolling plan benefits over to an IRA, which will give the person compete discretion over the stream of payments. This strategy also allows the individual to calculate the required minimum distribution under the discretionary payout rules as described in chapter 10. This method generally results in smaller distributions than under the annuity payment minimum distribution rules (at least for the first several years of payout), and therefore may better protect the individual from the excess distributions excise tax. In addition, in later years when payouts increase under the minimum distribution rules, the annual exemption for the excess distributions excise tax will have increased as a result of indexing for inflation.

Using the minimum distribution rules provides a further benefit in many cases since distributions are not required to begin until April 1 of the year subsequent to the year the annuitant reaches age 70 1/2. Annuity payments from most pension plans begin at normal retirement age, which is typically age 65. This deferral allows the indexed annual exemption to increase even further before distributions actually begin. The methods of maximizing deferrals under the discretionary method are covered more fully in chapter 10.

Deferring Distributions As Long As Possible

As mentioned above, taking the required minimum distributions is one method for both deferring distributions, at least until age 70 1/2, and minimizing the exposure to the excise tax on lifetime distributions. In addition, when a person is eligible for distributions because of plan termination or separation from service, he or she should consider rolling plan benefits over to IRAs or, if possible, other qualified plans. When permitted, a person who is separating from service should consider leaving plan benefits with the employer until normal retirement age or until age 70 1/2.

Preserving TEFRA Sec. 242(b) Elections

As discussed in chapter 10, employees who made an election under Sec. 242(b) of the Tax Equity and Fiscal Responsibility Act of 1982 (TEFRA) before January 1, 1984, continue to be exempt from the general rule that distributions must begin at age 70 1/2 even if the employee continues to work beyond that age. Preserving the Sec. 242(b) election allows the participant to delay payment of taxes as long as possible. Delaying the distributions allows the excess distributions excise tax threshold to increase with inflation.

The drawback of this technique is that a person is locked into the distribution plans made at the time of the election. Any change in an employee's election (other than the substitution or addition of a beneficiary) is considered a revocation. If an employee revokes the election, his or her benefit must commence and be distributed at least as rapidly as determined under the uniform required minimum distribution rules. According to proposed regulations, if a Sec. 242(b) election is revoked after a plan participant's required beginning date for distributions under the general rules, the plan must distribute, by the end of the calendar year following revocation, the amount not yet distributed that would have been distributed had the Sec. 242(b) election not been made. In addition, distributions must continue as though no election had been made.

Consequently revocation of a Sec. 242(b) election, especially after age 70 1/2, may force sizable distributions in the year subsequent to the revocation, which may trigger the excess distributions excise tax. If a person believes that the distribution election may not meet his or her objectives, he or she should revoke the election before reaching age 70 1/2 or as soon thereafter as possible to minimize exposure to the excess distributions excise tax on this "catch-up" distribution.

Taking Early Withdrawals

In some circumstances, the payout period can be extended and the required annual distributions thereby reduced by taking early withdrawals or by starting lifetime distributions early. Such situations occur, for example, when a person cannot defer the start of distributions or when a person's total qualified plan benefits and IRA balances are so large that deferral alone will not be sufficient to reduce annual distributions below the taxable threshold for lifetime excise tax purposes.

Certain types of plans, such as defined-benefit plans, prohibit distributions until such events as retirement, separation from service, or disability. However, certain other plans, notably profit-sharing plans, can permit withdrawals after a fixed number of years (but not less than 2 years) or the attainment of a stated age, as well as upon the usual events of retirement, disability, or separation from service.

The portion of any withdrawal that is attributable to aftertax contributions (the participant's investment in the contract) is not subject to either the regular income tax or the excess distributions excise tax. The portion of any such withdrawal that is subject to the regular income tax is also subject to the 10 percent early withdrawal penalty in certain circumstances. However, to the extent that an early withdrawal triggers the 15 percent excise tax, there is an offset for the amount of any 10 percent penalty tax imposed on the distribution.

The trade-off with this early withdrawal technique is that income taxes on the benefits are accelerated. The person forfeits the benefit of tax-deferred accumulation on the amounts distributed early. However, the loss of tax leverage on these early distributions may be more than offset by the elimination of the 15 percent tax that would otherwise be paid on future distributions.

Distributions before age 59 1/2 are generally subject to the 10 percent early withdrawal penalty, which, when applicable, significantly reduces the potential benefit of early withdrawals. However, persons may receive distributions without the imposition of the 10 percent penalty tax before age 59 1/2 if the distributions are (1) from a qualified plan or Sec. 403(b) annuity plan and are made on account of termination of employment after the age of 55, or (2) in the case of IRAs or qualified plan balances, taken in essentially equal annual payments based on the plan owner's life expectancy or the joint life expectancy of the owner and a beneficiary.

Once the person begins withdrawals he or she must continue until the later of age 59 1/2 or 5 years from the distribution starting date. The penalties for failing to do so are severe. All distributions prior to age 59 1/2 will become subject to the 10 percent penalty tax plus interest. For example, assume a person begins withdrawing money from an IRA at age 52 and the annual permitted withdrawal based on his or her life expectancy is $50,000 per year (adjusted upward for inflation if desired). If he or she withdraws more than $50,000 from the IRA in any year before reaching the age of 59 1/2, *all* distributions prior to age 59 1/2 become subject to the 10 percent penalty tax—not just the excess distribution in that year or just that year's withdrawal. Therefore steps should be taken when using this technique to assure that withdrawals do not inadvertently exceed the permitted amount.

Combining Lump-Sum Distributions with Installment Payouts

A second major strategy to reduce the effect of the excess distributions excise tax is to take both a lump-sum distribution with a 5- or 10-year averaging election from one plan and installment payouts from other plans. The excess distributions excise tax exemption is computed separately for lump-sum distributions and other regular annual distributions. In other words, a person may receive two exemptions in the same year if he or she receives both regular (non-lump-sum) payments from qualified plans and a lump-sum distribution where he or she elects to use forward averaging. In addition, the exemption for lump-sum distributions is equal to five times the applicable annual exemption for regular distributions.

Specifically a person who has not made the grandfather election could shelter up to $900,000 of distributions from the excess distributions excise tax in 1994 and later years (until the indexed annual exemption amount exceeds $150,000, at which time the amount that may be sheltered will increase). This amount is comprised of an exemption equal to $150,000 for regular (non-lump-sum) distributions and five times that amount, or $750,000, for a lump-sum distribution.

The total exemption in 1994 for a person who made the grandfather election is $891,000, comprised of $148,500 for regular distributions and $742,500 for a lump-sum distribution. In future years this total exemption amount will increase as the indexed annual exemption is adjusted upward for inflation.

For example, suppose that a person retires in 1996, when the estimated indexed annual exemption is $165,000 ($825,000 for a lump-sum distribution). Assume further that this person is entitled to a benefit under a pension with a present value of $825,000, and has account balances under a profit-sharing plan with an aggregate value of $1.7 million. This person will be able to avoid the 15 percent lifetime excise tax altogether by receiving the pension benefit in a lump-sum distribution and receiving profit-sharing benefits in a series of annual distributions not exceeding the indexed annual exemption equal to $165,000 a year. In contrast, if this person received an $80,000 annuity payment under the pension plan in addition to the $165,000 profit-sharing distribution, then the entire $80,000 pension plan distribution would be subject to the 15 percent tax (assuming no grandfather election).

Lump-sum distributions may often be particularly useful when a person has elected the 10 percent recovery method for grandfather amounts. In situations where an individual has participated in more than one type of qualified plan and has the opportunity to elect favorable 5- or 10-year averaging, he or she can capture significant excise tax savings and preserve a large portion of the grandfather amount by electing lump-sum treatment for one plan and then shifting to the 100 percent recovery rate in future years to shelter distributions from the remaining plans. This technique will be especially useful if a person wants the increased flexibility of taking sizable distributions later, when desired, or when required under the minimum distribution rules.

For example, assume that a person's grandfather amount based on August 1, 1986, benefit accruals in all plans is $1.2 million. Assume the current balance in his or her pension plan is $600,000 and the balance in his or her profit-sharing plan and IRAs is $1.1 million. In this particular case, if the person elects lump-sum averaging for the pension plan, he or she will incur no excise tax on the distribution (since the lump-sum exemption was $742,500 in 1994 and will be higher in future years). Only $60,000 (10 percent of the distribution) of the $1.2 million grandfather amount will be used up. This election will leave this person with a grandfather balance of $1.14 million—$40,000 more than the current balance in his or her other plans—and will preserve most of the original grandfather amount for future lifetime distributions and/or protection from the excess accumulations estate tax on excess retirement accumulations at death. If this person desires a large distribution in a future year (that is, one exceeding the indexed annual exemption), he or she may shift to the 100 percent recovery method and shelter all or most of the distribution. Alternatively he or she may keep annual distributions below the indexed annual exemption, continue to use the 10 percent recovery method, and save as much of the grandfather amount as possible to shelter the remaining retirement plan balances at death.

Note: In addition to the excise tax savings, lump-sum taxation may save federal income taxes. As discussed in chapter 9, taxation under the lump- sum rules may result in a lower rate. Consequently the use of lump-sum distributions now may provide both income and excise tax savings.

Depending on a person's qualified plan balances and the method he or she has elected for recovering grandfather amounts, combining lump-sum treatment with annual distributions may not always be the best technique. In particular, if a person has already elected to use the 100 percent recovery method, a lump-sum distribution will use up—and waste—a sizable portion of the grandfather amount.

The technique of combining a lump-sum distribution and annual distributions from multiple plans is available only to persons who have qualified plans with different employers or who have different types of plans (pension, profit-sharing, or stock bonus plans) with the same employer and who also qualify to use lump-sum averaging.

Shifting the Benefit Mix from Qualified to Nonqualified Retirement Plans

Distributions from nonqualified deferred-compensation plans are not taken into account for purposes of the excess distributions excise tax. From the perspective of the employee whose qualified plan benefits are large enough to trigger the excess distributions excise tax, this aspect makes nonqualified plans attractive. Nonqualified deferred compensation does not qualify for rollover treatment or averaging treatment, but if a person either has already used the one-time election for averaging after the age of 59 1/2 or has several plans and can, if he or she desires, elect averaging for one of those plans anyway, the loss of this tax planning flexibility may be an insignificant cost relative to the potential excise tax savings.

The principal drawback of this technique for the employee is the loss of benefits security. Nonqualified deferred-compensation arrangements are frequently unfunded and, even when they are funded, the funds must be subject to the claims of the employer's creditors. In the event that the employer becomes insolvent, the employee may never receive his or her nonqualified deferred compensation.

Nonqualified deferred-compensation plans are also more expensive from the employer's perspective than qualified plans since the employer's tax deduction is deferred until the employee includes the amounts in income. In addition, since amounts set aside to fund the benefits do not accumulate tax free as they would in qualified plans, the employer must set aside greater amounts in order to meet a given target benefit.

As an alternative to a nonqualified deferred-compensation arrangement, employers may wish to give key employees the bonus of additional income to compensate for the additional tax while their benefits continue to accrue under the qualified plan.

This technique has the highest potential for key executives who have some leverage in their contract negotiations and owner-employees of smaller companies, since they either are key decision makers or may influence decision makers on the type of compensation package they receive.

Shifting Contributions from Qualified Plans to Other Tax-advantaged Investments

A certain level of annual contributions is generally required for pension plans unless a plan is amended or terminated. However, voluntary aftertax contributions and contributions to profit-sharing and stock bonus plans, IRAs, and some forms of Keogh plans and SEPs are more or less discretionary. In the cases where discretion is allowed, a person who is likely to have a problem with the excess distributions excise tax should consider investing in tax-favored vehicles such as municipal bonds, commercial annuity contracts, life insurance policies, and even Series EE savings bonds rather than making additional contributions to the qualified plans.

The drawback of this strategy is the loss of the tax deduction on the original contribution and consequently the loss of income-tax-deferred compounding on the amount paid in tax. For example, a person who is in the 28 percent tax bracket and who would otherwise have $30,000 contributed to a qualified plan will have only $21,600 to invest after tax outside the plan (the amount left after paying a 28 percent tax on the $30,000). Consequently even if this person invests outside the plan in a tax-deferred vehicle such as an annuity, he or she forfeits the benefit of tax-deferred compounding on the $8,400 currently paid in income tax.

The lost opportunity cost of tax deferral rises as the period of deferral increases. When the period until the anticipated withdrawal is sufficiently long, the advantages of the deferral will offset the impact of paying the additional 15 percent tax. This means that a client can shoot himself or herself in the foot by avoiding qualified plan contributions just to dodge the excise tax.

The amount of time it takes to reach the crossover point depends on many factors, including the rate of return on investment, the persons's current and future income tax rates, and the proportion of any amount that is currently contributed to a qualified plan that will ultimately be subject to the 15 percent tax. For illustration, assume that a person is in the 28 percent income tax bracket and that amounts withdrawn from qualified plans in future years will also be taxed at a 28 percent rate. Assume further that each dollar currently contributed to the plan will ultimately be subject to the excess distributions excise tax when withdrawn and that a 9 percent tax-deferred rate of return on investment will be earned either inside or outside the plan. In this case the crossover point occurs in just under 12 1/2 years. If this person will begin to make withdrawals from the plan in less than 12 1/2 years and these withdrawals are at least equal to the amount of the current contribution in question, then he or she will be better off investing outside the plan. If withdrawals will not commence for more than 12 1/2 years, then he or she will be better off making contributions to the plan, despite also having to pay the 15 percent excise tax when those amounts are withdrawn.

Voluntary aftertax contributions to qualified plans may be eliminated and equivalent amounts invested in tax-favored investments outside the plans without any opportunity cost if the tax-deferred rate of return earned on the outside investment equals the rate that could be earned inside the plan. Consequently any person who is likely to pay the excise tax on distributions from or accumulations in qualified plans should cease all voluntary contributions to qualified plans and invest equivalent amounts in tax-deferred vehicles outside the plans.

Directing Benefits under a Qualified Domestic Relations Order

If a divorce is pending, the participant can negotiate to receive assets outside the qualified plans and to transfer to the spouse a portion of the retirement accumulation under a qualified domestic relations order (QDRO). Distributions and accumulations subject to a QDRO are not subject to the original participant's income and excise taxes. Instead, taxes on the amount subject to a QDRO are determined with regard to the alternative payee if the alternative payee is a former spouse.

Amending, Freezing, or Terminating Qualified Plans

Qualified plans that may be designed to permit early withdrawals, such as profit-sharing plans, should be amended to permit withdrawals if they do not currently do so. This will give participants maximum flexibility in timing their withdrawals to avoid the tax at little or no cost, other than the cost of redrafting the plan document. Along similar lines, plans can be amended to provide a wide variety of distribution options, including options to receive distributions beginning at age 70 1/2 under the uniform minimum distribution rules, to elect long guaranteed payment periods under single or joint and survivor annuity options, and to defer the starting date for annuities until age 70 1/2. There may be a substantial increase in both costs and administrative burdens as a result of providing broad flexibility in the election of distribution options. However, providing this flexibility may be a more economical way to help employees meet the need to minimize their exposure to the excise tax than other alternatives, such as nonqualified deferred-compensation plans or excise tax reimbursement plans.

Pension plans may be amended to reduce plan benefits. When amending plans, care must be taken to consider the impact of the change on all plan participants, not just the highly compensated who are trying to avoid the 15 percent excise tax. However, in many cases the contribution or benefit formula may be changed to reduce benefits for the highly compensated without similar reductions for the nonhighly compensated without a problem. If benefits for the highly compensated are reduced, the difference may often be made up by creating a nonqualified plan, increasing taxable compensation, or instituting an excise tax reimbursement plan.

The major drawbacks of reducing benefits are that redrafting the plan and complying with ERISA and other requirements may be expensive. In addition, the objectives of the highly compensated group may not be uniform, especially when the participants' ages and terms of service vary widely. Younger employees who may have years until their benefits will reach levels at which the excise tax will be a problem, and older employees with fewer years of service will probably be dissatisfied with any arrangement that reduces their qualified plan accruals. Therefore this technique generally will be effective only when the highly compensated group is homogeneous.

In extreme cases, in which the majority of the plan participants have accrued benefits to the point that additional contributions or benefit accruals are likely to increase their exposure to the excise tax when benefits are paid, terminating the plan may be a feasible alternative. Once again, this alternative should not be employed without fully considering the impact on employees for whom the excise tax is not and may never be a serious problem.

STRATEGIES TO REDUCE THE EXCESS ACCUMULATIONS ESTATE TAX

Many of the strategies that may be employed to minimize the excess distributions excise tax may increase a person's exposure to the excess accumulations estate tax at death. Specifically strategies that defer or reduce lifetime distributions, such as receiving distributions over life expectancy, having annual payments determined and paid on the basis of two lives rather than one, electing to receive payments under the uniform minimum distribution rules, and maintaining a TEFRA 242(b) election, will tend to preserve benefit balances. In addition, naming a person other than the spouse as the primary beneficiary may cause the 15 percent estate excise tax to be imposed when it could otherwise be avoided with a special election by the spouse.

Preserving qualified plan benefit balances may often be a desirable strategy, despite greater exposure to the 15 percent estate excise tax. First, as described above, the benefit of tax-deferred compounding, given a sufficient period of deferral, will outweigh the cost of the additional tax. Second, if a person's preferences lean towards the creation of a legacy for heirs rather than towards lifetime consumption, the imposition of an additional tax at death on a maximum bequest may be considered a reasonable trade-off. However, in these cases a person should explore all avenues for transferring wealth in more tax-advantaged ways. For example, using qualified plan benefits for one's lifetime consumption needs and making lifetime gifts—especially those qualifying for the $10,000

($20,000 joint) annual exclusion—from other sources may allow greater overall aftertax transfers of wealth to loved ones.

Finally, preserving qualified plan benefit balances may make tax and economic sense because of the estate tax deductibility of the excess accumulations estate tax. A person whose estate will be taxed at the maximum 55 percent rate will pay an effective excess accumulations estate tax of only 6.75 percent ([1 − 0.55] x 15 percent) as compared with the 15 percent excise tax on lifetime distributions. When this lower effective tax rate is used to determine the crossover point, if the benefit of income tax deferral on the amount in a qualified plan exceeds the cost of the additional tax that will be paid when the benefit is received, the crossover point is sharply reduced.

For example, assuming as above that a person is in the 28 percent income tax bracket and can earn a 9 percent rate of return on investment either inside the plan or in a tax-favored vehicle outside the plan, the crossover point occurs in just under 4 years and 9 months. In other words, in this case, if a person survives more than 4 years and 9 months, amounts retained in qualified plans will provide higher aftertax benefits to heirs than if the balances were withdrawn prior to death and invested for the benefit of the heirs in tax-favored vehicles earning the same rate of return as investments in the plan, despite the imposition of the estate excise tax. If one further takes into account that the survivor benefits of the qualified plan will usually be paid out over the beneficiary's lifetime or some other extended period of time, and that the survivor will continue to enjoy the benefit of tax deferral on the remaining balance, the crossover point is even shorter. Consequently, unless death is imminent or a person can structure transactions to avoid gift and estate taxes on amounts transferred, a person desiring to preserve as much of his or her estate as possible for the benefit of heirs should usually leave qualified plan benefit balances in place.

Some of the strategies for reducing the excise tax on lifetime distributions also help to reduce the likelihood of paying the excess accumulations estate tax at death. Specifically, electing the maximum survivor benefit under joint and survivor annuity options and choosing maximum period-certain guarantees will reduce the accumulations at death relative to what they would have been without such elections. Taking early withdrawals, combining a lump-sum distribution from one plan with installment payments from other plans, shifting the benefit mix from qualified plans to nonqualified deferred-compensation plans, reducing contributions to qualified plans and IRAs, terminating qualified plans, and transferring a portion of the retirement accumulation under a qualified domestic relations order in the event of a divorce settlement all either deplete the retirement benefits or reduce the rate of growth of accumulations.

The following strategies will also reduce the estate excise tax on excess retirement accumulations at death and in some cases help to reduce the potential excise tax on lifetime distributions.

Using Life Insurance in Qualified Plans

The value of any death benefits payable immediately after death with respect to the decedent are exempt from the estate excise tax to the extent that the sum of such death benefits plus other benefits payable exceeds the total value of benefits payable immediately prior to death. Consequently life insurance benefits within a plan that are payable at death are not subject to the estate excise tax to the extent that the death benefits exceed the amount the decedent could have received just prior to death if he or she had terminated or redeemed the policies. This means that only policy cash values are subject to the estate excise tax and that the net amount at risk (the pure protection element of the policies) is excludible.

The major drawbacks of using life insurance in qualified plans are that life insurance benefits are limited and the cost of the protection is treated as taxable income to the employee for the year in which deductible employer contributions or trust income is applied to purchase the life insurance protection. Life insurance benefits must be "incidental" to the primary purpose of the plan, which is to provide retirement benefits. In general, if the cost of providing current life insurance benefits is less than 25 percent of the cost of providing all the benefits under the plan, the incidental requirement is satisfied. The 25 percent rule is applied to the portion of the premium used to provide current life insurance protection (the cost of the amount at risk).

The 25 percent rule essentially becomes a 50 percent rule when ordinary life is the insurance instrument. Therefore a pension or profit-sharing plan that uses ordinary life insurance to provide the protection within the plan will generally satisfy the incidental requirement if less than half of the employer contribution credited each year to each participant's account is used to pay premiums. In the alternative, the plan will satisfy the incidental requirement if the face amount of insurance does not exceed 100 times the anticipated monthly benefit.

Only the cost of the pure amount at risk—generally the PS 58 costs—must be included in the gross income of the participant for the taxable year when so applied. The PS 58 costs are generally the one-year term rates published by the IRS. However, the cost is treated as an aftertax employee contribution that increases the employee's cost basis in the plan and which will be recovered tax free when benefits are paid from the plan at death if the employer has not surrendered the policies. If the employer surrenders the policies for their cash values to provide plan benefits when the employee retires, the IRS has ruled that the employee receives no credit for the PS 58 costs he or she was taxed on before retirement. In other words, the employee generally loses his or her cost basis attributable to the taxable cost of the insurance protection in the plan when the policies are surrendered for their cash values.

Despite current taxation of the amount paid for the pure cost of protection, using life insurance in qualified plans can provide significant net tax savings by providing excludible benefits at death for purposes of the excess accumulations estate tax. This benefit will be most useful if the plan provides postretirement death benefits and policies are kept in force after retirement. Postretirement death benefits in a pension plan are subject to the incidental limitation in the same way as preretirement death benefits are.

Making Charitable Donations during Lifetime rather than at Death

If a charitable bequest is contemplated from benefits held in a qualified plan, the benefit should be distributed to the participant over his or her lifetime and contributed to the charity as each distribution is made. A participant should avoid leaving large death benefit payments (directly from the plan) to the charity.

This strategy is necessary since charitable donations during lifetime are deductible for income tax purposes but will not reduce any excess accumulations estate tax payable on distributions. Also, the estate tax charitable deduction will not reduce the 15 percent excess accumulations estate tax.

Therefore when charitable contributions are contemplated, the best approach is to begin distributions after retirement (or any time after age 59 1/2 if allowed under the plan) in an amount up to the lifetime excise tax threshold ($150,000 annually). As distributions are made they can be contributed to the charity and deducted to offset the income tax consequences of the distribution. The stream of distributions should be large enough (if possible) to reduce benefits remaining in the plan to below the threshold for the estate excise tax at the time of the participant's death.

Taking Distributions in Anticipation of Death

Taking a large distribution equal to the remaining grandfather amount before death or taking a lump-sum distribution and electing to average can be an effective pre-mortem estate planning strategy. If a person takes a large distribution and uses up the remaining grandfather amount, he or she can reduce the accumulation that will be subject to the estate excise tax.

Similarly, if a person has more than one qualified plan, qualifies for a lump-sum distribution, and may elect to average, he or she may double up the exemptions by taking a lump-sum distribution before death. Although the estate could make the averaging election, doing so will generally provide no additional excise tax savings. The lump-sum distribution taken before death will receive an exemption equal to five times the applicable annual exemption and will reduce the amount that is otherwise subject to the excess accumulations estate tax.

Making the Special Spousal Election

TAMRA amended IRC Sec. 4980A, which now permits a surviving spouse in certain cases to elect not to have the 15 percent excess accumulations estate tax apply to the deceased spouse's benefit balances. In return, the deceased spouse's plans and IRAs are treated as the surviving spouse's for purposes of computing the survivor's own excess distributions and excess accumulations. The election is available only if the spouse is the beneficiary of at least 99 percent of all the deceased's interests.

The presence of this election impacts planning for qualified plan accumulations and distributions and for transfers before and after death. Unfortunately regulations have never been written on the operation of this election and several questions remain unanswered. For example, the law says that any grandfather amount remaining at the time of death is carried over to the spouse who makes the election. However, it is not clear whether the grandfather carryover amount may be recovered only against amounts independently accumulated by the remaining spouse. Also it is not clear how the remaining grandfathered amount is recovered if one participant had elected the 10 percent method while the other had already elected to accelerate to the 100 percent method. Since these issues have not yet been resolved, persons making the spousal election should probably avoid commingling their own funds with the funds of the deceased spouse.

In general, the spousal election will be warranted only if the excise tax that the surviving spouse is likely to pay over time as he or she receives the benefits attributable to the deceased spouse is less in present-value terms than the estate excise tax the deceased spouse would have paid.

Several factors should be considered when weighing this decision. First, if a person makes the spousal election, the deceased spouse's death exemption is forfeited. Consequently amounts that otherwise would be sheltered from the excise tax to the extent of the deceased spouse's death exemption will potentially be subject to excise tax in the hands of the electing surviving spouse.

Second, because the excess accumulations excise tax is deductible against the estate tax, the effective excess accumulations estate tax rate on the deceased spouse's benefits generally will be less than the 15 percent excess distributions excise tax rate that may be incurred as the benefits are paid over the surviving spouse's remaining lifetime. However, if the surviving spouse is in good health and the benefits will be paid over his or her remaining lifetime, the presumably increasing inflation-adjusted annual exemptions may add up to far more than the death exemption that was forfeited by making the spousal election.

In cases where the surviving spouse's own retirement benefit balances are not substantial, the spousal election generally will be desirable. However, if the spouse has IRAs and qualified plan balances of his or her own, the election could result in a greater overall tax.

OTHER RELATED PLANNING ISSUES

Annuity Valuation Rules

Planning for the impact of the excess accumulations excise tax is difficult because the calculation of the threshold amount uses a floating interest rate. This means that the threshold cannot be clearly pinpointed until death actually occurs.

As stated before, the applicable threshold amount is $150,000 multiplied by a hypothetical annuity purchase factor, based on the age of the individual at the time of death and using the 120 percent applicable federal mid-term rate in effect under Sec. 1274(d)(1) for the month in which the valuation date falls. The threshold amount will be volatile, as interest rates are bound to change over time. As a generalization, the threshold amount will vary approximately 5 percent for any one percent change in the applicable interest rate. Since interest rates and annuity values are inversely related, reductions in the interest rate will increase the threshold amount and vice versa.

Defective Spousal Rollovers

Certain spousal rollover accounts are not subject either to the excess distributions excise tax or the excess accumulations estate tax, if handled properly. This provision applies only to amounts that were subject to the estate tax in the deceased spouse's estate. In other words, it does not apply to amounts received under the spousal election to exempt the deceased spouse's benefits from the estate tax. To qualify, the surviving spouse must roll over the deceased spouse's qualified plan, tax-sheltered annuity, or IRA into a new IRA in the surviving spouse's own name and *no other contributions or transfers* can be made to the spousal rollover IRA. If the transfer is to an IRA that already contains contributions made by the surviving spouse or the spouse contributes any additional amounts to the account, the entire account is tainted. If the account is tainted, all later distributions from the account and the accumulation in the account will be subject to both taxes when the surviving spouse dies. Therefore care must be used to avoid this tax trap.

CONCLUSION

The excise taxes on excess distributions and excess accumulations affect all aspects of retirement accumulation and distribution planning. Since strategies to reduce the excess distribution excise tax may increase exposure to the excess accumulations estate tax and vice versa, advisers must consider a person's overall lifetime consumption and estate objectives when planning for these taxes. In addition, planning for the excise taxes cannot be done naively. Any strategy employed to minimize these taxes will usually involve income tax as well as estate and gift tax consequences. Planning cannot proceed without balancing the costs and benefits in all these areas.

12

Health Insurance Planning for the Older Client

Chapter Outline

In order to best help retired clients plan for their health care needs financial services professionals must be acutely aware of the ins and outs of the medicare system. But contrary to conventional consumer wisdom there is much more to retiree health care coverage than just medicare. For many clients, employer-provided health care benefits will help fill the gaps left unfilled by medicare. For others, medigap coverage may be useful to make up for the medicare shortfall. And for those retiring before medicare coverage kicks in, careful planning—usually using COBRA coverage—is required. Finally, one of the largest growing concerns involving health care for the older client is the use of long-term care insurance to meet nursing home needs. In this chapter we will explore each of these topics in a manner that will allow the planner to do comprehensive health care planning for the older client. One caveat: As we were writing this chapter health care reform was uncertain. For this reason we will for the most part ignore the ramifications of the various health care reform proposals.

MEDICARE

Any discussion of planning for a retiree's health care should start with an analysis of the medicare system. There are two parts to this federally run government program. "Part A" is the hospital portion of medicare. It provides benefits for expenses incurred in hospitals; skilled-nursing facilities; hospices (in limited circumstances); and for home-health care for a condition previously treated in a hospital or skilled-nursing facility. "Part B" is the supplementary medical insurance part of medicare. It provides benefits for physicians' and surgeons' fees, diagnostic tests, certain drugs and medical supplies, rental of certain medical equipment, and home-health service when prior hospitalization has not occurred. Let's take a closer look at the entire medicare system, starting with the question of eligibility.

Eligibility for Medicare

Most of your older clients will be eligible to receive health benefits under the federal government's medicare program. Part A is available *at no cost* to most persons aged 65 or older. Among those eligible are

- everyone 65 and over who is receiving a monthly social security retirement or survivor's benefit
- people aged 65 and over who have deferred receiving social security retirement benefits (these people must apply for medicare—others in "pay status" are automatically enrolled)
- 65-year-old civilian employees of the federal government who did not elect into the social security system under the 1983 law (see chapter 2)
- any spouse aged 65 and over of a fully insured worker who is at least aged 62

Any other people (aged 65 or older) who do not meet the requirements to receive Part A at no cost may voluntarily enroll by paying a premium, which may be as high as $261 in 1995 (less for people who have earned some quarters of coverage under social security).

Any person enrolled for Part A of medicare is eligible for Part B. However, a monthly premium of $46.10 (1995 figure) must be paid. This annually adjusted premium represents only about 25 percent of cost of the benefits provided. The remaining cost of the program is financed from the general revenues of the federal government.

YOUR FINANCIAL SERVICES PRACTICE:
MISCONCEPTIONS ABOUT MEDICARE ELIGIBILITY

Clients have several misconceptions about eligibility for medicare that must be corrected. It is important to point out the following:

- Those who retire early and elect to start social security at age 62 are *not* eligible for medicare until they reach age 65.
- Spouses who are younger than 65 and are married to a retiree over age 65 are *not* eligible for medicare until they turn age 65.
- Despite the Part B premiums, the system offers a relatively good value. In other words, rejecting Part B coverage to avoid paying premiums is not usually the best choice.

Signing Up for Medicare

Clients should contact their local social security office (see phone book for address) about 3 months before their 65th birthday to sign up for medicare, even if they are not planning to retire. Those who will be getting social security (at age 65 or earlier) will automatically be enrolled for medicare when they apply for social security benefits (note: early enrollment does not mean that medicare benefits start prior to age 65). In this case, the individual will receive a notice of automatic enrollment. If a client does not want Part B coverage, he or she must reject it in writing within 2 months of receiving the notice.

If a client is not automatically enrolled, he or she has a 7-month window for initially enrolling in Part B of medicare. It begins 3 months before attaining age 65 and ends 3 months after than month. In order to begin eligibility for benefits at the earliest possible date—the beginning of the month in which age 65 is reached—a person must enroll prior to the first day of that month. Signing up later will result in a one- to 3-month delay in eligibility. Anyone who rejects Part B or who does not enroll when initially eligible may later apply for benefits during a general enrollment period that occurs between January 1 and March 31 each year. However, because of the possibility of adverse selection, the monthly premium will be increased by 10 percent for each 12-month period during which the person was eligible but failed to enroll. This increase is waived, however, for those who do not enroll because they were covered under an employer plan considered primary to medicare.

Part A Benefits

Planners need to be aware of the benefits covered by Part A. Covered expenses fall into the following categories:

- hospital benefits
- skilled-nursing-facility benefits
- home-health care benefits
- hospice benefits

In addition, planners should be aware of benefits that are excluded under Part A.

Hospital Benefits

Part A pays for inpatient hospital services for up to 90 days in each *benefit period* (also referred to as a *spell of illness*). Benefit period is a key concept. A benefit period begins the first time a medicare recipient is hospitalized and ends only after the recipient has been out of a hospital or skilled-nursing facility for 60 consecutive days. A hospitalization after that 60-day period then begins a new benefit period. There is no limit on the number of benefit periods a person may have during his or her lifetime.

Example 1: Barbara goes into the hospital for 45 days, goes home for 2 weeks, and returns to the hospital for 80 days. Barbara's 125 days of hospitalization will be considered to be within one benefit period because there was not a gap of 60 days between hospital visits.

Example 2: Jake goes into the hospital for 80 days, goes home for 62 days, and returns to the hospital for 85 days. Both of Jake's stays are fully covered by Part A because they each fall within a different benefit period. In other words, Jake got a clean slate (and a new 90 days of coverage) because he was out for 60 consecutive days.

In addition to 90 days of hospital coverage each benefit period, medicare will cover an extra 60 days over an individual's lifetime. These days are referred to as *lifetime reserve days,* and are nonrenewable. In other words, once a lifetime reserve day is used it cannot be restored for use in future benefit periods.

Example 3: Remember Barbara in example 1. Barbara was covered for 90 days under the benefit period rule. In addition, Barbara chose to use 35 of her reserve days to cover the full amount of time she spent in the hospital (125 days). Note that Barbara has only 25 lifetime reserve days left. However, once she is out of the hospital for 60 days she will get 90 more days of coverage in the next benefit period in addition to the remaining lifetime reserve days.

Covered services for Part A hospital benefits include the following:

- Semi-private room and all meals (or private room if required for medical reasons)
- Regular nursing services
- Services of hospital's medical social workers
- Use of regular hospital equipment, supplies, and appliances, such as oxygen tents, wheelchairs, crutches, casts, surgical dressings, and splints
- Drugs and biologicals ordinarily furnished by the hospital
- Intensive care and coronary care
- Rehabilitation services, such as physical therapy
- Diagnostic or therapeutic items and services ordinarily furnished by the hospital
- Operating room costs, including anesthesia services
- Blood transfusions (after the first 3 pints of blood)
- Lab tests
- X-rays

What Is Not Covered. From a planning standpoint it is just as important to know what is not covered by Part A as to know what is covered. In each benefit period, covered hospital expenses are paid in full for 60 days, subject to an initial deductible of $716 (in 1995). This deductible is adjusted annually to reflect the increasing cost of care. Benefits for an additional 30 days of hospitalization are also provided in each benefit period, but the patient must pay a daily coinsurance charge ($179 in 1995). When using lifetime reserve days patients must also pay a daily coinsurance charge ($358 in 1995). In addition to copayment and deductibles, clients have to pick up the costs of such things as private rooms, private-duty nurses, and a phone or television in the room. Finally, clients should be aware that hospitals are not paid on the basis of actual charges, but are paid a flat fee for each medicare patient, based on the patient's diagnosis. This has encouraged hospitals to release patients "quicker and sicker." *Planning Point:* Hospitals must notify patients of their right to a written discharge plan that advises them about available health resources appropriate for their needs. In addition, patients can appeal premature discharges.

Skilled-Nursing-Facility Benefits

In many cases a patient may no longer require continuous hospital care but may not be well enough to go home. Consequently Part A provides benefits for care in a skilled-nursing facility. This coverage can be triggered only if a physician certifies that skilled-nursing care or rehabilitative services are needed for a condition that was treated in a hospital within the last 30 days. In addition, the prior hospitalization must have lasted at least 3 days.

When skilled-nursing-facility coverage is used, benefits are paid in full for 20 days in each benefit period and for an additional 80 days with a daily coinsurance charge ($89.50 in 1995). Covered expenses are the same as those described for hospital benefits.

One very important point should be made about skilled-nursing-facility benefits: Custodial care is not provided under any part of the medicare program unless skilled-nursing or rehabilitative service also are needed. With that being said, however, it is important to note that custodial care can be provided for 100 days in a skilled-nursing facility if your client needs skilled services.

What Are Skilled Services? A skilled-nursing facility may be a separate facility for providing such care or a separate section of a hospital or nursing home. The facility must have at least one full-time registered nurse, and nursing services must be provided at all times. Every patient must be under the supervision of a physician, and a physician must always be available for emergency care. *Planning Point:* A geriatric-care manager from the hospital will generally be available to inform patients and families of available skilled-nursing facilities in the area.

Home-Health-Care Benefits

If a patient can be treated at home for a medical condition, Part A will pay the full cost for an unlimited number of home visits by a home-health agency. Such agencies specialize in providing nursing services and other therapeutic services. To receive these benefits a person must be confined at home and be treated under a home-health plan set up by a physician. No prior hospitalization is required. The care needed must include either skilled-nursing services, physical therapy, or speech therapy. If one of these services is needed, Part A will also pay for the cost of part-time home-health aides, medical social services, occupational therapy, and medical supplies and equipment provided by the home-health agency. There is no charge for these benefits other than a required 20 percent copayment for the cost of durable medical equipment such as iron lungs, oxygen tanks, and hospital beds. Medicare does not cover home services furnished primarily to assist people in activities such as housecleaning, preparing meals, shopping, dressing, or bathing.

Hospice Benefits

Hospice benefits are available under Part A of medicare for terminally ill persons who have a life expectancy of 6 months or less. While a hospice is thought of as a facility for treating the terminally ill, medicare benefits are available primarily for hospice-type benefits provided to patients in their own homes. However, short-term (up to 5 days) inpatient care in a hospice is covered. The care is referred to as *respite care,* since it is intended to relieve the family providing home care. It can be provided in a facility, at the organization providing home treatment, or in a hospital or other facility with which that organization cooperates. In addition to including the types of benefits described for home-health care, hospice benefits include drugs, bereavement counseling, and the respite care described above. However, only drugs used primarily to relieve pain and control symptoms are covered. There are modest copayments for some services.

Hospice care benefits are limited 210 days unless the patient is recertified as terminally ill. In order to qualify for hospice benefits, a medicare recipient must elect such coverage in lieu of other medicare benefits, except for the services of the attending physician or services and benefits that do not pertain to the terminal condition.

Exclusions from Part A Medicare

In addition to the limitations, copayments, and deductibles described above, planners should be aware that there are some circumstances under which Part A of medicare will not pay benefits. In addition, there are times when medicare will act as the secondary payer of benefits. Exclusions under Part A include the following:

- services outside the United States and its territories or possessions. However, there are a few exceptions to this rule for qualified Mexican and Canadian hospitals. Benefits will be paid if an emergency occurs in the United States and the closest hospital is in one of these countries. Note also that a person living closer to a hospital in one of these countries than to a hospital in the United States may use the foreign hospital even if an emergency does not exist. Finally, there is coverage for Canadian hospitals if a person needs hospitalization while traveling the most direct route between Alaska and another state in the United States. However, this provision does not apply to persons vacationing in Canada.
- elective luxury services, such as private rooms or televisions
- hospitalization for services not necessary for the treatment of an illness or injury, such as custodial care or elective cosmetic surgery
- services performed in a federal facility, such as a veterans' hospital
- services covered under workers' compensation

Under the following circumstances, medicare is the secondary payer of benefits:

- when primary coverage under an employer-provided medical expense plan is elected by (1) an employee or spouse aged 65 or older or (2) a disabled beneficiary
- when medical care can be paid under any liability policy, including policies providing automobile no-fault benefits
- in the first 18 months for end-stage renal disease when an employer-provided medical expense plan provides coverage. By law, employer plans cannot specifically exclude this coverage during the 18-month period.

Medicare pays only if complete coverage is not available from these sources and then only to the extent that benefits are less than would otherwise be payable under medicare.

Part B Benefits

In addition to being aware of the benefits and exclusions under Part A of medicare, planners must be aware of what Part B of medicare covers and where it falls short for their clients.

Part B: In General

Part B of medicare provides benefits for the following medical expenses:

- physicians' and surgeons' fees. These fees may result from house calls, office visits, or services provided in a hospital or other institution. Under certain circumstances benefits are also provided for the services of chiropractors, podiatrists, and optometrists.
- surgical services including anesthesia
- diagnostic tests in a hospital or a physician's office
- physical or occupational therapy in a physician's office, or as an outpatient of a hospital, skilled-nursing facility, or other approved clinic, rehabilitative agency, or public-health agency
- drugs and biologicals that cannot be self-administered
- radiation therapy
- medical supplies, such as surgical dressings, splints, and casts
- rental of medical equipment, such as oxygen tents, hospital beds, and wheelchairs
- prosthetic devices, such as artificial heart valves or lenses needed after a cataract operation
- ambulance service if a patient's condition does not permit the use of other methods of transportation
- mammograms and Pap smears
- pneumococcal vaccine and its administration
- home-health services as described for Part A when a person does not have Part A coverage
- emergency room care
- X-rays

Part B Exclusions

Although the preceding list may appear comprehensive, there are numerous medical products and services not covered by Part B, some of which represent significant expenses for your elderly clients. They include the following:

- custodial care
- drugs and biologicals that can be self-administered (except drugs for osteoporosis)
- routine physical, eye, and hearing examinations (except mammograms)
- routine foot care
- immunizations (except pneumococcal vaccinations or immunizations required because of an injury or immediate risk of infection)
- cosmetic surgery unless it is needed because of an accidental injury or to improve the function of a malformed part of the body
- dental care unless it involves jaw or facial bone surgery or the setting of fractures
- eyeglasses or orthopedic shoes
- hearing aids

In addition, benefits are not provided to persons eligible for workers' compensation or to those treated in government hospitals. Benefits are provided only for services received in the United States, except for physicians' services and ambulance service rendered for a hospitalization that is covered in Mexico or Canada under Part A. Part B is also a secondary payer of benefits under the same circumstances described for Part A.

Amount of Benefits under Part B

With some exceptions Part B pays 80 percent of the approved charges for covered medical expenses after the satisfaction of a $100 annual deductible. Annual maximums apply to outpatient psychiatric benefits ($450) and physical therapy in a therapist's office or at the patient's home ($400). A few charges are paid in full without any cost sharing. These include (1) home-health services, (2) pneumococcal vaccine and its administration, (3) certain surgical procedures that are performed on an outpatient basis in lieu of hospitalization, and (4) diagnostic preadmission tests performed on an outpatient basis within 7 days prior to hospitalization.

Since 1992 the approved charge for doctor's services covered by medicare has been based on a fee schedule issued by the Health Care Financing Administration. A patient will be reimbursed for only 80 percent of the approved charges above the deductible—regardless of the doctor's actual charge. Since late 1990 doctors have been required to submit all bills directly to medicare regardless of whether they accept assignment of medicare benefits. Previously doctors could bill patients directly, which required the patients to file the medicare claims. Since 1991 there have been limits placed on the size of the fees in excess of approved charges that doctors can charge medicare patients. Nonetheless, balance billing does exist—this is the practice of charging medicare patients more than the reasonable and customary charge or in the case of new law more than 115 percent (see below).

YOUR FINANCIAL SERVICES PRACTICE:
LIMITATIONS ON PHYSICIAN CHARGES

Medicare has an assignment procedure whereby physicians can agree
to accept the medicare-approved charge amounts as payment in full.
(Note that medicare pays 80 percent and the doctor can still bill the
client for the remaining 20 percent.) However, there has been no way to
force all physicians to accept assignment. Now, however, federal law
restricts charges of physicians not agreeing to accept assignment to no
more than 115 percent of the medicare-approved charges in 1993 and
thereafter. In essence Congress is limiting even noncontracting physicians to a 15 percent surcharge on the medicare-approved charges for
medicare-covered patients. No surcharge is allowed by physicians who
have agreed to accept assignment under medicare.

These limitations on physician billing are designed to cut down on
the out-of-pocket expenses encountered by medicare patients. In many
localities it has become difficult if not impossible to find physicians who
accept assignment by medicare. Furthermore, many elderly report the
new law is ineffective in checking doctors' billing practices—in other
words, some physicians ask up front for additional compensation!

EMPLOYER-PROVIDED HEALTH BENEFITS

In addition to medicare, about one-third of Americans have employer-
provided health care coverage that continues after retirement. Lately these
benefits have been under assault because of an accounting change known as
Financial Accounting Standards Board (FASB) 106. FASB 106 has forced
employers to put liabilities for retiree health care benefits on the books.
Employers must make sound actuarial estimates of the eventual cost of providing
retiree health benefits, amortize the costs over a period of years, and take an
annual deduction against earnings. In response, some employers have been
modifying or eliminating retiree medical benefits in lieu of suffering adverse
consequences on the balance sheet. Not all employers, however, are decreasing
coverage immediately for current or new retirees. Rather, the decrease in benefits
may apply only to persons who will retire, for example, after 1998. A key
planning issue thus becomes this: Can your client's health benefits be dropped
or modified?

Will Client Benefits Continue?

Recently the issue of dropping or modifying retiree health care benefits has
been a hotly litigated topic. Rather than focus on a review of court decisions,

however, planners should focus on the following key factors. First, a decisive question is whether an employer has promised to provide retiree benefits. Contractual agreements (such as in a collective bargaining agreement) and other promises (such as in summary plan description) will obligate the employer to continue coverage. If, on the other hand, the employer explicitly retains the right to unilaterally modify or terminate the retiree health plan, most courts will permit the employer to carry out its stated intentions—despite the fact that from the retiree's perspective the employer had an "unspoken contract" to continue benefits. Ironically, retirees of bankrupt companies have a greater measure of benefit protection than retirees of solvent companies. The reason for this is that an employer who has filed under Chapter 11 can modify its retiree health plan only if it proves it needs to save the money to stave off liquidation.

A second key issue that planners must understand is that employers generally have the right to drop or eliminate retiree health benefits on a prospective basis for those employees who have not yet retired. That means current employees may find that retiree health care will not apply for them. This can be especially troublesome for retirees taking early retirement prior to medicare eligibility. One possible solution, however, is to negotiate for health care coverage if a golden handshake is available.

A third item to focus on is whether the employer plan has recently been or is in the process of being changed. Your client might have an outdated understanding of the program. Many programs have been cut back in the last few years and the summary plan description should be reviewed carefully. Check to see if certain employees have been excluded, if premiums and/or deductibles have been increased, if beneficiaries are still covered, or whether co-insurance has been added. Consider whether a third tier of health care protection such as medigap (discussed below) is needed because of these modifications.

YOUR FINANCIAL SERVICES PRACTICE:
TERMINATION OF RETIREE HEALTH CARE COVERAGE

When the group policyholder of a medigap policy terminates the policy and fails to replace it, a marketing opportunity arises. The insurer must offer individual policies to all group members. Clients have two choices:

- an individual policy that continues the benefits provided under the group policy
- a cheaper individual policy that is limited to the medigap minimum standard benefits

---

Types of Employer-Provided Retiree Health Care Plans

As described above, many employers have reduced or eliminated retiree health benefits. In the same vein, other employers have passed on to the retiring employee some (or all) of the costs of maintaining a program. Still, employer-sponsored retiree health benefit plans cover almost one-third of all workers. The types of plans provided by employers vary a great deal—some are quite generous and others pay only a small proportion of the retiree's medical expenses. If the retiring employee has to pay some or all of the premium for the plan, then he or she needs to decide whether to buy into the program or to pursue an individual medigap policy. Even if the coverage is provided without cost, both the adviser and the retiree must fully understand the extent of the coverage in order to determine whether additional medigap coverage is still necessary. The following briefly describes the types of retiree health care benefits commonly provided by the employer.

A Benefit Carve-Out Plan

This is the most common and frequently the least expensive approach for the employer. Generally this type of plan is designed around the same benefit program as applies to active employees. The amount paid by the insurer is calculated in two steps: first, the insurer determines how much of the claim it would pay for an active employee; second, that amount is reduced by the amount medicare will pay. For example, Felicia incurs $1,100 in medical expenses. The plan requires a $100 deductible and 20 percent copayment. Therefore for an active employee the plan would pay $800 ([$1,100 − $100] x .8 = $800) and the employee pays $300. Assume that medicare's allowable charge is $600, of which it pays 80 percent, or $480. The insurer will pay $320 ($800 − $480), medicare will pay $480, and Felicia pays $300.

Coordination Plan

This is the most generous (and therefore most expensive) approach that the employer can take. Under this type of plan, the insurer first calculates the applicable payment that it would make after applying the deductible and coinsurance payments. The insurer will actually pay this amount unless the insurer's payment plus medicare benefits actually exceeds the total expenses. If that is the case the payment is reduced so that the plan plus medicare equals total expenses. Using the same example as above, the insurer would pay $620 (the lesser of $800 and $1,100 less $480). Medicare still pays $480 and Felicia pays nothing.

Exclusion Plan

Also referred to as an *expense carve-out plan*, this approach only pays benefits based on the portion that medicare does not cover. Using the same example as above, medicare pays $480 of the $1,100 bill. The insurer applies the deductible ($100) and coinsurance (20 percent) to the remaining bill of $620 and pays $416 ([$620 − $100] x .8). Felicia is then responsible for paying $204.

Medigap

Some employers offer retirees regular medicare-supplement policies similar to those that individuals can buy on their own (as described in the next section). These plans are intended to pay for the specific deductibles and coinsurance amounts that medicare does not pay for.

Other Approaches

Another common approach is the expense account approach, in which the employer sets aside a sum of money for employees to spend on health care. The accounts can vary considerably in size, but generally are not sufficient to cover significant portions of postretirement medical expenses. Another approach is to provide a benefit similar to the medigap policies, but to cover considerably fewer benefits than provided under those plans—for example, a plan using this approach might cover only gaps in the Part A hospital insurance program.

MEDIGAP INSURANCE

For retired clients who do not have employer-provided insurance or who have inadequate amounts, there is medigap insurance. Medigap is a tool that can be used by private insurance planners to supplement the inadequacies of the medicare program and to relieve the elderly of part or all of their cost-sharing burden. In other words, as one expert puts it, medigap "eliminates the risk of unpredictable and uncontrollable bills by converting them into a predictable and affordable series of insurance payments."

How Medigap Works

Historically hundreds of variations in medigap policies were permitted under state laws. Duplicate coverage and confusion ensued. Today, however, medigap policies provide retirees with benefits that are not available under medicare. Medigap fills the "gaps" in medicare by dealing with the medicare system on its own terms. In other words, consistent definitions are used in both programs and medigap policies do not duplicate medicare benefits.

Medigap policies are regulated by both the state and the federal governments. Laws protect consumers and provide for the following:

- notice that no individual needs more than one medigap policy
- notice that medicaid-eligible individuals do not need a medigap policy
- easy comparison among rival policies
- basic care benefits using the same format and terminology offered by all insurers
- guaranteed renewability (can be cancelled in cases of material misrepresentation or nonpayment)
- 30-day refund periods during which the consumer can change his or her mind and receive a full refund
- automatic policy changes whenever medicare deductibles and coinsurance change

---

**YOUR FINANCIAL SERVICES PRACTICE:
REQUIREMENT THAT THE AGENT ASK IF THE POLICY IS A
REPLACEMENT**

Any agent selling medigap policies is now required to ask if the applicant already has medigap coverage in force. Agents must indicate on the application if the new policy is intended to replace an in-force policy. With the new standard forms there is no justification for an individual's having more than one medigap policy in force any longer than the brief time of overlap (a few days) needed to avoid a break in coverage. The federal law also prohibits high-pressure sales tactics in the selling process, but the statute is not specific in defining what constitutes high-pressure sales tactics. By leaving the term undefined, Congress has created a sort of catch-all provision that is open to a wide range of interpretations.

Legal Requirements

In general, people in poor health would be considered uninsurable for medigap purposes. The law guarantees, however, that for 6 months immediately following enrollment in medicare medical insurance (Part B) a person aged 65 or older cannot be denied medigap insurance because of health problems. To protect insurance companies, there is the possibility that a preexisting conditions clause will apply during the first 6 months of the policy's life. This clause, however, is the maximum insurer protection against adverse selection allowed under the new law.

At a minimum, a medigap policy must provide the following basic benefits:

- coverage for either all of the medicare Part A inpatient hospital deductible or none of it. Insurers are not permitted to pay just a part of the deductible.

- coverage for the Part A daily coinsurance amount for the 61st day through the 90th day of hospitalization in each medicare benefit period
- coverage for the Part A daily coinsurance amount for each of medicare's 60 nonrenewable, lifetime hospital inpatient reserve days used
- after all medicare hospital benefits are exhausted, coverage for the hospital charges that otherwise would have been paid by medicare for a lifetime maximum of 365 days
- reasonable costs of the first three pints of blood
- coverage for the Part B coinsurance amount after the policyowner pays the $100 Part B annual deductible

COMPARING MEDIGAP POLICIES

Under National Association of Insurance Commissioners (NAIC) direction, ten standard policy forms for medigap coverage have been created. These ten policies have been codified under federal law, and policies sold after July 1, 1992, must comply with their standards. The law does not require insurance companies to sell all the standardized forms. However, policies that are sold must conform to the standards and be identifiable as one of the ten forms.

Policy A is the standard for the base policy with the minimum coverage and the lowest premium. Every one of the other medicare supplement standard policy forms (B through J) must contain everything provided in policy A plus the additional coverage set forth for the specific standard form being complied with. Each insurance company is free to decide which standard forms it will offer in the market. Some insurers only sell policy A, while others make all ten variations (A through J) available. A significant number of medicare supplement insurers have decided to restrict their offering to fewer than all ten policy forms. Any insurance company selling more than one variation must sell policy A as one of the available choices.

Sample Annual Premiums and Other Information

To give you an idea of the cost involved, the following sample annual premiums can be used for reference purposes.

	Policy A	Policy D	Policy G	Policy H
California	$460−$ 800	$750−$1,100	$1,200−$1,400	$ 970−$1,200
Florida	$430−$1,300	$675−$1,300	$1,000−$1,500	$1,350−$1,800
New York	$400−$ 520	$700−$ 900	$ 850−$1,000	$ 900+

For more information, table 12-2 can be helpful to both you and your client.

TABLE 12-1
What the Ten Standard Medigap Policies Offer

● Policy offers this benefit　　　　○ Policy does not offer this benefit

Policy type	A	B	C	D	E	F	G	H	I	J
Basic benefits	●	●	●	●	●	●	●	●	●	●
Part A–hospital deductible	○	●	●	●	●	●	●	●	●	●
Part B–doctor deductible	○	○	●	○	○	●	○	○	○	●
20% co-insurance	●	●	●	●	●	●	●	●	●	●
Part B–% excess doctor bill	○	○	○	○	○	100%	80%	○	100%	100%
Additional 365 hospital days	●	●	●	●	●	●	●	●	●	●
Skilled-nursing coinsurance	○	○	●	●	●	●	●	●	●	●
At-home care	○	○	○	●	○	○	●	○	●	●
Prescription drugs	○	○	○	○	○	○	○	●	●	●
Preventive care	○	○	○	○	●	○	○	○	○	●
Health care abroad	○	○	●	●	●	●	●	●	●	●

THE PREMEDICARE GAP

One problem that is not solved by a medigap policy is the health gap that occurs after early retirement and before age 65 when medicare (and medigap) starts. Statistics show that slightly over 50 percent of those who retire early do not have employer-provided health insurance. For those in that group the effect can be devastating. A financial planning challenge awaits clients and planners alike, especially since poor health may have been the reason for early retirement in the first place. Let us take a closer look at what can be done.

COBRA Coverage

The Consolidated Omnibus Budget Reconciliation Act of 1985 (COBRA) established the option for a retiring employee to buy into the employer's group health plan. COBRA continuation coverage allows an employee to continue health benefits under the employer's plan for 18 months after retirement. The period is extended to 29 months in the case of retirement due to disability and 36 months if the insurance is through a spouse's plan and the spouse dies, the couple divorces, or the spouse becomes eligible for medicare.

TABLE 12-2
Medicare Supplement Insurance Counseling

State	Phone Number(s)	State	Phone Number(s)
California	(800) 927-4357	New Mexico	(800) 432-2080 (505) 827-7640
Delaware	(302) 739-4251	New York*	(518) 455-4312
Florida*	(904) 922-3132	North Carolina	(919) 733-0111
Idaho	(208) 334-2250	Ohio*	(800) 686-1526
Indiana*	(800) 622-4461 (317) 232-2395	Oregon*	(503) 378-4484
Iowa	(515) 281-5705	Tennessee*	(800) 252-2816 (615) 741-4955
Maryland	(800) 243-3425 (410) 225-1100	Texas	(512) 463-6515
Massachusetts	(617) 727-7750	Vermont*	(802) 828-3301
Michigan*	(517) 335-1702	Washington	(206) 753-2408
Missouri*	(800) 726-7390 (314) 751-2640	Wisconsin	(800) 242-1060 (608) 266-8944
New Jersey	(800) 729-8820 (609) 292-4303		

*Note: These states either do not include extensive one-on-one counseling or are in the process of establishing comprehensive counseling programs. The 800 numbers cannot be used to go outside state boundaries.

The COBRA requirements apply to all health care plans of employers (except for churches) with 20 or more employees. If the employer has a medical plan but COBRA does not apply, state law may provide for a similar continuation requirement. The continuation period varies; it may be as short as 3 months and as long as 18 months.

Under COBRA your client will take over the entire premium for coverage. This can equal the full cost of group coverage, and the employer can add an additional 2 percent for administrative charges. In many cases, the group coverage is a relative bargain, especially in cases of poor health or a preexisting condition, where comparable coverage is not available at any price. If the individual is healthy he or she may want to compare the price of an individual policy to the COBRA benefits to get the best possible deal.

YOUR FINANCIAL SERVICES PRACTICE:
CONVERSION SOLUTION

The Post-COBRA and Premedicare Gap. For clients who retire at age 62, COBRA coverage only protects them until age 63 1/2. Since medicare does not start until age 65, clients are often left scrambling for coverage in the interim. One solution is the automatic conversion privilege that is associated with much employer-provided group health insurance. What's more, planners will be pleased to know that this privilege still exists when COBRA coverage runs out. (Conversion to an individual policy with no evidence of insurability should be accomplished within 31 days of termination of the group coverage.) The downside may be the prohibitive costs associated with the individual policy. The upside is guaranteed coverage despite poor health or preexisting conditions.

Other Options

One solution to the premedicare heath care gap can be coverage under a spouse's plan. For couples who can keep one spouse in the workforce, this coverage offers the best solution possible. One problem, however, is that one reason for early retirement may be to perform care-giving services for a spouse. In such cases—and in other cases—spousal coverage may not be a viable solution. A second option is to purchase an individual policy. Surprisingly this can be a viable solution in some instances. It can also be problematic, however. Consider that it is often difficult to find coverage, that evidence of insurability may be required, and that costs may be prohibitive. For clients who are at or near the poverty level, medicaid may provide the answer. These state-run systems will provide health care coverage; however, coverage is available only to the poorest percentage of the population. Finally, many people choose to go uninsured. People in this group postpone health treatment, which ultimately jeopardizes their health and increases medicare costs. Elimination of this factor is one of the driving forces behind health care reform.

LONG-TERM CARE INSURANCE

The Need for Long-Term Care

The primary reason that long-term care (LTC) is a growing market is that our population is aging. The population aged 65 and over is the fastest-growing age group; today it represents about 11 percent of the population, a figure that is expected to increase to between 20 and 25 percent over the next 50 years. The segment of the population aged 85 and over is growing at an even faster rate. While less than 10 percent of the over-65 group is over 85 today, this percentage is expected to double over the next two generations.

Planners should keep in mind that the likelihood of a person needing to enter a nursing home increases dramatically with age. One percent of persons between the ages of 65 and 74 reside in nursing homes, and the percentage increases to 6 percent between the ages of 75 and 84. At ages 85 and over, the figure rises to approximately 25 percent.

A second reason for the rise in popularity of long-term care insurance is cost. Nearly $50 billion is spent each year on nursing home care. This cost is increasing faster than inflation because of the growing demand for nursing home beds and the shortage of skilled medical personnel. The cost of complete long-term care for a client can be astronomical, with annual nursing home costs of $30,000 to $50,000 not unusual.

A third reason for long-term care is the inability for families to provide full care. Traditionally long-term care has been provided by family members, often at considerable personal sacrifices and great personal stress. However, it is becoming more difficult for families to provide long-term care for the following reasons:

- the geographic dispersion of family members
- increased participation of women in the paid workforce
- fewer children in the family
- higher divorce rates
- the inability of family members to provide care because they, too, are growing old

The Legal Genesis of Long-Term Care Policies

In order to best understand how long-term care insurance works it is important to examine the NAIC model legislation regarding long-term care. Before proceeding with a summary of the major provisions of the NAIC model legislation, however, it is necessary to make three points. First, the model legislation establishes guidelines. Insurance companies still have significant latitude in many aspects of product design. Second, many older policies are still in existence that were written prior to the adoption of the model legislation or under one of its earlier versions. Third, not all states have adopted any or all of the model legislation.

The model legislation applies to any insurance policy or rider that provides coverage for not less than 12 consecutive months in a setting other than an acute care unit of a hospital for one or more of the following: necessary or medically necessary diagnostic, preventive, therapeutic, rehabilitative, maintenance, or personal services. The 12-month period has been the source of considerable controversy because, in effect, it allows policies to provide benefits for periods as short as one year. Many critics of long-term care insurance argue that coverage should not be allowed unless benefits are provided for at least 2 or 3 years. Statistics seem to support their views. Approximately 40 percent of all persons who enter nursing homes after age 65 have stays in excess of one year. This figure drops to about 15 percent for stays of 3 years or longer.

The model legislation focuses on two major areas—policy provisions and marketing. Highlights of the criteria for policy provisions include the following:

- Many words or terms cannot be used in a policy unless they are specifically defined in accordance with the legislation. Examples include *adult day care, home-health care services, personal care, skilled-nursing care,* and *usual and customary.*
- No policy can contain renewal provisions other than guaranteed renewable or noncancelable. Under neither type of provision can the insurance company make any unilateral changes in any coverage provision. Under a noncancelable provision, premiums are established in advance and cannot be changed. Under a guaranteed renewable provision, the insurance company is allowed to revise premiums on a class basis.
- Limitations and exclusions are prohibited except in the following cases:

  - preexisting conditions
  - mental or nervous disorders (but this does not permit the exclusion of Alzheimer's disease)
  - alcoholism and drug addiction
  - illness, treatment, or medical condition arising out of war, participation in a felony, service in the armed forces, suicide, and aviation if a person is a not fare-paying passenger
  - treatment in a government facility
  - services available under medicare and other social insurance programs

- No policy can provide coverage for skilled-nursing care only or provide significantly more coverage for skilled care in a facility than for lower levels of care.
- The definition of preexisting condition can be no more restrictive than to exclude a condition for which treatment was recommended or received within 6 months prior to the effective date of coverage. In addition, coverage can be excluded for a confinement for this condition only if it begins within 6 months of the effective date of coverage.
- Eligibility for benefits cannot be based on a prior hospital requirement or higher level of care.
- Insurance companies must offer the policyowner the right to purchase coverage that allows for an increase in the amount of benefits based on reasonable anticipated increases in the cost of services covered by the policy. The policyowner must specifically reject this inflation protection if he or she does not want it.

- A policy must contain a provision that makes the policy incontestable after 2 years on the grounds of misrepresentation alone. The policy can still be contested on the basis that the applicant knowingly and intentionally misrepresented relevant facts pertaining to the insured's health.

Provisions of the model legislation that pertain to marketing include the following:

- An outline of coverage must be delivered to a prospective applicant at the time of initial solicitation. This outline must contain (1) a description of the coverage, (2) a statement of the principal exclusions, reductions, and limitations in the policy, (3) a statement of the terms under which the policy can be continued in force or terminated, (4) a description of the terms under which the policy may be returned and the premium refunded, and (5) a brief description of the relationship between benefits and cost of care.
- A shopper's guide must be delivered to all prospective applicants.
- The policy must allow policyowners to have a free 30-day look.
- An insurance company must establish procedures to assure that any comparisons of policies by its agents or other producers will be fair and accurate and that excessive insurance is not sold or issued.
- The expected loss ratio under the policy must be at least 60 percent.
- Applications for insurance must be clear and unambiguous so that an applicant's health condition can be properly ascertained. The application must also contain a conspicuous statement near the place for the applicant's signature that says the following: "If your answers to this application are incorrect or untrue, the company has the right to deny benefits or rescind your policy." The purpose of these requirements is to control postclaim underwriting.
- No policy can be issued until the applicant has been given the option of electing a third party to be notified of any pending policy lapse due to nonpayment of premium. The purpose of this provision is to eliminate the problem of policy lapse resulting from a senile or otherwise mentally impaired person failing to pay the premium.
- If one long-term policy replaces another, the new insurer must waive any time periods pertaining to preexisting conditions and probationary periods for comparable benefits to the extent that similar exclusions were satisfied in the original policy.

The NAIC continues to discuss additional changes to the model legislation. One additional proposal would, if adopted, mandate the upgrading of old policies when newly improved policies are introduced. In other words, stay tuned for further developments.

Characteristics of Individual Policies

For many types of insurance, policies are relatively standardized. For long-term care insurance the opposite is true. Significant variations (and therefore differences in cost) exist from one insurance company to another. A policyowner also has numerous options with respect to policy provisions.

The discussion in this section focuses on issue age, benefits, renewability, and cost. The provisions and practices described represent the norm in that most policies fit within the extremes that are described. However, the norm covers a wide spectrum.

Issue Age

Substantial differences exist among insurance companies with respect to the age at which they will issue policies. At a minimum, a healthy person between the ages of 55 and 75 will be eligible for coverage from most insurance companies. Most companies also have an upper age of 80 or 85, beyond which coverage will not be issued. Coverage written at age 85 or older, if available, is often accompanied by restrictive policy provisions and very high premiums.

There is considerably more variation with respect to the youngest age at which coverage will be written. Some companies have no minimum age. Other companies sell policies to persons as young as age 20. Still other companies have minimum ages in the 40-to-50 age range. One reason for not issuing policies to persons under age 40 is the fear of the high number of potential claims resulting from AIDS.

YOUR FINANCIAL SERVICES PRACTICE:
THE BEST TIME TO SELL LTC INSURANCE

Many planners feel the best time to sell long-term care insurance is when clients are in their late 50s. One reason for this is that these clients have often recently undergone the experience of dealing with the long-term care needs of their parents. More important, however, the "numbers" seem to work well for this group compared to those in their mid- to late 60s since costs are more reasonable.

Benefits

Benefits under long-term care policies can be categorized by type, amounts, duration, the ability to restore benefits, and the degree of inflation protection.

Types. There are several levels of care that are frequently provided by long-term care policies:

- *skilled-nursing care*, which consists of daily nursing and rehabilitative care that can be performed only by, or under the supervision of, skilled medical personnel and must be based on a doctor's orders
- *intermediate care*, which involves occasional nursing and rehabilitative care that must be based on a doctor's orders and can be performed only by, or under the supervision of, skilled medical personnel
- *custodial care*, which is primarily to handle personal needs, such as walking, bathing, dressing, eating, or taking medicine, and can usually be provided by someone without professional medical skills or training
- *home-health care*, which is received at home and includes part-time skilled-nursing care, speech therapy, physical or occupational therapy, part-time services from home-health aides, and help from homemakers
- *adult day care*, which is received at centers specifically designed for the elderly who live at home but whose spouses or families are not available to stay home during the day. The level of care received is similar to that provided for home-health care. Most adult day-care centers also provide transportation to and from the center.

Most policies cover at least the first three levels of care, and many cover all five. Some policies also provide benefits for respite care, which allows occasional full-time care at home for a person who is receiving home-health care. Respite-care benefits enable family members who are providing much of the home care to take a needed break.

It is becoming increasingly common for policies to contain a bed reservation benefit. This benefit continues payments to a long-term care facility for a limited time (such as 20 days) if a patient must temporarily leave to be hospitalized. Without a continuation of payments, the bed may be rented to someone else and unavailable upon the patient's release from the hospital.

Some newer policies provide assisted-living benefits. These benefits are for facilities that provide care for the frail elderly who are no longer able to care for themselves but do not need the level of care provided in a nursing home.

Costs. Benefits are usually limited to a specified amount per day that is independent of the actual charge for long-term care. The insured purchases the level of benefit he or she desires up to the maximum level the insurance company will provide. Benefits are often sold in increments of $10 per day up to frequently found limits of $100 or $150 or, in a few cases, as much as $300. Most insurance companies will not offer a daily benefit below $30 or $50.

The same level of benefits is usually provided for all levels of institutional care. A high proportion of policies that provide home-health care limit the benefit to one-half the benefit amount payable for institutional stays. However, some insurers have introduced home-health care limits that are as high as 80 to 100 percent of the benefit for nursing homes.

Some policies are written on an indemnity basis and pay the cost of covered services up to a maximum dollar amount. For example, a policy may pay 80 to 100 percent of charges up to a maximum dollar amount per day.

Duration. Long-term care policies contain both an elimination (waiting) period and a maximum benefit period. Under an elimination period, benefit payments do not begin until a specified time period after long-term care has begun. While a few insurance companies have a set period (such as 60 days), most allow the policyowner to select from three or four optional elimination periods. For example, one insurance company allows the choice of 30, 90, or 180 days. Choices may occasionally be as low as 30 days or as high as 365 days. (*Planning Note:* The use of an elimination period often keeps policy costs down. Planners should recommend this type of self-insurance and make sure adequate assets are available for the period.)

The policyowner is also usually given a choice regarding the maximum period for which benefits will be paid. For example, one insurer offers durations of 2, 3, or 4 years; another makes 3-, 6-, and 12-year coverage available. At the extremes, options of one year or lifetime may be available. However, a policy with a lifetime benefit will be more expensive than one with a shorter maximum benefit limit. In some cases, the duration applies to all benefits; in other cases, the duration specified is for nursing home benefits, with home-health-care benefits covered for a shorter time.

A few insurers extend the maximum period (if it is less than a lifetime limit) by a specified number of days (such as 30 days) for each year the insured does not collect any benefit payments. Such an extension is usually subject to an aggregate limit, such as one or 2 years.

A few policies (usually written on an indemnity basis) specify the maximum benefit as a stated dollar amount, such as $50,000 or $100,000.

Restoration. A few policies provide for restoration of full benefits if the insured has been out of a nursing home for a certain time period, often 180 days. However, most policies do not have this provision, and maximum benefits for a subsequent claim will be reduced by the benefits previously paid.

Inflation Protection. Most long-term care policies offer some type of inflation protection that the policyowner can purchase. In some cases, the inflation protection is elected (for a higher premium) at the time of purchase; future increases in benefits are automatic. In other cases, the policyowner is allowed to purchase additional benefits each year without evidence of insurability.

Inflation protection is generally in the form of a specified annual increase, often 5 percent. This percentage may be on a simple interest basis, which means that each annual increase is a percentage of the original benefit. In other cases, the increase is on a compound interest basis, which means that each increase is based on the existing benefit at the time the additional coverage is purchased.

Some policies limit aggregate increases to a specified multiple of the original policy, such as two times. Other policies allow increases only to a maximum age, such as 85.

There are two approaches to pricing any additional coverage purchased. Some insurers base premiums on the insured's attained age when the original policy was issued; other insurers use the insured's age at the time each additional increment of coverage is purchased.

Inflation protection is usually less than adequate to offset actual inflation. The maximum annual increase in benefits is usually 5 percent. This is significantly below recent annual increases in the cost of long-term care, which have been in the double digits over the last decade.

Eligibility for Benefits

Almost all insurance companies now use a criterion for benefit eligibility that is related to several so-called activities of daily living. While variations exist, these activities often include eating, bathing, dressing, transferring from bed to chair, using the toilet, and maintaining continence. In order to receive benefits, there must be independent certification that a person is totally dependent on others to perform a certain number of these activities. For example, one insurer lists seven activities and requires total dependence for any three of them; another insurer requires dependence for two out of a list of six.

Newer policies contain a second criterion that, if satisfied, will result in the payment of benefits even if the activities of daily living can be performed. This criterion is based on cognitive impairment, which can be caused by Alzheimer's disease, strokes, or other brain damage. Cognitive impairment is generally measured through tests performed by trained medical personnel. Because eligibility for benefits often depends on subjective evaluations, most insurance companies use some form of case management. Case management may be mandatory, with the case manager determining eligibility, working with the physician and family to decide on an appropriate type of care, and periodically reassessing the case. Case management may also be voluntary, with the case manager making recommendations about the type of care needed and providing information about the sources for care.

Preexisting Conditions

The most common preexisting conditions provision specifies that benefits will not be paid for a long-term care need within the first 6 months of a policy for a condition for which treatment was recommended or received within 6 months prior to policy purchase. Policies with less restrictive provisions, and perhaps no such provision, are sometimes found but they are usually very strictly underwritten.

Exclusions

Most long-term care policies contain the exclusions permitted under the NAIC model act. One source of controversy is the exclusion for mental and nervous disorders.

Underwriting

The underwriting of long-term care policies, like the underwriting of medical expense policies, is based on the health of the insured. However, underwriting for the long-term care risk focuses on situations that will cause claims far into the future. Most underwriting is done on the basis of questionnaires rather than on the use of actual physical examinations. Numerous questions are asked about the health of relatives. For example, if a parent or grandparent had Alzheimer's disease, there is an increased likelihood that the applicant will get this disease in the future. In addition, the insurance company is very interested in medical events, such as temporary amnesia or fainting spells, that might be an indication of future incapacities.

Underwriting tends to become more restrictive as the age of an applicant increases. Not only is a future claim more likely to occur much sooner, but adverse selection can also be more severe.

Most insurers have a single classification for all acceptable applicants for long-term care insurance, but it is becoming more common to have three or four categories of insurable classifications, each with a different rate structure.

In the past, insurance companies were accused of "underwriting at the time of claims" by denying benefits because of restrictive policy provisions and supposed (or actual) misstatements in the distant past. The regulations of many states regarding preexisting conditions and the mandatory inclusion of an incontestability provision have caused this problem to become less severe over time. The current situation does, however, put many insurance companies in the position of having to underwrite more accurately prior to policy issuance.

Renewability

Long-term care policies currently being sold are guaranteed renewable, which means that an individual's coverage cannot be canceled except for nonpayment of premiums. While premiums cannot be raised on the basis of a particular applicant's claim, they can (and often are) raised by class.

Premiums

Premium Payment Period. The vast majority of long-term care policies have premiums that are payable for life and determined by the age of the insured at the time of issue. For example, a policy may have an annual cost of $800 at the time of purchase. Assuming the policy is guaranteed renewable, this premium will not change unless it is raised on a class basis. Long-term care policies of this nature are often advertised as being "level premium." This is misleading because premiums may be (and in a few cases have been) increased by class. As a result, the current NAIC model act prohibits the use of this term unless a policy is noncancelable, which means that rates cannot increase.

A few companies have guaranteed renewable policies with scheduled premium increases. These increases may occur as frequently as annually or as infrequently as every 5 years.

While most premiums are paid annually for the insured's lifetime, a few insurers offer other modes of payment. Lifetime coverage can sometimes be purchased with a single premium. Some insurers are now also beginning to offer policies that have premium payment periods of 10 or 20 years, after which time the premium is paid up.

Factors Affecting Premiums. Numerous factors affect the premium that a policyowner will pay for a long-term care policy. Even if the provisions of several policies are virtually identical, premiums will vary among companies. *Planning Note:* Shopping around for price and quality of company can result in rewards.

Age of Policyowner. Age plays a significant role in the cost of long-term care coverage, as shown by the rates in the table below. These figures demonstrate that long-term care coverage can be obtained at a reasonable cost if it is purchased at a young age.

TABLE 12-3 Comparison of Long-Term Care Premiums for Similar Policies			
Age	Company A	Company B	Company C
40	$ 680	$1,670	$1,220
45	850	2,000	1,370
50	1,090	2,450	1,440
55	1,440	3,060	1,830
60	2,010	4,200	2,370
65	2,900	5,750	3,250
70	4,300	7,660	4,650
75	6,290	11,300	6,630
79	9,530	14,710	10,180

Types of Benefits. The benefits provided under a policy have a significant bearing on the cost. Most policies cover care in a nursing home. However, many policies also cover home-health care and other benefits provided to persons who are still able to reside in their own homes. This broader coverage increases premiums by 30 to 50 percent.

Duration of Benefits. The longer the maximum benefit period, the higher the premium. The longer the waiting period, the lower the premium. With many insurers a policy with an unlimited benefit period and no waiting period will have a premium about double that of a policy with a 2-year benefit period and a 90-day waiting period.

Inflation Protection. Policies may be written with or without automatic benefit increases for inflation. All other factors being equal, the addition of a 5 percent compound annual increase in benefits will usually raise premiums by about 50 percent.

Waiver-of-Premium. Most long-term care policies have a provision that waives premiums if the insured has been receiving benefits under the policy for a specified period of time, often 60 or 90 days. The inclusion of this benefit usually increases premiums by about 5 percent.

Spousal Coverage. Most insurance companies offer a discount of 10 to 15 percent if both spouses purchase long-term care policies from the company.

CHECKLIST FOR COMPARING LONG-TERM CARE POLICIES

With the numerous variations in long-term care policies, it is very difficult for consumers, life insurance agents, and financial planners to compare policies. In the final analysis, two policies may have the same cost even though they may differ significantly. In other words, the one policy may be clearly superior in certain areas, while the second may have other more preferable provisions. In such cases a final selection decision is difficult and highly subjective. To make an informed choice, many factors must be compared as objectively as possible.

To facilitate such comparisons several states have prepared consumer guides that are usually available upon request. *The Consumer's Guide to Long-Term Care Insurance* prepared by the Health Insurance Association of America is also available. This guide contains a checklist for policy comparisons that is presented in table 12-4.

TABLE 12-4
Long-Term Care Policy Checklist

	Policy A	Policy B
1. What services are covered? Skilled care Intermediate care Custodial care Home health care Adult day care Other		
2. How much does the policy pay per day for: Skilled care? Intermediate care? Custodial care? Home health care? Adult day care?		

3. How long will benefits last?
 	
In a nursing home, for
    Skilled nursing care?
    Intermediate nursing care?
    Custodial care?
At home?		

4. Does the policy have a maximum lifetime benefit? If so, what is it? For nursing home care? For home health care?		
5. Does the policy have a maximum length of coverage for each period of confinement? If so, what is it? For nursing home care? For home health care?		
6. How long must I wait before pre-existing conditions are covered?		
7. How many days must I wait before benefits begin? For nursing home care? For home health care?		

TABLE 12-4 (Continued)
Long-Term Care Policy Checklist

	Policy A	Policy B
8. Are Alzheimer's disease and other organic mental and nervous disorders covered?		
9. Does this policy require: Physician certification of need? An assessment of activities of daily living? A prior hospital stay for: 　Nursing home care? 　Home health care? A prior nursing home stay for home health care coverage? Other?		
10. Is the policy guaranteed renewable?		
11. What is the age range for enrollment?		
12. Is there a waiver-of-premium provision? For nursing home care? For home health care?		
13. How long must I be confined before premiums are waived?		
14. Does the policy offer an inflation adjustment feature? If so: What is the rate of increase? How often is it applied? For how long? Is there an additional cost?		
15. What does the policy cost? Per year?　With inflation feature 　　　　　　Without inflation feature Per month?　With inflation feature 　　　　　　Without inflation feature		
16. Is there a 30-day free look?		

Reprinted from *The Consumer's Guide to Long-Term Care Insurance* by permission. Copyright 1993 by the Health Insurance Association of America.

13

Housing Issues Facing the Retiree

Chapter Outline

Housing issues facing the retiree vary from client to client. In this chapter we will address the major financial and tax concerns involving housing alternatives and relocation that can arise when planning for a retired client. Our focus, of course, will be financial. It is important to remember, however, that retirement is a time of change on many levels. It often means, among other things, adjusting to a new routine and reassessing one's identity. For this reason some clients cling to their home in retirement as the last bastion of status quo. Planners need to understand that the disposition of the family homestead and the decision of where to reside during the retirement years is, first and foremost, a personal choice with a different meaning for every client. In other words, the psychological attachment to the home in many cases far outweighs the financial and tax wisdom involved with thinking of the home as an asset. It is in this context that financial services professionals must deal with planning for the disposition of a retired client's home.

WHAT CLIENTS NEED TO KNOW ABOUT THE HOME AS A FINANCIAL ASSET

Despite the caveat raised in the opening paragraph, it is the planner's job to point out the following to his or her client:

- Although one's house remains the same, the character of the neighborhood will be changed during retirement by the deaths and departures of friends. In addition, development in the local area will change the essence of community that once was so familiar.
- The house that was suitable for raising a family may not be suitable for retirement. Instead of being close to schools in the best school district it might be more important to be close to medical care in a place with lower school taxes.
- The costs of heating, cooling, cleaning, and maintaining a house with empty rooms and a child-sized yard may be prohibitive.
- Even a mortgage-free house can be a financial drain that robs the retiree of income. Here's why: Besides the additional costs involved in maintaining a home, the equity that can be gained from its sale can be used to provide needed retirement income.

YOUR FINANCIAL SERVICES PRACTICE:
ILLUSTRATING THE STREAM OF INCOME AVAILABLE FROM THE SALE OF THE HOME

Clients need to understand the income that can be provided from any residual amount of money left after subtracting the purchase of the retirement residence from the sale of the preretirement residence. For this reason it can be a lucrative opportunity to illustrate the projected installment payout, life annuity, or joint and survivor annuity available from freed-up assets. The number crunching will help some clients to make a more informed decision, even if they choose not to cash in on the "home asset." For others, the income stream that can be provided by selling the home asset might mean the difference between just making ends meet and being able to enjoy retirement.

WHAT CLIENTS NEED TO KNOW ABOUT THE TAX OPPORTUNITIES INVOLVED WITH SELLING A HOME

One of the most important planning decisions facing a retired client is whether to take advantage of a one-time tax break on the sale of his or her home. In fact, in some circumstances the desire to gain this lucrative tax advantage drives the decision to sell the preretirement residence. Internal Revenue Code Sec. 121 specifies that up to $125,000 of the gain on the sale of a home can be excluded from tax if certain conditions are met. The ability to capitalize on the home as a tax-free retirement asset can mean tax savings of $35,000 for someone paying a 28 percent capital gains tax (.28 x $125,000). The gain from a sale is determined by subtracting basis from the net sales price (selling price less any selling expenses) of the house. For some homeowners the basis in the house is equal to the original purchase price they paid when they moved in. For others the basis of their house reflects the fact that they paid no tax when they moved from a less expensive residence. And for still others the basis is increased to include any improvements made to the house (for example, an addition or other substantial improvements to the house, but *not* expenses for home maintenance or repairs). IRS Publications 523 and 551 contain more information on the issues of basis and gain. In addition see the instructions to IRS Form 2119.

> *Example:* Dan and Jamie Johnson bought their house in 1975 for $40,000. In 1984 they added a porch at a cost of $5,000. No other capital improvements were made. The Johnson's basis in their house is therefore $45,000. They are selling the house today for $180,000. (Selling expenses are $10,000 so net sales price is $170,000.) The difference between the net sales price (in tax terms, the amount realized) and basis is therefore a gain of $125,000 ($170,000 minus $45,000). This gain can be shielded from tax if the Johnsons qualify to make a Sec. 121 election using IRS Form 2119.

To determine whether your client is entitled to make a Sec. 121 election, the following questions must be answered satisfactorily.

Has the Age 55 Requirement Been Met?

Your client must be aged 55 or over by the date of the sale of his or her home. A client can put his or her house on the market before attaining age 55 but cannot close on the sale before the date of his or her 55th birthday. In the case of a married couple, only one spouse needs to be 55 or over to take advantage of the $125,000 exclusion. For example, if Jack is 55 and Jill is 53 the couple can elect the exclusion when they file their joint tax return despite the fact that Jill is not yet aged 55.

Does the Client Meet the 3-out-of-5-Year Test?

In order to qualify for the $125,000 exclusion the house must have been owned and used by the client as a principal residence for at least 3 years out of the 5-year period ending on the date of sale. The years need not be consecutive, however. For example, Bruce lived at 10 Elm Street for all of 1989, 1990, and 1992. (For the year of 1991 his employer sent him to work in Japan.) At the end of 1993, Bruce sells his home. He can claim the exclusion because the 3-out-of-5-year rule has been satisfied.

Nursing Care Exception

An exception to the 3-out-of-5-year residency requirement applies to individuals who have moved into a nursing home because they are incapable of self-care. In this situation, a person who owned and used his or her house as a principal residence for at least one year will satisfy the residency requirements if he or she sells the property while living in the nursing facility. Technically, the exception applies if the sale is made at any time during the 5-year period ending on the date of sale, as long as the individual is living in the nursing facility at the time of sale and had resided in the house for at least one year during this period. *This means that for the individual residing continuously in nursing care, the exception will expire 4 years after moving into the facility.*

Does the Dwelling Meet the Principal Residence Test?

In most cases what constitutes a client's "principal" residence will be obvious—the single family home in which he or she lives. Clients who live in houseboats, mobile homes, condominiums, cooperatives, and so on can claim these dwellings as their principal residence. From a planning standpoint it can get tricky when a client owns more than one dwelling. Case law on this issue is extensive, and a thorough discussion of the myriad possibilities is beyond the scope of this book. Suffice it to say, however, that a summer home or vacation bungalow will not qualify as the principal residence when a permanent home is owned and extensively lived in by the client.

Has the Client Met the Once-in-a-Lifetime Requirement?

It is a relatively straightforward matter for a planner to determine whether or not a single client has previously elected the $125,000 exclusion. For married individuals, particularly where several previous marriages are involved, the question becomes more complex. As a general rule, husband and wife are treated as one person for purposes of the exclusion. If one spouse has already taken advantage of the exclusion before the marriage, both spouses cannot exclude the gain. In other words, if anyone filing the tax return has been a party to the exclusion (even from a prior marriage), both parties are deemed to have already used the exclusion.

Planning Point: This brings up an interesting planning opportunity when a marriage between two older people is involved. If two individuals aged 55 or older are contemplating marriage and each of them owns a home, it is best for each of them to sell his or her own home before the marriage so that each can take advantage of a full $125,000 exclusion (assuming neither party had a previous election). If the individuals decide to wait until after their marriage to sell their homes, then they will only be allowed one $125,000 exclusion between them. In addition, if one of the would-be newlyweds has already used the exclusion, the couple may decide to sell the other's home (taking the exclusion) before the marriage and live in the home of the one who had previously used the exclusion.

Should Your Client Elect to Exclude the Gain Now or Later?

Assuming your client is eligible to make the Sec. 121 election, the next question is when he or she should make it. In other words, would it be more advantageous to exclude gain when initially "downsizing" the home or to wait until late in retirement when the "downsized" home is sold (perhaps at the time when nursing home care begins)? To answer this question consider the following.

Loss of Unused Exclusion

If your client makes a Sec. 121 election right after attaining age 55, and the full $125,000 exclusion of gain is not utilized, any unused portion of the exclusion is lost forever and cannot be carried forward to a future election. For example, if Dan and Jamie Johnson sell their preretirement home for a net sales price of $95,000 ($100,000 sale price less $5,000 selling expenses) instead of $170,000 as in the previous example, their gain would be $50,000 (net sales price of $95,000 minus basis of $45,000). Assuming that the Johnsons make the election and exclude the $50,000 gain, they would wind up forfeiting the unused $75,000 portion of the exclusion and could not make another election at a future date.

Appreciation Issues

To continue with our example, suppose that several years pass and the Johnsons decide to sell their *downsized* home for a gain of $150,000. Since the Johnsons made a Sec. 121 election several years earlier to exclude the $50,000 gain from the sale of their preretirement home, they are not eligible to make another election. Under these circumstances, the Johnsons would probably have been better off if they had deferred making the election until the sale of their downsized home. Ignoring the effects of tax law and rate changes and the time value of money, if the Johnsons had waited to make the election they would have been able to utilize the full $125,000 exclusion.

Tax Changes

The ability of the downsized home to appreciate sufficiently (to significantly outgain the preretirement home) is a real concern. If this cannot reasonably be expected to happen, then the election should be taken at the time the preretirement home is sold. On the other hand, the retirement horizon may extend over a period of 30 years or more (age 55 to age 85 or higher). In addition, a client may move from a preretirement residence to a previously owned vacation home with plenty of existing equity. When the client converts the vacation home into his or her primary residence during retirement, the ability to "max out" the $125,000 exclusion may be very real, and may happen very quickly.

Another concern deals with the uncertainty of tax law in general. Some planners recommend that clients seize the opportunity to take a Sec. 121 election when it first becomes available (even if for a relatively small gain) because this tax break may not always be available in the future. Other planners point to the fact that Congress has taken upon itself to build in an ad hoc indexation to the exclusion. The exclusion started out in 1964 for $20,000 and was last changed in 1981 by the Economic Recovery Tax Act (ERTA) from $100,000 to $125,000.

Even if the $125,000 exclusion amount gain remains unchanged in the foreseeable future, clients also have to consider possible changes in capital-gains tax rates. To reinforce this point one only needs to pick up a newspaper to read about some politician promising to change tax rates.

Time Value of Money

Yet another concern is the time value of money. Because the client can invest any potential tax savings from taking the exclusion, the interest that would accrue on this amount must be factored against the client's ability to exclude a much larger gain sometime in the future. Since the client is only allowed to utilize the Sec. 121 exclusion once, he or she should select whichever alternative has the highest present value, all things being equal. In other words, from a purely monetary standpoint, the client should elect to take the Sec. 121 exclusion with the alternative that has the highest present value, whether that be the sale of the preretirement home now or the much later sale of the downsized retirement home.

An interesting exercise in this analysis is knowing how much gain the second home must generate at the point of its sale in order to justify not taking advantage of the Sec. 121 exclusion at the time of selling the first (or preretirement) home. Table 13-1 should enable us to calculate the amount of gain needed to break even.

Break-Even Analysis

The break-even point for determining when the tax savings on the delayed election will be greater than the tax savings and imputed interest on the first opportunity for making the election depends in part on the aftertax interest rate used for the imputed interest and the amount of time until the second opportunity for sale presents itself. Table 13-1 can be used to determine this break-even point. Assumptions underlying the table are that Code Sec. 121 will not be eliminated or changed in the future, the capital-gain tax rate will not change, and the client will not die before he or she can potentially capitalize on the sale of the second home.

TABLE 13-1
Break-even Table Indicating the Amount of Gain that the Second Home Must Generate to Delay Taking the Exclusion at the First Opportunity

Interest Rates	YEARS					
	5	10	15	20	25	30
4	1.216	1.480	1.800	2.191	2.666	3.243
5	1.276	1.629	2.079	2.653	3.386	4.322
6	1.338	1.791	2.396	3.207	4.292	5.743
7	1.402	1.967	2.759	3.869	5.427	7.612
8	1.469	2.159	3.172	4.661	6.848	10.062
9	1.538	2.367	3.642	5.604	8.623	13.267
10	1.610	2.593	4.177	6.727	10.843	17.449

For a given aftertax interest rate and time horizon, multiplying the number from the table by the gain from selling the first (or preretirement) home will tell you the amount of future gain that the sale of the second (or downsized) home must generate in order to break even and make it worthwhile to forgo the immediate tax savings from using a Sec. 121 election on the sale of the first home. To better understand how the break-even table works, let's look at an example.

Example: The Harts, who expect to realize a $50,000 gain on the sale of their current residence, plan to convert their vacation home into a residence, live in it for 10 years before selling it, and then move into a retirement community. If the Harts were to make a Sec. 121 election on the sale of the current home, they could invest the tax savings over a 10-year period at an annual aftertax rate of return of 6 percent. Should the Harts make the election now and use the tax exclusion on the gain from the sale of the current home, or should they wait until the subsequent sale of the former vacation home? Utilizing the break-even table, the Harts can calculate that the sale of the former vacation home must be able to generate a gain of at least $89,550 (1.791 x $50,000) before they can benefit by waiting 10 years to take the Sec. 121 tax exclusion. However, since the Harts anticipate that the gain on the sale of the former vacation home will undoubtedly be over $125,000, they should wait until its sale to take the Sec. 121 tax exclusion.

A word of caution is in order at this point. While we know what the gain is when the client sells the first (or preretirement) home and we are able to ascertain the amount of gain the client will need when selling the downsized second home (so as to break even and make it worthwhile to forgo the immediate tax savings from using a Sec. 121 tax exclusion with the sale of the first home), we do not know whether the client's second home will actually increase enough in value during the selected time frame to generate the gain needed (in other words, to break even). Moreover, as the client grows older and his or her chance of dying increases, we simply cannot determine whether the client will survive the time frame to sell the downsized second home and take advantage of a Sec. 121 tax exclusion. Any decision to forgo using the Sec. 121 tax exclusion with the sale of the first or preretirement home should be made with full knowledge of these risks.

What If Your Client Has More Than $125,000 in Gain?

Clients who take full advantage of a Sec. 121 election and who have a gain on the sale of their home that exceeds the $125,000 exclusion amount may be able to roll over the excess gain under Code Sec. 1034 if they purchase another home for use as their principal residence. Under Sec. 1034, any person who sells a home and buys another home is permitted to defer paying tax on the gain, provided the purchase price of the second home is at least as large as the net sales price of the first home. The 1034 tax break applies to homes bought within 2 years (either before or after) of the sale of the original home. Both the Sec. 1034 rollover and the Sec. 121 exclusion can be used in the same transaction if there is a gain of more than $125,000 and the requirements for both Code Sections are met. When these Code Sections are used together a person will be able to defer the excess gain over $125,000 as long as the home purchased is at least equal to the net sales price of the home sold less $125,000. If the purchase price of the home is less than this value, some or all of the excess gain will be subject to taxation.

Example: The Andersons, both aged 62, sell their home for a net sales price of $240,000. The home cost them $50,000 in 1970 and they have not made any capital improvements to it. Therefore, their gain from the sale is $190,000 (the net sales price of $240,000 minus the basis of $50,000). If the Andersons take advantage of the full $125,000 exclusion, they will reduce their potential taxable gain from the sale of the home to $65,000. If the Andersons subsequently buy another home within the requisite time period for $115,000 or more ($240,000 − $125,000), there will be no immediate tax consequences. The deferred gain will become subject to taxation on any future sale of the home to the extent that the gain is not again rolled over to yet another home.

PLANNING FOR THE CLIENT WHO MOVES

Up to this point the discussion has dealt with the tax implications of a retiree selling his or her home and before that the consideration of the home as a financial asset. This discussion has laid the groundwork for many planning opportunities. At the heart of each opportunity is the client's retirement decision either to remain in his or her current residence or to relocate to another. A discussion of these two options will consume the remainder of this chapter. First let us consider the client who changes residences.

As we have already seen, a common reason for changing residences at retirement is to downsize, that is, to purchase a retirement residence that costs less than the one being sold in order to transfer a portion of the gain (enhanced by tax breaks) into cash for retirement. At this point planners should also consider the two other principal reasons that retirees change residences. One reason is to avail themselves of living circumstances uniquely geared to the retired population. These new residences generally reflect changes in lifestyle that are thrust upon the retiree. The residences include life-care communities, alternative housing, and nursing homes. The final reason that retirees change residences is to relocate to an area where their dollars can be stretched further because the living costs are lower. In this situation the planner needs to consider the consequences of his or her client relocating to another state. Let us take a look at these issues starting with life-care communities.

Life-Care Communities

There are many varieties of life-care communities (sometimes called continuing-care retirement communities) throughout the United States. In fact, because of the number of options that exist it may be best to explain what life-care communities are by explaining what they are not. Life-care communities are not simply retirement villages where people over a specified age reside; nor are they simply nursing homes where elderly patients go for custodial and medical care. Life-care communities are a combination of these two extremes and a little bit of everything in between. Moreover, they are often mistakenly thought to be only for the wealthy. The truth is, however, that there are substantial variations in price among life-care communities, and the majority of them are nonprofit organizations.

How They Work

While it is true that facilities, fees, and services vary widely from one life-care community to the next, several common features do exist. Most frequently your clients will pay a one-time up-front fee that can range from $20,000 to $500,000 depending on the quality of the community and the nature of the contract. In some cases the fee is nonrefundable. In others the fee is fully refundable if the individual retiree, couple, or surviving spouse leaves. And in still other cases the fee is refundable based on an agreed-upon schedule. For example, 2 percent of the one-time up-front fee becomes nonrefundable for each month that your client is in residence. If your client leaves after 2 years (24 months) he or she will be entitled to a refund of 52 percent of the fee. In other words, your client will forfeit 48 percent of the fee.

In addition to a one-time up-front fee, residents generally pay a monthly fee that can range from under $1,000 per month up to and over $5,000 per month. In part the monthly fee depends on the dwelling unit chosen and any services rendered. A closer look at the disparity of fees is needed, however.

One reason for the great disparity in both the one-time up-front fee and the monthly fee is that in some cases they interrelate with each other and with any refund policy that applies to one-time up-front fee. In other words, there is a trade-off in these cases between the one-time up-front fee and the monthly fee. In other cases both types of fees are high because they go to pay for expensive medical benefits, such as long-term care, that are guaranteed in advance. In yet other cases, both the one-time up-front fee and the monthly fee vary widely because of the variety of services that are provided and the quality of the facility.

Planning Point: It is difficult to do an "apples to apples" comparison between two life-care communities; nonetheless, the planner must be able to assist the client in understanding their similarities and differences.

In return for the payment of fees, your client will get a life-lease contract (sometimes called a residential care agreement) that guarantees some level of living space, services, and lifetime health care. A closer look at these characteristics is in order.

Living Space. The residential accommodation may be a single-family dwelling or an apartment. It can change with the retiree's needs to a skilled-nursing facility or a long-term care facility. Most life-care communities point with pride to the safety of the facility and its accessibility to those who are suffering from one or more diseases associated with aging.

Services. Services may include the following:

- some level of housekeeping, including linen service
- some level of meal preparation (taking one or more meals in a common dining hall)

- facilities for crafts, tennis, golf, and other types of recreation
- transportation to and from area shopping and events
- supervision of exercise and diet
- skilled-nursing care (if needed)
- long-term care, including custodial care (if needed)

Lifetime Health Care.   One key element to the life-care contract is the guarantee of space in a nursing home if it becomes necessary. The guarantee of long-term care can be approached in several ways. One approach is to pay in advance for unlimited nursing home care at little or no increase in monthly payments (sometimes called an *extensive contract*). Another approach is to cover nursing home care up to a specified amount with a per diem rate paid by your client for usage over and above the specified amount (sometimes called a *modified contract*). A final approach is to cover only emergency and short-term nursing home care in the basic agreement and to provide long-term care on a per diem basis (sometimes called a *fee-for-service contract*).

YOUR FINANCIAL SERVICES PRACTICE:
COORDINATION OF LIFE-CARE COMMUNITY SELECTION WITH
LONG-TERM CARE INSURANCE AND MEDIGAP COVERAGE

Clients who are involved in a life-care community have definable needs for long-term care insurance and medigap coverage. Astute planners will best serve these clients by coordinating the medical and long-term care coverage provided by the life-care community with that provided by insurance policies. For example, a life-care community that provides long-term care for a specified period of time and then sets a rate for usage beyond that time can be coordinated with a long-term care insurance contract's waiting period and per diem allowance.

Additional Concerns

Many retirees enjoy life-care communities because of the opportunity for social interaction with people of like interests and ages. For example, they enjoy having a meal in a common dining room, and they appreciate being checked up on when they do not show up for dinner. Others are less enthusiastic about group living and the regimentation associated with their new "community." For these retirees it is a comfort to know that they can usually obtain a living unit with its own kitchen and that a coffee shop may be available for alternative dining.

Although no scientific evidence exists to support the contention that retirees who live in life-care communities live longer, many gerontologists share this belief because of the support-group mentality associated with the communities, the high-quality medical care provided, and the quality of life associated with social interaction.

Another concern with life-care communities deals with the above-mentioned Sec. 1034 rollover opportunity. The question arises as to whether the one-time up-front fee is actually the purchase of real estate that could qualify for Sec. 1034 treatment. Sadly in most cases the answer is no; Sec. 1034 treatment does not apply. With the exception of any life-care community organized like a condominium or cooperative, the life-care contract (or residence agreement) *cannot* be construed to be the purchase of real estate. For openers, in most cases no deed is transferred. Any possibility of refunding a portion of the one-time up-front fee takes away from a "purchase" agreement. And the interplay of the one-time up-front fee with the monthly fee or purchase of services makes it unlikely that the IRS will deem the one-time up-front fee as equivalent to the purchase of property.

The final concern deals with the tax deductibility of medical costs associated with the life-care contract. The astute planner will learn in advance the amount of the contract construed to be for medical expenses. Many life-care communities omit this fact from the contractual agreement. Inclusion, however, can go a long way in winning (or avoiding) an argument with the IRS regarding the cost of medical expenses.

Hidden Traps

Financial planners need to take special precautions when advising a client on the life-care community he or she should choose. Communities that have gone bankrupt have caused some retirees to lose the one-time up-front fee. Things to look for include whether long-term care costs are being self-insured or whether an outside carrier is involved. Special attention should be paid to how the community sets its fees and whether medical insurance on residents encourages overutilization of services. Also, planners should be wary of communities that undercharged their early residents and must make up the difference from their most recent residents. Planners who practice due diligence at the outset can save themselves from problems down the road.

Questions to Be Asked

Planners may want to ask the following questions when helping a client select a life-care community.

- Who manages the life-care community—owners or an outside profit agency? Third-party management is less desirable.
- Is there a powerful and active residence committee that can influence management decisions?

- What are the health care guarantees provided by the contract?
- What about amortization of the one-time up-front fee? Are the one-time up-front fees of current residents being used to pay current costs?
- How are fee increases determined?
- What is the refund policy for the one-time up-front fee?
- What are the minimum and maximum age requirements?
- What are the estate planning implications involved with the one-time up-front fee?

Alternative Housing Options

In addition to life-care communities, retirees have several other housing options that the planner should be aware of. These alternatives include

- accessory apartments—self-contained living units installed in the surplus space of a single-family home. (Be wary of local zoning laws.)
- echo housing or "granny flats"—removable housing units set up on the lot of a single-family home. (Once again, be wary of zoning laws.)
- residential-care facilities—adult homes that provide safety, shelter, and companionship. (They are not widely used.)
- retirement villages—age-restricted housing developments that often provide recreational opportunities and maintenance services for common ground.

YOUR FINANCIAL SERVICES PRACTICE:
RESIDENCE CHOICES LITERATURE

It may be a good idea to have literature on residence choices available for clients. AARP is a good source of information. In addition, local real estate professionals and life-care community managers can be of help. It is worth noting that these allied professionals can become a strong center of influence in your retirement planning practice.

Nursing Home Deductibility

A nursing home is a facility that provides residents with medical services and custodial care. The nuances of nursing home care and costs are covered thoroughly in this book's discussions of long-term care insurance. As far as a residence "choice," however, it is appropriate for the planner to consider the tax deductibility of nursing home costs.

As a general rule any medical costs incurred in a nursing home are considered medical expenses and are potentially deductible by the resident. The tax rule for deduction of medical expenses is that medical expenses are deductible to the extent that they exceed 7.5 percent of adjusted gross income. For example, Gertrude has an adjusted gross income of $40,000 and her medical expenses at the nursing home for skilled nursing and doctor care ran $4,000 (total nursing home cost is $25,000). Gertrude is therefore able to deduct $1,000 in medical expenses over and above her $3,000 threshold (.075 x $40,000 = $3,000). Planners for Gertrude and others like her, however, may be able to deduct the full amount of the nursing home bill. If this were the case for Gertrude, the total nursing home cost of $25,000 exceeds the $3,000 threshold by $22,000, which is the medical deduction.

It goes without saying that there is a huge tax advantage for clients who reside in nursing homes and are able to deduct the full amount of nursing home costs, not just the medical portion. Therefore the question is which clients can qualify to deduct the full amount of nursing home costs?

The quick answer to this question is that when the principal reason for a person's residing in a nursing home is that his or her condition warrants the availability of medical care, then meals, lodging, and most other custodial expenses are fully deductible as medical expenses. Conversely, if a person is in a nursing home for primarily personal or family reasons, then only medical expenses are deductible. The *principal reason test* is therefore an important planning issue.

To determine if the principal reason for a person's taking up residence at a nursing home is to receive medical care, the following factors need to be examined:

- the type and amount of medical care needed
- the percentage of lifetime care fees that are for medical expenses
- the person's physical and mental condition
- the type of services being provided
- statements from physicians
- admission requirements at the nursing home

Tax advice should be sought regarding your client's particular situation. Before you get to that point, however, it is wise to advise clients to create as large a paper trail as is ethically possible. Reports from doctors, a properly written nursing home contract, and other favorable records can go a long way in helping a client's cause. In many cases, awareness of the principal reason test is enough to allow the client and his or her family to do proper planning.

RELOCATION OUT OF STATE

The decision to relocate to another state is often motivated by such factors as climate, location of friends and relatives, and affection for the area itself. For clients considering such a move, some general advice is in order. First, weigh the decision cautiously because it is not easily reversible. Second, consider the prospect of dying in the new state. If one spouse should die, will the other want to cope with another uprooting? Third, consider establishing domicile in a state with lower death taxes. Domicile can be a choice if the client has more than one residence. Domicile is the intended permanent home of the client. Such factors as where the client spends his or her time, where he or she is registered to vote, where he or she has a driver's license, where his or her planner resides, and where his or her will is executed help to determine which residence is the client's permanent home. Fourth, consider state income taxes. Does the state tax base include pension income? Fifth, look carefully at property and transfer taxes. And finally, look to see if the state or local government provides specific tax breaks for the elderly. These tax breaks could include

- an additional exemption or standard deduction
- an income tax credit
- adjusted real estate taxes
- a deferral of real estate taxes until after the retiree's death (at which point the estate will pay the taxes from the sale of the home)
- an exemption of all or part of retirement pay from the state income tax base
- an exemption of all or part of social security from the state income tax base
- tax adjustments for renters (homestead credits)
- an exemption of all or part of unreimbursed medical expenses from the state income tax base
- frozen property tax levels for the year the retiree reaches age 65. (In other words, property taxes remain at age 65 rates until the home is sold by the retiree.)

PLANNING FOR CLIENTS WHO WANT TO REMAIN IN THEIR HOMES

A financial planner may look at a client's large, four-bedroom house and see unnecessary heating and maintenance costs. The client, on the other hand, sees the extra rooms as necessary for returning children and visiting relatives. This does not, however, preclude planning opportunities. If the client has decided that he or she will remain in the house throughout the retirement period the planner then needs to examine

- whether the house should be modified for elderly living
- the feasibility of a reverse annuity mortgage
- the opportunity for a sale leaseback

Modifying the House for Retirement Living

Elderly clients may want to modify their homes in the following ways to accommodate retirement living.

- add a stairlift
- add a downstairs bathroom
- widen doorways for wheelchair access
- install wheelchair ramps to the house

Planners should be aware of the possible tax deductibility of these actions as medical expenses and should seek to maximize tax deductions when possible.

Another reason for clients to modify their residences is to prepare their houses to receive tenants. A tenant may prove to be not only a valuable financial resource but also a companion for the retiree. Home modifications can provide a degree of privacy for both the tenant and the retiree.

Planning Point: Have your clients check zoning laws before renting out space. In some communities renting out a part of a home to tenants may not be permitted, or the town may impose restrictions on the types of modifications that can be made. In addition, your client should check his or her homeowner's insurance policy to see if additional coverage is necessary.

Reverse Annuity Mortgages and Look-alikes

For those clients who want to "age in place" but need to tap the equity in their homes because they are in need of finances to maintain their current standard of living, a reverse annuity mortgage (RAM) is available. There are many programs similar to RAMs and there is much nomenclature in this area. For this reason let us review the most common programs available.

Individual Reverse Annuity Mortgage

Under an individual RAM, a homeowner-client enters into an agreement with a lender to receive annuity payments (either single life or joint and survivor) in exchange for a secured interest in the equity in his or her home. Most commonly, the monthly annuity payments made by the lender are considered loans to the client. In return for these "loans" the lender receives a secured interest equal to the amount of the loans, the interest, and the agreed-upon portion of the appreciation and defers any repayment until such time as the client *either dies or moves*. If the client dies, it is up to the client's estate to pay back the loan, generally from the proceeds of the sale of the home. The amount of loan payments made to the client depends on the client's age (or clients' joint ages), the amount of equity the home currently has or is expected to have, and the interest rate that is being charged. Of importance from a planning standpoint is that if the client lives beyond his or her anticipated life expectancy, payments may exceed the value of the home. This represents a windfall for the client because the only asset that is security for the loan and that can be used for payback is the home. This opportunity for mortality gain and the knowledge that the client cannot outlive his or her income are both good reasons why a client would choose this type of program.

Although there are variations from lender to lender, the following factors usually can be found in this type of RAM.

- If your client dies shortly after the RAM contract is signed, his or her estate can repay the amount of the indebtedness without having to sell the house.
- The client is not taxed on the income he or she receives from the "annuity" because it is considered a loan.
- The value of the house is in the deceased client's estate.

YOUR FINANCIAL SERVICES PRACTICE:
REVERSE ANNUITY MORTGAGES AND LIFE INSURANCE

Often your client's children will object to the use of an individual reverse annuity mortgage because it typically means that the family home will be sold to repay the loan. When this situation arises the answer may be to have the *children buy second-to-die life insurance on their parents in the amount necessary to purchase the family home from the surviving parent's estate.*

Variation. A common variation of the individual reverse annuity mortgage involves the client selling a remainder interest in the home but retaining the right to occupy it until death. The purchaser of the remainder interest, whether it is a bank or financial institution, takes possession of the property after the homeowner's death (or the death of the homeowner's surviving spouse). The consideration for acquiring the remainder interest is that the purchaser agrees to make periodic payments to the client during the client's life. Other than this difference, many of the characteristics that apply to the individual reverse annuity mortgage apply here as well.

Home Equity Conversion Mortgage Demonstration

Another type of reverse annuity mortgage is one sponsored by the federal government. It allows a homeowner to borrow through a federally insured program known as the Home Equity Conversion Mortgage Demonstration.

How It Works

- Federal Housing Authority (FHA) approved lenders extend reverse annuity mortgages to owners of one-unit dwellings or condominiums.
- Clients must be 62 or over and own the home free and clear or have only minor liens.
- The client's risk is minimized because loans are insured by HUD against lender default. HUD will make payment if the bank does not.
- The loans are secured by a mortgage.
- Loan repayments cannot exceed the proceeds from the sale of the home, even if the amount of the principal and interest exceeds the amount of the sale.

Reverse Term Mortgage

Do not confuse a reverse term mortgage with a reverse *annuity* mortgage; the reverse term mortgage has no annuity element to the contract. Under a reverse term mortgage a client who owns his or her home is paid monthly installments in the form of a loan that is paid back when the "term" of the mortgage is over. The amount of the monthly installments depends on the amount of equity the client has in the home, the loan interest rate, and the term of the mortgage. Reverse term mortgages can range from a line of credit that lets the client decide the timing and amount of advances to monthly advances for a fixed term. Beware that at the end of a fixed term the house is usually sold to satisfy the debt. Therefore a planner who recommends that his or her client take a reverse term mortgage for a specified term should plan accordingly. Space in a long-term care facility or nursing home can be reserved to start at the end of the specified term.

One may ask why this arrangement is better than a straight home equity loan. The answer is that clients do not have to start payments immediately but can wait until the end of the term. The upside is that this frees up cash for retirement. The downside is that the interest deduction is delayed until it is paid, despite the fact that interest accrues during the whole period.

Special-Purpose Loans

A special-purpose loan does not have to be repaid until after the retiree dies, moves, or sells the home. These loans are available for limited purposes such as home repairs or property taxes. They typically are made by local government agencies to help low-income retirees remain in their homes. Most of your clients, however, will not be eligible for this type of loan because their incomes will exceed minimum levels.

YOUR FINANCIAL SERVICES PRACTICE:
QUESTIONS TO ASK WHEN A RAM OR RAM LOOK-ALIKE IS USED

When a RAM or RAM look-alike is used, the following questions should be considered:

- Does the monthly payment correspond favorably to the size of the home's equity, the client's life expectancy, and a fair rate of return?
- Is it truly an annuity?
- Is it available in your area?
- Does the financial institution require the client to get permission to make renovations?
- Does the financial institution require the client to maintain the property according to contractual specifications?
- Will the financial institution make periodic inspections?
- Are there closing costs involved?
- Is the client planning on moving soon?

Sale-Leaseback

Another means of unlocking the equity tied up in your client's home while allowing the client to remain in the residence is a sale-leaseback arrangement. Under a typical sale-leaseback arrangement, your client sells his or her house to an investor and then rents it back from the investor under a lifetime lease. Your client can thus garner extra retirement resources, make use of the $125,000 exclusion, and still remain in his or her home. In addition, the house is removed from the client's estate. The sale-leaseback agreement can specify future rents or can provide for how changes in the rental rate will be determined (for example, a periodic market value appraisal by a neutral third party).

The most desirable type of a sale-leaseback involves younger family members buying the client's home for investment purposes. The family relationship between the buyer and seller often makes the arrangement run more smoothly. Be cautious, however, because the IRS is sure to audit this type of intrafamily transaction and will expect that all facets of the transaction be conducted in an arm's-length manner. Regardless of who the buyer is, however, the responsibility of the new owner for paying property taxes, special assessments, insurance, and major maintenance and repairs should be clearly spelled out in the lease agreement.

Example: Jake and Peggy sell their house to their son for $100,000. They receive a down payment of $20,000 and take mortgage payments for 15 years from their son. Jake and Peggy are no longer subject to property taxes and major maintenance costs, their cash flow has improved, and they still have the security of living in "their" home. In the meantime, their son has acquired investment property and receives rental payments. Perhaps more important, however, the home will be kept in the family.

CONCLUDING REMARKS

We end this chapter where we began it, with a caveat about working within your client's emotional framework to help him or her make the best choices. Since home equity is often a major component of a retiree's wealth, planners often aspire to take their clients out of the position of being house rich and cash poor. The client's emotional and other nonfinancial needs must be factored in. Consider everything from caregiving responsibilities to housing needs and work with the client towards the best solution.

Formula for Determining Break-Even Life Expectancy

The formula for determining the break-even life expectancy is

$$(1) \quad N = 65 - \frac{\ln\{1 - [1 - 1/(f \times Ne)] \times [1 - (1 + i)^{\wedge} (Ne/12)]\}}{\ln(1 + i)}$$

where N = life expectancy where break even occurs
  i = real (inflation-adjusted) discount rate
  Ne = number of months before normal retirement age at which early retirement benefits begin to be paid
  $\wedge$ = exponential operator
  In = natural logarithm operator
  f = reduction factor that depends on the retirement classification of the person and is equal to

  — 0.0055556 for retiring worker
  — 0.0069444 for spouse
  — 0.00475 for surviving spouse aged 60 or over
  — 0.285/Ne for disabled surviving spouse between ages 50 and 60

This formula is derived by equating the present value of the reduced early retirement benefits with the present value of the difference between the reduced benefits and the full benefits that would otherwise be paid after normal retirement age (age 65) and solving for the number of years after normal retirement age.

The present value of the reduced early benefits (PVRED) is calculated using the formula for the present value of an annuity due with level monthly payments that are incremented by an inflation factor every 12 months. It is assumed that payments always start in January, so there are always 12 payments before the first inflation increment. (Changing the assumption that payments start in January to some other month makes almost no difference in the calculated break-even life expectancy values, but it does add undue complexity to the break-even formula.)

In order to use the present value of an annuity-due formula with monthly payments that are incremented by inflation only yearly, the level monthly payments must be converted to a yearly payment equivalent (PVLP). This is accomplished by applying the present value of an annuity-due formula to the 12 level payments, as follows:

417

(2) PVLP = $[1 - (1 + r/12)^{-12}] \times (1 + r/12)/(r/12)$

where r = the nominal annual discount rate

Now PVLP may be used as one yearly payment equivalent in the present-value calculation of the early benefits. The discount factor in the calculation for early benefits is the real rate of return, *i*, defined as

(3) $i = (r - I)/(1 + I)$

The logic behind this formula is straightforward. The yearly equivalent payment, PVLP, grows each year at the assumed inflation rate, *I*, because social security benefits are indexed for inflation once a year in January. Therefore the yearly PVLP in the second year is PVLP x $(1 + I)$. In the present-value formula this value is discounted at the nominal rate of return, *r*. Therefore the present value of this second-year amount is PVLP x $(1 + I)/(1 + r)$. Applying formula (3), this value becomes PVLP x $1/(1 + i)$. Discounting a stream of payments that grows at *I* per year with a discount rate of *r* is equivalent to discounting a level stream of payments with *i*. Therefore the present value of the reduced early benefits (PVREB) is computed using the present value of an annuity-due formula, as follows:

(4) PVREB = RBA x PVLP x $[1 - (1 + i)^{(-Ne/12)}] \times (1 + i)/i$

where RBA   = reduced benefit amount
      Ne   = number of months before age 65 that early benefits begin

The present value of the difference between the RBA and the PIA after normal retirement age is determined in a similar manner. First, the present value of the difference is computed as of age 65 using the present value of an annuity-due formula in the same manner as when calculating the present value of the reduced early benefits. Next, this value is discounted at the real rate of return back to the age when early benefits begin. The formula for the present value of the difference (PVD) is

(5) PVD = (PIA − RBA) x $[(1 + i)^{(-Ne/12)}] \times$ PVLP x $[1 - (1 + i)^{-B}] \times$
       $(1 + i)/i$

where B   = break-even number of years after age 65

When PVD and PVREB are equated, the terms $(1 + i)/i$ and PVLP cancel each other on each side of the equation, leaving

(6) RBA x $[1 - (1 + i)^{\wedge} (-Ne/12)]$ = (PIA − RBA) x $[(1 + i)^{\wedge} (-Ne/12)]$ x
$$[1 - (1 + i)^{\wedge} -B]$$

Dividing each side by $[(1 + i)^{\wedge} (-Ne/12)]$ gives us

(7) RBA x $[-1 + (1 + i)^{\wedge} (Ne/12)]$ = (PIA − RBA) x $[1 - (1 + i)^{\wedge} -B]$

RBA is itself a function of PIA, determined as follows for either retiring workers or surviving spouses:

(8) RBA = (1 − f x Ne) x PIA

where f   = benefit reduction factor and is equal to 0.555556 percent
              for the retiring worker and 0.475 percent for the surviving spouse.

Therefore, in these cases, equation (8) is substituted in equation (7) to derive

(9) (1 − f x Ne) x PIA x $[-1 + (1 + i)^{\wedge} (Ne/12)]$ = PIA x f x Ne x $[1 - (1 + i)^{\wedge}$
$$-B]$$

In the case of a spouse of a surviving retired worker,

(10) RBA = (1 − f x Ne) x 0.5 x PIA

But since PIA on the right side of equation (9) must also be multiplied by 0.5 in the case of the spouse's benefit, the 0.5 factor cancels out of the formula. Consequently the break-even formula for spouses is exactly the same as that for retiring workers and surviving spouses.

Dividing both sides of equation (9) by PIA x f x Ne and rearranging terms leaves us with

(11) $\{1 - [1/(f \text{ x } Ne)]\}$ x $[1 - (1 + i)^{\wedge} (Ne/12)]$ = $1 - (1 + i)^{\wedge} -B$

Multiplying each side of the equation by −1 and adding 1 to each side results in the following formula:

(12) $1 - [1 - 1/(f \text{ x } Ne)]$ x $[1 - (1 + i)^{\wedge} (Ne/12)]$ = $(1 + i)^{\wedge} -B$

Taking natural logarithms of both sides of equation (12) gives us

(13) $\ln\{1 - [1/(f \text{ x } Ne)]$ x $[1 - (1 + i)^{\wedge} (Ne/12)]\}$ = $-B$ x $\ln(1 + i)$

Dividing through by $-\ln(1 + i)$ gives us B. The break-even number of years after age 65 is

$$(14) \quad B = \frac{-\ln\{1 - [1 - 1/(f \times Ne)] \times [1 - (1 + i)\,\hat{}\,(Ne/12)]\}}{\ln(1 + i)}$$

Finally, adding 65 to the formula for B, we derive the break-even life expectancy formula, as provided in equation (1).

Annuity Tables

TABLE V Ordinary Life Annuities One Life—Expected Return Multiples					
Age	Multiple	Age	Multiple	Age	Multiple
5	76.6	42	40.6	79	10.0
6	75.6	43	39.6	80	9.5
7	74.7	44	38.7	81	8.9
8	73.7	45	37.7	82	8.4
9	72.7	46	36.8	83	7.9
10	71.7	47	35.9	84	7.4
11	70.7	48	34.9	85	6.9
12	69.7	49	34.0	86	6.5
13	68.8	50	33.1	87	6.1
14	67.8	51	32.2	88	5.7
15	66.8	52	31.3	89	5.3
16	65.8	53	30.4	90	5.0
17	64.8	54	29.5	91	4.7
18	63.9	55	28.6	92	4.4
19	62.9	56	27.7	93	4.1
20	61.9	57	26.8	94	3.9
21	60.9	58	25.9	95	3.7
22	59.9	59	25.0	96	3.4
23	59.0	60	24.2	97	3.2
24	58.0	61	23.3	98	3.0
25	57.0	62	22.5	99	2.8
26	56.0	63	21.6	100	2.7
27	55.1	64	20.8	101	2.5
28	54.1	65	20.0	102	2.3
29	53.1	66	19.2	103	2.1
30	52.2	67	18.4	104	1.9
31	51.2	68	17.6	105	1.8
32	50.2	69	16.8	106	1.6
33	49.3	70	16.0	107	1.4
34	48.3	71	14.3	108	1.3
35	47.3	72	14.6	109	1.1
36	46.4	73	13.9	110	1.0
37	45.4	74	13.2	111	.9
38	44.4	75	12.5	112	.8
39	43.5	76	11.9	113	.7
40	42.5	77	11.2	114	.6
41	41.5	78	10.6	115	.5

Table VI — Ordinary Joint Life and Last Survivor Annuities — Two Lives — Expected Return Multiples

AGES	51	52	53	54	55	56	57	58	59	60	61	62	63	64	65	66
51	38.2	...	...	...	...	...	...	...	...	...	...	...	...	...	...	...
52	37.8	37.3	...	...	...	...	...	...	...	...	...	...	...	...	...	...
53	37.3	36.8	36.3	...	...	...	...	...	...	...	...	...	...	...	...	...
54	36.9	36.4	35.8	35.3	...	...	...	...	...	...	...	...	...	...	...	...
55	36.5	35.9	35.4	34.9	34.4	...	...	...	...	...	...	...	...	...	...	...
56	36.1	35.6	35.0	34.4	33.9	33.4	...	...	...	...	...	...	...	...	...	...
57	35.8	35.2	34.6	34.0	33.5	33.0	32.5	...	...	...	...	...	...	...	...	...
58	35.5	34.8	34.2	33.6	33.1	32.5	32.0	31.5	...	...	...	...	...	...	...	...
59	35.2	34.5	33.9	33.3	32.7	32.1	31.6	31.1	30.6	...	...	...	...	...	...	...
60	34.9	34.2	33.6	32.9	32.3	31.7	31.2	30.6	30.1	29.7	...	...	...	...	...	...
61	34.6	33.9	33.3	32.6	32.0	31.4	30.8	30.2	29.7	29.2	28.7	...	...	...	...	...
62	34.4	33.7	33.0	32.3	31.7	31.0	30.4	29.9	29.3	28.8	28.3	27.8	...	...	...	...
63	34.2	33.5	32.7	32.0	31.4	30.7	30.1	29.5	28.9	28.4	27.8	27.3	26.9	...	...	...
64	34.0	33.2	32.5	31.8	31.1	30.4	29.8	29.2	28.6	28.0	27.4	26.9	26.4	25.9	...	...
65	33.8	33.0	32.3	31.6	30.9	30.2	29.5	28.9	28.2	27.6	27.1	26.5	26.0	25.5	25.0	...
66	33.6	32.9	32.1	31.4	30.6	29.9	29.2	28.6	27.9	27.3	26.7	26.1	25.6	25.1	24.6	24.1
67	33.5	32.7	31.9	31.2	30.4	29.7	29.0	28.3	27.6	27.0	26.4	25.8	25.2	24.7	24.2	23.7
68	33.4	32.5	31.8	31.0	30.2	29.5	28.8	28.1	27.4	26.7	26.1	25.5	24.9	24.3	23.8	23.3
69	33.2	32.4	31.6	30.8	30.1	29.3	28.6	27.8	27.1	26.5	25.8	25.2	24.6	24.0	23.4	22.9
70	33.1	32.3	31.5	30.7	29.9	29.1	28.4	27.6	26.9	26.2	25.6	24.9	24.3	23.7	23.1	22.5
71	33.0	32.2	31.4	30.5	29.7	29.0	28.2	27.5	26.7	26.0	25.3	24.7	24.0	23.4	22.8	22.2
72	32.9	32.1	31.2	30.4	29.6	28.8	28.1	27.3	26.5	25.8	25.1	24.4	23.8	23.1	22.5	21.9
73	32.8	32.0	31.1	30.3	29.5	28.7	27.9	27.1	26.4	25.6	24.9	24.2	23.5	22.9	22.2	21.6
74	32.8	31.9	31.1	30.2	29.4	28.6	27.8	27.0	26.2	25.5	24.7	24.0	23.3	22.7	22.0	21.4
75	32.7	31.8	31.0	30.1	29.3	28.5	27.7	26.9	26.1	25.3	24.6	23.8	23.1	22.4	21.8	21.1
76	32.6	31.8	30.9	30.1	29.2	28.4	27.6	26.8	26.0	25.2	24.4	23.7	23.0	22.3	21.6	20.9
77	32.6	31.7	30.8	30.0	29.1	28.3	27.5	26.7	25.9	25.1	24.3	23.6	22.8	22.1	21.4	20.7
78	32.5	31.7	30.8	29.9	29.1	28.2	27.4	26.6	25.8	25.0	24.2	23.4	22.7	21.9	21.2	20.5
79	32.5	31.6	30.7	29.9	29.0	28.2	27.3	26.5	25.7	24.9	24.1	23.3	22.6	21.8	21.1	20.4
80	32.5	31.6	30.7	29.8	29.0	28.1	27.3	26.4	25.6	24.8	24.0	23.2	22.4	21.7	21.0	20.2
81	32.4	31.5	30.7	29.8	28.9	28.1	27.2	26.4	25.5	24.7	23.9	23.1	22.3	21.6	20.8	20.1
82	32.4	31.5	30.6	29.7	28.9	28.0	27.2	26.3	25.5	24.6	23.8	23.0	22.3	21.5	20.7	20.0
83	32.4	31.5	30.6	29.7	28.8	28.0	27.1	26.3	25.4	24.6	23.8	23.0	22.2	21.4	20.6	19.9
84	32.3	31.4	30.6	29.7	28.8	27.9	27.1	26.2	25.4	24.5	23.7	22.9	22.1	21.3	20.5	19.8
85	32.3	31.4	30.5	29.6	28.8	27.9	27.0	26.1	25.3	24.5	23.6	22.8	22.0	21.2	20.4	19.6
86	32.3	31.4	30.5	29.6	28.7	27.9	27.0	26.1	25.3	24.4	23.6	22.8	21.9	21.1	20.4	19.6
87	32.3	31.4	30.5	29.6	28.7	27.8	27.0	26.1	25.3	24.4	23.5	22.7	21.9	21.1	20.3	19.5
88	32.3	31.4	30.5	29.6	28.7	27.8	27.0	26.1	25.2	24.4	23.5	22.7	21.9	21.1	20.3	19.5
89	32.3	31.4	30.5	29.6	28.7	27.8	26.9	26.1	25.2	24.4	23.5	22.7	21.8	21.0	20.3	19.5
90	32.3	31.3	30.5	29.5	28.7	27.8	26.9	26.1	25.2	24.3	23.5	22.7	21.8	21.0	20.2	19.4

Table VI — Ordinary Joint Life and Last Survivor Annuities — Two Lives — Expected Return Multiples

AGES	67	68	69	70	71	72	73	74	75	76	77	78	79	80	81	82
67	23.2	...	...	...	...	...	...	...	...	...	...	...	...	...	...	...
68	22.8	22.3	...	...	...	...	...	...	...	...	...	...	...	...	...	...
69	22.4	21.9	21.5	...	...	...	...	...	...	...	...	...	...	...	...	...
70	22.0	21.5	21.1	20.6	...	...	...	...	...	...	...	...	...	...	...	...
71	21.7	21.2	20.7	20.2	19.8	...	...	...	...	...	...	...	...	...	...	...
72	21.3	20.8	20.3	19.8	19.4	18.9	...	...	...	...	...	...	...	...	...	...
73	21.0	20.5	20.0	19.4	19.0	18.5	18.1	...	...	...	...	...	...	...	...	...
74	20.8	20.2	19.6	19.1	18.6	18.2	17.7	17.3	...	...	...	...	...	...	...	...
75	20.5	19.9	19.3	18.8	18.3	17.8	16.9	16.9	16.5	...	...	...	...	...	...	...
76	20.3	19.7	19.1	18.5	18.0	17.5	17.0	16.5	16.1	15.7	...	...	...	...	...	...
77	20.1	19.4	18.8	18.3	17.7	17.2	16.7	16.2	15.8	15.4	15.0	...	...	...	...	...
78	19.9	19.2	18.6	18.0	17.5	16.9	16.4	15.9	15.4	15.0	14.6	14.2	...	...	...	...
79	19.7	19.0	18.4	17.8	17.2	16.7	16.1	15.6	15.1	14.7	14.3	13.9	13.5	...	...	...
80	19.5	18.9	18.2	17.6	17.0	16.4	15.9	15.4	14.9	14.4	14.0	13.5	13.2	12.8	...	...
81	19.4	18.7	18.1	17.4	16.8	16.2	15.7	15.1	14.6	14.1	13.7	13.2	12.8	12.5	12.1	...
82	19.3	18.6	17.9	17.3	16.6	16.0	15.5	14.9	14.4	13.9	13.4	13.0	12.5	12.2	11.8	11.5
83	19.2	18.5	17.8	17.1	16.5	15.9	15.3	14.7	14.2	13.7	13.2	12.7	12.3	11.9	11.5	11.1
84	19.1	18.4	17.7	17.0	16.3	15.7	15.1	14.5	14.0	13.5	13.0	12.5	12.0	11.6	11.2	10.9
85	19.0	18.3	17.6	16.9	16.2	15.6	15.0	14.4	13.8	13.3	12.8	12.3	11.8	11.4	11.0	10.6
86	18.9	18.2	17.5	16.8	16.1	15.5	14.8	14.2	13.7	13.1	12.6	12.1	11.6	11.2	10.8	10.4
87	18.8	18.1	17.4	16.7	16.0	15.4	14.7	14.1	13.5	13.0	12.4	11.9	11.4	11.0	10.6	10.1
88	18.8	18.0	17.3	16.6	15.9	15.3	14.6	14.0	13.4	12.8	12.3	11.8	11.3	10.8	10.4	10.0
89	18.7	18.0	17.2	16.5	15.8	15.2	14.5	13.9	13.3	12.7	12.2	11.6	11.1	10.7	10.2	9.8
90	18.7	17.9	17.2	16.5	15.8	15.1	14.5	13.8	13.2	12.6	12.1	11.5	11.0	10.5	10.1	9.6

AGES	83	84	85	86	87	88	89	90
83	10.8	...	...	...	...	...	...	...
84	10.5	10.2	...	...	...	...	...	...
85	10.2	9.9	9.6	...	...	...	...	...
86	10.0	9.7	9.3	9.1	...	...	...	...
87	9.8	9.4	9.1	8.8	8.5	...	...	...
88	9.6	9.2	8.9	8.6	8.3	8.0	...	...
89	9.4	9.0	8.7	8.3	8.1	7.8	7.5	...
90	9.2	8.8	8.5	8.2	7.9	7.6	7.3	7.1

Table VI — Annuities for Joint Life Only — Two Lives — Expected Return Multiples

AGES	51	52	53	54	55	56	57	58	59	60	61	62	63	64	65	66
51	26.1	...	...	...	...	...	...	...	...	...	...	...	...	...	...	...
52	25.7	25.3	...	...	...	...	...	...	...	...	...	...	...	...	...	...
53	25.2	24.8	24.4	...	...	...	...	...	...	...	...	...	...	...	...	...
54	24.7	24.4	24.0	23.6	...	...	...	...	...	...	...	...	...	...	...	...
55	24.2	23.9	23.5	23.2	22.7	...	...	...	...	...	...	...	...	...	...	...
56	23.7	23.4	23.1	22.7	22.3	21.9	...	...	...	...	...	...	...	...	...	...
57	23.2	22.9	22.6	22.2	21.9	21.5	21.1	...	...	...	...	...	...	...	...	...
58	22.6	22.4	22.1	21.7	21.4	21.1	20.7	20.3	...	...	...	...	...	...	...	...
59	22.1	21.8	21.5	21.2	20.9	20.6	20.3	19.9	19.5	...	...	...	...	...	...	...
60	21.5	21.2	21.0	20.7	20.4	20.1	19.8	19.5	19.1	18.7	...	...	...	...	...	...
61	20.9	20.6	20.4	20.2	19.9	19.6	19.3	19.0	18.7	18.3	17.9	...	...	...	...	...
62	20.2	20.0	19.8	19.6	19.4	19.1	18.8	18.5	18.2	17.9	17.5	17.1	...	...	...	...
63	19.6	19.4	19.2	19.0	18.8	18.6	18.3	18.0	17.7	17.4	17.1	16.8	16.4	...	...	...
64	19.0	18.8	18.6	18.5	18.3	18.0	17.8	17.5	17.3	17.0	16.7	16.3	16.0	15.6	...	...
65	18.3	18.2	18.0	17.9	17.7	17.5	17.3	17.0	16.8	16.5	16.2	15.9	15.6	15.3	14.9	...
66	17.7	17.6	17.4	17.3	17.1	16.9	16.7	16.5	16.3	16.0	15.8	15.5	15.2	14.9	14.5	14.2
67	17.1	16.9	16.8	16.7	16.5	16.3	16.2	16.0	15.8	15.5	15.3	15.0	14.7	14.5	14.1	13.8
68	16.4	16.3	16.2	16.1	15.9	15.8	.15.6	15.4	15.2	15.0	14.8	14.6	14.3	14.0	13.7	13.4
69	15.8	15.7	15.6	15.4	15.3	15.2	15.0	14.9	14.7	14.5	14.3	14.1	13.9	13.6	13.3	13.1
70	15.1	15.0	14.9	14.8	14.7	14.6	14.5	14.3	14.2	14.0	13.8	13.6	13.4	13.2	12.9	12.6
71	14.5	14.4	14.3	14.2	14.1	14.0	13.9	13.8	13.6	13.5	13.3	13.1	12.9	12.7	12.5	12.2
72	13.8	13.8	13.7	13.6	13.5	13.4	13.3	13.2	13.1	12.9	12.8	12.6	12.4	12.3	12.0	11.8
73	13.2	13.2	13.1	13.0	13.0	12.9	12.8	12.7	12.5	12.4	12.3	12.1	12.0	11.8	11.6	11.4
74	12.6	12.6	12.5	12.4	12.4	12.3	12.2	12.1	12.0	11.9	11.8	11.6	11.5	11.3	11.2	11.0
75	12.0	12.0	11.9	11.9	11.8	11.7	11.7	11.6	11.5	11.4	11.3	11.1	11.0	10.9	10.7	10.5
76	11.4	11.4	11.3	11.3	11.2	11.2	11.1	11.0	10.9	10.9	10.8	10.6	10.5	10.4	10.3	10.1
77	10.8	10.8	10.8	10.7	10.7	10.6	10.6	10.5	10.4	10.3	10.3	10.2	10.0	9.9	9.8	9.7
78	10.3	10.2	10.2	10.2	10.1	10.1	10.0	10.0	9.9	9.8	9.8	9.7	9.6	9.5	9.4	9.2
79	9.7	9.7	9.7	9.6	9.6	9.6	9.5	9.5	9.4	9.3	9.3	9.2	9.1	9.0	8.9	8.8
80	9.2	9.2	9.1	9.1	9.1	9.0	9.0	8.9	8.9	8.9	8.8	8.7	8.7	8.6	8.5	8.4
81	8.7	8.7	8.6	8.6	8.6	8.5	8.5	8.5	8.4	8.4	8.3	8.3	8.2	8.1	8.0	8.0
82	8.2	8.2	8.1	8.1	8.1	8.1	8.0	8.0	7.9	7.9	7.8	7.8	7.7	7.6	7.5
83	7.7	7.7	7.7	7.6	7.6	7.6	7.6	7.5	7.5	7.5	7.4	7.4	7.3	7.3	7.2	7.1
84	7.2	7.2	7.2	7.2	7.2	7.1	7.1	7.1	7.0	7.0	7.0	6.9	6.9	6.8	6.8	6.7
85	6.8	6.8	6.8	6.7	6.7	6.7	6.3	6.2	6.2	6.2	6.2	6.2	6.1	6.1	6.0	6.0
86	6.4	6.4	6.3	6.3	6.3	6.3	6.3	5.9	5.9	5.9	5.8	5.8	5.8	5.8	5.7	5.6
87	6.0	6.0	6.0	5.9	5.9	5.9	5.9	5.9	5.9	5.8	5.8	5.8	5.4	5.4	5.3	5.3
88	5.6	5.6	5.6	5.6	5.6	5.5	5.5	5.5	5.5	5.5	5.5	5.4	5.4	5.1	5.0	5.0
89	5.2	5.2	5.2	5.2	5.2	5.2	5.2	5.2	5.2	5.2	5.1	5.1	5.1	5.1	5.0	4.7
90	4.9	4.9	4.9	4.9	4.9	4.9	4.9	4.9	4.9	4.8	4.8	4.8	4.8	4.8	4.7	4.7

Table VI — Annuities for Joint Life Only — Two Lives — Expected Return Multiples

AGES	67	68	69	70	71	72	73	74	75	76	77	78	79	80	81	82
67	13.5	...	...	...	...	...	...	...	...	...	...	...	...	...	...	...
68	13.1	12.8	...	...	...	...	...	...	...	...	...	...	...	...	...	...
69	12.8	12.5	12.1	...	...	...	...	...	...	...	...	...	...	...	...	...
70	12.4	12.1	11.8	11.5	...	...	...	...	...	...	...	...	...	...	...	...
71	12.0	11.7	11.4	11.2	10.9	...	...	...	...	...	...	...	...	...	...	...
72	11.6	11.4	11.1	10.8	10.5	10.2	...	...	...	...	...	...	...	...	...	...
73	11.2	11.0	10.7	10.5	10.2	9.9	9.7	...	...	...	...	...	...	...	...	...
74	10.8	10.6	10.4	10.1	9.9	9.6	9.4	9.1	...	...	...	...	...	...	...	...
75	10.4	10.2	10.0	9.8	9.5	9.3	9.1	8.8	8.6	...	...	...	...	...	...	...
76	9.9	9.8	9.6	9.4	9.2	9.0	8.8	8.5	8.3	8.0	...	...	...	...	...	...
77	9.5	9.4	9.2	9.0	8.8	8.6	8.4	8.2	8.0	7.8	7.5	...	...	...	...	...
78	9.1	9.0	8.8	8.7	8.5	8.3	8.1	7.9	7.7	7.5	7.3	7.0	...	...	...	...
79	8.7	8.6	8.4	8.3	8.1	8.0	7.8	7.6	7.4	7.2	7.0	6.8	6.6	...	...	...
80	8.3	8.2	8.0	7.9	7.8	7.6	7.5	7.3	7.1	6.9	6.8	6.6	6.3	6.1	...	...
81	7.9	7.9	7.7	7.5	7.4	7.3	7.1	7.0	6.8	6.7	6.5	6.3	6.1	5.9	5.7	...
82	7.5	7.4	7.3	7.2	7.1	6.9	6.6	6.7	6.5	6.4	6.2	6.0	5.9	5.7	5.5	5.3
83	7.1	7.0	6.9	6.8	6.7	6.6	6.5	6.4	6.2	6.1	5.9	5.7	5.5	5.4	5.2	5.1
84	6.7	6.6	6.5	6.4	6.4	6.3	6.2	6.0	5.9	5.8	5.7	5.5	5.3	5.2	5.1	4.9
85	6.3	6.2	6.2	6.1	6.0	5.9	5.8	5.7	5.6	5.5	5.4	5.3	5.1	5.0	4.9	4.7
86	5.9	5.9	5.8	5.8	5.7	5.6	5.5	5.4	5.4	5.3	5.1	5.0	4.9	4.8	4.6	4.5
87	5.6	5.6	5.5	5.4	5.4	5.3	5.2	5.2	5.1	5.0	4.9	4.8	4.7	4.6	4.4	4.3
88	5.3	5.2	5.2	5.1	5.1	5.0	5.0	4.9	4.7	4.7	4.6	4.5	4.4	4.4	4.2	4.1
89	5.0	4.9	4.9	4.8	4.8	4.7	4.7	4.6	4.5	4.5	4.4	4.3	4.2	4.1	4.0	3.9
90	4.7	4.6	4.6	4.6	4.5	4.5	4.4	4.4	4.3	4.2	4.2	4.1	4.0	3.9	3.8	3.8

AGES	83	84	85	86	87	88	89	90
83	4.9	...	...	...	...	...	...	...
84	4.7	4.6	...	...	...	...	...	...
85	4.6	4.4	4.2	...	...	...	...	...
86	4.4	4.2	4.1	3.9	...	...	...	...
87	4.2	4.1	3.9	3.8	3.6	...	...	...
88	4.0	3.9	3.8	3.6	3.5	3.4	...	...
89	3.8	3.7	3.6	3.5	3.4	3.2	3.1	...
90	3.7	3.5	3.4	3.3	3.2	3.1	3.0	2.9

Sources for Further Information

COURSES

Planning for Retirement Needs (HS 326)
    The American College, Bryn Mawr, PA   19010
    Telephone: (610) 526-1000

Advanced Pension and Retirement Planning I, II, and III (GS 814, GS 843, and GS 844)
    The American College, Bryn Mawr, PA   19010
    Telephone: (610) 526-1000

Executive Compensation (GS 842)
    The American College, Bryn Mawr, PA   19010
    Telephone: (610) 526-1000

Pension Fundamentals (C1 and C2)
    American Society of Pension Actuaries, 2029 K Street, NW, Washington, DC   20006
    Telephone: (202) 659-3620

Retirement Plans (Courses 2 and 3)
    International Foundation of Employee Benefit Plans
    Brookfield, WI   53008
    Telephone: (414) 786-6700

LOOSE-LEAF SERVICES

Bureau of National Affairs Pension Reporter
    BNA, 1231 25th Street, NW, Washington, DC   20037

Pension and Profit-Sharing Plans
    Prentice-Hall, Englewood Cliffs, NJ   07632

Pension Plan Guide
    Commerce Clearing House, 4026 W. Peterson Avenue
    Chicago, IL   60646

Pension Coordinator
>Research Institute of America, 90 Fifth Avenue
>New York, NY 10011

BOOKS

>*Pension Planning,* 7th ed., Allen, Melone, Rosenbloom, and Van Derhei.
>Irwin, 1992

>*Qualified Retirement and Other Employee Benefit Plans,* Canan.
>West Publishing Co., 1994 (published annually)

>*Retirement Planning for a Business and Business Owner,* 3d ed., Tacchino.
>The American College, 1993

>*Retirement Savings Plans,* Littell, Cardamone, and Gruszecki.
>John Wiley & Sons, Inc., 1993

PERIODICALS

>*Benefits Quarterly*
>International Society of Certified Employee Benefits Specialists
>>Brookfield, WI 53008

>*Tax Facts*
>The National Underwriter Company, Cincinnati, OH 45202

>*Employee Benefits Plan Review*
>Charles D. Spencer & Associates, Chicago, IL 60606

Calculating a Substantially Equal Periodic Payment

As discussed in chapter 8, the retirement planner may be involved in helping the client calculate how much must be distributed in order to satisfy the substantially equal periodic payment exception. Under IRC Sec. 72(t)(2)(A)(iv) the 10 percent tax does not apply to distributions that are part of a series of substantially equal periodic payments (not less frequently than annually) made for the life (or life expectancy) of the employee or the joint lives (or joint life expectancies) of the employee and his or her designated beneficiary. This exception applies to distributions from IRAs, qualified plans, and 403(b) plans. However, the exception will only apply to distributions from qualified plans and 403(b) annuity plans if the participant has separated from service.

THREE METHODS OF CALCULATION

IRS Notice 89-25 describes three methods (described below) that can be used for determining the amount of the withdrawal. Note that as prescribed under the first method, an individual retiring from an employer-sponsored plan may receive the benefit in almost any form of annuity, including a life annuity, a joint life annuity, or life annuity with a period certain; the benefit can even be received simply in installment payments, as long as the period does not exceed the joint life expectancy of the participant and a chosen beneficiary. In the alternative, an individual may choose to roll (or transfer) a lump-sum distribution from a qualified plan or 403(b) annuity into an IRA account and have the benefit distributed under any of the three methods.

The retirement planner is most likely to get involved in helping to determine the calculation under the scenario in which the benefit is being paid out of an IRA. The three methods provide for a great deal of flexibility. However, if the IRS ever questions the calculation, the individual should be able to demonstrate how the calculation complies with one of the methods described below.

Life Expectancy (or Minimum Distribution) Method

The annual payment is determined using a method that would be acceptable for purposes of calculating the minimum distribution required under IRC Sec. 401(a)(9). For an IRA this will usually be calculated using the minimum distribution account plan rules (see chapter 10 for more details). The simplest way to make this calculation is to divide the account balance (as of the last day of the previous year) by the participant's life expectancy (or the life expectancy of the participant and his or her beneficiary). The tables provided in Table V and VI of Treas. Reg. Sec. 1.72-9 will provide the applicable life expectancies (see appendix 2).

> *Example:*   Terri has an IRA account balance of $150,000 as of December 31, 1993. She is aged 56 in the distribution year; her life expectancy is therefore 27.7 years. The required distribution using this method is $5,415.

The life expectancy method will generally result in the smallest distribution. In the above example, the distribution calculated would have been even smaller if a joint life expectancy had been used. Under this method, as time goes on the payments will get larger because life expectancy is shorter. To fully appreciate the flexibility of calculating the distribution under this method, see chapter 10 for a complete discussion of the minimum distribution calculations.

Amortization Method

This approach is the same as amortizing a loan over the life expectancy of the participant. The amount to be distributed annually is determined by amortizing the taxpayer's account balance over a number of years equal to the life expectancy of the account owner or the joint life and last survivor expectancy of the account owner and beneficiary; an interest rate is used that does not exceed a reasonable interest rate on the date payments commence. Note that the calculation takes into consideration that the first "payment" is made at the beginning of the period, not as it normally is, at the end of the period. The rate of interest used to make the calculation must be reasonable (see discussion below).

> *Example:*   Begin with the same facts as above. In this case life expectancy can be determined using any reasonable actuarial table and a reasonable interest rate. Assuming the same life expectancy as used above, 27.7 years, and an interest rate of 5 percent, the required distributions are a level $9,637 per year. If instead an interest rate of 8 percent is used, the required annual distributions are $12,606.

Annuitization Method

The amount to be distributed annually is determined by dividing the taxpayer's account balance by an annuity factor (the present value of an annuity of $1 per year beginning at the taxpayer's age attained in the first distribution year and continuing for the life of the taxpayer). This annuity factor is derived using a reasonable mortality table and an interest rate that does not exceed a reasonable interest rate on the date payments begin. The results under this method and under the amortization method will yield the same results if the same interest and mortality assumptions are used. Presumably the IRS recognizes both methods separately because practitioners or taxpayers may have different sources of information available to do the mathematics.

REASONABLE RATES OF INTEREST

IRS guidelines have indicated that several rates of interest are acceptable. Each of the following has been approved at various times. Note, however, that the rate of interest needs to be reasonable at the time the first distribution is made.

- 120 percent of the federal long-term monthly rate in effect on the date of the initial distribution
- federal long-term monthly rate averaged over the past 12 months
- a rate determined with reference to Sec. 2619.41 of the Pension Benefit Guaranty Corporation regulations, Appendix B
- five percent, 8 percent and 9 percent, as deemed reasonable by the IRS in various rulings

Other Considerations

When determining the proper amount to satisfy the substantially equal periodic payment requirements, also consider the following:

- Withdrawals may begin at any age and for any reason.
- Payments may be made monthly, quarterly, or annually.
- Once payments begin they must continue until the later of 5 years from the first installment or attainment of age 59 1/2 unless the participant becomes disabled or dies before such date.
- Once the required number of payments has been made, withdrawals may be modified or stopped.
- Withdrawals may be taken from one plan (even if the individual is a participant in more than one plan), and the various plans do not have to be aggregated when making the calculation (IRS Letter Ruling 9050030).

Exclusion Ratio Calculations

CONVENTIONAL J & S ANNUITY (SURVIVOR BENEFIT RATIO LESS THAN 100 PERCENT)

The normal form of benefit for married participants is a conventional joint and survivor annuity with a survivor benefit ratio of between 50 percent and 100 percent (and no refund or guarantee feature). If the survivor benefit ratio is less than 100 percent and the annuity provides no refund feature or guaranteed payments, the exclusion ratio may be computed using the following form:

CONVENTIONAL J&S ANNUITY EXCLUSION RATIO FORM

1. The participant's single life expectancy for age at retirement from Table V (just as if the contract were a single life annuity) _____

2. Annual amount payable while participant lives _____

3. Participant's expected benefit (step 1 x step 2) _____

4. Joint and survivor expectancy from Table VI for the participant's and survivor beneficiary's ages _____

5. Subtract single life expectancy from joint life expectancy (step 4 − step 1) _____

6. Annual amount payable to survivor after participant's death _____

7. Survivor beneficiary's expected benefit (step 6 x step 5) _____

8. Total expected benefit (step 3 + step 7) _____

9. Investment in contract _____

10. Exclusion ratio (step 9 ÷ step 8) (rounded to three decimal places) _____

Example: Maureen Wagner is aged 65; her husband, Mike, is aged 68. Maureen is scheduled to receive monthly payments of $3,000 from her pension plan in the form of a joint and 50 percent survivor annuity. She has made $110,376 of aftertax contributions to the plan. The exclusion amount is calculated as follows:

CONVENTIONAL J&S ANNUITY EXCLUSION RATIO FORM

1.	The participant's single life expectancy for age at retirement from Table V (just as if the contract were a single life annuity)	20.0 years
2.	Annual amount payable while participant lives	$36,000
3.	Participant's expected benefit (step 1 x step 2)	$720,000
4.	Joint and survivor expectancy from Table VI for the participant's and survivor beneficiary's ages	23.8 years
5.	Subtract single life expectancy from joint life expectancy (step 4 − step 1)	3.8 years
6.	Annual amount payable to survivor after participant's death	$18,000
7.	Survivor beneficiary's expected benefit (step 6 x step 5)	$68,400
8.	Total expected benefit (step 3 + step 7)	$788,400
9.	Investment in contract	$110,376
10.	Exclusion ratio (step 9 ÷ step 8) (rounded to three decimal places)	14%

Therefore 14 percent of each payment is excluded from income until the entire $110,376 basis is recovered. While Maureen lives, the amount excludible each month is $420 ($3,000 x 0.14). If Maureen dies before Mike, Mike will exclude $210 of each $1,500 payment he receives.

FIRST-DEATH REDUCTION J&S ANNUITY WITH SURVIVOR BENEFIT RATIO LESS THAN 100 PERCENT

Many plans now offer a joint and survivor option that pays the lower survivor benefit after the first death, regardless of which person dies first. (Conventional J&S annuities pay the lower survivor benefit only if the participant dies first; if the nonparticipant dies first, the participant continues to receive the full amount until death.) In these cases the exclusion ratio may be computed using the following form:

**FIRST-DEATH REDUCTION J&S ANNUITY
EXCLUSION RATIO FORM**

1. Joint and survivor life expectancy for participant's and beneficiary's ages
   (Table VI)   _____

2. Annual amount payable after first death   _____

3. Multiply step 1 x step 2   _____

4. Joint life (first death) expectancy
   (Table VI)   _____

5. Annual amount payable while both live   _____

6. Subtract step 2 from step 5   _____

7. Multiply step 4 x step 6   _____

8. Expected return (step 3 + step 7)   _____

9. Investment in contract   _____

10. Exclusion ratio (step 9 ÷ step 8)
    (rounded to three decimal places)   _____

Example: Assume the facts are the same as in the previous example, except that the annuity pays 50 percent of the $3,000 monthly payment to the survivor regardless of whether Maureen or Mike dies first. The exclusion amount is calculated as follows:

While both Maureen and Mike live, $492 of each $3,000 payment is deductible (or $52 more than with the conventional J&S annuity described in the previous example). After the first death, the survivor will exclude $246 of each $1,500 payment (or $26 more than with a conventional J&S annuity).

FIRST-DEATH REDUCTION J&S ANNUITY EXCLUSION RATIO FORM

1.	Joint and survivor life expectancy for participant's and beneficiary's ages (Table VI)	23.8 years
2.	Annual amount payable after first death	$18,000
3.	Multiply step 1 x step 2	$428,400
4.	Joint life (first death) expectancy (Table VI)	13.7 years
5.	Annual amount payable while both live	$36,000
6.	Subtract step 2 from step 5	$18,000
7.	Multiply step 4 x step 6	$246,600
8.	Expected return (step 3 + step 7)	$675,000
9.	Investment in contract	$110,376
10.	Exclusion ratio (step 9 ÷ step 8) (rounded to three decimal places)	16.4%

Planning Note: The exclusion ratio for a first-death reduction joint and less-than-100 percent survivor annuity will always be higher than the exclusion ratio for a conventional J&S annuity with equivalent annual payments and survivor benefit ratio. Consequently the tax deductions are accelerated and the aftertax payments to the participant and beneficiary are always higher until the entire investment is recovered, all else being equal, as compared with the conventional J&S annuity. In addition, a given benefit balance at retirement will always provide higher annual benefits under a first-death reduction J&S annuity than under a conventional J&S annuity. Therefore, in the common case where the income needs of the survivor, regardless of who dies first, are less than the income needs while both live, choosing a first-death reduction J&S annuity, if available, rather than a conventional J&S annuity from the plan will almost always be the better choice.

SINGLE OR JOINT AND SURVIVOR ANNUITY WITH REFUND FEATURE

Refund features or a guaranteed number of payments under an annuity contract complicate the calculation of the exclusion ratio considerably. To compute the exclusion ratio one must first compute an adjusted investment in the contract. The adjusted investment is equal to the investment in the contract less the value of the refund feature. In the case of single life annuities the value of the refund feature may be computed with reference to Table VII—Percent Value of Refund Feature from IRC Reg. Sec. 1.72-9. In the case of joint and survivor annuities the value of the refund feature must be computed using a complicated formula (IRC Reg. Sec. 1.72-7(c)). Given the complexity of these rules the IRS has issued a simplified safe harbor method for calculating the taxable portion of annuity distributions from qualified retirement plans (Notice 88-118, November 15, 1988) that may be used in lieu of the regular rules, if so elected.

Form 4972 and Instructions

Form **4972**	**Tax on Lump-Sum Distributions**	OMB No. 1545-0193
Department of the Treasury Internal Revenue Service	From Qualified Retirement Plans ► **Attach to Form 1040 or Form 1041.** ► **See separate instructions.**	19**94** Attachment Sequence No. **28**
Name of recipient of distribution		Identifying number

Part I   Complete this part to see if you qualify to use Form 4972

			Yes	No
1	Did you roll over any part of the distribution? If "Yes," do not use this form	**1**		
2	Was the retirement plan participant born before 1936? If "No," do not use this form	**2**		
3	Was this a lump-sum distribution from a qualified pension, profit-sharing, or stock bonus plan? (See **Distributions That Qualify for the 20% Capital Gain Election or for the 5- or 10-Year Tax Option** in the instructions.) If "No," do not use this form	**3**		
4	Was the participant in the plan for at least 5 years before the year of the distribution?	**4**		
5	Was this distribution paid to you as a beneficiary of a plan participant who died?	**5**		
	If you answered "No" to both questions 4 **and** 5, do not use this form.			
6	Was the plan participant:			
a	An employee who received the distribution because he or she quit, retired, was laid off, or was fired? . .	**6a**		
b	Self-employed or an owner-employee who became permanently and totally disabled before the distribution?	**6b**		
c	Age 59½ or older at the time of the distribution? *(Caution: If "No," you may owe an additional tax. Get Form 5329 and its instructions for details.)*	**6c**		
	If you answered "No" to question 5 and **all** parts of question 6, do not use this form.			
7a	Did you use Form 4972 after 1986 for a previous distribution from your own plan? If "Yes," do not use this form for a 1994 distribution from your own plan	**7a**		
b	If you are receiving this distribution as a beneficiary of a plan participant who died, did you use Form 4972 for a previous distribution received for that plan participant after 1986? If "Yes," you may not use the form for this distribution	**7b**		

If you qualify to use this form, you may choose to use either Part II or Part III; OR you may choose to use both Part II and Part III.

Part II   Complete this part to choose the 20% capital gain election (See instructions.)

8	Capital gain part from box 3 of Form 1099-R	**8**	
9	Multiply line 8 by 20% (.20)	**9**	
	If you also choose to use Part III, go on to line 10. Otherwise, enter the amount from line 9 on Form 1040, line 39, or Form 1041, Schedule G, line 1b, whichever applies.		

Part III   Complete this part to choose the 5- or 10-year tax option (See instructions.)

10	Ordinary income from Form 1099-R, box 2a minus box 3. If you did not complete Part II, enter the taxable amount from box 2a of Form 1099-R	**10**	
11	Death benefit exclusion	**11**	
12	Total taxable amount. Subtract line 11 from line 10	**12**	
13	Current actuarial value of annuity (from Form 1099-R, box 8)	**13**	
14	Adjusted total taxable amount. Add lines 12 and 13. If this amount is $70,000 or more, **skip** lines 15 through 18, and enter this amount on line 19	**14**	
15	Multiply line 14 by 50% (.50), but **do not** enter more than $10,000 **15**		
16	Subtract $20,000 from line 14. If the result is less than zero, enter -0- **16**		
17	Multiply line 16 by 20% (.20) **17**		
18	Minimum distribution allowance. Subtract line 17 from line 15	**18**	
19	Subtract line 18 from line 14	**19**	
20	Federal estate tax attributable to lump-sum distribution	**20**	
21	Subtract line 20 from line 19	**21**	
	If line 13 is blank, skip lines 22 through 24 and go to line 25.		
22	Divide line 13 by line 14 and enter the result as a decimal	**22**	.
23	Multiply line 18 by the decimal on line 22	**23**	
24	Subtract line 23 from line 13	**24**	

For Paperwork Reduction Act Notice, see separate instructions.   Cat. No. 13187U   Form **4972** (1994)

Form 4972 (1994)   Page **2**

| **Part III** | 5- or 10-year tax option—CONTINUED |

25	Multiply line 21 by 20% (.20)	**25**	
26	Tax on amount on line 25. Use the Tax Rate Schedule for the 5-Year Tax Option in the instructions	**26**	
27	Multiply line 26 by five (5). If line 13 is blank, skip lines 28 through 30, and enter this amount on line 31	**27**	
28	Multiply line 24 by 20% (.20) **28**		
29	Tax on amount on line 28. Use the Tax Rate Schedule for the 5-Year Tax Option in the instructions **29**		
30	Multiply line 29 by five (5)	**30**	
31	Subtract line 30 from line 27. (Multiple recipients, see page 4 of the instructions.) . . .	**31**	
32	Add line 9 and line 31	**32**	
33	Multiply line 21 by 10% (.10)	**33**	
34	Tax on amount on line 33. Use the Tax Rate Schedule for the 10-Year Tax Option in the instructions	**34**	
35	Multiply line 34 by ten (10). If line 13 is blank, skip lines 36 through 38, and enter this amount on line 39	**35**	
36	Multiply line 24 by 10% (.10) **36**		
37	Tax on amount on line 36. Use the Tax Rate Schedule for the 10-Year Tax Option in the instructions **37**		
38	Multiply line 37 by ten (10)	**38**	
39	Subtract line 38 from line 35. (Multiple recipients, see page 4 of the instructions.) . . .	**39**	
40	Add line 9 and line 39	**40**	
41	Tax on lump-sum distribution. Compare lines 32 and 40. Enter the **smaller** amount here. Also, enter this amount on Form 1040, line 39, or Form 1041, Schedule G, line 1b, whichever applies . . . . ▶	**41**	

Left margin labels: 5-year tax option (lines 25–32); 10-year tax option (lines 33–40)

*U.S. Government Printing Office: 1994 — 375-390

Printed on recycled paper

Department of the Treasury
Internal Revenue Service

Instructions for Form 4972

Tax on Lump-Sum Distributions

From Qualified Retirement Plans

Section references are to the Internal Revenue Code.

Paperwork Reduction Act Notice

We ask for the information on this form to carry out the Internal Revenue laws of the United States. You are required to give us the information. We need it to ensure that you are complying with these laws and to allow us to figure and collect the right amount of tax.

The time needed to complete this form will vary depending on individual circumstances. The estimated average time is:

Recordkeeping . . . . . 33 min.
Learning about the law or the form . . . . . 26 min.
Preparing the form . . 1 hr., 27 min.
Copying, assembling, and sending the form to the IRS . . . . . . 35 min.

If you have comments concerning the accuracy of these time estimates or suggestions for making this form simpler, we would be happy to hear from you. You can write to both the IRS and the Office of Management and Budget at the addresses listed in the instructions for the tax return with which this form is filed.

General Instructions

Purpose of Form

The 20% capital gain election and/or the 5- or 10-year tax option are special formulas used to figure a separate tax on a qualified lump-sum distribution **ONLY** for the year in which the distribution is received.

You pay the tax only once. You do not pay the tax over the next 5 or 10 years. Once you choose your option and figure the tax, it is then added to the regular tax figured on your other income. The use of either option may result in a **smaller** tax than you would pay by including the taxable amount of the distribution as ordinary income in figuring your regular tax.

Related Publications

Pub. 575, Pension and Annuity Income (Including Simplified General Rule)
Pub. 721, Tax Guide to U.S. Civil Service Retirement Benefits
Pub. 939, Pension General Rule (Nonsimplified Method)

Who Can Use Form 4972

You can use Form 4972 if you received a qualified lump-sum distribution in 1994. To see if you qualify, you must first determine if your distribution is a qualified lump sum. See **What Is A Qualified Lump-Sum Distribution?** below. If you determine that your distribution is a qualified lump sum, you must **also** meet age and other requirements as outlined in **Distributions That Qualify for the 20% Capital Gain Election or for the 5- or 10-Year Tax Option** on this page.

What Is A Qualified Lump-Sum Distribution?

It is the distribution or payment in 1 tax year of a plan participant's entire balance from all of the employer's qualified plans of one kind (i.e., pension, profit-sharing, or stock bonus plans), in which the participant had funds. The participant's entire balance does not include deductible voluntary employee contributions or certain forfeited amounts. In addition, the distribution must have been made—

● Because of the participant's death, or

● After the participant reached age 59½, or

● Because the participant separated from service, or

● After the participant, if a self-employed individual, became permanently and totally disabled.

Distributions to Alternate Payees.— If you are the spouse or former spouse of a plan participant who was born before 1936 and you received a qualified lump-sum distribution as an

alternate payee under a qualified domestic relations order, you can use Form 4972 to figure the tax on that income.

If the distribution is a qualified distribution, you can use Form 4972 to make the 20% capital gain election and choose either the 5- or 10-year tax option to figure your tax on the distribution. See **How To Report the Distribution** on page 2.

Distributions That Qualify for the 20% Capital Gain Election or for the 5- or 10-Year Tax Option

The lump-sum distribution is qualified for the special tax option(s) **only if all** of the following conditions are met:

1. No part of the distribution was rolled over,

2. The plan participant was born before 1936, and

3. No earlier election to use either the 5- or 10-year tax option was made after 1986 for the same plan participant.

Caution: *If you received a distribution before the age of 59½, you* **may** *have to pay an additional tax. Get* **Form 5329,** *Additional Taxes Attributable to Qualified Retirement Plans (Including IRAs), Annuities, and Modified Endowment Contracts.*

Distributions That Do Not Qualify for the 20% Capital Gain Election or for the 5- or 10-Year Tax Option

The following distributions are not qualified lump-sum distributions and **do not** qualify for the 20% capital gain election or the 5- or 10-year tax option:

1. Distributions received if the plan participant was born after 1935.

2. U.S. Retirement Bonds distributed with the lump sum.

3. Any distribution made before the participant had been in the plan for 5 tax years before the tax year of the distribution, unless it was paid because the participant died.

Cat. No. 13188F

4. The current actuarial value of any annuity contract included in the lump sum (the payer's statement should show this amount, which you use only to figure tax on the ordinary income part of the distribution).

5. Any distribution to a 5% owner that is subject to penalties under section 72(m)(5)(A).

6. A distribution from an IRA.

7. A distribution from a tax-sheltered annuity (section 403(b) plan).

8. Redemption proceeds of bonds rolled over tax free to a qualified pension plan, etc., from a qualified bond purchase plan.

9. A distribution from a qualified pension or annuity plan if any portion of the distribution is rolled over tax free to another qualified pension or annuity plan or IRA.

10. A distribution from a qualified pension or annuity plan when the participant or his or her surviving spouse received an eligible rollover distribution from the same plan (or another plan of the employer required to be aggregated for the lump-sum distribution rules), and the proceeds of the previous distribution were rolled over tax free to an eligible retirement plan (including an IRA).

11. A corrective distribution of excess deferrals, excess contributions, or excess aggregate contributions.

12. A lump-sum credit or payment from the Federal Civil Service Retirement System (or the Federal Employees Retirement System).

How To Report the Distribution

If you qualify to use Form 4972, attach it to Form 1040 (individuals) or Form 1041 (estates or trusts). The payer should have given you a **Form 1099-R,** Distributions From Pensions, Annuities, Retirement or Profit-Sharing Plans, IRAs, Insurance Contracts, etc., or other statement that shows the separate amounts to use in completing the form. The following choices are available to you:

20% Capital Gain Election.—If there is an amount shown in Form 1099-R, box 3, you can use Part II of Form 4972. You are electing to apply a 20% tax rate to the capital gain portion. See **Capital Gain Election** on this page.

5- or 10-Year Tax Option.—You can use Part III to choose the 5- or 10-year tax option to figure your tax on the lump-sum distribution. You can choose either option whether or not you make the 20% capital gain election described earlier.

Page 2

Where To Report.—Depending on which parts of Form 4972 you choose to use, report amounts from your Form 1099-R either directly on your tax return (Form 1040 or Form 1041) or on Form 4972.

● If you choose **not** to use **any** part of Form 4972, report the entire amount from Form 1099-R, box 1 (Gross distribution), on Form 1040, line 16a and the taxable amount on line 16b (or on Form 1041, line 8). If your pension or annuity is fully taxable, enter the amount from Form 1099-R, box 2a (Taxable amount), on Form 1040, line 16b; **do not** make an entry on line 16a.

● If you choose **not** to use Part III of Form 4972, but you do use Part II, report only the ordinary income part of the distribution on Form 1040, lines 16a and 16b (or on Form 1041, line 8). The ordinary income part of the distribution is the amount shown in Form 1099-R, box 2a, minus the amount shown in box 3 of that form.

● If you choose to use Part III of Form 4972, do not include any part of the distribution on Form 1040, lines 16a and 16b (or on Form 1041, line 8).

The entries in other boxes on Form 1099-R may also apply in completing Form 4972:

● Box 6, Net unrealized appreciation (NUA). See **Net Unrealized Appreciation (NUA)** on this page for details on how to treat this amount.

● Box 8, Other, current actuarial value of an annuity.

If applicable, get the amount of Federal estate tax paid attributable to the taxable part of the lump-sum distribution from the administrator of the deceased's estate.

For more details, see Pub. 575.

How Often You Can Choose

After 1986, you may choose to use Form 4972 only once for each plan participant. If you receive more than one lump-sum distribution for the same plan participant in 1 tax year, you must treat all those distributions in the same way. Combine them on a single Form 4972.

If you make an election as a beneficiary of a deceased participant, it does not affect any election you can make for qualified lump-sum distributions from your own plan. You can also make an election as the beneficiary of more than one qualifying person.

Example. Your mother and father died and each was born before 1936. Each had a qualified plan of which you are the beneficiary. You also received a

qualified lump-sum distribution from your own plan and you were born before 1936. You may make an election for each of the distributions; one for yourself, one as your mother's beneficiary, and one as your father's. It does not matter if the distributions all occur in the same year or in different years. File a separate Form 4972 for each participant's distribution.

Note: *Even though you made an election on Form 4972 or Form 5544 for distributions received before 1987 while you were under age 59½, you may still be able to make an election for distributions received after 1986.*

When You Can Choose

You can file Form 4972 with either an original or an amended return. Generally, you have 3 years from the later of the due date of your tax return or the date you filed your return to choose to use any part of Form 4972.

Capital Gain Election

If your distribution includes capital gain, you can either **(a)** make the 20% capital gain election in Part II of Form 4972, or **(b)** treat the capital gain as ordinary income.

Only the taxable amount of distributions resulting from pre-1974 participation qualifies for capital gain treatment. The capital gain amount should be shown in Form 1099-R, box 3. If there is an amount from Form 1099-R, box 6 (net unrealized appreciation), part of it may also qualify for capital gain treatment. Use the NUA Worksheet on page 3 to figure the capital gain part of NUA if you make the election to include NUA in your taxable income.

You may elect to report the remaining balance of the distribution as ordinary income on Form 1040, line 16b (or Form 1041, line 8), or you may elect to figure the tax using the 5- or 10-year tax option. The remaining balance is the difference between Form 1099-R, box 3, and Form 1099-R, box 2a.

Net Unrealized Appreciation (NUA).—Normally, the net unrealized appreciation (NUA) in employer securities received as part of a lump-sum distribution is not taxable until the securities are sold. However, you can elect to include NUA in taxable income in the year received.

The total amount to report as NUA should be shown in Form 1099-R, box 6. Part of the amount in box 6 will qualify for capital gain treatment if there is an amount in Form 1099-R, box 3, and you elect to include the NUA in current income.

To figure the total amount subject to capital gain treatment including the NUA, complete the NUA Worksheet on this page.

Specific Instructions

Name of Recipient of Distribution and Identifying Number.—At the top of Form 4972, fill in the name and identifying number of the recipient of the distribution.

If you received more than one qualified distribution in 1994 for the same plan participant, add them and figure the tax on the total amount. If you received qualified distributions in 1994 for more than one participant, file a separate Form 4972 for the distributions of each participant.

If you and your spouse are filing a joint return and each has received a lump-sum distribution, complete and file a separate Form 4972 for each spouse's election, and combine the tax on Form 1040, line 39.

If you are filing for a trust that shared the distribution only with other trusts, figure the tax on the total lump sum first. The trusts then share the tax in the same proportion that they shared the distribution.

If the distribution is made to more than one beneficiary, follow the instructions under **Multiple Recipients of a Lump-Sum Distribution** on page 4.

Part II

See **Capital Gain Election** on page 2 before completing Part II.

Line 8.—Leave this line blank if your distribution does not include a capital gain amount, **or** you do not make the 20% capital gain election. Go to Part III.

To make the 20% capital gain election but **not take a death benefit exclusion** (see instructions for line 11), enter on line 8 the entire capital gain amount from Form 1099-R, box 3. However, if you elect to include NUA in your taxable income, use the NUA Worksheet on this page to figure the amount to enter.

To make the 20% capital gain election when you **are taking a death benefit exclusion,** use the Death Benefit Worksheet below to figure the amount to enter on line 8.

The remaining allowable death benefit exclusion should be entered on line 11, if you choose the 5- or 10-year tax option.

If any Federal estate tax was paid on the lump-sum distribution, you must decrease the capital gain amount by the amount of estate tax applicable to it. To figure the amount, multiply the total Federal estate tax paid on the lump-sum distribution by the decimal from line C of the Death Benefit Worksheet. The result is the portion of the Federal estate tax applicable to the capital gain amount. Then use that result to reduce the amount in Form 1099-R, box 3, if you don't take the death benefit exclusion, or reduce line F of the Death Benefit Worksheet if you do. Enter the remaining capital gain on line 8. If you elected to include NUA in taxable income, subtract the portion of Federal estate tax applicable to the capital gain amount from the amount on line G of the NUA Worksheet. Enter the result on line 8. Enter the remainder of the Federal estate tax on line 20.

Note: *If you take the death benefit exclusion **and** Federal estate tax was paid on the capital gain amount, the capital gain amount must be reduced by both the above procedures to figure the correct entry for line 8.*

Part III

Line 10.—If the payer of the distribution left box 2a (taxable amount) of Form 1099-R blank, you must first figure the taxable amount. For details on how to do this, see Pub. 575.

If you **made the 20% capital gain election,** enter only the ordinary income from Form 1099-R on this line. To figure this amount, subtract Form 1099-R, box 3, from Form 1099-R, box 2a. Enter the result on line 10. Add to that result the amount from line F of the NUA Worksheet if you included NUA capital gain in the 20% capital gain election.

If you **did not make the 20% capital gain election** and did not elect to include NUA in taxable income, enter the amount from Form 1099-R, box 2a. If you did not make the 20% capital gain election but did elect to include NUA in your taxable income, add the amount from Form 1099-R, box 2a, to the amount from Form 1099-R, box 6. Enter the total on line 10. On the dotted line next to line 10, write "NUA" and the amount of NUA included.

NUA Worksheet (keep for your records)
Complete only if you make the capital gain election.

A. Enter the amount from Form 1099-R, box 3	**A.**	_____
B. Enter the amount from Form 1099-R, box 2a	**B.**	_____
C. Divide line A by line B and enter the result as a decimal	**C.**	_____
D. Enter the amount from Form 1099-R, box 6	**D.**	_____
E. Multiply line C by line D (NUA subject to capital gain treatment) .	**E.**	_____
F. Subtract line E from line D (NUA that is ordinary income)	**F.**	_____
G. Add lines A and E (total part of distribution that can receive capital gain treatment). Enter the total here and on Form 4972, line 8	**G.**	_____
On the dotted line next to line 8, write "NUA" and the amount from line E above.		

Death Benefit Worksheet (keep for your records)

A. Enter the capital gain amount from Form 1099-R, box 3. If you elected to include NUA in taxable income, enter the amount from line G of the NUA Worksheet	**A.**	_____
B. Enter the taxable amount from Form 1099-R, box 2a. If you elected to include NUA in taxable income, add the amount from Form 1099-R, box 6, to the amount from Form 1099-R, box 2a, and enter the total here	**B.**	_____
C. Divide line A by line B and enter the result as a decimal	**C.**	_____
D. Enter your share of the death benefit exclusion*.	**D.**	_____
E. Multiply line D by line C	**E.**	_____
F. Subtract line E from line A. Enter the result here and on Form 4972, line 8	**F.**	_____

*If there are multiple recipients of the distribution, the $5,000 maximum death benefit exclusion must be allocated among the recipients in the same proportion that they share the distribution.

Page 3

Note: *Community property laws do not apply in figuring tax on the amount you report on line 10.*

Line 11.—If you received the distribution because of the plan participant's death, you may be able to exclude up to $5,000 of the lump sum from your gross income. If there are multiple recipients of the distribution not all of whom are trusts, enter on line 11 the full remaining allowable death benefit exclusion (after the amount taken against the capital gain portion of the distribution by all recipients—see the instructions for line 8) without allocation among the recipients. (The exclusion is in effect allocated among the recipients through the computation described below under **Multiple Recipients of a Lump-Sum Distribution.**) This exclusion applies to the beneficiaries or estates of common-law employees, self-employed individuals, and shareholder-employees who owned more than 2% of the stock of an S corporation. Pub. 575 gives more information about the death benefit exclusion.

Enter the death benefit exclusion on line 11. But see the instructions for line 8 if you made a capital gain election.

Line 20.—A beneficiary who receives a lump-sum distribution because of a plan participant's death must reduce the taxable part of the distribution by any Federal estate tax paid on the lump-sum distribution. The reduction is made by entering on line 20 the Federal-estate tax attributable to the lump-sum distribution. Also see the instructions for line 8.

Line 22.—Decimals should be carried to five places and rounded to four places. Drop amounts 4 and under (.44454 becomes .4445). Round amounts 5 and over up to the next number (.44456 becomes .4446).

Lines 26 and 29.—Use the following tax rate schedule to complete lines 26 and 29.

Tax Rate Schedule for the 5-Year Tax Option Lines 26 and 29

If the amount on line 25 or 28 is: Over—	But not over—	Enter on line 26 or 29:	Of the amount over—
$-0-	$22,750	- - - - - 15%	$-0-
22,750	55,100	$3,412.50 + 28%	22,750
55,100	115,000	12,470.50 + 31%	55,100
115,000	250,000	31,039.50 + 36%	115,000
250,000	- - - - -	79,639.50 + 39.6%	250,000

Lines 34 and 37.—Use the following tax rate schedule to complete lines 34 and 37.

Tax Rate Schedule for the 10-Year Tax Option Lines 34 and 37

If the amount on line 33 or 36 is: Over—	But not over—	Enter on line 34 or 37:	Of the amount over—
$-0-	$1,190	- - - - - 11%	$-0-
1,190	2,270	$130.90 + 12%	1,190
2,270	4,530	260.50 + 14%	2,270
4,530	6,690	576.90 + 15%	4,530
6,690	9,170	900.90 + 16%	6,690
9,170	11,440	1,297.70 + 18%	9,170
11,440	13,710	1,706.30 + 20%	11,440
13,710	17,160	2,160.30 + 23%	13,710
17,160	22,880	2,953.80 + 26%	17,160
22,880	28,600	4,441.00 + 30%	22,880
28,600	34,320	6,157.00 + 34%	28,600
34,320	42,300	8,101.80 + 38%	34,320
42,300	57,190	11,134.20 + 42%	42,300
57,190	85,790	17,388.00 + 48%	57,190
85,790	- - - - -	31,116.00 + 50%	85,790

Multiple Recipients of a Lump-Sum Distribution.—If you shared a lump-sum distribution from a qualified retirement plan when not all recipients were trusts (a percentage will be shown in Form 1099-R, boxes 8 and/or 9), figure your tax on Form 4972 as follows:

Step 1.—Complete Form 4972, Parts I and II. If you make the 20% capital gain election in Part II and also elect to include NUA in taxable income, see **Net Unrealized Appreciation (NUA)** on page 2 to determine the amount of NUA that qualifies for capital gain treatment.

Step 2.—Use this step **only** if you **do not elect to include NUA** in your taxable income or if you do not have NUA. If you elect to include NUA in taxable income, skip Step 2 and go to Step 3. (Box numbers used below are all from Form 1099-R.)

a. If you do not make the capital gain election, divide the amount shown in box 2a by your percentage of distribution shown in box 9. Enter this amount on Form 4972, line 10.

b. If you make the capital gain election, subtract the amount in box 3 from the amount in box 2a. Divide the result by your percentage of distribution shown in box 9. Enter the result on Form 4972, line 10.

c. Divide the amount shown in box 8 by the percentage shown in box 8. Enter the result on Form 4972, line 13.

Step 3.—Use this step **only** if you **elect to include NUA** in your taxable income.

a. If you do not make the capital gain election, add the amount shown in box 2a to the amount shown in box 6. Divide the result by your percentage of distribution shown in box 9. Enter the result on Form 4972, line 10.

b. If you make the capital gain election, subtract the amount in box 3 from the amount in box 2a. Add to the result the amount from line F of your NUA Worksheet. Then divide the total by your percentage of distribution shown in box 9. Enter the result on Form 4972, line 10.

c. Divide the amount shown in box 8 by the percentage shown in box 8. Enter the result on Form 4972, line 13.

Step 4.—Complete Form 4972 through line 39, except for line 32.

Step 5.—Complete the following worksheet twice (once to figure the entry for line 32 and once for line 40):

A. Enter your percentage of distribution from Form 1099-R, box 9 . . . .

B. Enter the amount from Form 4972, line 31 or 39 . . . .

C. Multiply line A by the amount on line B . . . .

D. Enter the amount from Form 4972, line 9 . . . . . .

E. Add lines C and D. Enter the total here and on Form 4972, line 32 or 40. Also, write "MRD" on the dotted line next to the entry space

*U.S. Government Printing Office: 1994 — 375-391

Inside Versus Outside Annuity: Time-Value Analysis

Whether a person will be better off taking a lump-sum distribution and using the aftertax proceeds to generate retirement income rather than taking a periodic distribution from the plan is a classic problem in time-value analysis. This problem incorporates most of the separate issues associated with distribution planning. These issues are as follows:

- calculating the tax on the lump sum
- determining whether 10-year or 5-year averaging is the more favorable method
- determining whether the person should elect capital-gain treatment for pre-1974 benefit accruals
- assessing which annuity form of payout pattern meets financial needs
- computing exclusion ratios

The principal advantages of the lump-sum distribution are the favorable up-front tax treatment and flexibility with respect to how proceeds are invested and ultimately consumed. The principal disadvantage of the lump-sum distribution is the loss of tax deferral. Although a person may pay more total tax by not electing a lump sum, the extra tax-sheltered earnings on the plan balances when a person does not take a lump sum may more than offset the additional tax payments. In many cases, despite paying more total taxes, a person who takes periodic payments from the plan will receive higher aftertax payments than could be generated by investing the aftertax lump-sum proceeds outside the plan.

In some circumstances a lump-sum distribution may be preferable to an annuity form of payout from the plan because an annuity form of payout is simply not the desired form of benefit. For example, a person who is terminally ill may not want a life annuity form of payment because he or she is unlikely to fully enjoy the benefits. But even in these circumstances a period-certain annuity from the plan for a relatively short period or discretionary withdrawals over time as needed from an IRA rollover account may be economically better on an aftertax basis than the lump-sum distribution.

Whether taking a lump-sum distribution is a better economic choice than taking periodic distributions from the plan (or an IRA rollover account) can be determined by calculating how much money a person would need to invest outside the plan to recreate the desired aftertax payout stream that is available from the plan (or IRA rollover account). If the amount so calculated is less than the aftertax proceeds from a lump-sum distribution, the lump-sum distribution is the

443

better choice because the aftertax proceeds could be used to generate even higher aftertax benefits than the plan provides. Conversely, if the amount so calculated exceeds the aftertax proceeds from a lump-sum distribution, the lump-sum distribution would be a poor choice because the aftertax proceeds would be insufficient to generate a benefit stream equal to that projected from the plan.

Whether a person will be better off taking a lump-sum distribution and using the aftertax proceeds to generate retirement income rather than taking periodic distributions from the plan can be determined as follows:

Step 1: Compute the aftertax proceeds from a lump-sum distribution using either 10-year or 5-year averaging, as appropriate, and the capital-gain provision, if appropriate and applicable.

Step 2: Determine the before-tax periodic benefit that will be paid from the plan under the desired payout option. Generally the plan administrator will indicate what benefit is payable under any available option. If a desired option is not available from the plan, funds can often be rolled over to an IRA, where the proceeds can be used to acquire a commercial annuity with the features desired. Alternatively a person can invest IRA assets at a reasonable assumed investment rate of return and make discretionary withdrawals as desired—in effect manufacturing his or her own customized payout stream. In this case, however, one must construct what is virtually an amortization schedule to determine when the benefit balance will be used up.

Step 3: Compute the aftertax periodic benefit payments that will be paid from the plan. To compute this amount a tax rate must be specified. When selecting the tax rate the amount of the person's anticipated taxable income after retirement from sources other than retirement benefits, as well as the amount of the retirement distributions, should be taken into account. Also, if the plan includes any nontaxable amounts, such as aftertax employee contributions, one must compute the amount that is excludable from each payment. In general, the exclusion amount is calculated by the plan trustee. However, since a person in certain circumstances may now elect to use either the regular method or the new safe harbor method for computing exclusion amounts and does not have to use the same method as the plan administrator, one should determine which method is best. This itself involves a separate time-value analysis. As a general rule, however, the safe harbor method will provide the higher aftertax economic benefit in most cases.

Step 4: Determine the present value of the aftertax payment stream from the plan. This present value may be computed in one of at least two ways, depending on how the person would actually invest the aftertax proceeds from a lump-sum distribution. The simplest method is to discount each aftertax payment back to the date of the lump-sum distribution, using a reasonable aftertax rate of return. The aftertax rate of return is determined by multiplying the before-tax rate of return one assumes a person could earn on the type of investment assets in which a lump-sum distribution would be invested by the sum of (1 − tax rate). A person's total annual taxable income during retirement will generally be less in this case than when distributions are paid annually from the plan because tax has already been paid on the lump-sum distribution. Consequently the appropriate tax rate for discounting the payment stream outside the plan may differ from that used to determine the aftertax payments from the plan.

However, in many cases, a person electing to receive a lump sum may also use the aftertax proceeds to purchase a commercial annuity with the desired payment stream. Earnings on the commercial annuity will be tax deferred until payments are received. The tax on each payment is determined using the regular method for computing the exclusion amount. (The safe harbor method for computing exclusion amounts is available only for distributions from qualified plans.) In general, unless a person has exceptional investment opportunities that are not available through commercial annuities, or the desired payout pattern cannot be reproduced by a commercial annuity (that is, the desired payout stream is not essentially level), an annuity, as a tax-sheltered vehicle, will be more economical than fully taxable alternatives.

To estimate the amount required to purchase a commercial annuity that will provide the same aftertax benefits as the plan, a present value must be calculated using the tax rules for annuities. Such a calculation is more complicated than a regular present-value calculation. Appropriate formulas are presented below.

FORMULAS FOR CALCULATING THE AMOUNT NECESSARY TO PURCHASE COMMERCIAL ANNUITIES WITH AFTERTAX PAYMENTS EQUAL TO THOSE PROJECTED FROM THE PLAN

General Case

The general case applies whenever the selected annuity is one of the following types:

- single life annuity with no guarantee or refund feature
- joint and survivor annuity with 100 percent survivor benefit and no guarantee or refund feature
- fixed-period annuity with no life contingency
- fixed-payment annuity with no life contingency

The formula for estimating the amount required to purchase a commercial annuity outside the plan that will provide the same aftertax retirement income as the plan is as follows:

Formula (1)

$$\text{Required amount} = \frac{(\text{Pmt x AF})}{[1 - t \times (1 - \text{AF/LE})]}$$

where Pmt = the amount payable from the plan after taxes
      t = the assumed tax rate on retirement benefit payments
    LE = the appropriate life expectancy or payment term factor
    AF = annuity factor
        = $[1 - (1 + i)^{\wedge}(-\text{LE})]/i$

       i = before-tax periodic interest rate
       $\wedge$ = exponential operator

Example 1: Find the amount required to acquire a commercial J&S 100 annuity paying $1,000 per month (aftertax) for a person aged 65 with a beneficiary aged 62, assuming a 9 percent before-tax rate of return and a 28 percent tax rate.

$$
\begin{aligned}
\text{Pmt} &= \$1,000 \\
t &= 0.28 \\
\text{LE} &= 26.5 \text{ (from Table VI) x } 12 = 318 \\
i &= 0.09/12 = 0.0075 \\
\text{AF} &= [1 - (1.0075)^{\wedge}(-318)]/0.0075 \\
&= [1 - 0.092912163]/0.0075 \\
&= .907087837/0.0075 = 120.945045
\end{aligned}
$$

$$
\begin{aligned}
\text{Required amount} &= (1,000 \text{ x } 120.945045)/[1 - 0.28 \text{ x} \\
&\quad (1 - 120.945045/318)] \\
&= \underline{\$146,335}
\end{aligned}
$$

A net amount of $146,335 used to purchase a single premium annuity paying 9 percent interest would provide a before-tax benefit of about $1,209.93 per month. The expected benefit for computing the exclusion ratio would be $384,757.74 (318 x $1,209.93). The exclusion ratio would be 38 percent ($146,335/$384,758). Therefore $750.16 (62% x $1,209.93) of each payment would be taxable at 28 percent. The tax would be $210 (28% x $750.16), leaving $1,000 ($999.89 rounded up) as the aftertax payment, which is equal to the aftertax benefit from the plan.

Example 2: Find the amount required to acquire a commercial annuity paying $1,000 per month after taxes for 15 years with no life contingency, assuming a 10 percent before-tax rate of return and a 31 percent tax rate.

$$
\begin{aligned}
\text{Pmt} &= \$1{,}000 \\
t &= 0.31 \\
\text{LE} &= 15 \text{ years x } 12 = 180 \\
i &= 0.10/12 = 0.008333 \\
\text{AF} &= [1 - (1.008333)\char`^(-180)]/0.008333 \\
&= 93.05744094
\end{aligned}
$$

$$
\begin{aligned}
\text{Required amount} &= (\$1{,}000 \text{ x } 93.05744094)/[1 - 0.31 \text{ x} \\
& \quad (1 - 93.05744094/180)] \\
&= \underline{\$109{,}445}
\end{aligned}
$$

A net amount of $109,445 used to acquire a term-certain annuity paying 10 percent before taxes would provide a before-tax benefit of $1,176.10 for 180 months. The expected benefit for computing the exclusion ratio is $211,698.00 ($1,176.10 x 180). The exclusion ratio is 51.7 percent ($109,445/$211,698). Therefore the amount subject to tax is $568.06 (48.3% x $1,176.10). The tax at 31 percent on this amount is $176.10, leaving $1,000 as the aftertax payment.

FORMULA FOR J&S ANNUITY WITH A SURVIVOR BENEFIT RATIO OF LESS THAN 100 PERCENT

Formula (1) may be used to estimate the amount required to acquire a J&S annuity with a survivor benefit ratio of less than 100 percent (with no guarantee or refund feature) if certain terms are redefined, as follows:

$$
\begin{aligned}
\text{AF} &= \text{R x AFL} + (1 - \text{R}) \text{ x AFF} \\
\text{R} &= \text{the survivor benefit ratio} \\
\text{AFL} &= \text{annuity factor for period until the last to die} \\
&= [1 - (1 + i)\char`^(-\text{LEL})]/i \\
\text{LEL} &= \text{joint and survivor life expectancy factor from Table VI} \\
& \quad \text{for annuitant's and beneficiary's ages at annuity} \\
& \quad \text{starting date} \\
\text{AFF} &= \text{annuity for period until the first to die} \\
&= [1 - (1 + i)\char`^(-\text{LEF})]/i \\
\text{LEF} &= \text{joint life (first death) expectancy factor from Table} \\
& \quad \text{VIA for annuitant's and beneficiary's ages at annuity} \\
& \quad \text{starting date} \\
\text{LE} &= \text{R x LEL} + (1 - \text{R}) \text{ x LEF}
\end{aligned}
$$

Example 3: Assume the same facts as in example 1 except that the desired annuity is a J&S 50 rather than a J&S 100 annuity.

$$
\begin{aligned}
\text{R} &= 0.50 \\
\text{Pmt} &= \$1{,}000 \text{ (until annuitant dies)}
\end{aligned}
$$

$$t = 0.28$$

$$\text{LEL} = 26.5 \times 12 = 318 \text{ (from Table VI)}$$

$$\text{LEF} = 15.9 \times 12 = 190.80 \text{ (from Table VIA)}$$

$$\text{LE} = (0.50 \times 318) + (0.50 \times 190.8) = 254.4$$

$$i = 0.09/12 = 0.0075$$

$$\text{AFL} = [1 - (1.0075)^{\wedge}(-318)]/0.0075 = 120.945045$$

$$\text{AFF} = [1 - (1.0075)^{\wedge}(-190.8)]/0.0075 = 101.2867098$$

$$\text{AF} = (0.5 \times 120.945045) + (0.5 \times 101.2867098) = 111.1158774$$

Required amount = $1,000 x 111.1158774)/[1 − 0.28 x
(1 − 111.1158774/254.4)]
= <u>$131,920</u>

The Complete Analysis

The four-step procedure described above can be used to determine whether your client will be better off taking distributions from the plan or taking a lump-sum distribution and using the aftertax proceeds to generate an income stream outside the plan. This process can best be described by example.

Example 4: Your client, aged 62, has a vested plan balance of $150,000 at retirement. His spouse is aged 58. No portion of the balance represents benefit accruals before 1974 qualifying for capital-gain treatment or aftertax amounts contributed by the client. The plan will pay $1,375.40 monthly if your client elects to receive from the plan a J&S two-thirds annuity with no guaranteed payments. The client's estimated tax rate on retirement distributions is 31 percent. The investment rate currently available on commercial annuities is 10 percent.

Step 1: Compute the aftertax lump-sum amount. Referring to table 9-3 we see that the tax on the lump-sum amount is $28,058 if 5-year averaging is used or $24,570 if 10-year averaging is used. Since using the 10-year method generates a lower tax, this is the method that should be used. This would leave your client with $125,430 of aftertax proceeds for investment outside the plan.

Step 2: The before-tax payments from the plan are $1,375.40 until your client dies and then 2/3 x $1,375.40, or $916.93, to the spouse after your client's death.

Step 3: Determine the aftertax periodic payout from the plan. At a tax rate of 31 percent, the aftertax payments are $949.03 (0.69 x $1,375.40) until your client dies and then $632.47 (0.69 x $916.63) to the spouse after your client's death.

Step 4: Determine the present value of the aftertax payment stream from the plan. To determine the amount necessary to acquire a commercial J&S annuity providing essentially the same aftertax benefit payments as those provided by the plan, use formula (1) with the modifications for a survivor benefit ratio less than 100 percent. The factors are

$$
\begin{aligned}
R &= 0.667 \\
Pmt &= \$949.03 \\
t &= 0.31 \\
LEL &= 29.9 \text{ (from Table VI) x } 12 = 358.8 \\
LEF &= 18.5 \text{ (from Table VIA) x } 12 = 222 \\
LE &= (0.667 \text{ x } 358.8) + (0.333 \text{ x } 222) = 313.2456 \\
i &= 0.10/12 = 0.008333 \\
AFL &= 113.8902817 \\
AFF &= 100.9863455 \\
AF &= 109.5932709
\end{aligned}
$$

$$
\begin{aligned}
\text{Required amount} &= (949.03 \text{ x } 109.5932709)/[1 - 0.31 \text{ x} \\
& \quad (1 - 109.5932709/313.2456)] \\
&= \underline{\$130,260}
\end{aligned}
$$

Since the estimated amount required to acquire the annuity outside the plan exceeds the aftertax proceeds available from a lump-sum distribution by over $4,830, your client clearly should take annuity payments from the plan. If he takes a lump-sum distribution, the aftertax proceeds will be insufficient to acquire a commercial J&S two-thirds annuity outside the plan that pays aftertax benefits equal to those he would receive from the plan.

Example 5: Your client, aged 64, is in poor health. The current balance in her plan is $250,000, of which no portion is attributable to pre-1974 participation or aftertax employee contributions. The client is single, but would like to leave as much of the benefit as possible to her son, after assuring that her own needs are satisfied until death. The before-tax investment rate of return is assumed to be 9 percent. The plan will pay monthly payments of $5,189.59 for 60 months, with no life contingency. With this level of payments the client's anticipated combined federal, state, and local tax rate on the payments will be 33 percent.

Step 1: Compute the aftertax lump-sum amount. Using the more favorable 10-year averaging, the aftertax proceeds would be about $199,230 ($250,000 − $50,770 tax).

Step 2: The before-tax payments from the plan are equal to $5,189.59 a month for 60 months, regardless of when the client dies.

Step 3: Determine the aftertax payment from the plan. At a tax rate of 33 percent, $3,477.03 is the aftertax amount.

Step 4: Determine the present value of the aftertax payment stream from the plan. The amount required to acquire a 60-month term-certain annuity is determined by using formula (1).

$$Pmt = \$3,477.03$$
$$t = 0.33$$
$$LE = 60$$
$$i = 0.09/12 = 0.0075$$
$$AF = [1 - (1.0075)^{\wedge}(-60)]/0.0075 = 48.17337352$$

$$Required\ amount = (\$3,477.03 \times 48.17337352)/[1 - 0.33 \times (1 - 48.17337352/60)]$$
$$= \underline{\$179,153.57}$$

In this case your client will be better off by more than $20,000 in present-value terms if she elects a lump-sum distribution and uses the aftertax proceeds to acquire a commercial annuity. With the $199,230 available after taxes from the lump-sum distribution, your client could acquire a 60-month term-certain annuity (assuming 9 percent before taxes) that pays about $4,136 a month before taxes ($199,230/ 48.17337352). The exclusion ratio on this annuity would be 80.3 percent ($199,230/(60 x $4,136). Therefore the amount subject to tax would be $814.79 ([1 − 0.803] x $4,136), the tax would be $268.88 (0.33 x $814.79), and the aftertax payments would be about $3,876 a month. This is about $390 more a month after taxes than would be paid from the plan.

accessory apartments • Self-contained living units installed in the surplus space of a single-family home.

account plan method of calculation • Under the minimum distribution rules, the account plan rules govern the calculation of the minimum distribution calculation for all account-type plans except when a commercial annuity is purchased.

active participant • An individual who is deemed to participate in an employer's retirement plan — but nonqualified plans are not counted. Active participant status affects the individual's ability to receive a deduction for contributions to an IRA.

activities of daily living • These are the criteria used to establish benefit eligibility under a long-term care contract — in other words, the telling signs of the need for nursing home care. They include eating, bathing, dressing, transferring from bed to chair, using the toilet, and maintaining continence.

adult day care • This is day care provided at centers specifically designed for the elderly who live at home but whose families are not available to stay at home for the day.

AIME • *See* average indexed monthly earnings.

AIR • *See* assumed investment rate.

ALE • *See* applicable life expectancies.

allocation formula • A profit-sharing plan formula that allows the employer to make discretionary contributions. Must contain a definitely determinable allocation formula. This formula determines how the contribution is allocated among the plan's participants.

amount of benefit • For minimum distribution calculations, the benefit amount of an IRA is the value of the benefit as of the last day of the year prior to the year for which the minimum distribution is being calculated.

annuity certain or term certain • An annuity payout over a specified period of time, for example 20 years.

annuity method of calculation • Under the minimum distribution rules, an annuity benefit payable from a defined-benefit plan or a commercial annuity purchased in any account-type plan must satisfy the annuity method of calculating the required minimum distribution.

applicable divisor • Under the minimum distribution rules, the applicable divisor is the number calculated under the MDIB rule, which is substituted for the ALE when the nonspousal beneficiary is more than 10 years younger than the participant.

applicable life expectancies • The minimum distribution calculation under the minimum distribution rules is based on the life expectancies of the participant and a chosen beneficiary. The ages used are generally based on the ages of those individuals as of the last day of the year for which the minimum distribution is calculated.

asset allocation • Process of setting the portfolio proportions for major asset categories.

assumed investment rate (AIR) • The rate of return that the investment portfolio must earn in a variable annuity in order for benefit payments to remain level.

average indexed monthly earnings (AIME) • An individual's wage history (capped at the taxable wage base and indexed for inflation) is averaged and the resulting average indexed monthly earnings are used to generate a person's primary insurance amount under social security.

basis • Basis is a complex term that refers to the amount of capital invested by the taxpayer plus any adjustments made under tax law. In theory, a taxpayer should pay taxes on gain only when property at an amount in excess of basis is sold. When it comes to the sale of a home, basis includes the purchase price (including adjustments from prior rollovers) and the cost of capital improvements made to the house. The cost of repairs and home maintenance is not included in basis.

beneficiary • Under the minimum distribution rules, applicable life expectancies are based on the lives of the participant and a beneficiary. The beneficiary is that individual chosen on the plan's election form to receive benefits as of the date of death (if death occurs prior to the required beginning date) or as of the required beginning date if the participant lives that long. Special rules apply if several beneficiaries have been elected or if a trust has been chosen as the beneficiary.

benefit carve-out plan • A way for an employer to provide retiree health care benefits. This plan is designed around the same benefit program that applies to active employees.

benefit period • Under the medicare system, a benefit period begins the first time a medicare recipient is hospitalized and ends only after the recipient has been out of the hospital or skilled-nursing facility for 60 consecutive days. There is no limit on the number of benefit periods a person may have during his or her lifetime, but medicare coverage is limited to 90 days in each benefit period.

benefit statement • A statement provided to plan participants notifying them of the dollar value of their benefits.

beta • A measure of the systematic risk of an asset or portfolio. Beta can be represented as either the mathematical ratio of the asset's covariance with the market divided by the variance of the market or as the slope of a regression line that relates the return of the asset to the return on the market.

bond default premium • The additional return received for the additional risk of investing in corporate bonds rather than government bonds of equal maturity.

bond maturity premium • The additional return received for the interest-rate risk incurred by investing in long-term government bonds rather than Treasury bills.

book-value purchase rights • Executive incentive plan, commonly used in closely held companies, in which the executive is offered the opportunity to purchase shares of stock, the price of which is determined by reference to book value.

"bottom-up" analysis • Investment approach concentrating on the individual company's characteristics, with less emphasis on economic/market and industry/sector factors.

break-even life expectancies • The point at which it is economically desirable to take full social security benefits at normal retirement age rather than reduced benefits at early retirement age.

capital asset pricing model (CAPM) • An extension of portfolio theory that contends that in an efficient market, investors should be compensated for incurring systematic risk, measured as beta, but not for incurring unsystematic risk since unsystematic risk can be eliminated through diversification.

capital-gains election • A special grandfather rule that applies to lump-sum distributions from qualified plans in the case of an individual born before 1936. The rule provides for a special 20 percent tax rate for the portion of the lump-sum distribution attributable to pre-1974 plan participation.

cash-out provision • Refers to a retirement plan provision that allows for the payment of a single-sum distribution upon termination of employment that occurs prior to attainment of normal retirement age, death, or disability.

COBRA • The Consolidated Omnibus Budget Reconciliation Act of 1985, which established health insurance continuation for employees changing jobs or retiring.

COLA • *See* cost of living adjustment.

contrarian investing • Investment approach in which the investor identifies a widely accepted view and then invests as if that view were incorrect.

conventional joint and survivor annuity • An annuity in which payments continue beyond the life of a participant to his or her chosen beneficiary, assuming that the beneficiary lives longer than the participant.

coordination plan • A way for an employer to provide retiree health care benefits. This plan factors in the amount the insurer would make after applying the deductible and coinsurance payments and then may reduce that amount so that the plan payments plus medicare payments are equal to total expenses.

cost of living adjustment (COLA) • Generally speaking, it refers to an increase in a payment stream typically based on the consumer price index (CPI). Under social security it refers to an increase in the CPI for the one-year period ending in the third quarter of the prior year. This is the amount by which social security benefits are typically increased to keep pace with inflation.

covariance • A measure of the degree to which random variables move in a systematic way relative to each other, either directly or inversely. In portfolio theory, reduction of risk is achieved more rapidly by combining assets that have small or even negative covariances with each other.

current assets future value factor • A factor that is determined by looking at the assumed rate of return on investments prior to retirement and the number of years until retirement.

decline in purchasing power (DIPP) • Assets that are not indexed for inflation will have a diminishing ability to buy goods and services over time. The DIPP fund is the amount saved to prevent this decline from happening.

defined-benefit pension plan • A category of qualified retirement plan that specifies a stated benefit to which eligible participants are entitled. The employer is responsible for making contributions in amounts sufficient to pay promised benefits.

defined-benefit present value factor • This is determined by looking at the assumed rate of return on investments after retirement and the expected duration of retirement.

defined-contribution plan • A category of qualified retirement plan in which participants' benefits are based simply on accumulated contributions and investment experience thereon.

DIPP • *See* decline in purchasing power.

disability insured • At a minimum, disability-insured status requires that a worker (1) be fully insured and (2) have a minimum amount of work under social security within a recent time period.

distribution year • Under the minimum distribution rules, a minimum distribution must be made for the calendar year in which a participant attains age 70 1/2 and for each subsequent year. Each year for which a distribution must be made is referred to as a distribution year.

diversifiable risk • Another name for unsystematic risk.

diversification • Spreading one's portfolio funds among many different assets in many different categories to reduce risk.

dollar-cost averaging • Process of adding a specified amount to the portfolio on a regular basis, regardless of whether the portfolio value is tending up or down; results in a lower average price per share since more shares are purchased when prices are low and fewer shares are purchased when prices are high.

domicile • The intended permanent home of a client. Important for state estate tax purposes, it is determined by such factors as where the person spends the majority of his or her time, where he or she is registered to vote, the state his or her driver's license is from, and where his or her will is executed.

early retirement reduction • Regarding social security retirement benefits, a reduction of 5/9 of one percent per month prior to the employee's normal retirement age.

early-distribution (Sec.72(t)) penalty tax • An additional 10 percent tax that applies to distributions made prior to attainment of age 59 1/2 from qualified plans, 403(b) plans, and IRAs.

earnings test • A restriction applied to people in social security pay status that earn over a threshold amount. These people will "lose" some of their social security benefit.

echo housing • Removable housing units set up on the lot of a single-family home.

efficient market hypothesis • The theory that new information is quickly incorporated into security prices.

employee stock ownership plan (ESOP) • A qualified plan that is categorized as a defined-contribution plan. The plan must invest primarily in securities of the sponsoring employer.

equity risk premium • The additional return received for the additional risk of investing in common stocks (as represented by the Standard & Poors 500 index) instead of investing in Treasury bills.

excess accumulations estate tax • A 15 percent additional estate tax that applies when accumulated retirement benefits exceed a specified threshold.

excess distributions excise tax • A 15 percent tax that applies to anyone who receives distributions from tax-sheltered retirement plans in excess of a specified threshold.

excess distributions grandfather election • Individuals with $562,500 in tax-sheltered retirement benefits on August 1, 1986, had the opportunity to make an election that may protect them from the full effect of the excess distributions and excess accumulations excise taxes.

excess-benefit plan • A nonqualified plan that provides benefits in excess of the maximum benefit or contribution limits of IRC Sec. 415.

exclusion plan • A way for an employer to provide retiree health care benefits. This approach pays benefits based only on the portion that medicare does not cover.

executive-bonus life insurance plan (Sec. 162 plan) • Employer pays a bonus to the executive for the purpose of purchasing cash value life insurance.

expense method • Measuring a person's financial need by using a retirement budget.

extensive contracts • A life lease contract that pays in advance for unlimited nursing home care at little or no increase in monthly payments.

family maximum • The maximum benefits that are paid out under the social security system when different types of benefits are paid to two or more members of a family.

FASB 106 • An accounting rule that requires employers to put future liabilities for retiree health care benefits on their current books.

fee-for-service contract • A life lease contract that covers only emergency and short-term nursing home care in the basic agreement. It typically, however, provides guaranteed space for long-term care on a per diem basis.

first-death reduction J&S annuity • An annuity in which payments are reduced at the first death, regardless of whether the participant or the beneficiary dies first.

first distribution year • The first year for which a distribution must be made under the minimum distribution rules. Generally a minimum distribution must be made for the year in which the participant attains age 70 1/2, even if the required beginning date is the following April 1.

5-year averaging • Special tax treatment for eligible lump-sum distributions from qualified plans.

Form SSA-7004 • Request for Earnings and Benefit Estimate Statement from the Social Security Administration.

401(k) plan • A profit-sharing type plan that allows employees to make salary-deferral-type contributions on a pretax basis.

403(b) plan • A tax-sheltered annuity program with similar tax advantages to those of qualified plans but that can be sponsored only by a tax-exempt organization or public school. The plan is similar to a 401(k) plan in that participants may make pretax contributions through salary deferral elections and the employer may make contributions on a discretionary basis.

full cash refund feature • A feature of an annuity in which a specified refund payment is made if the stream of annuity payments is less than a specified dollar amount.

fully insured • This term is used under social security to refer to a type of eligibility status. To be fully insured, an individual generally needs to complete 40 quarters of coverage.

fundamental analysis • Process of identifying investments that will have high risk-adjusted returns by evaluating their underlying economic factors.

growth rate • *See* step-up rate.

guaranteed renewable provision • In a long-term care contract, a provision that allows an insurance company to revise premiums on a class basis.

Home Equity Conversion Mortgage Demonstration Program • A reverse annuity mortgage program sponsored by the federal government.

hospice • A facility for treating the terminally ill. Medicare does, however, provide hospice care benefits for a person at home.

in-service distributions • Distributions from a qualified plan to a participant payable for any reason prior to termination from service.

incentive stock options (ISOs) • Options to purchase shares of company stock at a stated price over a limited period of time. Different from nonqualified stock options in that the rules governing ISOs are quite strict and the tax treatment is more favorable to the executive.

independence • In portfolio theory, independence refers to the absence of any relationship between the historical (or projected) periodic returns of two assets. Such assets would have no covariance with each other.

Index of Leading Economic Indicators • Set of eleven economic statutes that the government uses to forecast economic activity.

individual reverse annuity mortgage • A way to stay in the same home while capitalizing on the home's equity. The homeowner enters into an agreement with a lender to receive annuity payments in exchange for a secured interest in the equity in the home.

inflation bias • Tendency to overstate the degree to which one has a favorable personality trait.

individual retirement account (IRA) • A retirement plan established by an individual that receives special tax treatment.

IRC Sec. 1034 • The code provision allowing taxpayers to roll over gain from the sale of their principal residence in order to defer taxation. Under Sec. 1034, any person who sells a home and buys another is permitted to defer paying tax on the gain, provided the purchase price of the second home is at least as large as the net sales price of the first home. The 1034 tax break applies to homes bought within 2 years of the sale of the original home. It can be used in conjunction with the Sec. 121 one-time exclusion.

IRC Sec. 121 • The one-time $125,000 exclusion on the gain from the sale of a home.

IRS Form 1099R • The tax form that reports a payment from a qualified plan, IRA, SEP, or 403(b) plan to both the IRS and the participant.

ISO • *See* incentive stock options.

J&S annuity with pop-up feature • In contrast to the conventional J&S annuity, if the beneficiary dies before the participant, the monthly benefit pops up to what it would have been had the participant chosen a single-life annuity rather than the joint and survivor annuity.

junior stock • Restricted stock that is convertible at a one-to-one ratio into regular common stock shares of the company if specific performance goals are achieved.

Keogh plan • A qualified retirement plan sponsored by a partnership or self-employed individual.

LCI • *See* life-cycle investing.

life annuity • A stream of payments over the life of the participant.

life annuity with guaranteed payments • An annuity that pays benefits over the longer of the participant's lifetime or a specified time period.

life-care community • Sometimes called continuing-care retirement communities. These are villages that provide housing and services (including long-term care) to retired parties in exchange for up-front and monthly fees.

life-cycle investing (LCI) • Process of tailoring the investment portfolio to fit the individual's phase in the life cycle.

life-lease contract • Sometimes called a residential-care agreement, this is the contract issued by a life-care community. These contracts generally guarantee living space, services, and the availability of lifetime health care.

lifetime reserve days • Medicare coverage is provided for up to 90 days in each benefit period. Medicare recipients, however, are given 60 extra lifetime reserve days to tack on to the end of this period. These days are nonrenewable (use them and/or lose them).

long-term care insurance • Insurance that provides per diem allowances for nursing home costs.

lump-sum distribution • A distribution from a qualified plan that is eligible for special income tax treatment.

market portfolio • The theoretical portfolio of all assets, to which individual assets and portfolios can be compared in modern portfolio theory. Typically the Standard & Poors 500 or another broad-based stock market index is used as a surrogate for the market portfolio.

market risk • Another name for systematic risk.

market timing • Attempt to anticipate significant market movements and to make major changes in asset allocation accordingly.

matching maturities • Selecting an asset that matures at the same time that the funds will be needed

MDIB • *See* minimum distribution incidental benefits.

medigap insurance • Insurance that provides services not covered by medicare.

mental accounts • The set of information and experience that may cause an individual to select a financial alternative based on its relative, rather than absolute, monetary benefit.

min-max range • The range of returns for a specific asset type for a holding period of a specific length within a specific time frame. *Example:* The min-max range of returns for the Standard & Poors 500 stocks for all 5-year holding periods from 1926–1990 was 36.4 percent.

minimum distribution incidental benefits • The intent of the minimum distribution incidental benefit rule is to ensure that the participant who attains age 70 1/2 and begins retirement distributions does not defer payment of a large portion of the benefit until after his or her death. The rule applies only when the beneficiary is not the spouse and is more than 10 years younger than the participant.

minimum distribution rules • Rules that require payments from qualified plans, IRAs, SEPs, and 403(b) plans to begin within a specified period of time. The rules generally require that retirement benefits begin at age 70 1/2. The rules also specify how quickly distributions must be made after the death of the participant.

modern portfolio theory (MPT) • A set of quantitative approaches to explaining the risk-return relationship, portfolio diversification, and asset selection.

modified contract • A life-lease contract that provides a specified amount of nursing home care with a per diem rate paid for usage above the specified amount.

modified cash-refund annuity • A life annuity with the possibility of a refund to a chosen beneficiary if annuity payments have been less than a specified amount.

money-purchase pension plan • A defined-contribution type qualified plan in which the employer contribution is specified and benefits are based on the participant's accumulated account balance.

MPT • *See* modern portfolio theory.

noncancelable provision • In a long-term care contract, a provision for establishing premiums in advance that cannot be changed.

nonqualified retirement plan • An employer-sponsored deferred-compensation plan that does not receive the same special tax treatment as a qualified plan but that is subject to fewer restrictions. Generally these plans are established only for a small group of executives.

nonqualified stock options • Options granted by the company to the executive to purchase shares of company stock at a stated price over a given limited period of time.

OASDHI • Acronym for the old age, survivors, disability, and health insurance portions of social security.

Part A medicare • The hospital portion of the federal health insurance program for the elderly.

Part B medicare • The doctor and service provider portion of the federal health insurance program for the elderly.

passive investing • Attempt to duplicate the risk-reward characteristics of a well-known stock indicator series by creating a stock portfolio that is nearly identical to that implied by the indicator series.

pay-as-you-go • Current payroll taxes are used to pay current benefits.

pension plan • Certain qualified retirement plans are considered pension plans. Pension plans must state the level of contributions or benefits provided. Such plans are not allowed to make distributions except upon death, disability, termination of employment, or attainment of the plan's retirement age.

performance shares • Contingent performance award granted in the form of a fixed number of common shares of stock. The amount payable is contingent upon meeting established performance goals.

performance unit/performance cash • Award granted to the executive in the form of a contingent number of units or as a contingent cash award. Payment is contingent upon meeting established performance goals.

phantom stock • The employer promises to pay the executive the value of some stated number of shares of stock at some later specified date. The stock is not actually set aside, only entered as a promise, and payment may be in cash or possibly in shares of stock.

PIA • *See* primary insurance amount.

preference reversal • Change in a client's ranking of alternatives depending on how the alternatives are presented.

preretirement inflation factor • This is determined by looking at the assumed annual inflation rate prior to retirement and the number of years until retirement.

primary insurance amount (PIA) • A benefit amount that is used to determine most social security benefits. The primary insurance amount is determined by applying a formula to the individual's AIME.

principal residence • The place where a person lives as distinguished from a vacation residence. It is the exclusive permanent home.

profit-sharing plans • Certain qualified retirement plans, including profit-sharing plans, ESOPs, stock bonus plans, and 401(k) plans, are considered profit-sharing-type plans. These plans may allow for discretionary employer contributions, but the contributions must be allocated in a specified way. Distributions may be made at termination of employment but in-service distributions are permitted if certain conditions are met.

provisional income • A taxpayer's adjusted gross income plus tax-exempt interest income plus 1/2 of social security income.

put option • When an ESOP or stock bonus plan is sponsored by a company whose stock is not publicly traded, the company must offer to buy back any stock distributed to participants. This buy-back offer is called a put option.

qualified domestic relations orders (QDRO) • A court order as part of a divorce proceeding that requires the plan administrator to pay benefits to an alternate payee, who can be the participant's former spouse, child, or other dependent.

qualified retirement plan • An employer-sponsored retirement plan eligible for special tax treatment. Common types of qualified plans include profit-sharing plans, defined-benefit plans, and money-purchase pension plans. Special tax treatment includes employer deduction at the time contributions are made to the plan's trust, no income tax on the trust, and deferral of taxation to the employee until the time of distribution to the employee.

qualified joint and survivor annuity (QJSA) • The required form of payment for any benefits paid from a qualified plan to a married plan participant.

qualified preretirement survivor annuity (QPSA) • The required preretirement death benefit payable to the spouse of a married plan participant.

quarter of coverage • This is the measuring stick used for social security eligibility. In 1995 a worker receives credit for one quarter of coverage for each $630 in annual earnings on which social security taxes are paid.

question framing • Manner in which a question is posed, which often influences the client's response.

random walk hypothesis • The theory that security prices move in a manner that cannot be predicted by prior price changes.

real riskless rate • The rate of return on Treasury bills, adjusted for inflation, as measured by the consumer price index.

recalculation of life expectancies • When making minimum distribution calculations under the account plan rules, recalculating a life expectancy means determining the individual's age as of the last day of the given distribution year.

replacement ratio approach • Measuring a person's financial need as a percentage of final salary.

replacement ratio • Level of income stated as a percentage of final salary.

required beginning date • Under the minimum distribution rules, this is the latest date that the minimum distribution must begin. Generally it is the April 1 of the year following the calendar year in which the participant attains age 70 1/2.

residential care facilities • Adult homes that provide safety, shelter, and companionship.

residual risk • Another name for unsystematic risk.

restricted stock • Stock payments from the company to the executive that are nontransferable and forfeitable until some future specified date. Forfeiture usually occurs if the executive ceases employment prior to retirement age or some other specified age.

retirement income shortfall (RIS) • The result of subtracting the projected annual need from existing sources stated in terms of annual income provided at retirement.

retirement needs present value factor • This is determined by looking at the assumed annual inflation rate after retirement, the expected duration of retirement, and the assumed rate of return on investments after retirement. First subtract the assumed investment rate after retirement from the assumed inflation rate after retirement; then look at the duration of retirement.

retirement villages • Age-restricted housing developments that often provide recreational opportunities and maintenance services for common ground.

reverse annuity mortgage • *See* individual reverse annuity mortgage.

reverse term mortgage • A reverse mortgage with no annuity element to it. A person enters into an agreement with a lender to be paid monthly installments based on the equity the person has in the home. The loan is paid back *after* the term of the mortgage is over.

RIS • *See* retirement income shortfall.

risk premium • The additional return received for the risk incurred by investing in a given asset category rather than a safer alternative.

risk tolerance • Willingness to incur risk, especially in monetary matters.

risky shift • Tendency for a group decision to be riskier than the decisions of the individuals in the group.

salary reduction plan • A nonqualified retirement plan that allows participants to defer current salary with the objective of deferring taxation until a later date.

sale leaseback • An arrangement under which a person sells the home to an investor and rents it back. The seller/renter gets the advantage of removing the home from the estate and freeing up equity from the home.

SAR • *See* stock appreciation rights.

savings rate factor • This is determined by looking at the number of years until retirement, the average annual rate of return expected, and the savings step-up rate.

security market line • The linear relationship between systematic risk (beta) and expected return according to the capital asset pricing model.

SERP • *See* supplemental executive retirement plan.

simplified employee pension plan (SEP) • Employer-sponsored retirement plan in which contributions are made to the IRA of each participant. The SEP is an alternative to profit-sharing plan or a 401(k) plan, since employee pretax contributions may be made.

skilled-nursing facility • A facility for patients who no longer require continuous hospital care but are not well enough to go home. The facility must have at least one full-time registered nurse, and nursing services must be provided at all times. Patients must generally be under the supervision of a physician.

small stock premium • The additional return received for the additional risk of investing in small capitalization stocks rather than investing in Standard & Poors 500 stocks.

social desirability bias • Tendency to overstate the degree to which one has a favorable personality trait.

special-purpose loan • A special-purpose loan does not have to be repaid until after the retiree dies, moves, or sells the home.

special situation analysis • Identification of investments with high potential returns and lower-than-commensurate risk due to market inefficiencies; usually associated with financially troubled companies.

SPD • *See* summary plan description.

spell of illness • Another term for benefit period.

spousal benefit • Social security retirement benefit paid to a nonworking spouse. The benefit is based on the primary insurance amount (PIA) of the working spouse.

spousal consent • Refers to the consent required for a participant to elect out of the qualified joint and survivor annuity or the qualified preretirement survivor annuity.

spousal IRA • A separate individual retirement plan for a married individual who does not receive employment income (and therefore cannot maintain his or her own IRA).

step-up rate • This is the rate by which savings are increased each year. The rate usually parallels expected salary increases.

stock appreciation rights (SARs) • A benefit program that gives participants the right to receive cash or stock in the amount of the stock's appreciation over a limited period of time.

substantially equal periodic payments • Refers to an exception to the early distribution penalty tax whereby payments are paid over the life expectancy of the participant.

summary plan description (SPD) • A brief, easy-to-read document summarizing the terms of a retirement plan that must be given to participants of any plan covered by ERISA.

supplemental executive retirement plan (SERP) • A nonqualified retirement plan paid for by the company and intended to supplement other retirement income.

"sure thing" principle • Tendency for people to put too much emphasis on selecting a choice with a certain outcome and too little emphasis on choices that have outcomes of moderate or high probability.

systematic risk • The part of risk that is related to the market as a whole and cannot be diversified away. As investors add assets to their portfolios, they diversify away the unsystematic risk. If investors continue to diversify, the portfolio will eventually resemble the market portfolio and will retain the risk that is inherent in the market portfolio—systematic risk. Systematic risk can also be represented as the relative tendency for an asset's return to track the market's return—beta.

target replacement ratio (TRR) • This is postretirement annual income divided by the preretirement annual income, where each income provides the same standard of living.

target-benefit pension plan • A qualified retirement plan categorized as a defined-contribution pension plan that is a hybrid between a defined-benefit and a money-purchase pension plan. The plan has a stated benefit formula that is used to determine annual contributions. However, the actual benefit is based on accumulated contributions and actual investment experience—not the stated benefit in the plan.

taxable wage base • A 6.2 percent tax is levied on both the employer and employee to fund the OASDI portions of social security up to the taxable wage base. The taxable wage base for 1995 is $61,200.

technical analysis • Process of identifying underpriced investments by looking at the market itself and especially at supply and demand for the investment.

temporary annuity • An annuity that expires at the earlier of death or a specified period of time.

10-year averaging • Special tax treatment for eligible lump-sum distributions from qualified plans available only for individuals born before 1936.

three-legged stool • The need for social security, employer-sponsored retirement programs, and personal savings in order for a client to succeed in retirement.

thrill seeker • Personality type that is prone to take risk in all categories of life situations.

"top-down" analysis • Fundamental analysis approach in which analyst evaluates sequentially (1) economic and market factors, (2) industry/sector factors, and (3) company characteristics.

TRR • *See* target replacement ratio.

trust fund • All funds to pay for social security are deposited into one of four trust funds: an old age and survivors fund, a disability fund, and two medicare funds.

unrealized appreciation • A term used to describe a special tax rule that applies to lump-sum distributions from qualified retirement plans. The rule allows the benefit recipient to defer paying taxes on the appreciation on the value of distributed employer securities.

unsystematic risk • The part of an asset's total risk that is independent of movements in the general market. In practice, unsystematic risk represents investment-specific characteristics. For a stock investment, such factors include the company's relative reliance on government contracts, potential foreign currency losses, potential competition, management depth, financial leverage, and a myriad of other factors. Unsystematic risk, also called diversifiable risk and residual risk, can be reduced by diversifying among many assets.

variable annuity • An annuity that may provide fluctuating benefit payments based upon the rate of return of underlying assets.

variable life annuity • Type of life annuity in which the periodic payments depend on the performance of an underlying asset, such as a stock portfolio.

Index